The Thirties
in America

The Thirties in America

Volume I
Academy Awards—
Good Neighbor Policy

Editor
Thomas Tandy Lewis
St. Cloud State University

SALEM PRESS
Pasadena, California
Hackensack, New Jersey

Editor in Chief: Dawn P. Dawson

Editorial Director: Christina J. Moose   *Photo Editor:* Cynthia Breslin Beres
Project and Development Editor: R. Kent Rasmussen   *Production Editor:* Andrea E. Miller
Manuscript Editor: Christopher Rager   *Graphics and Design:* James Hutson
Acquisitions Editor: Mark Rehn   *Layout:* William Zimmerman
Research Supervisor: Jeffry Jensen

Title page photo: *President Franklin D. Roosevelt throws out the ceremonial first pitch of the baseball season at Griffith Stadium, home of the Washington Senators. Roosevelt continued the tradition throughout the decade, hurling the first pitch for the Senators from 1933 to 1941.* (©Bettmann/CORBIS)

Cover images: (pictured clockwise, from top left): The *Hindenburg* disaster (The Granger Collection, New York); Superman comic book (The Granger Collection, New York); Babe Ruth trading card (The Granger Collection, New York); "Migrant Mother," by Dorothea Lange (The Granger Collection, New York)

Library of Congress Cataloging-in-Publication Data

The thirties in America / editor, Thomas Tandy Lewis.
    p. cm.
Includes bibliographical references and index.
    ISBN 978-1-58765-725-2 (set : alk. paper) — ISBN 978-1-58765-726-9 (vol. 1 : alk. paper) — ISBN 978-1-58765-727-6 (vol. 2 : alk. paper) — ISBN 978-1-58765-728-3 (vol. 3 : alk. paper)
    1. United States—Civilization—1918-1945—Encyclopedias. 2. United States—History—1933-1945—Encyclopedias. 3. Nineteen thirties—Encyclopedias. I. Lewis, Thomas T. (Thomas Tandy)
    E169.1.T475 2011
    973.917—dc22

    2010049260

■ Table of Contents

Publisher's Note ix
Contributors xiii
Complete List of Contents xxi

Academy Awards 1
Adams, Ansel 4
Addams, Jane 5
Adler Planetarium 6
Adventures of Robin Hood, The. 6
Advertising in Canada 7
Advertising in the United States 8
African Americans 12
Agricultural Adjustment Acts 17
Agriculture in Canada 18
Agriculture in the United States 20
Aid to Dependent Children 24
Air mail route scandal 25
Air pollution 26
Airships 27
Akron disaster 29
Alcatraz Federal Penitentiary 30
Alcoholics Anonymous 32
All Quiet on the Western Front 33
American Federation of Labor 34
American Gothic 35
American Liberty League 36
Amos 'n' Andy 37
Anderson, Marian 39
Anti-Racketeering Act of 1934 41
Anti-Semitism 42
Apple Mary 43
Archaeology 44
Archambault Report 46
Architecture 47
Armstrong, Edwin H. 50
Armstrong, Louis 51
Art movements 52
Asia 54
Asian Americans 56
Astaire, Fred 59
Astor, Mary 60
Astronomy 61
Atherton Report 64
Auto racing 65
Automobiles and auto manufacturing 66
Aviation and aeronautics 70
Awake and Sing! 73

Bank holiday 75
Bank of United States failure 75
Banking 77
Banking Act of 1935 79
Barker Gang 80
Barrow, Clyde, and Bonnie Parker 82
Baseball 83
Basie, Count 87
Basketball 88
Bathysphere 90
Beard, Charles A. 90
Beatty, Clyde 92
Bennett, Richard Bedford 92
Benny, Jack 95
Benton, Thomas Hart 96
Berkeley, Busby 97
Bethune, Mary McLeod 98
Bingo 99
Birth control 100
Black, Hugo L. 102
Black Empire 104
Black hole theory 105
Black Monday 106
Black No More 107
Blondie comic strip 107
Blondie films 108
Blood banks 110
Bonus Army March 111
Book publishing 112
Boulder Dam 115
Boxing 117
Braddock, James J. 120
Brains Trust 121
Brandeis, Louis D. 122
Breadlines and soup kitchens 123
Breedlove v. Suttles 125
Bringing Up Baby 125
Broadway musicals 127
Brown v. Mississippi 129
Brownlee, John Edward 130
Buck, Pearl S. 131
Budge, Don 133
Business and the economy in Canada 134
Business and the economy in the
    United States 136
Butler, Smedley 139
Byrd, Richard 140

Cagney, James	142
Calder, Alexander	143
Caldwell, Erskine	145
Canada, U.S. investments in	146
Canada and Great Britain	148
Canadian minority communities	151
Canadian regionalism	153
Cancer	155
Capone, Al	157
Capra, Frank	160
Car radios	161
Carter family	162
Carter v. Carter Coal Co.	164
Chaplin, Charles	164
Charlie Chan films	166
Chemistry	168
Chicago World's Fair	171
Children's Hour, The	173
Christie Pits riot	173
Chrysler Building	174
City Lights	175
Civil rights and liberties in Canada	176
Civil rights and liberties in the United States	178
Civilian Conservation Corps	181
Cleveland "torso" murders	182
Cohan, George M.	183
Coinage	184
Collier, John	185
Comic strips	187
Commodity Credit Corporation	189
Communism	189
Congress, U.S.	192
Congress of Industrial Organizations	196
Consumers Union of the United States	197
Contract bridge	198
Corrigan's wrong-way flight	199
Coughlin, Charles E.	199
Crane, Hart	202
Crater disappearance	203
Credit and debt	204
Crimes and scandals	207
Curry, John Steuart	210
Curtis, Charles	211
Cyclotron	212
Dance	215
Davis, Bette	217
Day, Dorothy	218
Day of the Locust, The	219
DC-3	220
Dean, Dizzy	220
De Jonge v. Oregon	221
Demographics of Canada	222
Demographics of the United States	226
Design for Living	229
Destry Rides Again	230
Dewey, John	232
Diary of a Country Priest, The	233
Dick Tracy	234
Dillinger, John	235
Dionne quintuplets	236
Dorsey, Tommy	238
Dracula	239
Drive-in theaters	240
Dubinsky, David	241
Du Bois, W. E. B.	242
Dust Bowl	243
Dutch elm disease	247
Earhart, Amelia	249
Ecstasy	251
Education	252
Einstein, Albert	256
Elections, Canadian	258
Elections of 1930, 1934, and 1938, U.S.	261
Elections of 1932, U.S.	264
Elections of 1936, U.S.	267
Electric razors	269
Electron microscope	270
Elixir sulfanilamide scandal	271
Ellington, Duke	272
Empire State Building	274
Erie Railroad Co. v. Tompkins	276
Europe	276
Evian Conference	280
Export-Import Bank of the United States	281
Fads	282
Fair Labor Standards Act of 1938	285
Fallingwater house	286
Farmer-Labor Party of Minnesota	287
Farmers' organizations	288
Farnsworth, Philo T.	289
Fascism in Canada	291
Fascism in the United States	292
Fashions and clothing	295
Father Divine	298
Faulkner, William	300

Federal Communications Commission. 302
Federal Emergency Relief
    Administration 304
Federal Food, Drug, and Cosmetic Act
    of 1938 305
Federal Housing Administration 306
Federal National Mortgage Association 308
Federal Power Commission 309
Federal Reserve Board 310
Federal Theatre Project 311
Federal Trade Commission 315
Federal Writers' Project 316
Fetchit, Stepin 317
Fibber McGee and Molly 318
Field Guide to the Birds 319
Fields, W. C. 319
Film. 321
Film serials 324
Fireside chats. 326
Fitzgerald, Ella 328
Fitzgerald, F. Scott 329
Flash Gordon 330
Fleming, Victor 331
Flint sit-down strike 332
Floyd, Pretty Boy. 333
Fluorescent lighting 334
Food processing 335
Food stamps 337
Football. 339
Ford, Henry 342
Ford, John 343
Ford Foundation. 344
Foreign Agents Registration Act of 1938 345
Foreign policy of Canada 346
Foreign policy of the United States. 348

Fortune magazine. 352
Forty-second Street 353
Four Horsemen vs. Three Musketeers 355
Foxx, Jimmie. 356
Frankenstein films. 357
Freaks 360
Freon 360
Frost, Robert 361
Frozen-food marketing 363
Functions of the Executive, The 364
Fundamentalist-Modernist conflict. 365

Gable, Clark 368
Gambling. 369
Gangster films 370
Garbo, Greta 372
Garner, John Nance 373
Gehrig, Lou 375
General Theory of Employment, Interest and
    Money, The. 377
Geneva Disarmament Conference 378
George VI's North American visit 379
George Washington Bridge 381
German-American Bund 382
Germany and U.S. appeasement 384
Gershwin, George 386
Glass-Steagall Act of 1933 387
"God Bless America". 388
Goddard, Robert H. 389
Gold Clause Cases 390
Gold Reserve Act of 1934 390
Golf. 391
Gone with the Wind 393
Good Earth, The. 395
Good Neighbor Policy. 395

■ Publisher's Note

The three volumes of *The Thirties in America* constitute an encyclopedic reference work covering the most important people, institutions, events, and developments of all types in the United States and Canada between the years 1930 and 1939. This set is the seventh in Salem Press's Decades in America series, which now encompasses every decade from the 1930's through the 1990's and soon will add sets on the 1920's and the first decade of the twenty-first century. Librarians and teachers have acclaimed this series for its ability to help students understand the most significant aspects of each decade's history.

Although essays in *The Thirties in America* have been written to meet the needs of high school students and college undergraduates, the set's clear and innovative approach to the decade and authoritative articles should also make it useful to more advanced students and scholars. Its 670 essays cover the full breadth of North American history and culture throughout the decade, and its supporting features include 15 appendixes and such helpful finding aids as end-of-article cross-references, detailed indexes, and a list of articles by subject category.

Scope and Coverage

Almost every decade of the twentieth century is closely identified with at least one landmark event, turning point, or fundamental change. The key event of the 1930's was the Great Depression, a nearly decade-long economic cataclysm that devastated not only the United States and Canada but also the entire world. Within the United States, the Depression prompted the social and political revolution of President Franklin D. Roosevelt's New Deal programs, which left an indelible stamp on American economic and social history.

It should not, however, be thought that the Great Depression was the only significant development of the 1930's. One of the fascinating aspects of Salem's decades sets is what they reveal about the many unique events and contributions to history of each decade. In *The Thirties in America*, for example, readers will find articles on such subjects as the discovery of Pluto, the invention of radar, the birth of Canada's famous Dionne quintuplets, the Bonus Army March, the Dust Bowl, the notorious Scottsboro trials, and Orson Welles's *War of the Worlds* radio broadcast. The 1930's also saw the end of Prohibition and the development of large-scale organized crime and such infamous criminals as Al Capone, John Dillinger, Pretty Boy Floyd, the Barker Gang, and Clyde Barrow and Bonnie Parker—the "Bonnie and Clyde" of folk legend.

On the world stage, the 1930's saw the breakdown of the 1919 peace settlement that had come out of World War I. Under Adolf Hitler's National Socialist regime, Germany rearmed and began expanding its territory. At the same time Japan was building its military forces and beginning to expand its domination in the Pacific and on mainland Asia. By 1939, the last year of the decade, World War II had begun in both Europe and Asia. Meanwhile, the growing strength and interest in expansionism of the Soviet Union's communist regime was causing increasing anxiety in Canada and the United States.

Despite the horrendous impact of the Great Depression and the movement toward a new world war, the developments of the 1930's were not all negative. Fostered in part by U.S. government programs, the decade saw a flowering of literature and the arts, particularly in the field of jazz music. The 1930's also saw the coming of age of the film industry. Aided by the advent of sound films and successful experiments with color and feature-length animated films, the decade is remembered as the beginning of a brief "Golden Age" of Hollywood. Indeed, the year 1939 is regarded as one of the greatest in film history and is remembered for such classics as *Gone with the Wind*, *Stagecoach*, and *The Wizard of Oz*.

The full breadth of the set's essays can be seen in this selection from the many categories under which the essays fall:

- African Americans
- Agriculture
- Architecture & Engineering
- Art & Photography
- Business & Economics
- Canada
- Civil Rights & Liberties

- Communications
- Courts & Court Cases
- Crime & Scandals
- Dance
- Demographics
- Diplomacy & International Relations
- Disasters
- Education & Scholarship
- Environmental Issues
- Fads & Fashions
- Film
- Government & Politics
- Great Depression
- Health & Medicine
- Journalism
- Labor
- Laws & Treaties
- Literature
- Military & War
- Music
- New Deal
- Products & Inventions
- Radio
- Recreation & Entertainment
- Religion
- Science & Technology
- Sports
- Theater
- Transportation & Travel
- Women's Issues

The appendix section at the end of volume 3 contains the complete list of category headings, followed by the articles to which they apply.

Like Salem's other decade sets, *The Thirties in America* mixes long overview essays on broad subjects with shorter articles discussing people, books, films, fads, inventions and scientific discoveries, and other events and important topics representative of the decade. Every article focuses on its subject within the context of the 1930's, devoting only such attention to what happened before and after that decade as is needed to place the subjects within their fuller historical contexts.

Organization and Format

Ranging in length from 1 to 6 pages, each article in *The Thirties in America* begins with a concise title followed by a brief definition or description of the person, organization, work, concept, or event.

Headwords are selected to help users find articles under the titles they expect, but extra help is provided in the form of textual cross-references. For example, users looking for an article under the heading "Hays Code" are referred to the article titled "Motion Picture Production Code." Additional help in locating topics can be found in the extensive List of Entries by Category, and Personage and Subject Indexes in volume 3.

After their titles, articles provide a variety of ready-reference top matter tailored to the individual topics. For example, articles on individual persons provide brief identifications and their subjects' birth and death dates and places. Articles on events give brief descriptions of the events and their dates and places. Other types of articles provide similar information.

The main body of each article concludes with an "Impact" section that reviews the subject's broader importance during the 1930's. "See also" cross-references following every article direct readers to additional articles on closely related and parallel subjects. Every article also offers bibliographical notes, which include annotations in articles of 1,000 or more words, and every article is signed by its contributor. The affiliations of the contributors can be found in the list following this note.

Special Features

A rich selection of 312 evocative photographic images illustrate the articles in *The Thirties in America*. The subjects of these photographs are listed in a special index in volume 3. In addition, 16 maps and 70 sidebars—lists, time lines, tables, graphs, and textual extracts—highlight interesting facts and trends from the decade.

Volume 3 contains 15 appendixes providing additional information about films, Academy Award winners, Broadway plays and theatrical awards, radio programs, best-selling books and literary awards, popular musicians and top-selling recordings, winners of sports events, U.S. legislation, and U.S. Supreme Court decisions. The appendixes also include a glossary of new words and slang that arose during the 1930's, a detailed time line, and an extensive annotated general bibliography.

The encyclopedia also contains a number of useful tools to help readers find entries of interest. A complete list of all essays in *The Thirties in America* appears at the beginning of each volume. A list of entries sorted by category appears at the end of volume 3. In addition to a photo index, volume 3 has personage and comprehensive subject indexes.

Online Access

Salem Press provides access to its award-winning content both in traditional, printed form and online. Any school or library that purchases *The Thirties in America* is entitled to complimentary access to a fully supported online version of the set. Online features include a simple, intuitive interface, user-profile areas for students and patrons, sophisticated search functionality, and complete contents, including appendixes. Access is available through a code printed on the inside cover of the first volume, and that access is both unlimited and immediate. Salem's online customer service representatives are happy to help with any questions at (800) 221-1592. E-books are also available.

Acknowledgments

The editors of Salem Press would like to thank the 326 scholars who contributed essays and appendixes to *The Thirties in America*. Their names and affiliations are listed in the front matter to volume 1. The editors especially wish to thank Professor Thomas Tandy Lewis of St. Cloud State University in Minnesota for serving as the project's Editor and for bringing to the project his special expertise on North American history.

■ Contributors

Randy L. Abbott
University of Evansville

Michael Adams
CUNY Graduate Center

Patrick Adcock
Henderson State University

Linda Adkins
University of Northern Iowa

Richard Adler
University of Michigan—Dearborn

Emily Alward
Henderson, Nevada, District Libraries

Stephanie A. Amsel
University of Texas at San Antonio

David E. Anderson
Seymour, Indiana

Jacob M. Appel
New York University

Erica K. Argyropoulos
University of Kansas

Colin Asher
Society of Professional Journalists

Mary Welek Atwell
Radford University

Charles Lewis Avinger, Jr.
Washtenaw Community College

Charles F. Bahmueller
Center for Civic Education

Jane L. Ball
Yellow Springs, Ohio

David Barratt
Montreat College

Jonathan Bean
Southern Illinois University

Keith J. Bell
Western Carolina University

Eric T. Bellone
Suffolk University

James R. Belpedio
Becker College

Alvin K. Benson
Utah Valley University

Jill Stapleton Bergeron
University of Tennessee

Milton Berman
University of Rochester

R. Matthew Beverlin
University of Kansas

Cynthia A. Bily
Adrian, Michigan

Margaret Boe Birns
New York University

Pegge Bochynski
Salem State College

David Boersema
Pacific University

Delbert S. Bowers
Sherman Oaks, California

Susan Roth Breitzer
Fayetteville, North Carolina

Robert A. Britt-Mills
Florida State University

John A. Britton
Francis Marion University

Marc D. Brodsky
Virginia Tech

Howard Bromberg
University of Michigan Law School

Stefan Brooks
Lindsey Wilson College

David M. Brown
Jackson State University

Stephen W. Brown
Alliant International University

Thomas Buchanan
Ancilla Domini College

Tony Buell
Northeastern University

Michael A. Buratovich
Spring Arbor University

Michael H. Burchett
Limestone College

Hugh Burkhart
University of San Diego

William E. Burns
George Washington University

Patrick Callaway
University of Montana Western

Jennifer L. Campbell
Lycoming College

Kimberlee Candela
California State University, Chico

William Carney
Cameron University

Thomas Gregory Carpenter
Lipscomb University

Henry L. Carrigan, Jr.
Northwestern University

Keith Carson
Atlantic Cape Community College

Alexandra Carter
University of California, Los Angeles

Frederick B. Chary
Indiana University Northwest

Dennis W. Cheek
Ewing Marion Kauffman Foundation

Michael W. Cheek
Kennett Square, Pennsylvania

John L. Clark, Jr.
Connecticut College

Joseph F. Clark III
Embry-Riddle Aeronautical University

David W. Cole
University of Wisconsin Colleges

Stacy Cole
South Pasadena, California

Michael Conklin
College of New Jersey

Michael Coronel
University of Northern Colorado

Patricia Coronel
Colorado State University

Tyler T. Crogg
Southern Illinois University, Carbondale

Brian T. Crumley
Indiana University—Southeast

Robert L. Cullers
Kansas State University

Michael D. Cummings, Jr.
Madonna University

Dolores Amidon D'Angelo
American University

Eddith A. Dashiell
Ohio University

Anita Price Davis
Converse College

Jennifer Davis-Kay
Education Development Center, Inc.

Rhea Davison-Edwards
Minnesota State University, Mankato

Frank Day
Clemson University

Bruce J. DeHart
University of North Carolina, Pembroke

Peng Deng
High Point University

James I. Deutsch
Smithsonian Institution

Joseph Dewey
University of Pittsburgh-Johnstown

Thomas E. DeWolfe
Hampden-Sydney College

Marcia B. Dinneen
Bridgewater State College

Cecilia Donohue
Madonna University

Natalie Dorfeld
Thiel College

Thomas Du Bose
Louisiana State University at Shreveport

Val Dusek
University of New Hampshire

Wilton Eckley
Colorado School of Mines

K Edgington
Towson University

George R. Ehrhardt
Durham, North Carolina

Howard C. Ellis
Millersville University of Pennsylvania

Robert P. Ellis
Worcester State College

Linda Eikmeier Endersby
Missouri State Museum

Nancy Enright
Seton Hall University

Victoria Erhart
Strayer University

Jill Eshelman
Northeastern University

Mauricio Espinoza-Quesada
Ohio State University

Jack Ewing
Boise, Idaho

Thomas R. Feller
Nashville, Tennessee

Ronald J. Ferrara
Middle Tennessee State University

Susan M. Filler
Chicago, Illinois

Paul Finnicum
Arkansas State University

Gerald P. Fisher
Georgia College and State University

Dale L. Flesher
University of Mississippi

George J. Flynn
SUNY—Plattsburgh

Joseph Francavilla
Columbus State University

Timothy C. Frazer
Western Illinois University

Alan Frazier
University of North Dakota

Jean C. Fulton
Landmark College

Hannah Schauer Galli
University of Hawaii at Manoa

Gary Galván
LaSalle University

Janet E. Gardner
University of Massachusetts at Dartmouth

Karen S. Garvin
American Military University

Brandon Kyle Gauthier
Fordham University

Camille Gibson
Prairie View A&M University

Jay Gilliam
University of Illinois, Springfield

Richard A. Glenn
Millersville University

N. Michael Goecke
The Ohio State University

Sheldon Goldfarb
University of British Columbia

Melissa Ursula Dawn Goldsmith
Nicholls State University

M. Carmen Gomez-Galisteo
Universidad de Alcala

Bonnye Busbice Good
Seymour, Indiana

Nancy M. Gordon
Amherst, Massachusetts

Sidney Gottlieb
Sacred Heart University

William Crawford Green
Morehead State University

Johnpeter Horst Grill
Mississippi State University

Tim Gruenewald
Hong Kong University

Scot M. Guenter
San Jose State University

Larry Haapanen
Lewis-Clark State College

Michael Haas
College of the Canyons

Fusako Hamao
Santa Monica, California

Randall Hannum
New York City College of Technology, CUNY

Patricia King Hanson
American Film Institute

Dennis A. Harp
Texas Tech University

P. Graham Hatcher
Shelton State Community College

Bernadette Zbicki Heiney
Lock Haven University of Pennsylvania

Tammy Heise
Florida State University

L. Daisy Henderson
SUNY at Buffalo

Howard V. Hendrix
California State University, Fresno

Joyce E. Henry
Ursinus College

Mark C. Herman
Edison College

Wendy L. Hicks
Loyola University, New Orleans

Randy Hines
Susquehanna University

Matthew Hoch
Shorter College

Paul Hodge
University of Washington

Aaron D. Horton
University of Arkansas at Little Rock

Shaun Horton
Florida State University

John C. Hughes
Saint Michael's College

Ski Hunter
University of Texas at Arlington

Raymond Pierre Hylton
Virginia Union University

Margaret R. Jackson
Troy University

Carolyn Janik
Eckerd College

Jeffry Jensen
Glendale Community College

Bruce E. Johansen
University of Nebraska at Omaha

Sheila Golburgh Johnson
Santa Barbara, California

Yvonne J. Johnson
St. Louis Community College, Meramec

David M. Jones
University of Wisconsin—Oshkosh

Joseph E. Jones
University of Illinois at Urbana-Champaign

Ramonica R. Jones
Austin, Texas

Susan E. Jones
Palm Beach Atlantic University

Mark S. Joy
Jamestown College

George B. Kauffman
California State University, Fresno

Steven G. Kellman
University of Texas at San Antonio

Lisa Kernek
Western Illinois University

Paul M. Klenowski
Thiel College

Bill Knight
Western Illinois University

Grove Koger
Boise State University

David B. Kopel
Independence Institute

Ludwik Kowalski
Montclair State University

Beth Kraig
Pacific Lutheran

Jeanne L. Kuhler
Auburn University

P. Huston Ladner
University of Mississippi

Wendy Alison Lamb
South Pasadena, California

Timothy Lane
Louisville, Kentucky

Julia del Palacio Langer
Columbia University

Eugene Larson
Los Angeles Pierce College

Jennifer Leigh Lasswell
Indiana University of Pennsylvania

J. Wesley Leckrone
Widener University

Joseph Edward Lee
Winthrop University

Jennie MacDonald Lewis
University of Denver

Leon Lewis
Appalachian State University

Thomas Tandy Lewis
St. Cloud State University

Jing Li
Duquesne University

Roy Liebman
California State University, Los Angeles

Victor Lindsey
East Central University

Ellen Lippert
Thiel College

Alar Lipping
Northern Kentucky University

L. Keith Lloyd
McMurry University

Donald W. Lovejoy
Palm Beach Atlantic University

M. Philip Lucas
Cornell College

Eric v. d. Luft
SUNY Upstate Medical University

Arthur J. Lurigio
Loyola University Chicago

R. C. Lutz
Madison Advisors

Roxanne McDonald
New London, New Hampshire

Thomas McGeary
Champaign, Illinois

James Edward McGoldrick
Greenville Presbyterian Theological Seminary

S. Thomas Mack
University of South Carolina, Aiken

Rachel Maines
Cornell University

Martin J. Manning
U.S. Department of State

Andrew R. Martin
Inver Hills College

James I. Matray
California State University, Chico

Laurence W. Mazzeno
Alvernia College

Joseph A. Melusky
Saint Francis University

Scott A. Merriman
Troy University

Beth A. Messner
Ball State University

Eric W. Metchik
Salem State College

Julia M. Meyers
Duquesne University

Michael R. Meyers
Pfeiffer University

Matthew Mihalka
University of Minnesota, Twin Cities

Steven P. Millies
*University of South Carolina—
Aiken*

Randall L. Milstein
Oregon State University

Christian H. Moe
*Southern Illinois University at
Carbondale*

B. Keith Murphy
Fort Valley State University

Daniel P. Murphy
Hanover College

Alice Myers
Bard College at Simon's Rock

John E. Myers
Bard College at Simon's Rock

Michael V. Namorato
University of Mississippi

Jerome Neapolitan
Tennessee Technological University

Steve Neiheisel
St. Mary's University

Leslie Neilan
*Virginia Polytechnic Institute and State
University*

William Nelles
*University of Massachusetts—
Dartmouth*

Elizabeth M. McGhee Nelson
Christian Brothers University

Caryn E. Neumann
*Miami University of Ohio at
Middletown*

Norma C. Noonan
Augsburg College

Myron C. Noonkester
William Carey University

William E. O'Brien
Florida Atlantic University

William A. Paquette
Tidewater Community College

Robert J. Paradowski
Rochester Institute of Technology

David Peck
Laguna Beach, California

Amanda M. Pence
University of Kansas

Sadie Pendaz
*Century College and Normandale
Community College*

Michael Penkas
Chicago, Illinois

Mark E. Perry
*North Georgia College & State
University*

Barbara Bennett Peterson
University of Hawaii

John R. Phillips
Purdue University Calumet

Allene Phy-Olsen
Austin Peay State University

Bethany E. Pierce
Bridgewater State College

Anastasia Pike
Columbia University Teachers College

Julio César Pino
Kent State University

Troy Place
Western Michigan University

Michael Polley
Columbia College

Mark D. Porcaro
Wichita State University

David L. Porter
William Penn University

Judy Porter
Rochester Institute of Technology

Edmund D. Potter
Mary Baldwin College

Victoria Price
Lamar University

April L. Prince
University of Texas, Austin

Aaron D. Purcell
Virginia Tech

Steven J. Ramold
Eastern Michigan University

Kevin B. Reid
Henderson Community College

H. William Rice
Kennesaw State University

Mark Rich
Cashton, Wisconsin

Betty Richardson
Southern Illinois University at Edwardsville

Robert Ridinger
Northern Illinois University

Gina Robertiello
Felician College

Russell Roberts
Bordentown, New Jersey

O. Nicholas Robertson
SUNY at Buffalo

James L. Robinson
University of Illinois at Urbana-Champaign

April J. Robson
University of Arkansas, Little Rock

Stephen F. Rohde
Rohde & Victoroff

Carol A. Rolf
Rivier College

Carl Rollyson
Baruch College, CUNY

Francine S. Romero
University of Texas at San Antonio

Sandra Rothenberg
Framingham State College

Robert Rubinson
University of Baltimore School of Law

Joseph R. Rudolph, Jr.
Towson University

Richard J. Rundell
New Mexico State University

Virginia L. Salmon
Northeast State Community College

Daniel Sauerwein
University of North Dakota

Kurt M. Saunders
California State University, Northridge

Timothy Sawicki
Canisius College

Edward J. Schauer
Prairie View A&M University

Lisa Scoggin
Saint Anselm College

Shawn Selby
Kent State University, Stark

Chrissa Shamberger
Ohio State University

Emily Carroll Shearer
Eastern Kentucky University

Jennifer Hardiman Shearer
Winchester, Kentucky

Chenliang Sheng
Northern Kentucky University

Martha A. Sherwood
Eugene, Oregon

R. Baird Shuman
University of Illinois at Urbana-Champaign

Julia A. Sienkewicz
Smithsonian American Art Museum

Charles L. P. Silet
Iowa State University

Donald C. Simmons, Jr.
Dakota Wesleyan University

William M. Simons
SUNY, College at Oneonta

Richard Simonton
Simonton Film & Radio

Paul P. Sipiera
William Rainey Harper College

Amy Sisson
Houston Community College

Douglas D. Skinner
Texas State University, San Marcos

Billy R. Smith, Jr.
Anne Arundel Community College

Roger Smith
Portland, Oregon

Tom Smith
New Mexico State University

Joanna R. Smolko
University of Pittsburgh

Christy Jo Snider
Berry College

Sonia Sorrell
Pepperdine University

Joseph L. Spradley
Wheaton College

Brian Stableford
Reading, United Kingdom

Mark Stanbrough
Emporia State University

James Stanlaw
Illinois State University

Jennifer Stephenson
Longview Community College

Robert E. Stoffels
St. Petersburg, Florida

Theresa L. Stowell
Adrian College

Eric S. Strother
University of Kentucky

Cynthia J. W. Svoboda
Bridgewater State College

Patricia E. Sweeney
Shelton, Connecticut

Peter Swirski
University of Hong Kong

James Tackach
Roger Williams University

Charlotte Templin
University of Indianapolis

Joanna L. Thaler
University of Texas at Austin

John M. Theilmann
Converse College

Monica G. Tibbits
TransitWorks

Kelly Amanda Train
Ryerson University

Anh Tran
Wichita State University

Paul B. Trescott
Southern Illinois University

Monica Tripp-Roberson
Anne Arundel Community College

Richard Tuerk
Texas A&M University-Commerce

Dwight Vick
West Texas A&M University

Charles L. Vigue
University of New Haven

Brenda Vose
University of North Florida

William T. Walker
Chestnut Hill College

Spencer Weber Waller
Loyola University Chicago School of Law

Mary C. Ware
SUNY, College at Cortland

Megan E. Watson
Duke University

Shawncey Webb
Taylor University

Thomas A. Wikle
Oklahoma State University

Fay V. Williams
Prairie View A&M University

LaVerne McQuiller Williams
Rochester Institute of Technology

Tyrone Williams
Xavier University

Bradley R. A. Wilson
University of Cincinnati

Jan Doolittle Wilson
University of Tulsa

Nathan Wilson
University of Tulsa

Maureen Moffitt Wilt
University of Central Missouri

Gregg Wirth
Bloomsburg, Pennsylvania

Scott Wright
University of St. Thomas

Scott D. Yarbrough
Charleston Southern University

Cynthia Gwynne Yaudes
Indiana University, Bloomington

Tung Yin
Lewis & Clark Law School

William Young
University of North Dakota

■ Complete List of Contents

Volume I

Contents. v
Publisher's Note ix
Contributors xiii
Complete List of Contents xxi

Academy Awards 1
Adams, Ansel 4
Addams, Jane 5
Adler Planetarium 6
Adventures of Robin Hood, The 6
Advertising in Canada 7
Advertising in the United
    States. 8
African Americans. 12
Agricultural Adjustment Acts . . . 17
Agriculture in Canada. 18
Agriculture in the United
    States 20
Aid to Dependent Children. . . . 24
Air mail route scandal. 25
Air pollution 26
Airships 27
Akron disaster 29
Alcatraz Federal Penitentiary . . . 30
Alcoholics Anonymous 32
All Quiet on the Western Front 33
American Federation of
    Labor 34
American Gothic. 35
American Liberty League 36
Amos 'n' Andy. 37
Anderson, Marian 39
Anti-Racketeering Act of
    1934. 41
Anti-Semitism 42
Apple Mary 43
Archaeology 44
Archambault Report 46
Architecture 47
Armstrong, Edwin H. 50
Armstrong, Louis 51
Art movements 52
Asia. 54
Asian Americans. 56
Astaire, Fred 59
Astor, Mary. 60
Astronomy 61
Atherton Report. 64

Auto racing 65
Automobiles and auto
    manufacturing 66
Aviation and aeronautics 70
Awake and Sing! 73

Bank holiday. 75
Bank of United States
    failure. 75
Banking 77
Banking Act of 1935. 79
Barker Gang 80
Barrow, Clyde, and Bonnie
    Parker. 82
Baseball 83
Basie, Count 87
Basketball 88
Bathysphere 90
Beard, Charles A. 90
Beatty, Clyde 92
Bennett, Richard Bedford . . . 92
Benny, Jack. 95
Benton, Thomas Hart. 96
Berkeley, Busby 97
Bethune, Mary McLeod. 98
Bingo. 99
Birth control 100
Black, Hugo L.. 102
Black Empire. 104
Black hole theory 105
Black Monday 106
Black No More 107
Blondie comic strip 107
Blondie films 108
Blood banks 110
Bonus Army March 111
Book publishing 112
Boulder Dam 115
Boxing 117
Braddock, James J. 120
Brains Trust 121
Brandeis, Louis D. 122
Breadlines and soup
    kitchens 123
Breedlove v. Suttles 125
Bringing Up Baby 125
Broadway musicals 127
Brown v. Mississippi 129

Brownlee, John Edward 130
Buck, Pearl S.. 131
Budge, Don. 133
Business and the economy in
    Canada 134
Business and the economy in
    the United States 136
Butler, Smedley. 139
Byrd, Richard. 140

Cagney, James 142
Calder, Alexander 143
Caldwell, Erskine. 145
Canada, U.S. investments in . . . 146
Canada and Great Britain 148
Canadian minority
    communities 151
Canadian regionalism 153
Cancer 155
Capone, Al 157
Capra, Frank 160
Car radios. 161
Carter family 162
Carter v. Carter Coal Co.. 164
Chaplin, Charles 164
Charlie Chan films 166
Chemistry. 168
Chicago World's Fair. 171
Children's Hour, The. 173
Christie Pits riot 173
Chrysler Building 174
City Lights. 175
Civil rights and liberties in
    Canada 176
Civil rights and liberties in
    the United States 178
Civilian Conservation Corps. . . 181
Cleveland "torso" murders. . . . 182
Cohan, George M. 183
Coinage. 184
Collier, John 185
Comic strips 187
Commodity Credit
    Corporation. 189
Communism 189
Congress, U.S. 192
Congress of Industrial
    Organizations. 196

Consumers Union of the
United States 197
Contract bridge 198
Corrigan's wrong-way flight . . . 199
Coughlin, Charles E.. 199
Crane, Hart. 202
Crater disappearance 203
Credit and debt 204
Crimes and scandals 207
Curry, John Steuart 210
Curtis, Charles 211
Cyclotron 212

Dance. 215
Davis, Bette 217
Day, Dorothy 218
Day of the Locust, The 219
DC-3. 220
Dean, Dizzy. 220
De Jonge v. Oregon 221
Demographics of Canada 222
Demographics of the United
States 226
Design for Living. 229
Destry Rides Again 230
Dewey, John 232
Diary of a Country Priest, The . . . 233
Dick Tracy 234
Dillinger, John 235
Dionne quintuplets 236
Dorsey, Tommy. 238
Dracula 239
Drive-in theaters 240
Dubinsky, David 241
Du Bois, W. E. B. 242
Dust Bowl. 243
Dutch elm disease 247

Earhart, Amelia 249
Ecstasy. 251
Education. 252
Einstein, Albert. 256
Elections, Canadian 258
Elections of 1930, 1934, and
1938, U.S. 261
Elections of 1932, U.S. 264
Elections of 1936, U.S. 267
Electric razors 269
Electron microscope. 270
Elixir sulfanilamide scandal . . . 271
Ellington, Duke 272

Empire State Building 274
Erie Railroad Co. v. Tompkins . . . 276
Europe 276
Evian Conference 280
Export-Import Bank of the
United States 281

Fads. 282
Fair Labor Standards Act of
1938 285
Fallingwater house 286
Farmer-Labor Party of
Minnesota. 287
Farmers' organizations 288
Farnsworth, Philo T. 289
Fascism in Canada 291
Fascism in the United
States 292
Fashions and clothing 295
Father Divine 298
Faulkner, William 300
Federal Communications
Commission. 302
Federal Emergency Relief
Administration 304
Federal Food, Drug, and
Cosmetic Act of 1938 305
Federal Housing
Administration 306
Federal National Mortgage
Association 308
Federal Power Commission . . . 309
Federal Reserve Board. 310
Federal Theatre Project 311
Federal Trade
Commission. 315
Federal Writers' Project 316
Fetchit, Stepin 317
Fibber McGee and Molly 318
Field Guide to the Birds. 319
Fields, W. C. 319
Film. 321
Film serials 324
Fireside chats. 326
Fitzgerald, Ella 328
Fitzgerald, F. Scott 329
Flash Gordon. 330
Fleming, Victor. 331
Flint sit-down strike 332
Floyd, Pretty Boy 333
Fluorescent lighting 334

Food processing 335
Food stamps 337
Football. 339
Ford, Henry 342
Ford, John 343
Ford Foundation. 344
Foreign Agents Registration
Act of 1938 345
Foreign policy of Canada 346
Foreign policy of the United
States 348
Fortune magazine 352
Forty-second Street 353
Four Horsemen vs. Three
Musketeers 355
Foxx, Jimmie 356
Frankenstein films 357
Freaks 360
Freon 360
Frost, Robert 361
Frozen-food marketing 363
Functions of the Executive, The. . . 364
Fundamentalist-Modernist
conflict 365

Gable, Clark 368
Gambling. 369
Gangster films 370
Garbo, Greta 372
Garner, John Nance 373
Gehrig, Lou 375
General Theory of Employment,
Interest and Money, The 377
Geneva Disarmament
Conference 378
George VI's North American
visit 379
George Washington Bridge . . . 381
German-American Bund. 382
Germany and U.S.
appeasement 384
Gershwin, George 386
Glass-Steagall Act of 1933 387
"God Bless America" 388
Goddard, Robert H. 389
Gold Clause Cases 390
Gold Reserve Act of 1934 390
Golf 391
Gone with the Wind 393
Good Earth, The 395
Good Neighbor Policy 395

Volume II

Contents xxxiii
Complete List of
    Contents xxxvii

Goodman, Benny 397
Graham, Martha 398
Grand Coulee Dam 399
Grand Hotel 400
Grapes of Wrath, The. 401
Graves v. New York ex rel.
    O'Keefe 403
Great Depression in
    Canada 404
Great Depression in the
    United States 408
Great New England
    hurricane 413
Green Pastures, The 414
Greenfield Village 416
Gropius House 416
Grosjean v. American
    Press Co. 417
Gross national product 418
Group Theatre 421
Grovey v. Townsend 422
Gunther, John 422
Guthrie, Woody 423

Hague v. Congress of Industrial
    Organizations 425
Hairstyles 425
Haiti occupation 427
Hammett, Dashiell 428
"Happy Days Are Here
    Again" 429
Harlem on the Prairie 430
Harlem Renaissance 431
Harlow, Jean 433
Hatch Act 434
Hawk's Nest Tunnel disaster . . . 435
Hawley-Smoot Tariff Act of
    1930 436
Health care 437
Hearing aids 441
Heart-lung machine 441
Heat wave of 1931 442
Hell's Angels 443
Hellman, Lillian 445
Hellzapoppin' 446
Hemingway, Ernest 447
Hepburn, Katharine 448

Hindenburg disaster 449
Hobbies 451
Holiday, Billie 454
Home Building and Loan
    Association v. Blaisdell 456
Home furnishings 457
Homelessness 460
Homosexuality and gay
    rights 462
Hoover, Herbert 463
Hoovervilles 466
Horror films 468
Horse racing 469
House Committee on Un-
    American Activities 471
Housing in Canada 473
Housing in the United
    States 475
How to Win Friends and
    Influence People 478
Hughes, Charles Evans 479
Hughes, Howard 481
Hull, Cordell 482
Humphrey's Executor v. United
    States 483
Hutton, Barbara 484

I AM movement 486
Ice hockey 487
Ickes, Harold 489
I'd Rather Be Right 491
Imitation of Life 491
Immigration to Canada 493
Immigration to the United
    States 495
Income and wages in
    Canada 500
Income and wages in the
    United States 502
Indian Reorganization Act . . . 505
Inflation 507
Informer, The 509
Instant coffee 510
Insull Utilities Trusts
    collapse 511
Inter-American Conference
    for the Maintenance of
    Peace 512
International trade 513
Inventions 516
Invisible Man, The 519

Isolationism 520
It Happened One Night 522

Japanese American Citizens
    League 524
Japanese military
    aggression 524
Jews in Canada 526
Jews in the United States 527
Jim Crow segregation 529
John Muir Trail 530
Johnson, Robert 531
Johnson v. Zerbst 532
Joliet prison riot 533
Joy of Cooking, The 533

Karloff, Boris 535
Kaufman, George S., and
    Moss Hart 536
Kelly, Machine Gun 537
King, William Lyon
    Mackenzie 538
King Kong 541

Labor Day hurricane 544
Labor strikes 545
La Guardia, Fiorello Henry . . . 549
Landon, Alf 550
Lange, Dorothea 551
Last Mile, The 553
Latin America and the
    Caribbean 553
Latinos 556
Laurel and Hardy 559
Leadbelly 561
League of Nations 563
Lee, Gypsy Rose 564
Let Us Now Praise Famous
    Men 566
Lewis, John L. 566
Lewis, Sinclair 567
Life Begins at Forty 568
Life magazine 569
L'il Abner 570
Lincoln Continental Mark I . . . 571
Lindbergh, Anne Morrow 572
Lindbergh baby kidnapping . . . 573
Literature in Canada 574
Literature in the United
    States 578
Little Caesar 582

Little Orphan Annie 583
Lobotomy 584
London Economic
    Conference 585
London Naval Treaty 586
Long, Huey 587
Long Beach earthquake 590
Look magazine 591
Louis, Joe 591
Lovell v. City of Griffin 593
Luce, Henry 594
Luciano, Lucky 594
Ludlow amendment 596
Lynching 596

MacArthur, Douglas 599
McDaniel, Hattie 600
MacLeish, Archibald 601
Magazines 603
Man Who Came to Dinner,
    The 605
Manchuria occupation 606
Marathon dancing 607
Marble, Alice 608
March of Dimes 609
Marihuana Tax Act of 1937 . . . 610
Marquand, John P. 611
Marx Brothers 613
Massie trial 615
Medicine 616
Memorial Day Massacre 618
Mencken, H. L. 619
Merry Widow, The 620
Mexico 621
Micheaux, Oscar 624
Mickey Mouse 626
Migrations, domestic 627
Migratory Bird Hunting and
    Conservation Stamp Act
    of 1934 631
Miller, Glenn 631
Missouri ex rel. Gaines v.
    Canada 632
Modern Corporation and Private
    Property, The 633
Modern Times 634
Monopoly 636
Moody, Helen Wills 637
Morgenthau, Henry T., Jr. 638
Morro Castle disaster 639
Motion Picture Production
    Code 639
Mount Rushmore National
    Memorial 641

Mr. Deeds Goes to Town 642
Mr. Moto films 643
Mr. Smith Goes to Washington . . . 644
Muni, Paul 645
Music: Classical 646
Music: Jazz 650
Music: Popular 654
Mutiny on the Bounty 657
Muzak 658

Nancy Drew novels 659
Nation of Islam 660
National Association for the
    Advancement of Colored
    People 662
National Association of
    Manufacturers 665
National Baseball Hall of
    Fame 666
National Council of Negro
    Women 667
National debt 668
National Film Act of 1939
    (Canada) 669
National Firearms Act of
    1934 670
National Industrial Recovery
    Act of 1933 670
National Labor Relations Act
    of 1935 672
National Labor Relations Board v.
    Jones and Laughlin Steel
    Corp. 674
National Negro Congress 675
National parks 676
National Recovery
    Administration 679
National Wildlife
    Federation 681
National Youth
    Administration 682
Native Americans 683
Natural disasters 687
Natural Gas Act of 1938 689
Natural resources 690
Naval forces 692
Near v. Minnesota 695
Nebbia v. New York 696
Nebraska unicameral
    legislature 697
Negro Leagues 697
Ness, Eliot 700
Neutrality Acts 701
Neutron star theory 704

New Deal 705
New State Ice Co. v. Liebmann . . . 709
New York World's Fair 710
Newspapers, Canadian 712
Newspapers, U.S. 713
Nitti, Frank 716
Nixon v. Condon 718
Nobel Prizes 719
Nonpartisan League 723
Norris-La Guardia Act of
    1932 724
Northrop, John Howard 725
Nuclear fission 726
Nye Committee 728
Nylon 729

Odets, Clifford 732
Ohio Penitentiary fire 733
Ohio River flood 734
Oklahoma Welfare Act of
    1936 735
Olympic Games of 1932
    (Summer) 736
Olympic Games of 1932
    (Winter) 738
Olympic Games of 1936
    (Summer) 740
Olympic Games of 1936
    (Winter) 742
100,000,000 Guinea Pigs 744
O'Neill, Eugene 746
Organized crime 748
Ott, Mel 751
Ottawa Agreements 752
Our Town 753
Owens, Jesse 754

Palko v. Connecticut 757
Panama Refining Co. v. Ryan . . . 757
Panay incident 759
Parking meters 760
Patterns of Culture 760
Pauling, Linus 762
Peace movement 763
Pearson, Drew 765
Pendergast, Thomas Joseph . . . 766
People's Forests, The 768
Perkins, Frances 768
Petrified Forest, The 770
Philippine Independence Act
    of 1934 771
Philippine Islands 772
Philosophy and
    philosophers 775

Photography 778
Physics 781
Pittman-Robertson Act of
    1937 784

Pluto discovery 785
Polio 786
Porgy and Bess 787
Pornography 788

Positron discovery 790
Post, Wiley 790
Postage stamps 792
Prohibition repeal 793

Volume III

Contents xlix
Complete List of Contents liii

Psychology and psychiatry 797
Public Utilities Act 800
Purge of 1938 800

Quarantine speech 802

Race riots 804
Racial discrimination 805
Radar, invention of 809
Radio astronomy 810
Radio in Canada 811
Radio in the United States 814
Radio trust 818
Rand, Sally 819
Ranger, USS 820
Rayburn, Sam 820
Recession of 1937-1938 821
Reciprocal Trade Agreements
    Act of 1936 823
Reconstruction Finance
    Corporation 824
Recording industry 825
Recreation 827
Refrigerators 830
Religion in Canada 831
Religion in the United
    States 835
Reorganization Act of 1939 . . . 838
Resettlement
    Administration 840
Reuther, Walter P. 841
Revenue Acts 842
Rice, Elmer 844
Richter scale 846
Riggs, Bobby 847
Roberts, Owen J. 848
Robeson, Paul 849
Robinson, Edward G. 851
Robinson, Joseph Taylor 852
Robinson-Patman Act of
    1936 853
Rockefeller Center 853

Rockefeller Center Rivera
    mural 855
Rocketry 855
Rogers, Will 857
Rooney, Mickey 858
Roosevelt, Eleanor 859
Roosevelt, Franklin D. 860
Roosevelt assassination
    attempt 863
Roosevelt's court-packing
    plan 864
Roosevelt's first one hundred
    days 866
Rural Electrification
    Administration 867
Ruth, Babe 868

St. Lawrence Seaway Treaty . . . 870
St. Louis incident 870
San Francisco Bay bridges 871
Sarazen, Gene 873
*Schechter Poultry Corp. v. United
    States* 873
Schultz, Dutch 875
Schuyler, George S. 876
Science fiction 877
Scottsboro trials 879
Screwball comedy 882
Seabiscuit 884
Securities and Exchange
    Commission 885
Serenade 886
Sex and sex education 887
Sexually transmitted
    diseases 890
Shaw, Artie 892
Sherwood, Robert E. 892
Shore, Eddie 893
Simpson, Wallis 894
Since Yesterday 896
Sinclair, Upton 897
Smith, Alfred E. 899
Smith, Bessie 900
*Snow White and the Seven
    Dwarfs* 901

Soap operas 902
Soccer 904
Social Security Act of 1935 905
Socialist parties 908
Soil Conservation Service 909
Sons of the Pioneers 910
Soviet Union 911
Spanish Civil War 913
Sparling, Gordon 916
Sports in Canada 917
Sports in the United States . . . 920
Squalus sinking 923
Stagecoach 924
"Star-Spangled Banner" 925
Statute of Westminster 926
Steinbeck, John 927
Stimson, Henry L. 929
Story of Philosophy, The 930
Stromberg v. California 931
Studs Lonigan trilogy 932
Supermarkets 933
Supreme Court, U.S. 935

Tarzan films 939
Taylor Grazing Act of 1934 . . . 940
Telephone technology and
    service 941
Television technology 944
Temple, Shirley 945
Tennessee Valley Authority . . . 947
Tennis 949
Texas school explosion 951
Thalberg, Irving 953
Theater in Canada 954
Theater in the United
    States 956
Thin Man, The 960
Thomas, Norman 961
Thousand Islands Bridge 962
Tilden, Bill 963
Timberline Lodge 964
Tobacco Road 964
Todd, Thelma 965
Top Hat 966
Townsend Plan 967

Tracy, Spencer 968
Trail Smelter dispute. 969
Trans World Airlines 970
Transportation 971
Travel 974
Triborough Bridge 977
Twentieth Amendment 978
Typhus immunization 980

Ultramares Corporation v.
    Touche 982
Ulysses trial 982
Unemployment in Canada . . . 983
Unemployment in the United
    States 985
Unionism 989
United States v. Butler 992
United States v. Carolene
    Products Co. 993
United States v. Curtiss-Wright
    Export Corp. 994
Urbanization in Canada 995
Urbanization in the United
    States 997
U.S.A. trilogy 1000

Vanderbilt custody trial 1002
Vander Meer, Johnny 1004
Vending machines 1004
Veterans Administration 1006
Voting rights 1007

Wagner, Robert F. 1011
Wagner-Steagall Housing Act
    of 1937 1012

Walker, James J. 1013
Wallace, Henry A. 1013
War of the Worlds, The radio
    broadcast 1014
Weissmuller, Johnny 1016
West, Mae 1017
West, Nathanael 1018
West Coast Hotel Co. v.
    Parrish 1019
Western films 1020
Wheeler-Lea Act of 1938 1022
Whitney Museum of
    American Art 1023
Wilder, Laura Ingalls 1024
Wilderness Society 1025
Winter War 1026
Wizard of Oz, The 1027
Wolfe, Thomas 1029
Wood, Grant 1030
Works Progress
    Administration 1032
World War I debts 1035
World War II and Canada . . . 1036
World War II and the United
    States 1039
Wray, Fay 1042
Wright, Frank Lloyd 1044

Xerography 1046

Yearling, The 1047
You Can't Take It with You 1047
Young Mr. Lincoln 1049

Zangara, Giuseppe 1050

Appendixes
Drama: Major Broadway
    Plays and Awards 1053
Entertainment: Academy
    Awards for Films 1057
Entertainment: Major Films
    of the 1930's 1060
Entertainment: Major Radio
    Programs 1068
Legislation: Major U.S.
    Legislation 1078
Legislation: Major U.S.
    Supreme Court
    Decisions 1084
Literature: Best-Selling Books
    in the United States 1089
Literature: Major Literary
    Awards 1092
Music: Popular Musicians . . . 1095
Music: Top-Selling U.S.
    Recordings 1101
Sports: Winners of Major
    Events 1105
Time Line 1113
Bibliography 1125
Glossary 1140
List of Entries by Category . . . 1144

Indexes
Photo Index 1159
Personage Index 1163
Subject Index 1173

The Thirties
in America

A

■ Academy Awards

Definition   Awards by the Academy of Motion Picture Arts and Sciences

The Academy Awards (also known as the Oscars) are given by film professionals who are academy members to acknowledge achievement in various categories (such as best actor and best director) of technical and creative fields in the business. In addition, the awards tend generally to reflect popular taste in the films; receiving an Oscar usually increases a film's exposure and its box-office take.

The first Academy Awards were held in 1928. During the 1930's, they underwent modifications, which included the expansion of categories. By the end of the decade, the awards had more or less the same format as they did at the start of the twenty-first century. The biggest expansion during the 1930's was implemented to accommodate the emergence of sound in film in the late 1920's. At first, Hollywood traditionalists thought sound in film was a fad. However, most in the industry soon realized that sound was going to transform the medium. Dialogue in screenplays became more important as actors began to talk. Scores and individual song categories were added to the awards, and sound was included in the special-effects category. The addition of Special Oscars and the Irving G. Thalberg Memorial Award provided recognition not directly associated with specific films. During the 1930's, the Academy Awards became an integral part of the motion-picture business.

The Pre-1930's Academy   The 1928 Academy Awards had eleven categories, with the best film divided into two: best production and best artistic quality of production; there was a separate category for best comedy direction. The ceremony gave an honorary Oscar to the first sound film, *The Jazz Singer* (1927),

which was not allowed to compete with the silent films. Charles Chaplin also received an award for writing, acting, directing, and producing *The Circus* (1928). In 1929, the artistic quality of production, comedy direction, title writing, and engineering effects awards were discarded, and the sound recording award was added the following year. By 1930, the basic categories had been established: best production (later best picture), best direction, best actor,

Claudette Colbert (right) accepts the 1935 Academy Award for best actress for her role in It Happened One Night *from child star Shirley Temple.* (Hulton Archive/Getty Images)

Best Picture Awards, 1930-1939

The 1930's winners of the most coveted of the Academy's awards, "Best Picture" (known as "Best Production" until 1931) are listed below.

Year	Film	Production Company (Producer)
1930	*All Quiet on the Western Front*	Universal (Carl Laemmle, Jr.)
1931	*Cimarron*	RKO Radio (William LeBaron)
1932	*Grand Hotel*	Metro-Goldwyn-Mayer (Irving Thalberg)
1933	*Cavalcade*	Fox (Winfield Sheehan)
1934	*It Happened One Night*	Columbia (Harry Cohn)
1935	*Mutiny on the Bounty*	Metro-Goldwyn-Mayer (Thalberg with Albert Lewin)
1936	*The Great Ziegfeld*	Metro-Goldwyn-Mayer (Hunt Stromberg)
1937	*The Life of Emile Zola*	Warner Bros. (Henry Blanke)
1938	*You Can't Take It with You*	Columbia (Frank Capra)
1939	*Gone with the Wind*	Selznick International Pictures, Metro-Goldwyn-Mayer (David O. Selznick)

best actress, best cinematography, best writing, best art direction, and best sound.

The Early 1930's Academy In 1931, the Academy Awards had five nominations in four categories: best picture, best director, best actor, and best actress. Listings for best supporting actor and actress did not yet exist. The best screenplay award was divided into original and adapted screenplays. Best cinematography, best art direction, and best sound completed the categories. In 1932, categories in three short subjects (cartoon, comedy, and novelty) were added, and best cinematography was restricted to films shot in the United States. In the following year, the same restriction was placed on the category of art direction.

Longtime studio actors such as Lionel Barrymore, Fredric March, Adolphe Menjou, Marlene Dietrich, Irene Dunne, and Marie Dressler, many of whom had been associated with silent films, were nominated in 1930; Dressler and March were also nominated the following year. Katharine Hepburn won her first award in 1933. Not until that year did the newest batch of directors, such as George Cukor, Frank Capra, and W. S. Van Dyke—all of whom helped shape sound films—began to receive academy recognition.

The Mid-1930's Academy In 1934, categories were added for best editing, best song, and best score, and directors became ineligible for the writing awards. The following year, the best dance direction category was included. In the same year, *It Happened One Night* won best picture, best director, best screenplay, best actor, and best actress, representing the first time one film won all the major awards. In 1935, Metro-Goldwyn-Mayer (MGM) launched the first studio campaign, lobbying for *Ah, Wilderness!* The number of best picture nominations continued to vary throughout the decade, but by 1936, five candidates became the standard in the other major categories. Shirley Temple won an Honorary Oscar in 1934, and silent-film director D. W. Griffith received one in 1935.

Clark Gable and Claudette Colbert received the 1934 awards for best actor and best actress for their roles in *It Happened One Night*. The two were nominated in 1935 also, along with Charles Laughton, Merle Oberon, Hepburn, and Bette Davis, who won the best actress Oscar. In 1936, Gary Cooper, Spencer Tracy, William Powell, and Paul Muni earned best actor nominations, while Irene Dunne, Carole Lombard, and Norma Shearer earned nominations for best actress. By the middle of the decade the stars who dominated the awards for the following two decades had emerged. Prominent directors emerged as well: Capra won for best director in 1934 for *It Happened One Night* and in 1936 for *Mr. Deeds Goes to Washington*; John Ford won in 1935 for *The Informer.*

The Late 1930's Academy In 1936, the categories of best supporting actor and actress first appeared, and picture, acting, editing, and writing Oscars were opened to all English-language films. The Irving G. Thalberg Memorial Award, given for humanitarian work, was created in 1937 to commemorate MGM's head of production, who died at the age of thirty-six. Directors were again allowed to compete for writing awards, and the academy changed the rules for nominating and voting. In 1938, the best score and best original score replaced the best score award, and awards for assistant director and dance direction were eliminated. In 1939, the academy added the best special effects award; directors were allowed only one nomination; and, in recognition of changing film technology, the best cinematography award split into black-and-white and color categories.

Many of the usual actors were nominated for awards in the later years of the 1930's. Luise Rainer won consecutive Oscars and made her last appearance in 1937. March, Muni, Tracy, Dunne, Greta Garbo, and newcomer Barbara Stanwyck all appeared the same year. In 1938, Tracy won for the second year, Davis won another, and Shearer was nominated again. James Stewart, Greer Garson, and Vivien Leigh earned nominations in 1939. As in previous years, the acting nominations followed along studio lines. William Wellman, Michael Curtiz, King Vidor, and William Wyler, as well as Ford and Capra, were nominated by the end of the decade.

In 1938, at which time the best foreign film category did not exist, Jean Renoir's *Grand Illusion* became the first foreign-language film to be nominated for best picture. In 1939, a remarkable number of important films were released. The academy honored several of them: *Dark Victory*; *Goodbye, Mr. Chips*; *Mr. Smith Goes to Washington*; *Ninotchka*; *Stagecoach*; *The Wizard of Oz*; *Wuthering Heights*; and *Gone with the Wind*, which won ten awards, including best picture, a special Oscar for color art direction, and the Thalberg for David O. Selznick. Hattie McDaniel became the first African American nominated and the first to even attend the ceremonies. Also, because the *Los Angeles Times* published a list of the winners before the awards dinner, for future cer-

emonies, the academy decided to hire the accounting firm of Price Waterhouse to tabulate the results and keep them secret until the ceremonies.

Impact During the 1930's, the Academy of Motion Picture Arts and Sciences became a force in the film industry, providing publicity for and cachet to Hollywood films. At the beginning of the decade the ceremonies were held in an intimate dinner club setting and paid homage to silent-film stars and technicians; however, by the end of the decade the ceremonies had expanded to include exposure to the wider moviegoing public. The awards began to emphasize the quality in films, which helped Americans view filmmaking as an art form and not mere entertainment.

During the 1930's, the academy did not generally reward socially progressive films; in fact, Hollywood did not produce many. Although many of the writers, directors, actors, and technicians were progressive, the studio executives were not. The few films with leftist leanings tended not to get much attention from the academy.

Charles L. P. Silet

Further Reading

Harkness, John. *The Academy Awards Handbook: Winners and Losers from 1927 to Today!* New York: Pinnacle Books, 1999. Handy listing of the nominees and winners by year.

Levy, Emanuel. *All About Oscar: The History and Politics of the Academy Awards.* New York: Continuum, 2003. Examination of what happened behind the glitz of the awards.

Matthews, Charles. *Oscar A to Z: A Complete Guide to More than Twenty-four Hundred Movies Nominated for Academy Awards.* New York: Doubleday, 1995. Listing of the film, studio, and individual nominees and winners by category.

Osborn, Robert. *Seventy Years of the Oscars: The Official History of the Academy Awards.* New York: Abbeville Press, 1999. Authoritative history of the Oscars written by one of Hollywood's insiders.

Pickard, Roy. *The Oscar Movies.* New York: Facts On File, 1994. A comprehensive look at the films that have won or been considered for the Oscar.

See also Capra, Frank; Chaplin, Charles; Davis, Bette; Film; Ford, John; Garbo, Greta; *Gone with the Wind*; Hepburn, Katharine; McDaniel, Hattie; *Wizard of Oz, The*.

Act to Prevent Pernicious Political Activities.
See **Hatch Act**

■ Adams, Ansel

Identification American photographer and
  environmentalist
Born February 20, 1902; San Francisco, California
Died April 22, 1984; Carmel, California

Adams was one of the most respected technical photographers of the 1930's, publishing many manuals and developing the "zone system" of photography. In addition, he advanced the cause of environmentalists by presenting the beauty of national parks such as Yosemite through his photography and speaking engagements.

During the 1930's, Ansel Adams became a major figure in both photography and environmentalism. As a young man, he was not successful in school and pursued music before developing an interest in photography. He loved Yosemite National Park and spent time there nearly every year of his life from 1916 to his death.

Adams worked for the Sierra Club during his youth and began to publish his photographs in its publications. His connection with the Sierra Club both helped him realize that he could support himself via photography and nurtured his environmental interests.

Adams was a great collaborator, working with Mary Austin to produce "Taos Pueblo" in 1930. He sought out the experts in photography and worked, wrote, and shared ideas with them, advancing his view of "straight," or unmanipulated, photography and his passion for the landscapes of the West.

Adams found a benefactor in Albert M. Bender, whose support and encouragement allowed him to work full time as a photographer. In 1932, Adams and Edward Weston formed Group f/64, which supported a West Coast view of photography.

In 1933, Adams met Alfred Stieglitz on his first visit to New York, and their correspondence inspired both of them. During the 1930's, Adams spent a great deal of time in New York, and his connection with Stieglitz was important for his success at that time. Also in 1933, he had his first New York exhibition, at the Delphic Gallery. His first technical articles were published in 1934, and his first book, *Making a Photograph*, which received major recogni-

tion, was published in 1935. In 1936, Stieglitz gave Adams a one-man show at An American Place.

The Great Depression affected Adams despite his success. He wrote to many of his colleagues and friends that the pressure to make enough money to live forced him to do "commercial" photography instead of the art that he loved. He managed to balance the two competing pressures and was eventually successful both commercially and artistically. He struggled financially during the 1930's, however.

Adams played an important role in the establishment of the first museum department of photography at the Museum of Modern Art in New York. He continued to support environmentalism and photography as art throughout the rest of his life. He also was a sought-after speaker on photographic issues, the West, and environmental causes.

His technical photographic expertise helped him become a major photographic consultant to camera companies such as Polaroid and Hasselblad. He wrote ten volumes of technical manuals on photography, which many consider among the most influential books written on this subject.

Eventually, Adams's photographs became a symbol of the American national parks, the Sierra Club, and nature photography in general. His black-and-white photographs expressed "wilderness" in their composition. Some have said that his photographs were even more powerful than the real objects that he photographed.

Impact Adams was a well-loved photographer, but he was also an activist, working for the preservation of wilderness spaces. He was the author of many books of photographs, technical manuals for photographers, and treatises on the environment.

Mary C. Ware

Further Reading
Adams, Ansel, and James Alinder. *Classic Images*. Ansel Adams, 1986.
Adams, Ansel, and Mary S. Alinder. *Ansel Adams: An Autobiography*. Boston: Little, Brown, 1984.
Adams, Ansel, and Andrea Gray Stillman. *Ansel Adams: Four Hundred Photographs*. Boston: Little, Brown, 2007.
Newhall, Nancy. *Ansel Adams: The Eloquent Light*. Rev. ed. New York: Aperture Foundation, 1980.

See also John Muir Trail; National parks; Photography; Wilderness Society.

■ Addams, Jane

Identification   American social reformer and
  pacifist
Born   September 6, 1860; Cedarville, Illinois
Died   May 21, 1935; Chicago, Illinois

*Addams started the Settlement House movement in the
United States. She and Ellen Gates Starr founded Hull
House in Chicago in 1889. A tireless worker on behalf of
world peace, Addams was the first woman in the United
States to receive the Nobel Peace Prize.*

Jane Addams was the leader of the Settlement House
movement and was elected the first head of the National Federation of Settlements in 1911, a position
she held until her death in 1935. In 1929, she and
her friends and coworkers celebrated the fortieth
anniversary of the founding of Hull House, a center
designed to assist Chicago's working class, many
members of which were European immigrants. In the same year, she was elected
president for life of the Women's International League for Peace and Freedom;
she had served as the founding president
since 1919. In 1930, at the age of seventy,
she published her eleventh book, *The Second Twenty Years*, a sequel to her famous
Twenty Years at Hull House (1910). The
former book focused on her disappointment in the lack of internationalism and
the restrictions on immigration during
the 1920's in the United States.

In early 1931, Addams was the keynote
speaker at an international peace conference in Washington, D.C. In October of
that year, she returned to the U.S. capital
to present to President Herbert Hoover a
worldwide petition advocating international disarmament. More than 200,000
American women had signed the petition. In November of that year, she and
Nicholas Murray Butler were selected to
receive the Nobel Peace Prize. She was
unable to attend the award ceremony in
Oslo, Norway, because she was hospital-
ized for the removal of a tumor on the
same day that she was to receive the
award. During the next four years,
Addams continued to write articles and
make speeches, and she began her last

book, a partially completed manuscript entitled *My
Friend Julia Lathrop* (1935). She died of cancer on
May 21, 1935, and her funeral was held in the court-
yard of Hull House.

Impact   Although Addams was the target of criticism for her pacifist views and activities, she remained a steadfast supporter of international peace
organizations. Her writings and speeches undoubtedly influenced the structure of the United Nations.

Yvonne J. Johnson

Further Reading

Davis, Allen F. *American Heroine: The Life and Legend of
  Jane Addams*. Chicago: Ivan R. Dee, 2000.
Linn, James Weber. *Jane Addams: A Biography*. Chi-
  cago: University of Illinois Press, 2000.

See also   Nobel Prizes; Peace movement; Philosophy and philosophers.

Jane Addams. (Library of Congress)

■ Adler Planetarium

Identification   First American planetarium
Also known as   Adler Planetarium and
   Astronomical Museum of Chicago
Date   Opened on May 12, 1930
Place   Chicago, Illinois

The Adler Planetarium was the first public planetarium opened in the United States. It served as an example for a number of planetariums, such as those in Los Angeles, New York, and Philadelphia, that were opened across the United States during the 1930's and 1940's.

In 1928, Chicago business leader Max Adler invested $500,000 to build the first modern planetarium in the Western Hemisphere. He had learned of an optical projection device designed by the firm of Carl Zeiss in 1923, and he brought one to Chicago. Zeiss's device, positioned at the center of a hemispherical room, used self-produced light to project images of celestial objects onto the inner surface of the dome. While the planetarium was the main feature of Adler's building, numerous astronomy exhibits surrounded it.

Adler built the museum on Northerly Island, an artificial land mass in Lake Michigan that was the first of a series of artificial islands stretching southward. The South Park Commissioners (later the Chicago Park District) agreed to maintain and operate the planetarium. They connected the island to the mainland permanently soon after the opening of the planetarium, which formed what became a popular complex with the nearby Field Museum of Natural History and Shedd Aquarium. The average daily attendance at the Adler in its first two years was more than seventeen hundred.

The lights for opening night of the Chicago World's Fair were turned on by light from the star Arcturus that was converted into electrical signals and sent to the Adler. The planetarium became one of the main features of the fair. The fair also contributed to the long-term sustainability of the Adler when its president donated $16,000.

Impact   The Adler Planetarium influenced the development of numerous planetariums in the United States, of which there were more than two hundred by 1960. Adler obtained historical artifacts to form one of the most important astronomy collections in the world. The planetarium also became a leader in science education.

Linda Eikmeier Endersby

Further Reading

Fox, Philip. *Adler Planetarium and Astronomical Museum.* Chicago: Fred J. Ringley, 1937.

Marché, Jordan D. *Theaters of Time and Space: American Planetaria, 1930-1970.* New Brunswick, N.J.: Rutgers University Press, 2005.

Webster, Roderick S., Marjorie Webster, and Sara Schechner. *Western Astrolabes.* Chicago: Adler Planetarium and Astronomy Museum, 1998.

See also   Astronomy; Chicago World's Fair; Pluto discovery.

Administrative Reorganization Act. See **Reorganization Act of 1939**

■ *Adventures of Robin Hood, The*

Identification   Romantic film adaptation of a
   classic English folktale
Directors   William Keighley and Michael Curtiz
Date   Released on May 14, 1938

A romantic epic, The Adventures of Robin Hood *was a product of the Hollywood studio system, providing a classic but modernized story line to a mass public tired of economic displacement and wary of rising political unrest in the world.*

In the spring of 1938, Warner Bros. released *The Adventures of Robin Hood* to general audiences across the United States, three months after deadline and with production costs of more than $2 million. The film combined acting, writing, production, musical, technical, and directorial talent into a modern, romantic retelling of a popular English folk legend. Reviews were nearly uniformly positive. The film received Academy Awards for best art direction, best editing, and best original score.

Although screenwriter Norman Reilly Raine, in conjunction with Seton I. Miller, incorporated traditional elements of the legendary Robin Hood ballads, such as Robin's quarterstaff duel with Little John, he modernized the story by depicting Robin as a charismatic, heroic individual committed to social equality while cheerfully exhibiting personal contempt toward the illegitimacy of authoritarian Norman usurpers. With a faithful conformity to the script, director William Keighley cast Errol Flynn as Sir Robin of Locksley. Flynn's swashbuckling performance was complemented by an all-star supporting cast, featuring the graceful beauty Olivia de Havilland as Lady Marian Fitzwalter; Basil Rathbone as the conniving, duplicitous Sir Guy of Gisbourne; and Claude Rains as the villainous Prince John.

Because the film was overbudget and off schedule, Warner Bros. replaced director Keighley in November, 1937, with the Hungarian workhorse director Michael Curtiz, who finished production. The film was produced in Technicolor, using a three-color dye transfer process that was richly hued. Erich Wolfgang Korngold composed the original, romantic orchestral score, for which he won an Academy Award.

Impact By 1938, the United States was slowly beginning to emerge from the worldwide economic depression precipitated by the stock market crash of 1929. As the nations of the world transitioned out of the Great Depression, they were awakened to the dangers of emergent authoritarianism in the form of fascism in Germany and Italy and totalitarianism in the Soviet Union. *The Adventures of Robin Hood* romanticized the American virtues of individualism, social equality, and antiauthoritarianism. The work set the filmmaking standard for the Hollywood studio system.

Keith Carson

Further Reading

Knight, Stephen, ed. *Robin Hood: Anthology of Scholarship and Criticism.* Cambridge, England: D. S. Brewer, 1999.

Nollen, Scott Allen. *Robin Hood: A Cinematic History of the English Outlaw and His Scottish Counterparts.* Jefferson, N.C.: McFarland, 1999.

Nugent, Frank S. "The Screen: Errol Flynn Leads His Merry Men to the Music Hall in *The Adventures of Robin Hood.*" *The New York Times*, May 13, 1938, p. 17.

Potter, Lois, ed. *Playing Robin Hood: The Legend as Performance in Five Centuries.* Newark: University of Delaware Press, 1998.

See also Academy Awards; Film; *Merry Widow, The*; Motion Picture Production Code; *Snow White and the Seven Dwarfs*; *Wizard of Oz, The.*

Advertising Act. See Wheeler-Lea Act of 1938

■ Advertising in Canada

The 1930's was an important if schizophrenic time for Canadian advertising. While advertising techniques had become highly refined and efficient, the Great Depression made it difficult to promote goods and services to a population with a significant percentage of unemployed individuals simply struggling to survive.

In the first three decades of the twentieth century, Canada experienced tremendous economic growth. From 1896 to 1914, a sustained and highly successful governmental print and poster campaign called "The Last Best West" had attracted tens of thousands of new immigrants to settle on free, 160-acre farmlands in the Prairie Provinces. An economic surge following World War I, which was the result of industrialization and growth in the mining, agricultural, and timber industries, brought new prosperity across the nation. A great wave of consumerism swept across Canada, resulting in skyrocketing sales of clothing, appliances, cars, radios, and other goods advertised in print, on billboards and posters, and especially in mail order catalogs targeted at rural audiences. Under the direction of campaign-tested professional ad agencies that knew how to skillfully meld copy and art, advertising began to acquire a distinctive Canadian identity, separate from the American promotional efforts. Employing scientific analysis and precise media placement, Canadian ad mavens built effective appeals based upon pride in national icons, such as the maple leaf, the beaver, ice hockey, and the unspoiled character of the vast, sparsely populated land.

In 1929, the American stock market crashed. Within four years the Canadian economy, closely tied to that of the United States, shrank by 40 percent. One in five Canadians was out of work, and in some communities one-half of the population was living on government relief. Many advertiser-sponsored magazines and newspapers, the mainstays of the Canadian marketing industry, folded as manufacturers downsized or went out of business and as consumers let subscriptions lapse and saved their money for bare essentials.

In the depth of the Depression, advertising received a major boost from the addition of a new medium: radio. Though limited broadcasts had begun in 1923 under the auspices of the Canadian National Railway, radio was not a sustainable commercial medium until 1932, when the Canadian Radio Broadcasting Company was formed. Only after the formation of the Canadian Broadcasting Corporation (CBC) in 1936, when the economy had started to recover, did advertising revenues become more available. By this point, Canadians had purchased or built sufficient quantities of radio sets; thus, radio advertising became a powerful influence on buying habits.

An unexpected, and highly exploitable, source of advertising revenue was the 1934 birth of the uniquely Canadian Dionne quintuplets. Thousands of people flocked daily to a compound dubbed "Quintland" to observe the five infant girls and to purchase souvenirs. For a number of years after the mid-1930's, the quintuplets were the most readily recognized symbol of Canada, as they were portrayed on or associated with a variety of products, including syrup, cereal, condensed milk, toothpaste, and other consumer goods.

Impact Depression-era advertising practices and fortunes in Canada paralleled those of the United States. After a severe slump during the early years of the 1930's following the stock market crash, conditions gradually improved throughout the decade as employment and disposable income rose in tandem. Advertising revenues, supplemented by the addition of commercial radio, increased incrementally toward pre-Depression levels by the end of the decade. The outbreak of World War II in Europe in 1939 caused not only a sudden rise in productivity that signaled the end of the Depression but also a shift in advertising emphasis in Canada. Because many manufacturing facilities were retooled for military rather than consumer products, advertising was aimed more at citizen participation and support of the Allied war effort. Canadian advertising agencies in particular benefited during the war years, as the federal government invested more than $30 million in ten separate and successful campaigns to promote the sale of Victory Bonds.

Jack Ewing

Further Reading

Johnston, Russell Todd. *Selling Themselves: The Emergence of Canadian Advertising.* Toronto: University of Toronto Press, 2001.

Rose, Jonathan. *Making Pictures in Our Heads: Government Advertising in Canada.* Santa Barbara, Calif.: Praeger, 2000.

Tuckwell, Keith J. *Canadian Advertising in Action.* Toronto: Pearson Education Canada, 2008.

See also   Agriculture in Canada; Business and the economy in Canada; Dionne quintuplets; Great Depression in Canada; Immigration to Canada; Income and wages in Canada; Radio in Canada; Unemployment in Canada; World War II and Canada.

■ Advertising in the United States

During the Great Depression, the advertising industry suffered throughout the United States, as companies could barely afford to keep their employees or promote their goods and services through paid advertising. One of the few areas to show advertising revenue growth was the medium of broadcast radio.

On the eve of the 1929 stock market crash, advertising expenditures in the United States were approaching $3.5 billion annually. After the crash, advertising evaporated almost as quickly as businesses. More than 100,000 American businesses were forced to close between the crash and 1933. In that year, the amount spent on advertising was less than one-half of what it had been in 1929. So severe was the Depression that unemployment hit 25 percent in the early 1930's. The lack of jobs and incomes led to a reduced demand for many goods and services that used to be advertised in newspapers, magazines, billboards, and radio commercials.

Colorful, lavish magazine advertisements were replaced with black-and-white ads, often with lots of text and exaggerated claims. Time-consuming and expensive illustrations were often reduced to quicker and cheaper photographs during the Depression years. Advertising budgets shrank, and many companies tried to save money by moving their accounts to in-house agencies. Advertising was often packaged with newly designed public-relations staffs within large corporations in another attempt to cut expenses. Public-relations departments opened at Bethlehem Steel, General Motors, and U.S. Steel, for example, often to defend their advertising. Ads were often scaled back from the dramatic flair that developed during the preceding decade of growth and grandeur.

Radio Advertising Versus Other Media　By 1931, one-half of American households owned radios. The decade is often considered the golden age of radio. The Radio Act of 1927 created the Federal Radio Commission, which was expanded in 1934 to become the Federal Communications Commission (FCC). Such action allowed Americans to hear radio stations and their commercials better through expansion of the broadcast band and elimination of most static. Radio networks were already in place by 1930; thus, advertising messages could be carried across the country with the flip of a switch. People in rural areas were able to listen to radio with more regularity. However, because of the need for advertising revenue, most stations served urban areas in which businesses were located. By the end of the decade, more than 80 percent of radio stations were affiliated with networks. Many national radio programs were sponsored by major companies. Among musical programs during the 1930's were the *General Motors Family Party*, the *General Motors Promenade Concerts*, and *The Palmolive Hour*. Another type of sponsored radio program was soap operas. Mainly appealing to housewives, the "soaps" were so named because their sponsors were primarily household-cleaning-product companies. The first soap opera aired in the early 1930's from station WGN in Chicago.

President Franklin D. Roosevelt's radio fireside chats originated on March 12, 1933. These informal broadcasts helped to keep downcast listeners focused on a better future. The chats ushered in an era in which radio became a national mass medium that delivered timely news, entertainment, and sports at an affordable price thanks to paid advertising commercials. American citizens had little money for other types of entertainment; therefore, the living room became the focal point as the family gathered around the radio set. During the 1930's, manufacturers began producing radio cabinets, which became major pieces of furniture in homes. Unlike print publications, radio brought together disparate social, economic, and ethnic groups to hear the same message at the same time. While print publications suffered advertising declines, advertising revenue for radio stations continued to grow as larger audiences turned to this medium. Radio earned $18.7 million in advertising revenue in 1929; ten years later the figure was more than $80 million. One study determined that newspaper advertising revenue dropped 40 percent between 1929 and 1933. During the same time, radio advertising jumped 112 percent.

The leading product category for magazine ads during the 1930's was automobiles and auto-related products, such as gas, oil, and tires. In fact, that category grew from 27 percent of advertising content during the 1920's to 35 percent during the 1930's. Celebrities and athletes were often used in print advertisements during the 1930's. Babe Ruth, for example, appeared in magazine advertisements hawking Old Gold Cigarettes, Red Rock Cola, and Babe Ruth Underwear. Magazines had a slight recovery in revenue starting in the mid-1930's. Although feminist ideals were sometimes advanced in advertising during the decade, most women were depicted

Film star Jean Harlow promotes Lucky Strike cigarettes in this 1932 magazine advertisement. (The Granger Collection, New York)

within the home. Ads in *Time* and *Life*, for example, placed women in the kitchen, getting dinner ready for when their employed husbands returned from work.

Billboards, an inexpensive and increasingly effective medium of advertising because of the rising number of automobiles on American roads during the 1920's, continued to feature various products and services. Chewing tobacco, cigarettes, automobiles, motor oil, motels, restaurants, and tourist destinations were frequently topics of roadside signs. Thanks to the low cost of outdoor advertising during tough economic times, the medium was eventually able to rebound from its decade-low revenue of $20 million in 1932 to $37 million by 1938. However, this figure was substantially short of the 1927 amount of $50 million.

Growth of the Consumer Movement The election of Democrat Roosevelt as president in 1932 brought with it an antibusiness, antiadvertising mind-set among labor unions, political activists, and a growing national consumer movement. Advertising came under scrutiny for making outlandish claims and encouraging poor behavior among women, such as smoking, according to the swelling ranks of its critics. Advertising called for spending at a time when consumers needed to save money, according to its foes. The consumer movement received an added incentive for action from a May 25, 1931, Supreme Court ruling in *Federal Trade Commission v. Raladam Co.* The Court determined that the commission could not stop false advertising unless it injured a business competitor, totally ignoring the average citizen's possible injury from such deception. Raladam promoted Marmola, an obesity cure with unsubstantiated claims, but no individuals were said to be harmed. The ruling upheld the Federal Trade Commission's authority to regulate advertising that harmed a competitor, but not any that injured consumers.

Because the media were dependent on advertising for their own survival, they often ignored consumer discontent. However, that did not dissuade

Major American companies such as Coca-Cola, Chevrolet, and Wrigley's promote their products with colorful and eye-catching advertisements in Times Square in New York City. (Archive Photos/Getty Images)

consumerists from taking their antiadvertising messages to the American public. Several books were critical of advertising, including: *100,000,000 Guinea Pigs: Dangers in Everyday Foods, Drugs, and Cosmetics* (Arthur Kallet and Frederick John Schlink; 1933); *Eat, Drink and Be Wary* (Schlink; 1935); *American Chamber of Horrors: The Truth About Food and Drugs* (Ruth deForest Lamb; 1936); and *Your Money's Worth: A Study in the Waste of the Consumer's Dollars* (Stuart Chase and Schlink; 1931). *Ballyhoo*, a men's magazine with parodies of popular ads, started during the 1930's. Research organizations were established to gauge the accuracy of advertising claims. Among them were the ACNielsen, Consumers' Research, and George Gallup polling services. Consumers Union began publishing *Consumers*

Union Reports in 1935, which later became known as *Consumer Reports.* Consumer-inspired, truth-in-advertising laws were passed in several states. A few bills were introduced on the national level to control advertising, but they failed, as the ad industry made efforts to regulate itself. In 1934, radio came under government control with the formation of the FCC.

Consumers in 1930 started a drive for stiffer enforcement of the Pure Food and Drug Act, originally passed in 1906, to include advertising and the labeling of such products. Amid four years of controversy and lobbying, nothing was adopted to regulate advertising beyond the product's label on the shelf. In 1938, the Wheeler-Lea Act was passed, however, redefining the original 1914 Federal Trade Commission Act to include false and deceptive advertising as a form of unfair competition. Thus, the FTC was able to protect consumers by prohibiting certain advertisements, without showing proof of unfairness to another company. Cease-and-desist orders and stiff fines strengthened the implementation of the amendment, much to the relief of the consumer movement. Another 1938 piece of legislation was finally pushed successfully by the consumer movement. The Copeland Bill expanded the Food and Drug Administration's authority to regulate food, drugs, and, eventually, cosmetics.

Business Defends Advertising   Corporations did not acquiesce to such restrictions and criticism from Congress and consumers. With the persuasive power of advertising and public relations, the business community attempted to partner with the U.S. family to overcome the Great Depression together. Another important front in the battle between government and business was the public school classroom, which had been exposed to the consumer argument. Major industries were encouraged to provide pro-business and pro-advertising materials to budget-deficient classrooms that were often short on teaching materials. When school funds were not available to purchase the industry-supported learning aids, businesses often donated them. Primary audiences for such advertising materials were schoolchildren, their parents, and educators, especially home-economics teachers.

The National Association of Manufacturers, formed in 1895, was one of the major defenders of corporate advertising. During the latter half of the 1930's, this trade organization unleashed its Ameri-can Way campaign to demonstrate how its members' products and services could assist the public during these difficult times. The argument was made that advertising could lift the spirits of all Americans in the decade. A 1931 comment by Franklin D. Roosevelt, then the governor of New York, was revived by the advertising profession. He had said, "If I were starting life over again . . . I would go into the advertising profession in preference to almost any other."

Advertisements in support of the free enterprise system were seen repeatedly after 1936, when the American Way campaign officially began. Corporations tried to portray themselves as friendly, empathetic, and compassionate to counter the antibusiness messages from the U.S. government. The message was simple: Businesses built the United States, and they would see it through the Depression. Advertisers had a difficult task in trying to persuade the American people because of Roosevelt's New Deal platform and the critical finger-pointing at the business community. The widespread campaign, using a variety of willing business-owned media options, included billboard ads with the slogans "There's No Way Like the American Way" and "World's Highest Standard of Living." Likewise, individual companies felt compelled to continue advertising so they would not be forgotten when the economy recovered. For example, Lifebuoy soap, in the light of the Depression, switched its advertising emphasis from the luxury of beauty care to the prevention of body odor.

Impact   Advertising felt the economic sting of the Great Depression, as did American citizens. The industry cut back, made adjustments, and, in the case of radio, experienced advertising revenue growth during the 1930's. Advertising survived and was ready to thrive by the time World War II began.

Randy Hines

Further Reading

Goldsborough, Robert. *The Crain Adventure: The Making and Building of a Family Publishing Company.* Lincolnwood, Ill.: NTC Business Books, 1992. Traces advertising in the publishing field prior to, during, and after the Great Depression.

Marchard, Roland. *Advertising the American Dream: Making Way for Modernity, 1920-1940.* Berkeley: University of California Press, 1986. Nice overview of changes in print advertisements before and during the Great Depression.

St. John, Burton, and Ana Timofte. *Restoring the Primacy of Industry: Psychological Action, Propaganda, and Advertising During the Depression Era.* Boston: Association for Education in Journalism and Mass Communications, 2009. Chronicles the successful pro-advertising movement started during the Great Depression by the National Association of Manufacturers.

Spring, Joel H. *Educating the Consumer-Citizen: A History of the Marriage of Schools, Advertising, and Media.* Mahwah, N.J.: Lawrence Erlbaum Associates, 2003. Discusses how home-economics courses developed housewives into dedicated consumers, thanks in part to sponsored products and advertisements in the classroom.

Stole, Inger L. *Advertising on Trial: Consumer Activism and Corporate Public Relations in the 1930's.* Urbana: University of Illinois Press, 2005. Thorough examination of the economic situation leading up to the 1930's, with a detailed response by the advertising industry to the consumer movement.

See also   Business and the economy in the United States; Federal Food, Drug, and Cosmetic Act of 1938; Federal Trade Commission; Magazines; National Association of Manufacturers; Newspapers, U.S.; *100,000,000 Guinea Pigs*; Radio in the United States; Unemployment in the United States; Wheeler-Lea Act of 1938.

AFL. See **American Federation of Labor**

■ African Americans

African Americans made up nearly 10 percent of the total U.S. population during the 1930's. During the Great Depression in the United States, unemployment peaked at 16 million persons; African Americans composed approximately 21 percent of this total. Because of racial prejudice in much of the nation, African Americans experienced legal and illegal discrimination in practically every aspect of their daily lives. Despite such obstacles, they made significant contributions to the United States during the decade.

In 1930, nearly 12 million African Americans resided in the United States, more than 78 percent of whom were living in the fourteen southern states:

Alabama, Arkansas, Florida, Georgia, Kentucky, Louisiana, Maryland, Mississippi, North Carolina, Oklahoma, South Carolina, Tennessee, Texas, and Virginia. Only about 32 percent resided in urban areas; two-thirds were either sharecroppers or wage laborers. The sharecropping system kept cotton-growing tenants perpetually in debt to landowners and severely curtailed opportunities to expand or diversify crops to make profits. Wage laborers were usually unskilled workers paid lower wages than their white counterparts, working different and longer hours.

Living Conditions   Between 1920 and 1930, the "boom" years after World War I, approximately 700,000 African Americans left the South for jobs in northern cities. By 1932, nearly one-half of the entire African American population was unemployed; thus, African Americans once again started migrating to northern states in large numbers. About 175,000 headed to Harlem, a three-square-mile, predominantly black, New York City neighborhood, that soon became the largest black community in the United States and the largest concentration of black people in the world. Though Harlem offered a welcoming haven, by 1935 50 percent of its residents were unemployed.

President Franklin D. Roosevelt's New Deal, begun in 1933, started the country's recovery from the Depression. The Works Progress Administration (WPA) and the Civilian Conservation Corps (CCC) were two programs providing young men with work, such as constructing or renovating schools, hospitals, libraries, bridges, and sewage systems and protecting, improving, and increasing natural resources by planting trees; building roads, trails, cabins, and campgrounds; and fighting forest fires. CCC wages were only about $40 a month, $25 of which was sent home to dependents. These jobs provided room and board for the young men and a dependable income for their families. The WPA supported more than one million African Americans through relief and taught many to read and write. Black professionals and artists were provided employment opportunities in their areas of expertise. Nearly 10 percent of all federal government employees—postal clerks, mailmen, unskilled laborers, and janitors—were black.

Of the 116,000 professional jobs held by African Americans, two-thirds of them were as teachers or

Agricultural workers, most of them African American, wait in line to be paid after a day in the fields. (Library of Congress)

preachers. During this era the National Association for the Advancement of Colored People (NAACP) succeeded in getting teacher salaries equalized in some parts of the nation. In Maryland, for example, the salaries of white teachers were nearly twice as much as those of African Americans teaching the same grades.

The average annual income for black tenant farmers and wage laborers in the South was $278, compared to the $452 Caucasians earned. Thirty-three percent of African Americans living in the South in the early years of the decade were on relief, while only 11 percent of Caucasians were. In addition to working on farms, African Americans in the South worked as drivers; teamsters; maintenance men; domestic servants; menials in wholesale or retail trades, banking, brokerage houses, and insurance; launderers; and iron and steel laborers. Fewer than 2 percent of oil- and gas-production field jobs were held by African Americans. Some 50 percent of northern African Americans were on relief compared to only 13 percent of Caucasians. About 10

percent of automobile-industry-related jobs were held by African Americans. As jobs all over the South and North decreased, African Americans began migrating to the West, increasing the African American population there by 2.1 percent during the decade.

As the nation's economy improved, its citizens' conditions improved. By 1939, the annual income of black men was approximately $460, and a black female could make around $246. White males, however, could earn $1,112 and white females, $676. By the end of the decade African Americans, numbering nearly 13 million, were 9.8 percent of the total population. Most lived in southern rural areas, although the number employed as agricultural workers dropped from 1.1 million in 1930 to fewer than 800,000; the total black rural farm population had decreased 4.5 percent.

Racial Discrimination and Segregation Racial prejudice was widespread in much of the country during the 1930's. Housing, education, entertainment, and employment were all areas in which lines were drawn to separate the races. Laws permitted entities to prohibit African Americans from participating in politics, thus preventing them from changing their circumstances legally. In Texas in 1932, for example, the Democratic Party was legally allowed to set its own rules for its primaries, and it stipulated that only white Democrats could participate in them. By 1939, Oklahoma had manipulated its laws to require that nonregistered voters must register within a twelve-day period or be forever barred from the polls. The U.S. Supreme Court eventually ruled that this statute violated the Fifteenth Amendment.

Education for African Americans was poorly supported or funded. Ten southern states spent fewer than twenty dollars on each black pupil in elementary and secondary schools but almost fifty dollars on each white pupil. Black teachers usually had more pupils in their classes, fewer sources for student transportation, worse facilities, and fewer days per term to teach than white teachers did.

Federal government programs were created to supply equitable work opportunities to all citizens, black or white, but the individual state governments had unfair hiring and wage policies that short-changed black workers. Federal officials, such as African American Robert Clifton Weaver, race adviser and special assistant to Secretary of the Interior Harold Ickes, advocated economic and social reforms, addressing and often ameliorating some of the prevailing inequities. Even so, as late as 1939, racial discrimination was still so prevalent that the Daughters of the American Revolution, owners of Constitution Hall in Washington, D.C., refused to allow noted black concert singer Marian Anderson to sing in their auditorium. Secretary Ickes quickly arranged for Anderson to present her memorable Easter concert on the steps of the Lincoln Memorial.

Lynchings, particularly shameful illegalities, occurred on a fairly regular basis, mostly in the South but in other regions as well. African Americans were hanged, shot, burned at the stake, castrated, dismembered, and maimed both to punish perceived wrongdoers and to warn others who might challenge the status quo. In 1932, an antilynching bill passed the U.S. House of Representatives but not the Senate. During the decade, 119 African Americans were lynched; the highest number by year was 24 in 1933, the lowest was 2 in 1939. The Scottsboro trials of 1931 publicized the unfair treatment of African Americans by the ostensibly legal processes in the

southern states. Nine black youths were accused by several white youths of raping two white girls. Over a period of years and several trials, the African Americans were condemned to death or long prison terms, even though they got poor legal representation and solid evidence against them was never presented. Numerous civil rights organizations united to help defend the boys, and after six years, four boys were released; the others got severe sentences. Finally, all the "Scottsboro Boys" were freed in 1950.

In 1935, African Americans rioted in Harlem when they mistakenly thought police had beaten a black youth to death for stealing. The riot may have erupted because African Americans were frustrated and resentful of white businesspeople who did not want African Americans to work in their Harlem stores. A black boycott forced the businesses to hire some African Americans, but they got an injunction through the Sherman Antitrust Act and fired them, setting off anger and resentment.

Achievements and Achievers Though the decade's horrendous economic conditions and widespread discrimination were dire for African Americans, outstanding individuals and encouraging events made the era memorable and even progressive. In the arts, sports, entertainment, religion, and even politics, African Americans made significant contributions.

The Nation of Islam was started in 1930 by Wallace Dodd Fard. The Black Muslims, as the followers of the tenets of the Nation of Islam came to be known, encouraged African Americans to believe in their self-worth and deny their status as second-class citizens. The organization was almost always controversial but was instrumental in raising black awareness.

Several civic and political organizations came into prominence during the decade: the NAACP, the National Council of Negro Women, and the National Negro Congress. Each brought the racial situation in the United States to the attention of the nation and the world. The groups proposed antilynching legislation, tried to get African Americans appointed as deputy administrators in states with large black populations, and campaigned for equitable federal funding for African Americans' educations. Among the many politically minded African Americans advancing the cause of black Americans were Mary McLeod Bethune, a member of

(continued on page 16)

African American Population by State, 1930 and 1940

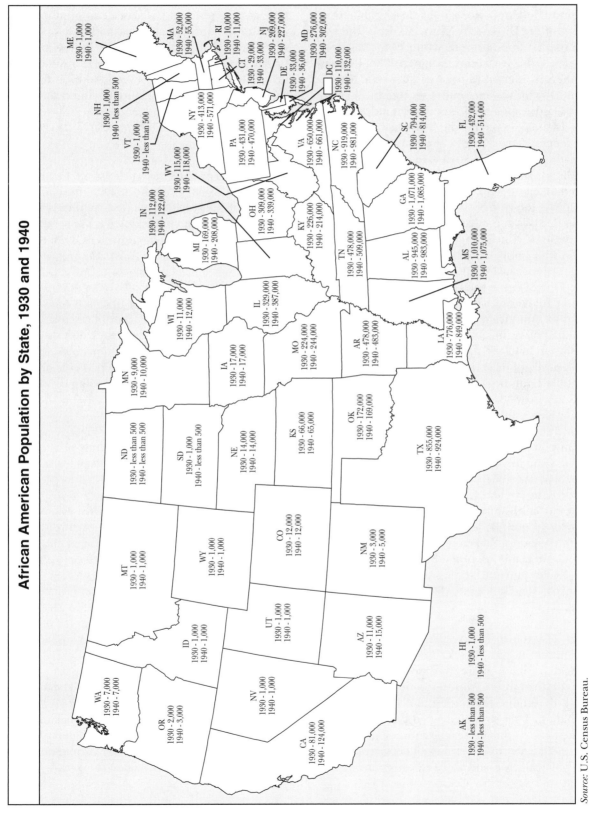

ME
1930 - 1,000
1940 - 1,000

MA
1930 - 52,000
1940 - 55,000

RI
1930 - 10,000
1940 - 11,000

NJ
1930 - 209,000
1940 - 227,000

MD
1930 - 276,000
1940 - 302,000

NH
1930 - 1,000
1940 - less than 500

CT
1930 - 29,000
1940 - 33,000

DE
1930 - 33,000
1940 - 36,000

DC
1930 - 110,000
1940 - 132,000

VT
1930 - 1,000
1940 - less than 500

NY
1930 - 413,000
1940 - 571,000

PA
1930 - 431,000
1940 - 470,000

VA
1930 - 650,000
1940 - 661,000

NC
1930 - 919,000
1940 - 981,000

SC
1930 - 794,000
1940 - 814,000

FL
1930 - 432,000
1940 - 514,000

WV
1930 - 115,000
1940 - 118,000

IN
1930 - 112,000
1940 - 122,000

OH
1930 - 309,000
1940 - 339,000

KY
1930 - 226,000
1940 - 214,000

GA
1930 - 1,071,000
1940 - 1,085,000

MI
1930 - 169,000
1940 - 208,000

TN
1930 - 478,000
1940 - 509,000

AL
1930 - 945,000
1940 - 983,000

MS
1930 - 1,010,000
1940 - 1,075,000

WI
1930 - 11,000
1940 - 12,000

IL
1930 - 329,000
1940 - 387,000

MO
1930 - 224,000
1940 - 244,000

AR
1930 - 478,000
1940 - 483,000

LA
1930 - 776,000
1940 - 849,000

MN
1930 - 9,000
1940 - 10,000

IA
1930 - 17,000
1940 - 17,000

KS
1930 - 66,000
1940 - 65,000

OK
1930 - 172,000
1940 - 169,000

ND
1930 - less than 500
1940 - less than 500

SD
1930 - 1,000
1940 - less than 500

NE
1930 - 14,000
1940 - 14,000

TX
1930 - 855,000
1940 - 924,000

MT
1930 - 1,000
1940 - 1,000

WY
1930 - 1,000
1940 - 1,000

CO
1930 - 12,000
1940 - 12,000

NM
1930 - 3,000
1940 - 5,000

ID
1930 - 1,000
1940 - 1,000

UT
1930 - 1,000
1940 - 1,000

AZ
1930 - 11,000
1940 - 15,000

HI
1930 - 1,000
1940 - less than 500

WA
1930 - 7,000
1940 - 7,000

OR
1930 - 2,000
1940 - 3,000

NV
1930 - 1,000
1940 - 1,000

CA
1930 - 81,000
1940 - 124,000

AK
1930 - less than 500
1940 - less than 500

Source: U.S. Census Bureau.
Notes: Alaska and Hawaii did not become states until 1959; numbers rounded to the nearest thousand.

President Franklin D. Roosevelt's "black cabinet" as director of the Division of Negro Affairs of the National Youth Administration; Arthur Wergs Mitchell, elected to Congress from Chicago in 1934; Charles W. Anderson, elected to the Kentucky state legislature in 1936 for six consecutive terms; and William Henry Hastie, appointed U.S. district judge in the Virgin Islands, becoming the first black appointed to the federal bench. Crystal Bird Fauset became the first black woman elected to a state legislature, while Jane Matilda Bolin became the first black woman appointed to a judgeship.

In sports, the 1936 Berlin Summer Olympics were memorable for the outstanding performances by black athletes. Nine of the ten black track-and-field athletes who competed in Berlin won gold medals, much to the chagrin of German chancellor Adolf Hitler. One of them, the redoubtable Jesse Owens, won four gold medals. In boxing, Henry Armstrong, an African American, was the only boxer to hold three championships and three world titles simultaneously. He held the featherweight, welterweight, and lightweight championships in 1937. Heavyweight Joe Louis began his successful ten-year boxing career in 1938, becoming one of the most admired athletes, black or white, in American sports history.

Numerous African Americans achieved both success and fame in art and entertainment. Music had singers such as Anderson, Paul Robeson, Dorothy Maynor, Billie Holiday, Ella Fitzgerald, Ethel Waters, and Bessie Smith and instrumentalists such as Louis Armstrong, Count Basie, and Duke Ellington. Stage and screen had Stepin Fetchit, Hattie McDaniel, Oscar Micheaux, and Josephine Baker. Literature had Zora Neale Hurston, Langston Hughes, Ralph Ellison, Chester Himes, and Richard Wright, among others.

Impact The Great Depression caused distress for most Americans, but African Americans may have felt the deprivations more than any other group because they had to deal with not only economic setbacks but also injustices connected with racial discrimination. They struggled against the inequities, and their efforts, and those of significant numbers of white Americans on their behalf, brought about many political, civic, and social advances during the decade.

African Americans increased in number, improved their educational levels, and developed advanced work skills, making their usefulness and importance to the nation obvious. African Americans during the 1930's laid the groundwork for the group's gradual acceptance into the American mainstream.

Jane L. Ball

Further Reading

Biles, Roger. *The South and the New Deal.* Lexington: University Press of Kentucky, 2006. Examines the effects of Roosevelt's New Deal on the rural and urban South when the region was the most disadvantaged and racially prejudiced in the nation.

Cripps, Thomas. *Slow Fade to Black: The Negro in American Film, 1900-1942.* New York: Oxford University Press, 1993. A history of African Americans in American films during the first four decades of the twentieth century. Chapter 11 discusses black actors working during the Great Depression.

Hill, Laban C. *Harlem Stomp! A Cultural History of the Harlem Renaissance.* Boston: Little, Brown, 2009. A history, beginning in 1900, discussing conditions leading to the Harlem riots in 1935. Includes drawings and photos.

Lewis, David L. *When Harlem Was in Vogue.* New York: Penguin, 1997. A sociological study of Harlem's people, places, and events and its place in black culture.

Maxwell, William J. *New Negro, Old Left: African American Writing and Communism Between the Wars.* New York: Columbia University Press, 1999. Discusses the role of communism in shaping African American literature, the Scottsboro case, and lynchings.

Taylor, Quintard. *In Search of the Racial Frontier: African Americans in the American West, 1528-1990.* New York: Norton, 1999. Includes a chapter devoted to African Americans in the urban West between 1911 and 1940.

See also Civil rights and liberties in the United States; Harlem Renaissance; Jim Crow segregation; Lynching; Nation of Islam; National Association for the Advancement of Colored People; National Council of Negro Women; National Negro Congress; Race riots; Racial discrimination; Scottsboro trials.

■ Agricultural Adjustment Acts

Identification   Federal legislation that provided
government subsidies to farmers
Also known as   AAA
Date   First law enacted on May 12, 1933; second
law enacted on February 16, 1938

In an attempt to balance the surplus of agricultural goods that was an effect of the Great Depression, the first Agricultural Adjustment Act (AAA) created agricultural scarcity by plowing under crops and destroying livestock. It also authorized the president to adjust currency prices. The act was greeted by widespread criticism, but agricultural prices rose in response. After the Supreme Court declared the Agricultural Adjustment Act unconstitutional in 1936, Congress passed a second law that reinstated many of the subsidies and other aspects of the first Agricultural Adjustment Act.

The United States officially entered the Great Depression in 1929 with the crash of the stock market. Farmers, who earlier had been encouraged to expand their crop production, had suffered from dropping commodity prices during the decade following World War I. Their plight was exacerbated by the onset of the Depression, as thousands of farmers could not meet the debt on their mortgaged properties. In 1933, more than 5 percent of the nation's farms were foreclosed because the farmers could not pay the taxes on their property. In 1931, midwestern farmers organized the Farmers' Holiday Association in an attempt to force prices up. They withheld grain and livestock from the market, and dairy farmers dumped thousands of gallons of milk in Iowa and Wisconsin to protest the price drop to $0.02 a quart. Furthermore, farmers across Oklahoma, Texas, Kansas, Colorado, and New Mexico suffered an extended drought, and resulting dust storms caused the topsoil in the region to blow away. Thousands of "Okies" packed their meager belongings and left for the West Coast, where they hoped to find work.

One of the first laws passed during Franklin D. Roosevelt's New Deal was the AAA. The Emergency Farm Mortgage Act was passed with the AAA in an effort to forestall the many foreclosures of farms across the United States. The Agricultural Adjustment Administration under Secretary of Agriculture Henry A. Wallace used four methods designed to raise farm income: restricting farm production

and removing surpluses from the market, paying farmers for taking acreage out of production, charging a tax on food processors to raise funds to pay for farm benefits, and creating agreements between farm co-ops and the food processors.

Under the provisions of the law, Wallace ordered the destruction of more than 10 million acres of cotton and the slaughter of 6 million baby pigs. However, many people in the nation were unemployed and hungry; therefore, they criticized the AAA for its creation of artificial scarcity. While farm prices rose somewhat, the AAA was not a cure-all. Farmers were never required to reduce acreage, and many took government payments for not planting portions of their land while continuing to plant and harvest their best acres.

On January 6, 1936, the Supreme Court declared portions of the AAA unconstitutional because some of its production control measures abrogated the powers of the states. The court especially targeted the processing taxes. According to the decision of the Court, only the legislative branch of government has the power to levy taxes. In 1938, Congress passed a second Agricultural Adjustment Act that was designed to control production and conserve the soil. Farmers were paid to grow crops that would not damage the soil and to allow land to lay fallow. Quotas were set on certain crops and, in return, farmers could receive commodity loans. As Congress had removed the processing tax from this law, the Supreme Court raised no objection.

Impact   The first Agricultural Adjustment Act did little to ease the plight of the farmer, although farm prices rose. The AAA benefited the large commercial farmer, but the demand for more production during World War II brought a return of prosperity to both large and small farmers. The principles established by the second AAA, tightening government control over production, were to determine agricultural policy for most of the remainder of the twentieth century.

Yvonne J. Johnson

Further Reading

Badger, Anthony J. *The New Deal: The Depression Years, 1933-1940.* Chicago: Ivan R. Dee, 2002.
Leuchtenberg, William E. *Franklin D. Roosevelt and the New Deal, 1932-1940.* New York: Harper Perennial, 2009.

McElvaine, Robert S. *The Great Depression: America, 1929-1941.* New York: Times Books, 1993.

See also Agriculture in the United States; Great Depression in the United States; Wallace, Henry A.

■ Agriculture in Canada

Canada is the largest country in the Western Hemisphere and is dominated by its geography, stretching from the Atlantic Ocean to the Pacific Ocean. The range of topographic and climatic conditions varies from the Maritime Provinces in the northeast to British Columbia in the west; this disparity has required a variety of agricultural systems adapted to the geography.

In Canada, agricultural activity has always been dominated by the climate prevailing in the area. In the northeast, the provinces of Nova Scotia, New Brunswick, and Prince Edward Island were among the first to attract European settlers. The draw was initially largely the ocean fisheries off the Atlantic coast. As the European population grew, the fisheries of the Maritime Provinces provided a substantial amount of the foodstuffs of Europe. As the fisheries declined in the twentieth century, the inhabitants were forced to earn their living from the land, and it proved to be less than bountiful. Only 5.2 percent of the land in the Maritime Provinces is suitable for agriculture.

The two central provinces, Quebec and Ontario, have 23.9 percent of Canada's agricultural land located within their boundaries. The early French settlers of Quebec were peasants who set up their plots mostly along the St. Lawrence River. Technical advances have managed to improve agricultural output in Quebec; however, the small holdings have made deriving a comfortable living from growing crops difficult. Ontario, the province just west of Quebec, which includes the land just north of Lake Ontario, has a better agricultural climate, and it has had a viable agricultural sector throughout the two centuries since settlement.

The most important agricultural zone of Canada is the vast prairie stretching from just west of Lake Superior to the Rocky Mountains. Almost 70 percent of Canada's agricultural land is located in the three provinces of Manitoba, Alberta, and Saskatchewan. Contained within these three provinces is Canada's Wheat Belt, enclosed within a triangle that borders the United States to the south and stretches northward at least one hundred miles to the boreal forest. The climate limits the variety of crops that can be grown in this area, but wheat grows in abundance. Canada is one of the five largest wheat-producing countries in the world.

West of Saskatchewan, the Rocky Mountains reach more than ten thousand feet and separate the most westerly of Canada's provinces, British Columbia, from the rest. Although British Columbia has some valuable lands along the Pacific coast and includes a major Pacific harbor, its land is mostly rugged. Agriculture is possible only in the valleys, where specialized crops can be grown. It has just 2.3 percent of Canada's agricultural land but it has one enormously profitable crop, trees, which grow along the coast to immense sizes and provide a significant amount of the lumber used in the United States.

The Wheat Belt Comprising the three Prairie Provinces, Canada's Wheat Belt was settled at the end of the nineteenth century and the early years of the twentieth century. Several factors made possible the settlement of the Prairie Provinces. The Dominion government passed laws similar to the U.S. Homestead Act, surveyed the prairie into townships, and established a preemption provision that allowed for more than one million individual farmers to buy and cultivate land on the prairie. The spread of railroads to the area helped to market the wheat of the prairie land. During World War I, Canada's Prairie Provinces became one of the five breadbaskets of the world.

During the 1920's production of wheat soared in the Canadian prairie, and the world market for wheat grew to the benefit of the wheat farmers. However, fortunes changed during the 1930's, and the wheat farmers were the major sufferers of the economic downturn. By 1930, Canada was producing more wheat than the world wanted to buy. Furthermore, severe drought then impacted the prairie, notably in Saskatchewan, so that fields that had once been bountiful were unable to grow much of anything. Canada's per-acre wheat output had been much more than 10 bushels, and in many places, as much as 15 bushels per acre. However, during the 1930's, it fell to below 10 bushels; Saskatchewan produced only 2.6 bushels per acre. The common Canadian practice of "summer fallow," in which land was not sowed with any crop on a regular rotation, left the land open to ravages by the wind, so that much of the prairie was shrouded in a fog of dust; comparable conditions existed in many parts of the United States.

The peak of the drought occurred in 1933, signifying the low point for the Wheat Belt. Over the following three years, the climate improved and production increased, but a renewed drought in 1937 put many wheat farmers out of business. Numerous farmers lost all of the investment they had made in their farms during the productive and profitable decade of the 1920's. It became clear that government intervention was needed.

The Wheat Board   The Canadian Wheat Board was first created in 1919 to provide centralized marketing of Canada's wheat crop in the turmoil of the international market. As things stabilized the board was abandoned, only to be resurrected in 1935 in an effort to deal with the inability of Canada's wheat farmers to market their crop. Wheat farmers re-

ceived an initial payment in the form of "participation certificates" and subsequent payments after the wheat had been marketed, much like in the system established in the United States. During the drought years the board was able to sell off virtually all the crop, though at a price well under one dollar per bushel during most of the 1930's. It also undertook the marketing of related grains such as oats and barley, in the hope of encouraging farmers to switch to other crops. In 1939, the Dominion government proposed abolishing the wheat board, but the proposal proved widely unpopular and was dropped. The government then authorized the creation of voluntary pools, but the oversupply of wheat in relation to the world market, except during wartime, continued to make the wheat board essential.

Other Crops   Canadian farmers did learn to produce other crops. Apples had been an important crop for two areas outside the wheat zone, British Columbia and Nova Scotia, but the European mar-

Canadian wheat field in 1935. Wheat has long been a staple of Canadian agriculture, but the economic depression of the 1930's caused the price of the commodity to decline drastically. (Hulton Archive/Getty Images)

ket for these dried up during World War II. Farmers in the wheat zone turned to the production of beef cattle; substantial numbers of these were exported to the United States, though the numbers dropped dramatically during the early 1930's. During the last half of the decade, production rose again to as many as three million head, and Canada was able to export to the United States once again.

During the first part of the twentieth century, Canada's dairy products were consumed entirely by Canadians; most of it was produced in Ontario and Quebec. However, as refrigeration techniques improved, exportation of the products became possible.

Impact During the 1930's, Canada was a huge country with a rather modest population considering its geographic size. Its northerly climate limited what could be grown on its land. However, Canada became a world leader with its gargantuan wheat crop. The droughts of the decade decreased the production of wheat dramatically, but Canada remained one of the world leaders in growing wheat.

Nancy M. Gordon

Further Reading

Britnell, G. E., and V. C. Fowke. *Canadian Agriculture in War and Peace, 1935-50.* Stanford, Calif.: Stanford University Press, 1962. Inclusive and fact-filled account of Canadian agriculture. Despite the dates in the title, it covers the early years of the twentieth century also.

Malenbaum, Wilfred. *The World Wheat Economy, 1885-1939.* Cambridge, Mass.: Harvard University Press, 1953. Comprehensive account of Canada's wheat production in the context of the world market.

Marr, William L., and Donald G. Paterson. *Canada: An Economic History.* Toronto: Macmillan of Canada, 1980. Provides a broad background of the Canadian economy in the twentieth century.

Watkins, M. H., and H. M. Grant, eds. *Canadian Economic History: Classic and Contemporary Approaches.* Ottawa: Carleton University Press, 1993. Collection of articles, including several relevant to the Canadian agricultural sector.

See also Agriculture in the United States; Business and the economy in Canada; Demographics of Canada; Farmers' organizations; Food processing; Great Depression in Canada; Income and wages in Canada; Unemployment in Canada.

■ Agriculture in the United States

The 1930's were a difficult time for agriculture in the United States, as prices and incomes plummeted and many farmers lost their farms. The federal government intervened into the field of agriculture for the first time. Farm numbers peaked during this decade and declined afterward because of consolidation and increased technology.

Agriculture encompasses a diverse range of plants and animals, each with differing requirements. In the United States, agriculture varies across the country depending primarily on the climate and soils. In 1930, fourteen different agricultural regions were recognized: These included the Cotton Belt from Virginia to Texas; the Corn Belt from western Ohio to eastern Nebraska; a corn and winter-wheat belt from Maryland to Kansas; two wheat regions, featuring spring wheat in the Dakotas and parts of Montana and winter wheat in Kansas and the panhandles of Texas and Oklahoma; the Dairy Belt from Maine to Minnesota; a grazing and irrigated-crops region in the Western states; and several coastal regions. During the 1930's, the main agricultural commodities were wheat, corn, cotton, pork, beef, and dairy. Soybeans were a minor crop, mostly used as green manure to improve depleted soils. However, in 1931, a process was developed to remove a disagreeable odor from soybean oil, and the soybean began its ascent to a major agricultural commodity.

The first two decades of the twentieth century were a heyday for U.S. agriculture. From 1910 to 1914, the incomes of farmers and nonfarmers were in balance. During World War I, farmers increased production for export to the war-devastated countries of Europe. However, after the war, as those countries recovered, surpluses led to a severe fall in prices for agricultural commodities. While most of the 1920's were a boom time for the country, farmers were generally left out of this prosperity. Farm bankruptcies peaked in 1925. Farmers organized and held sporadic strikes to call attention to their plight; these actions persisted into the 1930's. Proposals were repeatedly made in Congress to respond to the situation; these generally consisted of cooperative marketing of agricultural commodities, foreign dumping of surplus production, or a combination of the two. Cooperative marketing would have given farmers the opportunity to form a cartel to better control the prices of their products. However, this would have required the farmers to curtail production, and farmers had little enthusiasm for doing so. Foreign dumping of surplus commodities would have involved a two-tiered system: higher prices in the domestic market and lower prices in the export market, and compensation for the lower export prices and likely tariffs to prevent foreign competition in the domestic market. However, no laws were enacted until the end of the decade, when the Agricultural Management Act of 1929, the first direct intervention of the federal government into agricultural marketing, was passed and signed by President Herbert Hoover.

Government Agricultural Programs The Agricultural Management Act of 1929 established the Federal Farm Board, which was allocated a $500 million revolving fund to buy and sell major commodities, such as wheat, corn, cotton, tobacco, livestock, eastern fruits and vegetables, and California fruit. Ostensibly, the board would buy commodities when in surplus and sell them when in deficit, thus stabilizing prices. However, in the summer of 1929, a bumper crop of wheat was produced, lowering prices. Following the October, 1929, stock market crash, prices fell further. In 1930, the board bought 250 million bushels of wheat, one-third of the previous year's crop, at $1.18 per bushel and urged farmers to decrease wheat acreage by 10 percent in 1930 and 25 percent over the following three years. Without authority to compel compliance, no reduction in wheat planting occurred. The price of wheat dropped to 90 cents per bushel in 1930. The board made a further attempt to stabilize prices in early 1931, but it exhausted its allocation and stopped its attempts at price support in the middle of 1931; prices dropped to 61 cents per bushel in 1931 and to

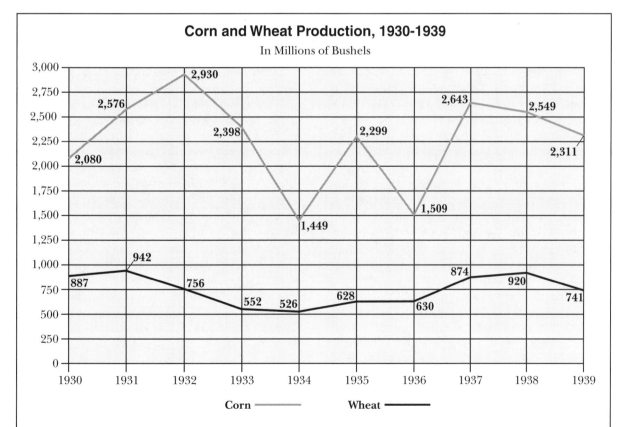

Source: Historical Statistics of the United States: Colonial Times to 1970. Washington, D.C.: U.S. Department of Commerce, Bureau of the Census, 1975, p. 511.
Note: Corn is for all purposes; wheat is for grain.

Filipino agricultural workers cutting lettuce in California in 1935. (The Granger Collection, New York)

49 cents per bushel in 1932. The board liquidated its stocks in 1933, mainly abroad. In the context of the worldwide depression, it had failed dismally to achieve price stabilization for wheat.

The cotton situation differed in details but not in the end result. Cotton was largely dependent on exports, and its price collapsed after the stock market crash. The board tried to keep prices above 16 cents per pound with crop loans, but the prices fell to 7 cents per pound. The board made purchases in an attempt to maintain prices, but by 1931 it had no more funds and had to stop. It had also failed to stabilize cotton prices. Overproduction was the fundamental problem: Pleas to farmers to voluntarily reduce planted acres were unsuccessful, and in 1931, carryover of cotton equaled the average annual production. The board did successfully stabilize prices for California grapes. However, this was based on contractual reduction in production, aided by climatic and disease problems that decimated the crop in some years.

When President Franklin D. Roosevelt took office in 1933, he asserted that the federal government had a responsibility to place a floor under farm incomes. The Agricultural Adjustment Acts of 1933 and 1938, as well as other laws and executive orders,

had that goal. The net effect was that the federal government began to make payments to farmers for commodities and for taking land out of production. The Commodity Credit Corporation was authorized to make nonrecourse loans; crops would be accepted for payment of crop loans when the prices were lower than the loan rate. The program was for cotton, wheat, hogs, corn, and tobacco. The price support program for dairy products was more complicated because of the perishable nature of liquid milk.

The programs involved idling acres, including plowing up those already planted, and slaughtering young pigs and breeding stock to reduce future supplies. Some stockpiles of commodities were made available for distribution to the urban poor.

The programs also established a base acreage allocated to a farmer for growing a covered crop. This number was established by considering production in the previous five years. Contracts based on reduced production specified a percentage of that base acreage. Once allocated, the acreage was retained by the owner, who could pass it on when the land was sold. With some commodities, the base acreage set in 1933 persisted into the twenty-first century. This had the unintended consequence of permanently favoring those who were assigned a base acreage at that time.

After 1936, with the Dust Bowl and the droughts of 1930, 1934, and 1936 in mind, commodity programs focused on soil conservation. In the Soil Conservation Act (1935), commodity support was made dependent on soil conservation measures undertaken by farmers. The Taylor Grazing Act (1934) provided for the regulation of grazing on public lands to improve rangeland conditions and to regulate their use.

The Emergency Farm Mortgage Act (1933) allowed farmers five additional years to pay off their mortgages at an interest rate of 4.5 percent. While farm bankruptcies were prevalent during the 1930's, the number was one-half that of the 1920's because of this act and other programs. Furthermore, the Agricultural Adjustment Act of 1938 included a federal crop insurance program for wheat, which was soon expanded to other crops.

By the end of the decade, farmers were receiving government payments for cutting production, subsidies for conservation practices, price support for five commodities, and crop insurance protection. Large farms received the same percentage as small farms, a policy that favored bigger farms. The benefits flowed to farm owners but not necessarily to farmworkers or tenant farmers. While the agricultural sector benefited from these government programs, the benefits were not uniformly distributed.

Changes in Agricultural Demographics and Production During the decade, the farm population decreased from 25 percent of the total national population in 1930 to 18 percent in 1940. The proportional decline in the farm population persisted to the end of the twentieth century, when less than 2 percent of the country's population lived on farms. During the 1930's, tenants operated around 40 percent of farms. (The percentage was much higher in the Cotton Belt.) While many tenants were displaced during this decade, others became tenants when their farms were foreclosed. In 1940, 2.5 million farmworkers were unable to secure agricultural employment.

Farm numbers peaked in 1935, at around 6.8 million, and decreased into the twenty-first century. Cropland harvested, however, remained fairly constant, at around 350 million acres, throughout the twentieth century. Average farm size grew from 157 acres in 1930 to 175 in 1940 and increased the remainder of the century. During the 1930's, farms were not specialized; each farm produced five different commodities on average. Interest payments took an average of 16 percent of farm income during the early 1930's, and taxes were also high. Net real farm income per farm was the lowest in the early 1930's. While farm income was 60 percent of what nonfarm income was from 1910 to 1914, it dropped to 40 percent during the 1920's and to 23 percent in the early 1930's. Farm share of retail food dollars was about forty cents during the 1920's, fell to thirty-two cents in the early 1930's, and returned to forty cents during the 1940's.

The use of mechanization on farms started during the 1920's. From a peak of 26 million horses and mules in 1918, the number fell to 19 million in 1930 and to 15 million in 1940. In 1924, International Harvester introduced the Farmall, the first successful all-purpose tractor. Tractor numbers increased to 1 million in 1930 and to 1.7 million in 1940, reaching a peak of 6.5 million during the 1960's. Wheat and corn farmers were the first to adopt mechanization. Farms with milking machines increased from 100,000 in 1930 to 175,000 in 1940. While yields of wheat and corn per acre were depressed during droughts, they otherwise remained fairly constant during the 1930's. Yield of milk per cow also remained constant during the decade; commercial artificial insemination of dairy cattle began in 1938, but its impact on milk yield did not become evident until the 1950's.

The Rural Electrification Act (1936) increased electrical power to farms from less than 10 percent to more than 30 percent during the decade. This raised the standard of living by bringing indoor plumbing, hot-water heaters, refrigerators, and electric irons and stoves. Electrification also enhanced farm efficiency as various technologies, such as milking machines, electric cream separators, feed grinders, and feed heaters, became available.

Impact The 1930's were a time of great upheaval in U.S. agriculture. While productivity was relatively constant, except during droughts, the income from agriculture was much lower than it had been in other decades and in comparison to the rest of the economy. Many farmers lost their farms, and many more farmworkers were displaced as a result of the precarious farm situation, droughts, and technology. The decade was marked by the first interventions into the field by the federal government and was a transitional period from a largely traditional agriculture to one based on technology.

James L. Robinson

Further Reading

Bovard, James. *The Farm Fiasco*. San Francisco: Institute for Contemporary Studies Press, 1991. Provocative and critical assessment of agricultural policies instituted during the 1930's.

Conklin, Paul K. *A Revolution down on the Farm: The Transformation of American Agriculture Since 1929*. Lexington: University Press of Kentucky, 2008. History of U.S. agriculture based on facts and personal recollections. One chapter deals with the government interventions of the 1930's.

Drache, Hiram M. *History of U.S. Agriculture and Its Relevance to Today.* Danville, Ill.: Interstate, 1996. Well-illustrated history of U.S. agriculture, with a section dealing with developments from 1914 to 1954.

Gardner, Bruce L. *American Agriculture in the Twentieth Century: How It Flourished and What It Cost.* Cambridge, Mass.: Harvard University Press, 2002. Readable text with many graphs, placing U.S. agriculture of the 1930's in its twentieth century context.

Hurt, R. Douglas. *Problems of Plenty: The American Farmer in the Twentieth Century.* Chicago: Ivan R. Dee, 2002. Readable and balanced examination of the agricultural events of the 1930's in the context of the demographics, economics, and legislation of the twentieth century.

Pillsbury, Richard, and John Florin. *Atlas of American Agriculture: The American Cornucopia.* New York: Simon and Schuster Macmillan, 1996. With graphs, maps, and pictures, this volume details the variation in U.S. agriculture over time in different regions and for numerous commodities.

See also Agricultural Adjustment Acts; Commodity Credit Corporation; Dust Bowl; Farmers' organizations; Great Depression in the United States; Heat wave of 1931; National Recovery Administration; Rural Electrification Administration; Soil Conservation Service; Taylor Grazing Act of 1934; *Tobacco Road*; Urbanization in the United States; Wallace, Henry A.

■ Aid to Dependent Children

The Law   Federal law providing financial support to poor families

Date   Enacted August 14, 1935

Part of the Social Security Act of 1935, Aid to Dependent Children inaugurated a federal program that provided assistance to poor women and their families through federal matching of state expenditures.

Aid to Dependent Children (ADC) was enacted as part of the Social Security Act of 1935. Original proponents of ADC were primarily female social reformers who argued that New Deal social programs did not address the needs of poor women and their families. At the time of its enactment, ADC earned little notice given the rush of social-reform projects initiated during the New Deal and the controversies generated by other provisions of the Social Security Act.

The intent of ADC was to provide cash assistance to families who no longer had the financial support of fathers. The program was consistent with state social welfare programs at the time: Beneficiaries were meant to be the "deserving poor," primarily widows, and the program required moral worthiness as a criterion for eligibility. An operating assumption was that the program would enable women to fulfill their role as nurturers and not be forced to enter the workforce. ADC was to achieve these goals by providing federal matching funds for state expenditures. Initially, this match was one dollar of federal money for every two dollars of state funds spent to aid dependent children. In 1939, the federal match was increased to one dollar in federal money for every one dollar in state expenditures.

Impact   ADC provided increasing support to poor mothers and children. At the time of the program's enactment in 1935, 300,000 children were receiving benefits under state programs. By 1939, ADC was providing benefits for 700,000 children.

Although ADC received scant attention at the time of its passage, it became both increasingly important and controversial after World War II. Its basic operation—federal matching of state expenditures accompanied by a measure of federal oversight—became a model for numerous federal programs, such as those related to housing, medical care, and education. ADC also initiated the idea of a federal welfare program, which, particularly after World War II, continued to generate intense public debate.

Robert Rubinson

Further Reading

Blau, Joel. *The Dynamics of Social Welfare Policy.* New York: Oxford University Press, 2004.

Patterson, James T. *America's Struggle Against Poverty, 1900-1994.* Cambridge, Mass.: Harvard University Press, 1994.

See also   Food stamps; Great Depression in the United States; Health care; Income and wages in the United States; New Deal.

■ Air mail route scandal

The Event In a series of meetings in Washington, D.C., the postmaster general divided routes and airmail contracts among four major airlines. His unilateral moves were later criticized for driving many smaller airlines out of business

Date May 15 to June 9, 1930

Postmaster General Walter Folger Brown used his power over airmail contracts to dramatically reshape the airline industry in the United States. During his tenure, transcontinental mail delivery and passenger service were greatly streamlined. Although the airmail contracts Brown awarded were later deemed illegal, the system he created had a major influence on mail delivery and air travel throughout the twentieth century.

In 1925, Congress passed the Air Mail Act, also known as the Kelly Act. This act mandated the privatization of airmail service through the process of competitive bidding. This goal was accomplished by 1927; however, it soon became apparent that many of the contract airmail operators existed only because of the government airmail subsidy and were unwilling to commit to the expense of developing passenger service. A major premise of the airmail service had been that it would demonstrate the feasibility of regularly scheduled, long-distance airline service, which would ultimately result in the establishment of passenger service throughout the country.

When President Herbert Hoover was elected in 1928, he appointed Brown as postmaster general. After studying the existing airmail system, Brown concluded that it had to be redesigned in order to be efficient. However, the Air Mail Act of 1925 limited the authority of the postmaster general to mandate changes in the system. Late in 1929, Brown began his effort to streamline the entire air-transportation network. First, he refused to renew the five airmail contracts that were scheduled to expire, electing to extend them for six months. Brown openly expressed his dissatisfaction with the existing patchwork of routes and companies involved in the industry.

On October 9, 1930, Congress passed the third amendment to the Air Mail Act. Called the McNary-Watres Act, the amendment was crafted by Brown himself with the assistance of William P. Mac-Cracken, Jr., a former assistant secretary of commerce and airline-industry lobbyist. This act revised the manner in which airlines were paid for carrying mail and gave the postmaster general virtually dictatorial power over the industry. The postmaster general's prerogative was to determine which bidders for airmail contracts were considered responsible and what actions would best serve the public interest. The act also included the provision that only airlines that had flown a daily schedule of at least 250 miles for six months were eligible to bid; this immediately eliminated many of the smaller airlines.

With his power firmly established, Brown called a meeting in May, 1930, with a select group of airline executives. At this meeting, called the "spoils conference," Brown imposed his will on the industry and created three transcontinental routes operated by three large, well-financed airlines. Those who objected to his provisions were threatened with the denial of airmail contracts, the lifeblood of the industry. Brown forced a number of unwilling participants to merge, thus establishing American Airlines and Trans World Airlines (TWA), which in turn were awarded transcontinental mail routes. He used his authority to extend postal routes and adjust rates.

Brown also imposed a requirement that pilots have experience flying at night, a provision that was not part of the McNary-Watres Act but that Brown argued best served the public interest. In order to silence the objections of some smaller airlines such as Southwest Air Fast Express, Brown went so far as to encourage one of his favored airlines to buy out the troublemakers. In the case of Southwest Air Fast Express, the purchase price was twice the value of the airline.

The details of Brown's meetings were uncovered by a Hearst newspaper reporter. Based on the reporter's evidence, Democratic senator Hugo L. Black initiated a congressional investigation. Black and the Democratic administration elected in 1932 were certain that they had uncovered evidence of collusion and illegal activities under Brown. The new postmaster, James Farley, and Black persuaded President Franklin D. Roosevelt to cancel the contracts and use the Army Air Corps to fly the mail. This move was a disaster, as twelve Army pilots were killed in the seventy-eight days before the contracts were returned to the airlines.

Impact Brown, in imposing his vision of the ideal air transportation system, favored large, well-financed corporations over smaller airlines. His methods were dictatorial and ultimately resulted in the bankruptcies or forced mergers of many smaller, pioneer operators. The big four airlines—United, TWA, American, and Eastern (or their subsidiaries)—were awarded nearly all of the available airmail contracts at the spoils conference. Regardless of Brown's methods, however, he created an effective mail and passenger air-transportation system. Brown transformed the system, creating thirty-four subsidized mail routes that covered more than 27,000 miles and carried 474,000 passengers by 1932. The cost to the post office of delivering airmail decreased from $1.10 to $0.54 per mile. The airline industry was on the brink of self-sufficiency when the contracts were canceled. The air-transportation program developed by Brown became the model for the system used throughout the rest of the twentieth century.

Ronald J. Ferrara

Further Reading

Allen, Oliver E. *The Airline Builders*. Alexandria, Va.: Time-Life Books, 1981. Provides a basic history of the development of airlines in the United States.

Brady, Tim, ed. *The American Aviation Experience: A History*. Carbondale: Southern Illinois University Press, 2000. A well-written history of aviation in the United States; includes a number of interesting illustrations.

Christy, Joe, and Leroy Cook. *American Aviation: An Illustrated History*. New York: Tab Books, 1994. A detailed history of aviation in the United States with valuable treatment of the airmail situation in the 1930's.

Ferrara, Ronald. "Legalized Murder: The Army Flies the Mail." *American Aviation Historical Society Journal* 54, no. 1 (2009): 45-52. Describes the airmail scandal of the 1930's, using primary sources from the Herbert Hoover Presidential Library.

See also Aviation and aeronautics; Black, Hugo L.; Business and the economy in the United States; DC-3; Elections of 1932, U.S.; Hoover, Herbert; New Deal; Trans World Airlines; Transportation.

■ Air pollution

Definition Degradation of physical and chemical air quality, usually the result of human activities

Most Americans did not see air pollution as a significant problem during the 1930's. Primarily caused by coal smoke, air pollution was becoming a health hazard in a few eastern cities but did not pose the environmental risks that it did in the latter part of the twentieth century.

Americans who lived in certain cities during the 1930's were aware that coal smoke often led to an unpleasant haze on some days. Medical practitioners even connected continued exposure to coal smoke with respiratory problems. Smoke and the resulting air pollution were connected to industrial production by many Americans during the 1930's even though home heating with coal also contributed to air pollution. In some areas the decline in industrial production that came from the Great Depression led to less air pollution early in the decade.

Sources of Air Pollution Burning fossil fuels has always generated smoke as a result of combustion. Burning coal in particular generates several harmful pollutants, such as sulfur dioxide and nitrogen oxides, that produce acid deposition when these compounds interact with water vapor in the atmosphere. By the late twentieth century, sulfur dioxide and nitrogen oxides were classified as major contributors to air pollution. During the 1930's, few Americans were aware of these hazards, but they did notice that clothes left on an outdoor clothesline in an area with extensive coal smoke often took on a grayish tinge. These pollutants also created lung problems for many Americans, especially in the winter, when atmosphere inversions led to smoke settling along the ground for extended periods of time.

Metal smelting also contributed to air pollution. Copper smelting in particular produced large amounts of sulfur dioxide in the air. In places such as Copper Hill, Tennessee, the sulfur dioxide emitted into the atmosphere destroyed all of the vegetation in the region, producing a terrain that looked like a moonscape.

In some areas people were more concerned with noxious odors than smoke. People who lived near meatpacking plants and stockyards in such cities as Chicago often complained of the odors. In other areas chemical or rubber plants emitted odors that nearby residents found objectionable. People may have been less aware of the chemical pollutants coming from these plants, but toxic chemicals, heavy metals, sulfur dioxide, and particulate matter were also part of the mix in the air near many of these plants. Even though nearby residents complained of headaches, they were not fully aware of the long-term health hazards in their air, hazards could cause lung cancer and other respiratory problems.

Agriculture also contributed to air pollution during the decade. The severe drought in the Great Plains region that had started during the 1920's made growing crops in many parts of the region impossible. Without any ground cover the wind could easily blow the topsoil high into the atmosphere. The resulting dust storms occurred in an area of little industrial production but produced many respiratory problems for anyone near. Some of these dust storms lasted for days, often burying small buildings and killing cattle. The dust from the Great Plains even found its way to the East Coast and darkened the skies in cities such as Washington, D.C.

The Effects of Air Pollution   During the 1930's, air pollution had a negative impact on the United States, even if most people did not consider it to be a problem. One negative impact visible in some older cities was the damage done by sulfur and nitrogen oxides. When acid rain fell on limestone buildings, the resulting chemical reaction led to the gradual destruction of the limestone.

Air pollution can produce numerous health problems, both short- and long-term. Irritated eyes and runny noses resulting from exposure to coal smoke were often taken to be normal wintertime occurrences. Sensitive people, however, also might experience bronchitis or weakened resistance that could lead to colds or pneumonia. Long-term exposure to some chemical pollutants could cause cancers or reduced lung function.

The massive dust storms that swept across the plains produced allergic reactions and more severe respiratory problems. Because keeping the fine dust out of buildings was nearly impossible, the dust storms affected people who stayed indoors. In a few cases, the volume of the dust in the air even killed people or animals that were exposed for lengthy periods of time.

Impact   Coal and chemical pollution continued to be growing factors in American life, especially as in-

dustry resumed production. Some cities, such as Chicago and Cincinnati, had passed smoke reduction ordinances in the nineteenth century. By 1940, fifty-two cities and three counties had smoke reduction ordinances. Even by the end of the 1930's smoke was considered to be a local problem; therefore, there were no state or national laws governing air pollution. The local laws were almost exclusively smoke-reduction laws that did not deal with the chemical components of coal smoke or other forms of chemical air pollution.

John M. Theilmann

Further Reading
Davis, Devra Lee. *When Smoke Ran Like Water: Tales of Environmental Deception and the Battle Against Pollution.* New York: Basic Books, 2000. Good account of smoke pollution and the fight against it.
Merchant, Carolyn. *American Environmental History: An Introduction.* New York: Columbia University Press, 2007. Parts of several chapters deal with various pollution issues of the 1930's.
Portney, Paul R. "Air Pollution Policy." In *Public Policies for Environmental Pollution,* edited by Paul R. Portney. Washington, D.C.: Resources for the Future, 1990. Good summary of early air-pollution legislation.
Wirth, John. *Smelter Smoke in North America: The Politics of Transborder Pollution.* Lawrence: University Press of Kansas, 2000. Discusses pollution from metal smelters.
Worster, Donald. *Dust Bowl.* Rev. ed. New York: Oxford University Press, 2004. Examines various impacts of the Dust Bowl.

See also   Cancer; Dust Bowl; Natural resources.

■ Airships

Definition   Type of aircraft held aloft by lighter-than-air gas stored in large internal cavities; usually steered by rudders under thrust provided by propellers

Because airships were the first vehicles capable of transporting heavy loads via air and also offered the first luxury air travel, their popularity in the United States grew quickly among the military and civilians, particularly during the 1930's. This period of airship development later helped the United States effectively utilize small blimps to detect enemy submarines during World War II.

Following a lengthy period of development beginning as far back as the late eighteenth century, airships enjoyed a tremendous surge in popularity in the United States between World War I and World War II. This popularity culminated during the 1930's, when transoceanic airship travel was considered the height of luxury and the U.S. military sought ways to enhance its air power. Three types of airships were used throughout this period: smaller nonrigid airships, also called blimps; semirigid airships, which were slightly larger vehicles with some internal structure; and rigid airships, which had extensive internal skeletons and the largest cargo and passenger capacities.

Arrival of Airships in the United States   During World War I, the U.S. government, intrigued by German and English advances in airship capabilities, decided to pursue this line of technology, in part as defense against German submarines. In 1917, the Goodyear Tire and Rubber Company purchased land near Akron, Ohio, to build a plant for its newly formed subsidiary, the Goodyear Zeppelin Company, which signed a contract to produce nonrigid

airships for the U.S. military. The end of World War I in 1918 led to renewed cooperation between Germany and the United States, the latter of which received the German-built zeppelin the USS *Los Angeles* in 1924. This allowed Goodyear a close look at the Germans' rigid airship technology, leading to an additional contract for Goodyear Zeppelin to build two rigid airships for the U.S. Navy.

Triumphs and Tragedies   On August 8, 1931, the USS *Akron* was christened by First Lady Lou Hoover in front of a cheering crowd. For the next two years, the *Akron* participated in a series of exercises, demonstrating its ability to act as an airborne aircraft carrier for five reconnaissance fighter planes. The *Akron*'s performance was impressive but was marred by a series of minor accidents over the following several months. The airship was joined on March 11, 1933, by its sister ship, the *Macon*, but only a month later, the *Akron* was lost in a catastrophic accident, killing seventy-three of the seventy-six people aboard.

With the loss of the *Akron*, the *Macon* was joined by the *Los Angeles*, which was brought out of retirement. The *Macon* survived only two years. However, when the ship was lost on February 12, 1935, there were only two deaths because it had been outfitted with life jackets and inflatable rafts following the loss at sea of the *Akron*. The *Los Angeles* remained in service until 1939, when it was retired a second time.

In the meantime, Germany had launched the *Graf Zeppelin* in 1928 and the *Hindenburg* in 1936, which together became known as the fastest and most comfortable means of crossing the Atlantic Ocean. In addition to passengers, these zeppelins transported cargo and mail among Europe, North America, and South America. In 1933, the *Graf Zeppelin* made a brief stop at the Chicago World's Fair, thus fueling American's interest in these magnificent airships. However, on May 6, 1937, the *Hindenburg* burst into flames while landing in Lakehurst, New Jersey, killing thirty-five people.

Naval personnel sorting through the wreckage of the airship USS Akron after it crashed off the coast of New Jersey in 1933. Airships were plagued by a series of unfortunate occurrences during the 1930's, and their military and public popularity declined as the decade progressed. (AP/Wide World Photos)

The *Graf Zeppelin* was retired a month later amid safety concerns, in spite of its perfect safety record.

The loss of three of the five best-known airships within a span of only four years caused a tremendous loss of confidence from which the airship industry could not recover. In the meantime, advances in traditional airplane technology meant that persevering through the airships' safety and operational issues was not imperative, and the industry dwindled to only a fraction of its former glory.

Impact   In spite of the decline of airship transportation by the end of the 1930's, the quiet, graceful vehicles never entirely lost their hold on the public's imagination. In addition, the Allied forces in World War II successfully utilized the smaller, nonrigid blimps in antisubmarine operations. After World War II, companies such as Goodyear and MetLife continued to use blimps for tourism and advertising. The aviation industry has explored the possibility of reintroducing airships for military and commercial use, taking advantage of technological advances that would reduce the possibility of catastrophic incidents.

Amy Sisson

Further Reading

Crouch, Tom D. *Lighter than Air: An Illustrated History of Balloons and Airships.* Baltimore: Johns Hopkins University Press, 2009. Describes the development of pressure airships and their various uses during the first half of the twentieth century.

De Syon, Guillaume. *Zeppelin: Germany and the Airship, 1900-1939.* Baltimore: Johns Hopkins University Press, 2007. Primarily addresses the wartime origins and culture surrounding zeppelins but contains a chapter detailing how airship culture and travel came of age during the period from 1933 to 1939.

Dick, Harold G., and Douglas H. Robinson. *Graf Zeppelin and Hindenburg: The Golden Age of the Great Passenger Airships.* Washington, D.C.: Smithsonian Institution Press, 1985. Based on photographs, notes, diaries, and other materials collected by Dick, an American Goodyear engineer who worked at the Zeppelin Company in Germany from 1934 to 1938. Gives a first-person perspective into the relationship between the two most important companies in airship history.

Payne, Lee. *Lighter than Air: An Illustrated History of the Airship.* Rev. ed. New York: Orion Books, 1991. Notable for its extensive quotes by eyewitnesses to key events, gleaned from radio broadcasts, newspaper articles, and personal interviews.

Topping, Dale. *When Giants Roamed the Sky: Karl Arnstein and the Rise of Airships from Zeppelin to Goodyear.* Akron, Ohio: University of Akron Press, 2001. This illustrated volume traces the history of rigid airships in the United States by following the work of Karl Arnstein, who played key roles in both the German company Zeppelin and the American company Goodyear.

See also   *Akron* disaster; Aviation and aeronautics; *Hindenburg* disaster; Naval forces; Transportation.

■ *Akron* disaster

The Event   Crash of a U.S. Navy airship
Date   April 3, 1933
Place   Off the New Jersey coast

The Akron, *one of the largest man-made objects ever to fly, was part of the early history of U.S. naval aviation. The Navy commissioned the ship to help it develop a lighter-than-air aviation program, but the crash of the* Akron *prompted the U.S. government to move toward a fleet of heavier-than-air ships such as airplanes.*

The *Akron*, officially known as the ZRS-4, was 785 feet long and 133 feet in diameter and had a top speed of 78 miles per hour. Akron, an industrial city in Ohio, had been hard hit by the Depression, and the naming of the ZRS-4 was an effort to instill some cheer. The ship, which Goodyear Tire and Rubber Company built in two years at the cost of more than $5 million, launched in 1930. A rigid airship, the *Akron* could launch and recover airplanes in flight, provide reconnaissance, and help rescue sailors.

The airship departed from the U.S. Naval Air Station at Lakehurst, New Jersey, at 7:38 P.M. on April 3, 1933. Frank C. McCord served as captain, with Herbert V. Wiley as his executive officer. Rear Admiral William A. Moffett, first head of the U.S. Bureau of Aeronautics and arguably the father of naval aviation, was also on board. The *Akron* soon encountered thunderstorms that accompanied a cold front from the west. Trying to dodge the storms, McCord guided the *Akron* over the Atlantic Ocean. About midnight, the ship went into the sea tail first, killing seventy-three people; only Wiley and two enlisted men survived. A German tanker rescued the survivors. The *Akron* carried no life jackets. The cause of the crash was never determined. Both structural failure and down currents from the storm cells were suspected. To add to the tragedy, the nonrigid airship J-3 crashed while searching for *Akron* survivors, killing two crew members.

Impact When the *Akron*'s sister ship, the *Macon*, crashed in 1935, the Navy's rigid airship program ended. Congress did authorize two hundred blimps, all nonrigid, for the Navy in 1940, as preparation for World War II. However, the ships proved too fragile for anything more than monitoring U-boats.

Caryn E. Neumann

Further Reading

Topping, Dale. *When Giants Roamed the Sky: Karl Arnstein and the Rise of Airships from Zeppelin to Goodyear.* Akron, Ohio: University of Akron Press, 2001.

Vaeth, J. Gordon. *They Sailed the Skies: U.S. Navy Balloons and the Airship Program.* Annapolis, Md.: Naval Institute Press, 2005.

See also Airships; Aviation and aeronautics; *Hindenburg* disaster; Naval forces; Transportation; World War II and the United States.

■ Alcatraz Federal Penitentiary

Identification First maximum security prison
Also known as America's Devil's Island; Hellcatraz; The Rock
Date Opened on August 22, 1934; closed on March 21, 1963
Place San Francisco Bay, California

Alcatraz Federal Penitentiary, designated a National Historic Landmark in 1986, is a significant monument of the 1930's. As a result of the prison's status as a park, hundreds of people tour the island each day. It housed some of the most notorious criminals and gangsters from the 1930's, including Al Capone, George "Machine Gun" Kelly, Alvin Karpis, and Robert Franklin Stroud.

Established in 1934, the Alcatraz federal prison was the first super-maximum facility to provide a high level of security for notorious criminals and gangsters. During the early 1930's, there was a dramatic increase in crimes and gangs, a trend attributable to

the negative effects of the Great Depression, which impacted the social and economic landscape of the country. In response to the massive rise in crime, both the public and the government adopted a more punitive approach to the treatment of the notorious offenders. Therefore, Alcatraz federal prison was supposed to demonstrate to the offenders and the general public that the government was serious in addressing the issue of violent crimes.

This federal prison was located on Alcatraz Island, which is in the San Francisco Bay, California. The island was discovered in 1775 by Juan Manuel del Ayala, a Spanish explorer, who named the island, La Isla de los Altraces (The Island of the Pelicans). Many considered the island to be an ideal location for a prison because it was essentially composed of a large rock that was surrounded by cold and swirling tides infested with white sharks. Historically, the island had been used as a military prison for several groups of people, such as Confederate sympathizers, Union soldiers, and Native Americans.

In 1934, the Federal Bureau of Prisons converted the facility to provide maximum security through solitary confinement for criminals and gang members. The prison had a capacity of 600 inmates, but the average inmate population was 204. Inmates had committed a range of crimes, from kidnapping to bank robbery, tax evasion, murder and other violent crimes, drug violations, and gang membership.

Life at Alcatraz federal prison was rigid. Officials afforded inmates only the basic requirements for survival: clothing, shelter, food, and medical care. There were three main cell blocks used on a regular basis. The sizes of the cells were 5 feet by 9 feet and each contained a bed, a sink, a toilet, and a writing desk. Privileges such as employment, recreation, library access, visits, and personal correspondence had to be earned.

The daily activities were rigid and regimental; body counts were conducted several times each day. The inmates worked five days per week for eight hours each day. They were required to be up at 7:00 A.M. and have lights out at 9:30 P.M. Three meals were provided each day, and whatever was taken had to be eaten. The work assignments included laundry, tailoring, gardening, standard labor, and employment in the metal shop. Inmates who exhibited sustained good behavior could be assigned to work with the guards' families.

Recreation was also provided for the inmates, but

In 1934, railroad cars transported by ferry deliver prisoners, including gangster Al Capone, to Alcatraz Federal Penitentiary in the San Francisco Bay. (AP/Wide World Photos)

each inmate was quarantined upon arrival for thirty days. Once per month a film was shown, and inmates could also have a supervised visit. Physical exercise was available through organized games such as baseball and handball. Table games were also available. The inmates also had access to recreation on the weekends and on public holidays.

Inmates were expected to obey the rules, avoid contraband, and perform well on their work assignments. They also had the opportunity to earn "good time," which could shorten their sentences. Disciplinary action resulted in loss of privileges, such as recreation, and could require assignment to special cells where the inmate could be left naked, without blankets and with limited food.

The average stay at Alcatraz was eight years, although most prisoners became eligible for a transfer to a less restricted facility after five years. This was contingent on the inmate's behavior and his ability to follow rules. One of the positive aspects of the

Alcatraz federal prison was that it afforded inmates some degree of privacy and reduced the likelihood of abuse by others.

Although Alcatraz was considered escape-proof, there were several escape attempts during the 1930's. However, most were unsuccessful because the inmates were either recaptured, shot, or went missing and were presumed drowned.

Alcatraz federal prison closed operations in 1964 because of the high operating costs and the deteriorating conditions of the prison. The provision of solitary confinement in individual cells made the operating costs of Alcatraz approximately three times higher than the operating costs of most other prisons. Another factor that may have contributed to the high operating costs was the low 1:5 ratio of officers to inmates.

Impact Alcatraz federal prison was the first attempt to provide maximum security for prisoners. Although the prison was closed after twenty-nine years, it nevertheless made a significant contribution to penology. Several films and video games were developed based on prison life in and escape attempts from Alcatraz. It remains an important landmark and tourist attraction in San Francisco.

Fay V. Williams

Further Reading

Allen, Harry E., et al. *Corrections in America: An Introduction.* 10th ed. Upper Saddle River, N.J.: Pearson Education, 2004.

Schmalleger, Frank, and John Ortiz Smykla. *Corrections in the Twenty-first Century.* New York: McGraw-Hill, 2001.

Ward, David A., and Gene G. Kassebaum. *Alcatraz: The Gangster Years.* Berkeley: University of California Press, 2009.

Welsh, Michael. *Corrections: A Critical Approach.* 2d ed. New York: McGraw-Hill, 2004.

See also   Capone, Al; Kelly, Machine Gun; National parks; Native Americans.

■ Alcoholics Anonymous

Identification   Autonomous mutual-help organization fostering abstinence and recovery from alcoholism for members
Also known as   AA
Date   Founded on June 10, 1935

Alcoholics Anonymous revolutionized the treatment of addiction by synthesizing elements of medicine, religion, and philosophy in a manner that had never before been tried with alcoholics. Originally applied to treatment of alcohol and drug addiction, the twelve steps proved successful for a variety of other disorders.

Alcoholics Anonymous did not legally exist until April of 1939. However, members trace the organization's founding to June 10, 1935. On this date, two severe sufferers of alcoholism clinched their agreement to apply a synthesis of medicine, first century Christianity, and pragmatism in order to achieve permanent sobriety. Until their deaths, neither William G. Wilson nor Robert Smith touched another drink of alcohol.

Between 1935 and 1939, Wilson and Smith spent most of their time promoting their program of absti-

nence to other alcoholics in hospitals and sanatoriums. Wilson formulated these principles into a coherent twelve-step method of spiritual conversion in the fall of 1938. This method was particularly inspired by the philosopher William James, the psychologist Carl Jung, Judeo-Christian principles of the Oxford Group (later Moral Rearmament), and the medical conception of alcoholism inspired by William D. Silkworth of Towns Hospital in New York. Alcoholics Anonymous is a uniquely American religious movement in that the twelve-step program does not require members to adhere to any particular denomination, or adhere to any religion at all. It simply requires an attitude of tolerance toward religious matters. Wilson, a bankrupted Wall Street financier, spent nearly all his life devoted to the work of helping other alcoholics and guided Alcoholics Anonymous to become a self-sustaining organization. Smith, however, quickly regained his prominence as a highly respected proctologist and was not nearly as involved in the development of the organization.

Originally, two groups existed. One group was in Akron, Ohio, the other in Brooklyn, New York. The groups were associated with the residences of Smith and Wilson, respectively. A third autonomous group, led by Clarence Snyder, formed slowly between 1935 and 1939 in Cleveland, Ohio. The characteristics of these groups varied, but each was led by the idea of members sharing personal biographies with one another to achieve sobriety. These regular meetings were usually held at the homes of Wilson, Smith, or Snyder. Biographies shared during meetings emphasized what life was like while drinking, what happened at the point of sobriety, and what life was like after sobriety. This method of sharing helped new members to identify as alcoholics and presented them with practical suggestions for sobriety.

By the time of publication of the book *Alcoholics Anonymous* (1939), membership numbered one hundred. This represented an approximate 5 percent success rate. Members of the fellowship nicknamed the text "The Big Book," based on its abnormal size. For Wilson, this book represented as much of a publicity attempt as it did a written program of recovery for members. Although in later years this book was a cornerstone in the growth of the fellowship, initially it gained virtually no external recognition.

By the end of 1939, Alcoholics Anonymous was

struggling both financially and publicly, despite minor but laudable articles about the group published in the *Cleveland Plain Dealer* newspaper and *Liberty* magazine and a book review in *The New York Times*. Although the group experienced early tribulations, membership grew steadily during the decade, and the organization had planted seeds that proved fruitful in later decades.

Impact The Alcoholics Anonymous fellowship expanded around the globe to include more than two million members. In the United States, groups can be found in every metropolis and a majority of rural areas. Although membership has expanded and receded at various points in the organization's history, the group has never displayed symptoms of collapse. The twelve-step program articulated by Wilson has proven effective for recovery from a variety of substance-abuse disorders and other obsessive-compulsive disorders, including compulsive gambling, sex addiction, and eating disorders.

Tony Buell

Further Reading

Alcoholics Anonymous. *Alcoholics Anonymous.* 4th ed. New York: Alcoholics Anonymous World Services, 2004.

Cheever, Susan. *My Name Is Bill: Bill Wilson—His Life and the Creation of Alcoholics Anonymous.* New York: Simon & Schuster, 2004.

James, William. *The Varieties of Religious Experience.* New York: Touchstone, 2004.

Kurtz, Ernest. *Not-God: A History of Alcoholics Anonymous.* 2d ed. Center City, Minn.: Hazelden Educational Services, 1980.

See also Great Depression in the United States; Philosophy and philosophers; Psychology and psychiatry; Religion in the United States; Unemployment in the United States.

AA's Twelve Steps

Alcoholics Anonymous adopted the Twelve Steps in 1939, and they have been a crucial part of the organization ever since.

1. We admitted we were powerless over alcohol—that our lives had become unmanageable.
2. Came to believe that a Power greater than ourselves could restore us to sanity.
3. Made a decision to turn our will and our lives over to the care of God *as we understood Him.*
4. Made a searching and fearless moral inventory of ourselves.
5. Admitted to God, to ourselves, and to another human being the exact nature of our wrongs.
6. Were entirely ready to have God remove all these defects of character.
7. Humbly asked Him to remove our shortcomings.
8. Made a list of all persons we had harmed, and became willing to make amends to them all.
9. Made direct amends to such people wherever possible, except when to do so would injure them or others.
10. Continued to take personal inventory and when we were wrong promptly admitted it.
11. Sought through prayer and meditation to improve our conscious contact with God as we understood Him, praying only for knowledge of His will for us and the power to carry that out.
12. Having had a spiritual awakening as the result of these steps, we tried to carry this message to alcoholics, and to practice these principles in all our affairs.

Source: Alcoholics Anonymous World Services, *Big Book*, 4th ed. (New York: Author, 2001).

■ All Quiet on the Western Front

Identification Film about German students who volunteer to serve during World War I
Director Lewis Milestone
Date Released on April 21, 1930

During the early 1930's, when an era of renewed militaristic nationalism dawned in Europe, All Quiet on the Western Front *was Hollywood's strongest antiwar statement. The film was a critical and financial success and won two Academy Awards, including best picture and best director.*

All Quiet on the Western Front was a film adaptation of German author Erich Maria Remarque's 1928 antiwar novel of the same title. By 1930, the novel had already been translated into more than twenty languages and had sold more than 25 million copies. Carl Laemmle, Jr., produced the film, and Lewis Milestone directed it.

All Quiet on the Western Front begins with a military parade in a small German town in 1914 followed by a passionate speech by a warmongering professor in a schoolroom. The teacher indoctrinates his students with nationalism and calls on them to volunteer for war service in defense of Germany. Enthusiastically, seven naive students follow their teacher's appeal, among them Paul Bäumer (Lew Ayres) and some of his close friends. Their disillusionment begins early, during basic training, and is solidified during the first night in the trenches when one of them is first blinded by shrapnel and then killed by gunfire. The terror of the incessant shelling gradually erodes the sanity of those who survive. One by one, the boys are wounded and killed. In the end, only Paul is still alive. In the film's famous final scene, Paul reaches for a butterfly as a shot is heard; Paul's hand drops, indicating his death.

Impact   *All Quiet on the Western Front* distinguishes itself from other major Hollywood war films as it is told from the perspective of the United States' eventual World War I enemy, yet the viewer identifies with the young German soldiers. Thus, the film emphasizes the common humanity across battle lines. The film features stark realism, depicting man-to-man combat and, in particular, World War I trench warfare, and is considered to be one of the most important American antiwar films.

Tim Gruenewald

Further Reading

Hark, Ina Rae. *American Cinema of the 1930's*. New Brunswick, N.J.: Rutgers University Press, 2007.

Kelly, Andrew. *Cinema and the Great War*. London: Routledge, 1997.

_____. *Filming "All Quiet on the Western Front."* London: I. B. Tauris, 1998.

See also   Academy Awards; Film; Geneva Disarmament Conference; Peace movement.

■ American Federation of Labor

Identification   Coalition of labor unions
Date   Established in December, 1886

The American Federation of Labor (AFL) was the major labor organization in the United States at the beginning of the 1930's. It suffered significant membership loss during the 1920's and early 1930's, but it was revived after New Deal legislation gave more legal protection to labor unions. During the mid-1930's, the AFL experienced a major schism over the issue of organizing workers in mass-production industries. This split led to the creation of the Congress of Industrial Organizations (CIO) in 1938.

Since its founding under Samuel Gompers in 1886, the AFL had emphasized craft or trade unionism—the organization of skilled workers into unions for each particular job specialty or craft. These skilled workers felt little solidarity with unskilled workers. As mass-production industries grew, however, more and more factory workers did not practice any particular craft. Many workers felt that only industrial unions, representing all the workers in a particular industry no matter their job or skill level, could represent the needs of such workers. When Gompers died in 1924, William Green became president of the AFL. Green had been part of the United Mine Workers and had declared support for industrial unionism earlier in his career. However, as head of the AFL, he continued Gompers's emphasis on organizing skilled craft workers.

Organized labor suffered significant losses in membership during the early years of the Great Depression. In 1933, union membership was less than three million. President Franklin D. Roosevelt's more sympathetic approach to organized labor and the passage of important legislation, such as the Norris-La Guardia Act of 1932 and section 7a of the National Industrial Recovery Act of 1933 (later incorporated into the Wagner-Connery Act of 1935), gave new impetus to the labor movement. While union membership began to grow again, a conflict existed within the AFL between the trade unionists and the industrial unionists. This controversy, which raged from 1935 to 1938, eventually led to the creation of the CIO under John L. Lewis, the president of the United Mine Workers.

Rather than create industry-wide unions covering all workers in a particular industry, traditionalists within the AFL wanted to maintain the jurisdiction of the traditional craft unions, ignoring the fact that many workers in mass-production jobs did not fall clearly into any job specialty or trade. As worker militancy grew and strike activity became more frequent, the AFL leadership continued to pursue a more conservative course, at times accepting federal intervention instead of calling strikes. Finally in 1938, the industrial unionists, who were generally also the more militant activists, left the AFL to form the CIO. While the CIO soon rivaled the AFL in size, both organizations continued to grow during the late 1930's and then grew dramatically when war production started to revive industrial manufacturing during the 1940's.

Under Gompers and Green, the AFL had usually held to a nonpartisan position, aligning with no political party but agreeing to support candidates who promised to work for the good of labor. The CIO became more clearly associated with the Democratic Party. The traditionalists within the AFL may not have liked this trend, but neither did they react against it. During the New Deal era the identification of organized labor with the Democratic Party became more pronounced.

Impact   The internal struggles within the AFL during the 1930's illustrated the two diverging concepts of labor organization in the United States: trade unionism as opposed to industrial unionism. Despite the struggles and schism, both the AFL and the CIO continued to grow during the late 1930's; by 1937, union membership was more than seven million, about twice what it had been in 1932.

As a more conservative, probusiness atmosphere arose in the United States after World War II, the differences between the approaches of the AFL and CIO seemed to be less important than a unified stand for labor. In 1955, the two bodies merged, creating a labor organization representing more than sixteen million workers.

Mark S. Joy

Further Reading

Galenson, Walter. *The CIO Challenge to the AFL: A History of the American Labor Movement.* Cambridge, Mass.: Harvard University Press, 1960.

Kennedy, David. *Freedom from Fear: The American People in Depression and War, 1929-1945.* New York: Oxford University Press, 1999.

Sinyai, Clayton. *Schools of Democracy: A Political History of the American Labor Movement.* Ithaca, N.Y.: Cornell University Press, 2006.

See also   Congress of Industrial Organizations; Labor strikes; Lewis, John L.; National Industrial Recovery Act of 1933; *National Labor Relations Board v. Jones and Laughlin Steel Corp.*; Unionism.

■ American Gothic

Identification   Iconic painting of a rural midwestern couple
Painter   Grant Wood
Date   Painted in 1930

The Regionalist style of the 1930's was sandwiched between abstracted and often inaccessible movements such as Surrealism and Abstract Expressionism. The painting American Gothic *is often cited as the best example of Regionalism because of its simple style and return to early American ideals.*

Grant Wood's *American Gothic* has become a national icon. Wood's inspiration for the painting came when he saw a gothic-styled farmhouse and attempted to envision the people who lived within it. The result of Wood's vision is a painting depicting a midwestern couple clad in provincial attire. The farmer, modeled after Wood's dentist, wears denim overalls and a jacket. The pitchfork he holds has a prominent position in the center of the image and repeats the rigid vertical lines on the farmhouse. The female figure, modeled after Wood's sister, who has been interpreted as both the wife of the farmer and his spinster daughter, is wearing an apron over a modest blouse fastened high on her throat with a broach. The farmer's rigid pitchfork is a reference to masculine roles in early American society, while the curvilinear designs on the woman's apron and the plants over her shoulder refer to feminine roles.

The man and woman have dour expressions, and their faces are aged and haggard, characteristics that have caused critics and viewers to criticize Wood for providing a pessimistic and simplified view of American Midwest citizens. What perhaps increases this negative perception is that the painting is done in the Regionalist style of the 1930's. As a member of the Regionalist movement, Wood, along with Thomas Hart Benton and John Steuart Curry, rejected the abstracted and modern art of the cities

One of the most iconic paintings ever produced in the United States, American Gothic *(1930) is the masterpiece of Regionalist artist Grant Wood.* (The Granger Collection, New York)

and instead celebrated the rural locations of the United States, which they viewed as the true representation of the country.

Impact   *American Gothic* is one of the few paintings in history to have achieved an iconic status and readily recognizable familiarity. The numerous parodies of this work suggest that it has touched a nerve in American culture, despite its seemingly simple subject. Exactly what about the painting people have continued to respond to is unclear. Perhaps it is that the couple, depicted in such a straightforward and undemanding style, represents the physical, spiritual, economic, and social aspects of Americans.

Ellen Lippert

Further Reading

Biel, Steven. *"American Gothic": A Life of America's Most Famous Painting.* New York: W. W. Norton, 2005.

Corn, Wanda. "The Birth of a National Icon: Grant Wood's *American Gothic.*" In *Reading American Art,*

edited by Marianne Doezema and Elizabeth Milroy. New Haven, Conn.: Yale University Press, 1998.

See also   Art movements; Benton, Thomas Hart; Curry, John Steuart; Wood, Grant.

■ American Liberty League

Identification   Nongovernmental organization opposing the New Deal
Also known as   Liberty League
Date   Established on August 15, 1934

In the interests of business, the American Liberty League opposed the New Deal policies of President Franklin D. Roosevelt. It engaged in an extensive public-relations campaign to convince the American public that Roosevelt was subverting the Constitution and the free market system. Democrats were successful in portraying the group as representing the same forces that caused the Great Depression.

Many business leaders opposed President Roosevelt's New Deal from the beginning of his administration in 1933. However, there was no single organization that united the various segments of the business community to publicly oppose the president. This changed on August 15, 1934, with the formal pronouncement of the founding of the American Liberty League.

The organization described itself as a nonpartisan group founded to protect the Constitution and preserve liberty. To reinforce this nonpartisanship, the leadership of the American Liberty League was composed of three prominent Democrats (including the 1924 and 1928 nominees for president, John W. Davis and Alfred E. Smith) and three Republicans. Nevertheless, from the start, the fact that the group was composed of conservative politicians and business interests that opposed the policies of Roosevelt was apparent. Undergirding this opposition was a belief in free markets, personal responsibility, and private property. The American Liberty League argued that the New Deal was unconstitutional and would lead to socialism and the demise of private enterprise. To stop the perceived threat of the New Deal, the league's primary objective became defeating Roosevelt in his bid for reelection in 1936.

Leadership of the American Liberty League sought to build a broad-based organization that incorporated all facets of American society. Its goal was a mass membership of three to four million people. However, the league never had more than seventy-five thousand members and remained primarily an organization of prominent members of the business community.

Described as a "Who's Who" of American business leadership, the league's members helped fund an expensive campaign to defeat Roosevelt. They created a sophisticated public-relations system to relate their agenda to the press and ultimately the American public. From the league's inception until the 1936 presidential election, the league sent to media outlets more than five million copies of 177 publications that they had produced. These publications, along with frequent editorials, consistently carried the theme of the organization: Roosevelt was presiding over the demise of the American way of life and leading the country toward a nightmarish future of governmental control.

Roosevelt and the Democratic Party were able to use the affluence of the American Liberty League against it. They portrayed the league's members as the cause of the economic failures that led to the Great Depression and claimed that its ideas of laissez-faire economics and small government were rooted in its own economic self-interest rather than the interest of the common person.

Ultimately the league came to be viewed by the public as out of touch with the economic realities of the 1930's. This perception was crystallized when Smith gave a speech before an affluent crowd of league supporters at the exclusive Mayflower Hotel in Washington, D.C., on January 25, 1936. Smith implied that members of the Roosevelt administration were more in tune with Karl Marx and the Soviet Union than with the founders of the United States. His speech received widespread attention and the extreme views voiced were ultimately seen as helping the cause of the New Deal and marginalizing the American Liberty League politically.

The overwhelming reelection victory of Roosevelt in 1936 signaled the beginning of the end for the American Liberty League. Stung by its massive defeat, the leadership of the league ended its attempts to persuade public opinion. It cut its staff and focused on providing Congress with analyses of New Deal legislation. The group hung on for several more years but disbanded in September, 1940, when the last of its major funders withdrew support.

Impact The American Liberty League was the most vocal and well-financed lobbying group of the 1930's. Backed by prominent businessmen, the organization labeled New Deal legislation as contrary to traditional views of the Constitution, the role of government in society, and personal responsibility. The group never gained public support because its objectives ran counter to the public opinion of the 1930's.

J. Wesley Leckrone

Further Reading

Archer, Jules. *The Plot to Seize the White House: The Shocking True Story of the Conspiracy to Overthrow FDR.* New York: Skyhorse, 2007.

Wolfskill, George. *All but the People: Franklin D. Roosevelt and His Critics, 1933-39.* New York: Macmillan, 1969.

_____. *The Revolt of the Conservatives: A History of the American Liberty League, 1934-1940.* Boston: Houghton Mifflin, 1962.

See also Business and the economy in the United States; Elections of 1936, U.S.; Great Depression in the United States; New Deal; Smith, Alfred E.

■ *Amos 'n' Andy*

Identification A radio program about two black laborers from the South who migrate to Chicago

Dates Broadcast on radio from 1928 to 1960

Amos 'n' Andy was one of the first serial comedies broadcast on radio, originally airing on WMAQ in Chicago. It also was the longest-running program in radio history. At the height of its popularity in the early 1930's, it claimed an audience of approximately 40 million listeners.

Amos 'n' Andy was created by Freeman Fisher Gosden and Charles Correll, two white minstrel performers who began working together in radio in the mid-1920's. The program had its roots in *Sam 'n' Henry,* an earlier radio serial that the duo created for Chicago's WGN radio station in 1926. Gosden and Correll not only wrote the scripts for *Amos 'n' Andy* but also played most of the show's male characters, including the title roles.

The characters Amos Jones and Andy Brown were farmworkers from Georgia. Like many African Americans during the period, they had migrated north to Chicago after World War I, hoping to land better jobs and strike it rich. Amos was an uneducated, naive, but diligent and honest man who was determined to improve his lot in life. By contrast, Andy was an egotistical know-it-all, who was not particularly fond of hard work. Gosden and Correll carefully crafted these characters. They were highly nuanced, unlike the rough stereotypes often used to portray African Americans. The writers took similar care with other characters. For example, Ruby, Amos's girlfriend and later his wife, was a confident, educated young woman. The program's supporting cast also featured black doctors, lawyers, police officers, secretaries, and judges. Nonetheless, some characters did display stereotypical qualities, including "Kingfish"

Stevens, a larger-than-life hustler, and Sapphire, his domineering wife.

Over the following decade, audiences followed Amos and Andy's escapades in nightly fifteen-minute installments. They listened as the pair established the "Fresh Air Taxi Company" and then moved from Chicago's west side to Harlem, New York. Amos's seven-year courtship of his beloved Ruby and the subsequent birth of their daughter, Arbadella, kept audiences riveted. Andy's ill-fated schemes to make money and the pair's involvement with Kingfish and the Mystic Knights of the Sea Lodge also were commonly featured story lines.

As the 1930's ended and the United States entered World War II, *Amos 'n' Andy*'s ratings declined. In response, the program shifted to a weekly, thirty-

Amos and Andy, played by blackfaced actors Freeman Gosden (left) and Charles Correll, race through traffic in the 1930 film Check and Double Check. *(The Granger Collection, New York)*

minute format performed by a full cast of actors before a live audience. More important, Gosden and Correll were joined and eventually replaced by a team of comedy writers who transformed the once complex characters into exaggerated stereotypes. Slowly, the intimacy and texture of the original serial was replaced with broad slapstick and outlandish story lines that critics perceived as demeaning to African Americans. This transformation continued when a televised version of the program was introduced on the Columbia Broadcasting System (CBS) network in 1951, providing even more ammunition for the program's critics.

Despite *Amos 'n' Andy*'s popularity with both black and white audiences, the show was the target of criticism. Leading the initial charge was the *Pittsburgh Courier*, the second-largest black newspaper in the United States. In 1931, the *Courier* began an unsuccessful campaign denouncing the show's racial stereotypes. Black leaders continued to attack the show throughout its broadcast history, but it was the demeaning imagery evident in the televised version of *Amos 'n' Andy* that reignited a national protest in 1951. This protest, led by the National Association for the Advancement of Colored People (NAACP), failed to convince the network to discontinue the program, but the show's slumping ratings did eventually prompt its cancellation in 1953. The program continued to air in television syndication until 1966, making it the longest-running show in broadcast history.

Impact *Amos 'n' Andy* became embedded in the American consciousness. Competitors attempted to capitalize on the show's success by creating similar programs employing ethnic humor. Department stores and movie theaters aired the program on their public address systems to keep customers in their establishments. Manufacturing plants modified their work shifts to oblige faithful listeners. Even President Calvin Coolidge left state dinners to listen to the show. Merchandisers sold *Amos 'n' Andy* toys, candy bars, card games, and novelty products. Additionally, the show contributed several popular catchphrases to the national lexicon, including "I'se regusted!" and "Buzz me, miss Blue!"

Beth A. Messner

Further Reading

Andrews, Bart, and Ahrgus Juilliard. *Holy Mackerel! The Amos 'n' Andy Story*. New York: E. P. Dutton, 1986.

Ely, Melvin P. *The Adventures of Amos 'n' Andy: A Social History of an American Phenomenon*. New York: The Free Press, 1991.

McLeod, Elizabeth. *The Original Amos 'n' Andy: Freeman Gosden, Charles Correll, and the 1928-1943 Radio Serial*. Jefferson, N.C.: McFarland, 2005.

See also African Americans; Jim Crow segregation; Migrations, domestic; National Association for the Advancement of Colored People; Racial discrimination; Radio in the United States.

■ Anderson, Marian

Identification Singer of classical music
Born February 27, 1897; Philadelphia, Pennsylvania
Died April 8, 1993; Portland, Oregon

Anderson was a brilliant vocalist and an advocate for the struggle against racial discrimination. Her captivating performances brought people of all races together.

Marian Anderson displayed an interest in music at an early age. Before she was two years old, she would sit at her toy piano, playing original melodies and singing them back. By the time Anderson was four, her family had become aware of her gift for singing. During her teenage years, she participated in every musical opportunity. She was heavily involved in the Stanton Grammar School choir and the Union Baptist Church choir. She received rudimentary music training because her parents could not afford to give her music lessons. The first professional musician to recognize Anderson's extraordinary vocal ability was Alexander Robinson, Union Baptist Church's choir director. Robinson found it unusual for a child as young as Anderson to have a mature voice that extended upward almost three octaves. Anderson credited Robinson for stimulating her love of singing.

Anderson encountered racial discrimination throughout her life. During one instance in 1914, she tried to receive formal training at the Philadelphia Music Academy, but she was rejected because of the color of her skin. During the 1920's, Anderson and her accompanist, Billy King, booked tours to churches and black colleges. During their travels they experienced racial discrimination. They could not eat at certain restaurants, and they were turned

Marian Anderson (left) shakes hands with Secretary of the Interior Harold Ickes, after the conclusion of her 1939 concert at the Lincoln Memorial in Washington, D.C. (Library of Congress)

away from hotels. Anderson learned that living in the United States as a black classical artist was not easy. Black classical artists had sparse musical opportunities; those they did have were confined to churches, semiprofessional choral societies, and black schools and colleges.

Anderson often traveled to Europe in order to study, as most serious musicians did. While in Europe from 1930 to 1931, she presented concerts and found enthusiastic audiences. She did not experience the racial tension that she did in the United States. She felt personal and musical freedom. When she returned to the United States, she was a more confident and skilled musician.

Her tours during the early 1930's numbered more than thirty. During this time, ticket sales were few and the audiences were sparse because of the economic depression. Despite these obstacles, Anderson believed she could be recognized as an

American singer. She knew the odds were long as a black woman singing predominantly white music.

Anderson did not let her race or gender hinder her. She performed in numerous venues, such as New York's Town Hall, before some of the most intimidating critics. She won first prize in a singing competition sponsored by the New York Philharmonic orchestra and was given an opportunity to perform in a concert with the orchestra. She received rave reviews from both audiences and music critics.

The most pivotal moment in Anderson's life was in 1939, when she performed in a concert on the steps of the Lincoln Memorial. Prior to this concert, the Daughters of the American Revolution refused to allow Anderson to sing before an integrated audience in Constitution Hall. As a result of this discrimination, First Lady Eleanor Roosevelt and other members resigned from the Daughters of the American Revolution and the National Association for the Advancement of Colored People became involved. It persuaded Secretary of the Interior Harold Ickes to arrange an open-air concert for Anderson on the steps of the Lincoln Memorial. The concert took place on Easter Sunday. She sang "My Country, 'Tis of Thee." More than seventy-five thousand people of various races and ethnicities were present for the successful event.

Anderson toured and performed until she retired in 1965. Following her retirement, she continued to make public appearances. She received many awards throughout her lifetime. Some of these awards include the United Nations Peace Prize, the Congressional Gold Medal, the Kennedy Center Honors, and a Grammy Lifetime Achievement Award. In 1984, she was the first recipient of the Eleanor Roosevelt Human Rights Award of the City of New York. Anderson died in 1993 from congestive heart failure.

Impact   Through her ability as a classical singer, Anderson was one of numerous African Americans of the 1930's to disprove long-held racial stereotypes. Working in a field regarded as off limits to African Americans, she symbolized an emerging class of nonwhite Americans who gained prominence on the national stage and helped pave the way for subsequent generations of minority artists and entertainers.

Monica Tripp-Roberson

Further Reading

Anderson, Marian. *My Lord, What a Morning: An Autobiography.* Urbana: University of Illinois Press, 2002.

Arsenault, Raymond. *The Sound of Freedom: Marian Anderson, the Lincoln Memorial, and the Concert That Awakened America.* New York: Bloomsbury Press, 2009.

Keiler, Allan. *Marian Anderson: A Singer's Journey.* Urbana: University of Illinois Press, 2000.

See also   African Americans; Bethune, Mary McLeod; Jim Crow segregation; Music: Classical; Racial discrimination; Roosevelt, Eleanor.

Anti-Chain-Store Act. See **Robinson-Patman Act of 1936**

■ Anti-Racketeering Act of 1934

Identification   Federal legislation protecting trade and commerce from organized crime groups
Also known as   ARA
Date   Enacted June 18, 1934

Passed to protect American labor efforts from exploitation from organized crime syndicates, the Anti-Racketeering Act of 1934 made purposely interfering with commerce and trade practices illegal.

The Anti-Racketeering Act of 1934 was enacted at a time when Congress was concerned about racketeering activities stemming from organized crime. Despite these concerns, the act was written in broad language, never mentioning or defining what was meant by racketeering. The principal congressional committee working on the act determined that the word "racket" had for some time been used freely to describe every conceivable kind of behavior or activity that was problematic, unethical, fraudulent, or even detested, whether criminal or not. The committee opted to develop its own working definition

of racketeering but chose not to incorporate this definition into the act.

The law made it illegal to obtain, or attempt to obtain, money or property through force or threat of force across state lines. It was created in large part to protect legitimate businesses and their workers from predatory Mafia gangs, groups that earned celebrity status during the late 1920's and the early 1930's, largely from bootlegging, gambling, and involvement with labor unions. Thus, the intentions of this federal law were both to address and to cope with nefarious actions associated with organized crime figures such as Al Capone, Dutch Schultz, and Legs Diamond. For example, it prohibited the use of violence, intimidation, and injury to extort money or other items of value from individuals or to force individuals to join or make payments to organizations against their will.

The original bill was enacted in 1934 and passed by the Senate without debate; however, it contained no specific mention of legitimate labor or wages. It did outline a basic prohibition against violence or coercion in connection with racketeering and interstate commerce. Subsequently, when fear was expressed by the American Federation of Labor, the first organized federation of American unions, regarding the vague language of the act and how it might result in serious harm to legitimate activities of American businesses, including activities of actual labor unions, the bill was redrafted to make an exception for legitimate workers engaged in legitimate activities.

Noting that the clear language of the statute protected only lawful actions of the unions, courts soon interpreted the act as protecting violence and intimidation by unions during strikes on the grounds that strikes are legal and are carried out to achieve legal ends such as improvements for American workers. The Supreme Court made this understanding of the law official in its ruling in *United States v. Local 807, International Brotherhood of Teamsters* (1942). Congress reacted promptly to that decision by enacting the Hobbs Act in 1946. With the passage of the Hobbs Act, Congress stated that union acts of violence, extortion, and intimidation that cross state lines, not just similar acts carried out by organized crime syndicates, would be deemed illegal by the federal government. However, the federal courts did not agree with Congress. In fact, federal judges continued to apply the *Local 807* decision in various cases of union violence and intimidation during strikes, permitting unions to engage in such acts as robbery, arson, and assault without repercussions of federal law. The Supreme Court took a firm stance on issues concerning union immunity to federal antiracketeering laws in 1973 with its ruling in *U.S. v. Enmons.*

Impact   This Anti-Racketeering Act of 1934 became a pivotal federal law in combating the influence of organized crime on American businesses. Additionally, the act laid the foundation for union rules, rights, and guidelines in the United States.

Paul M. Klenowski

Further Reading

Cohen, Andrew W. *The Racketeer's Progress: Chicago and the Struggle for the Modern American Economy, 1900-1940.* New York: Cambridge University Press, 2004.
Jacobs, James. *Mobsters, Unions, and Feds: The Mafia and the American Labor Movement.* New York: New York University Press, 2006.

See also   National Labor Relations Act of 1935; New Deal; Organized crime; Prohibition repeal; Unionism.

■ Anti-Semitism

Definition   Hostility to or dislike of Jews based on reasons of ethnicity or religion

Anti-Semitism achieved its most powerful expression in the United States during the 1930's and was practiced even by well-established individuals and venerable institutions. Restrictions and quotas against Jews were widely and blatantly imposed, and in some large cities, Jews were physically attacked.

Several trends during the 1920's promoted the wave of anti-Semitism that swept over the United States during the 1930's. There was more anti-Semitic literature published in the country than in any other period of history, led partly by the national automobile magnate, Henry Ford, in his weekly newspaper, *The Dearborn Independent.* Only in 1927, under intense economic and legal pressure, did Ford apologize for the slanders, but by then, the damage had been done. In 1920, Prohibition came into force, outlawing the sale or manufacture of intoxicating bever-

ages, but Jews were granted exemption because of the use of wine during religious rituals. Mobsters, impoverished rabbis, and unscrupulous impostors took the opportunity to sell wine for nonritual purposes, an activity that proved lucrative. The repeal of Prohibition was enacted in 1933, but the publicity disclosing illicit sales of wine only confirmed in the minds of many the association of Jews with corrupt practices.

Charles E. Coughlin, a Roman Catholic priest, won a large following during the 1930's with his anti-Semitic rhetoric. From his base in Detroit, Coughlin disseminated his anti-Semitism in a weekly radio show broadcast to an audience that reached into the millions; his inflammatory periodical, *Social Justice,* which included false information, was sold throughout the United States. The peddlers who sold this journal were members of the priest's Christian Front, which turned into the largest and most threatening of anti-Semitic fraternities and was particularly active in New York and other eastern cities.

After World War I, anti-Semitism in the United States and abroad grew and was accelerated by the Great Depression. Universities such as Harvard, Yale, Princeton, Columbia, Johns Hopkins, Cornell, and Duke, as well as many state universities, found ways to limit the number of their Jewish students. Jews also faced restrictions in fraternities, clubs, hotels, and resorts. Bigoted practices and "restrictive covenants" excluded Jews from some of the most desirable neighborhoods in New York, Chicago, Washington, D.C., Los Angeles, Miami, Denver, Boston, Baltimore, and Cleveland. Physical violence against Jews increased in the late 1930's, particularly in cities where German Americans sympathetic to the policies of Adolf Hitler took to the streets and where the Christian Front was influenced by the pro-Nazi Coughlin.

Impact   By working together, Jews were able to counter the restrictions raised against them. Differences among them were ignored in this difficult period, and Jews hired and patronized other Jews, linking employers, employees, consumers, and suppliers in one commercial network. Jews also founded alternatives to exclusion: They created fraternities, sororities, country clubs, and resorts that were primarily Jewish, with some admitting Gentiles as well. When they were often unable to gain acceptance to such universities as Harvard and Princeton, they

At this 1938 gathering in New York City, five thousand people protest the atrocities perpetrated by Nazi Germany against Jews and members of other ethnic minorities. (AP/Wide World Photos)

flooded into City College of New York. Segregation created Jewish neighborhoods similar to those of their gentile counterparts. During the 1930's, most Jews lived segregated from the non-Jewish population.

Sheila Golburgh Johnson

Further Reading

Marcus, Jacob Rader. *The Dynamics of American Jewish History: Jacob Rader Marcus's Essays on American Jewry.* Boston: Brandeis University Press, 2004. Particularly valuable are the essays "Zionism and the American Jew," written in 1933, and "Mass Migrations of Jews and Their Effects on Jewish Life," written in 1940.

Sarna, Jonathan D. *American Judaism: A History.* New Haven, Conn.: Yale University Press, 2004. A view of American Jewish history that is both scholarly and accessible to students.

Teller, Judd L. *Strangers and Natives: The Evolution of the American Jew from 1921 to the Present.* New York: Delacorte, 1968. Strong on social themes of the 1930's and afterward.

See also   Coughlin, Charles E.; Ford, Henry; Germany and U.S. appeasement; Jews in Canada; Jews in the United States.

■ Apple Mary

Identification   Newspaper comic strip
Artist   Martha Orr
Date   First published on October 29, 1934

Apple Mary *became a popular newspaper feature during the Great Depression, when the comic strip offered hope in trying times. It is credited as the first "soap opera" strip. Its creator, Martha Orr, was one of the first female comic-strip artists and is recognized as the first woman to expand the repertoire of women cartoonists beyond strips aimed at children.*

Apple Mary, one of the first newspaper comic strips to use Depression-era events in its plots, had a journalism lineage: Its creator Orr was the niece of Pulitzer Prize-winning journalist Carey Orr, its inspiration came from newspaperman Damon Runyon, its longtime writer was a former newsman.

Loosely derived from Runyon's short story "Madame la Gimp"—which also inspired the character Apple Annie in the films *Lady for a Day* (1933) and *Pocketful of Miracles* (1961)—the term "apple Mary" also can be traced to the 1870's as the name usually given to women who sold apples on the street.

First published in 1934 and syndicated by Publishers Syndicate, *Apple Mary* focused on an old widow who sold apples on the street and humbly gave people advice about their woes. "Comic strips such as *Little Orphan Annie*, *Annie Rooney*, and *Apple Mary* (later called *Mary Worth*) described the plight of the dispossessed middle classes, who moved from security, even affluence, to poverty," wrote Barry D. Karl in *The Uneasy State: The United States from 1915 to 1945* (1983).

Mary had such troubles, too. Her late Wall Street-tycoon husband, Jack Worth, lost everything, and their grandson, Dennie, was crippled and needed an operation to regain the use of his legs. Other characters included a friendly beat cop, a greedy landlady, and a network of neighbors whose gossip provided Mary with the background for her involvement with their lives.

As the decade moved on and the country emerged from the Depression, *Apple Mary*'s relevance began to wane. In 1938, Orr quit the strip, which was taken over by writer Allen Saunders and Orr's assistant, artist Dale Conner, together credited as "Dale Allen." Saunders later said he added the subtitle *Mary Worth's Family* to *Apple Mary*, and by 1942, its title was *Mary Worth*, written by Saunders, drawn by Ken Ernst, and syndicated by King Features. However, King Features (which eventually absorbed Publishers Syndicate) disputes the connection between *Mary Worth* and *Apple Mary* despite the double title, the same writer, and same character name.

Saunders, a former reporter for the Toledo, Ohio, *News-Bee*, contended that he was given the strip and developed it to accommodate female newspaper readers attracted to soap-opera-style story lines. A veteran of other continuity strips that he termed "open-ended novels," Saunders said he re-

vised the character by restoring her family fortune and moving Mary from a New York tenement to a condo in fictional Santa Royale, California.

Impact   *Apple Mary* had the immediate effect of soothing troubled newspaper readers in need of an escape from the uncertainty of the times. It eventually proved that readers enjoyed continuity comic strips with domestic instead of action themes.

Bill Knight

Further Reading

Horn, Maurice. *The World Encyclopedia of Comics.* Edgemont, Pa.: Chelsea House, 1999.

O'Sullivan, Judith. *The Great American Comic Strip.* Boston: Bulfinch Press, 1990.

Ridgeway, Ann. "Allen Saunders." *The Journal of Popular Culture* 5, no. 2 (1971): 385-420.

Strickler, Dave. *Syndicated Comic Strips and Artists, 1924-1995: The Complete Index.* Cambria, Calif.: Comics Access, 1995.

Walker, Brian. *The Comics: Before 1945.* New York: Harry N. Abrams, 2004.

See also   *Blondie* comic strip; Comic strips; *Dick Tracy*; *Flash Gordon*; Great Depression in the United States; *L'il Abner*; *Little Orphan Annie*; Newspapers, U.S.; Soap operas; Unemployment in the United States.

■ Archaeology

Definition   Study of human habitation through the excavation of buildings and other physical remnants of past occupation

During the 1930's, federally funded employment projects created opportunities for archaeologists to excavate and preserve important archaeological sites and to develop techniques for dating, classifying, and reporting archaeological discoveries. In an era when many Americans were without work, the 1930's proved to be a decade of opportunity and advancement for archaeologists and the field of archaeology.

The financial pall cast upon the nation by the Great Depression might have suspended all archaeological activities were it not for the federally funded public-works projects created for the purpose of keeping Americans at work. Many of these projects involved the construction of dams and highways, which necessitated archaeological survey, excavation, and salvage activities, with archaeologists often working just ahead of the contractors. Other federally funded projects involved the preservation of historical sites, which required archaeological excavation, stabilization, and reconstruction, often with the goal of opening the historic sites to the public. Whether in rescue and salvage or preservation and restoration, archaeologists were employed in record numbers throughout the 1930's.

Government Programs and Agencies President Franklin D. Roosevelt's New Deal provided countless opportunities for archaeologists. In 1933, the Historic American Building Survey, in cooperation with the National Park Service (NPS), began recording the U.S. built environment, including prehistoric indigenous, colonial, and subsequent eras' sites. In that same year, the Civil Works Administration's archaeology program was established to locate, excavate, preserve, and protect U.S. archaeological heritage. Also in that year, the Civilian Conservation Corps was founded to carry out conservation projects in national and state parks, and the Department of the Interior and the NPS were designated to oversee historic and archaeological sites across the United States.

In 1935, the Works Progress Administration was established, which funded numerous archaeological projects, and the Historic Sites Act declared the government's responsibility to protect the nation's archaeological heritage. In 1939, the National Research Council (NRC) established an advisory committee to enhance and support the federal government's archaeological efforts. Throughout the decade, federal and state governments assumed increasing stewardship over the nation's cultural heritage.

Archaeological Achievements The 1930's brought American archaeology to public, private, and professional attention. Almost every geographic area within the United States was affected by archaeological discoveries and efforts, whether in the form of rescue and salvage operations or in excavation and preservation projects. Federally and privately funded excavations, restorations, and reconstructions were undertaken at the historic sites of Yorktown in Virginia and Morristown in New Jersey. The reconstructed Governor's Palace and Capitol at Colonial Williamsburg were officially opened in 1934, giving the public an opportunity to experience what daily life was like in colonial America.

Other federally funded projects included major excavations at the Missouri Basin Project along the Missouri River, the Ocmulgee National Monument in Georgia, the Chickamauga Basin and the Tennessee Valley Authority areas in Tennessee, Marksville in Louisiana, and Somerset County and the Susquehanna Valley in Pennsylvania. In each of these projects, local workers participated as part of the archaeological team, thereby gaining a greater understanding of their communities and a deeper appreciation for their own cultural heritage.

In the Southwest, archaeologists began intensive excavations of prehistoric and historic Native American sites in New Mexico and Arizona. Their discoveries helped to give Native Americans a renewed sense of identity that had all but vanished after the government's assimilation policy had forcibly dismantled their tribal system and mandated their integration into American culture. With each discovery across the country, Americans everywhere gained an increased sense of self and identity. The archaeological evidence produced not only information about the past but also connections with the present.

Impact The 1930's laid the foundation for the establishment of archaeology as a discipline worthy of governmental, institutional, and public support. By the close of the decade, scores of archaeologists had gained firsthand field experience that led to a better understanding of peoples and cultures within their historical contexts. Many of those archaeologists went on to be leaders in their field and to train subsequent generations of archaeologists who found work in the departments of archaeology that arose in universities and museums across the United States. The decade helped mold the perception of archaeology as it changed from a solely academic activity carried out by individual scholars in remote locales for entirely esoteric purposes to a local community activity with the potential to engage members of the general public in the discovery and preservation of their own ethnic, cultural, and national heritage.

Sonia Sorrell

Further Reading
Chapman, Janet, and Karen Barrie. *Kenneth Milton Chapman: A Life Dedicated to Indian Arts and Artifacts.* Albuquerque: University of New Mexico

Press, 2008. An insightful look at the Southwest Native American's struggle to overcome the federal government's policy of assimilation.

Fagette, Paul. *Digging for Dollars: American Archaeology and the New Deal.* Albuquerque: University of New Mexico Press, 1996. Investigation into the interdependence of archaeology, government, and academia during the 1930's.

Guthe, Carl E. "The Basic Needs of American Archaeology." *Science* 90 (1939): 528-530. Article delineating the NRC committee's recommendations for improved field operations; reflects on the challenges faced by archaeologists during the 1930's.

Lyon, Edwin. *A New Deal for Southeastern Archaeology.* Tuscaloosa: University of Alabama Press, 1996. Discussion of the role of governmental agencies in archaeological excavation and preservation in the southeastern United States.

McManamon, Francis, et al., eds. *Archaeology in America: An Encyclopedia.* Santa Barbara, Calif.: Greenwood Press, 2008. A compilation of more than 350 articles, providing an accessible and comprehensive overview of archaeology in North America.

Merriman, Nick, ed. *Public Archaeology.* New York: Routledge, 2004. Examines the interaction between archaeology and public relations and discusses the importance of educational archaeology.

See also   Civilian Conservation Corps; Great Depression in the United States; National parks; Native Americans; Roosevelt, Franklin D.; Tennessee Valley Authority; Works Progress Administration.

■ Archambault Report

Identification   Comprehensive investigation on the Canadian penal system

Also known as   Report of the Canada Royal Commission to Investigate the Penal System of Canada

Date   April 4, 1938

Place   Ottawa, Canada

As a result of this report, Canadian prisons changed from a retributive to a rehabilitative system. Therefore, the report played a critical role in facilitating widespread reform and tremendous changes within the penal system.

Historically, the prison system in Canada was based on the Auburn model practiced in the United States. In this model, prisoners were forced to be silent even when congregated for work. The physical conditions in the Canadian prisons were harsh and brutal. The cells were small and overcrowded. The lighting was poor, and there were no proper toilet facilities. The prison guards were not qualified and had little formal training. As punishment, prisoners were often whipped, shackled in darkened cells, and placed in solitary confinement. The deplorable situation in the prisons resulted in tension and several riots that influenced the Royal Commission to undertake a comprehensive evaluation of the Canadian penitentiary system.

The investigations occurred over a two-year period beginning in 1936 and included visits to approximately 116 penal institutions, including several in Europe, the United Kingdom, and the United States. The studies were based on information obtained from private and public meetings, letters, and formal documentation. A wide cross section of persons, including inmates, judges, correctional officers, and community members, were interviewed.

The overall goal of the report was to reduce recidivism and to facilitate rehabilitation of the prisoners. Other important recommendations were to centralize the prison system under the federal government and establish a prison commission. The report also urged a reorganization of the staff and the establishment of a formal training school for officers. Furthermore, it suggested the establishment of an educational program for the inmates and the employment of qualified tutors.

A recommendation for better management and enhanced rehabilitation of women, the young, and the reformable offender was the creation of a classification system to divide prisoners into specific groups. Also, the report highlighted the importance of physical and mental examinations, which would allow mental and/or physically ill prisoners to be sent to mental or medical institutions for treatment. It also recommended maximum security for hardened offenders in order to reduce the likelihood of those prisoners influencing others.

Impact   The Archambault Report resulted in major reforms. New penitentiaries were built with separate facilities for young offenders, and formal training programs for penitentiary officers were established.

Prisoners were allowed to have educational programs taught by trained individuals, better access to chaplains, and involvement in recreational activity.

Fay V. Williams

Further Reading

Goff, Colin. *Corrections in Canada.* Cincinnati, Ohio: Anderson, 1999.

Gosselin, Luc. *Prisons in Canada.* Montreal: Black Rose Books, 1982.

McMahon, Maeve W. *The Persistent Prison? Rethinking Decarceration and Penal Reform.* Toronto: University of Toronto Press, 1992.

Topping, Coral W. *The Royal Commission on the Penal System of Canada.* Ottawa: J. O. Patenaude, 1938.

See also   Brains Trust; Crimes and scandals; Great Depression in Canada; Immigration to Canada.

■ Architecture

During the 1930's, architecture was used by a variety of groups to promote their vision of what the United States was and could be. From the more traditional New Deal constructions and early automobile-based suburbs to the "modern" skyscrapers, theaters, and commercial buildings, each structure sought to present a positive alternative to the Depression.

In a financial downturn, construction is often one of the first areas of the economy to suffer; however, despite the Great Depression, the United States continued to build, and its architects continued to design. The continued architectural development was made possible partly by a significant investment made by the federal government. The New Deal left a tangible legacy, which can be found in thousands of courthouses and post offices throughout the United States.

By the start of the 1930's, the Office of the Supervising Architect, a division of the Treasury, had designed and overseen the construction of federal buildings for more than seventy-five years. The office was joined by the newly created Section of Fine Arts in 1934. As the New Deal expanded, the office's role changed from actual designing to supervising. The structures that were built and decorated under its supervisor tended to fall into two categories. The first, such as Paul Philippe Cret's Federal Reserve Board Building in Washington, D.C., utilized a stripped-down style, which was popular in both Nazi Germany and the Soviet Union; the second group tended to be versions of Colonial Revival, with red brick and white columns or pilasters.

New Deal Support for American Architecture   President Franklin D. Roosevelt's New Deal also made a sizable investment in architectural preservation. Founded in 1933, the Historic American Building Survey hired unemployed architects to document not only the structures that belonged to important individuals but also old vernacular buildings. These men and women cataloged more than thirty-five thousand structures before the start of World War II. In 1935, Roosevelt signed the Historic Sites Act, which made preserving the country's built environment government policy. Together, these New Deal programs provided vital tools for the preservation movement.

Another means of federal involvement in the built environment came through the Civilian Conservation Corps (CCC) and the Works Progress Administration (WPA). Starting in 1933, the CCC employed young men in forestry and soil projects. Additionally, for many state parks they built campground facilities still in use in the twenty-first century. The WPA built more impressive structures, such as Timberline Lodge, which was constructed within the Mount Hood National Forest between 1936 and 1938. Many of these facilities utilized local materials, creating a rustic look that celebrated American pioneer heritage.

While the New Deal and the WPA often receive credit for government investment in the built environment, the earliest efforts date to the Hoover administration. One of the most significant is Hoover Dam (originally the Boulder Dam). Begun in 1931, the dam was completed ahead of schedule in 1936. Originally conceived as simply an engineering project, the dam incorporated architectural elements that were added as the work progressed. The resulting structure has many of the features that define 1930's federal architecture: monumentality, limited decoration, and references to classical design in form and proportion.

Housing and Residential Architecture   During the 1930's, the federal government entered the housing market for the first time. In 1932, President Hoover signed the Federal Home Loan Bank Act, which was designed to reduce the number of foreclosures, increase home ownership, and encourage construction. Because of it, many Americans were able to buy their first houses. During Roosevelt's New Deal, the government created three model residential developments: Greenhills, Ohio; Greendale, Wisconsin; and the most famous, Greenbelt, Maryland. These self-sufficient communities were conceived by the U.S. Resettlement Administration in 1935 for the growing federal workforce.

Many architects and entrepreneurs tried to use the home construction market to help the overall economy. Robert W. McLaughlin and Howard T. Fisher, among others, sought to create prefabricated houses using industrial materials. Frank Lloyd Wright's Usonia homes were conceived as a means to bring good architecture within the reach of average Americans. In 1932, Wright, running short of clients, had founded his own architecture school. Four years later, Herbert and Katherine Jacobs asked the famous architect if he could design a house that could be built for $5,000. Wright produced an L-shaped ranch structure, which became the model for the Usonian Houses. However, Wright used a flat roof, which led the Federal Housing Administration to deem the structures nonresidential and thus deny numerous mortgage applications.

For the most part, the rest of residential architecture of the 1930's was not nearly as adventurous. Suburbs had existed since the mid-nineteenth century, but during the 1920's, they took on a new form. No longer were developers restricted to building near a railway or street-car line. The automobile opened up the potential of vast, untapped areas for middle- and upper-class housing. The Depression discouraged some of this suburban expansion, but it did not end it. For those who could afford it, the homes built during the 1930's were created with some of the highest-quality materials and craftsmanship ever seen in the residential market. High unemployment and low wages allowed builders to hire the best. The resulting structures included some of the most traditional architecture created during the decade. Americans wanted to feel secure; thus the movement toward traditional, historic American architecture. Many residential architects were influenced by the opening of Colonial Williamsburg in 1932. It provided many models for those wanting a brick or clapboard dwelling. Others looked to the Southwest and created Spanish Revival haciendas, which appeared somewhat out of place in New England or the Midwest.

Commercial Architecture: Art Deco and Bakelite
Two related misconceptions associated with commercial construction during the 1930's exist. First, with the exception of a few highly visible projects such as the Chrysler Building, the Empire State Building, and Rockefeller Center, few commercial structures were built during the Depression. Second, most new structures were designed in the Art Deco style. Because all the aforementioned projects were located close to one another in New York City, they indicated to the public what was possible even in an economic downturn. Likewise, they all used the Art Deco style, which had been developed in the mid-1920's, in an attempt to merge a modern interest in abstract geometric shapes with classical forms. The resulting buildings relied on sculpture and the use of multiple types of building materials.

Such design elements were out of the price range of many developers, especially during the Depression. Instead, Americans appeared to be inspired by the early plastic Bakelite, which became popular during the 1920's. The substance was nonconductive and strong, but it could not be easily molded into square corners. The rounded edge became a dominant form in many commercial products, and this came to be seen by the public as a symbol of "the modern." Architects embraced this design aesthetic and employed it in everything from the Hecht department store in Washington, D.C., to the Hollywood headquarters of the National Broadcasting Company. Like the International Style promoted by the European avant-garde, this form of modern architecture stressed the use of horizontal lines and large expanses of windows. Unlike its European rivals, American Depression structures tended to employ more traditional building materials such as brick, rather than rely on reinforced concrete.

The one area in which Art Deco continued to be a leading force in architecture was in the design of movie theaters. Hollywood introduced talking pictures at the end of the 1920's. During the Depression, films offered an opportunity to escape from everyday life for the cost of five to ten cents. Also, movie theaters were some of the first buildings in American small towns to offer air-conditioning. Competition for patrons was high, and architecture became a means to attract them. The largest and one

Despite the economic downturn of the Great Depression, many important architectural structures were added to New York City's skyline, including (from left to right) the Lincoln Building, the Leftcourt Colonial Building, and the Johns-Manville Building. (Hulton Archive/Getty Images)

of the most spectacular of these movie palaces was Radio City Music Hall, which opened in 1932. Edward Durell Stone designed the building, and Donald Deskey created the interior spaces. While these buildings were loved by the public, they were not always seen as true architecture by some critics.

The International Style: Europe's Influence Frank Lloyd Wright is considered a giant in modern architecture. Nonetheless, his position in the canon of great architects was questioned early in the decade. Philip Johnson, the first curator of architecture of the Museum of Modern Art, produced a traveling exhibition on the latest trends in design in 1932. He included Wright only in passing because he believed that the architect had passed his prime and was no longer an innovator. Instead, he and architectural

historian Henry-Russell Hitchcock sought to promote what they coined the International Style of the European avant-garde. The show traveled throughout the United States for two years, promoting the pair's agenda with little effect. Only with the rise of Adolf Hitler in 1933 did many of these architects of the International Style begin to flee Germany.

Walter Gropius, founder of the Bauhaus art school in Germany, was one of the first of the avant-garde to arrive in the United States in 1937. He became a professor at Harvard, and the next year he designed his own dwelling, the Gropius House. The International Style architect created excitement within the press by designing a modern building using a mixture of regional and industrial materials. Despite early interest, Gropius was eclipsed by other architectures, such as Ludwig Mies van der Rohe, who went to France and Britain and then came to the United States at the start of World War II. Therefore, despite the best efforts of Gropius, Johnson, and Hitchcock, the International Style did not become an important architectural force in the United States until after World War II.

Impact Following World War II, many proponents of modernism in architecture became dismissive of the buildings of the 1930's. On one hand, critics compared the buildings to structures built in Nazi Germany and Communist Russia. On the other hand, many considered these structures too provincial. While it is true that government architects in Russia, Germany, and the United States all used stripped-down designs, this style was not new. Beginning with Charlemagne, rulers have used classical forms in order to assert their rightful place as rulers. Americans generally welcomed New Deal construction. It not only brought jobs but also left fiscal proof that the government was trying to do something about the Great Depression. Following World War II, government investment in architecture continued with such programs as urban renewal. As to the second charge, most American architects did consciously draw on local or regional themes in their design. Using the past as a reference allowed Americans to challenge the notion put forward by some that the Depression was proof that there was something wrong with the fundamental philosophies of the United States.

Edmund D. Potter

Further Reading

Butler, Sara Amelia. *Constructing New Deal America: Public Art and Architecture and Institutional Legitimacy.* Charlottesville: University of Virginia, 2001. Provides important insights into the expansion of government construction during the New Deal.

Gebhard, David. *The National Trust Guide to Art Deco in America.* New York: Diane, 1996. Illustrates the diverse use of Art Deco during the 1930's.

Greif, Martin. *Depression Modern: The Thirties Style in America.* New York: University Books, 1976. Greif was one of the first to show that 1930's American architecture was not just Art Deco and International Style buildings.

Grossman, Elizabeth Greenwell. *The Civic Architecture of Paul Cret.* New York: Cambridge University Press, 1996. Cret set an important model for civic architecture throughout the New Deal.

Jandl, H. Ward, John A. Burns, and Michael J. Auer. *Yesterday's Houses of Tomorrow: Innovative American Homes, 1850 to 1950.* Washington, D.C.: National Trust for Historic Preservation, 1991. Summary of attempts to make the home a more livable space.

Korom, Joseph J. *The American Skyscraper, 1850-1940: A Celebration of Height.* Boston: Branden Books, 2008. Provides a building-by-building analysis of the skyscraper's development.

See also Boulder Dam; Chrysler Building; Empire State Building; Grand Coulee Dam; Gropius House; Housing in the United States; Timberline Lodge; Works Progress Administration; Wright, Frank Lloyd.

■ Armstrong, Edwin H.

Identification Electrical engineer and inventor
Born December 18, 1890; New York, New York
Died January 31, 1954; New York, New York

Armstrong made numerous contributions to the development of radio, radar, and television electronics. Of particular note is his invention of the frequency-modulated (FM) broadcasting system.

While attending Columbia University, Edwin H. Armstrong invented the regenerative circuit that led to the development of regenerative amplifiers and oscillators. In 1918, he invented the superheterodyne radio receiver circuit, which is the basic circuit of almost all modern radio receivers. Beginning in 1925, he investigated the use of modulating the frequency of the carrier wave to transmit communication signals instead of the well-established amplitude-modulation (AM) method.

After much experimentation, Armstrong introduced a wideband FM system in 1933. Field tests showed its clear reception of signals, offering high-fidelity sound even during violent thunderstorms. Because of the economic conditions associated with the Great Depression, Armstrong found stiff resistance to his efforts to encourage the radio industry to implement use of the FM broadcasting system. On December 26, 1933, he was granted a patent on wideband FM, but it required litigation that extended beyond his lifetime to win a battle with the Radio Corporation of America (RCA) and others for his rightful claim to the patent.

On June 17, 1936, Armstrong demonstrated the superior sound quality of FM when he played a jazz record over conventional AM radio from the headquarters of the Federal Communications Commission followed by an FM broadcast of the record. Armstrong and his FM system were heralded in headlines nationwide. In 1937, he financed the construction of the first FM radio station, W2XMN, in Alpine, New Jersey. Radio signals could be heard clearly 100 miles away using less power than an AM radio station. Known for his perseverance and work ethic, Armstrong was one of the most prominent pioneers of electronic communications. He was inducted into the National Inventors Hall of Fame in 1980.

Impact Through his development of regenerative feedback, the superheterodyne receiver, and FM broadcasting, Armstrong helped lay the foundation for the field of telecommunications. His FM invention made high-fidelity broadcasting possible by overcoming the problem of static noise. It is used in radio sets, microwave relay links, and space communications.

Alvin K. Benson

Further Reading

Armstrong, Edwin H. *Five Basic Engineering Papers from the Proceedings of the Institute of Radio Engineers.*

Washington, D.C.: Smithsonian Institution/Division of Electricity and Nuclear Energy, 1972.

Brodsky, Ira. *The History of Wireless: How Creative Minds Produced Technology for the Masses.* St. Louis, Mo.: Telescope Books, 2008.

See also Car radios; Federal Communications Commission; Inventions; Physics; Radar, invention of; Radio astronomy; Radio in the United States; Radio trust; Television technology.

■ Armstrong, Louis

Identification African American jazz trumpeter, vocalist, and film actor
Born August 4, 1901; New Orleans, Louisiana
Died July 6, 1971; New York, New York
Also known as Satchmo; Pops

During the 1930's, Armstrong, who had established himself internationally as one of the greatest of all jazz musicians during the 1920's, continued to make prolific musical recordings, appeared in Hollywood films, and maintained a rigorous touring schedule entertaining audiences worldwide.

Louis Armstrong. (AFP/Getty Images)

Louis Armstrong grew up in poverty on the streets of New Orleans, where he began playing the cornet at the age of eleven. He spent as much time as he could learning from the city's best musicians, including Bunk Johnson, Kid Ory, and his mentor Joe "King" Oliver. Armstrong moved to Chicago in 1922 and began to produce important recordings under his own name in 1925, including his famous Hot Five and Hot Seven records. In 1929, Armstrong established a performance model he employed until 1947, which consisted of fronting established big bands, particularly that of Luis Russell.

In 1935, Joe Glaser, who had alleged ties to the Chicago mob, became Armstrong's manager. Glaser helped Armstrong resolve legal issues and successfully promote his career. During this period, Armstrong was sometimes criticized for the low quality of his bands. Nevertheless, he became increasingly significant as a singer of popular songs, influencing almost every jazz and pop vocalist, including Bing Crosby, Frank Sinatra, Ella Fitzgerald, and Sarah Vaughn. Armstrong also appeared in several Hollywood films during the 1930's, including *Pennies from Heaven* (1936) with Bing Crosby.

Impact Armstrong is widely acknowledged as one of the most influential musical artists in the history of the United States. In later years, he performed extensively with a small group billed as Louis Armstrong and His All Stars and became known as "Ambassador Satch" during his successful diplomatic U.S. State Department tours in Africa, Asia, and Europe. In 1964, he became the oldest artist in history to have a top single on the American pop charts when he knocked the Beatles from the *Billboard* Hot 100's number-one slot with his version of "Hello, Dolly!"

N. Michael Goecke

Further Reading

Brothers, Thomas. *Louis Armstrong's New Orleans.* New York: W. W. Norton, 2007.

_____, ed. *Louis Armstrong in His Own Words: Selected Writings.* New York: Oxford University Press, 2001.

See also Basie, Count; Ellington, Duke; Film; Fitzgerald, Ella; Holiday, Billie; Music: Jazz; Music: Popular; Smith, Bessie.

■ Art movements

Definition Trends and innovations in the visual arts

During the Great Depression, the U.S. government provided programs and financial support to American artists who had suffered economically from the lack of patronage from private collectors and art museums. Because the government employed artists to create work, the production of art during this period flourished. While much art of the decade is of the realist style, abstraction also continued as an art form.

During the 1930's, artists were employed by the art-related economic relief projects of President Franklin D. Roosevelt's New Deal, which legitimized the role of American art in the United States. The New Deal appropriated $35 million for art-related programs that employed more than twelve thousand artists, who created 3,350 public murals, 18,000 sculptures, 108,000 easel paintings, and 250,000 prints. The murals were large public art projects, and many decorated U.S. post offices. In 1933, the Public Works of Art Project (PWAP) of the Civil Works Administration was the first of the government agencies to support art projects. The PWAP employed artists at hourly wages to create murals, sculptures, paintings, and prints to decorate public buildings. This agency lasted only six months; however, in 1934, a second agency, the Section of Painting and Sculpture (later the Section of Fine Arts), administered through the U.S. Treasury, took over this role and was joined the following year by the Treasury Relief Art Project and the Federal Arts Project of the Works Progress Administration (FAP/WPA). With the establishment of the FAP/WPA, an artists' trade union, known as the Artists' Union, was founded to act as the bargaining agent for artists employed by the federal government.

The American Scene Artists The American scene artists reflected the shared social and economic experience of the Depression through their subject matter. Their work, stylistically realist, was accessible to a wide audience; the group was opposed to the stylistic tradition of European modernism. A group of painters known as the Regionalists depicted the rural and small-town aspects of the United States during this time period. Three of the best-known artists of the movement were Thomas Hart Benton from Missouri, Grant Wood from Iowa, and John Steuart

Curry from Kansas. In 1924, *Time* magazine wrote an article on American Regionalism, mentioning Benton and Wood and heralding this style as an authentic American art form. Organized in 1934, Associated American Artists sold original lithographs and etchings by Regionalist and American scene artists for five dollars in department stores and by mail order, making American art accessible to the public at large. The periodical *The Art Digest* also supported these artists and the notion that art should reflect the American way of life.

Benton viewed art as an agent of social change. This was reflected in his images of American workers, both agricultural and industrial. Through the dynamic rhythms and overlapping forms of the figures in his paintings, Benton symbolized the key American values of hard work and community. In 1930 and 1931, Benton was employed to create a mural entitled *American Today* for the New School for Social Research in New York, a piece that reflected themes of community as its subject matter.

In 1930, Wood created one of the most iconic images of American art during this period, the painting *American Gothic*, which symbolized American national identity through midwestern archetypal imagery. Utilizing a crisp handling of paint and realistic, descriptive detail, Wood painted the portrait of a stoic farmer and his daughter, which depicted the resilience of the American spirit in a rural world slowly disappearing. Wood also painted landscapes that celebrated the fecundity and abundance of the agrarian United States.

Curry also portrayed scenes of human interactions with the land and midwestern life and values, where he often depicted the struggle of man against nature. In contrast to the scenes of agrarian richness in the rural United States, Texas Regionalist Alexandre Hogue painted scenes of drought-ridden landscapes that reflected the bitter reality of the period.

Urban American Scene Artists Depicting daily life in the metropolitan United States, the urban American scene painters were also referred to as the social realists. Many artists of this group had studios in New York City in the neighborhood around Fourteenth Street and Union Square. A number of them had also been the students of Kenneth Hayes Miller at the Art Students League. These artists depicted the lives of women—often shoppers, office workers, and sales girls—in New York. Miller created images of solidly built, matronly, middle-class shoppers. His student Isabel Bishop portrayed modestly dressed female office workers in intimate conversations on the street. Another of Miller's students, Reginald Marsh, became known for his densely cluttered, many-figured compositions that included images of sexually alluring women who worked as taxi dancers and in burlesque halls. Walt Kuhn used bright colors and loose, expressive paint handling to paint show-girls and the acrobats and clowns of the flashy world of urban entertainment. Paul Cadmus created a scandal with his painting *The Fleet's In!*, which featured images of sexually provocative women. The painting, depicting women cavorting with sailors, was removed from a PWAP art exhibition at the Corcoran Gallery in Washington, D.C., because some considered it to be a defamatory portrayal of the American sailor.

The artists and brothers Raphael, Isaac, and Moses Soyer illustrated the grim reality of the period with isolated, melancholy figures grappling with issues such as finding work and surviving in the urban landscape. The well-known artist Edward Hopper also tapped into the mood of alienation and isolation in urban life by depicting figures alone in interiors, such as in the painting *New York Movie* (1939), in which a female usher stands pensively alone in a corner of a darkened movie theater.

Some other artists communicated more overtly sociopolitical messages through their art. Philip Evergood, a president of the Artists' Union and thus actively involved in the labor struggle, took a more political stance in his paintings. His work *American Tragedy* (1937) portrays a real-life incident from a demonstration for higher wages at Republic Steel in Chicago in which the police opened fire on the striking workers and innocent people were killed and injured. As a Lithuanian immigrant to the United States, Ben Shahn was interested in exploring the experiences of other immigrants. His most famous work, the twenty-three gouache paintings entitled *The Passion of Sacco-Vanzetti*, was created in 1932 and 1933. In it, he sympathetically portrays the story of the Italian immigrant anarchists Nicola Sacco and Bartolomeo Vanzetti, who were accused of armed robbery and murder and tried unfairly to a guilty verdict. Although somewhat abstract in his flat, colorfully patterned style, African American artist Jacob Lawrence also communicated a strong social

message though his art. In the late 1930's, Lawrence painted a series devoted to African Americans—such as Harriet Tubman, Frederick Douglass, and Toussaint L'Ouverture—who escaped from slavery and subsequently fought to free others.

Abstract Artist While much of the work created during the 1930's was social realist art that reflected the realities of the United States during this time, abstract art still thrived. However, it was often criticized as irrelevant, elitist, and unintelligible. Abstract artists countered that abstract art worked on a deeper, more universal level and spoke directly to aesthetic sensibilities. For these artists, social realist art was aligned with a political agenda, specifically with Marxist models.

Stuart Davis, though not affiliated with any group, was one of the best known of the abstract painters of the period. As with most American painters making art in the abstract style, Davis drew from the stylistic influences of European modernism. In fact, Davis went to Paris in 1928 and came back to the United States more committed to his graphic style of large, flat planes of bright color. To make these works reflect the energy of American life, Davis interspersed lettering taken from signboards with glimpses of forms signifying American shop fronts and streets. The other famous abstract American artist of the 1930's was Alexander Calder, who divided his time between the United States and Paris. Drawing on European modernist models and sculpture, Calder synthesized the black, red, and white colors used by Dutch artist Piet Mondrian with the biomorphic shapes of Spanish artist Joan Miró. Calder translated these colors and shapes into cantilevered sculptural forms made of sheet metal and metal rods, called stabiles, that moved and drifted according to air currents.

In 1937, American Abstract Artists, a cooperative exhibition society of twenty-two abstract artists, was founded in New York. These artists employed a hard-edged, geometric style. The group included spokesperson George L. K. Morris and Burgoyne Diller (who directed the mural division), Harry Holtzman, Albert Swindon, Rosalind Bengelsdorf, and Gertrude and Balcomb Greene. Abstract artists working in New York City during the 1930's, not all of whom were part of the American Abstract Artists society, included a culturally diverse, foreign-born group; members included Josef Albers and Ilya

Bolotowsky from Eastern Europe; Arshile Gorky and László Moholy-Nagy; and women such as Irene Rice Pereira, Suzi Freylingshuysen, and Charmion Von Wiegand. These artists were all aware of the European modernist style and read about European artistic developments in the periodical *Cahiers d'Art*. A number of abstract artists including Gorky, Diller, Bolotowsky, Balcomb Greene, and Davis worked on FAP/WPA mural projects, including the Williamsburg Housing Project murals in Brooklyn.

Impact Though the United States was in the throes of a major financial crisis during the 1930's, the art industry thrived. For the first time in American history, the U.S. government was a patron of the arts, developing programs to give artists the financial means to produce art. A sense of artistic community developed because of these programs. The WPA was important to the abstract expressionist artists who emerged during the 1940's and 1950's. In fact, about 80 percent of the artists who gained recognition during the 1940's and 1950's were supported by the government funds of the FAP/WPA. In 1931, the Whitney Museum of American Art, founded by Gertrude Vanderbilt Whitney, opened. Later in the decade, the Museum of Non-Objective Painting (which became known as the Solomon R. Guggenheim Museum) was founded. Thus, the climate of the 1930's in the United States formed the basis for the later developments in art that made American art an important international force.

Sandra Rothenberg

Further Reading

Baigell, Matthew. *The American Scene: American Painting of the 1930's*. New York: Praeger, 1974. Overview of the American scene painters focused on a number of artists who painted in this style.

Doss, Erika. *Twentieth-Century American Art*. New York: Oxford University Press, 2002. Succinct but thorough overview of the art of the period.

Haskell, Barbara. *The American Century: Art and Culture, 1900-1950*. New York: Whitney Museum of American Art, 1999. Excellent overview of American art written by the curator of early American art at the Whitney Museum of Art in New York.

Hunter, Sam. *American Art of the Twentieth Century*. New York: Harry N. Abrams, 1972. Classic overview of American art.

Knott, Robert. *American Abstract Art of the 1930's and 1940's: The J. Donald Nichols Collection*. New York: Harry N. Abrams, 1998. Introduction to the abstract art of this period.

Leuchtenburg, William E. "Art in the Great Depression." In *A Modern Mosaic: Art and Modernism in the United States*, edited by Townsend Ludington. Chapel Hill: University of North Carolina Press, 2000. An interdisciplinary collection of essays with an excellent chapter on art during the Great Depression.

Pohl, Francis K. *Framing America: A Social History of American Art*. New York: Thames and Hudson, 2002. Sociopolitical overview of American art, focusing on neglected groups such as women and minorities.

Shapiro, David, ed. *Social Realism: Art as a Weapon*. New York: Frederick Unger, 1973. Includes a good overview essay on social realism with primary-source documents of statements by artists and of exhibition reviews.

See also *American Gothic*; Benton, Thomas Hart; Calder, Alexander; Curry, John Steuart; Whitney Museum of American Art; Wood, Grant.

■ Asia

The relationship between the United States and Imperial Japan was the most significant foreign relationship in Asia that the United States had during the 1930's. The United States also had interactions with other Asian countries, such as China and the Philippines. As the decade continued, Japan became aggressive toward China, and the professed neutrality of the United States became hard to maintain; conflict seemed almost inevitable.

The United States had a historical relationship with Asia that was far different from its relationship with Europe. Unlike U.S. interests in Europe, which were essentially based on trade and finance, the United States had territory in the western Pacific Ocean and East Asia that was a part of the U.S. empire. In addition to the preferential treatment and economic benefits received in the treaty ports in China, the United States held sovereignty over the Philippines, Hawaii, and smaller islands. These possessions were under varying degrees of American control; Hawaii and the Philippines had military installations on them. This Pacific Ocean network contributed to U.S. trade with the Far East, which made the expansion of Japanese imperial power unwelcome in American business and military circles. The United States had national pride, international prestige, and financial gain at stake in its Asia-Pacific possessions. Despite these factors, the American response to Japanese expansion during the 1930's was initially muted; the administration of President Franklin D. Roosevelt was inhibited by American isolationism and problems in Europe. In the late 1930's, however, American policy shifted away from nonintervention, as the United States moved closer to war with Japan.

Imperialism in Asia   U.S. interest in China began in the mid-nineteenth century, when, after a series of wars and military ventures, the European and American governments forced treaties upon a weak and unstable China. The so-called unequal treaties, among other things, opened many Chinese ports to foreign trade and gave the Western imperial powers opportunities and privileges on Chinese soil. American interests in the Asia-Pacific region were strengthened by the U.S. acquisition of Spanish colonies in the region after the Spanish-American War (1898) and by the American annexation of Hawaii at the behest of wealthy businessmen in that same year. By the beginning of the twentieth century, Japan had experienced an impressive and swift transformation from a feudal society to a modern, industrialized nation. In 1876, Japan forced Korea to open to foreign trade and soundly defeated China in the Sino-Japanese War (1894-1895). Therefore, the United States considered Japan to be the most immediate threat to its imperial holdings in Asia during the period between World War I and World War II. Of the U.S. possessions in Asia, the Philippines was the largest and closest to mainland Asia and, thus, integral to U.S. strategic aims and capitalist ambitions in the region. The United States had fought a protracted guerrilla war in the Philippines from the time it gained control of the archipelago. This established a major American military presence in the Philippines. It also gave American businesses a great opportunity, as the U.S. administrators of the islands dismantled the Roman Catholic Church and parceled out its vast holdings to U.S. companies. In 1937, when the Philippines was a semi-independent commonwealth, the president of the Philippines requested that General Douglas MacArthur supervise the creation of the Philippine army because of the growing threat of the Japanese Empire.

The United States was not the only latecomer to the imperialists' table in East Asia: Japan, too, made territorial gains in the region beginning in the late nineteenth century. After defeating the Russian Empire in the Russo-Japanese War (1904-1905), the Japanese acquired enormous international prestige. Japan's power in Asia grew in the absence of the chastened Russians, with the annexation of Korea in 1911, and through the acquisition of the German possessions in China and the Pacific during World War I. Though fascism never took root in Japan as it did in European countries, the extreme nationalists in Japan had a similar worldview, one that was based on racial superiority and conquest of lesser peoples (particularly other Asians), the elimination of Bolshevism, and a militarized society in service to one leader: the emperor. In September, 1931, rogue elements in the Japanese army tasked with guarding the South Manchurian Railroad staged an incident near Mukden (now Shenyang) and used it as a pretext to occupy all of Manchuria. This was done without the knowledge or consent of the Japanese civilian government in Tokyo and began a pattern in Imperial Japan of military-led foreign policy decisions.

American Foreign Policy Reactions   The Manchuria incident prompted U.S. secretary of state Henry L. Stimson to send a message to both China and Japan in January, 1932. The Stimson Doctrine stated that the United States would not recognize any territory that Japan took by force. This was a continuation of basic U.S. foreign policy but, more to the point, emphasized American nonrecognition of any "treaty or agreement" that impinged upon, abrogated, or otherwise negatively affected U.S. rights in China. Despite the League of Nations' condemnation of Japan as the aggressor in Manchuria, nothing was done by the international community. None of the Western nations wanted to go to war over China, much less one of its provinces.

The protection of American interests in Asia was not the focal point of Roosevelt's foreign policy. The Neutrality Acts, passed by an isolationist U.S. Congress, were in response to events in Europe, not Asia. Roosevelt was not as strictly isolationist as the U.S. Congress; he disliked the sweeping design of the legislation, which banned U.S. aid to any belligerent in wartime and actually hurt the victims of aggression more than the aggressors. Roosevelt had followed the Stimson Doctrine in regard to Manchuria, but in July, 1937, when war broke between Japan and China, he gave a speech about "quarantining" aggressor nations through economic pressure instead of staying neutral while friends and allies suffered. The speech had an effect opposite to the one intended on the American public. Finally, after two years of war in China, the United States implemented measures that made direct conflict with Japan inevitable. In July, 1939, the Roosevelt administration declared that in six months the United States would end its commercial treaty with Japan, which began an increasingly restrictive embargo of essential war materials, cutting off Japanese access to aviation parts, scrap metal, and eventually even oil. The embargo of these vital materials drove Japan to wage war on the British, Dutch, and American possessions in the Pacific in the hope of gaining enough raw materials to fight its primary war in China.

Impact The United States had an uneasy relationship with Imperial Japan, Asia's dominant power, and an unequal one with China. American territorial and financial interests in the western Pacific Asia were threatened by growing Japanese power and ambition. American colonial possessions in the Pacific were integral parts of U.S. trade and geopolitical strategy by the 1930's. Constrained, however, by the Neutrality Acts, Roosevelt had limited reaction to Japan's imperial expansion. American isolationism encouraged bellicose Japanese military planners to escalate the conflict in China in 1937, because they believed that the United States would not get involved in the affairs of other nations. This noninvolvement inadvertently encouraged Japan to pursue its war against China. By 1939, the U.S. government was seeking, belatedly, to curb Japanese ambitions with numerous restrictive embargoes, but the action had the opposite effect. The sanctions propelled both nations toward a conflict that neither really wanted, but because of mutual distrust and a lack of understanding, neither was able to stop war from coming.

Megan E. Watson

Further Reading

Barnhart, Michael. *Japan Prepares for Total War: The Search for Economic Security, 1919-1941.* Ithaca, N.Y.: Cornell University Press, 1987. Half of the chapters focus on U.S. policies; the mixture of diplomatic and economic history provides a solid comprehension of the missteps and misunderstandings on both sides.

Iriye, Akira. *The Globalizing of America, 1913-1945.* New York: Cambridge University Press, 1993. Part of a series; survey of U.S. foreign relations and the uniquely American considerations that guided American decision makers during the interwar period.

_____, ed. *Pearl Harbor and the Coming of the Pacific War: A Brief History with Documents and Essays.* New York: St. Martin's, 1999. Overview of international relations during the 1930's, with a section devoted to primary sources.

Nimmo, William F. *Stars and Stripes Across the Pacific: The United States, Japan, and the Asia/Pacific Region, 1895-1945.* Westport, Conn.: Praeger, 2001. Chronological history of U.S. involvement in the region, with an emphasis on relations with Japan.

Ninkovich, Frank A. *The United States and Imperialism.* Malden, Mass.: Blackwell, 2001. Thought-provoking interpretation of the topic; author deftly fleshes out his theory in chapters on the Philippines and China.

Rhodes, Benjamin D. *United States Foreign Policy in the Interwar Period, 1918-1941: The Golden Age of American Diplomatic and Military Complacency.* New York: Praeger, 2001. Thorough study of the people and polices of the interwar years; essential reading for serious students of U.S. foreign relations.

See also Foreign policy of the United States; Isolationism; Japanese military aggression; League of Nations; Manchuria occupation; Naval forces; *Panay* incident; Philippine Independence Act of 1934; Quarantine speech; World War II and the United States.

■ Asian Americans

Identification Americans of full or partial Asian descent

During the 1930's, Asian American communities survived both economic challenges and Caucasian hostility. Second-generation American-born Asian Americans were frustrated that their pursuit of the American Dream through hard work and education was thwarted by Caucasian refusal to let them integrate into professional mainstream society.

During the 1930's, the nation's Asian American population declined, the only decade in the history of the United States that this has been the case. Anti-Asian immigration restrictions in place since 1924 and the net loss of about twelve thousand Japanese Americans as conflict intensified between Japan and the United States contributed to the decline. The 1930 U.S. Census listed 264,766 Asian Americans, although that term was not yet used for people of full or partial Asian descent. Asian Americans constituted a minority of 0.22 percent of the total U.S. population of 122,775,046. According to the U.S. Census of 1940, the Asian American population declined to 254,918 people, accounting for only 0.19 percent of the 131,669,275 million persons living in the United States. At the end of the 1930's, about 98 percent of all Asian Americans were of either Japanese, Chinese, or Filipino heritage.

In San Francisco's Chinatown a man holds a one-hundred-year-old pipe, while a woman lights it. (AP/Wide World Photos)

Japanese Americans Face Pressures in the United States In 1930, the Japanese American population of 138,834 had an almost even gender balance, and children accounted for roughly one-half of the number. Because of racist naturalization laws barring all Asian immigrants from becoming U.S. citizens, the first-generation Japanese Americans, called Issei, placed their hopes in their children. These children, called Nisei, had American citizenship because they had been born in the United States. In 1930, the Japanese American Citizens League was founded with the goal of promoting loyalty and patriotism to the United States as a means of persuading Caucasians to accept Asian Americans.

Nisei grew into adulthood during the 1930's. However, upon graduating from school and college, they were excluded from professional jobs. By 1935, only one-fourth of Japanese American college graduates held jobs in line with their education, and only 5 percent were employed in Caucasian-owned businesses in Los Angeles, for example. Many had no choice but to work in the family agriculture businesses that supplied the majority of California's fresh vegetables.

Pressures exerted by Caucasian exclusionary politics persuaded thousands of Japanese Americans to leave the United States. The trend was exacerbated by international conflict, as the United States objected to Japanese aggression in China. During the 1930's, the Japanese American population declined by twelve thousand people.

Chinese Americans Survive the Great Depression Because Chinese Americans, who generally lived in "Chinatown" communities, were largely self-sufficient and frugal, they handled the challenges of the Great Depression relatively well. They also organized against unfair business practices. In 1933, when Caucasian businesses planned to destroy the Chinese laundries in New York City with a spurious set of municipal codes, the Chinese Hand Laundry Alliance formed and thwarted the ordinances. However, American-born Chinese Americans faced the same prejudices as Japanese Americans and were barred from professional jobs outside Chinatown. College-educated Chinese Americans of both genders often ended up working in family restaurants.

A few Chinese Americans prospered during the 1930's by organizing tours of the Chinatowns of San Francisco, Los Angeles, and New York City. These tours blatantly catered to Caucasian prejudices: residents staged fake tong wars, opium dens, and brothels. Hollywood, too, bought into the stereotypes.

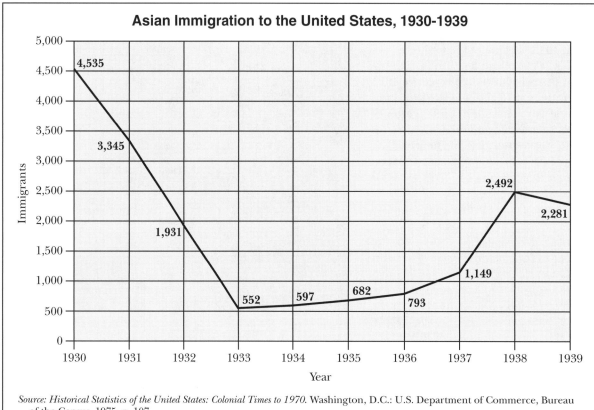

Asian Immigration to the United States, 1930-1939

Source: *Historical Statistics of the United States: Colonial Times to 1970.* Washington, D.C.: U.S. Department of Commerce, Bureau of the Census, 1975, p. 107.

While Chinese American cinematographer James Wong Howe succeeded, the greatest Chinese American star of the decade, Anna May Wong, lost the leading role in the China-based film *The Good Earth* (1937) to a Caucasian actor.

When Japan attacked China in 1937, Chinese Americans supported the Nationalist government of China, and American public opinion became more sympathetic toward them. Conflict with Japanese Americans increased, and the annual "Rice Bowl" football match between Chinese and Japanese American athletes in San Francisco became fraught with political overtones.

Filipino Americans Encounter Setbacks and Successes Because the Philippines was a U.S. trusteeship, Filipinos were able to immigrate to the United States, where the vast majority worked in agriculture and domestic services. Apart from small family communities around East Coast naval bases, Filipinos on the West Coast were overwhelmingly male and single. The relationships between Filipino men and Caucasian women triggered the Watsonville, California, anti-Filipino race riots in January, 1930, that killed one Filipino. The event was symptomatic of similar conflicts throughout the decade brought on by Caucasian sexual jealousy.

Filipino agricultural workers stood up against exploitative labor conditions in California and organized the Filipino Labor Union in 1933. Caucasians sought legal ways to deport Filipino workers. In 1934, U.S. Congress set a time line for Philippine independence and offered to pay the passage for any Filipino American to return to the Philippines. Only 2,190 Filipinos accepted this dubious offer. In 1936, Filipino American persistence in the labor struggle paid off when the Filipino-Mexican farmworkers union was granted a charter by the American Federation of Labor.

Impact Asian Americans survived the 1930's despite Caucasian racist harassment, noticeably by the

California Joint Immigration Committee and organizations such as the American Legion Navy Post No. 278 in Los Angeles. Japanese and Chinese Americans raised children who worked and studied hard to be part of the mainstream society only to face severe job discrimination. The conflict between Japan and China, the latter of which was supported politically by the United States, began to cast its shadow on Japanese Americans, the only group of Asian Americans to leave the United States in significant numbers during the 1930's.

R. C. Lutz

Further Reading

Ancheta, Angelo N. *Race, Rights, and the Asian American Experience*. 2d ed. New Brunswick, N.J.: Rutgers University Press, 2006. Academic study of Asian American struggle with racial discrimination in the United States.

Chan, Sucheng. *Asian Americans: An Interpretive History*. Boston: Twayne, 1991. Survey of Asian immigrant experience in the United States; covers the 1930's.

Chang, Iris. *The Chinese in America*. New York: Viking, 2003. Excellent historical work; chapter 12 offers in-depth coverage of all aspects of the Chinese American experience during the 1930's.

Okihiro, Gary Y. *The Columbia Guide to Asian American History*. New York: Columbia University Press, 2005. Comprehensive scholarly work. Useful time line of key events for Asian Americans during the 1930's.

Takaki, Ronald. *Strangers from a Different Shore: A History of Asian Americans*. Rev. ed. Boston: Back Bay, 1998. Widely available standard work about the Asian American experience; the 1930's are presented based on analysis of primary sources, interviews, and official statistics. Covers the experience of Japanese, Chinese, Filipino, Korean, and Asian Indian Americans.

See also Asia; Charlie Chan films; Demographics of the United States; *Good Earth, The*; Japanese American Citizens League; Japanese military aggression; Manchuria occupation; Mr. Moto films; Philippine Independence Act of 1934; Philippine Islands.

■ Astaire, Fred

Identification American Broadway and film actor, singer, dancer, and choreographer
Born May 10, 1899; Omaha, Nebraska
Died June 22, 1987; Los Angeles, California

One of the most beloved personalities in the history of the musical, Astaire excelled as a singer and dancer first on the Broadway stage and later as one of the most prominent figures of the Hollywood musical. His choreographic invention and fresh directorial concepts revolutionized the genre.

Fred Astaire, born Frederick Austerlitz, began his career in vaudeville in 1905, paired alongside his sister Adele. They shared in a successful premiere of Sigmund Romberg's revue *Over the Top* (1917), which led to a host of stage endeavors throughout the early 1920's. These included *The Bunch and Judy* (1922), *For Goodness Sake* (1923), and *Stop Flirting* (1923). By 1926, the Astaires had debuted in London and soon gained international fame. However,

Film and dance star Fred Astaire rehearsing in 1937. (Hulton Archive/ Getty Images)

Adele married in 1932 and ceased her profession as a stage actor.

After retiring from the Broadway stage in 1932, Astaire embarked upon a career in Hollywood at RKO Pictures. The company lent him to Metro-Goldwyn-Mayer for a short sequence in his first film, *Dancing Lady* (1933). Astaire was reluctant to enter into another male-female partnership; he craved autonomy as a performer after nearly three decades of working with his sister. Nonetheless, he continued his Hollywood career by entering into one of the most successful pairings in film history with singer, dancer, and actor Ginger Rogers. They collaborated in a total of ten iconic and lucrative films, nine of which were produced during the 1930's: *Flying Down to Rio* (1933), *The Gay Divorcee* (1934), *Roberta* (1935), *Top Hat* (1935), *Follow the Fleet* (1936), *Swing Time* (1936), *Shall We Dance* (1937), *Carefree* (1938), and *The Story of Vernon and Irene Castle* (1939). Katharine Hepburn famously quipped that Astaire gave Rogers class, and in return, she gave him sex appeal. The films of Rogers and Astaire popularized many celebrated songs written by famous Broadway composers, including George Gershwin, Cole Porter, Jerome Kern, and Irving Berlin. The latter penned the famous song "Cheek to Cheek" for Astaire, who debuted the number in *Top Hat*. The ballad brilliantly showcases Astaire's clearly annunciated and pleasant vocals and was subsequently recorded by a host of other artists. In 1935, Astaire recorded the song with the Leo Reisman Orchestra, and the track was inducted into the Grammy Hall of Fame in 2000.

Impact   Gene Kelly, who proved a mammoth influential figure in the film musical during the 1940's, said: "The history of dance on film begins with Astaire." Astaire's lively choreography and charming persona paved the way for many aspiring performers. His most important contribution to the development of the film musical was his innovative idea of the stationary camera. While many directors had utilized multiple angles to film lengthy dance scenes, Astaire insisted that the dancer remain in full view at all times with little or no movement of the camera, noting that the dancer's job was to create interest through his or her own changing positions. Additionally, Astaire helped to integrate the Hollywood musical, insisting that song and dance be utilized to advance the plot rather than inhibit its momentum. Over the years, prominent choreogra-

phers have frequently acknowledged Astaire's tremendous influence, including Jerome Robbins, who paid homage to the elder Astaire in a 1983 tribute at the New York City ballet. In 1999, the American Film Institute named Astaire the fifth greatest male star in history. While the Hollywood musical declined during the 1950's, Astaire's films and his partnership with Rogers continue to be enjoyed by millions of fans around the globe.

Erica K. Argyropoulos

Further Reading

Astaire, Fred. *Steps in Time*. New York: Harper Press, 1959.

Gallafent, Edward. *Astaire and Rogers*. New York: Columbia University Press, 2002.

See also   Broadway musicals; Dance; Film; Gershwin, George; Music: Popular; *Top Hat*.

■ Astor, Mary

Identification   American actor
Born   May 3, 1906; Quincy, Illinois
Died   September 25, 1987; Woodland Hills, California

Astor, who became an actor in her teens, came into prominence in the mid-1920's. Despite a troubled personal life, she rose to become a preeminent supporting player throughout the 1930's and into the 1940's during a stage, film, radio, and television career that spanned more than forty years.

Mary Astor was born Lucile Vasconcellos Langhanke, the only child of a German immigrant, Otto Langhanke, and an American, Helen de Vasconcellos. Astor was an attractive child, with expressive eyes, and her ambitious, social-climbing parents began exploiting her attractiveness from a young age. Astor was homeschooled. Her father taught her how to play the piano. From her mother, a frustrated thespian, she learned drama and elocution. Her parents entered her photograph in beauty contests. When Astor began to attract professional attention, her parents moved to Chicago, New York, and Hollywood to keep Astor at the center of the entertainment industry. Until well into Astor's adult years, the elder Langhankes maintained tight control of her finances.

Astor debuted on film in the early 1920's and was a bit player until John Barrymore cast her as his costar in *Beau Brummel* (1924). Astor appeared in dozens of silent films and eventually succeeded in sound after 1930, though initially the distinctive low-pitched timbre of her voice surprised some. From 1932 to 1941, she was particularly productive; she starred in such popular films as *Red Dust* (1932), *The Kennel Murder Case* (1933), *Dodsworth* (1936), *The Prisoner of Zenda* (1937), and *The Hurricane* (1937). She earned a best supporting actress Oscar for her work in *The Great Lie* (1941) and is best remembered for her role as Brigid O'Shaughnessy, opposite Humphrey Bogart, in *The Maltese Falcon* (1941).

Despite on-screen success, Astor had off-screen problems that interrupted and nearly derailed her acting career. Astor's first husband, Kenneth Hawks—brother of famous director Howard Hawks—was killed in 1930 in a midair plane collision while filming over the Pacific Ocean. Subsequently, Astor had a nervous breakdown and attempted suicide. In 1931, she married Franklyn Thorpe, the psychologist who treated her, and they had a daughter, Marylyn. Their marriage disintegrated after five years, fueled by Astor's adultery, which was revealed in a court custody battle that featured tame excerpts from Astor's supposedly sizzling diary, detailing her affair with playwright George S. Kaufman. Two successive marriages, to insurance salesman Manuel del Campo, which produced a son, Tono, and stockbroker Thomas Gordon Wheelock, did not last.

Other problems inhibited Astor's success, namely her alcoholism, which worsened throughout the 1930's, and the deteriorating relationship with her manipulative parents. In 1925, the elder Langhankes had purchased—with Astor's earnings—a palatial Hollywood mansion called Moorcrest and for years thereafter lived lavishly on her income while doling out a small allowance to her. In 1933, Astor took her parents to court and won: Their monthly $1,000 stipend (an extravagant amount at the time) was reduced to $100, and Moorcrest was sold at auction for $21,000, a tenth of its value, to settle debts incurred from making expensive improvements to the place.

Though Astor's star began to wane after 1943, as the result of a long-term contract with Metro-Goldwyn-Mayer that relegated her to mediocre roles, she continued acting until retiring in 1964. In addition to performing more than 120 film and oc-

casional theater roles, she was a frequent guest on popular television shows after 1954, including *Studio 57*, *Robert Montgomery Presents*, *Studio One*, *Alfred Hitchcock Presents*, *Playhouse 90*, *Rawhide*, *The Defenders*, and *Ben Casey*. Her last film role was in *Hush . . . Hush, Sweet Charlotte* (1964). In 1959, she published a best-selling autobiography, *My Story*, which detailed her personal life. During the 1960's, she published five novels, and in 1971, she released another nonfiction best seller about her acting career, *A Life on Film*. In her later years, she lived at the Motion Picture and Television House and Hospital, where she died at the age of eighty-one.

Impact   The sordid public disclosures of Astor's private life did not particularly damage her reputation in a decade filled with such events of import as the Depression; the Lindbergh kidnapping; the exploits of bandits such as Bonnie Parker, Clyde Barrow, and John Dillinger; and the rumblings of war in Europe. By the late 1930's, Astor had weathered several personal crises and was heading into one of the most productive and satisfying periods of her acting career, when she had critically acclaimed performances both in film and on stage.

Jack Ewing

Further Reading

Astor, Mary. *A Life on Film.* New York: Dell, 1972.

Kinn, Gail, and Jim Piazza. *The Academy Awards: The Complete History of Oscar.* New York: Black Dog and Leventhal, 2002.

See also   Academy Awards; Film; Hammett, Dashiell; Kaufman, George S., and Moss Hart; Theater in the United States.

■ Astronomy

Definition   Study of celestial objects and phenomena

The decade of the 1930's was a relatively busy period for astronomy in North America in spite of the Great Depression. The universe of galaxies had been discovered, and its existence was recognized as a new field of research to develop. Exciting observational discoveries were made about the universe, and theoretical developments arose through the application to the cosmos of Albert Einstein's theory of general relativity.

Astronomy in the United States at the beginning of the 1930's was conducted mostly at a few well-funded private observatories and at large universities by a select group of people. Nonetheless, some of the advances in the previous decade, especially Edwin Powell Hubble's discovery of the vast universe of galaxies, had opened a new realm of exploration that catalyzed growth of the science of astronomy. A notable increase in research activity occurred during the 1930's. By the end of the decade the prospects for the future looked bright: The giant Palomar telescope was under construction, the physics of stellar interiors were becoming understandable, and the field of radio astronomy had emerged.

Solar System The decade began with a remarkable discovery: a new planet. In 1930, Clyde William

Astronomer Clyde Tombaugh, twenty-four years old in this 1930 picture in which he stands with his Newtonian telescope. Tombaugh discovered Pluto, then considered to be the ninth planet in the solar system but later reclassified as a dwarf planet. (©Bettmann/CORBIS)

Tombaugh, a young astronomer at the Lowell Observatory, revealed that he had found a faint object beyond Neptune that had a planetary-shaped orbit. Named Pluto, this planet was unlike the other planets in the distant solar system: It was small, similar to the Earth's moon in size, and it was apparently a solid body, not a gaseous giant such as Jupiter and the other distant planets. Pluto remained an enigma until the early twenty-first century, when many similar objects were discovered, and Pluto was deemed one of a new class of asteroids in the Kuiper Belt.

Jupiter and it neighbors were also a major topic during the 1930's. Yale astronomer Rupert Wildt showed that the atmosphere of Jupiter contains both methane and ammonia; he correctly inferred that the major atmospheric constituent is hydrogen gas. Furthermore, he speculated that a layer of "metallic" hydrogen exists in the interior of Jupiter and its fellow giant planets, where hydrogen atoms are pressed together so much that they act like a metal. Scientists also examined the atmosphere of Venus and found a high concentration of carbon dioxide, which is the cause of Venus's greenhouse effect and its intense surface heat. Scientists at the Mount Wilson Observatory in California examined the infrared radiation emitted by Mercury and found the planet to be even hotter than Venus, with a surface temperature of 350 degrees Celsius.

Stellar Astrophysics Although planetary science developed during the 1930's, stellar astronomy showed the most growth during the decade. Most of the programs using the large telescopes in Canada and the United States were devoted to stellar astrophysics, using spectrographs to penetrate the atmospheres of the stars to examine their physical properties. Primary research concerned the physics of stellar interiors, atmospheres, and compositions as well as the nature of variable and peculiar stars.

In 1930, astronomers understood the basic properties of normal stars, but many mysteries remained, some of which were solved in the following ten years. The source of a star's energy, a fundamental property, was unknown. Scientists debated this topic futilely until 1938, when Hans Albrecht Bethe and his colleagues discovered the proton-proton cycle, a series of nuclear reactions that convert protons (hydrogen nuclei) into helium, releasing large amounts of energy. This is the principal source of energy for most stars.

The source of the opacity of a star's gaseous interior was also a mystery. Astronomers were able to calculate the process by which radiation from the hot central area passes outward to the surface, but they found that there was a mysterious substance that made the gas more opaque than they could account for. The mystery was solved in 1939, when Wildt proposed that the darkness was caused by the presence of a negative hydrogen ion, consisting of a proton with two electrons orbiting it.

The brilliant Indian astronomer Subrahmanyan Chandrasekhar, who moved to the University of Chicago in 1937, made several fundamental contributions to the theoretical understanding of stars in terms of their interior structure, atmospheres, evolution, and dynamics. He was also an early contributor to the subject of black holes.

Milky Way Galaxy During the 1930's, most scientific work on the Milky Way, the Earth's local galaxy, was part of an endeavor to unscramble the confusing distribution of stars near the Sun. A common method of investigation was to examine photographs of the sky by eye to count the number of stars of different brightnesses. Because, on average, the brightness of a star is related to its distance from the observer, the star counts could give statistical evidence about the distribution of stars in that particular direction. This process gave at least a hint of the Galaxy's structure near the Sun, but the larger structure, including the spiral arms, was not detected for another ten years.

The study of star clusters in the Galaxy was more successful. The pioneering work in this field was performed by the Lick Observatory astronomer Robert Julius Trumpler, who measured the distances to "open" clusters, groups of stars located in the thickly populated parts of the Milky Way. Trumpler found that distant clusters were farther away than their stars' brightnesses indicated, which led to the realization that the Galaxy was heavily obscured by interstellar dust. This, in turn, showed that the size of the Galaxy had been grossly underestimated.

A tentative but important step in a new direction occurred in 1933, when Karl G. Jansky at Bell Telephone Laboratories (Bell Labs) detected radio noise that he showed to be emission from outside the solar system. Grote Reber, a radio amateur, followed up on this discovery by building a radio telescope in his backyard, detecting cosmic signals from the Milky Way in 1938. Scientific understanding of this remarkable discovery did not come until the following decade.

External Galaxies Mount Wilson astronomer Hubble, after his groundbreaking discoveries of the 1920's, whereby he proved the existence of external galaxies and the immense universe beyond our Milky Way, continued his careful work on galaxies, concentrating on a classification system and on the apparent expansion of the extragalactic universe. In 1931, he and colleague Milton Humason published a data analysis showing that the so-called Hubble law, which relates the velocity of expansion to the distance of galaxies, is linear out to distances of 250 million light-years. These observations led to a blossoming of theoretical cosmological models, mostly by scientists in the United Kingdom and Europe.

In 1938, Harvard astronomers Martha Dowse and Rebecca Jones detected two peculiar objects. Named Sculptor and Fornax after the constellations in which they lie, the two objects were eventually found to be nearby galaxies of exceedingly faint luminosity. Analysis by Henrietta Hill Swope and Harlow Shapley, also at Harvard, placed the objects' distances at only a few hundred light-years. These were the first dwarf elliptical galaxies, believed to be the most common type in the universe, to be discovered.

Impact The astronomical discoveries of the 1930's opened up several important fields of exploration. Astronomers discovered that the universe is expanding and extends to incredible distances. The Milky Way Galaxy was explored, and its deeply obscuring dust was detected, which implied it was much larger than previously known. Also in the decade, radio astronomy was born. The physical nature of stars, including their structure and the source of their energy, was discovered. Furthermore, scientists made advances in understanding the atmospheres of the planets. A whole new class of solar system inhabitants, called dwarf planets, was detected when Pluto was discovered.

Paul Hodge

Further Reading

Hoskin, Michael, ed. *The Cambridge Concise History of Astronomy.* New York: Cambridge University Press, 2008. Chapters that deal with developments in the first part of the twentieth century give the context of the astronomical discoveries of the 1930's.

Srinivasan, G. *From White Dwarfs to Black Holes: The Legacy of S. Chandrasekhar.* University of Chicago Press, 2000. Biography of the scientist whose brilliant theoretical papers ranged over many of the topics first developed during the 1930's.

Tyson, Neil deGrasse. *The Pluto Files: The Rise and Fall of America's Favorite Planet.* New York: W. W. Norton, 2009. Overview of the history of human's knowledge and research of Pluto; begins in the 1930's.

See also Astronomy; Black hole theory; Neutron star theory; Nobel Prizes; Physics; Pluto discovery; Radio astronomy.

■ Atherton Report

Identification Grand jury report on members of the San Francisco police department's involvement with illegal activities
Dates November 21, 1935, through March 16, 1937
Place San Francisco, California

The Atherton Report was one of the nation's first deep investigations into police corruption in an American city. Investigators determined that San Francisco was facing an epidemic of illegal activities perpetrated and permitted by some of its own policemen and public officials. More than fifty officers and officials were indicted for involvement in numerous schemes that occurred throughout the decade.

During the early 1930's, vice was prominent in large eastern and midwestern cities such as New York, Philadelphia, and Chicago and on the West Coast in large cities such as San Francisco. In fact, Angelo Joseph Rossi, who served as mayor of San Francisco from 1931 to 1944, asked for and appropriated $70,000 to investigate corruption in his city. Rossi's reasons for the investigation stemmed from both a Bureau of Internal Revenue grand-jury investigation of a San Francisco police captain who was suspected of bribery and tax evasion and Rossi's overwhelming desire to rid San Francisco's streets of vice, especially prostitution and gambling.

Both the Bureau of Internal Revenue and the Federal Bureau of Investigation (FBI) suggested to Matthew Brady, the city's district attorney, that Edwin Atherton, a private investigator and former FBI agent, be hired to open and conduct a grand-jury investigation into the long-standing and well-publicized levels of corruption and graft connected to the San Francisco Police Department. In 1935, Atherton began his investigation by enlisting other former federal agents and local police officers to assist him in investigating the alleged illegal activities of members of the police department.

After a lengthy investigation of sixteen months, Atherton convened a special grand jury to determine whether or not there was enough evidence to indict police officers and other public officials. The grand jury amassed thousands of documents that were used to indict more than fifty police officers and public officials. In his final report, dubbed the Atherton Report, Atherton named a total of sixty-seven San Francisco police officers and twenty-four local- and state-level government officials, including city council members, judges, a district attorney, and other notable public officials.

Names of four police captains were forwarded in connection to payoff monies received from 135 brothel owners in the greater San Francisco Bay Area. Additionally, the final report mentioned two well-known San Francisco citizens, Peter and Tom McDonough, brothers who were deemed the "overlords" of San Francisco, responsible for a high percentage of illegal rackets, which included bribery and graft of police officers, in and around the Bay Area. The McDonough brothers ran a local saloon on the corner of Clay and Kearny Streets and a successful bail bonds operation. From 1910 to 1941, they were central figures in various illegal rackets, including gambling, prostitution, extortion of unions, the corrupting of public officials, suborning of witnesses, and controlling the San Francisco police through bribery and kickbacks. Known Italian crime figures such as Al Capone attempted for many years to infiltrate the lucrative San Francisco Bay Area but could not gain entry and acceptance into the McDonough brothers' corrupt realm. Since the McDonoughs were extremely organized and offered generous opportunities to other, low-level California crime syndicates, their tight-knit operation became virtually impenetrable to outside mobsters. Furthermore, anyone who attempted to violate McDonoughs' rules either would be arrested by corrupt police officers or would be found dead.

Impact   The Atherton Report was a groundbreaking investigation into the dark world of police corruption. This lengthy report persuaded other cities to investigate their own police officers and public officials.

Paul M. Klenowski

Further Reading

Clayborn, Hannah. *Historic Photos of San Francisco Crime.* Nashville, Tenn.: Turner, 2009.

Nelli, Humbert. *The Business of Crime: Italians and Syndicate Crime in the United States.* Chicago: Chicago University Press, 1976.

See also   Anti-Racketeering Act of 1934; Crimes and scandals; Gambling; Organized crime; Pornography.

■ Auto racing

Identification   The sport of racing automobiles

Auto racing grew during the 1930's as its focus areas shifted from the Northeast and Midwest to the South and the West, regions where the sport built strong followings. The relative ease of holding races in warmer climates provided the backdrop for much of its increase in popularity.

Most auto-racing events were held as preliminary races, often ten to fifteen laps in length, with the winners meeting in the main race. Those races were short compared with today's standards; twenty-five laps often decided a winner. The exceptions to this format were the Indianapolis 500 and coast-to-coast events. The appeal of all types of racing grew along with Americans' love of the automobile and the desire to travel fast. The sport built a loyal following as races were held at numerous tracks around the country.

The Racing Tracks and Vehicles   For most of the decade, two types of cars were used for racing. The most notable car was the open-cockpit vehicle used on tracks that ranged from as small as 0.5 mile in length to the 2.5-mile Indianapolis Motor Speedway. The latter track was not the norm; most tracks tended

Year	Driver	Finishing Time
1930	Billy Arnold	4:58:39.72
1931	Louis Schneider	5:10:27.93
1932	Fred Frame	4:48:03.79
1933	Louis Meyer	4:48:00.75
1934	Bill Cummings	4:46:05.20
1935	Kelly Petillo	4:42:22.71
1936	Louis Meyer	4:35:03.39
1937	Wilbur Shaw	4:24:07.80
1938	Floyd Roberts	4:15:58.40
1939	Wilbur Shaw	4:20:47.39

Indianapolis 500 Winners, 1930-1939

Note: Finishing time is measured in hours, minutes, seconds, and tenths of seconds.

to be less than one mile in length. Almost all of these tracks had dirt surfaces and were surrounded by fencing. As a result, fans felt part of the action, as dirt flew from the cars outward. However, these conditions also proved problematic because of safety issues. On-track fatalities were relatively common.

The Indianapolis 500 became the grand annual event in American auto racing. Though the purse for the race dropped precipitously during the 1930's because of the Depression, the race remained a marquee event. However, the number of fatalities at Indianapolis had a negative effect on the racing community. Between 1931 and 1935, fifteen drivers died there because of the increased speeds of the cars. As a result, the track's trademark bricks were paved over.

In 1933, at Hughes Stadium in Sacramento, California, a new type of car began to gain attention. At first called midget or sprint cars, these vehicles were smaller than the ones that had been in use. These also had open cockpits with exposed wheels; however, they were smaller than the traditional type. Midget cars engendered a different style of racing because they could run on small tracks. Therefore, races could be held indoors. These cars became known as "doodlebugs."

Toward the end of the decade another type of racing car emerged: the stock car. As a lumbering, closed-cockpit, covered-wheel vehicle, the stock car called for a different style of racing, one in which the focus was on straight-line speed. The rise of stock-car racing provided the foundation for the incorporation of the National Association of Stock Car Automobile Racing (NASCAR) during the 1940's.

Sanctioning Bodies and Promoters   Three organizations governed the sport during the 1930's. The American Automobile Association (AAA) was the largest and best known. Based in New York, the AAA oversaw the Indianapolis 500 and most large-scale events. The Central States Racing Association, based in Dayton, Ohio, focused on both stand-alone events and those held at fairs. The third organization, the International Motor Contest Association (IMCA), was formed in response to the perceived inflated rates charged by the AAA. The IMCA focused its efforts on sanctioning races at fairs. In contrast to these large organizations, small groups sanctioned many races in California, and the relative independence of these groups gave them an "outlaw" appeal. All three of the major organizations, usually working independently, sped the evolution of competitive racing, establishing rules, encouraging safety measures, and working with promoters, owners, and drivers to sell tickets.

The promoters, not the drivers, developed and carried the sport forward. The notable promoters of the era were Ralph Hankinson, Walter Stebbins, and J. Alex Sloan. These three men helped the sport grow. Hankinson, who worked with Southern Speedways, provided backing to racing in the South. The Lakewood Speedway in Atlanta became a hub of activity during its Independence Day races. Similarly, tracks in Florida also experienced a surge in activity; more drivers raced in the South as temperatures cooled in the North.

Impact   American auto racing experienced arguably more change during the 1930's than it has in any other decade. The rise of midget- and stock-car racing offered new avenues for both fans and drivers. In addition, the moves to the South and West, where the temperate climate provided longer seasons for racing, helped to solidify the sport in American culture.

P. Huston Ladner

Further Reading
Fabritz, Earl C., and Allan G. Krause. *Wooden Rails and Rooster Tails: An Auto Racing Anthology.* Zionsville, Ind.: Pitstop Books, 2003. Provides a survey of American auto racing, and how it has moved from racing on wooden tracks to a modern spectacle.

Hall, Randal L. "Carnival of Speed: The Auto Racing Business in the Emerging South, 1930-1950." *North Carolina Historical Review* 84, no. 3 (2007): 245-275. Hall's article details how the racing industry moved southward, shaping NASCAR.

Martin, J. A., and Thomas F. Saal. *American Auto Racing: The Milestones and Personalities of a Century of Speed.* Jefferson, N.C.: McFarland, 2004. Covers the growth of auto racing from its humble beginnings to its place among major American sports.

Radbruch, Don. *Dirt Track Auto Racing, 1919-1941: A Pictorial History.* Jefferson, N.C.: McFarland, 2004. Photographs provide a visual context for the racing that transpired in the early part of the twentieth century.

See also   Automobiles and auto manufacturing; Recreation; Sports in Canada; Sports in the United States.

■ Automobiles and auto manufacturing

The automotive industry was hard-hit by the Great Depression, suffering significant losses in sales. On the long road to economic recovery, the number of manufacturers dwindled, paving the way for the emergence of the "big three" manufacturers in the industry.

For the automotive industry, the 1930's was a decade of catastrophic decline and slow recovery, one in which only the strongest manufacturers were able to survive the steep losses in sales brought on by the Great Depression. The output of an industry that had produced more than 5.6 million cars and trucks in 1929 plummeted to 1.3 million vehicles by 1932. While Americans continued to drive, they did not buy new vehicles, largely because so many people lacked the financial resources to do so. Before the stock market crash of 1929 forty-four American companies were manufacturing automobiles; a decade later the list had dwindled to fewer than twelve, and 90 percent of sales were made by the big three: General Motors, Chrysler, and Ford. While sales increased gradually from the low point in 1932, the industry still produced only 3.6 million vehicles in

Promotional photograph focusing on the trunk of a car large enough to hold multiple luggage items for travelers going on long trips. (Archive Photos/Getty Images)

1939. The decline in sales during these tough times required companies to be innovative and ruthless, and only those who exhibited both qualities managed to be in business at the end of the decade.

Industry Response to Economic Catastrophe The initial shock of the Great Depression was felt in the automotive industry almost immediately. General Motors stock lost two-thirds of its value in October, 1929; other publicly traded companies fared no better. Auto manufacturers large and small found it necessary to severely curtail their production activities. Some plants were shuttered, and workers were laid off. At other facilities, shifts were reduced, and any temporary rise in demand required remaining employees to work overtime.

How quickly each manufacturer reacted to the drop in sales during 1930 and 1931 was not consistent, however. Initially, Henry Ford was certain that the catastrophe would be short-lived. Only months after the stock market crash, he announced plans to increase wages and to invest $25 million in plant expansion. One year later, however, he was forced to abandon those plans, and the Ford Motor Company joined other companies in scaling back operations. Dealers, too, were hard hit, as many found themselves holding inventory that they could not sell. By 1930, auto sales fell by as much as two-thirds for smaller manufacturers such as Hudson and Willys-Overland. The severity of the problem was evident in the downturn in sales of low-priced models during 1931. In that year, only Chrysler experienced a small increase in sales, largely because its new Plymouth model was heavily promoted and seemed truly innovative. Chevrolet sales were down 25 percent, while Ford sales declined 40 percent. Companies found it necessary to adjust their production schedules and sales techniques to weather the economic storm.

In addition to curtailing expenses, automobile manufacturers tried to deal with the economic downturn by becoming more innovative. At General Motors, chief executive Alfred P. Sloan insisted that the company continue to conduct annual model changes, improve vehicle quality, and introduce technical and stylistic innovations for each of its product lines. Thus, potential customers were offered new choices each year at various price points designed to allow Americans to consider purchasing new automobiles regardless of their level of income. In 1931, General Motors added a six-cylinder Chevrolet to its product line, offering a car with more horsepower than those models offered by their competitors. Henry Ford also believed Americans would eventually return to purchasing automobiles, especially inexpensive ones that showed some innovation in design. The initial success of his Model A, introduced in 1928, persuaded him that weathering

the financial crisis was possible by making cutbacks in production until sales improved. In 1932, Ford introduced the V-8, an economy car with an eight-cylinder engine. Walter P. Chrysler was more attuned to the need for constant improvements in both style and technical efficiency. Throughout the decade, the Chrysler company maintained a strong engineering division, allocating millions to research in product design.

In 1931, Ford's company pioneered several engineering innovations, including a "floating" power system for engine mounting that produced a smoother ride. Introduced in 1934, Chrysler's new "Airflo" body design did not catch on. However, Chrysler's advances in the design of its high-end Imperial forced both General Motors and Ford to revamp their luxury Cadillac and Lincoln models and eventually forced Ford to increase its product line to compete at every price range with its major competitors.

Government Intervention and Unionization During the first three years of the Great Depression, the automotive industry was largely left on its own to deal with the economic crisis. The inauguration of Franklin D. Roosevelt in 1933 changed the relationship

The 1938 Phantom Corsair featured a sleek, futurist design. (Archive Photos/Getty Images)

between these private businesses and the federal government drastically. One of the first initiatives of the new administration was to intervene directly in managing the economic crisis in the country. Central to that initiative was passage of the National Industrial Recovery Act (NIRA). Under this legislation, businesses involved in the same industry were required to create codes for fair competition and set up wage and price guidelines. The latter were designed to stop companies from further lowering prices simply to make sales, so that the economy would not continue in a deflationary spiral. This move caused serious concern for the automotive industry, in which lowering prices while providing additional features to customers had become the standard practice for increasing sales volume. General Motors, Chrysler, and many smaller manufacturers agreed reluctantly to participate in enforcement of the industry codes and guidelines established by their trade association. Ford refused to cooperate, even though the federal government threatened to withhold contracts with his company. Two years later, the Supreme Court declared NIRA unconstitutional, and auto manufacturers were allowed to return to competitive practices that had made them successful before 1929.

A second challenge to auto manufacturers' autonomy had lasting effects. As part of its plan for assuring fair treatment for workers in all industries, the Roosevelt administration was committed to unionization. Before the 1930's unions were virtually nonexistent in automobile factories. Men such as Ford and Sloan were vehemently opposed to allowing workers to organize, considering the practice bad for business. Passage of the National Labor Relations Act (NLRA) of 1936, however, guaranteed workers the right to organize and choose a bargaining agent. The new law prompted renewed efforts by many activists to infiltrate the largest industry in the United States, none with greater zeal than the United Auto Workers (UAW). Shortly after the passage of the NLRA, union organizers persuaded workers at the General Motors plant in Flint, Michigan, to strike.

In February, 1937, after serious and sometime volatile negotiations, General Motors management agreed to accept the UAW as the bargaining agent for General Motors workers. Two months later, management at Chrysler also came to terms with the UAW, virtually guaranteeing that union shops would

become the norm throughout the automotive industry. Once again, Ford was the lone holdout. He ordered the head of his services division, Harry Bennett, to marshal resources to combat any attempt to unionize Ford Motor Company workers. Bennett ran what amounted to the largest private police force in the country, and he routinely used it to intimidate workers at Ford into working more efficiently and keeping quiet about problems within the company. In 1932, Bennett's group effectively quelled a protest against employment practices at Ford. In May, 1937, Ford workers and union officials demonstrating to support unionization were brutally attacked by men hired by Bennett to disrupt their efforts. Several more years passed before Ford Motor Company management agreed to recognize the UAW as the bargaining agent for Ford workers.

Changes in Leadership Another significant change occurred during the 1930's, not so much a result of the Depression but rather because of the inevitable passage of time. During the decade, several key industry leaders either died or retired, most notably Chrysler in 1935 and Sloan in 1937. While both men retained a hand in strategic management of their companies, responsibilities for handling day-to-day operations were passed to capable successors. The transition of power at Chrysler and General Motors demonstrated that companies built on sound management principles with a strong leadership infrastructure and quality products could survive even in times of dire financial stress. The continuing slide of Ford Motor Company, as the aging Ford dictated policy often in an erratic and counterproductive fashion, was the exception, and it proved the wisdom of the management philosophies developed at the other two automotive giants.

Impact During the 1930's, the automobile industry demonstrated that in times of crisis, firms that can produce new products or improve older ones can still find buyers for their goods and can maintain a loyal client base. It also proved that in an industry in which significant capital investment is necessary for continued operations, only those companies with the financial wherewithal can sustain significant, long-term downturns in consumer sales. Nevertheless, the eventual success that General Motors and Chrysler showed by weathering the Depression, and the ability of smaller firms to stay afloat by changing business plans and achieving key mergers, represents the industry's resiliency during the decade. On the other hand, dozens of automobile manufacturers went bankrupt during this time. Of lasting significance, too, was the change in labor-management relationships brought about by government pressure on auto manufacturers to allow unions into their factories. Since the 1930's, the prices of American automobiles have been affected by the costs companies incurred in providing higher wages and improved benefits packages to their workers.

Laurence W. Mazzeno

Further Reading

Brinkley, Douglas. *Wheels for the World: Henry Ford, His Company, and a Century of Progress.* New York: Viking Press, 2003. Chronicles the accomplishments and mistakes at Ford Motor Company during the 1930's, a period in which the company fell to third among the "big three" U.S. auto manufacturers.

Curcio, Vincent. *Chrysler: The Life and Times of an Automotive Genius.* New York: Oxford University Press, 2000. Explains how Chrysler positioned his company to overtake Ford as the second largest auto manufacturer during the 1930's.

Lichtenstein, Nelson. *The Most Dangerous Man in Detroit: Walter Reuther and the Fate of American Labor.* New York: Basic Books, 1995. Describes the efforts of unions to establish a foothold in the automotive industry and explains tactics union leaders used to bring management to the bargaining table.

Pelfrey, William. *Billy, Alfred, and General Motors.* New York: AMACOM, 2006. Traces the growth of General Motors, emphasizing its unique place among auto manufacturers as a conglomerate of formerly independent manufacturers; explains why the company became the dominant player in the market by the 1930's.

Rae, John B. *The American Automobile Industry.* Boston: Twayne, 1984. General history of the growth of the automobile industry in the United States; describes the reasons for the emergence of the "big three" auto companies during the 1920's and 1930's.

See also   Car radios; Chrysler Building; Congress of Industrial Organizations; Ford, Henry; Labor strikes; Lincoln Continental Mark I; National Labor Relations Act of 1935; Reuther, Walter P.; Transportation; Unionism.

■ Aviation and aeronautics

Definition   Industry and science of artificial flight

During the 1930's, aviation and aeronautics developed in the shadow of larger events. After World War I, countries slashed their defense spending. Research funds were limited; thus, aviation developments tended to be focused on small improvements to previous designs rather than on major advances. The Great Depression limited the amount of funds available for research, equipment, and travel. Only the most necessary or economically viable projects received funding.

The biggest change in aviation was in the types of materials and production methods used. The wood and fabric biplanes of World War I persisted into the 1920's, reflecting the necessity for simple and light materials because of the limited engines of the day. By the 1930's, however, engine technology made faster and longer flights possible. In 1927, for example, the engine on the *Spirit of St. Louis* that carried Charles A. Lindbergh on his transatlantic flight produced only 223 horsepower, giving a top speed of 133 miles per hour. Only eight years later, however, a typical engine, such as the Pratt and Whitney R-1830, produced at least 1,200 horsepower.

The Evolution of the Military Aircraft   The heavier weight and power of the new engines meant that aircraft needed new construction methods and types of materials. Wood and fabric gave way to all-metal construction with steel framing, load-bearing components, and a fuselage covered with lightweight aluminum. An example of this was the Boeing P-26 fighter, the "Peashooter," which first flew in 1932. The P-26 featured a 500-horsepower Pratt and Whitney engine that produced a top speed of 240 miles per hour. The Peashooter had a single wing, unlike World War I biplanes, but its heavy bracing, open cockpit and fixed landing gear hark back to the biplane. By the end of the 1930's, advanced fighters, such as the Curtiss P-40 Warhawk, with its 1,400-horsepower Alison 1710 engine, could fly at nearly 400 miles per hour with three times the firepower of the P-26. The P-40 had little in common with the World War I biplane. It had a single wing, was all-metal construction, and featured an enclosed cockpit and retractable landing gear.

The high operating ceiling of the P-26 indicated that high-altitude and long-distance abilities were also elements of the new aircraft designs. During the

1920's, a multiengined aircraft meant two engines, one on each wing. The Martin B-10 bomber, first flown in 1932, followed this pattern with its two 775-horsepower Wright R-1820 engines, enabling it to fly 1,200 miles at 213 miles per hour at 24,000 feet. However, the new metal airframes, along with the need for a longer range at higher altitudes, meant that multiengine aircraft soon got much larger. First flown in 1935, the legendary Boeing B-17 Flying Fortress was the first all-metal, four-engine bomber to enter service and was nearly twice the size of the B-10. The prototype B-17 also had Wright R-1820 engines but was uprated to 1,200 horsepower for each engine, allowing the plane to fly faster, farther, and higher than its predecessor. High altitude caused problems, though. High-flying planes required oxygen systems and electrically heated suits for the aircraft crews to survive the thin air and frigid temperatures. The planes also needed complex and expensive navigational equipment and bombsights to locate and accurately hit targets far below them.

Aircraft Weaponry The military aircraft of the 1930's utilized the same weapons of World War I aircraft with only relatively slight improvements. A World War I biplane carried only two light machine guns or a small bomb load; aircraft of the 1930's carried similar weapons but with a larger capacity. Fighter planes dispensed with the light machine guns in favor of heavy ones, such as the Browning .50 caliber machine gun. Whereas earlier fighters carried only two guns, 1930's fighters carried up to eight Brownings. Alternative armaments were cannons in the 20- to 30-millimeter caliber, which did damage if the shells struck their targets; however, the cannons fired at a slower rate and carried fewer rounds than machine guns did, and aircraft could not carry as many of the heavier cannons.

Bombs remained largely the same, except aircraft could carry larger ones or more of the earlier types. The most significant change was how they were delivered. In addition to traditional horizontal bombing, air forces adopted dive bombing, in which an

Before ushering in regular pan-Pacific travel, the Pan American China Clipper *goes on a test run over the San Francisco Bay in 1935.* (AP/Wide World Photos)

"Miss Air Travel" Jean McClandish (second from the left) and federal aviation officials promote the first week of October, 1936, as National Air Travel Week. (Library of Congress)

aircraft enters a nearly vertical dive from high altitude to low altitude and dives the bomb directly into the target before pulling up and flying away. This technique gained favor because it did not require an expensive bombsight or an extra crew member to operate it. The U.S. Navy in particular embraced the technique, acquiring a specialized dive bomber, the Douglas SBD Dauntless, in 1939.

Civilian Air Transportation Civil aviation, which flourished during the 1920's, languished during the 1930's, as the Great Depression made owning a private aircraft difficult. Cessna and Piper, companies that later became giants in the civil aviation industry, both initially went bankrupt during the 1930's before reemerging in the latter part of the decade. With few civilian pilots, civil aviation during the 1930's meant little commercial travel was provided by the airlines. International travel was arduous because, although aircraft were faster, the vast distances to foreign des-

tinations meant long travel times and multiple stops. A trip from the United States to Europe, for example, required at least one stop in Greenland, Ireland, or the Azores. Trips to Asia meant astronomical distances with stops in primitive and undeveloped islands along the way. The answer to the problem was a large flying boat, a craft big enough to carry a lot of fuel and passengers but capable of landing and taking off from the water, which made facilities and runways unnecessary in places where they were not available anyway. In 1935, Pan American Airlines introduced its first massive Martin M-130 flying boat, better known as the "China Clipper." The M-130's could carry thirty-six passengers, but with a top speed of only 180 miles per hour, the clippers took seven days to cross the Pacific Ocean.

Air travel within the United States was simpler and more reliable than international air travel. The first passenger airlines started operation during the 1920's, but service was unpredictable. The airlines made more money moving the mail than they did moving people, so flights were often irregular and schedules were virtually nonexistent, which made planning a trip by air difficult for the average traveler. Moreover, airports were relatively few and far between. Cities were hesitant to devote public resources to airports for commercial use by private companies. The lure of travelers and business opportunities, however, prompted many cities to invest in municipal airfields, and the number of major airports grew by the end of the 1930's. Large airports that either began or completed construction during the 1930's include Midway Airport in Chicago, National Airport (now the Ronald Reagan Washington National Airport) in Washington, D.C., and La-Guardia Airport in New York.

Civil air transportation also increased when aircraft improved. The most common civilian airliner at the start of the decade was the Ford 3AT, better known as the Trimotor, which could carry up to seventeen passengers but offered only a minimum of comfort. The aircraft had no climate control, and lack of insulation meant the aircraft's engine noise roared in the cabin. By the end of the decade, however, Boeing introduced its superior DC-2 and DC-3 models. These aircraft carried up to twenty-eight passengers at an increased speed and with considerably more comfort. The DC-3 featured soundproofing, cabin heating, and bathroom facilities.

Assisting with passenger comfort were the first flight attendants. In 1933, American Airlines hired the first female flight attendants, who initially were nurses who assisted with flight-sick passengers; the attendants soon found themselves catering to the passengers' comfort. Thanks to the improved reliability and comfort of the airplanes, airline travel boomed during the 1930's despite the Great Depression. U.S. airlines carried 474,000 passengers in 1932, and that number nearly tripled in six years to 1,178,000 in 1938.

Impact   Aeronautical advancements of the 1930's helped to bring the world closer together. For the first time, a traveler could reach the far corners of the world at a relatively fast speed and in a reasonable amount of comfort. The development of better engines and aircraft seemed to offer a bright future, but the same technology was soon applied to military aircraft during World War II.

Steven J. Ramold

Further Reading

Berry, Kathleen, and Daniel J. Walkowitz. *Femininity in Flight: A History of Flight Attendants.* Durham: Duke University Press, 2007. As the face of civil aviation during the 1930's, flight attendants were the symbol of the new airline industry.

Garvey, William. *The Age of Flight: A History of America's Pioneering Airline.* Greensboro, N.C.: Pace Communications, 2001. History of United Airlines; many of United's struggles and advances were similar to those of other fledgling airlines during the 1930's.

Sullivan, Mark P. *Dependable Engines: The Story of Pratt and Whitney.* Reston, Va.: American Institute of Aeronautics and Astronautics, 2008. Discusses Pratt and Whitney's innovations, which powered the new age of flight.

Trautman, James. *Pan American Clippers: The Golden Age of Flying Boats.* Boston: Boston Mills Press, 2007. Account of the importance of the clippers in opening up transpacific travel, paving the way for modern global travel.

Underwood, Jeffrey S. *The Wings of Democracy: The Influence of Air Power on the Roosevelt Administration, 1933-1941.* College Station: Texas A&M University Press, 1992. Study of how President Franklin D. Roosevelt perceived air power as a cheap means of defending the United States from foreign threats.

See also   Airships; *Akron* disaster; DC-3; Earhart, Amelia; *Hindenburg* disaster; Naval forces; Post, Wiley; Rocketry; Trans World Airlines; Travel.

■ *Awake and Sing!*

Identification   Play about tensions in a Jewish family during the Depression
Author   Clifford Odets
Date   First produced February 19, 1935

One of six plays by Clifford Odets that catapulted him to fame in the last half of the 1930's and made his name synonymous with radicalism and social protest. The play was later seen as a sensitive study of family dynamics and the immigrant experience rather than as a serious call to revolution.

Early in 1935, after the success of Odets's first produced play, *Waiting for Lefty* (1935), the Group

Theatre mounted the first production of *Awake and Sing!*, advertising it as a new play by the author of *Waiting for Lefty*. However, *Awake and Sing!* was written before *Waiting for Lefty*. Moreover, whereas *Waiting for Lefty*, a one-act play about a taxi strike, was primarily a propaganda vehicle, *Awake and Sing!* was a full-length, three-act play that at the time was compared by some commentators to the works of the nineteenth century Russian playwright Anton Chekhov.

Odets had begun writing *Awake and Sing!* (then called *I Got the Blues*) in 1932, but the directors of the Group Theatre, a troupe with which Odets had been associated since 1931, at first declined to produce it, finding it too pessimistic and too narrowly Jewish. The play was performed in part at a summer camp, but the theater's directors encouraged Odets to revise the play, which he did, introducing the optimism that characterizes the ending of the play. He also modified the character of Bessie, the mother, to make her less harsh, and removed most of the Yiddish expressions that were found in the original version. However, the play remains a depiction of the Jewish milieu during the Depression. The pessimism of the original version remains in the revised one, mixing uneasily with the closing optimism, which for some commentators does not fit with the rest of the play.

Odets produced an ensemble piece in which several characters have important roles: Bessie, the domineering Jewish mother who will not let her son marry a poor orphan and who is obsessed with respectability; Jacob, her father, an old socialist who talks about revolution and listens to records of Enrico Caruso; Myron, Bessie's ineffectual husband, who talks about how things were better in the past when Theodore Roosevelt was president; Uncle Morty, who has become a successful dress manufacturer; and Ralph, Bessie and Myron's son, who wishes life did not have to depend on money. There is also the strange couple of Moe Axelrod, the one-legged bookie who pursues Ralph's sister, Hennie, and Hennie herself, who complains about being forced by Bessie into a loveless marriage so that she can have a father for her illegitimate child.

Commentators have praised the play for its use of dialogue; its conjuring of the lower-middle-class milieu of the Jewish community of the Bronx, New York; and its exploration of the tensions among the various family members, especially between Bessie and her children and between Bessie and Jacob. Some commentators suggest that the play depicts a mixture of love and hate toward the institution of the family; it is a lovingly created portrayal of a family that also includes rebellion against the very nature of family, as in Hennie's decision to run away with Moe, leaving her baby and husband behind, and in Jacob's quotation from Karl Marx to the effect that such families should be abolished.

The play is also seen as an examination of the American Dream. Uncle Morty seems to embody the dream, but Jacob insists he is an exception; most of the rest of the characters struggle to survive the economic woes of the Depression.

Impact   Although some commentators see *Awake and Sing!* as a topical play about the economic hardships of the Depression, most see the Depression as simply the backdrop to a more universal exploration of family conflicts. The play is also seen as a forerunner in its portrayal of Jewish American life and of the immigrant and minority experience more generally, influencing such later Jewish writers as Arthur Miller, Philip Roth, and Saul Bellow and even African American writers such as James Baldwin.

Sheldon Goldfarb

Further Reading

Cantor, Harold. *Clifford Odets: Playwright-Poet.* 2d ed. Lanham, Md.: Scarecrow Press, 2000.

Murray, Edward. *Clifford Odets: The Thirties and After.* New York: Frederick Ungar, 1968.

Novick, Julius. *Beyond the Golden Door: Jewish American Drama and Jewish American Experience.* New York: Palgrave Macmillan, 2008.

See also   Communism; Great Depression in the United States; Group Theatre; Immigration to the United States; Jews in the United States; Literature in the United States; Odets, Clifford; Theater in the United States.

B

■ Bank holiday

The Event Federal legislation associated with the reorganization of insolvent banks following the banking crisis of 1933

Date March 6, 1933

In response to a string of bank failures in late 1932 and early 1933, President Franklin D. Roosevelt declared that all banks in the United States would be closed until the U.S. Treasury could verify their financial stability. Followed by Congress's creation of the Emergency Banking Relief Act, the closing of financial institutions was a step in the direction of tighter federal control of American financial institutions.

Because of the economic chaos following the stock market collapse of 1929 and several subsequent years of ineffective government measures to mitigate the collapse of banks, President Roosevelt called a joint session of the Congress in March, 1933, to pass the Emergency Banking Relief Act. The government established the right to certain emergency powers over financial institutions. For example, it could declare that banks could not open during times of emergency—"bank holidays." The federal government could take control of insolvent banks and reorganize them.

Further, recognizing the need for consumer trust, the government introduced several measures designed to discourage depositors from withdrawing and hoarding hard currency such as gold. The Emergency Banking Relief Act and, later, the Gold Reserve Act of 1934 allowed the federal government the right to request the return of privately held gold. In return, the act also established the commitment of the federal government to insure depositor funds—a promise to Americans that they would never again lose their life savings because of the closing of a bank.

Impact The response to Roosevelt's Banking Act was a remarkable show of trust and faith in a president's leadership. When President Roosevelt al-

lowed American banks to open after the four-day Bank Holiday, depositors reentered their neighborhood banks in large numbers to redeposit their savings. In only two weeks, almost 50 percent of withdrawn currency had been returned to depositor accounts. Further, when stock trading resumed on March 15, 1933, the New York Stock Exchange closed with the largest one-day rise in stock prices ever recorded.

Julia M. Meyers

Further Reading

Kiewe, Amos. *FDR's First Fireside Chat: Public Confidence and the Banking Crisis.* College Station: Texas A&M University Press, 2007.

Silber, William L. "Why Did FDR's Bank Holiday Succeed?" *Federal Reserve Bank of New York Economic Policy Review* (July, 2009).

See also Banking; Banking Act of 1935; Gold Reserve Act of 1934.

■ Bank of United States failure

The Event The Bank of United States closes, increasing the atmosphere of panic as the Great Depression sets in

Date December 11, 1930

Place New York City

The largest bank failure of its time led to increased currency withdrawal and worsened the ongoing economic downswing.

In December, 1930, the Bank of United States (BUS) closed in the midst of a heavy run. In September, 1929, the bank had $238 million in deposits and was the twenty-eighth-largest commercial bank in the country. The numerous bank failures during the 1920's generally were small banks and had little impact on money and credit. However, in November, 1930, bank suspensions escalated sharply with the closing of large banks in the Southeast.

The BUS was established in 1913 by Joseph Marcus, a Russian-born Jew and successful clothing manufacturer. The bank was well managed and successful, sharing in the boom in New York City bank stocks that led their prices to double between 1924 and 1927. The stock prices rose because the banks were able to generate rapid growth in earnings by creating securities affiliates that were active in marketing new securities issues, conducting brokerage operations, and holding securities for capital gains. In July, 1927, Marcus died, and control of BUS passed to his son, Bernard Marcus, who assembled a management team that included Saul Singer, C. Stanley Mitchell, Isidor J. Kresel, and Simon Kugel. The BUS created a securities affiliate named City Financial Corporation in August, 1927, and a much larger one named Bankus in December, 1928. By then the bank was aggressively conducting mergers, absorbing five other banks with $170 million of deposits beginning in May, 1928. BUS was also heavily involved in real estate lending. The affiliates and the management team invested heavily in BUS stock.

After April, 1929, the value of BUS stock began to decline, even though New York bank stocks in general continued to rise. BUS insiders sold stock because they were able to observe serious flaws in management, particularly favoritism toward some borrowers, failure to pay taxes, violations of real estate regulations, and the extreme vulnerability of earnings connected to stocks and real estate. BUS management became desperate to prop up the stock's price, selling stock with a promise to buy it back on demand at the issue price—a promise the bank failed to keep.

Between April, 1929, and June, 1930, BUS stock fell more than 80 percent. Revenues from financial services and capital gains were vanishing. A corps of 129 bank examiners worked on BUS records from June until September, 1930. They concluded that BUS was in serious difficulty and recommended it be rescued by a merger. Frantic negotiations broke down, and the banking authorities closed the bank in December.

The banking authorities determined that the bank's liabilities totaled $189 million, of which $161 million were deposits. By the end of 1931, liquidators had repaid $21 million ($19 million to the Federal Reserve), allowed $33 million of offsets, and paid depositors $61 million directly. Additional repayments to depositors followed at irregular intervals, until the process was completed May 16, 1944. Nonpreferred depositors recovered about three-fourths of their money. Stockholders lost their entire investments.

The BUS was the only major New York City bank to fail between 1929 and 1933, suggesting the problem arose from its mismanagement rather than from the generally poor economic environment. Marcus and Singer were convicted of criminal violations of the banking laws and served prison terms of twenty-three months, beginning in March, 1933.

A civil suit against the BUS management filed in August, 1931, sought $60 million for wrongful actions, including "fake and fictitious" systems of bookkeeping and illegal side payments to insiders. In June, 1934, the court issued a judgment of $28.5 million against twelve officers and directors. Only about $1 million was actually collected.

Impact   The 400,000 BUS depositors lost the use of $161 million in funds, but much of this was later repaid. BUS borrowers lost access to credit. The BUS failure led to a sharp rise in currency withdrawal from the banks. By the end of December, 1930, currency issued by the Federal Reserve Bank of New York was $66 million above the preceding December, and by June, 1931, the increase was $102 million. The atmosphere of panic was enhanced by publicity: Between December 11, 1930, and July 2, 1931, *The New York Times* carried at least one BUS story on every day but two. The currency withdrawal reduced the reserves of the surviving banks and led them to curtail lending.

Paul B. Trescott

Further Reading

Friedman, Milton, and Anna J. Schwartz. "The Failure of the Bank of United States: A Reappraisal. A Reply." *Explorations in Economic History* 23, no. 2 (April, 1986): 199-204.

Richardson, Gary, and Patrick Van Horn. *Intensified Regulatory Scrutiny and Bank Distress in New York City During the Great Depression.* Cambridge, Mass.: National Bureau of Economic Research, 2008.

Trescott, Paul B. "The Failure of the Bank of United States, 1930." *Journal of Money, Credit and Banking* 24, no. 3 (August, 1992): 384-399.

See also   Bank Holiday; Banking; Business and the economy in the United States; Credit and debt; Great Depression in the United States.

■ Banking

Drastic changes occurred during the 1930's to the structure and regulation of the U.S. banking industry. The banking system supplied most of American money in the form of bank deposits. A large number of bank failures occurred during the downswing of 1929 to 1933, reducing the money supply and adding to deflation.

At the end of 1929, about twenty-four thousand commercial banks, holding $51 billion in deposits, existed in the United States. Most were small organizations operating only one office. About 70 percent of commercial bank loans went to business firms, and commercial banks accounted for about 30 percent of the debts of noncorporate businesses and farms. The large Wall Street banks in New York City were also extensively involved in the securities business. Several established securities affiliates that engaged in brokerage marketed new issues of stocks and bonds, held securities for income and capital gains, and made numerous margin loans on stock collateral. They also managed large sums of personal trust funds.

About 15 percent of bank loans in 1929 were to farmers. The farm economy had gone through rough times during the 1920's, and defaults on farm loans led to a high rate of failure among small rural banks. Several states had experimented with deposit guarantee programs, and these had mostly been wiped out by the losses of the 1920's. There was no federal deposit insurance program.

Bank Failures in the Downswing   As the economy moved into recession late in 1929, the rate of bank failures escalated. Larger banks were involved, notably the Bank of United States in New York City, which failed in December, 1930, with nearly $200 million in deposits. The bank had made high-risk loans on securities and real estate. Bank failures meant that depositors lost the use of their money, though some of the money was ultimately repaid. Furthermore, failed banks could not renew loans for their ongoing borrowers. Repeated rounds of bank failures contributed a large deflationary force to the economic downswing. Depositors withdrew currency from the banks, reducing the bank's reserves and lending power. Deteriorating business led to loan defaults and more bank failures. The Federal Reserve, which had been created in 1913 to eliminate bank panics,

did not take sufficient expansionary action to stop the disaster. Some emergency loans to banks were extended by the Reconstruction Finance Corporation, established in 1932. Some nine thousand banks failed from 1930 through 1933. As a result, the public's money supply (currency plus bank deposits) declined from $45 billion at the beginning of 1930 to $30 billion in mid-1933. The number of commercial banks fell from twenty-four thousand in 1929 to fourteen thousand in 1933.

Emergency Actions in 1933   Immediately after his inauguration in March, 1933, President Franklin D. Roosevelt ordered all the banks to close. They were to be examined, and those in sound condition reopened as soon as possible. At the same time, the gold standard was terminated, and people were required to sell their gold coins to the government. This bank holiday put an end to the panic. Currency flowed back into the banks.

The Banking Act of 1933 (also known as the Glass-Steagall Act) established the Federal Deposit Insurance Corporation (FDIC). Initially, each deposit was insured up to $2,500, but this was soon increased to $5,000. As banks reopened, almost all joined the FDIC, which extended federal bank supervision to virtually the entire banking system. FDIC maintained rigorous standards and virtually eliminated bank failures for the remainder of the decade.

In March, 1933, the government created the Farm Credit Administration and expanded the number and variety of farm lending agencies. These assisted the banks by providing a market to which banks could sell mortgages and other farm loans. In a similar fashion, the Home Owners' Loan Corporation, created in June, 1933, purchased more than $1.2 billion worth of mortgages from commercial banks. The Federal Housing Administration, established June 27, 1934, insured long-term, amortized home mortgages. This created a category of low-risk, long-term loans suitable for banks and other lenders.

Numerous new regulations were imposed on the banks. The Banking Act of 1933 prohibited banks from most activities involved in the issue of new securities or trading in existing securities. Also, the Securities Exchange Act of 1934 authorized the Federal Reserve Board to require minimum margins (down payments) for lending to finance purchases of securities. Requirements averaging about 30 percent

American Bankers Association officials, including President Philip A. Benson (third from the left in front) visit President Franklin D. Roosevelt in 1938, assuring him of their cooperation with attempts to remedy banking problems. (Library of Congress)

The number of banks stabilized to around fifteen thousand after 1934. Regulatory authorities were reluctant to authorize new banks, and investors had little motivation to establish them. The combination of the extended panic and the numerous new regulations made the banks strongly risk-averse. The money supply grew vigorously from $30 billion in mid-1933 to $51 billion in late 1939. Commercial-bank deposits increased by $20 billion over that period. Monetary growth was generated by the U.S. Treasury's purchase of gold, which flowed into the country in response to the increase in gold price in 1934. Banks also created deposits by purchasing the U.S. Treasury securities, the supply of which increased to finance the deficits arising from expanded government spending.

In 1939, the total volume of commercial-bank loans was less than one-half of what it had been in 1929, falling from $36 billion to $16 billion. However, the dollar volume of consumer and home-mortgage loans was higher in 1939 than it had been ten years before. Demand for loans by business firms was weak. Also, risk-averse attitudes led banks to maintain large excess reserves and invest heavily in U.S. government securities, despite the low interest rates.

came into effect in October, 1934. Statutory fixed reserve requirements for member-bank deposits had been in effect since 1917. The Thomas amendment to the Agricultural Adjustment Act of 1933 authorized the Federal Reserve Board to increase reserve requirements to double the previous levels. This authority was broadened in the Banking Act of 1935. However, the Federal Reserve Board first used this power to raise requirements significantly in 1936 and 1937, contributing to the onset of the recession of 1937. Finally, the Banking Act of 1933 prohibited banks from paying interest on demand deposits. The law authorized the Federal Reserve Board to set maximum interest rates on time deposits. Beginning November, 1933, these were set at 3 percent and reduced to 2.5 percent in February, 1935. While theoretically intended to reduce risky behavior by banks, the real motive was to reduce competition among the banks.

Impact Creation of federal deposit insurance was perhaps the most important policy change affecting banks. The dollar extent of insurance coverage was steadily enlarged, reaching $10,000 in 1950 and climbing all the way to $100,000 in 1980. For many years, the number of bank failures remained low. However, after the large expansion of coverage in 1980, deposit insurance became increasingly a method for encouraging risky behavior by banks, with the burdens of losses falling on FDIC and the taxpayers.

The stringent regulations imposed on the banking system during the 1930's were steadily liberalized in later years. Banking deregulation during the 1980's removed interest-rate ceilings from time deposits and permitted interest payment on some types of checking deposits. After reaching high levels during World War II, reserve requirements were steadily scaled back.

Paul B. Trescott

Further Reading

Chandler, Lester V. *America's Greatest Depression, 1929-1941.* New York: Harper & Row, 1970. Simple overview; banking developments are stressed in chapters 5 and 9.

Eccles, Marriner. *Beckoning Frontiers.* New York: Knopf, 1951. Autobiographical memoir by a prominent banker appointed to the Federal Reserve Board in 1934; discusses policy making.

Mishkin, Frederic S. *The Economics of Money, Banking, and Financial Markets.* 9th ed. New York: Addison-Wesley, 2009. This college text provides abundant historical perspective and up-to-date information on the banking system.

Trescott, Paul B. *Financing American Enterprise: The Story of Commercial Banking.* New York: Harper, 1963. Written for the general reader; deals at length with the banking developments of the 1920's and 1930's.

White, Eugene N. "The Legacy of Deposit Insurance: The Growth, Spread and Cost of Insuring Financial Intermediaries." In *The Defining Moment: The Great Depression and the American Economy in the Twentieth Century,* edited by Michael D. Bordo, Claudia Goldin, and Eugene N. White. Chicago: University of Chicago Press, 1998. Argues that banking regulation diminished the share of banks in financial business and opened the way for risk-enhancing policies for many types of financial firms.

See also Bank Holiday; Bank of United States failure; Banking Act of 1935; Business and the economy in the United States; Credit and debt; Federal Reserve Board; Glass-Steagall Act of 1933; Great Depression in the United States; Recession of 1937-1938.

Banking Act of 1933. See **Glass-Steagall Act of 1933**

■ Banking Act of 1935

The Law Federal legislation that changed and strengthened the Federal Reserve system
Date Enacted August 23, 1935

The Banking Act of 1935 reformed the Federal Reserve system by making the Federal Deposit Insurance Corporation (FDIC) permanent, by allowing the secretary of the Treasury to purchase FDIC stock, by replacing the Federal Reserve Board with a seven-member board of governors, by authorizing the board to set reserve requirements, and by restructuring the Federal Open Market Committee.

In 1913, the U.S. Congress passed the Federal Reserve Act, which created the Federal Reserve system. A significant improvement over the national banking system of the Civil War days, the Federal Reserve Act divided the country into twelve regional districts with a regional bank in each, set up a Federal Reserve Board with reserve requirements and rediscount rate powers, and stabilized the U.S. banking system overall. All national banks had to join, while state banks could join the Federal Reserve Board if they chose to do so. Despite the fact that the Federal Reserve Board had done fairly well during World War I, its actions, or inactions, during the 1920's, especially in terms of the stock market, demonstrated a need to reform the banking system again.

In 1933, Congress passed the Glass-Steagall Act, which created the FDIC, separated investment and savings banks, and passed Regulation Q, which prohibited banks from competing over interest rates. Glass-Steagall was a major accomplishment for the U.S. banking system. Nonetheless, there were some, such as Marriner Eccles, who felt that the banking industry needed to be more centralized. Eccles, head of the Federal Reserve, worked on a bill to accomplish more centralization. The House passed it, but in the Senate, Carter Glass, founder of the Federal Reserve System, opposed it. Attacking the Eccles bill mercilessly, Glass thought he had gutted it. The truth, however, was that the Banking Act of 1935 remained a major advance for the U.S. banking structure.

As a result of the law, the president could appoint the seven-member board of governors to fourteen-year terms each. The board had more control over member banks, more control over reserve requirements and rediscount rates, and more authority in the Federal Open Market Committee (FOMC), which was composed of seven board members and five members of reserve banks. All large banks had to join the Federal Reserve Board, and the law made FDIC a permanent establishment with secure funding. While more laws and changes came after 1935, especially after World War II, the U.S. banking system was stable, secure, and capable of handling national and international financial intermediary functions. Finally, credit for the Banking Act of 1935 goes to Eccles and, to an extent, Glass as well.

Impact   The Banking Act of 1935 did much to reform and strengthen the Federal Reserve system. It made FDIC a permanent establishment, established a new board of governors for the system, and centralized the FOMC. It also disqualified the comptroller of the currency and the secretary of the Treasury from serving on the board. Its long-term impact was measured in how it sustained public confidence in the U.S. banking institutions.

Michael V. Namorato

Further Reading

Dwyer, Gerald, Jr. "The Effects of the Banking Acts of 1933 and 1935 on Capital Investment in Commercial Banking." *Journal of Money, Credit, and Banking* 13, no. 2 (May, 1981): 192-204.

Eccles, Marriner. *Beckoning Frontiers: Public and Personal Recollections.* Edited by Sidney Hyman. New York: Alfred A. Knopf, 1951.

Hyman, Sidney. *Marriner Eccles: Private Entrepreneur and Public Servant.* Stanford, Calif.: Graduate School of Business, Stanford University, 1976.

Phillips, Ronnie. *The Chicago Plan and New Deal Banking Reform.* New York: M. E. Sharpe, 1995.

Smiley, Gene. *Rethinking the Great Depression.* Chicago: I. R. Dee, 2002.

See also   Bank Holiday; Banking; Business and the economy in the United States; Credit and debt; Federal Reserve Board; Glass-Steagall Act of 1933; Morgenthau, Henry T., Jr.; New Deal; Nye Committee; Roosevelt, Franklin D.

■ Barker Gang

Identification   Criminal gang that committed bank robberies, burglaries, murders, and kidnappings

Date   Operated from mid-1931 until 1936

During the early 1930's, the criminal band commonly known as the Barker, or Barker-Karpis gang, after its central leaders, engaged in a widely publicized and often murderous crime spree that terrorized the Midwest until its principal members were killed or arrested. The gang's association with a woman known as "Ma" Barker, the mother of several of the gang's leaders, won the gang notoriety and helped it enter folk mythology.

The history of the Barker gang's leadership is not fully established and consequently subject to mythologizing. Through its brief existence, it may have had as many as eighteen different members. Ironically, Ma Barker, the person most closely associated with the gang, may not even have been a true member. Born Arizona Clark in Missouri during the 1870's, Arizona, or Kate, Barker, was the mother of four criminal sons: Herman, Lloyd, Arthur, and Fred Barker. In popular representations of the gang's criminal spree during the early 1930's, she was depicted as the gang's ruthless mastermind. More likely, however, she simply traveled with the gang, looking after her sons between their criminal jobs but otherwise having no involvement in their crimes.

Arizona Clark became Arizona Barker in 1892, when she married a farmhand named George Barker in Aurora, Missouri. It was to him she bore the four sons who would grow up as juvenile delinquents and eventually become hardened criminals. In 1915, the Barkers resettled in Oklahoma. By the early 1920's, the sons were being arrested frequently for crimes such as highway robbery, car theft, and bank robbery. Some of their crimes led to murder. By the end of the decade, all the sons either were in prison or had served time, and their father had left the family. In 1927, Herman Barker committed suicide when facing possible arrest on a murder charge. By the following year, the boys' father, George Barker, had left the family for good. Sometime afterward, Arizona Barker became involved with a man named Arthur Dunlop, whom she may have later married.

Formation of the Gang   Meanwhile, the surviving sons were joined by a man known as Alvin Karpis a Canadian, who would later rank as "public enemy number one" on the Federal Bureau of Investigation's (FBI) most-wanted list, after John Dillinger and George "Baby Face" Nelson were killed. Karpis had been stealing since at least the age of sixteen and quickly advanced to murder. He and Fred Barker met as both were serving time in the Kansas State Penitentiary. After he met the rest of the Barkers at the family's primary base in Tulsa, Oklahoma, he and Arthur Barker became coleaders of the gang that would soon gain national notoriety. Karpis was apparently feared and hated by his criminal associates, but adored by "Ma" Barker.

In early 1931, Karpis and Fred Barker were arrested for burglary in Oklahoma. Barker avoided incarceration, but Karpis was sentenced to four years in prison. Not long afterward, Karpis was paroled, and the gang began the crime spree that would make it famous. Toward the end of the year, Barker and Karpis killed Arkansas and Missouri law-enforcement officers. A string of bank and payroll robberies that drew the gang through states ranging from Minnesota to Kansas and Nebraska led to more killings in 1932 and 1933, as gang members shuffled in and out of prisons.

In June, 1933, the gang took up a new and more profitable line of crime: kidnapping. Its kidnapping of a member of the Hamm's Brewery family netted a big ransom, though it is possible that the gang had to share the money with the Chicago mob leader Frank Nitti for using Chicago as its hiding place. The gang staged another successful kidnapping in early 1934 and continued its crime sprees throughout the year. The turning point for the gang came in early 1935. On January 8, Arthur Barker was arrested in Chicago. Eight days later, Fred and Ma Barker were killed during a six-hour gun battle with the FBI in Florida. Ma Barker's death in that dramatic event contributed to her reputation as the gang's leader, although it is not certain she was even handling a weapon. The circumstances of her death on January 16, 1935, left many with the impression that her son Arthur had given law enforcement the information that led the FBI to Florida. Meanwhile, Karpis narrowly escaped capture during a shootout with police.

Arthur Barker was eventually given a life term in the Alcatraz federal penitentiary in San Francisco Bay for his role in one of the gang's kidnappings. Other members of the gang also received prison sentences. Karpis was the last leader of the gang to be captured. After committing several more violent crimes, he was arrested in New Orleans, Louisiana, in May, 1936, and later sentenced to life imprisonment in Alcatraz.

Impact   The Barker-Karpis gang had a bold and bloody reign that fascinated a nation during the early 1930's, as the charismatic FBI director J. Edgar Hoover and his federal agents pursued them. By 1936, however, the gang was gone. The surviving leaders of the gang met dramatic ends. In 1939, Arthur Barker was killed while attempting to escape from Alcatraz. Ten years later, his brother Lloyd was killed by his wife after he had served his prison sentence. Karpis was paroled from prison in 1969 and deported back to Canada. In 1979, he died under suspicious circumstances in Italy. The gang lived on in folklore and would later become the subject of a number of Hollywood films, including the 1996 production *Public Enemies*, in which Theresa Russell starred as Ma Barker.

Camille Gibson and the Editors

Further Reading

Ernst, Robert R. *Robbin' Banks and Killin' Cops: The Life and Crimes of Lawrence DeVol and His Association with Alvin Karpis and the Barker-Karpis Gang.* Baltimore: PublishAmerica, 2009. Study of one of the many members of the Barker Gang.

Karpis, Alvin, with Robert Livesey. *On the Rock: Twenty-five Years in Alcatraz—The Prison Story of Alvin Karpis.* Rev. ed. Oakville, Ont.: Little Brick Schoolhouse, 2008. First published in 1980, this autobiography by the Barker Gang's most ruthless leader provides some insights into the gang's history.

Koch, Michael. *A Murder in Tulsa: The Sherrill Murder Case and the Rise of the Barker-Karpis Gang.* Baltimore: PublishAmerica, 2009. Detailed history of one of the Barker Gang's most sensational crimes.

Prassel, Frank Richard. *The Great American Outlaw: A Legacy of Fact and Fiction.* Norman: University of Oklahoma Press, 1993. Fascinating attempt to separate truth from myth about famous criminals, with a useful section on the Barker Gang.

Strunk, Mary Elizabeth. *Wanted Women: An American Obsession in the Reign of J. Edgar Hoover.* Lawrence: University Press of Kansas, 2010. This study of the first FBI director's special interest in female criminals helps to explain how Ma Barker earned her exaggerated reputation.

See also Alcatraz Federal Penitentiary; Barrow, Clyde, and Bonnie Parker; Capone, Al; Crimes and scandals; Dillinger, John; Gangster films; Nitti, Frank; Organized crime.

■ Barrow, Clyde, and Bonnie Parker

Identification American couple who robbed banks during a brief crime spree

Clyde Barrow
Born March 24, 1909; Telico, Texas
Died May 23, 1934; near Gibsland, Bienville Parish, Louisiana

Bonnie Parker
Born October 1, 1910; Rowena, Texas
Died May 23, 1934; near Gibsland, Bienville Parish, Louisiana

Barrow and Parker symbolized the fascination that Americans have with crime and law enforcement. The couple also helped to popularize the culture of gangs in the United States.

In 1930, Bonnie Parker met Clyde Barrow in Texas. She was an ambitious student who liked poetry and was already married. He had dropped out of high school and had already been in and out of jail. Barrow had been able to use his charm and wit to avoid prison sentences until he was arrested for car theft and burglaries in 1930. He was sentenced to two years in prison but escaped. Once he was recaptured, he was sentenced to fourteen years but only had to serve two. During Barrow's time in prison, Parker remained loyal and wrote to him every day. Once Barrow was released from prison, he joined Parker, and they began their crime spree by stealing a car. Parker was apprehended and served time in a Texas jail. While she was in jail, Barrow began to rob banks and gas stations. During this time he also committed his first murder, killing the owner of a jewelry store that he was robbing.

After Parker was released from jail, she and Barrow met in Oklahoma. There, Barrow murdered two police officers who were investigating suspicious activity inside Barrow's car. During this time, Barrow and Parker continued to commit robberies, some of which ended in murder.

Parker and Barrow began to add members to their gang. The first to join was W. D. Jones, followed by Marvin "Buck" Barrow, Barrow's brother, and his wife Blanche in 1933. This group of outlaws became known as the Barrow gang. The gang was hiding in Joplin, Missouri, when the police, believing the gang was making illegal alcohol, raided their apartment. During the raid, Barrow and Jones were shot but survived. However, the Barrow gang killed two officers.

After the Barrow gang escaped from Missouri, they fled to Texas. While in Texas, Parker was severely injured after the stolen car she was in careened off a bridge and caught fire, pinning her underneath. Her leg was permanently damaged. While Parker was still pinned, a group of farmers attempted to rescue her until they saw all of the guns

Clyde Barrow (left) and Bonnie Parker. (Library of Congress)

and ammunition in the car. When they tried to contact the police, the Barrow gang ambushed them and took them hostage. Two policemen were killed in the process and a few of the farmers were wounded. The Barrow gang escaped and moved back to Missouri.

While in Missouri, the gang engaged in a gun battle with police officers at a rented cabin. In the crossfire, Buck was shot in the forehead and Blanche suffered injuries to her eyes. The entire gang escaped to Iowa, where a witness spotted them engaging in suspicious activity and reported them to the police. The police officers shot at the Barrow gang's car and hit Buck several times. While Parker, Barrow, and Jones were able to escape, Buck was apprehended and later died at a local hospital. Blanche was arrested and sentenced to prison in Missouri. In the following few months, Jones abandoned the Barrow gang and was eventually captured in Texas.

In January of 1934, Parker and Barrow helped Raymond Hamilton and Henry Methvin escape from prison in Texas. During the escape another police officer was killed. Over the following months, the Barrow gang robbed several banks. Within the next month, Hamilton left the gang and was eventually executed for the death of the police officer who had been shot during Hamilton's escape. After Hamilton left, the Barrow gang killed two more police officers in Texas and killed an officer and took a police chief hostage in Oklahoma. After the Texas governor hired a special agent, Barrow proceeded to kill three more police officers.

The special agent, Frank Hamer, devised a setup using Methvin's father, who knew a place that the Barrow gang frequented and helped the police. A group of men surrounded the scene and waited for Parker and Barrow to arrive. At around 9:10 A.M., their car pulled up, and police officers ordered them to stop. After Barrow and Parker failed to comply, the group of men opened fire, shooting 167 rounds of bullets into the car, killing both Barrow, twenty-five, and Parker, twenty-three. Afterward, the car became a traveling attraction across the United States for the remainder of the 1930's. Hundreds of people attempted to catch a glimpse of their bodies, and thousands stood in line to see the car full of bullet holes.

Impact   Barrow and Parker changed the way Americans viewed criminals. Many glorified their actions,

and others were simply fascinated by the couple and their legend. Despite their crimes, the iconic couple has come to represent an American archetype of star-crossed love and rebellion, later romanticized in the 1967 film *Bonnie and Clyde*, starring Warren Beatty and Faye Dunaway.

April J. Robson

Further Reading

Guinn, Jeff. "Notorious." *Smithsonian* 40, no. 1 (2009): 12-14.

Hunter, Stephen. "Clyde and Bonnie Died for Nihilism." *Commentary* 128, no. 1 (2009): 77-80.

See also   Automobiles and auto manufacturing; Barker Gang; Capone, Al; Crimes and scandals; Dillinger, John; Kelly, Machine Gun.

■ Baseball

Baseball was primarily a summer recreation for boys and young men, while the professional sport served as an entertainment for families. Fans who could not attend the games, which were nearly always played in the afternoon, often could listen to radio broadcasts. At the end of the decade, the game was first televised.

During the 1930's, as in previous decades, baseball attracted boys in neighborhoods and schools and some young men in colleges. The game was played on vacant lots, and even college teams rarely had well-maintained fields. Restrictive academic schedules meant that seasons could be only a few weeks long, especially in northern states, and college teams traveling south in late winter or early spring was almost unheard of. Semiprofessional teams abounded; on these teams, only a few key players were paid. In 1939, Little League baseball began, but it did not become a prominent institution for several years. A baseball league for women did not begin until 1943; some girls and women played softball but seldom as part of school or college programs.

The Minor Leagues and the Negro Leagues   Though minor league professional baseball began in the 1880's, during the 1930's, it assumed its modern incarnation as "boot camps" and breeding grounds for Major League Baseball. Branch Rickey, at the time the general manager of the St. Louis Cardinals, was most responsible for this development and for many other innovations in the game. Under Rickey, the Cardinals built a farm system comprising hundreds of players at six different levels, indicated by letters from AAA to D. Rickey's system was soon imitated by most other major league executives. The great majority of minor league players never reached the major leagues; however, their contracts were controlled by the major league team, and unless they retired or were traded, they had no choice but to play for the organization that owned their services. Some capable minor leaguers owned by well-stocked organizations had limited opportunities. Older players who had once performed in the major leagues also continued to play in the minors, especially in the Pacific Coast League, a AAA league with long seasons and warm climates. The Newark Bears of the AAA International League, owned by the New York Yankees, are considered to be one of the best minor league teams of the decade, but only a few of the team's players succeeded in the majors.

There was no place in organized professional baseball for African Americans. Black players, some of superlative ability, had to be content with playing in the Negro Leagues, as they were called. These leagues were not as organized as the major and minor leagues, and records were kept inconsistently. For these reasons, and because black teams played against white teams only in freelance or "barnstorming" games, measuring the quality of these leagues and teams is difficult. There is no doubt, however, that the best black players—men such as catcher Josh Gibson, outfielder Cool Papa Bell, and pitcher Satchel Paige—were among the greatest players of all time. African Americans did not appear in modern Major League Baseball until 1947, and most of the early black major leaguers played little or not at all in the Negro Leagues of the 1930's. One exception was Paige, who played in the Negro Leagues throughout the 1930's and joined the Cleveland Indians in 1948 at the age of forty-two; he continued to

Earl Averill of the Cleveland Indians jumps over catcher Al Lopez of the Boston Bees on his way to home plate in a 1939 game. (Getty Images)

Major League Baseball Statistical Leaders, 1930-1939

Year	Player	Home Runs	Player	RBI	Player	Batting Average
1930	Hack Wilson	56	Hack Wilson	191	Bill Terry	.401
1931	Lou Gehrig Babe Ruth	46	Lou Gehrig	184	Al Simmons	.390
1932	Jimmie Foxx	58	Jimmie Foxx	169	Lefty O'Doul	.368
1933	Jimmie Foxx	48	Jimmie Foxx	163	Chuck Klein	.368
1934	Lou Gehrig	49	Lou Gehrig	165	Lou Gehrig	.363
1935	Jimmie Foxx Hank Greenberg	36	Hank Greenberg	170	Arky Vaughan	.385
1936	Lou Gehrig	49	Hal Trosky	162	Luke Appling	.388
1937	Joe DiMaggio	46	Hank Greenberg	183	Joe Medwick	.374
1938	Hank Greenberg	58	Jimmie Foxx	175	Jimmie Foxx	.349
1939	Jimmie Foxx	35	Ted Williams	145	Joe DiMaggio	.381

Sources: Baseball Almanac and Baseball Reference.

pitch impressively. He even pitched three scoreless innings in an American League game in 1965, when he was fifty-nine. During the 1930's, black teams existed in every city except Boston then represented by Major League Baseball; teams also existed in a few southern cities.

Major League Conditions and Events Although the demography of the nation was changing, the sixteen teams of Major League Baseball were confined to the same ten cities from 1903 throughout the 1930's. Despite shifts in population toward the West and South, St. Louis remained the southernmost and westernmost home of Major League Baseball. Transportation was the main reason for this; teams did not yet travel by plane, and railroad trips longer than from Boston to St. Louis, for example, were forbidding. Team revenues, which fell during this period, also diminished chances of expansion. The Philadelphia Athletics, pennant winners for three consecutive years from 1928 to 1930, were a prime illustration of a team that suffered financially. Forced to sell most of its best players, the Athletics dropped to last place by the middle of the decade and for years thereafter finished seventh or eighth.

Some Major League Baseball parks were old and barely adequate, but teams persisted with what they had. A commitment to night baseball, which eventually helped improve the situation of club owners, appeared by the end of the decade. Most of the teams were owned by individuals, who were sometimes industrialists, but not by industrial organizations. These owners exerted a tight control on team expenses; ballplayers basically had to accept what was offered them. In 1930, Babe Ruth was offered the highest salary, $80,000, up to that time. Informed that he was making more than President Herbert Hoover, Ruth quipped that he had had a better year.

The all-star game, featuring American League stars versus National League stars, began in 1933. Another baseball highlight from the 1930's was night baseball, which had been played early in the minor leagues but did not happen in the majors until 1935. Larry MacPhail, the general manager of the Cincinnati Reds, eager to stimulate attendance in the depths of the Depression, persuaded President Franklin D. Roosevelt to push a button in the White House that would light up Crosley Field for a game between the Reds and the Philadelphia Phillies. Many observers contended that the game should be played only in daylight, but by the end of the decade, night baseball had become a part of the game.

In 1939, Major League Baseball opened the National Baseball Hall of Fame and Museum in Cooperstown, New York. The year and location for the establishment of the hall of fame were based on the long-held belief—which has since been proved erroneous—that baseball had been invented there exactly one hundred years earlier. The best retired players were to be honored by inclusion, with the ceremony taking place each summer. In the same year, the first telecast of a major league game occurred. Interestingly, a collegiate baseball game between Princeton and Columbia had already been televised earlier that season. Again the Cincinnati Reds, usually considered the first professional baseball team, were involved. The game was played between the Reds and the Brooklyn Dodgers at Ebbets Field in Brooklyn. Both of these games were seen by only a handful of people over an experimental station, W2XBS. Another decade passed before games were televised widely. During the 1930's, a fan could see the best teams and players perform only briefly in movie-theater newsreels.

Outstanding Teams and Players   Both the American and National Leagues consistently fielded eight teams throughout the decade. Two teams had risen to prominence during the 1920's: the New York Yankees of the American League, buoyed by the great Ruth, and the St. Louis Cardinals, who began to dominate the National League, particularly because of Rickey. Both teams continued to stand out during the 1930's. The Yankees, boosted by the addition of outstanding young players to supplement the aging Ruth, won the pennant in 1932 and in the final four years of the decade. The team's field manager throughout the 1930's, a decade in which the Yankees won five World Series, was Joe McCarthy. The Cardinals won pennants in 1930, 1931, and 1934, with an exciting group of players that became known as the Gashouse Gang. The Chicago Cubs and New York Giants also won three National League pennants each in the decade. The Giants' Bill Terry was a player-manager, a combination of duties fairly common at the time but unusual after the 1950's.

The baseball heroes of the 1930's tended to be home-run hitters. Ruth had made the home run a prominent feature of the game in the previous decade, when the greatest stars had been famous for hitting consistency and for superlative baserunning abilities. Stolen bases remained important, but none of the base stealers of the 1930's appealed to fans as much as home-run hitters such as Ruth, Lou Gehrig,

Jimmie Foxx, Hank Greenberg, Hack Wilson, and Mel Ott did.

The greatest pitcher of the decade was Lefty Grove, who won thirty-one games in 1931, a total unmatched through the first decade of the twenty-first century, and averaged twenty wins per season over the entire decade, while pitching for the Athletics and the Red Sox of the American League. Dizzy Dean of the St. Louis Cardinals starred as the dominant winner and strikeout pitcher in the National League before his career was shortened by injury while he was still in his twenties.

Of the stars whose careers began later in the decade, Joe DiMaggio of the Yankees and Ted Williams, of the Red Sox, proved most outstanding. Bob Feller, who began playing for the Cleveland Indians at the age of seventeen in 1936, with no minor league experience, became a pitching celebrity by 1939. Perhaps the saddest baseball event of the decade was Lou Gehrig Appreciation Day at Yankee Stadium on July 4, 1939. Gehrig had played in 2,130 consecutive games, but amyotrophic lateral sclerosis (still commonly known as Lou Gehrig's disease) had ended his career. In a short speech, Gehrig claimed that despite his mortal illness he considered himself "the luckiest man on the face of the earth."

Impact   Like much of the entertainment that captivated Americans during the 1930's, baseball provided relief from the troubles of the Depression. At the same time, it exhibited serious deficiencies. Its players were economic captives of their teams' owners. More seriously, black players, including all Latino and Native American players with dark skin, were denied access to the major and minor leagues. Professional baseball was not the entrepreneurial giant it became, nor did it reflect the population of the nation, which it began to resemble in the decades following World War II.

Robert P. Ellis

Further Reading

James, Bill. *The New Bill James Historical Baseball Abstract.* New York: Free Press, 2001. Chapters on the 1930's and the Negro Leagues and analysis of outstanding players of the era.

Lanctot, Neil. *Negro League Baseball: The Rise and Ruin of a Black Institution.* Philadelphia: University of Pennsylvania Press, 2004. In addition to supplying information about the game itself, the author

makes important points about the social and economic conditions of black players.

Vincent, Fay. *The Only Game in Town: Baseball Stars of
the 1930s and 1940s Talk About the Game They Loved.*
New York: Simon & Schuster, 2006. Former baseball commissioner's interviews with players display their strengths and their weaknesses.

Ward, Geoffrey C. *Baseball: An Illustrated History.* New
York: Alfred A. Knopf, 1994. Treats baseball by decades, with seventy pages on the 1930's. Outstanding photographs.

See also   Dean, Dizzy; Foxx, Jimmie; Gehrig, Lou;
National Baseball Hall of Fame; Negro Leagues; Ott,
Mel; Ruth, Babe; Vander Meer, Johnny.

Baseball Hall of Fame. See **National Baseball
Hall of Fame**

■ Basie, Count

Identification   Jazz pianist, bandleader, arranger,
and composer
Born   August 21, 1904; Red Bank, New Jersey
Died   April 26, 1984; Hollywood, Florida

*Basie led one of the top jazz bands, the Count Basie Or-
chestra, of the 1930's and helped establish and popularize
swing music through tours, recordings, and national
broadcasts. As a pianist, Basie created a signature economical style that later influenced bebop and cool-jazz musicians.*

Born into a musical family in New Jersey, William
"Count" Basie received his first music lessons from
his pianist mother, Lillian. He later studied with Fats
Waller, a New York stride pianist, and performed
with various New York bands from 1923 to 1926. In
1927, Basie was stranded in Kansas City after the
vaudeville troupe with which he was touring disbanded; he remained in the city playing piano in
silent-film theaters. During the 1920's and 1930's,
Kansas City served as a center for several jazz bands
that toured the area known as the "territories,"
which consisted of cities in the Midwest and Southwest. Basie performed with several such bands, serving as the pianist for Walter Page's Blue Devils from
1928 to 1929 and as a pianist and arranger for
Bennie Moten's orchestra from 1929 to 1935. Musi-

Count Basie in 1936. (AP/Wide World Photos)

cians from these two groups eventually provided the
core for Basie's own group, the Barons of Rhythm,
which was formed after Moten's death in 1935.

The Barons of Rhythm was a nine-member group
that began an extended engagement at the Reno
Club in Kansas City in 1935. Through its local radio
broadcasts from the club, the group gained the attention of record producer John Hammond and
eventually signed a recording contract with Decca
Records in 1936. That same year, the group expanded to fourteen members and toured Chicago
and New York, the latter replacing Kansas City as the
band's home base. At this point known as the Count
Basie Orchestra, the group became one of the most
successful big bands of the 1930's with hits such as
"One O'Clock Jump" in 1937 and "Jumpin' at the
Woodside" in 1938, both written by Basie. During the
late 1930's, the Count Basie Orchestra had several
notable engagements in New York City, including
performing at the Apollo Theatre with Billie Holiday in March of 1937 and a four-month residency at
the Famous Door from July to November of 1938.
The Famous Door concerts were broadcasted nationally on Columbia Broadcasting System (CBS) radio

stations, enhancing the group's popularity and leading to the group's first cross-country tour in 1939.

After the decline of swing music during the 1940's, Basie temporarily led a smaller group of musicians, but otherwise the Count Basie Orchestra continued to perform and record big band music after the 1930's. After returning to the big band format in 1952, the Count Basie Orchestra made several tours of Europe and served as the backing band for a number of prominent vocalists, such as Ella Fitzgerald, Frank Sinatra, and Tony Bennett. Basie led the group until his death in 1984, after which the group continued under the leadership of several different directors.

Impact Along with Duke Ellington's big band, Basie and his group helped popularize swing music to the extent that it became the most popular style of not only jazz music but also popular music in general during the period from 1935 to 1945. Also, the light, responsive rhythm section of the Count Basie Orchestra, led by Basie on piano, changed the approach to jazz accompaniment. Basie's simpler approach to jazz accompaniment granted greater freedom to the band's notable soloists, such as saxophonist Lester Young and trumpeter Buck Clayton. While known primarily for his contributions as bandleader, Basie was also innovative as a pianist. He developed a blues-influenced, minimalist style of piano playing that was frequently fragmentary. He occasionally contributed solos that consisted of short musical phrases but primarily utilized his spare approach to piano playing to lead his band and cue soloists.

Matthew Mihalka

Further Reading

Basie, Count. *Good Morning Blues: The Autobiography of Count Basie as Told to Albert Murray.* New York: Da Capo Press, 2002.

Dance, Stanley. *The World of Count Basie.* New York: Charles Scribner's Sons, 1980.

Horricks, Raymond. *Count Basie and His Orchestra: Its Music and Its Musicians.* New York: The Citadel Press, 1957.

Vail, Ken. *Count Basie: Swingin' the Blues, 1936-1950.* Lanham, Md.: Scarecrow Press, 2003.

See also Armstrong, Louis; Ellington, Duke; Fitzgerald, Ella; Goodman, Benny; Holiday, Billie; Miller, Glenn; Music: Jazz.

■ Basketball

During the 1930's, basketball became a popular diversion because it requires little in the way of equipment and because the Public Works Administration built so many high school and college basketball facilities. As a result of its increasing popularity during this period, the rules of the game were codified and regularized.

From its inception in the nineteenth century, basketball experienced slow and rather uneven development in terms of rules; the women's game featured far more structure than the men's. During the 1920's, men's and women's basketball increased in popularity at the high school and collegiate levels because its modest equipment and personnel requirements allowed small schools to field teams to compete with large interscholastic rivals. By 1930, basketball was arguably the most popular winter sport, but the men's game was largely viewed as a way for high school and college football players to remain fit during the off-season. However, barnstorming teams such as the New York-based Original Celtics and the Edmonton Grads, a women's touring team from Canada, brought the game to cities across the United States; this ensured a steady increase in popularity for the game. With the advent of the Great Depression, basketball experienced increasing interest as a spectator sport at both the interscholastic and professional levels, which led to the regularization of rules at all levels of the game.

Interscholastic Basketball The New Deal featured the Public Works Administration, which put the unemployed to work building schools, parks, and government buildings and making improvements to preexisting structures. During the 1930's, this agency constructed or renovated high school and college gymnasiums, essentially doubling the seating capacity for basketball games. Many schools were unable to field football programs at this time, but they found that basketball was far less expensive to facilitate. As a result, by 1937, basketball was played in approximately 95 percent of American high schools and became so popular at the collegiate level that officials started to discuss holding a national championship.

Using as a prototype Amos Alonzo Stagg's National Interscholastic Basketball Tournament (1917-

1930), an invitational tournament for high schools held at the University of Chicago, the National Association of Intercollegiate Basketball tournament was organized in 1937 and the National Invitation Tournament was organized a year later. Although women's collegiate athletes were not offered the same championship opportunities, the Amateur Athletic Union (AAU) chose its annual all-America team from 1929 through the 1960's to recognize female collegiate and "industrial league" basketball stars.

The men's team at Long Island University was widely considered the best team in the country until it met Stanford University in 1936. Stanford featured the guard play of Hank Luisetti, who had scored an unprecedented fifty points in a game that year. Luisetti employed one-handed shots and behind-the-back passes and led Stanford to victory in the game against Long Island. Soon, coaches from colleges across the country were teaching these moves to their players and, because of the fan interest in this style of play, the AAU and the National Collegiate Athletic Association instituted a number of rule changes to quicken the pace of the game. The center jump after every basket and foul shot was eliminated. During the 1935 season, the Pacific Coast Conference had experimented with this change and reported that fans were extremely happy with the rule. Also, officials increased the number of time-outs from three to four, allowing for more substitutions. The final new rule was that the ball had to be advanced past midcourt within ten seconds.

Men's basketball received another boost in fan support as a feature of the 1936 Olympic Games in Berlin. Although the games were played outdoors on lawn tennis courts and often in torrential rain, a U.S. team composed of collegiate stars, most of whom were from the University of California, Los Angeles, beat Canada for the gold medal. Twenty-three nations entered the Olympic basketball tournament, making it the largest team sport tournament at the 1936 games.

Similar changes occurred in the women's game. At the beginning of the decade, women's basketball used the Spalding rules, which divided the basketball court into three separate areas and forbade players from moving out of their designated zone. Players had to pass the ball after a possession of only three seconds. Limited substitutions were allowed and a player could not reenter the game after leaving. The rules for the women's game changed over the course of the decade to mirror much of what had been adopted in the men's game.

Professional Basketball Despite the increasing popularity of basketball throughout the 1930's, the professional version of the game was a minor sport compared with professional baseball and football. Numerous men's and women's teams barnstormed around the country, often playing up to 170 games per year. The teams were usually unsalaried and were paid a percentage of ticket sales. Many of the teams were organized around ethnic or racial lines. The Harlem Globetrotters and the Harlem Renaissance Big Five (the "Rens") were African American teams. The Philadelphia Warriors, which entered the ill-fated American Basketball League in 1931, only to see the league fold in 1934, were promoted as a Jewish team. Women's teams were typically organized around a "gimmick" such as the red wigs worn by members of the All-American Red Heads. Babe Didrikson Zaharias, an Olympic gold medalist at the 1932 games, and Hazel Walker both had great success leading women's barnstorming teams in the middle of the decade.

Impact Because of basketball's minimal equipment and personnel requirements, the game was ideally suited for the Great Depression era. As a result, the sport attracted a number of participants in interscholastic and recreational settings. As fan interest increased, the governing bodies of both men's and women's basketball instituted modifications and outright changes to the rules of the game to make it faster-paced and more appealing to fans, which modernized the game and strengthened its institutions.

William Carney

Further Reading

Baldwin, Douglas O. *Sports in North America: A Documentary History. Volume Eight. Sports in the Depression, 1939-1940.* Gulf Breeze, Fla.: Academic International Press, 2000.

Caponi-Tabery, Gena. *Jump for Joy: Jazz, Basketball, and Black Culture in 1930s America.* Amherst: University of Massachusetts Press, 2008.

Great Athletes: Basketball. Pasadena, Calif.: Salem Press, 2010.

See also Olympic Games of 1932 (Summer); Olympic Games of 1936 (Summer); Sports in the United States.

■ Bathysphere

Definition   Device for deep-sea study

First-hand scientific exploration of the deep ocean took place for the first time in the 1930's.

Little was known scientifically about the ocean depths prior to the 1930's. The naturalist William Beebe became the first scientist to use a diving helmet to explore the ocean, but only in fairly shallow depths. While pondering the design of a vehicle for even deeper exploration, he was introduced to a young engineer, Otis Barton, who had already designed such a craft, and the two made plans to build it.

The bathysphere, as Beebe named it, was a 5,000 pound tethered sphere with a diameter of 4.75 feet and steel walls 1.5 inches thick. It had four windows, a water spotlight, oxygen tanks for breathing, a telephone for communication with the surface, and a steel door that was bolted closed prior to descent. The device was lowered by steel cable from a winch on a surface ship.

Three seasons of dives were made in the Atlantic Ocean near Nonsuch Island off Bermuda. The first manned dive, on June 3, 1930, proved that the device worked and yielded useful observations. A final dive that year descended to 1,425 feet. A dive conducted on September 22, 1932, was broadcast live by the National Broadcasting Company and reached a depth of 2,200 feet. On August 15, 1934, during the final season, a record dive of 3,030 feet was made. Beyond the depth records, the dives established that light disappeared while descending by color according to wavelength, as scientists had predicted, and that many new and exotic species of luminescent fish and jellyfish lived in the hostile blackness of the deep.

Impact   Beebe and Barton had descended farther than any other living humans and had uncovered a largely unsuspected deep-sea ecosystem. The public was fascinated by the reports of the dives, published in *National Geographic* and other magazines and in Beebe's own popular account, *Half Mile Down* (1934). However, the bathysphere had limitations: It could move vertically only; its use in deeper dives required more steel cable, which called for larger and more expensive ships; and no escape mechanism existed in the event of a catastrophic leak. These fac-

tors meant that future exploration had to be made using submarines and other nontethered submersible craft.

George R. Ehrhardt

Further Reading

Beebe, William. *Half Mile Down*. New York: Harcourt, Brace, 1934.

Gould, Carol Grant. *The Remarkable Life of William Beebe: Explorer and Naturalist*. Washington, D.C.: Island Press, 2004.

Matsen, Bradford. *Descent: The Heroic Discovery of the Abyss*. New York: Pantheon Books, 2005.

Welker, Robert Henry. *Natural Man: The Life of William Beebe*. Bloomington: Indiana University Press, 1975.

See also   Inventions; Physics; Radio astronomy; Rockefeller Center.

Bay Bridge. See **San Francisco Bay bridges**

■ Beard, Charles A.

Identification   American progressive historian
Born   November 27, 1874; near Knightstown, Indiana
Died   September 1, 1948; New Haven, Connecticut

In his 1933 presidential address to the American Historical Association, Beard asserted that historians are the product of the age in which they write and, therefore, bring contemporary concerns to the writing of history. As such, history reflects the spirit of the age in which it is written.

Charles A. Beard was the "father of history" to a generation of American historians who came of age during the 1930's. In both *An Economic Interpretation of the Constitution of the United States* (1913) and *Economic Origins of Jeffersonian Democracy* (1915), Beard focused on economic factors influencing the early development of the United States.

Beard taught at Columbia University, although he resigned his professorship in October, 1917, because of ideological policing by the university's board of trustees and the firings of James McKeen Cattell and Henry Wadsworth Longfellow Dana. Beard returned to Columbia in 1939 as a visiting professor of government.

Joseph O'Mahoney (left) and Charles A. Beard conversing after Beard addressed the Senate Judiciary subcommittee regarding corporate concentration of wealth. (Library of Congress)

Beard cowrote with Mary R. Beard *The Rise of American Civilization* (1927), in which he extended his earlier economic interpretation to the whole of American history. Published as a one volume college edition in July, 1930, this single work was hugely influential in the education of waves of American students of higher education. *The Rise of American Civilization* was revised and published in 1934, 1964, and 1966.

The American Historical Association elected Beard president in 1933. In his presidential address, titled *Written History as an Act of Faith,* Beard asserted that historians are the product of the age in which they write and, therefore, bring contemporary concerns to the writing of history. As such, history reflects the spirit of the age in which it is written.

Beard supported President Franklin D. Roosevelt and the New Deal: He applauded government planning initiatives aimed at providing for the collective good of society and viewed national relief measures as necessary for the preservation of American de-

mocracy in the face of the severe socio-economic challenges caused by the Great Depression.

Beard split with the Roosevelt administration on international policy and foreign relations. He was critical of the government's lend-lease program, and he disliked the internationalist ambitions and idealism of Roosevelt's foreign policy. He disapproved of imperialism and hoped for the preservation of American neutrality. In 1939, he accused Roosevelt of "blundering into war" and worried that global conflict would curtail civil liberties and undermine democracy.

The third volume of *The Rise of American Civilization,* titled *America in Midpassage* (1939), closed the Beards' materialist analysis of American history from President Warren G. Harding's "return to normalcy" to Roosevelt's April 29, 1938, message to Congress on the "problem of . . . the growing concentration of economic and financial power."

Impact Alternately decried and heralded as an activist, dabbler, isolationist, pacifist, populist, progressive, reactionary, reformer, relativist, and other labels too numerous to list, Beard defied easy categorization. To be sure, Beard's influence looms large in the story of twentieth century historiography and beyond: His work as an historian set the standard until his death in 1948, and his scholarship foreshadowed the ideological divides—between idealists and materialists—that historians in the United States and elsewhere have wrestled with ever since.

Keith Carson

Further Reading

Barrow, Clyde W. *More than a Historian: The Political and Economic Thought of Charles A. Beard.* New Brunswick, N.J.: Transaction, 2000.

Beard, Charles A., and Mary R. Beard. *America in Midpassage, Volumes I and II.* New York: Macmillan, 1939.

_____. *The American Spirit.* New York: Macmillan, 1942.

_____. *The Rise of American Civilization.* Rev. ed. New York: Macmillan, 1930.

Beard, Charles A., and George H. E. Smith. *The Open Door at Home: A Trial Philosophy of National Interest.* New York: Macmillan, 1934.

Hofstadter, Richard. *The Progressive Historians: Turner, Beard, and Parrington.* Chicago: University of Chicago Press, 1969.

Nore, Ellen. *Charles A. Beard: An Intellectual Biography.* Carbondale: Southern Illinois University Press, 1983.

Thomas, Brook. *The New Historicism and Other Old-Fashioned Topics.* Princeton, N.J.: Princeton University Press, 1991.

See also Dewey, John; Education; Isolationism; London Economic Conference; Neutrality Acts; Nye Committee; Philosophy and philosophers; Roosevelt, Franklin D.; Roosevelt's first one hundred days; Wallace, Henry A.

■ Beatty, Clyde

Identification American animal trainer and circus performer

Born June 10, 1903; Bainbridge, Ohio

Died July 10, 1965; Ventura, California

The epitome of the wild-animal trainer and circus performer, Beatty brought to the steel arenas of the American circus a revolutionary act: Armed with chair, whip, and blank-firing pistol, he put forty lions and tigers through their paces.

Clyde Beatty left home in his midteens to work as a cage cleaner on the Howes Great London Shows. From then until he reached the Hagenbeck-Wallace Circus in 1925, he sought to develop an act based on an apparent conflict between man and animal. Because he knew his animals and his audiences, Beatty was able to make the conflict seem even more dangerous than it was. Reflecting a feisty cockiness that did much to create his battling image, Beatty entered the arena with great flair. With the sleeves of his white shirt rolled up, he would pivot around, waving his chair, cracking his whip, and occasionally firing his pistol. That he could bring order to chaos seemed miraculous to the audience.

Each summer, Beatty traveled from coast to coast, putting his act before thousands of circus fans. He also joined Ringling Brothers and Barnum and Bailey Circus for its annual openings at Madison Square Garden in New York. His status as the top animal trainer in the country gained him Hollwood contracts. He acted in two films and a serial: *The Big Cage* (1933), *The Lost Jungle* (1934), and *Darkest Africa* (1936). In 1935, Beatty joined two noted circus managers, Jesse Adkins and Zack Terrell, to build a new circus to be called Cole Brothers Circus with Clyde Beatty. In 1938, he left to build a zoo in Florida and to put a circus of his own on the road.

Impact Beatty had all the trappings of a folk hero, particularly at a time when the nation was looking for such. When Beatty outstarred his famous lion Nero, he did not seek domination. In the process, Beatty earned his place on the list of circus greats.

Wilton Eckley

Further Reading

Goldsack, Bob. *A Pictorial History of the Clyde Beatty Cole Bros. Circus.* Nashua, N.H.: Midway, 2004.

Joys, Joanne Carol. *The Wild Animal Trainer in America.* Boulder, Colo.: Pruett, 1983.

Wilkie, Katharine E. *Clyde Beatty: Boy Animal Trainer.* Indianapolis, Ind.: Bobbs-Merrill, 1968.

See also Film; *King Kong*; Tarzan films.

■ Bennett, Richard Bedford

Identification Canadian prime minister, 1930-1935

Born July 3, 1870; Hopewell Hill, New Brunswick, Canada

Died June 26, 1947; Mickleham, Surrey, England

Bennett became prime minister of Canada just as the Great Depression entered its most severe phase. His various responses to the disaster failed to please voters, and he lost the following election.

Richard Bedford Bennett overcame the disadvantages of a poverty-stricken childhood to become a successful lawyer and a millionaire industrialist and reach the highest elective office of his country. The main influence on his childhood was his mother, a stern Wesleyan Methodist, who inculcated in him the values of hard work, diligence, self-denial, and charity.

At the age of sixteen, after attending Fredericton Normal School in New Brunswick, Bennett began teaching. In four years, he saved enough money to attend Dalhousie University Law School, Halifax. He then became junior partner in a law firm in Chatham. In 1897, seeing greater opportunity in the West, Bennett accepted an offer to join a Calgary law firm. He soon had a busy and profitable practice and joined his clients in successful business enterprises that made him the wealthiest of Canadian prime ministers.

Active in the Alberta Conservative Party, Bennett was elected to the territorial legislature in 1898, the Alberta provincial legislature in 1909, and the House of Commons in 1911. In 1916, he became head of the Canadian National Service Board. In 1920, he became minister of justice, only to be defeated in 1921 when the Conservatives lost the general election. By 1925, Bennett was back in the Commons, serving as minister of finance during the Conservatives' three months in power in 1926.

Party Leader   When the leader of the Conservative Party resigned, the party's national convention chose Bennett in October, 1927. In 1928, he divested himself of corporate directorships and blocks of stock that might raise conflict of interest questions.

As party leader Bennett headed the 1930 Conservative campaign, running against William Lyon Mackenzie King's Liberals. He proved a most effective campaigner. His dynamic speaking style suited the newly useful medium of radio. Neither he nor King realized the significance of the economic downturn and expected prosperity to return shortly. However, where King proposed to continue his cautious fiscal policies, Bennett promised action. He insisted that raising tariffs would encourage Canadian manufacturing and create new jobs and that public works programs would reduce unemployment. Conservatives swept the July 28, election, winning 137 seats against 91 for the Liberals and 17 for all other parties.

Prime Minister of Canada   Bennett had promised action, and he acted immediately, calling a special session of the Canadian parliament for September, which in two weeks enacted record tariffs and appropriated $20 million for public works. In October, he was in London trying unsuccessfully to convince the British to grant Canada preferential treatment in the British market in return for preferences in Canada. At the 1932 Ottawa Conference, Bennett's hard bargaining produced greater concessions for Canada than it gave Great Britain.

However, other countries also raised tariffs, and international trade declined sharply. Demand for Canada's vital wheat and minerals exports fell. Wheat prices began declining during the late 1920's and reached catastrophic levels just as drought afflicted the Prairie Provinces. Mines closed or laid off workers. Textile manufacturers profited under the Ottawa Agreements, but not workers—some mills paid as low as nine cents per hour. Unemployment, which stood at 300,000 when Bennett took office, reached 675,000 in 1932.

Bennett increased appropriations for public works. He began direct federal relief of individuals, establishing work camps in 1932 for unemployed single men, who received board and lodging and twenty cents per day for their labor. Fearing radical unrest, Bennett placed camps far from urban centers and put them under the control of the Department of National Defence. Aware that economic conditions encouraged agitation, Bennett increased undercover activities by the Royal Canadian Mounted Police. His Department of Justice convicted nine top leaders of the Canadian Communist Party in 1931 for violating the law against unlawful assembly.

To encourage trade with the United States, Bennett began negotiating a reciprocity treaty in 1932 that was signed one month after he lost the 1935 election. A treaty to jointly build a St. Lawrence Seaway failed to be ratified in the U.S. Senate. Bennett also created the predecessor of the Canadian Broadcasting Corporation in 1932, preparing the way for an outstanding public radio and television network.

Bennett's most productive year as prime minister was 1934. To aid farmers, parliament passed an agricultural marketing bill giving the government power to set prices and quotas. A farm credit bill provided bankruptcy protection, permitting farmers to avoid foreclosure and remain on their farms. A companies act aimed at preventing future price bubbles on the stock exchange was initiated. A central Bank of Canada was created to manage the currency, despite vigorous opposition by major banks.

Historians praise Bennett's efforts in 1934, but the electorate seemed less impressed. Facing the expiration of the Canadian parliament's five-year-term in 1935, Bennett decided on a major policy shift. In a January, 1935, radio broadcast, he proposed his New Deal, clearly modeled on that of Franklin D. Roosevelt in the United States. He called for a minimum wage, an eight-hour day, a forty-eight-hour work week, unemployment insurance, old-age pensions, and debtor relief. Bennett's biographers believe that although his rhetoric had become increasingly radical, the program was consistent with his paternalistic personal and political attitudes. Others termed it hypocrisy, a deathbed conversion as he faced electoral defeat.

Bennett's plan divided Conservatives, while King kept Liberals together by not taking any stand. He expected the Depression to defeat Bennett, and it did. The Liberals took 173 seats, the largest majority on record; Conservatives won 40 seats. However, Liberals received only 45 percent of the popular vote, about the same as 1930; the drop in support for Conservatives and the shift of 20 percent of the electorate to new radical parties created a rout of the Conservatives.

Bennett remained the Conservative leader until 1938 before retiring to Mickleham, Surrey, England. Lord Beaverbrook's lobbying of Winston Churchill garnered Bennett the title Viscount Bennett of Mickleham and a seat in the House of Lords in 1941. Bennett died of a heart attack and was buried in Mickleham churchyard.

Impact   Rejected by the electorate in 1935, Bennett was widely considered a failure. He woefully underestimated the impact of the Depression and promised too much during the 1930 campaign. His claim that an increased tariff would end unemployment had no chance of succeeding. Bennett provided work and direct relief for the unemployed, but he did so grudgingly, failing to convince the public that he actually wanted to help. His work camps for unemployed single men closely resembled Roosevelt's Civilian Conservation Corps (CCC). The CCC paid thirty dollars a month, twenty-five dollars of which was sent home, giving the men the feeling they were doing something worthwhile for their families. Bennett's derisory twenty cents a day had the opposite effect on morale. In June, 1935, inmates of the government camps on the West Coast began a protest march on Ottawa. Bennett ordered police to stop it; on July 1, a pitched battle broke out in Regina, Saskatchewan, that left a policeman and a marcher dead and dozens wounded.

Bennett's biographers call him a partial success, arguing things could have been much worse. No democratic leader anywhere in the world was able to reduce unemployment substantially by 1935. He left a permanent mark on Canadian life with his effective agricultural relief program in 1934, starting the Canadian Broadcasting Corporation, and inaugurating the Bank of Canada, which proved invaluable during World War II. Bennett's paternalistic belief in private charity belies his public image as a cold, arrogant corporation lawyer insulated from economic reality by his wealth and insensitive to the plight of the unemployed.

Milton Berman

Further Reading

Allen, Ralph. *Ordeal by Fire: Canada, 1910-1945*. Toronto: Doubleday Canada, 1961. Readable narrative focusing on people and events; weak on policy issues.

Beaverbrook, Lord William Maxwell Aitken. *Friends: Fifty Years of Intimate Personal Relations with Richard Bedford Bennett*. London: Heinemann, 1959. Favorable description of Bennett's personality and politics.

Bothwell, Robert. *The Penguin History of Canada*. Toronto: Penguin Canada, 2006. Valuable for the general background of Bennett's public life.

O'Brien, Anthony Patrick, and Judith A. McDonald. "Retreat from Protectionism: R. B. Bennett and the Movement to Freer Trade in Canada, 1930-1935." *Journal of Policy History* 21, no. 4 (2009): 331-365. Critique of Bennett's economic policy.

Watkins, Ernest. *R. B. Bennett: A Biography*. London: Secker and Warburg, 1963. Full-scale examination of Bennett's life and career.

Wilbur, Richard. *The Bennett Administration, 1930-1935*. Ottawa: Canadian Historical Association. 1969. Brief and careful evaluation of Bennett's policies.

See also   Agriculture in Canada; Business and the economy in Canada; Canada and Great Britain; Elections, Canadian; Great Depression in Canada; King, William Lyon Mackenzie; Ottawa Agreements; Radio in Canada; Unemployment in Canada.

■ Benny, Jack

Identification   American radio and television
   comedian
Born   February 14, 1894; Chicago, Illinois
Died   December 26, 1974; Beverly Hills,
   California

*Benny is widely regarded as one of the greatest comedy enter-
tainers of the twentieth century. His popularity for more
than five decades was fueled by his mastery of the well-timed
pause and simple expressions. Both his radio and television
programs were instrumental in the development of the situation comedy.*

Prior to serving in the Navy during World War I, Jack
Benny, born Benjamin Kubelsky, toured on the
vaudeville circuit as a violinist. While on tour, he
discovered his comic ability. After the war, he became a well-known and respected vaudeville comedian. Soon enough, Hollywood executives discovered Benny, and he was given a five-year contract
with Metro-Goldwyn-Mayer (MGM). After two films,

*Comedian Jack Benny, admiring a photograph of himself with his wife,
Mary Livingstone, in 1937, in his Beverly Hills home.* (Archive Photos/
Getty Images)

MGM no longer provided him with scripts, and the
studio eventually released him from his contract. At
this time, Benny accepted a costarring role in the
vaudeville-style show the *Vanities*. In the latter part
of 1931, Benny left the *Vanities* to pursue a career in
radio.

In March of 1932, Benny appeared on the Ed
Sullivan radio show, where he was heard by an advertising account executive for Canada Dry. Soon
Benny was emceeing *The Canada Dry Ginger Ale Program*, twice each week on Columbia Broadcasting
System (CBS). Benny's star was beginning to rise. In
1932, radio editors voted him the most popular comedian on the air. In spite of all this success, Benny
still faced challenges.

After Benny poked fun at the sponsored product
during the program, *The Jack Benny Show* was
dropped from *The Canada Dry Ginger Ale Program* in
January of 1933. However, Benny's tremendous popularity with both the public and the critics was undeniable, and the show was soon picked up by General
Motors for *The Chevrolet Program*. However, this show
was dropped on April 1, 1934. General Motors president William Signius Knudsen decided that Benny was no longer funny. Five
days later General Tire announced it would
sponsor the show. During this brief relationship with General Tire, Don Wilson, who became Benny's longtime announcer, joined
the show.

For the 1934-1935 season, *The Jack Benny
Show* was sponsored by General Foods. The
company recognized that Benny had the star
power to reintroduce to American consumers its floundering product Jell-O; therefore, Benny's program received the coveted
7:00 P.M. time slot on Sundays. By the end of
the 1934-1935 season, Benny was third in the
ratings, ahead of well-known acts such as
Amos 'n' Andy and Ed Wynn.

At this point, the cast of characters on the
show was taking shape. Harry Conn, one of
the writers, suggested adding a small-town
girl as Benny's on-air foil. Benny's wife, Sadie
Marks, who had already established herself
in vaudeville with Benny, auditioned for the
part of Mary Livingstone and became an instant hit. Marks became so identified with
her character that she eventually changed
her legal name to Mary Livingstone.

The Jack Benny Show continued to grow in size and popularity throughout the decade. By 1939, the regular cast included Benny, Marks, Wilson, Kenny Baker, Phil Harris, and Eddie Anderson as Benny's long-suffering valet, Rochester Van Jones. At the end of the 1939 season, Baker departed the show and was replaced by Dennis Wilson.

Throughout the 1930's, Benny was a major star on radio. He cultivated a successful career in films during the same period. He appeared in numerous films, including *Transatlantic Merry-Go-Round* (1934) and *Man About Town* (1939), confirming his versatile star power.

Impact   Benny achieved his greatest fame as a radio performer. *The Jack Benny Show*, first introduced in 1932, was heard weekly for twenty-four years. Benny successfully transferred his program to television during the 1950's. The program continued on television through 1965. Although his on-air persona was that of an egotistical penny pincher who never surpassed the age of thirty-nine, Benny was well known for his generosity and modest personality.

Michael D. Cummings, Jr.

Further Reading

Benny, Jack, and Joan Benny. *Sunday Nights at Seven: The Jack Benny Story.* New York: Warner Books, 1990.

Leannah, Michael, ed. *Well! Reflections on the Life and Career of Jack Benny.* Albany, Ga.: BearManor Media, 2007.

See also   *Amos 'n' Andy; Fibber McGee and Molly;* Marx Brothers; Radio in the United States.

∎ Benton, Thomas Hart

Identification   American Regionalist painter
Born   April 15, 1889; Neosho, Missouri
Died   January 19, 1975; Martha's Vineyard, Massachusetts

Thomas Hart Benton was a key member of the American Regionalist art movement during the 1930's. In contrast to the abstracted, urbane, and often elitist modernist aesthetic of the time, Benton's works focus on simple midwestern subjects presented in a visually accessible manner. He was drawn to the Midwest because he believed that American identity lay in the rural center of the country rather than in the modernized city.

Thomas Hart Benton was the grandnephew of the well-known Missouri senator of the same name. Rather than follow in his granduncle's political footsteps, Benton decided to pursue a career in art. He began attending the Art Institute of Chicago in 1907 but soon left for Paris and the Académie Julian in 1909. Despite his European training, Benton achieved fame as a key member of the Regionalist style, along with artists Grant Wood and John Steuart Curry. Regionalism, also known as American scene painting, rejected the idea that true American art was found in cosmopolitan centers and could only be expressed through the increasingly elitist modern art. These Regionalist painters turned their attention to the Midwest and the simplified life of those in the rural United States.

Benton began his career in the modernist Synchromist style—he had met the Synchromist painter Stanton Macdonald-Wright in Paris—but turned to more recognizable and accessible subject matter. Benton's style retains the simplified forms and bold colors of Synchromism, but his style is more visually accessible. His distinctive elongated and rubbery figures represent readily recognizable types, and his bold colors and large scale give his works a cinematic quality that enhances their accessibility.

Though Benton did many paintings of New York and Martha's Vineyard, as well as of the American South, he is best known for his paintings of the Midwest. Among his best known works is the mural he completed for the Missouri state capitol building entitled *A Social History of the State of Missouri* (1936). Here, Benton combines positive aspects of Missouri's background with its more negative historical realities of slavery and vigilante lynchings. In so doing, Benton does not idealize his state but provides an accurate description of its history.

Impact   After the Regionalist's emphasis on the American Midwest began to wane, Benton continued painting and teaching, first at the Art Students League of New York and then at the Kansas City Art Institute, where he met his most famous student, Jackson Pollock. Pollock later founded the revolutionary abstract expressionist movement, which at first glance appears to be in direct contrast to Benton's style. However, recent scholarship has suggested that Benton's forms and subject matter were influential to Pollock.

Ellen Lippert

Further Reading

Adams, Henry. *Thomas Hart Benton: An American Original*. New York: Alfred A. Knopf, 1989.

_____. *Tom and Jack: The Intertwined Lives of Thomas Hart Benton and Jackson Pollock*. New York: Blooms-bury Press, 2009.

Benton, Thomas Hart. *An Artist in America*. Columbia: University of Missouri Press, 1983.

See also   *American Gothic*; Art movements; Curry, John Steuart; Rockefeller Center Rivera mural; Wood, Grant.

■ Berkeley, Busby

Identification   Film and theater director and choreographer
Born   November 29, 1895; Los Angeles, California
Died   March 14, 1976; Palm Desert, California

Berkeley's style of directing and choreography became so well known that the term "busby berkeley" was coined and appears in the American Thesaurus of Slang *to describe an elaborate dance number. His overhead camera shots, forming dancers into kaleidoscopic patterns, and dazzling dance sequences, featuring scantily clad women, are characteristics of his musical film productions.*

Born William Berkeley Enos, Busby Berkeley was the son of show people. He made his stage debut in New York at the age of five and, as an adult, appeared in musicals and began staging musical numbers. However, Broadway was not the sole influence on his development as an artist. When the United States entered World War I in 1917, he enlisted. While stationed in Europe, he created large-scale parade drills for troops and later served as an aerial observer with the Air Corps. After the war, he returned to Broadway, and his first job as a dance director was in the musical *Holka Polka* in 1925. Subsequently, he staged numbers for more than twenty shows, building a reputation as an innovator in the genre of musical comedy. His work caught the attention of Samuel Goldwyn who invited him to Hollywood in 1930. During the 1930's, Berkeley's body of work as a dance director changed the look of the Hollywood musical.

Berkeley's first film for Goldwyn was *Whoopee* (1930), starring Eddie Cantor. Quick to see the advantages of using a camera, Berkeley designed dance numbers that were different from those for the theater. He invented a camera mounted on a monorail; consequently, the camera could be suspended above the dances, providing an "aerial" viewpoint of the dancers. Also drawing from his military experience, he emphasized the dancers as a troupe, rather than as isolated individuals.

In 1933, Berkeley was hired by Warner Bros., which offered a big budget for his increasingly large and spectacular routines. At Warner Bros. he created the films that made him famous. His first big musical was *Forty-second Street* (1933), starring Ruby Keeler. A box-office hit, it rescued the studio from bankruptcy and revived the film musical format. In-

Dancers perform an elaborate routine choreographed by Busby Berkeley for the 1933 musical film Footlight Parade. *(Hulton Archive/Getty Images)*

tricate dance numbers included "Shuffle Off to Buffalo" and "Forty-second Street," with the dancers manipulating banners and flags in such a way as to create a kaleidoscope of movement.

The opening number of *Gold Diggers of 1933* (1933) featured dancers wearing strategically placed coins; later in the show Berkeley used sixty female dancers, holding neon-lighted violins. In the "By a Waterfall" scene in *Footlight Parade* (1933) Berkeley developed geometric shapes, formed by women's legs, spread wide, displayed on a fountain. As Berkeley's routines became larger and more elaborate, the way he positioned the dancers became more sexually explicit. Dance numbers were also lengthy, many running more than ten minutes.

When Warner Bros. lost interest in producing big musicals, Berkeley went to Metro-Goldwyn-Mayer (MGM). There he directed three Mickey Rooney and Judy Garland films: *Babes in Arms* (1939), *Strike Up the Band* (1940), and *Babes on Broadway* (1941). By the mid-1940's, Berkeley-style musicals were beginning to be replaced by musicals in which the songs and dances did not stand outside the plot but were integrated into the action. His two water-ballet films, *Million Dollar Mermaid* (1952) and *Easy to Love* (1953), both starring Esther Williams, included outstanding examples of his style, but the days of the Hollywood musicals were waning. Berkeley retired in 1954, but in 1962, he created numbers for the circus film *Jumbo*. Renewed interest in Berkeley's dance extravaganzas led to the Broadway revival of 1925's *No, No, Nanette* in 1971, with Berkeley supervising the production.

Impact As Berkeley once stated, his aim during an era of breadlines, Depression, and war, was to make people happy. This he did through creating spectacles: over-the-top dance numbers that were often the most significant parts of the films. With innovative camera angles, over-large props, dancers in risqué costumes, and extended dance routines, Berkeley's style was stamped on the film musicals of the 1930's. During the decade, the energetic and creative Berkeley directed fourteen pictures, most of them musicals, and choreographed the musical numbers for twenty-one more. Berkeley provided entertainment during a time when a grim economic reality made his escapist visions a temporary relief for filmgoers.

Marcia B. Dinneen

Further Reading

Rubin, Martin. *Showstoppers: Busby Berkeley and the Tradition of Spectacle.* New York: Columbia University Press, 1993.

Siegel, Marcia B. "Busby Berkeley and the Projected Stage." *Hudson Review* 62, no. 1 (2009): 106-112.

Thomas, Tony, and Jim Terry. *The Busby Berkeley Book.* Greenwich, Conn.: New York Graphic Society, 1973.

See also Broadway musicals; Dance; *Forty-second Street.*

■ Bethune, Mary McLeod

Identification Educator; activist for minorities, women, and children; and presidential adviser
Born July 10, 1875; Mayesville, South Carolina
Died May 18, 1955; Daytona Beach, Florida

By the 1930's, Bethune was a well-known figure in the field of education, especially southern education. She was considered an expert in this area and influenced the quality of education for all children. In addition, she advised political figures about the African American community and its needs.

Mary McLeod Bethune's influence reached beyond southern education and into politics. A Republican, Bethune nevertheless supported Franklin D. Roosevelt in his run for president by encouraging the African American community, which was mostly Republican, to vote for him. Bethune's relationship with Eleanor Roosevelt granted her access to the president. The First Lady and Bethune became good friends and remained so until Bethune's death. President Roosevelt had African American advisers in several of his departments, and Bethune united them in a group referred to as the black cabinet (formally the Federal Council of Negro Affairs). Bethune would inform Roosevelt about the group's discussions.

During the 1930's, Bethune was extremely active. She was president of Bethune-Cookman College from 1932 to 1942 (and again from 1946 to 1947). In 1935, she founded the National Council of Negro Women in New York City to integrate African American women into their communities socially, politically, culturally, and economically. Bethune was the council's president from 1935 to 1949. In 1936, President Roosevelt appointed Bethune as an assistant in the National Youth Administration, and she later became the group's director of the Division of Negro Affairs. For her work, Bethune received several honorary degrees, medals, and decorations.

Impact The effect Bethune had on the education of African American youth is immeasurable, and her lasting legacy is Bethune-Cookman University. She worked tirelessly for the betterment of African American women and children and advised the Roosevelts on matters pertaining to the African American community. She was the first African American woman to have such influence and to use it well.

Linda Adkins

Further Reading

Holt, Rackham. *Mary McLeod Bethune: A Biography.* Garden City, N.J.: Doubleday, 1964.

Johnston, Lissa Jones. *Mary McLeod Bethune: Empowering Educator.* Mankato, Minn.: Capstone Press, 2007.

McKissack, Pat. *Mary McLeod Bethune: A Great American Educator.* Chicago: Children's Press, 1985.

See also Civil rights and liberties in the United States; Education; Elections of 1932, U.S.; Hoover, Herbert; Ickes, Harold; National Council of Negro Women; National Youth Administration; Racial discrimination; Roosevelt, Eleanor; Roosevelt, Franklin D.

Bingo became a fund-raising technique for many churches and religious organizations during the 1930's. In this 1938 image, Jersey City, New Jersey, mayor Frank Hague's parish priest, Father John Sullivan (center) presides over a bingo game. (Time & Life Pictures/Getty Images)

■ Bingo

Definition Game in which players try to match five numbers in a row on a square card to numbered balls selected randomly

Bingo had a major impact on the recreational culture of the 1930's. The game was immediately successful because of two main factors: Bingo allowed Americans to participate in a game that required little to no payment, and it presented the possibility of winning a prize.

Edwin Lowe, the creator of Bingo, stumbled upon the game by accident. While on a business trip, Lowe stopped at a carnival. Most of the carnival was shutting down; however, Lowe noticed a booth at which participants were playing a game called "beano." This early version of Bingo was played with a pitchman who called out numbers printed on wooden discs. Players used cards with numbers made by rubber stamps. Lowe noticed the enthusiasm of the people as they won the game. He began to construct his own version. In one early trial of the game's commercial viability, a woman became so excited about winning the game that she stammered "Bingo!" The name stuck, and Lowe released Bingo at one dollar to two dollars a game, depending on how many cards came with the set.

Just a month after Bingo was released, a priest from Pennsylvania complained to Lowe that the game was causing financial problems in his church. The priest had originally planned to use Bingo as a way to raise funds; but because the game could only have up to twenty-four cards, there could be up to ten winners. As a result, Lowe hired Carl Leffler, a mathematics professor, to create six thousand Bingo cards without repeated number groupings. Once Leffler completed this task, many more religious congregations held weekly Bingo meetings because of the profit involved.

Impact   Bingo had a significant financial and cultural impact on the United States during the 1930's. By 1934, ten thousand Bingo games were played on a weekly basis. It was also played in movie theaters. Movie theater owners used "Bingo night" as a way to lure customers. Because of Bingo's ties to gambling, judiciary measures across the country were taken in order to control "bank night," another name for Bingo. Nonetheless, the game continued to thrive throughout most of the 1930's.

Jennifer Stephenson

Further Reading

Currell, Susan. *The March of Spare Time: The Problem and Promise of Leisure in the Great Depression.* Philadelphia: University of Pennsylvania Press, 2005.

Dulles, Foster Rhea. *A History of Recreation: America Learns to Play.* New York: Meredith, 1965.

Kaye, Marvin. *The Story of Monopoly, Silly Putty, Bingo, Twister, Frisbee, Scrabble, Et Cetera.* New York: Stein and Day, 1973.

See also   Advertising in the United States; Fads; Hobbies; Recreation; Religion in the United States.

■ Birth control

Definition   Ability of parents to better manage the number of children they have by diminishing the chances of conception

The public fight for birth control led to federal court decisions allowing legal dispersal of information and methods, resulting in personal and professional opportunities for women and improved financial circumstances for struggling families during the Great Depression.

The birth control movement in the United States evolved with the growing interest in women's suffrage, socialism, and other contemporary progressive movements. Millions of poor and middle-class women appealed unsuccessfully to doctors and nurses for information and devices to limit the number of births in their families. During the Great Depression, this need became more urgent because of unemployment, starvation, and the perils of childbirth. While many upper-class women received birth control information discreetly from their doctors, the majority of American women did not. At the beginning of the 1930's, distribution of birth control and instructions pertaining to it were illegal.

Margaret Sanger's Contribution to the Movement Margaret Sanger coined the term "birth control," and her life became synonymous with the American birth-control movement. As a nurse, she received countless requests from women and men for birth control information. She lobbied for the abolition of the restrictive 1873 Comstock Law, which had outlawed the distribution of information or items pertaining to birth control sent through the U.S. mail system. The Comstock Law prevented distribution of Sanger's pre-1930's publications, *The Woman Rebel* and *The Birth Control Review,* and prevented the dispensation of birth-control devices to physicians.

Sanger founded the American Birth Control League in 1921 but left it in 1929 for the Birth Control Clinical Research Bureau (formerly the Clinical Research Bureau). In 1939, the two organizations merged to form the Birth Control Federation of America, which later became Planned Parenthood Federation of America.

Religious Reactions to Birth Control   Both Roman Catholic and many Protestant church organizations objected to birth control. Pope Pius XI chastised the notion in his 1930 encyclical *Casti Connubii,* which discussed the idea of Christian and chaste marriage using Catholic theology. Secularly, the *Journal of American Medical Association* promoted abstinence as the only effective method of limiting childbearing, although men could legally receive devices to prevent sexually transmitted diseases.

In 1933, the calendar rhythm method of birth control became well known after Leo J. Latz created fertility calendars based on the research of scientists Kyusaku Ogino and Hermann Knaus, who studied ovulation and fertility independently of each other during World War I. Using no barriers or chemicals, the rhythm method and its reliance on abstinence, was approved by the Catholic Church.

In spite of social and religious opposition, some churches such as the Anglican endorsed the concept of birth control, and Americans began speaking

The Supreme Court Legalizes Doctor-Approved Birth Control

Reproduced below is a portion of the U.S. Supreme Court's 1936 decision in United States v. One Package of Japanese Pessaries, *which allowed women to receive birth control from their doctors. One year later, the American Medical Association endorsed birth control.*

While it is true that the policy of Congress has been to forbid the use of contraceptives altogether if the only purpose of using them be to prevent conception in cases where it would not be injurious to the welfare of the patient or her offspring, it is going far beyond such a policy to hold that abortions, which destroy incipient life, may be allowed in proper cases, and yet that no measures may be taken to prevent conception even though a likely result should be to require the termination of pregnancy by means of an operation. It seems unreasonable to suppose that the national scheme of legislation involves such inconsistencies and requires the complete suppression of articles, the use of which in many cases is advocated by such a weight of authority in the medical world.

---

more freely about the controversial topic. Sanger and her fellow proponents had pushed for legalization for several years by this point, so many Americans became more sympathetic and less shocked by the idea of birth control. Supporters during the 1930's included First Lady Eleanor Roosevelt and American Birth Control League board member Katharine Martha Houghton, also known as the mother of actor Katharine Hepburn.

Economic Impact on Burgeoning Birth Control Industry In 1935, a federal court ruled that contraceptives could be advertised and sent through the mail, leading to a rash of advertising for "feminine products" in women's magazines such as *McCall's*. Interest in birth control led to a multimillion-dollar industry for companies discreetly touting birth-control products to married women. As the result of a lack of federal oversight or industry regulations, many of these methods did not work or were actually harmful to the women who used them; some caused chemical burns or death. Although the Federal Trade Commission could monitor claims, few companies were penalized for inaccurate advertising. For other methods of birth control, chemical and rubber advancements allowed for increased production and required less medical oversight.

Court Decisions Legalizing Birth Control In 1936, a U.S. Circuit Court of Appeals' decision in the *United States v. One Package of Japanese Pessaries* stated that

the Comstock Law was not authorized to interfere with medical information. Since pregnancy was characterized as a disease, women were legally allowed to obtain birth control from their physicians. The American Medical Association endorsed birth control in 1937.

Impact The legalization of birth control during the 1930's allowed families to plan for children, resulting in greater health and financial opportunities. Women no longer had to fear the toll of constant childbirth and vastly shortened life spans and were instead able to work longer and to provide better for their families . Family planning proved beneficial during World War II, when women were exhorted by the government to work in factories and other traditionally male jobs, which in turn led to the women's movement of the 1960's.

Bonnye Busbice Good

Further Reading

Gray, Madeline. *Margaret Sanger: A Biography of the Champion of Birth Control.* New York: Richard Marek, 1979. Details Sanger's professional efforts and private life as she became the major public proponent of legalized birth control.

Landmark Decisions of the Supreme Court, Vol. V. New York: Excellent Books, 1995. Follows judicial decisions on legalization of birth control.

Page, Cristina. *How the Pro-Choice Movement Saved America: Freedom, Politics and the War on Sex.* New

York: Basic Books, 2006. Measures impact of birth control movement on modern society, business, and economy.

Sanger, Alexander. *Beyond Choice: Reproductive Freedom in the Twenty-first Century.* New York: Public Affairs, 2004. Offers easily understood discussions of court cases regarding birth control during the 1930's.

Tone, Andrea, ed. *Controlling Reproduction: An American History.* Wilmington, Del.: Scholarly Resources, 1997. Collection of essays about accessibility of birth control in various demographics throughout movement's history; outlines Comstock Law.

See also Federal Trade Commission; Health care; Religion in the United States; Sex and sex education; Socialist parties.

■ Black, Hugo L.

Identification U.S. senator from Alabama who became an associate justice of the Supreme Court
Born February 27, 1886; Harlan, Alabama
Died September 25, 1971; Bethesda, Maryland

Black was Roosevelt's first appointment to the U.S. Supreme Court. He served for more than thirty years, during which time he was an avid advocate for First Amendment freedoms.

Before Hugo L. Black was elected U.S. senator as a Democrat from Alabama in 1926, he had experience as a police court judge, as a county prosecutor, and as a member of the executive committee of the American Bar Association. After Franklin D. Roosevelt won the presidency in 1932, Black established a reputation as a strong supporter of New Deal legislation. In at least one case, Black went beyond Roosevelt's agenda for economic recovery by proposing a bill that would require a thirty-hour week for any workers whose industries engaged in interstate commerce. Although Black's bill was not passed by Congress, Black supported most of Roosevelt's relief and recovery efforts, including the National Industrial Recovery Act (NIRA), the Agricultural Adjustment Administration, the Social Security Act, the Tennessee Valley Authority, and the National Labor Relations Act. Black's endorsement of the New Deal was consistent with some of his long-standing political philosophies. Even during his years in Alabama, Black had opposed concentrations of wealth and, unlike many of his fellow southerners, he believed that government could be an instrument for improving people's lives.

In 1937, after Roosevelt was reelected, he surprised many members of Congress by proposing legislation to expand the number of justices on the Supreme Court. The "court-packing" bill was provoked by Roosevelt's frustration with rigidly conservative justices who had declared several major New Deal laws, including the NIRA and the Agricultural Adjustment Administration, unconstitutional. Black was a quiet supporter of the proposal, which failed in the Senate. A vacancy on the Court arose, however, when Justice Willis Van Devanter, one of Roosevelt's critics, resigned his seat in May, 1937. Senator Joseph Taylor Robinson, who many believed was Roosevelt's first choice for the appointment, died suddenly of a heart attack. At that point, the president chose Black as his nominee for associate justice.

The Senate confirmed Black quickly after a brief debate. However, before the Court convened and Black took his seat, the *New York Times* broke the story that the new justice had been a member of the Ku Klux Klan (KKK). Black responded that he had resigned from the KKK before his election to the Senate and suggested that his membership in the group had been a youthful indiscretion. The extent of his allegiance to the KKK remained controversial. Some claimed that Black was an ardent participant in KKK activities between 1923 and 1926. Others argued that for Black, as for many young men of his class and region, KKK membership was a professional necessity. As most juries consisted of Klansmen, it would be foolhardy for a young lawyer with political ambitions to challenge them. Black's enthusiasm for Prohibition would also have been consistent with the Klan's position. On the other hand, his public record on racial issues was more mixed. Although he had opposed federal antilynching legislation, as an attorney he had successfully defended a number of black clients.

Despite the KKK controversy, Black took his seat as an associate justice in October, 1937, and remained on the Supreme Court until his retirement in 1971, only a week before his death at the age of 85. During that long tenure, Black was known for his outspoken defense of civil liberties, especially

Hugo L. Black (center) in June, 1938, visiting the U.S. Senate for the first time since joining the Supreme Court. He is welcomed by Alabma senators John H. Bankhead (left) and Lister Hill, who filled the seat from which he resigned. (Library of Congress)

the freedom of expression guaranteed in the First Amendment. He was a serious student of the Constitution and often referred to it as his "legal Bible." Black argued that the Fourteenth Amendment incorporated the entire Bill of Rights. Although that view did not prevail with his fellow justices, the Court ruled that the Fourteenth Amendment selectively incorporated most of the provisions of the Bill of Rights. Conversely, Black did not believe that unwritten rights, such as the right to privacy, were implied by the Constitution.

Impact As a strong civil libertarian, Black supported many decisions that reversed policies of racial segregation, including *Brown v. Board of Education* in 1954. At the same time, he believed the Court should defer to legislatures regarding economic issues.

Mary Welek Atwell

Further Reading

Abraham, Henry. *Justices, Presidents, and Senators: A History of United States Supreme Court Appointments from Washington to Bush II.* Lanham, Md.: Rowman and Littlefield, 2007.

Dunne, Gerald T. *Hugo Black and the Judicial Revolution.* New York: Simon and Schuster, 1977.

Frayer, Tony, ed. *Justice Hugo Black and Modern America.* Tuscaloosa: University of Alabama Press, 1990.

Irons, Peter. *A People's History of the Supreme Court: The Men and Women Whose Cases and Decisions Have Shaped Our Constitution.* New York: Penquin, 2006.

See also Civil rights and liberties in the United States; New Deal; Racial discrimination; Roosevelt's court-packing plan; Supreme Court, U.S.

■ *Black Empire*

Identification   Serialized science fiction novel
   imagining the triumph of black nationalism
   across the world
Author   George S. Schuyler, using the pseudonym
   Samuel I. Brooks
Date   Serialized from 1936 to 1938; published in
   book form in 1991

Originally published as two sequential serials in the Pittsburgh Courier, Black Empire *is a science-fiction adventure story about an African American genius who builds
an organization and uses advanced science to retake Africa
from its European colonizers. Among the first science-
fiction stories written by an African American, the tales
provided African Americans with a cathartic response to Italy's violent conquest of Ethiopia—the last black African-
ruled domain to be occupied by white Europeans. Although
the tales satirized Marcus Garvey's Back-to-Africa movement, their popularity suggests that African Americans
found in these fantasies of worldwide black power justifica-
tions for resurgent racial pride.*

Between November, 1936, and July, 1937, the journalist George S. Schuyler published "The Black
Internationale: Story of Black Genius Against the
World" under the pen name Samuel I. Brooks in the
nationally distributed black newspaper *Pittsburgh
Courier* in thirty-three weekly installments. In response to the popularity of that serial among readers, Schuyler followed with a twenty-nine-chapter sequel, "Black Empire: An Imaginative Story of a Great
New Civilization in Modern Africa." It ran in the *Courier* from October, 1937, to April, 1938. Afterward,
both serials were essentially forgotten, along with
the identity of their author, until 1991, when the editors of the Marcus Garvey Papers at the University of
California at Los Angeles arranged for the stories'
publication under the single title, *Black Empire.*

In "The Black Internationale," Carl Slater, a newspaper reporter, is kidnapped by a black organization
when he observes the murder of a white woman by a
black man, who turns out to be the organization's
leader, Dr. Henry Belsidus. Slater is gradually introduced to the international dimensions of the organization, which is dedicated to destroying the United
States. Almost all the social problems plaguing African Americans—theft, murder, even poverty—turn
out to be part of a grand scheme to fund the organi-

zation's build-up of weapons, planes, and a variety of
advanced, science-fiction-type military weapons. At
the same time, Slater observes the systematic murder and torture of traitors. After subduing the
United States, the Black Internationale turns its attention to repopulating the West African nation of
Liberia with African Americans, a reference to the
country's origins as a nineteenth century haven for
free African Americans and former slaves from the
United States.

"Black Empire" picks up where the previous serial
ends. The Internationale consolidates its power
across the African continent by imposing draconian
regulations regarding religious worship, diet, and
clothing. At the same time, diseased rats and cyclo-
tron-bearing airplanes are unleashed on Europe,
devastating the population across the continent and
allowing Belsidus's organization to seize control of
the African continent.

Impact   "The Black Internationale" and "Black Empire" did not have an immediate influence on the
burgeoning field of science fiction. However, their
commentary on the fascist underpinnings of all
forms of nationalism, including Garvey's program,
was prophetic. Schuyler's stories exposed the authoritarianism underlying religious and secular nationalism that would later be embodied in the Nation of Islam and the Black Panthers.

Tyrone Williams

Further Reading

Ferguson, Jeffrey B. *The Sage of Sugar Hill: George S.
   Schuyler and the Harlem Renaissance.* New Haven,
   Conn.: Yale University Press, 2005.
Hill, Robert A., and R. Kent Rasmussen. "After-
   word." In *Black Empire*, by George S. Schuyler. Bos-
   ton: Northeastern University Press, 1991.
Neptune, Harvey. "At Sea: The Caribbean in 'Black
   Empire.'" *Small Axe: A Caribbean Journal of Criti-
   cism* 20 (June, 2006): 269-275.
Tal, Kali. "That Just Kills Me." *Social Text* 20, no. 2
   (Summer, 2002): 65-83.

See also   African Americans; Airships; *Black No
More*; Civil rights and liberties in the United States;
Cyclotron; Literature in the United States; Nation of
Islam; Schuyler, George S.; Science fiction.

■ Black hole theory

Definition   Theory outlining a region of space where the gravitational field is so powerful that no matter or radiation can escape

The theory of black holes, emerging from Albert Einstein's general theory of relativity, predicted that regions in space exist where gravity is so strong that everything surrounding the region, including light, is pulled inward. Since no light is emitted from black holes, they cannot be seen directly. Their existence must be inferred by studying their effect on the motion of surrounding objects.

In 1916, astronomer Karl Schwarzschild found the first exact solution to Einstein's general relativity equations. It demonstrated the possible existence of a nonrotating, spherically symmetrical black hole. Between 1925 and 1930, white dwarf stars were found. A white dwarf has a mass similar to the Sun, but is only about the size of the Earth. In 1930, physicist Subrahmanyan Chandrasekhar determined that the maximum possible mass of a white dwarf was 1.44 times the mass of the Sun. Based on this model, he further demonstrated that the formation mechanism for black holes was the collapse of more massive stars.

In 1934, Walter Baade and Fritz Zwicky predicted that the star collapse proposed by Chandrasekhar would strip the electrons from the atoms that make up the star. This would pack the nuclei together to form a neutron star. Neutron stars would be ten to fifteen miles in diameter, with densities approaching a billion tons per cubic inch. Using these results and those of Chandrasekhar, J. Robert Oppenheimer and others predicted in 1939 that stars with masses exceeding three solar masses would collapse into black holes once their thermonuclear sources of energy were exhausted. This work refocused physicists and astronomers on developing improved models of black holes and on looking for evidence of their existence in the Milky Way Galaxy and beyond.

Impact   The developing theory of black holes led astronomers to look for evidence that they really exist. As time progressed and better astronomical tools emerged, both theoretical and experimental evidence demonstrated their existence. Indications were that massive black holes formed by the collapse of great clusters of stars exist at the center of galaxies. Sharp imaging of nearby large galaxies by the Hubble Space Telescope confirmed that most of these galaxies do have supermassive black holes at their centers.

Alvin K. Benson

Further Reading

Melia, Fulvio. *Cracking the Einstein Code: Relativity and the Birth of Black Hole Physics.* Chicago: University of Chicago Press, 2009.

Vishveshwara, C. V. *Einstein's Enigma or Black Holes in My Bubble Bath.* New York: Springer, 2006.

See also   Astronomy; Einstein, Albert; Neutron star theory; Physics; Radio astronomy.

Indian American astrophysicist Subrahmanyan Chandrasekhar, pictured in 1939, was a leading figure in the development of the black hole theory. (©Bettmann/CORBIS)

■ Black Monday

The Event Date on which the U.S. Supreme
Court struck down three major pieces of New
Deal legislation
Date May 27, 1935

*The Black Monday decisions overturned the Frazier-Lemke
Farm Bankruptcy Act and the enforcement power of the National Recovery Administration (NRA).*

On May 27, 1935, the U.S. Supreme Court issued
unanimous rulings in three important cases. Chief
Justice Charles Evans Hughes had hesitated to an-
nounce three such decisions on one day, but Justice
Louis D. Brandeis advised him to go ahead.

In *Humphrey's Executor v. United States*, the Court
had to deal with President Franklin D. Roosevelt's
October, 1933, removal of William Humphrey from
the Federal Trade Commission because of political
disagreements. Roosevelt justified his action on the
basis of the 1926 decision *Myers v. United States* (upholding the removal of a postmaster) and the 1903
decision *Shurtleff v. United States* (upholding the removal of an appraiser). Humphrey had died, but his
executor continued the case. Reflecting Brandeis's
dissent in *Myers*, Sutherland ruled Roosevelt's action
unconstitutional because it violated the separation of
powers put in the Constitution to prevent autocracy.

Sutherland argued that the postmaster in *Myers*
was an executive appointee and that the appraiser in
Shurtleff, though he theoretically could not be removed without proper cause, did not have a specific
term. By contrast, the Federal Trade Commission
(FTC) was structured by Congress as an independent agency with specific, staggered seven-year
terms for its commissioners. Sutherland also argued
that the FTC's role was partly legislative and judicial,
further underscoring the need for independence.

In *Louisville Joint Stock Land Bank v. Radford*, the
Court overturned the Frazier-Lemke amendment to
the Federal Farm Bankruptcy Act of 1934. This had
allowed the government to take over farm mortgages if farmers were unable to make payments. The
Court ruled this to be a violation of the Fifth Amendment ban on taking private property when applied
to existing mortgages. Brandeis pointed out that the
government should instead have bought the mortgage using eminent domain.

In *Schechter Poultry Corp. v. United States*, the Court
ended the enforcement power of the NRA. The
Schechter brothers were poultry dealers in Brooklyn who ignored the NRA's labor codes and were also
accused of selling sick chickens. The government
sued to compel them to obey the NRA codes, winning in the lower courts.

Hughes pointed out that the Schechter brothers
were neither directly involved in interstate commerce nor directly affected it; thus, they were not
subject to federal supervision. He also pointed out
that the statute creating the NRA, the National Industrial Recovery Act, delegated too much authority
too vaguely to the president, failing even to define
what "fair competition" meant. Finally, Hughes argued that an emergency such as the Depression did
not create extra government power.

Justice Benjamin N. Cardozo, joined by Justice
Harlan Fiske Stone, wrote a concurring opinion in
Shechter harshly criticizing the vague language and
excessive delegation in order to explain overruling
the NRA in *Shechter* after he had been the lone dis-
senter in *Panama Refining Co. v. Ryan*, the previous
case overturning an NRA code. He was also wary of
Hughes's constitutional distinction between direct
and indirect effects on interstate commerce.

Impact The Black Monday decisions eliminated
the NRA as well as certain bankruptcy provisions.
This forced Congress to pass new laws, such as the
National Labor Relations Act, designed to accomplish similar goals by constitutional means. President Roosevelt was angry about the use of the interstate commerce clause in the *Schechter* case and the
implication that he abused his power in removing
Humphrey. Black Monday thus helped set the stage
for the court-packing struggle of 1937.

Timothy Lane

Further Reading

Arkes, Hadley. *The Return of George Sutherland: Restor-
ing a Jurisprudence of Natural Rights.* Princeton,
N.J.: Princeton University Press, 1994.
Pusey, Merlo J. *Charles Evans Hughes.* Vol. 2. New
York: Macmillan, 1951.
Urofsky, Melvin J. *Louis D. Brandeis: A Life.* New York:
Pantheon Books, 2009.

See also Agriculture in the United States; Brandeis, Louis D.; Federal Trade Commission; Hughes,
Charles Evans; *Humphrey's Executor v. United States*;
National Recovery Administration; New Deal; *Schechter Poultry Corp. v. United States*; Supreme Court, U.S.

■ *Black No More*

Identification   Novel about a black scientist who creates a formula to turn black people white
Author   George S. Schuyler
Date   Published in 1931

Black No More was published in the wake of the demise of the Harlem Renaissance and at the onset of the Great Depression. Its themes of race obsession, class warfare, and cynical opportunism undercut the foundation of racial pride at the center of the renaissance while heralding the political and labor unrest that defined the Depression.

When Harlem resident Max Disher is rejected by a white woman, Helen Givens, at a nightclub, he vows revenge. He reads a news story about a black scientist, Dr. Junius Crookman, who has created a formula to turn black people white. Despite his misgivings, Disher decides to be converted. As Matthew Fisher, he is exposed to undisguised white racism. Shocked, he moves south to exploit white labor organizations and white business owners, pitting them against one another. He also exploits Christian fundamentalism, through the figure of Reverend Givens, Helen's father, to stifle political unrest among the poor Caucasians. After marrying Helen, Fisher discovers that the Negro Social Equality League (modeled after the National Association for the Advancement of Colored People) is working with the Knights of Nordica (modeled after the Knights of Labor) and the Anglo-Saxon Association of America (modeled after the Ku Klux Klan) to destroy Crookman's wildly successful business. At the novel's conclusion, Helen's pregnancy and a coalition of black and white organizations threaten to expose Fisher as a double agent in multiple senses of the phrase.

Impact   *Black No More* was one of several novels of the 1930's that predicted the intensification of racial and class warfare. The novel faded from public view during the resurgence of black racial pride during the 1960's and 1970's. Its republication at the end of the twentieth century signaled that African Americans, more or less secure within the fabric of American society, could once again laugh at themselves and, most important, analyze racial shibboleths from a disinterested critical perspective.

Tyrone Williams

Further Reading

Joo, Hee-Jung Serenity. "Miscegenation, Assimilation, and Consumption: Racial Passing in George Schuyler's *Black No More* and Eric Liu's *The Accidental Asian*." *MELUS* 33, no. 3 (Fall, 2008): 169-190.

Kuenz, Jane. "American Racial Discourse, 1900-1930: Schuyler's *Black No More*." *Novel: A Forum on Fiction* 30, no. 2 (Winter, 1997): 170-192.

See also   *Black Empire*; Communism; Great Depression in the United States; Harlem Renaissance; Labor strikes; Literature in the United States; Lynching; National Association for the Advancement of Colored People; Schuyler, George S.

■ *Blondie* comic strip

Identification   Humorous newspaper comic strip focusing on domestic situations
Artist   Murat "Chic" Young
Date   Launched in 1930

One of the most popular comic strips of the decade, Blondie *successfully blended elements of romance and domestic comedy. The title character's move from 1920's-style flapper to housewife and her husband Dagwood's fall from rich scion to working stiff mirrored American life in the Depression.*

Blondie, which debuted September 8, 1930, originally centered around a flighty young woman named Blondie Boopadoop (the strip predated the cartoon character Betty Boop) and her suitors, including the young playboy Dagwood Bumstead. Its creator, writer, and artist, Murat "Chic" Young, was a specialist in "pretty girl" strips; he had abandoned the successful *Dumb Dora* for *Blondie*.

As the Depression tightened its grip, Blondie's frivolity and Dagwood's wealthy lifestyle lost their appeal to hardworking, economically stressed Americans. Young responded by giving the strip a domestic turn: Blondie and Dagwood fell in love, and their relationship became more serious. In 1933, Blondie and Dagwood married, and Dagwood was disowned by his wealthy family and forced to take a job in the construction company of skinflint boss J. C. Dithers. The loss of Dagwood's parents—typical comic-strip tycoons—as characters meant that fantasy elements, such as the elder Bumsteads' enormous mansion, disappeared. Blondie and Dagwood's marriage was a highly publicized event, as was the birth of their first child, Alexander, the following year. Avoiding some of the cliches of the "comic-strip marriage" genre, such as the henpecked husband and domineering wife of George McManus's *Bringing up Father*, *Blondie* successfully portrayed a happily married couple dealing with everyday problems such as bills and the neighbors.

Blondie was syndicated by King Features. Like other successful strips of the time, *Blondie* reached into other media, including radio, comic books, and films. Along with other King strips, it first appeared in a comic book in 1937, in *Ace Comics* number one. The first *Blondie* film, titled *Blondie*, came out in 1938, and three more followed the next year.

Impact   *Blondie* is one of the longest-running comic strips in history. Its simple formula of a husband and wife, two children, a dog, and neighbors proved adaptable over decades of social, cultural, technological, and economic change.

William E. Burns

Further Reading

Walker, Brian. *The Comics Before 1945*. New York: H. N. Abrams, 2004.

Young, Dean, and Rick Marschall. *Blondie and Dagwood's America*. New York: Harper & Row, 1981.

See also   *Apple Mary*; *Blondie* films; Comic strips; *Dick Tracy*; *Flash Gordon*; Hairstyles; *L'il Abner*; *Little Orphan Annie*; Newspapers, Canadian; Newspapers, U.S.

■ *Blondie* films

Identification   Series of low-budget films based on a popular comic strip
Creator   Murat "Chic" Young
Director   Frank R. Strayer
Dates   Syndicated from 1938 to 1950

Columbia's Blondie *series consisted of twenty-eight feature films—the most in motion-picture series history. The films presented a comic take on a typical American family as the United States was emerging from the Great Depression, entering World War II, and going through postwar changes that characterized the middle of the twentieth century in the United States.*

Like the King Syndicate comic strip created by Chic Young in 1931, the Columbia Pictures *Blondie* series

centered on the foibles of a middle-class, small-town American family. While Blondie Bumstead (Penny Singleton) was the titular main character, her hapless spouse, Dagwood (Arthur Lake), was also central to the series' comedy, which was personified in his plaintive signature cry, "Blondeeeee," that opened every film.

Stock situations that were transferred from the comic strip to the films included Blondie perpetually urging Dagwood to ask for a raise from Mr. Dithers (Jonathan Hale), his crabby boss at a construction company; Dagwood's ineptness at household chores; his need for long naps and his chronic tardiness; his enormous sandwiches; his unfortunate financial endeavors; and his loving, if inept, attempts to accomplish almost anything. Although a kind and loving wife and mother, Blondie constantly struggles to improve the family's social and economic condition, often leading Dagwood into confusing turns of events. Both characters frequently create comic webs of lies to cover up problems, but everything turns out well by the end of each film. As the film series progressed into the 1940's, the films shifted their emphasis from the economic challenges of the 1930's to deal with changes in American society precipitated by World War II.

In contrast to many of the long-running film series of the 1930's and 1940's, *Blondie* retained its three principal cast members, Singleton, Lake, and Larry Simms, who played Dagwood "Baby Dumbling" Bumstead, Jr., throughout the series. Singleton, who started her film career during the mid-1930's as a brunette named Dorothy McNulty, changed her name and dyed her hair blonde for the series. She appeared in few other films during the course of the series and made only one film after it ended, *The Best Man* (1964). Lake, however, had acted in many films prior to the series, and occasionally acted in non-*Blondie* films. His last feature film appearance was the series finale, but he revived the Dagwood character in 1957 for a short-lived National Broadcasting Company (NBC) television series. At the same time they were making the *Blondie* films, Lake and Singleton recreated their roles on the long-running *Blondie* radio series.

Hale portrayed Dagwood's boss, Mr. Dithers, in fourteen of the films, offering a more dignified and somewhat less stern alternative to the character in the comic strip. Irving Bacon was the perfect embodiment of Mr. Beasley, the frustrated and often

In a scene from the 1939 film Blondie Takes a Vacation, *Blondie, played by Penny Singleton (left), speaks with her son (Larry Simms).* (Hulton Archive/Getty Images)

blindsided neighborhood mail carrier, in thirteen of the pictures.

In line with many of the major studios' low-budgeted B-pictures, the *Blondie* films ran between sixty to seventy-five minutes in length and were made by a regular group of directors and writers. They also utilized some of Columbia's rising stars such as Rita Hayworth, Janet Blair, and Larry Parks. Only two of the films did not include the name "Blondie" in their titles—*It's a Great Life* and *Footlight Glamour,* both made in 1943 when Columbia reportedly was losing interest in the films. The series resumed in 1945 with *Leave It to Blondie,* and the final entry was *Beware of Blondie* (1950), released at a time in which the burgeoning television industry was about to become the primary source for family-centered comedies.

Impact   *Blondie* was one of several series produced by the major Hollywood studios from the mid-1930's to the 1950's that centered on the lives of characters who were promoted as average American families. Metro-Goldwyn-Mayer had the successful A-budgeted *Hardy Family* series, Paramount had *The Aldrich Family,* Fox *The Jones Family,* and Republic *The Higgins Family.* Studio series films, especially those centering on family life, were the forerunners of the television domestic situation comedies that flourished during the 1950's and 1960's. *Blondie* presented a comic prototype of American family life. Its quirky stock characters, bumbling father, social-climbing mother, and precocious children have continued as staples of television into the twenty-first century.

Patricia King Hanson

Further Reading

Young, Chic. *Twenty-five Years with Blondie: A Silver Anniversary Volume.* New York: Simon & Schuster, 1958.

Young, Dean. *Blondie: The Bumstead Family History.* New York: Thomas Nelson, 2007.

See also *Apple Mary*; *Blondie* comic strip; *Dick Tracy*; Film; Film serials; *L'il Abner.*

■ Blood banks

The Event Establishment of the first facility for collecting and storing blood plasma for use in blood transfusions
Date March 15, 1937
Place Cook County Hospital, Chicago, Illinois

Although scientists have done research into the properties of blood since the Middle Ages, the ability to extract, store, and transfuse human blood into other persons was not developed until the early twentieth century, and this technology gave rise to the creation of storage facilities known as "blood banks." In 1937, the first American blood bank was established at the Cook County Hospital in Chicago, Illinois.

An essential fluid for human life, blood cannot be synthesized outside a living human body. However, blood from a healthy person can often be used effectively by another person who is in need of this life-sustaining fluid. Every day, many sick and injured people need blood or blood products in order to stay alive and heal. In times of disaster and war, the need for blood and blood products increases dramatically. A blood bank is a health-care process in which a healthy person deposits a small portion of his or her blood, usually about one pint, in a sanitary blood-drawing process. The blood is then stored under sanitary conditions for a period of time. Later, the blood is transfused into another person.

The ability to store human blood and preserve it so that it can be transfused into patients rested on nineteenth and early twentieth century research developments and discoveries, such as the existence of fibrinogen, fibrin, the Rh factor, and enzymes. Safeguarding blood for transfusion has always been a central problem. The precious liquid is unstable, and fresh supplies need to be available for unforeseen medical emergencies.

The use of stored blood was begun in 1918 by Oswald H. Robertson, a World War I physician, who found blood could be kept virtually intact for several days by storing it at low temperatures, from 35.6 to 39.2 degrees Celsius. John Lundy, the director of anesthesiology at the Mayo Clinic in Rochester, Minnesota, began storing blood for later use at that facility in 1935. However, the first large blood bank was established at the Cook County Hospital in Chicago in 1937 by Bernard Fantus, the director of therapeutics at the hospital.

Impact Since the development of the first permanent blood bank during the 1930's, the process of collecting, storing, and transfusing human blood has made major contributions to the advancement of medicine. Blood banks and their products have saved countless lives. Also, research conducted with human blood has led to many medical discoveries that have helped save many lives and have helped improve the quality of life for millions of people.

David M. Brown

Further Reading

Hillier, Christopher D., et al. *Blood Banking and Transfusion Medicine.* New York: Elsevier, 2002.

Rabbits, J. A., et al. "Mayo Clinic and the Origins of Blood Banking." *Mayo Clinic Proceedings* 82, no. 9 (2007): 1117-1118.

Starr, Douglas P. *Blood: An Epic History of Medicine and Commerce.* New York: Knopf, 1998.

Wailoo, Keith. *Drawing Blood: Technology and Disease Identity in Twentieth Century America.* Baltimore: Johns Hopkins University Press, 1999.

See also Health care; Heart-lung machine; March of Dimes; Medicine; Polio; Typhus immunization.

Bonnie and Clyde. See **Barrow, Clyde, and Bonnie Parker**

■ Bonus Army March

The Event   Depression-era movement of World
War I veterans who sought government relief
through the early payment of cash bonuses that
had been promised them for their wartime
service

Date   1932

Place   Washington, D.C.

The Bonus Army March contributed to Franklin D. Roose-velt's election and planted the seeds for New Deal programs such as the Civilian Conservation Corps and the Service-men's Readjustment Act of 1944 (also known as the G.I. Bill of Rights).

The "Bonus movement" was a grassroots effort by
veterans hoping to force the U.S. government to pay
bonuses for military service. The group marched in
Washington, D.C., to pressure the government,
which, in turn, used the U.S. Army to disperse the
marchers. This tactic was a public-relations disaster
for the Hoover administration.

In the post-World War I economic downturn
many felt that soldiers had suffered an unreasonable
economic burden. While workers' wages had risen
during the war, those who had enlisted out of patriotism or been drafted earned low wages. In the early
1920's, Congress introduced bills for providing soldiers with monetary compensation for these "lost
wages" that veterans would have
received if they had not served.
This "adjusted compensation"
required additional taxes, a prospect that was anathema to the
fiscally conservative Republican
government. These bonus bills
were opposed by both Presidents
Warren G. Harding and Calvin
Coolidge. In 1924, supporters
passed the Adjusted Compensation Act of 1924 over a presidential veto. This created a fund for
compensation of $1 per day for
those who did not go overseas (to
a maximum of $500 per veteran)
and $1.25 for those who served
overseas (to a maximum of $625
per veteran). Fiscal conservatives
demanded that these monies be
largely issued as certificates to be

redeemed when they matured in 1945. Additionally,
each veteran was to receive $50 and could get loans
against 22.5 percent of the remaining "adjusted
compensation." While this compensation was called
a "bonus," it really was more akin to an insurance or
retirement policy.

Organizing the Bonus Expeditionary Forces   The
bonus generally satisfied veterans until the Great Depression's financial strains caused widespread unemployment and repossessions. Among the unemployed and homeless were many veterans whose
compensation certificates constituted their final
asset. Many called for an early issuance of the bonus to either pay off their debts or to start over. In
March, 1932, an unemployed veteran from Oregon
named Walter W. Waters proposed that veterans go
to Washington, D.C., and hold a march to underscore their plight and generate political pressure for
a bill to allow veterans to cash in certificates in 1932.
To highlight their patriotic credentials, the marchers called themselves the Bonus Expeditionary
Forces (BEF), an allusion to American forces in
World War I, which were called the American Expeditionary Forces.

While most Americans were sympathetic to the
BEF, Hoover's administration was hostile. The head
of the Bureau of Investigation (later the Federal Bureau of Investigation) insisted that the BEF was filled

Bonus Marchers fighting with police in Washington, D.C. (NARA)

with communists. Waters demanded discipline within the BEF and expelled radical marchers. Between May and July, 1932, more veterans arrived in Washington, D.C.; they built a temporary camp in the Anacostia Flats area south of the city. Between twenty thousand and twenty-five thousand marchers, including wives and children, lived in either the camp or in abandoned buildings downtown.

Hoover's Response The BEF marched repeatedly to support pro-bonus bills in Congress. On June 17, 1932, a bill previously passed by the House was defeated in the Senate. Rising tensions resulted in a scuffle with police on July 28, in a BEF-occupied building in Washington, D.C. Hoover's garbled instructions to Major General Douglas MacArthur, the U.S. Army's chief of staff, concerning this skirmish were to order the Army to disperse the BEF. Tanks, cavalry, bayonets, and tear gas were turned on the BEF, and as soldiers swept through the camp, the temporary shelters were burned. The numerous photographers and reporters on hand publicized this so-called Battle of Anacostia Flats.

Impact While MacArthur later claimed that his swift action had forestalled armed revolt, the images of tanks and tear gas turned on loyal veterans was damning. Hoover's tepid responses to the deepening Depression virtually guaranteed defeat in 1932, and the suppression of the BEF significantly benefited Roosevelt's campaign. While Roosevelt also vetoed bonus legislation, he understood the BEF's grassroots appeal. One of the most popular organizations formed from Roosevelt's New Deal policies was the Civilian Conservation Corps, which ultimately employed many veterans. In World War II many pro-bonus congressmen worried that the postwar future of the United States would be hurt by similar bonus movements. To avoid this, Congress passed the G.I. Bill of Rights to institutionalize policies to prepare veterans for an easier reintegration into civilian life and preempt the claim that wartime service disadvantaged U.S. soldiers.

Kevin B. Reid

Further Reading

Barber, Lucy G. *Marching on Washington: The Forging of an American Political Tradition.* Berkeley: University of California Press. 2002. Illustrates how the BEF introduced the tradition of marching on the nation's capital for political change.

Daniels, Roger. *The Bonus March: An Episode of the Great Depression.* Westport, Conn.: Greenwood, 1971. The standard treatment of the BEF's misadventures in Washington, D.C.

Dickson, Paul, and Thomas B. Allen. *The Bonus Army: An American Epic.* New York: Walker, 2004. Accessible narrative, emphasizing the BEF's interracial composition.

Keene, Jennifer. *Doughboys, the Great War, and the Remaking of America.* Baltimore: Johns Hopkins University Press, 2001. Insightful chapter on the BEF in this analysis of how World War I transformed the United States.

Lisio, Donald J. *The President and Protest: Hoover, Conspiracy, and the Bonus Riot.* New York: Fordham University Press, 1994. This work investigates Hoover's fears of the BEF and the consequences of MacArthur's actions.

See also Civilian Conservation Corps; Communism; Congress, U.S.; Elections of 1932, U.S.; Great Depression in the United States; Hoover, Herbert; MacArthur, Douglas; Roosevelt, Franklin D.; Unemployment in the United States.

■ Book publishing

By the 1930's, book publishing was an established industry in the United States, and books continued to be major sources of entertainment in hard economic times. During the early years of the decade, publishers sought ways to reduce the size of their lists, prices, and production costs; to adjust sales policies with bookstores in order to grow and thrive in the face of new economic pressures; and to continue to provide the public with affordable and entertaining books.

In spite of the tough economic times ushered in by the stock market crash of 1929 and the ensuing Depression that dogged many Americans through the 1930's, many Americans escaped the travails of their own times by escaping to other cultures or to other historical periods in the pages of popular books. In 1931 and 1932, Pearl S. Buck's *The Good Earth* (1931), a story about missionaries in China, sat atop the fiction best-seller lists. One year later, Hervey Allen's twelve-hundred-page epic of the Napoleonic era, *Anthony Adverse*, knocked Buck out of first place and stayed at the top of the list for two years, selling more than 700,000 copies by 1936. The biggest seller by far during the 1930's was Margaret Mitchell's epic tale of love and loss in the Civil War, *Gone with the Wind* (1936). It sold for three dollars when first published and sold more than one million copies in six months; sales were so brisk that in one day alone the novel sold more than fifty thousand copies. The book was number one on the best-seller lists for 1936 and 1937 and has never been out of print.

Other best-selling fiction of the decade reflected the preoccupations of American culture. James Hilton's *Lost Horizon* (1933) presented a utopian fantasy about an ideal and carefree world called Shangri-La, while his *Goodbye, Mr. Chips* (1934) captured the sentimental nostalgia for an earlier time and place. Lloyd Douglas's *Magnificent Obsession* (1932) and *Forgive Us Our Trespasses* (1932) as well as Willa Cather's *Shadows on the Rock* (1931) reflected the culture's deepening interest in religion. As the decade drew to a close, John Steinbeck's *The Grapes of Wrath* (1939), his epic tale of Dust Bowl migration, looked at the environmental crisis, its place within the legacy of the Depression, and its effects on class structure.

In 1930, the nonfiction best sellers reflected the preoccupation with ideas and the lives of great historical figures, which carried over from the 1920's. However, readers quickly turned their attention to popular games such as bridge, reading the *Contract Bridge Blue Book* (1931) by Ely Culbertson and others that covered the subject. Also popular were books on American history and democracy such as James Truslow Adams's *The Epic of America* (1931), which was on best-seller lists from 1931 through 1932. Adams' two-volume *The March of Democracy* (1932 and 1933) stayed on the lists from 1932 through 1933. Frederick Lewis Allen's *Only Yesterday* (1931) was another popular nonfiction book. By the end of the decade, readers were turning their thoughts away from the American scene and looking toward international events. John Gunther's *Inside Europe* (1936) and *Inside Asia* (1939) provided a glimpse into the larger historical, political, and economic structures of geopolitically relevant areas of the world. In 1939, Americans were so fascinated with Germany's new chancellor, Adolf Hitler, that they catapulted his *Mein Kampf* (1925-1926; English translation, 1939) onto best-seller lists. Although publishers faced various challenges during the 1930's, the depth and breadth of the books that they continued to publish reflected their success in providing entertainment and information for a growing reading public.

Trends in Publishing   Many of the challenges that publishers faced during the 1930's were comparable to those faced by publishers in the twenty-first century. During the 1930's, publishers had to assess how many people would read a particular book to determine how many copies of the book they should print. Since the publishers seldom sold the books directly to customers themselves, they sold to book departments of major department stores, which then set their own selling price on the books. The advent of book clubs, such as the Book-of-the-Month Club, while often guaranteeing the wide distribution of particular titles, raised issues regarding fair and equitable discounts to retailers.

Between the end of World War I and 1930, the total number of new titles published was more than ten thousand, a notable increase from earlier periods. Numerous publishers recognized that the growth of the publishing industry could only be sustained by maintaining a healthy margin between production and distribution costs and the retail price of books. The growth of book clubs and the advent of independently owned book shops, such as the Brentano's chains, gave many publishers hope that multiple channels would enable them to sell more books. The increased number of retail outlets allowed for greater price control as well. However, by the early 1930's, publishers recognized that one response to the economic crisis was to publish fewer books; thus many publishers did begin to trim their lists. Nonetheless, most publishers remained optimistic, even as the economic crisis deepened, and looked for ways to reduce prices, to advertise more broadly, and to get their books into the small bookshops, drug stores, and department stores.

A number of publishers recognized that reducing prices on their books was the key to publishing success, not only because they were concerned about the future of their businesses in an uncertain economy but also because Americans continued to buy books in spite of the economic crisis; publishers understood that reduced prices would result in more sales. In 1930, three publishers—Simon and Schuster, Coward-McCann, and Farrar and Rinehart—announced a variety of pricing strategies for new titles to enable the publishers to compete for readers; that began a decade-long debate regarding pricing.

In addition, the retail prices at which the publishers sold their books were as low as the retail prices of magazines; the publishers were thus encouraging readers to buy books rather than magazines as their reading material. For example, Simon and Schuster announced that it would sell its top fiction titles for the fall season at one dollar, rather than the previously announced two dollars or two dollars and fifty cents, and it instituted generous returns policies for booksellers.

Even as individual publishers sought to regulate their practices in order to ensure success, the National Association of Book Publishers (NABP) appointed Oliver H. Cheney to conduct an economic survey of the book industry. In 1932, the Cheney Report recommended numerous reforms in book publishing, encouraging the book industry to engage in smarter business practices to bring it in line with other major industries. Among other recommendations, the report called for better systems of record-keeping among publishers and bookstores, the standardization of manufacturing materials, the elimination of best-seller advertising, campaigns to encourage rental library readers to buy books, the elimination of inside deals and consignment plans (long a feature of inequitable distribution practices in the publishing industry), and the elimination of the practice of price-cutting by booksellers. While some publishers responded negatively to the sarcastic and sensational nature of the report, others such as Alfred A. Knopf and Alfred Harcourt announced that they would study the report and perhaps adopt some of its recommendations. Overall, book publishing in the United States during the 1930's succeeded relatively well because it maintained a healthy margin between costs and profits by keeping administrative and production costs low and retail prices in line with the market value of the books. By 1939, book-publishing companies were prepared to meet the challenges that the early years of World War II brought to the industry.

New Publishers and University Presses In spite of the economic crises of the 1930's, a number of new book publishers opened for business, a testimony to the liveliness of the book business in general and to the American hunger for books in particular. Zondervan Publishing House, the unofficial publishing arm of the Dutch Reformed Church, opened in 1931 and first published books of biblical inter-

pretation and commentary. In 1933, Sheed and Ward, a well-known British publisher, opened an office in New York. Founded by Roman Catholic activist Maisie Ward and Frank Sheed, the company published a number of important Catholic writers, such as Léon Bloy, Hilaire Belloc, Jacques Maritain, and François Mauriac. These writers probed not only deep religious questions but also philosophical and literary matters, all in an elegant literary style. In 1935, Paul Grabbe established Basic Books and published important books—such as Marian Lockwood and Arthur Draper's *Earth Among the Stars* (1935)—for thirty-five cents each.

James Laughlin started one of the most famous publishing houses of the 1930's when he launched New Directions Press in a stable in Norfolk, Connecticut. While at Harvard, Laughlin began publishing *New Directions Anthology*, a compilation of writing by modernist and avant-garde writers. A prolific letter writer, Laughlin corresponded with most of the twentieth century's most famous writers about the nature of literature and other matters. He published, among other writers, William Carlos Williams, Ezra Pound, Delmore Schwartz, and Tennessee Williams. When the standard print run for small presses was around thirty-five hundred, he sold more than seventy thousand copies of Thomas Merton's *New Seeds of Contemplation* (1961) and fifteen thousand copies of Williams's *A Streetcar Named Desire* (1947). Among other prominent publishers that opened during or soon after the 1930's were Stackpole Books (1936), Watson-Guptill (1937), Schocken Books (1938), and Pantheon Books (1941).

In spite of the uncertain economy, twelve new university presses opened during the 1930's: the University of Michigan Press (1930); MIT Press, Dartmouth College Publications, and Brown University Press (1932); University of New Mexico Press (1933); LSU Press (1935); Rutgers University Press and the University of Pittsburgh Press (1936); the University of Wisconsin Press (1937); the University of Georgia Press, the Press of Western Reserve University, and the Middlebury College Press (1938); and the Catholic University of America Press (1939). Older established university presses launched new initiatives during the decade. Yale University Press published Carl L. Becker's *The Heavenly City of the Eighteenth Century Philosophers* (1932), John Dewey's *A Common Faith* (1934), and Robert M. Hutchins's

The Higher Learning in America (1936). Harvard University Press acquired the Loeb Classical Library in 1933 and established the series of books by Greek and Latin authors as standards of classical scholarship. Columbia University Press published the *Columbia Encyclopedia* in 1935, a landmark event in publishing; this was the first-ever one-volume encyclopedia to be compiled in the United States. Recognizing that their contributions to society could grow beyond the scholarly community, numerous university presses launched regional books that often sold thousands of copies.

Impact Although it faced substantial economic challenges during the 1930's, the book-publishing industry in the United States creatively and consistently addressed those financial issues to sustain itself and develop new strategies for becoming more profitable, more efficient, and more productive. During the 1930's, Americans bought books of wide-ranging subject matter. Popular genres included nostalgic fiction, as in *Gone with the Wind*; self-help, as in *How to Win Friends and Influence People* (1937) by Dale Carnegie; recreation, as in Culbertson's *Contract Bridge Blue Book*; and spirituality, as in *The Importance of Living* (1937) by Lin Yutang.

Henry L. Carrigan, Jr.

Further Reading

Dickstein, Morris. *Dancing in the Dark: A Cultural History of the Great Depression.* New York: W. W. Norton, 2009. Demonstrates that novels and films helped both expose and assuage the national trauma of the Depression.

Epstein, Jason. *Book Business: Publishing Past, Present, and Future.* New York: W. W. Norton, 2001. Although not directly about book publishing during the 1930's, Epstein's account of the evolution of the publishing industry provides a helpful overview of perennial publishing issues from the perspective of an industry veteran.

Kazin, Alfred. *Starting Out in the Thirties.* Boston: Atlantic Monthly Press, 1965. Memoir from one of greatest American literary critics, offering electrifying insight into what it meant to grow up as an omnivorous reader in the Depression.

Schiffrin, André. *The Business of Books: How International Conglomerates Took Over Publishing and Changed the Way We Read.* London: Verso, 2000. Part memoir and part history of publishing that offers a long view of the history of publishing.

Tebbel, John. *A History of Book Publishing in the United States. Volume II: The Golden Age Between Two Wars, 1920-1940.* New York: R. R. Bowker, 1978. Standard and indispensable guide to the history of American book publishing.

See also Literature in Canada; Literature in the United States; Magazines; Newspapers, Canadian; Newspapers, U.S.

■ Boulder Dam

The Event Construction of a large, multipurpose dam on the Colorado River
Also known as Hoover Dam
Dates Built 1931-1936
Place near Boulder City, Nevada

Boulder Dam, later known as Hoover Dam, was a primary facilitator of the development of the Southwest, particularly Southern California, but was also a central force in ameliorating the economic impact of the Great Depression.

The development of the semiarid Southwest was aided by the construction of numerous large dams, such as Arizona's Roosevelt Dam, completed in 1911. In 1922, two California congressmen, Senator Hiram Warren Johnson and Representative Philip D. Swing, introduced legislation for the construction of a dam in Boulder Canyon on the Arizona-Nevada border. It received the support of Secretary of Commerce Herbert Hoover but failed to pass into law. It finally passed in 1928 and was signed on December 28, by President Calvin Coolidge.

Construction did not begin until 1931, when Hoover was president. The previous year, Secretary of the Interior Ray Lyman Wilbur formally designated the dam as "Hoover Dam," a first for an incumbent president. By then, the Great Depression was well underway, and the project was considered to be a jobs-creation endeavor.

A new town, Boulder City, Nevada, was constructed for the many workers and soon became the third largest city in Nevada. For geological reasons the dam's site was changed from Boulder Canyon to Black Canyon, eight miles farther down the Colorado River. With the election of Franklin D. Roosevelt in 1932 and the creation of the New Deal, activity on the dam increased as part of the Works Progress Administration (WPA), which provided

Boulder Dam

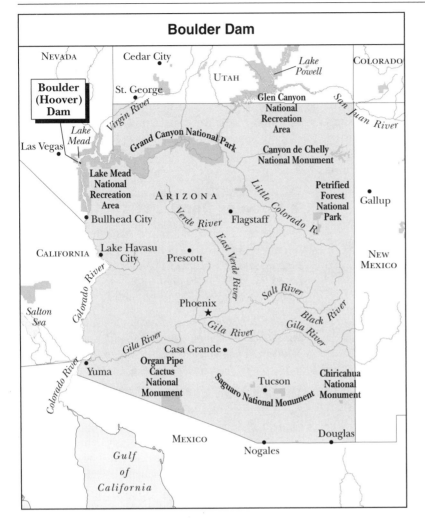

270 miles to Los Angeles. The Metropolitan Water District constructed the Colorado River Aqueduct, at a cost of $220 million, which brought water to Southern California. The All-American Canal provided water to the lower Colorado River basin to the Coachella and Imperial valleys.

Johnson and Hoover, both California Republicans, were bitter political foes, and when Harold Ickes, a Johnson ally, was named secretary of the interior under Roosevelt, the Hoover Dam was renamed Boulder Dam in 1933. In 1947, after World War II, Congress voted unanimously to rename it Hoover Dam.

Encouraged by the federal government, Boulder Dam became a major tourist destination. In 1937, Ickes's WPA established the United States Travel Bureau to boost recreational travel. During the construction of the dam, viewing platforms were provided so that spectators could watch the transformation of the river and the desert. The waters behind the dam formed Lake Mead, named for Elwood Mead, who was head of the U.S. Bureau of Reclamation during the dam's construction. The location was designated the Boulder Dam National Recreation Area in 1936 under the National Park Service. This was done to bring tourists to the site for recreation. Campsites and cabins were constructed, and boating, fishing, and swimming facilities were provided. The 1930's was the era of the automobile, and the Boulder Dam Service Bureau provided free maps. It also showed a free film that chronicled the construction of the dam.

$38 million in funds. Construction concluded in 1936, two years ahead of the predicted date. More than fifty-two hundred workers were employed by the federal government on the project, and more than one hundred died during the construction. When finished, the dam was the world's largest concrete facility; it rises 726 feet above the Colorado River and is 1,244 feet long. The construction cost was $49 million.

Initially, the dam was to be in an unadorned architectural style. However, in the end, it had an Art Deco style, with Native American motifs in the walls and the floors. Two million horsepower of electricity were produced by the dam's turbines and generators, and the Boulder Power Transmission System, built by the Los Angeles Department of Water and Power at a cost of $23 million, brought electricity

Impact Hoover Dam is not only a great American icon of construction and engineering but also a symbol of the American ability to transform challenging environments. However, with the rise of the environmental movement, by the 1980's, the dam and its associated projects were criticized as encouraging too much population growth and development, far beyond the capacity of the natural environment of the semidesert Southwest.

Eugene Larson

Further Reading

Duchemin, Michael. "Water, Power, and Tourism: Hoover Dam and the Making of the New West." *California History* 86, no. 4 (Fall, 2009).

Dunar, Andrew J. *Building Hoover Dam: An Oral History of the Great Depression.* New York: Twayne, 1993.

Hiltzik, Michael A. *Colossus: Hoover Dam and the Making of the American Century.* New York: Free Press, 2010.

See also   Architecture; Empire State Building; Grand Coulee Dam; Great Depression in the United States; Hoover, Herbert; Ickes, Harold; Natural resources; Tennessee Valley Authority; Travel; Works Progress Administration.

■ Boxing

Following the excitement and excess of the Roaring Twenties, the Great Depression adversely affected virtually all segments of American society, from industry to sports. During the early 1930's, boxing, although long a perennially popular sport, suffered subpar attendance and often lackluster competition. However, it rebounded after the middle of the decade, thanks primarily to the heroics of several larger-than-life fighters.

With the stock market crash of 1929, the first golden age of boxing—an era of huge audiences, million-dollar prizes, and big-name fighters such as Jack Dempsey, Jess Willard, and Gene Tunney—came to a sudden end. Though promotional money became scarce, attendance dropped, and purses grew smaller than before, the sport remained active even during the worst years of the economic slump. Through the depths of the decade, boxing retained its popularity, as evidenced by numerous, generally well-received boxing films released during the time, bookended by *The Champ* (1931) and *Golden Boy* (1939). Though individuals scrimping to afford the basics of food and shelter could not afford to attend events, the rise of radio as a broadcast medium allowed them to gather in public places; listen to free, blow-by-blow ringside accounts of matches; and perhaps place small wagers on the outcome.

Making Ends Meet During the Depression   Desperate times meant resorting to desperate measures for talented competitors and would-be pugilists. With no other marketable skills and few alternative jobs available, known boxers were forced to compete more frequently than they had previously to earn a living. Even the aging former heavyweight champion Jack Johnson came out of retirement to fight occasionally during the 1930's on what was called "the tank-town circuit." Fairs and carnivals of the period often featured experienced former prizefighters ready to take on anyone willing to risk injury for the chance to win a few dollars by staying upright for a specified length of time.

Fight clubs sprang up, pitting supposed amateurs against one another for token honors; professional boxers sometimes fought under false names to supplement their incomes. Winners of the typically three-round bouts were awarded gold-plated watches that could be sold back to management for cash. Amateurs and professionals in disguise could box several times a week, and if they were triumphant and stayed healthy, might take home as much as forty dollars per week—reasonable wages during the depths of the Depression, a time when tens of thousands of unemployed Americans subsisted on public relief.

Young African Americans, particular victims of high unemployment during the Depression, were especially attracted to boxing as a means of earning money. In the Deep South, they were fodder for promoters who staged popular "battle royals": brutal free-for-alls in which few rules applied and the fighter left standing at the end was declared winner. For the enjoyment of mostly white audiences, black competitors were sometimes blindfolded in the "battle-blind," a demeaning, slapstick form of entertainment that was mercifully short-lived.

Amateur Boxing   If professional boxers despaired during the early years of the Great Depression, amateurs thrived. Boxing was seen as a respectable diversion for unemployed young persons who could learn about daily training regimens, diet, discipline and other concepts that might be profitably applied once the economy improved. For those fortunate enough to attend college, there were hotly contested, national-team boxing championships sponsored by the National Collegiate Athletic Association (NCAA) after 1932. For elite amateur athletes capable of competing on an international level, there was boxing at the 1932 and 1936 Summer Olympics. Begun in Chicago and New York during the late 1920's, the Golden Gloves tournaments blossomed, expanding to many geographical venues by the mid-1930's. Numerous professionals came from the amateur ranks of Golden Glove boxers during the decade of the 1930's and afterward; these boxers included 1929's 126-pound national champion Barney Ross; the 175-pound champ of 1934, Joe Louis; and the 160-pound champion of 1939, Ezzard Charles.

Professional Boxing Although fights in the light- and middleweight divisions were seldom as popular with spectators as heavyweight bouts during the De-

pression, they often produced exciting, entertaining matches featuring precedent-setting white, African American, and Latino athletes. Tony Canzoneri, Ross, and Henry Armstrong each won world championships in three different weight divisions during the 1930's. Armstrong, an African American considered one of the best fighters ever, held world titles at three different classifications simultaneously, a feat that will never be duplicated because modern boxing rules do not permit a single person to hold multiple championships at different weights. Also in these weight divisions were the first world champions from Cuba, junior lightweight and featherweight Eligio "Kid Chocolate" Sardiñas, and Puerto Rico, bantamweight Sixto Escobar, crowned in 1931 and 1934, respectively.

The heavyweight division did not attract much interest during the early years of the Depression. Com-

Max Baer (left) boxing with Joe Louis at New York City's Yankee Stadium in a 1935 fight. (AP/Wide World Photos)

bined ticket sales for seven heavyweight championship bouts fought in the United States between 1930 and 1935 could not equal the box-office receipts of the 1927 Dempsey-Tunney fight. Despite reduced ticket prices at Madison Square Garden, average gates for boxing events in 1933 were one-third of what they had been in 1928.

Symptomatic of the difficulties of drawing audiences to heavyweight matches was the 1930 title fight. Vacated in 1928, the championship was contested between German fighter Max Schmeling and Jack Sharkey, a National Boxing Association-sanctioned contender. Sharkey was disqualified for a low blow, and Schmeling was declared champion—the first heavyweight titleholder to win on a foul. In 1932, Sharkey reclaimed the championship from Schmeling, winning on points in a dull, fifteen-round bout.

Heavyweight prospects began to improve in 1933 with the introduction and skillful promotion of the huge, Italian-born former circus strongman Primo Carnera, nicknamed the "Ambling Alp." He knocked out Sharkey to claim the championship amid rumors that the fight, and several of his subsequent title defenses, were fixed to rig betting odds. In 1934, the colorful, high-living Jewish fighter Max Baer—sporting a Star of David on his boxing trunks—demolished Carnera over eleven rounds to take the heavyweight title. Carnera's meteoric but brief career would later inspire the 1959 boxing film *The Harder They Fall*, in which Humphrey Bogart had his last film role, as a bogus boxer's promoter.

In 1935, journeyman boxer James J. Braddock, who had earlier retired from competition after breaking his hand, became the symbol of the embattled working man struggling to survive in troubled times. A family man forced to go on public relief while working part time as a longshoreman, Braddock returned to the ring. After a couple of victories, he was given a shot at the heavyweight championship and made good, beating Baer in a unanimous decision and earning the nickname "Cinderella Man." Braddock retained the title until 1937, when Louis knocked him out to claim the world championship. Louis's victory would set the stage for one of the most anticipated title bouts in history, a rematch against German Schmeling, who had defeated Louis in a nontitle fight in 1936. Though the two men were actually friends, the fight was billed as a combat of American democracy versus the forces of German Nazism, a war between good and evil, and a test of racial superiority. The actual fight, staged on June 21, 1938, before more than sixty thousand screaming fans in Yankee Stadium, was anticlimactic: Louis knocked out Schmeling in the first round.

Impact   Like the global economy, boxing slumped during the early years of the Depression but recovered strongly before World War II. Heavyweight champion Louis, the best-known, best-loved boxing icon of the decade and a symbol of American strength and African American pride, successfully defended his title numerous times. Before retiring from the ring in 1947, he served as a major contributing factor in keeping boxing an important part of American culture. By that time, television had begun to supplement radio in bringing the excitement of prizefighting to an ever-increasing audience, which helped set the stage for the highly promoted, big-money international matches that characterized later eras of boxing.

Jack Ewing

Further Reading

Boddy, Kasia. *Boxing: A Cultural History*. London: Reaktion Books, 2009. Collection of short studies gathered from many sources. Presents a comprehensive overview of the history of boxing from its earliest days to the early twenty-first century from a variety of viewpoints: writers, spectators, and competitors. Illustrated.

Fleischer, Nat, Sam Andre, and Nigel Collins. *An Illustrated History of Boxing*. New York: Citadel, 2002. Covers the most outstanding representatives from every weight class over the entire history of professional boxing.

Page, Joseph S. *Primo Carnera: The Life and Career of the Heavyweight Boxing Champion*. Jefferson, N.C.: McFarland, 2010. Biography of one of the most colorful and controversial individuals ever to wear the heavyweight boxing championship belt.

Roberts, Randy. *Joe Louis: Hard Times Man*. New Haven, Conn.: Yale University Press, 2010. Written by a Pulitzer Prize-nominated biographer and professor of history. Well-researched biography of the boxer who became an American hero.

Schaap, Jeremy. *Cinderella Man: James J. Braddock, Max Baer, and the Greatest Upset in Boxing History*. Boston: Houghton Mifflin, 2005. Inspiring story of an obscure Depression-era fighter who overcame incredible odds to become world heavyweight champion.

Schulberg, Budd. *Ringside: A Treasury of Boxing Reportage.* Lanham, Md.: Ivan R. Dee, 2007. Illustrated collection of stories, biographies, and articles from a variety of sources.

See also African Americans; Braddock, James J.; Gambling; Great Depression in the United States; Income and wages in the United States; Louis, Joe; Olympic Games of 1932 (Summer); Olympic Games of 1936 (Summer); Racial discrimination; Radio in the United States; Sports in the United States.

■ Braddock, James J.

Identification American boxer who held world heavyweight title from 1935 to 1937

Born June 7, 1905; New York, New York

Died November 29, 1974; North Bergen, New Jersey

During the Depression, Americans craved, paradoxically, both hard truth and escapism in film, literature, and sport. No sport captured that duality better than boxing, then America's favorite sport, and no champion better represented the people and his time than Braddock. His comeback to win the heavyweight championship, against the longest odds, is a great "Cinderella story." He gave Americans hope and inspiration when they desperately needed it.

At the age of twenty, James J. Braddock, born James Walter Braddock, was New Jersey's amateur light-heavyweight and heavyweight champ. His manager, Joe Gould, changed Braddock's middle initial to "J" in homage to past champions. Braddock's pro career was uneven, mostly because he broke his right hand repeatedly. Nonetheless, before the stock market crash of 1929, Braddock had a promising future.

In 1929, Braddock lost his life savings when the banks failed, and he began losing more fights than he won. His winning purse had once been as high as seventeen thousand dollars per fight; as the Depression set in, he was sometimes paid less than two hundred dollars for a fight. In 1933, he broke his hand again and was forced to retire. He walked up to twelve miles a day looking for work, toiling as a longshoreman whenever possible. His destitute family lived in a basement, at times without utilities. He was forced to register for government relief, receiving twenty-four dollars a month, and sent his children to live with relatives.

Gould hounded boxing promoters until Braddock was given a chance against rising star John "Corn" Griffin in June, 1934. Braddock's hard labor had transformed him into a rock-solid 191 pounds; he won by technical knockout. Five months later, Braddock fought John Henry Lewis and delivered another upset. This led to another stunning win against Art Lasky in March, 1935. In three fights, Braddock went from welfare recipient to heavyweight contender. After German champion Max Schmeling passed on the bout, Braddock was named challenger to the heavyweight champion, Max Baer.

Baer was younger, taller, and heavier than Braddock and reportedly had killed two men in the ring. He was also an unmotivated, undisciplined boxer and Hollywood film star known as "the playboy clown." As Braddock trained seriously, sportswriters wrote about his life on the dole, making him a national hero. Nonetheless, the ten-to-one odds against him were the longest in boxing history.

On June 13, 1935, Braddock's relentless ability to take and throw a punch wore down the lethargic Baer in fifteen rounds. Braddock won the heavyweight championship by unanimous decision, earning the nickname "Cinderella Man" from sportswriter Damon Runyon. The inspiring champion bought a house for his family and paid back the $367 in relief money he had received—a remarkable gesture that cemented his popularity during his two-year reign.

On June 22, 1937, Braddock faced the youngest challenger to the heavyweight crown, twenty-three-year-old phenomenon Joe Louis. Although Braddock was only the second man (after Schmeling) to knock down Louis, Louis knocked out Braddock in the eighth round—the only time he was ever counted out. Louis's victory was a seminal moment in African American history, and many consider him to be the greatest heavyweight of all time. Louis called Braddock the most courageous man he ever fought.

In 1938, Braddock retired with his body and popularity intact. In 1954, he received boxing's James J. Walker Award in recognition of his long and meritorious service to the sport. He was inducted posthumously into the International Boxing Hall of Fame in 2001. His final boxing record includes eighty-six fights, forty-five wins (twenty-seven by knockout), twenty-three losses, eleven no decisions, five draws, and two no contests.

Impact Americans have always looked to the underdog for inspiration and affirmation of their cultural belief that hard work, self-reliance, and perseverance can be personally transformative. In 2005, Braddock's story was revived in the Oscar-nominated film *Cinderella Man*, starring Russell Crowe. The film introduced a new generation to his inspiring life.

Eric T. Bellone

Further Reading

DeLisa, Michael C. *Cinderella Man: The James J. Braddock Story.* Wrea Green Preston, Lancashire, England: Milo Books, 2005.

Margolick, David. *Beyond Glory: Joe Louis vs. Max Schmeling, and a World on the Brink.* New York: Alfred A. Knopf, 2005.

Schaap, Jeremy. *Cinderella Man: James J. Braddock, Max Baer, and the Greatest Upset in Boxing History.* Boston: Houghton Mifflin, 2005.

See also Boxing; Great Depression in the United States; Louis, Joe; Sports in the United States.

■ Brains Trust

Identification Scholarly group formed to advise Roosevelt during the 1932 presidential campaign

The Brains Trust served a vital function in the 1932 presidential campaign by educating Franklin D. Roosevelt on the problems caused by the Great Depression facing the American economy. The group's ideas, discussions, memorandums, and speech writing helped Roosevelt to better formulate his later New Deal program.

The use of university professors or experts to help a political candidate or officeholder is an established tradition in the United States. Woodrow Wilson, for example, used academic advisers to help him with the Versailles Conference. Later, John F. Kennedy formed his famous Brains Trust to help formulate his New Frontier programs in 1960 and 1961.

Roosevelt is most credited with the idea of developing a Brains Trust to help him in his presidential bid in 1932. The concept was first suggested by Samuel Rosenman in March, 1932, and was carried out by Doc O'Connor, Roosevelt's law partner, and Raymond Moley, a political science professor at Columbia University. Moley selected individuals for the trust, and Rosenman held individual interviews before a candidate was brought to Roosevelt. Moley used this arrangement to bring to Roosevelt two Columbia University professors—Rexford Guy Tugwell, a professional economist and expert on agricultural affairs, and Adolf A. Berle, Jr., who was best known for his publication *The Modern Corporation and Private Property* (1932), with Gardiner C. Means. Moley, Tugwell, and Berle served as the original Brains Trust throughout the 1932 presidential campaign.

The Brains Trust worked closely with Roosevelt throughout the prenomination campaign, the nominating convention, and the electoral campaign. Each worked on different aspects of the American economy and the Great Depression to educate Roosevelt and to help him formulate possible programs to be implemented should he be elected. Tugwell, for example, served as the specialist on agricultural matters, suggesting to the candidate the importance of considering domestic allotment as a possible program for the American farmers. Moley worked on a number of issues, ranging from international affairs to domestic policy, the latter with Berle. All three wrote memorandums and speeches, held extensive discussions with Roosevelt, and offered ameliorative programs to resolve the Great Depression.

During the nominating convention, the roles of the Brains Trust were diminished; political experts such as Louis McHenry Howe and James Aloysius Farley instructed Roosevelt on what to say and to do. After the campaign began, the Brains Trust worked again to educate Roosevelt on as many issues as needed. By election day, its work proved fruitful, as Roosevelt won the presidency.

Although the election was over and the Brains Trust disbanded, each of the original three members helped Roosevelt with the New Deal. Moley went into the State Department and stayed there until the London Economic Conference, at which point his views were no longer in agreement with Roosevelt's. Moley became one of Roosevelt's harshest critics. Tugwell, on the other hand, remained part of the New Deal staff in the Department of Agriculture and later the Resettlement Administration. Berle was more of an outside consultant to Roosevelt during the New Deal years and later.

Others claimed to be Brains Trusters or associate members. The list of such individuals was incredibly long. However, among the more important members of the later group were Tom Corcoran and Ben Cohen, both of whom played vital roles in Roosevelt's implementation of the second New Deal in 1935.

Impact The Brains Trust had a significant influence on Roosevelt and his New Deal. Moley, Tugwell, and Berle not only helped educate the Democratic candidate on economic issues but also played vital roles in the implementation of New Deal policy. The idea of the Brains Trust resurfaced when Kennedy put together his own group.

Subsequent presidents have had academic advisers who give advice and develop policy programs. All of these academic political advisers are the inheritors of the 1930's academics who assisted Roosevelt.

Michael V. Namorato

Further Reading

Namorato, Michael. *Rexford G. Tugwell: A Biography.* New York: Praeger, 1988.

Rauchway, Eric. *The Great Depression and the New Deal: A Very Short Introduction.* New York: Oxford University Press, 2008.

Schwarz, Jordan. *The New Dealers: Power Politics in the Age of Roosevelt.* New York: Vintage Press, 1994.

Tugwell, Rexford. *The Brains Trust.* New York: Viking Press, 1968.

See also Agricultural Adjustment Acts; Bank Holiday; Blood banks; Dust Bowl; Elections of 1932, U.S.; Federal Food, Drug, and Cosmetic Act of 1938; Great Depression in the United States; London Economic Conference; *Modern Corporation and Private Property, The*; National Industrial Recovery Act of 1933; New Deal.

■ Brandeis, Louis D.

Identification U.S. Supreme Court justice
Born November 13, 1856; Louisville, Kentucky
Died October 5, 1941; Washington, D.C.

Possessing a diverse combination of experiences rare in the annals of American law, Brandeis was a successful lawyer in private practice, an advocate for social justice, and an influential U.S. Supreme Court justice. As a member of the Supreme Court, he transformed his sympathy for the plight of average working people into clearly articulated principles of law guaranteeing personal constitutional rights.

The son of Jewish immigrants, Louis D. Brandeis entered Harvard Law School at the age of nineteen. In 1879, he settled in Boston, and in 1890, he and his law partner, Samuel Warren, wrote one of the most quoted law-review articles in history, "The Right to Privacy," published in the *Harvard Law Review.* Brandeis's great success as a private lawyer afforded him the opportunity to work on social causes, generally without compensation.

In 1907, Brandeis agreed to defend Oregon's maximum-hour law for women. He wrote a Supreme Court brief that devoted less space to legal precedents and more to empirical data reflecting the eco-

Louis D. Brandeis (left) and his wife on the porch of their home on the occasion of Brandeis's eighty-third birthday on November 13, 1939. (Library of Congress)

nomic and social realities that supported the legislation. This style of legal writing became known as a "Brandeis Brief" and influenced the fundamental nature of legal argumentation in the Supreme Court and other appellate courts. In early 1908, a unanimous Supreme Court upheld the Oregon law in *Muller v. Oregon.*

Although Brandeis was not a religiously observant Jew, he became a committed Zionist dedicated to the creation of a Jewish state in Palestine. During the European Holocaust of the 1930's, he donated more than $250,000 to that cause from the wealth he had amassed while practicing law. Meanwhile, in 1916, he became the first Jew nominated to the U.S. Supreme Court. His nomination by President Woodrow Wilson drew vigorous opposition from probusiness senators and corporate leaders, who feared that he would bring his progressive, prolabor views to the Court. His confirmation battle was also stained by anti-Semitic attacks, which were disguised as inquiries into his "fitness" to serve. Both *The New York Times* and *The Wall Street Journal* opposed his nomination, and former U.S. president and later chief justice of the United States William Howard Taft called his nomination "an evil and a disgrace." Six former presidents of the American Bar Association and the president of Harvard University denounced his nomination. Nevertheless, Brandeis was confirmed by the Senate in a 47-22 vote.

After being seated on the Court, Brandeis became first a protégé and later the able ally of the legendary justice Oliver Wendell Holmes, Jr. Together they dissented from efforts by the Court's majority to second-guess state legislatures on social and economic regulations and to limit individual constitutional rights. In the 1927 case of *Whitney v. California,* Brandeis opposed a California antisyndicalism law that suppressed free speech and gave eloquent voice to the historic meaning and purpose of the First Amendment. Brandeis also recognized a right to privacy in *Olmstead v. United States* (1928), in which he cited as evidence the founders of the Constitution in their effort to protect beliefs, thoughts, and emotions of Americans.

During the 1930's, Brandeis generally supported President Franklin D. Roosevelt's policies. However, in 1935, he joined a unanimous Court in striking down the National Industrial Recovery Act because he found that Congress had exceeded its constitutional authority. This did not signal that Brandeis had become an economic conservative. Rather, he thought the act was poorly drafted and overly broad. After 1936, Brandeis consistently supported Roosevelt until he retired from the Court in 1939. He died two years later.

Impact   Brandeis remained on the Court for nearly twenty-three years and left a legacy as one of the most celebrated and forward-thinking justices who has ever served. He was deeply committed to the Constitution as a source of personal liberty and justice.

Stephen F. Rohde

Further Reading

Purcell, Edward A., Jr. *Brandeis and the Progressive Constitution: Erie, the Judicial Power, and the Politics of the Federal Courts in Twentieth Century America.* New Haven, Conn.: Yale University Press, 2000.

Strum, Phillipa. *Brandeis: Beyond Progressivism.* Lawrence: University Press of Kansas, 1993.

Urofsky, Melvin I. *Louis D. Brandeis: A Life.* New York: Pantheon Books, 2009.

See also   Anti-Semitism; Civil rights and liberties in the United States; *Erie Railroad Co. v. Tompkins*; Jews in the United States; Roosevelt's court-packing plan; Supreme Court, U.S.

■ Breadlines and soup kitchens

Definition   Centers for the distribution of free food to the hungry

With millions homeless or without income during the Great Depression, simple and direct measures for the relief of hunger sprang up in various cities. Although these measures were criticized as stopgaps, they eased the plight of many desperate people.

Providing free food to impoverished citizens has been seen as a duty by numerous civilized societies. At various times, this work has been done by government entities, religious or civic groups, labor unions, and, occasionally, by individuals. During the 1930's, breadlines and soup kitchens became a feature of most urban landscapes.

Typically, breadlines formed outside a given location, with the operators handing out bread of varying quality and sometimes other basic foodstuffs. Recipients took the food home or, sometimes, ate on the spot. Soup kitchens served simple meals, usually

Unemployed men form a breadline during the Depression. (Library of Congress)

in indoor facilities. Soup was the default choice for menus because it is economical and expandable. Large quantities can be cooked and served with a minimum of utensils, and soup recipes can be stretched or varied depending upon what donations come in. The Depression-era cooks at the kitchens were adept at making hot meals from a variety of inexpensive ingredients. Hot dishes such as macaroni and cheese, casseroles, and simple sandwiches were often served. Coffee, tea, or fruit drinks and desserts such as cake or pastries were added when available.

Any place preparing and serving meals to large numbers of people requires a kitchen for food preparation, certain hygiene precautions, and several people to manage, cook, and serve the meals. For this reason, soup kitchens were usually run by established groups. Food was obtained from donations, government commodity banks, retail outlets' surpluses, and community gardens. Although the majority of sponsoring groups were nonprofit and well

established, some unexpected operators also ran food programs. The gangster Al Capone set up a soup kitchen in Chicago that served around three thousand meals per day. The meals there were said to be excellent.

Many impoverished people were ashamed to take free food. Men hid their faces when photographed in breadlines. On the other hand, at least one Depression survivor wrote a essay about the camaraderie of waiting in a local breadline on Saturday afternoons. Neighbors exchanged gossip and jokes and, after a few hours in line, collected high-quality bread, milk, butter, and cheese to take home to their families. Songs, stories, and other popular lore circulated about the experience.

Impact   Some criticize soup kitchens as "band-aid" measures or say they undercut self-reliance. However, the reasons for feeding the hungry often outweigh the objections. Feeding the hungry is not only a tenet of most religions but also a tactic for combating social unrest. The Depression-era soup kitchens provided a model for future relief projects during hard times. Breadlines that handed out basic foodstuffs later mutated into a large government-commodities program that distributes surplus food items to both schools and individuals. In the midst of economic distress, food pantries and their predecessors continue to aid the impoverished.

Emily Alward

Further Reading

Marchant, John, et al. *Bread: A Slice of History.* Charleston, S.C.: History Press, 2009.

Terkel, Studs. *Hard Times: An Oral History of the Great Depression.* New York: The New Press, 2000.

See also Aid to Dependent Children; Capone, Al; Federal Emergency Relief Administration; Food stamps; Unemployment in Canada; Unemployment in the United States.

■ *Breedlove v. Suttles*

The Case U.S. Supreme Court ruling upholding a state poll tax as a condition to voting

Date December 6, 1937

Poll taxes were a common tool used by southern states to limit political participation of African Americans, as well as poor Caucasians, from the late nineteenth century until the mid-twentieth century. The Breedlove *decision gave the policy of exclusion constitutional support.*

Payment of a tax as a condition for registering to vote had been widespread when the Constitution was written but had largely fallen out of favor by the time the Fourteenth Amendment was added in the wake of the American Civil War. Revival of the practice in southern states late in the nineteenth century was part of a broader movement to disenfranchise African American voters, many of whom were poor and could not afford the tax.

Georgia required proof of payment as a condition to register to vote for men between the ages of twenty-one and sixty. Women who did not vote and the blind were exempted from the tax. When election officials refused to register a white man for failure to pay the tax, he brought suit challenging the law under the privileges and immunities and equal protec-

tion clauses of the Fourteenth Amendment, as well as under the Nineteenth Amendment that had granted women the right to vote. A unanimous Supreme Court rejected these claims, finding the law did not impose arbitrary burdens on male voters.

Impact Because the plaintiff was white, the issue of race discrimination in voting was not directly raised. However, the practice of imposing poll taxes was widely understood to be a means of diminishing African American political participation. The Twenty-fourth Amendment to the Constitution banned poll taxes for federal elections after 1964. Two years later, in *Harper v. Virginia Board of Elections*, the Supreme Court overruled *Breedlove*, declaring poll taxes to violate the equal protection clause of the Fourteenth Amendment. By then, only four states maintained a poll tax.

John C. Hughes

Further Reading

Lawson, Stephen F. *Black Ballots: Voting Rights in the South, 1944-1969.* New York: Columbia University Press, 1976.

McDonald, Laughlin. *A Voting Rights Odyssey: Black Enfranchisement in Georgia.* New York: Cambridge University Press, 2003.

See also African Americans; Civil rights and liberties in the United States; Supreme Court, U.S.; Voting rights.

■ *Bringing Up Baby*

Identification Comedy film about a scatterbrained heiress and a scholarly paleontologist

Director Howard Hawks

Date 1938

One of Howard Hawks's zaniest films, Bringing Up Baby *refueled the screwball comedy craze that began in 1934. It gave Depression audiences an escape into comic nonsense with a plot that involved a loony upper class. Though Katharine Hepburn had to leave RKO Pictures after the film's disappointing box-office results, Cary Grant earned the reputation as a screwball virtuoso; he later starred in several additional notable screwball comedies.*

Bringing Up Baby is the definitive screwball-comedy prototype: The scatterbrained rich heiress (Hep-

Katharine Hepburn (left) and Cary Grant in a scene from the 1938 screwball comedy Bringing Up Baby. (The Granger Collection, New York)

burn) chases the passive, confused, and irritated scientist (Grant), convincing him that he really loves her and their wild misadventures. The film takes a nonsensical, farcical look at romance. Its repeated line—"The love impulse in men frequently reveals itself in terms of conflict."—could be a slogan for virtually all screwball comedies. An additional source of laughter in the film is the blurring of identities fostered by substitution and interchangeability of objects such as golf balls, purses, cars, leopards, and fiancés.

Impact Despite its initial box-office failure, *Bringing Up Baby* has come to be considered the quintessential screwball comedy and influenced many directors, such as Peter Bogdonovich, whose *What's up, Doc?* (1972) was a successful remake of the original. *Bringing Up Baby* has a breathless pace, a zany supporting cast, absurd misadventures, a combina-tion of pratfalls and verbal wit, and smooth special effects that set a standard that few subsequent screwball comedies attained.

Joseph Francavilla

Further Reading

Cavell, Stanley. *Pursuits of Happiness: The Hollywood Comedy of Remarriage.* Cambridge, Mass.: Harvard University Press, 1984.

Mast, Gerald. *Bringing Up Baby: Howard Hawks, Director.* New Brunswick, N.J.: Rutgers University Press, 1988.

Salamensky, S. I. "Screwball and the Con of Modern Culture." In *Film Analysis: A Norton Reader,* edited by Jeffrey Geiger and R. L. Rutsky. New York: W. W. Norton, 2005.

See also Film; Hepburn, Katharine; Motion Picture Production Code; Screwball comedy.

■ Broadway musicals

Definition   Musical plays staged in New York City's Broadway district

During the 1930's, the economic slump of the Great Depression took an artistic toll on Broadway, compromising the musical-theater culture of New York that thrived during the 1920's. Many of the major Broadway composers and lyricists left New York for employment in Hollywood. Lavish Ziegfeld-style revues and European-influenced operettas were not financially sustainable. Nevertheless, a steady stream of work was produced in New York throughout the decade.

During the 1930's, many Broadway musicals continued the aesthetics of the previous decade. Two of the most prominent writing teams of the 1920's—Richard Rodgers and Lorenz Hart and George and Ira Gershwin—continued to dominate in the 1930's, producing a steady stream of musical comedies. Jerome Kern, who worked mostly in Hollywood during the first part of the decade, contributed several works, and Cole Porter and Irving Berlin rose to greater prominence. Ethel Merman, Mary Martin, George Balanchine, George Abbott, Howard Lindsay, and Russel Crouse began their illustrious careers, while Kurt Weill and Harold Rome wrote their first shows for Broadway. Kay Swift wrote *Fine and Dandy* (1930), the first Broadway score ever written by a woman.

Great Achievements from Familiar Names   During the 1930's, Rodgers and Hart wrote some of their finest shows for the Broadway stage. *On Your Toes* (1936) was a production on which the duo collaborated with director George Abbott and choreographer George Balanchine and was noteworthy for its major ballet component and integration of music and plot. *The Boys from Syracuse* (1938) was a musical adaptation of William Shakespeare's *Comedy of Errors*, and *Babes in Arms* (1937) endures as one of Rodgers and Hart's most popular scores, containing the hits "Where or When," "My Funny Valentine," "The Lady Is a Tramp," and "Johnny One Note."

Berlin's *As Thousands Cheer* (1933) was a unique revue that used newspaper headlines as a springboard for a series of musical tableaus that commented on current events of the time. The most popular show of the decade, however,

was *Anything Goes* (1934) by Porter. With a book by Guy Bolton, P. G. Wodehouse, Howard Lindsay, and Russel Crouse, *Anything Goes* was a vehicle for Merman, who premiered "Blow, Gabriel, Blow," "I Get a Kick out of You," and the title number.

Political Works   While the Gershwins continued to specialize in lighthearted musical comedies, several of their works featured political themes and a satirical edge. These works included *Strike Up the Band* (1930), *Of Thee I Sing* (1931), and *Let 'Em Eat Cake* (1933), an unsuccessful sequel to *Of Thee I Sing*. *Of Thee I Sing*, the most famous and enduring of these three works, featured a book by George S. Kaufman and Morrie Ryskind and is distinguished as the first musical in history to be awarded the Pulitzer Prize for Drama.

In 1938, Marc Blitzstein premiered *The Cradle Will Rock* (1938), a left-wing attack on capitalism that was funded by the Federal Theatre Project. Accused

Clockwise from the top left: Ira Gershwin, George Gershwin, Morrie Ryskind, and George S. Kaufman, creators of some of the most beloved Broadway musicals of the decade, in 1931. (The Granger Collection, New York)

The Golden Age of Broadway

Listed in chronological order are some of the most important Broadway musicals of the 1930's.

Year	Title	Composer(s)
1930	Strike Up the Band	George Gershwin and Ira Gershwin
	Fine and Dandy	Kay Swift and Paul James
	Girl Crazy	Gershwin and Gershwin
1931	The Cat and the Fiddle	Jerome Kern and Otto Harbach
	Of Thee I Sing	Gershwin and Gershwin
1932	Face the Music	Irving Berlin
	Music in the Air	Kern and Oscar Hammerstein II
1933	As Thousands Cheer	Berlin
	Let 'Em Eat Cake	Gershwin and Gershwin
1934	Anything Goes	Cole Porter
1935	Porgy and Bess	Gershwin, Gershwin, and Du Bose Heyward
	Jumbo	Richard Rodgers and Lorenz Hart
1936	On Your Toes	Rodgers and Hart
	Johnny Johnson	Kurt Weill and Paul Green
1937	Babes in Arms	Rodgers and Hart
	I'd Rather Be Right	Rodgers and Hart
	Pins and Needles	Harold Rome
1938	The Cradle Will Rock	Marc Blitzstein
	Hellzapoppin'	Sammy Fain and Charles Tobias
	Leave It to Me!	Porter
	The Boys from Syracuse	Rodgers and Hart
1939	Very Warm for May	Kern and Hammerstein
	DuBarry Was a Lady	Porter

and DuBose Heyward. *Porgy and Bess* was an operatic version of the Heywards' play, with recitatives replacing dialogue. Although *Porgy and Bess* opened at the Alvin Theatre and the score was laden with a jazz influence, its composition and demands upon the singers categorized the work as a full-fledged opera, as opposed to a musical. This unique hybridity is precisely why *Porgy and Bess* has such enduring appeal. "Summertime," "I Got Plenty o' Nuttin," "My Man's Gone Now," "It Ain't Necessarily So," and "Bess, You Is My Woman Now," are some of the finest numbers in the Gershwins' catalog.

Exile to Hollywood In 1927, Hollywood introduced the first "talkies," films with sound, and the major Hollywood studios began producing numerous film musicals. While Broadway suffered during the 1930's, the film industry thrived. As the Great Depression loomed over Broadway, many composers and lyricists headed to California, where they found work in Hollywood. Perhaps no film composer was more eminent throughout the decade than Kern. He adapted many of his Broadway musicals and operettas for Hollywood. Some of these include *The Cat and the Fiddle* (1934), *Music in the Air* (1934), *Sweet Adeline* (1934), *Roberta* (1935), and *Show Boat* (1936). Kern often wrote additional songs for the film adaptations. He also wrote scores for new films, such as *Swing Time* (1936); *High, Wide and Handsome* (1937); and *Joy of Living* (1938).

Berlin was also prolific, writing the scores for *Top Hat* (1935), *Follow the Fleet* (1936), *On the Avenue* (1937), *Alexander's Ragtime Band* (1938), *Carefree* (1938), and *Second Fiddle* (1939). Rodgers and Hart collaborated on the film musicals *Love Me Tonight* (1932), *The Phantom President* (1932), *Hallelujah, I'm*

of promoting communism, Blitzstein's work was banned by the U.S. government before its first performance. The performers and audience, however, relocated to another theater and gave a premiere performance of the work without scenery, costumes, props, or an orchestra. The curious circumstances of this first performance helped elevate *The Cradle Will Rock* to cult status in Broadway history.

Porgy and Bess In 1935, the Gershwins wrote a musical adaption of *Porgy*, a 1927 play by Dorothy *a Bum* (1933), *Evergreen* (1934), and *Mississippi* (1935). Hart also wrote an English adaptation of the film version of *The Merry Widow* (1934), the famous operetta by Franz Lehár.

Porter wrote the scores for *Born to Dance* (1936) and *Rosalie* (1937) and adapted *Anything Goes* (1936) for Hollywood. The Gershwins' most famous film scores are *Shall We Dance* (1937), *A Damsel in Distress* (1937), and *The Goldwyn Follies* (1938). Harry Warren and Al Dubin also contributed many scores to Hollywood, including *Forty-second Street* (1933), *Gold Diggers of 1933* (1933), *Footlight Parade* (1933), *Roman Scandals* (1933), *Wonder Bar* (1934), *Dames* (1934), *Gold Diggers of 1935* (1935), *Go into Your Dance* (1935), and *Gold Diggers of 1937* (1937).

Impact In some ways the 1930's was the least significant decade of Broadway's "golden age." Because of the financial climate, far fewer shows were produced than in the decades of the 1920's and the 1940's. Nevertheless, many of the shows that premiered during this decade endure as either some of the most significant or frequently performed works in the history of Broadway. Many of the more successful shows continued the musical comedy formula of the 1920's, but some shows reflected greater social awareness, exhibited marked technical innovation, or challenged the well-established genres of revue, musical comedy, and operetta. The decade also represents some of the finest work of Broadway's greatest luminaries: the Gershwins, Rodgers and Hart, and Porter.

Matthew Hoch

Further Reading

Block, Geoffrey. *Enchanted Evenings: The Broadway Musical from Show Boat to Sondheim.* New York: Oxford University Press, 2004. Concerns the creative process behind fourteen of the most significant shows in Broadway history.

Bloom, Ken. *The Routledge Guide to Broadway.* New York: Routledge, 2006. Designed to be a student resource for Broadway theater in general, focusing on major performers, writers, directors, plays, and musicals.

Everett, William A., and Paul R. Laird. *Historical Dictionary of Broadway Musicals.* Lanham, Md.: Scarecrow Press, 2008. This dictionary is valuable not only for its entries devoted to composers, lyricists, performers, and terminology but also for its de-tailed historical time line, bibliography, and plot summaries of important shows.

Green, Stanley, and Kay Green. *Broadway Musicals: Show by Show.* 6th ed. New York: Hal Leonard, 2007. A single-volume, chronological reference work of virtually every significant show in Broadway history. Excerpts from opening-night reviews are included. A seven-volume companion collection of sheet music is sold separately.

Kantor, Michael, and Laurence Maslon. *Broadway: The American Musical.* New York: Bulfinch Press, 2004. The companion volume to Maslon's six-hour PBS documentary on the history of Broadway. The 470-page tome is packed with photographs and essays from every era of Broadway.

McLarmore, Allyson. *Musical Theater: An Appreciation.* Upper Saddle River, N.J.: Prentice Hall, 2004. McLarmore's book is a single-volume, chronological survey of the musical as an art form, starting with its European roots. History is presented within a social-political context, and each chapter is complete with listening examples and analyses of specific song lyrics.

Mordden, Ethan. *Sing for Your Supper: The Broadway Musical in the 1930's.* New York: Palgrave Macmillan, 2005. This seven-volume history of the Broadway musical is perhaps the best work on the subject. This 270-page volume is devoted exclusively to the 1930's. Mordden is erudite while remaining accessible and humorous.

See also Federal Theatre Project; Gershwin, George; Group Theatre; Hellman, Lillian; Kaufman, George S., and Moss Hart; Marx Brothers; *Porgy and Bess*; Theater in the United States.

■ *Brown v. Mississippi*

The Case U.S. Supreme Court ruling on the admissibility of physically coerced confessions

Date Decided February 17, 1936

In this case, as with Powell v. Alabama *(1932), which concerned the right to appointed counsel in death-penalty cases, the Supreme Court applied the due process clause of the Fourteenth Amendment to provide some minimum standards of fairness in state criminal-court proceedings. Here, the Court ruled invalid convictions based solely on confessions obtained by severe beatings.*

In this landmark ruling, the Supreme Court overturned the convictions of three African American sharecroppers in Mississippi for the murder of a white plantation owner. None of the three had any apparent connection to the killing. The "interrogation" was conducted both by law enforcement and by white civilians in the presence of law enforcement and consisted of beatings so severe that the Court termed them torture. One of the defendants was hung twice, and all of the defendants were whipped until they were gravely injured. During the two-day trial, the only evidence presented against the three was the coerced confessions. In undisputed testimony, several witnesses admitted to the brutal circumstances by which the confessions were obtained. Still, the men were convicted and sentenced to death; that judgment was upheld by the Mississippi Supreme Court.

The U.S. Supreme Court declared that the Fourteenth Amendment's due process clause, which provides that states may not deprive any person of "life, liberty, or property, without due process of law," prohibited the use of the confessions as evidence. Allowing the convictions to rest upon the strength of confessions procured by such "extreme brutality" was a "wrong so fundamental that it made the whole proceeding a mere pretense of a trial." Thus, admitting the confessions into evidence was a "clear denial of due process."

Impact This case and *Powell v. Alabama* informed the southern states during the 1930's that there were limits to the autonomy of their criminal courts. Violations of fundamental principles of justice would not be allowed. *Brown* was the first in a series of cases overturning convictions on issues related to confessions, culminating in the famous case of *Miranda v. Arizona* (1966) that found its legal footing in the Fifth Amendment's privilege against self-incrimination. The precedent established in *Brown*, that confessions are inadmissible in court unless they are voluntarily given, remains valid law.

Kimberlee Candela

Further Reading

Cortner, Richard C. *A "Scottsboro" Case in Mississippi: The Supreme Court and Brown v. Mississippi.* Jackson: University Press of Mississippi, 2005.

Dripps, Donald A. *About Guilt and Innocence: The Origins, Development, and Future of Constitutional Criminal Procedure.* Santa Barbara, Calif.: Praeger, 2002.

See also Civil rights and liberties in the United States; Jim Crow segregation; Lynching; National Association for the Advancement of Colored People; Racial discrimination; Scottsboro trials.

■ Brownlee, John Edward

Identification Canadian statesman and premier of Alberta, 1925-1934
Born August 27, 1883; Port Ryerse, Ontario, Canada
Died July 15, 1961; Calgary, Alberta, Canada

On June 19, 1930, with support from the United Farmers of Alberta (UFA), Brownlee was reelected premier of Alberta. During his terms in office, Brownlee negotiated an agreement that transferred the control of natural resources in the province from the federal government to Alberta. Also, he supported farm organizations and served on the Royal Commission that created the central bank. A personal scandal forced his resignation in 1934.

John Edward Brownlee was the premier of Alberta when the 1929 stock market crashed and ensuing Depression struck. The government and the citizens of the largely agrarian province became financially strapped by the sudden drop in wheat prices. Seed costs became higher than the value of harvested wheat. Grasshoppers, drought, and dust storms further decimated the land, leaving poverty and unemployment throughout the area. Poor economic conditions also created social unrest, including marches, riots, and suicides. Brownlee and his administration were unprepared for the economic and social blows that befell them during the Depression.

Some people lost their homes and livelihood, and others were in need of an infusion of money to plant new crops and to install better irrigation methods. Brownlee approved loan credit programs that were established to aid farmers, but the programs did not prevent banks from repossessing farms and equipment. A premier and leader of the UFA, Brownlee was a conservative whose fiscal restraints in handling the economic woes frustrated many people. They wanted more government assistance, but the UFA government was not prepared to provide adequate relief from the Great Depression.

Crowds of people waited and cheered for Brownlee when he returned to Alberta in 1929 with the news that the province's natural resources would be turned over to provincial control. The province became the proprietor of its own forests, coal reserves, minerals, and potential hydroelectric power. This enthusiasm soon waned; the Depression and personal scandal shook people's confidence in Brownlee. In July, 1930, Brownlee met Vivian MacMillan, a young, attractive friend, for lunch, a drive, and a dance. MacMillan soon became a good family friend and a junior stenographer for the attorney general. On September 22, 1933, MacMillan and her father, Allan MacMillan, filed a seduction suit against Brownlee, who denied the charges. The trial, which began in June, 1934, was front-page news in the United States and in Canada. Neil D. MacLean, a liberal lawyer, represented MacMillan; A. L. Smith was the counsel for Brownlee.

In early July, 1934, an all-male jury awarded MacMillan and her father $15,000 in damages and costs, but the judge reversed the decision and ruled that the MacMillans were to pay Brownlee's expenses. On July 10, Brownlee resigned as premier but stayed on as a private member of the Alberta legislature. The suit continued, and the Court of Appeals upheld the lower court judge's decision. On March 1, 1937, the Supreme Court of Canada again reversed the decision and ordered the damages be paid to the MacMillans. The Judicial Committee of the Privy Council upheld this decision in 1940 that Brownlee pay the damages.

Impact   Brownlee was a major proponent and voice for the UFA. During his career he signed drought relief legislation, supported highway construction, sold the province's financially crippling railroad services, improved health and education services, and transferred resources to the province. He also served as the only nonbanker in the Royal Commission on Banking and Currency. The Great Depression, the debilitating effects of natural phenomena on the land, and seduction charges ended both his career and the majority lead of the UFA. The organization was defeated by the Social Credit Party on August 22, 1935. Brownlee's reputation and political career were tarnished. He eventually became both president and general manager of the United Grain Growers Limited. His wife, Florence Agnes, supported Brownlee in court. The couple had two sons, John Edy and Alan Marshall. Brownlee died in Alberta on July 15, 1961. Edmonton, Alberta named a provincial government building in Brownlee's honor.

Cynthia J. W. Svoboda

Further Reading

Foster, Franklin Lloyd. *John E. Brownlee: A Biography.* Lloydminster, Alta.: Foster Learning, 1996.

Palmer, Howard, and Tamara Palmer. *Alberta: A New History.* Edmonton, Alta.: Hurtig, 1990.

Payne, Michael, Donald Wetherell, and Catherine Cavanaugh, eds. *Alberta Formed, Alberta Transformed.* Edmonton: University of Alberta Press, 2006.

See also   Agriculture in Canada; Canadian regionalism; Dust Bowl; Farmers' organizations; Income and wages in Canada; Unemployment in Canada.

■ Buck, Pearl S.

Identification   American author and winner of the Nobel Prize in Literature; also a political activist and humanitarian

Born   June 26, 1892; Hillsboro, West Virginia

Died   March 6, 1973; Danby, Vermont

Buck broke new ground in American literature by writing about ordinary peasants in China and unglamorous women from different countries with profound understanding, compassion, and authenticity. In 1938, she became the first American woman to win the Nobel Prize in Literature. She actively participated in the major social and political movements of the 1930's, including racial equality, equal rights for women, children's welfare, and world peace, all topics she covered in her writing.

During the 1930's, Pearl S. Buck emerged as one of the most popular and prolific American writers. Within a decade, she published eight novels, three plays, two biographies, twenty-two short stories, and fifty-nine articles, exploring a wide range of topics, from a Chinese peasant's everyday life to the worldwide struggle against fascism. During the same period, she published her translation of *Shui Hu Zhuan*, one of the four most famous classical novels in China. Buck's translation, entitled *All Men Are Brothers* (1933), was the first complete English version of this novel.

Buck's first novel, *East Wind: West Wind*, appeared in 1930 in the United States while she was still living in China. It introduces an American audience to a Chinese family caught in an agonizing clash between the ancient Confucian tradition and twentieth century ideas influenced by the West. In 1931, Buck's most famous novel, *The Good Earth*, was published. Set in Anhui, China, during the turbulent years of the early twentieth century, the novel depicts with minute details the eventful life of a peasant, Wang Lung, and his family, who survive war and famine and prosper through endurance, thrift, and toil in the field.

Buck's realistic portrayal of her characters' strengths, weaknesses, and struggles through tough times allowed readers to develop an affinity for the characters. During the Great Depression, readers empathized with the characters because of their own struggles: high unemployment and low income, long breadlines, and falling crop prices. *The Good Earth* was an instant success. It was chosen for the Book-of-the-Month Club, the Pulitzer Prize, and the

The Good Earth *author Pearl S. Buck.* (Edward Steichen/ Courtesy, George Bush Presidential Library and Museum)

William Dean Howell Medal. In 1938, this novel and Buck's biographies of her parents, *Fighting Angel* and *The Exile*, won her the Nobel Prize in Literature.

Buck wrote two sequels to *The Good Earth*, *Sons* (1932) and *A House Divided* (1935). The first sequel depicts the different paths Wang Lung's three sons choose against their father's wishes. None of them chooses to till the land. The second dramatizes the struggle of a grandson of Wang Lung trying to reach a compromise between the suffocating yet familiar traditional way of life and the exciting yet dangerous life of a revolutionary.

Throughout the 1930's, Buck not only wrote profusely but also generously devoted time, energy, and money she earned from her writings to the causes that promoted the ideals she wrote about. Affiliated with no political party, she was fiercely independent and fearlessly outspoken on issues such as missionary work in China, racial discrimination, equal rights for women, disadvantaged children welfare, and war and peace.

During the debate over foreign missions that intensified after the 1920's, Buck, a missionary herself, voiced her disenchantment with her overseas colleagues and their performance. She criticized many of them for their narrow-mindedness and insensitivity, for their contempt for any civilization different from their own, and for their interest in counting the number of converts. She urged her fellow missionaries to approach the Chinese as equals. Her criticisms and her call for action were presented clearly in a 1932 address she made to a large audience at the Astor Hotel in New York. Her address was immediately printed as a pamphlet by John Day and in the January, 1933, issue of *Harper's* magazine under the title "Is There a Case for Foreign Missions?"

After returning to the United States from China in 1934, Buck continued to serve as a bridge across the Pacific. She watched closely the major events developing in her foster country—the civil war between the nationalists, led by Chiang Kai-shek, and the communists, headed by Mao Zedong, and the united front they formed against Japanese aggression. She openly supported the Chinese resistance by writing such articles as "China Against Japan" (1936) and "Arms for China Democracy" (1938). She exposed and condemned Japanese atrocities against Chinese civilians in *Asia* magazine. She also wrote about these events and their effects on ordinary people in her novel *The Patriot* (1939).

Principal Works of Pearl S. Buck, 1930-1939

- *East Wind: West Wind* (1930)
- *The Good Earth* (1931)
- *East and West and the Novel* (1932)
- *Sons* (1932)
- *The Young Revolutionist* (1932)
- *All Men Are Brothers* (1933)
- *The First Wife, and Other Stories* (1933)
- *The Mother* (1934)
- *A House Divided* (1935)
- *House of Earth* (1935)
- *The Exile* (1936)
- *Fighting Angel: Portrait of a Soul* (1936)
- *This Proud Heart* (1938)
- *The Chinese Novel* (1939)
- *The Patriot* (1939)

While following developments in China, Buck championed various causes in the United States. She urged an end to racial segregation in her public speeches and in her writings. She demanded equal opportunity for women in employment. She denounced discriminatory laws against interracial children and Chinese immigration. She opposed the practice of manipulating cultural differences into a hierarchy of races and advocated cross-cultural understanding at home and abroad.

Impact Buck changed the way many Americans viewed the Chinese by presenting realistic images of ordinary people in China instead of perpetuating stereotypes. Her political and humanitarian activism helped to end racial segregation, to raise women's social status, and to repeal the Chinese Exclusion Act in 1943. It also led to the founding of the East and West Association in 1943 and the Welcome House in 1949. Her writings about her foster country have become invaluable historical records of China.

Chenliang Sheng

Further Reading

Buck, Pearl S. *My Several Worlds: A Personal Record.* New York: John Day, 1954. Describes Buck's years in China and their impact on her life and work. She discusses her family in detail.

Conn, Peter. *Pearl S. Buck: A Cultural Biography.* Cambridge, Mass.: Cambridge University Press, 1996. An expansive biography covering her writing and social activism.

Doyle, Paul A. *Pearl S. Buck.* Rev. ed. New York: Twayne, 1980. A close examination of Buck's most significant works.

Harris, Theodore F. *Pearl S. Buck: A Biography.* New York: John Day, 1969. Selections from letters and speeches, highlighting her sympathy and compassion for those who sought her out.

Leong, Karen J. *The China Mystique: Pearl S. Buck, Anna May Wong, Mayling Soong, and the Transformation of American Orientalism.* Berkeley: University of California Press, 2005. Looks at three prominent women with ties to China; looks at how each shaped Americans' ideas about China.

Liao, Kang. *Pearl S. Buck: A Cultural Bridge Across the Pacific.* Westport, Conn.: Greenwood Press, 1997. Focuses on Buck's work in altering Americans' views of China and Chinese people.

Stirling, Nora B. *Pearl Buck: A Woman in Conflict.* Piscataway, N.J.: New Century, 1983. Chronicles Buck's final years and her continued activism.

See also Asian Americans; Civil rights and liberties in the United States; *Good Earth, The*; Immigration to the United States; Japanese military aggression; Literature in the United States; Peace movement; Racial discrimination.

■ Budge, Don

Identification American tennis player
Born June 13, 1915; Oakland, California
Died January 26, 2000; Scranton, Pennsylvania

Budge emerged in the middle of the decade as the world's best tennis player. In 1938, he became the sport's first Grand Slam winner by capturing the Australian, French, U.S. National, and Wimbledon titles.

A Californian, Don Budge took up tennis as a teenager and quickly mastered the game, winning junior tournaments across his home state. In 1933, he won the U.S. National Juniors Championship.

Six-feet one-inch tall, lean, and red-haired, Budge possessed a strong serve and powerful forehand, but his signature stroke was a backhand that he developed playing baseball as a left-handed hit-ter. Budge used those weapons to earn a place on the 1935 U.S. Davis Cup team.

In 1937, Budge won singles titles at Wimbledon and the U.S. Nationals. For his court achievements that year, Budge won the James E. Sullivan Award, as the nation's best amateur athlete, and the Associated Press Athlete of the Year Award. Budge excelled the following year, winning the tennis Grand Slam. From 1936-1938, Budge ranked as the top tennis player in the world. During that period, he also won several major doubles and mixed-doubles titles.

Budge is also remembered for winning one of the most thrilling tennis matches of the twentieth century. In Davis Cup competition in 1937, Budge faced Gottfried von Cramm, the German champion. The match took place the summer after the Berlin Olympics, in which Jesse Owens had won four gold medals while Adolf Hitler watched, and the summer before Joe Louis knocked out German boxing champ Max Schmeling. Von Cramm won the first two sets, but Budge won the next two. In the deciding set, von Cramm jumped to a 4-1 lead, but Budge stormed back to beat the German, 8-6. The U.S team went on to win its first Davis Cup in a decade. In 1938, after completing the Grand Slam, Budge turned professional, which, as per the rules at the time, eliminated him from competition in Grand Slam tournaments.

Impact   Budge emerged in the mid-1930's as the world's greatest player after American Bill Tilden had dominated tennis during the 1920's. Budge completed the first Grand Slam in history. He was elected to the International Tennis Hall of Fame in 1968.

James Tackach

Further Reading

Budge, Don. *Don Budge: A Tennis Memoir.* New York: Viking, 1969.

Fisher, Marshall Jon. *A Terrible Splendor: Three Extraordinary Men, a World Poised for War, and the Greatest Tennis Match Ever Played.* New York: Crown, 2009.

See also   Louis, Joe; Owens, Jesse; Tennis; Tilden, Bill.

■ Business and the economy in Canada

Canada's business sector was vital to the overall health of the country's economy. As a "staples economy," a term coined by historian Harold Inglis, the leading businesses of Canada were those engaged in producing the raw materials that enjoyed robust demand in the world market of the 1920's. However, the 50 percent drop in world trade that resulted from the Great Depression severely impacted those Canadian businesses that mined or produced the raw materials from which finished goods were made. Canada is a resource-rich land, and its ability to produce and sell minerals to other manufacturers, especially in the industrialized countries, played a major role in Canada's prosperity during the 1920's.

The market for agricultural products was vital in Canada. During the prosperous years of the 1920's, Canada had built up its capacity to produce wheat, for which the wide open spaces of its prairies were ideally suited. By the end of the 1920's, Canada's wheat output rivaled that of the United States, Australia, and Argentina. In 1928, Canada earned $500 million from wheat exports; but exports earnings fell to $300 million in 1929 and drifted downward after that. At that point, Canadian wheat had to be sold into a market in which supply exceeded demand by several hundred million bushels. Many prairie farmers went bankrupt because of the combination of the drought that occurred during the early years of the decade and heavy debt.

Natural Resources   The market for minerals, of which Canada produced a significant amount, fell along with the 50 percent drop in world trade. Canada produced about 90 percent of the world's gold in 1930. Although the price of gold fell along with other prices, the world continued to need Canada's gold. Canada was also one of the major world producers of nickel, which was used to manufacture specialty metals; the nickel operations in Sudbury continued to function, though at a reduced rate. The iron mines on Cape Breton in Nova Scotia had to reduce their operations with the falling world market. The asbestos industry, supplied by mining chiefly in Quebec, was pulled back as industrial building construction fell. Reduced world demand had a powerful effect on Canada's mining industry.

Because of Canada's vast geography, railroads

were a major factor in the production of both agricultural products and industrial raw materials. During the 1920's, the Canadian Pacific Railway had built numerous branch lines to enable wheat to move from the fields of the prairies to the ports of both the Great Lakes and the Atlantic coast. As demand dropped with the global economy, the railroads became overextended. The eastern railroads that had merged into the Canadian National Railway had received substantial investment at the expense of the national government and carried a heavy burden of debt. The Dominion government had to spend a significant portion of its tax revenue on servicing this debt.

During the 1920's, Canada's vast forests of softwood trees had fueled the creation of a major pulpwood industry that supplied a large portion of the newsprint used in the United States and in Great Britain. Large pulpwood processors were developed that nearly bankrupted the industry. Suddenly, the industry produced newsprint at only 50 to 60 percent of its capacity, which led to significant consolidation.

Canadian geography led to the development of important sources of hydroelectricity, chiefly in the Arctic. In turn, this made possible low-cost manufacturing. Although only a portion of the potential output of electricity had been captured by the 1930's, the generation of electricity became an important part of industrial production in Canada.

Industry and Banking   Although Canada's car market was small, branches of the American car industry had developed in the Canadian hinterland of Detroit. While only a portion of the cars produced in Windsor and Oshawa, Ontario, were sold in Canada, the jobs the branches provided were important to Canadians.

Canada had a number of private banks, called "chartered" banks, located in regional centers. However, Canada passed legislation in 1934 that created the Bank of Canada, which controlled the issuance of currency and, through its ability to rediscount loans, the money supply. The new bank, established in 1935, regulated the amount of reserves that the smaller private banks were required to hold. The Bank of Canada was also empowered to purchase securities from private firms and had the authority to discount commercial paper, giving it effective control of Canada's economy.

During the later years of the 1930's, the Dominion government created several public corporations, known as Crown corporations, that served a public need not met by private firms. In 1937, Trans Canada Airlines was set up to conduct all air transportation in Canada. Another Crown corporation, Trans Pacific Airlines, carried passengers and freight across the Pacific Ocean. Radio broadcasting was also assigned to a publicly owned corporation.

Impact   The drop in international trade following the 1929 stock market crash in the United States affected Canadian business profoundly, not only in the substantial decrease in world markets for Canadian products but also in the financing of Canadian business. Many Canadian businesses had relied on foreign investment, chiefly from the United States but also from Great Britain. Much of this investment dried up during the 1930's. Businesses survived, but they pulled back during this bleak period.

Nancy M. Gordon

Further Reading

Bliss, Michael. *Northern Enterprise: Five Centuries of Canadian Business.* Toronto: McClelland and Stewart, 1987. Excellent survey of business in Canada with many details of individual firms.

Creighton, Donald Grant. *Dominion of the North: A History of Canada.* Boston: Houghton-Mifflin, 1944. Although the book is a survey of all of Canada's history, the last segment contains useful information about the events of the 1930's.

Horn, Michiel. The *Great Depression of the 1930's in Canada.* Ottawa: Canadian Historical Association, 1984. Small pamphlet that brings together useful data about the 1930's.

Safarian, A. E. *The Canadian Economy in the Great Depression.* Toronto: Toronto University Press, 1959. Based on many statistics, the book gives useful details of the effects of the Depression.

Thompson, John Herd, and Allen Seager. *Canada, 1922-1939: Decades of Discord.* Toronto: McClelland and Stewart, 1985. Contrasts the 1920's with the 1930's and, thus, brings out the negative effects of the economic downturn.

See also   Agriculture in Canada; Canada and Great Britain; Demographics of Canada; Great Depression in Canada; Income and wages in Canada; King, William Lyon Mackenzie; Radio in Canada; Unemployment in Canada.

■ Business and the economy in the United States

The decade was dominated by the Great Depression, which was characterized by a powerful downswing from 1929 to 1933, an incomplete recovery process followed by a painful recession in 1937, and a stronger upswing through 1939. The Depression inflicted hardships on millions through unemployment, bankruptcies, and property foreclosures. It brought a drastic political shift and the creation of a vast array of government policies and agencies.

After a decade of peace and prosperity, the economy was entering a downswing at the beginning of 1930. The immediate cause was decline in aggregate demand for goods and services, as measured by the gross national product (GNP) in current prices. From a peak value of $104 billion in 1929, the GNP declined steadily to a low of $56 billion in 1933.

Consequences of Declining Demand The decline in expenditures brought a corresponding drop in the sales receipts of business firms. Many cut back on production and laid off workers. The quantity of national output declined by about one-fourth. As a result, unemployment, at only 3 percent of the labor force in 1929, rose to 25 percent by 1933. No system of unemployment compensation existed, so the loss of a job meant the loss of income. Many others found their working hours reduced. Personal income totals fell from $85 billion in 1929 to $47 billion in 1933. As a result, consumer spending dropped from $77 billion to $46 billion over the same period.

The decrease in expenditures to buy goods and services led many firms to reduce the prices of their products and services. Price declines were especially extreme for agricultural products. Prices received by farmers declined by more than one-half. Farm output did not decline significantly, so farm incomes fell in proportion to the drop in prices.

The drop in product prices and business revenues led to an increase in the burden of debt. Business firms, farmers, and home buyers defaulted on their debts in large numbers and consequently lost their properties to foreclosures. Business profits evaporated—by 1933, corporations as a group lost more than $1 billion. Borrower defaults aggravated the vast number of bank failures. The disappearance of corporate profits drove down the market value of corporate stocks.

Federal government responses to the downswing included a major increase in tariff rates on imports in 1930 and increase in tax rates in 1932 to try to reduce the budget deficit. In 1932, Congress created the Reconstruction Finance Corporation as a source of emergency loans to distressed borrowers.

Causes of the Downswing Numerous factors combined to produce the downswing. Initially, the process was no different from earlier, milder downturns resulting from overbuilding of housing and some industrial sectors such as automobiles. The Federal Reserve had slowed the growth of the money supply. The decline in stock prices that began in October, 1929, reduced people's perceived wealth and raised the cost of capital. American lending to foreign countries slackened, leading to decreases in their purchases of American products.

A mild slump escalated with a wave of bank failures in 1930, primarily in response to excessive lending for stock and real estate ventures. The bank failures led to accelerated withdrawals of currency and to build-up of excess reserves by wary banks. There was no federal deposit insurance, so depositors in failed banks lost the use of their money. Bank lending declined. The Federal Reserve was reluctant to pursue expansionary measures, alarmed by the prospect that the nation's stock of monetary gold would be withdrawn.

Abrupt Reversal in 1933 Public distress was reflected in the overwhelming victory of Franklin D. Roosevelt in the presidential election of 1932. Immediately following his inauguration in March, 1933, Roosevelt declared a national bank holiday to stem the wave of bank failures. All banks were to be examined, and only those of unquestioned solvency would be allowed to reopen. The panic demand for currency subsided, but the nation lost twenty-seven hundred banks in 1933. At the same time, the government went off the gold standard. Gold coins were withdrawn from circulation. Gold-based limitations on the money supply were removed. The Banking Act of 1933 effectively eliminated banking panics by creating a system of federal deposit insurance.

Two major government measures aimed at promoting recovery were adopted in 1933, the Agricultural Adjustment Act and the National Industrial Recovery Act (NIRA). Both were aimed at increasing prices by restricting supply, and both were deemed to be unconstitutional in 1935 and 1936. However, pieces of both were reenacted. Programs to boost farm prices by reducing output were adopted in February, 1936, and in February, 1938. Elements of the NIRA reappeared in the National Labor Relations Act (Wagner Act of 1935) and the Fair Labor Standards Act of 1938, establishing a federal minimum wage. The Wagner Act protected the right of workers to form labor unions and to bargain collectively. More effective in boosting aggregate demand were measures to m1ake direct payments ("relief") to the needy and the unemployed and to expand publicworks programs. Prominent among these programs was the Works Progress Administration (WPA), created in 1935.

The expansion of federal programs brought expansion of federal government expenditures. Budget expenditures went from $4.6 billion in fiscal 1933 to $6.6 billion the following year. Another major increase took them to $8.4 billion in fiscal 1936. However, the potential expansion of aggregate demand was largely lost by steady increases in tax rates.

With the end of the financial panic in 1933, aggregate demand began a vigorous expansion. From a low of $56 billion in 1933, nominal GNP rose to $83 billion by 1936. Prices increased slightly, especially for farm products. The chief effect was to stimulate higher production. National output increased by 37 percent and the unemployment rate declined from 25 percent to 17 percent. Public approval for the government's interventions was reflected in Roosevelt's landslide reelection in 1936.

The Recession of 1937-1938 The economy's march toward recovery was interrupted in 1937, responding to shifts in government policies. Roosevelt, eager to balance the budget, reduced federal spending at the same time that a new wage tax (to finance Social Security) was going into effect. Also, the Federal Reserve increased the reserve requirements against bank deposits. GNP expenditures, which had reached $90 billion in 1937, which was still far below the 1929 number, fell by 6 percent; even in 1939, GNP ex-

penditures were no higher than in 1937. Unemployment increased from 14 percent in 1937 to 19 percent in 1938 and 17 percent in 1939.

Thus, in 1939, the economy remained seriously depressed. Nominal GNP was still about 10 percent below 1929. However, because prices had declined, the amount of real output was slightly higher in 1939. Nonetheless, more than eight million workers remained unemployed. The outbreak of war in Europe in September, 1939, accelerated a vigorous economic expansion. Not until 1940, however, did the number of employed workers reach the level of 1929.

Structural Changes Government programs brought about major structural changes. The Wagner Act of

This never-to-be-finished hotel in Vincennes, Indiana, symbolizes the overall stagnation experienced in the business sector as a result of the Great Depression. (Library of Congress)

1935 provided a great stimulus to the growth in labor-union membership, which increased from about three million in 1933 to nearly nine million in 1939. Union efforts to achieve recognition often provoked strong resistance from employers, and violence often resulted. "Sit-down" strikes in 1937, involving workers seizing employer facilities, led to union recognition by leading automobile manufacturers.

Between 1929 and 1939, the American labor force increased by 12 percent, reaching 55 million in 1939. Despite the Depression, labor productivity increased about one-fourth. These developments hindered the reduction of unemployment. The rise in productivity made possible a rise in real-wage rates by about 10 percent. At the same time, higher labor costs impeded job creation.

The decade brought major changes to the financial sectors. The number of banks decreased as a reflection of widespread failures. At the end of 1929, 24,600 banks existed; a decade later only 15,000 did. Changes in banking legislation forced banks out of most investment banking operations. Virtually all of the surviving banks were covered by federal deposit insurance, and the rate of bank failure had become small. Securities markets had come under the Securities and Exchange Commission (appointed June, 1934). The Federal Housing Administration was created in 1934 to insure long-term home mortgages.

The Social Security Act of 1935 created a network of government income supplements. The first was a national system of old-age pensions to be financed by a wage tax. However, the tax become effective before the benefits began to be paid, so the effect was severely deflationary. The second was a combined federal-state system of unemployment compensation. The third was a system of means-tested welfare programs, providing income support for the blind, the aged, and families with dependent children.

The Reciprocal Trade Agreements Act of 1934 set up the United States as leaders in negotiations with other countries on mutual reduction of trade restrictions. By 1937, there were sixteen agreements in effect, covering one-third of American trade.

Technological Advances   Despite the decade's economic hardships, technological improvements brought many benefits. The proportion of homes with electric power increased from 68 percent in 1930 to 77 percent in 1939. The increase was most notable for farm families, affected by the rural elec-

trification program adopted by the government in 1936. The number of households with radio sets doubled between 1930 and 1939, surpassing 27 millions. The number and variety of network broadcasts increased greatly and featured soap operas, adventure serials for children, comedy, big band music, sporting events, and President Roosevelt's fireside chats. The eyewitness broadcast report of the burning of the dirigible *Hindenburg* became immortalized. Motion pictures moved from silence to sound and from black-and-white to color. Frozen foods became a consumer staple. Visitors to the 1939 New York World's Fair could witness demonstrations of television. DuPont introduced nylon and synthetic rubber.

Major discoveries of petroleum led to abundant supplies and declining prices, to the distress of producers. Automobile registrations initially dipped as business worsened but recovered as the economy improved; by 1939, there were three million more cars than in 1930. The cars were vastly improved—electric self-starters replaced the crank, and heaters and car radios became common. Commercial air travel expanded, spurred by the introduction of the DC-3 in 1936. Passenger railroads tried to fight their desperate financial troubles by introducing streamlined trains such as the Burlington Zephyr and the Super Chief.

Impact   The hardships of the Depression brought a decline in the birthrate. Although the population grew from 122 million in 1929 to 131 million in 1939, the number of children under age fifteen declined from 38.5 million to 35.6 million. However, life expectancy at birth increased from sixty years in 1930 to sixty-four years in 1939. Hard times on the farm led to a decrease of one million in agricultural employment.

The economic role of the federal government was greatly expanded. Federal civilian employment grew from 500,000 in 1930 to 900,000 in 1939. This did not include the people on work relief programs such as WPA, which employed more than three million people in November, 1938.

The size and influence of labor unions increased greatly under the protection of the Wagner Act. Unionization was particularly noteworthy in mass production industries such as steel and automobiles, where it had hardly existed before 1933.

For all the vigor of its actions, the New Deal administration of Franklin D. Roosevelt failed to get the country out of the Depression. Adverse effects on business confidence and investment spending resulted especially from tax increases and the promotion of labor unions. It took the upsurge of aggregate demand associated with World War II to restore full employment.

Paul B. Trescott

Further Reading

Atack, Jeremy, and Peter Passell. *A New Economic View of American History from Colonial Times to 1940.* New York: W. W. Norton, 1994. Explains the contraction of the economy during the 1930's and the eventual recovery.

Bordo, Michael D., Claudia Goldin, and Eugene N. White, eds. *The Defining Moment: The Great Depression and the American Economy in the Twentieth Century.* Chicago: University of Chicago Press, 1998. Stresses the radical transformation of the role of government, highlighting monetary and fiscal policies, agriculture, labor unions, Social Security, and the international economy.

Chandler, Lester V. *America's Greatest Depression.* New York: Harper & Row, 1970. Brief and cogent review of economic conditions. Reviews causes and consequences of the Depression and the major policy innovations.

Mitchell, Broadus. *Depression Decade.* New York: Rinehart, 1947. Detailed, lively reflections on the decade.

Shlaes, Amity. *The Forgotten Man: A New History of the Great Depression.* New York: HarperCollins, 2007. Emphasizes the failures of federal government policies and why the Depression lasted so long and why it was so deep.

Stein, Herbert. *The Fiscal Revolution in America.* Chicago: University of Chicago Press, 1969. The first seven chapters describe the evolution of attitudes toward balancing the budget and deficit finance under presidents Herbert Hoover and Roosevelt.

See also Banking; Credit and debt; Great Depression in the United States; Gross national product; Income and wages in the United States; International trade; Recession of 1937-1938; Social Security Act of 1935; Unemployment in the United States; Unionism.

■ Butler, Smedley

Identification U.S. Marine Corps general
Born July 30, 1881; West Chester, Pennsylvania
Died June 21, 1940; Philadelphia, Pennsylvania

Butler was a controversial figure who upset many military and political leaders by supporting World War I veterans in their struggle to receive a promised bonus, criticizing the influence on military campaigns by big business, and endorsing isolationism.

Major General Smedley Darlington Butler, "Old Gimlet Eye," remains among the most illustrious officers in U.S. Marine Corps history. One of only two Marines to be awarded the Medal of Honor twice, he participated in virtually every major Marine Corps action between the Spanish-American War and World War II.

Outside the Marine Corps, he was controversial. He was almost court-martialed for criticizing Italian

Former Marine commander Smedley Butler (foreground) appears before the Senate Naval Affairs Committee in 1938 to discuss his opposition to a proposed naval expansion bill. (Library of Congress)

dictator Benito Mussolini in 1931. After Butler's retirement that year, he argued publicly that the United States should not maintain military personnel beyond its borders nor naval vessels more than two hundred miles off its shores. He particularly incensed business and political leaders by publishing a pamphlet entitled *War Is a Racket* in 1935. It denounces war profiteering and blames the government for sending Marines to countries such as Nicaragua, Mexico, and Haiti simply to enforce business interests and not for national security, as if the Marines were glorified mobsters. To the consternation of President Herbert Hoover, Butler gave speeches in support of the Bonus Army March, which consisted of World War I veterans seeking payment of a promised service bonus.

Most controversial of all, however, was Butler's claim before a congressional committee in 1934 that a cabal of business leaders and politicians tried to hire him to lead a mercenary army to occupy Washington, D.C., and his related claim that the cabal was planning to subvert the power of President Franklin D. Roosevelt. The committee suppressed some of Butler's testimony and generally downplayed the rest.

Impact   Historians debate how serious the "Business Plot" really was, yet Butler's testimony reinforced the public's suspicion of business leaders, already in low repute because of the Great Depression. Although *War Is a Racket* had little influence on American military policy, it did become an influential document in the rising isolationist and pacifist movements.

Roger Smith

Further Reading

Brady, James. *Why Marines Fight.* New York: St. Martin's Press, 2007.

Butler, Smedley D. *War Is a Racket.* New ed. Los Angeles: Feral House, 2003.

See also   American Liberty League; Bonus Army March; Isolationism; Naval forces; Peace movement; Roosevelt, Franklin D.; Veterans Administration.

■ Byrd, Richard

Identification   Arctic explorer, pilot, and adventurer

Born   October 25, 1888; Winchester, Virginia

Died   March 11, 1957; Boston, Massachusetts

Byrd was a well-publicized national hero, aviator, and explorer, famous for his flights to the Arctic and Antarctic and associated ever after with the Antarctic Little America bases and Byrd expeditions.

Richard Byrd's earlier career involved naval service, innovations in airplane navigation, a claimed flight over the North Pole, and a transatlantic flight that was beaten by Charles A. Lindbergh. However, Byrd began the 1930's as a nationally renowned hero. He had just returned from a successful first Antarctic expedition, which he had organized. During the expedition he had flown over or near the South Pole. The expedition made numerous geological and meteorological observations.

Byrd's ships returned to New York City in June, 1930, and his team rode in a ticker-tape parade. Byrd spent the next day at the White House with President Herbert Hoover. A few days later, he and his expedition crew were conveyed on a Navy destroyer up the Hudson River to visit his friend and New York governor Franklin D. Roosevelt. This week constituted the high point of Byrd's career. A few months later, Byrd published *Little America* (1930).

Afterward, the public admiration for Byrd diminished, a fact probably attributable to the shift in interests and priorities brought on by the Depression. Byrd decided, mistakenly, that he could become a political figure. He supported cutting or eliminating veterans' pensions. The National Economy League, of which Byrd was a member, thought that the way out of the Depression was through cutting government spending. Byrd supported the attack on the Bonus Army marchers and campaigned for a government economy drive. This offended many but gained support from economic conservatives and the industrial leaders whom Byrd had cultivated to support his expeditions.

Byrd turned from his unsuccessful foray into politics for a second Antarctic expedition of 1933. President Roosevelt supported the expedition, both to get Byrd out of politics and to pursue future claims on Antarctic territory. The expedition included scientists studying Antarctic geology, glaciology, weather, and biology. Byrd secretly planned to spend the Antarctic winter inland, alone, in a small, specially constructed hut. He thought this would outdo all previous Arctic explorers. This project was harmful to his physical and mental health but did yield publicity and a book. During Byrd's retreat the expedition members at the home base began to fight, experience low moral, and drink. Byrd's radio transmissions became strange, and the crew decided to rescue him. After two failed attempts the crew arrived at Byrd's hut. Byrd had been poisoned by fumes from his stoves; this affected his mental and physical health and left him undernourished, depressed, and weak. The rescuers spent two months nursing him back to health at the hut before he was well enough to return to base. He was aged, pale, and thin on return. Byrd claimed to be less vain and more humble thereafter. Despite the physical and mental breakdown, Byrd published *Alone: The Classic Polar Adventure*, a popular book about his ordeal, in 1938.

Richard Byrd's expedition plane in 1933. (Library of Congress)

Upon returning to the United States, Byrd turned again to politics. He became involved in peace movements, including the No Foreign War Crusade. Byrd supported the Ludlow amendment, calling for a national referendum before entering a war. This alienated Roosevelt. Byrd associated with Thomas J. Watson, Sr., of the International Business Machines Corporation (IBM), praised Nazi Germany, and engaged in violent strikebreaking, all of which diminished his popularity. After his peace campaign failed, he turned back to exploration.

In 1939, Byrd embarked on his third Antarctic expedition, the U.S.-sponsored Antarctic Service Expedition. Byrd left the expedition in 1940 for military service, but the expedition had a large scientific output and was considered a success.

Impact Byrd was a public hero in the early 1930's and remained a hero to readers of boys' adventure accounts in succeeding decades. His name is synonymous with Antarctic exploration, and the scientific results of the expeditions he effectively organized were a foundation for subsequent Antarctic research.

Val Dusek

Further Reading

Byrd, Richard. *Alone: The Classic Polar Adventure.* Washington, D.C.: Island Press, 2003.

Rink, Paul. *Admiral Byrd: Alone in the Antarctic.* New York: Sterling, 2006.

Rose, Lisle. *Explorer: The Life of Richard E. Byrd.* Columbia: University of Missouri Press, 2008.

See also Aviation and aeronautics; Bonus Army March; Ludlow amendment; Naval forces; Newspapers, U.S.; Peace movement; Roosevelt, Franklin D.; Veterans Administration.

■ Cagney, James

Identification   American film actor
Born   July 17, 1899; New York, New York
Died   March 30, 1986; Stanfordville, New York

Cagney was one of the world's most recognized film stars for his portrayals of gangsters and tough-guy characters throughout the 1930's. In 1938, Cagney received the first of his three Academy Award nominations for best actor for his signature performance in Angels with Dirty Faces *(1938).*

Actor James Cagney, known during the decade primarily for his roles in gangster films, leaps into the air while on a set during the early 1930's. He would later win his only Academy Award playing song-and-dance man George M. Cohan in the 1942 film Yankee Doodle Dandy. *(Hulton Archive/Getty Images)*

James Francis Cagney, Jr., was born on the lower East Side in New York City to Carolyn and James Cagney, Sr. His parents were of Norwegian and Irish descent, and his family lived in poverty above his father's saloon. He was one of seven children, two of whom died as infants. As a young man growing up in the slums of New York City, Cagney learned quickly how to take care of himself. Among his many talents were boxing, tap dancing, and baseball.

Cagney graduated from high school in 1918 and took on a variety of jobs to help support his family. His first experience with acting came as a last-minute replacement for his older brother. In 1919, Cagney auditioned for a dancing part in a musical spoof in which male servicemen dressed as women. Cagney played a chorus girl. The ability to perform in this role assured him that he could play any part. This was the beginning of Cagney's ten-year career on Broadway and the vaudeville stage. In this environment, he met his future wife, Frances Willard Vernon. Their marriage lasted for more than sixty-four years, ending only with his death in 1986.

More than one-half of Cagney's films were made between 1930 and 1939. Although Cagney is best remembered as the stereotypical tough guy, his versatile performance skills gave him the ability to appear in a variety of roles that included comedy, musicals, and dramas. In films such as *The Public Enemy* (1931), *Angels with Dirty Faces*, and *The Roaring Twenties* (1939), his vivid portrayal of life in the slums of New York gave the moviegoing public insight into the darker side of American life. Perhaps his most defining scene was in *The Public Enemy* when, as the character Tom Powers, he smashes a grapefruit into the face of his girlfriend, played by actor Mae Clarke. Many film critics consider this particular scene to be responsible for changing the way heroes and leading men were portrayed in subsequent films. Occasionally, Cagney took on roles that were clearly a departure from what the public expected from him. A good example of this is the Western film *The Oklahoma Kid* (1939), in which Cagney and Humphrey Bogart both looked terribly uncomfortable on the backs of horses.

Impact Cagney's acting career made a huge impact on the American film industry both on and off the screen. Cagney played the hero at a time when the American public desperately needed one. Perhaps his greatest performance came in the role of George M. Cohan in *Yankee Doodle Dandy* (1942). This patriotic film was released shortly after U.S. entry into World War II, and it helped raise the spirit of the American public. For his performance Cagney was honored with the Academy Award for best actor in 1942.

Paul P. Sipiera

Further Reading

McCabe, John. *Cagney.* New York: Alfred A. Knopf, 1997.

Nollen, Scott Allen. *Warners Wiseguys: All 112 Films That Robinson, Cagney, and Bogart Made for the Studio.* Jefferson, N.C.: McFarland, 2008.

Schickel, Richard. *James Cagney: A Celebration.* Boston: Little, Brown, 1985.

See also Academy Awards; Broadway musicals; Cohan, George M.; Gangster films; Great Depression in the United States; Organized crime.

■ Calder, Alexander

Identification American sculptor
Born July 22, 1898; Lawnton (now part of Philadelphia), Pennsylvania
Died November 11, 1976; New York, New York

As an artist familiar with American and European modern artists and styles, Calder combined fine art with industrial materials and engineering to become the first American artist to produce monumental sculpture in the form of the kinetic mobile and the fixed stabile.

Alexander Calder's formal training in art and engineering provided the backbone for his artistic work during the 1930's. The time he spent in Paris and New York from 1926 to 1933 after his academic training was critical to his artistic innovations. From 1926 to 1931, Calder worked on wire dioramas, many of which displayed his early engineering training. Us-

ing a circus as subject matter, he incorporated mechanized movement into his acrobatic figures. As ringmaster, he presented a three-ring performance known in the United States as "Calder's Circus." In recognition of Calder's previous work in wire and his circus performances, in 1930, Calder was invited by the Harvard Society for Contemporary Art to exhibit *Wire Sculpture by Alexander Calder* and performed his circus for an educated American audience.

In the same year, Calder realized that the artist Piet Mondrian's arrangement of shapes, forms, and colors implied a mass that was absent in his wire sculptures. With further exposure and encouragement from other European artists, Calder explored movement of forms in space with abstract constructions and kinetic sculpture that relied on chance motion. To achieve natural movement through space, he experimented with delicate balances of weights and counterweights of various shapes placed at the ends of wire frames. By placing weights and balances sufficiently off-center, Calder demonstrated that gentle movements by currents of air were possible. From 1930 to 1931, he incorporated motorized movement and wind movement in his sculptures, coined "mobiles" by artist Marcel Duchamp. His mobiles broke from sculptural convention when he hung works from the ceiling rather than securing them to a floor or pedestal base.

Significant American recognition of his work came in 1931, when he was one of the youngest artists invited to participate in a group exhibition, *Painting and Sculpture by Living Americans*, at the Museum of Modern Art in New York. The following year, his first "mobile" exhibitions were displayed in Galerie Vignon in Paris and Julien Levy Gallery in New York.

In 1933, Calder purchased an old farmhouse on eighteen acres in Roxbury, Connecticut, which allowed him the space to work on large-scale sculpture. There Calder began cutting shapes out of large sheets of metal and bolting them together to make his first monumental "stabiles," a term first used by the artist Jean Arp in 1931 when describing Calder's abstract wire constructions. In 1935, Calder installed workbenches and a system of pulleys in his farm studio that facilitated development of the large-scale mobiles that characterized his later work. They featured a succession of bent wires of unequal length freely connected to one another and ending with curvilinear plates of painted metal.

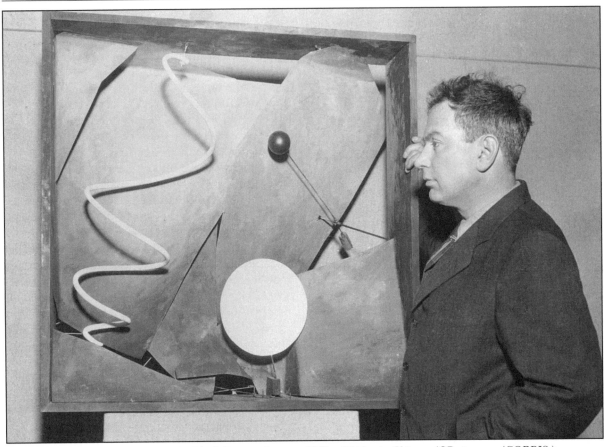

Alexander Calder, showing his Black Frame *piece at a 1935 exhibition in Chicago.* (©Bettmann/CORBIS)

Calder created other abstract works in which all parts were contained within a rectangular frame or placed before a panel. Each could move laterally, perpendicularly, or rotarily at different speeds. In the United States these works were included in theatrical commissions. Calder supplied mobile panels for two Martha Graham productions—*Panorama* (1935) at Bennington School of Dance in Vermont and *Horizons* the following year in New York. In 1936, he provided the mobile settings for Erik Satie's *Socrate* at the First Hartford Festival in Connecticut. Calder's largest audience for a theater performance was *Water Ballet* at the pool of the Consolidated Edison Building at the New York World's Fair in 1939. The decade culminated for the artist when he won first place in the Museum of Modern Art's Plexiglas sculpture competition.

Impact   Calder brought to American art during the 1930's large-scale sculpture made of industrial mate-

rials, engineered to be both movable and fixed, ground or ceiling attached, and designed for diverse public indoor and outdoor spaces. His innovations led the way for later American artists to explore new materials, architectural scale, and nonconventional space.

Patricia Coronel and Michael Coronel

Further Reading

Bourbon, David. *Calder: Mobilist, Ringmaster, Innovator.* New York: Macmillan, 1980.

Calder, Alexander. *Calder.* New York: Pantheon, 1966.

Giménez, Carmen, and Alexander S. C. Rower, eds. *Calder: Gravity and Grace.* London: Phaidon, 2003.

Rosenthal, Mark. *The Surreal Calder.* New Haven, Conn.: Yale University Press, 2005.

See also   *American Gothic*; Art movements; Benton, Thomas Hart; Curry, John Steuart; Graham, Martha; Wood, Grant.

■ Caldwell, Erskine

Identification   American writer
Born   December 17, 1903; White Oak, Georgia
Died   April 11, 1987; Paradise Valley, Arizona

Caldwell dramatized the desperate plight of the U.S. agrarian underclass in violent and frequently lurid stories and novels, attracting a large readership, dividing critics, and sometimes precipitating legal action.

Georgia-born Erskine Caldwell had already worked as a reporter by the time he enrolled in the University of Virginia in 1923. He married Helen Lannigan in 1925 and, the following year, moved with her to Maine, where he ran a bookstore for a time. Caldwell hoped to be a creative writer and had published a short novel and a handful of stories by the beginning of the 1930's.

Scribner's magazine featured two stories by Caldwell in 1930, and noted editor Maxwell Perkins accepted a story collection, *American Earth*, for publication by Scribner's Sons the following year. Caldwell returned to Georgia to refresh his memories and observe the devastating impact of the Great Depression on his native state. The novel into which he poured his impressions, *Tobacco Road*, was published by Scribner's Sons in 1932. Although it would rank as one of his best works, *Tobacco Road* was not an immediate success. Readers and critics alike were dismayed by its tragicomic descriptions of chronically poor individuals who had lost everything except the will to survive and the urge to reproduce. However, Jack Kirkland's 1933 dramatization—which ran for more than seven years in New York City—made Caldwell's name familiar to a larger public and secured him a measure of financial independence.

When Scribner's Sons rejected Caldwell's next novel, which was set in Maine, Caldwell offered a story collection, *We Are the Living* (1933), and an entirely new novel, *God's Little Acre* (1933), to Viking Press. Although its concluding story, "A Country Full of Swedes," won a Yale Review prize of $1,000, *We Are the Living* itself made little impact. *God's Little Acre* was a different matter. Describing the situation of Ty Ty Walden, a hapless Georgia farmer who spends his time and energy searching vainly for gold rather than raising crops, it quickly attracted the attention of the New York Society for the Suppression of Vice. The resulting charges of pornography were dismissed, but the publicity fueled Caldwell's growing fame. Critics also found the novel an advance over *Tobacco Road*.

The novel *Journeyman* (1935) dealt with an itinerant preacher and was both a bitter attack on fundamentalism and a meditation on the nature of evil. It also marked the beginning of what became an increasingly important concern in Caldwell's works: the plight of African Americans. That concern was also evident in *Kneel to the Rising Sun* (1935), a collection whose title story—an account of a lynching—has been recognized not only as Caldwell's best single work but also as one of the most powerful American short stories ever written.

In 1936, Caldwell toured the South with fledgling photographer Margaret Bourke-White. The immediate result was the moving photo-essay *You Have Seen Their Faces* (1937), for which Caldwell wrote the text and Bourke-White supplied the illustrations. Next, the two visited eastern Europe, producing another collaboration, *North of the Danube* (1939). Despite the praise of critics, neither work sold well. In the meantime, Caldwell's wife had divorced him in 1938, and he and Bourke-White were married in 1939.

Impact   Caldwell's marriage to Bourke-White ended in 1942, and he married twice more over the ensuing years. He continued writing prolifically until the end of his life, but the 1930's were the most successful decade of his career. Among Caldwell's later works, some critics have praised the genial novel *Georgia Boy* (1943), but the consensus has been that Caldwell was unable to expand his range beyond a limited number of themes, situations, and character types. A generous contract that he signed with paperback publisher New American Library in 1953 also proved problematic, for although the publisher's many reprints of Caldwell's books sold well, their frequently lurid covers contributed to the popular view of him as a writer of "cheap" drugstore paperbacks.

Grove Koger

Further Reading

Caldwell, Erskine. *Tobacco Road*. Reprint. Athens: University of Georgia Press, 1995.

Devlin, James E. *Erskine Caldwell*. Boston: Twayne, 1984.

McDonald, Robert L., ed. *Reading Erskine Caldwell: New Essays*. Jefferson, N.C.: McFarland, 2006.

Stevens, C. J. *Storyteller: A Life of Erskine Caldwell.* Phillips, Maine: John Wade, 2000.

See also Agriculture in the United States; Faulkner, William; Great Depression in the United States; Literature in the United States; Lynching; Racial discrimination; Steinbeck, John; Theater in the United States; *Tobacco Road*; Wolfe, Thomas.

■ Canada, U.S. investments in

From its earliest days of settlement, Canada has welcomed foreign investments as a means of stimulating the economy. The United States, Canada's nearest neighbor, both geographically and culturally, has served as a major trading partner since the nineteenth century, and American businesses have found Canada a profitable place to invest their capital.

Canada has long been an attractive market for both U.S. trade and American private enterprise. The relationship between the two nations similar in culture, ethnicity, geography, language, lifestyle, and philosophy has been mutually beneficial.

For the United States, easy access to a wealth of Canadian natural resources, such as fishing grounds, furs, timber for pulp and paper, agricultural products, minerals and petroleum, and water and hydroelectric power, was of primary importance in establishing public and private trade arrangements beginning during the 1850's. Favorable laws governing taxes, patent leasing arrangements, incorporation and ownership, and proximity to waterways and rail systems for the transportation of goods have all proven highly advantageous.

Meanwhile, Canada has been able to draw on the usually robust American economy for cash and credit infusions that make expansion and modernization possible. In general, the United States has had a huge and eager consumer market for Canadian products. American expertise in technology, management, and marketing has also produced a generally high standard of living in Canada.

Twentieth Century U.S. Investments in Canada During the early twentieth century, a period of great economic growth in both the United States and Canada took hold as a result of industrialization. One of the early instances of the modern Canadian-American business relationship was the 1898 Standard Oil of New Jersey takeover of the Imperial Oil Limited of Canada. That transaction and others like it began a period of massive U.S. investment in Canada, and money from American businesses flowed in great quantities into the country. Before World War I, American investments in Canada exceeded $400 million annually. Although the war, and a brief inflationary period afterward, slowed the stream of money to Canada, the pace soon picked up again. By 1920, American investments were found in virtually every segment of the Canadian economy, from shoes to liquor, and from shipbuilding to sugar. Americans boasted controlling interests (50 percent or more ownership) in Canadian manufacturing industries such as copper and smelting, drugs and chemicals, patent medicines, automobiles and accessories, paint and varnish, and abrasives.

In 1923, Americans invested $2.4 billion in Canadian enterprises. The balance sheets of U.S. entrepreneurs showed major holdings in Canadian public securities, general industries, forests, paper and pulp processing and sawmills, mining, public utilities and services, and railways in addition to significant investments in fisheries, banking and insurance, and land.

During the 1920's, dozens of American companies established branches in Canada to serve the provincial markets, which not only eliminated shipping costs, import duties, and capital gains issues but also allowed the Canadian-made goods to achieve preferential tariff rates when sold to other countries in the British Empire. International Nickel, International Harvester, International Paper, B.F. Goodrich Rubber Company, Goodyear, General Electric, the Aluminum Company of America, Ford Motor Company, General Motors, Singer Manufacturing, and other U.S.-based companies set up Canadian subsidiaries. While exact figures are difficult to ascertain because some investments were direct, others were portfolio purchases, and still others were set up with Canadians at the helm, at least six hundred and as many as sixteen hundred Canadian companies received sizable investments from American entrepreneurs during the late 1920's and early 1930's. American interests also absorbed many Canadian firms, notably the Montreal Locomotive Works and the Canadian Consolidated Rubber Company. Continental Baking Corporation of New York bought out six of Canada's leading baking companies.

Although some Canadians expressed concern that their homeland had become the country with the highest percentage of foreign ownership in the world and that it was becoming too dependent on American financing, their fears were drowned in a wave of prosperity. Productivity was high: Between 1922 and 1929, the Canadian gross national product grew at an annual rate approaching 5 percent. Unemployment was low: less than 4 percent during the same period. Consumerism during the boom was rampant: The number of registered, privately owned automobiles rose from 300,000 in 1918 to 1.9 million in 1929 as Canadians enjoyed an unprecedented standard of living.

U.S. Investments and the Great Depression Between 1922 and 1931, the total of all annual American foreign investments nearly doubled, from about $8 billion to more than $15 billion, with some 50 percent of the total going to countries in the Western Hemisphere. In 1931, Americans invested almost $4 billion in Canada alone, as the United States supplanted Great Britain as Canada's top supplier of private funding for business.

The onset of the Depression in late 1929 slowed the rate of cumulative American foreign investments. For a time, the 1930 Hawley-Smoot Tariff Act greatly reduced exports from Canada to the United States, until the 1934 Reciprocal Trade Agreements Act ameliorated tariffs and renewed trade; a second act signed in 1938 cut tariffs again and increased imports and exports between the two countries. While American investments in Canada fell precipitously during the first few years of the Depression, the proportion of American investments in Canada actually increased. Throughout the Depression, about 60 percent of all foreign capital in Canada came from American investors, and two-thirds of all imports into Canada originated in the United States.

U.S. investors continued to look to Canada for profits. In 1930, Dominion Gas and Electric Company, a subsidiary of the American Commonwealth Power Corporation, bought a network of Canadian utilities. That same year, the American firm Sparks-Worthington, a manufacturer of equipment for transportation, electronics, communication, and defense industries, formed Sparton of Canada to introduce a line of Canadian-made radios. In fact, in 1930, American firms set up forty-two branch offices in Canada, a number that compares favorably with

the 1929 pre-Depression peak of fifty. In 1931, another twenty-seven American branch offices were established in Canada, and in 1932, during the worst year of the Depression, an additional twenty-six American-owned branch operations were founded. Most of the new American-owned enterprises were concentrated in food, textiles, public utilities, mining, and metal processing.

Impact Throughout the long joint history in business between Canada and the United States, the relationship between the two countries has been mostly amicable, though there have been occasional squabbles over tariff rates. Because of the high percentage of imports and exports to and from the United States, Canada periodically frets over its overdependence on American trade and its vulnerability to U.S. trade policies. Despite such reservations, the economic relationship between the United States and Canada has remained strong, in both public and private arenas.

Jack Ewing

Further Reading

Easterbrook, W. T., and M. H. Watkins, eds. *Approaches to Canadian Economic History*. Montreal: McGill-Queen's University Press, 2003. Collection of essays examining Canada's economic history, tracing the development and impact of the country's traditionally strong industries: fish, fur, timber, minerals, and oil.

Harris, Richard G., ed. *North American Linkages: Opportunities and Challenges for Canada*. Calgary: University of Calgary Press, 2003. Part of a series. Includes essays from many international economic experts regarding the history, development, and significance of relationships and policies among Canada's major trading partners.

Levitt, Kari. *Silent Surrender: The Multinational Corporation in Canada*. Reprint. Montreal: McGill-Queen's University Press, 2003. Examines the history of foreign, particularly American, investments in Canada and their effects on Canadian economy and society.

Martin, Joe. *Relentless Change: A Casebook for the Study of Canadian Business History*. Toronto: University of Toronto Press, 2009. Presents case histories relating to the development of more than one dozen specific Canadian businesses across a variety of industries from the nineteenth century to the twenty-first century. Traces the evolution of

Canada's largest companies during the twentieth century.

Safarian, A. E. *The Canadian Economy in the Great Depression.* 3d ed. Montreal: McGill-Queen's University Press, 2009. Covers the period before, during, and after the Depression, showing the causes and effects of the boom and slump on Canada and relating the era to the economic crisis of the early twenty-first century.

Studer-Noguez, Isabel. *Ford and the Global Strategies of Multinationals: The North American Auto Industry.* London: Routledge, 2001. Case study of the Ford Motor Company, focusing on its investments in the automobile industries of Canada and Mexico.

See also   Agriculture in Canada; Business and the economy in Canada; Great Depression in Canada; Hawley-Smoot Tariff Act of 1930; Income and wages in Canada; International trade; Ottawa Agreements; Reciprocal Trade Agreements Act of 1936.

■ Canada and Great Britain

As Canada emerged from World War I, its independence as a nation became increasingly obvious. This meant readjusting its legal ties with Great Britain as well as finding proper relationships with the other members of the British Commonwealth. Such a relationship was considered an essential counterbalance to the increasingly close trade ties Canada had with the United States. The Depression era distorted and exposed this tension between Britain and both its Commonwealth and the United States.

After World War I, Canada had shown itself worthy of consideration as a fully independent nation rather than a dominion of the British Commonwealth whose foreign relations and treaty commitments were still largely determined by the mother country. During the 1920's, Canada was working out de facto independence. Increasingly, though, Canada felt the need to make this a de jure independence. The Statute of Westminster, signed by the British parliament in 1931, was the legal document finally agreed upon by Great Britain and the independent nations of the Commonwealth. In Canada's case, because French Canadians had suspicions that the Supreme Court of Canada was to be lodged in Ottawa, the agreement stipulated that the final court of appeal was to remain the Privy Council of the British parliament.

Commonwealth Preferences   During the 1920's, the Liberal Party government of William Lyon Mackenzie King wished to maintain strong ties with Britain and preferred British trade over American trade. The Wall Street crash of 1929 and the following economic Depression complicated this desire. For one, the American policy was to protect its own industries by imposing trade barriers against other countries by the use of increased import tariffs, effectively hindering any possible expansion of Canadian trade with the United States. Also, there was less to trade, and Canada's balance of payments began to suffer. Also, the King government was defeated in 1930 and replaced by the Conservative Party government of Richard Bedford Bennett, a prime minister much more open to dealing with the United States. His undersecretary of state, O. D. Skelton, had a deep distrust of Britain and encouraged this openness.

At the Imperial Conference in London in 1930, Canada took a lead in calling for a Commonwealth conference to stimulate trade between members. This conference was finally held in Ottawa in the summer of 1932. By then, the British government had changed and was much more protectionist, willing to put up its own tariff walls against non-Commonwealth countries. A large number of items had duties removed from them in import-export trade between the Commonwealth nations. There was not sufficient unanimity for an overarching agreement, but a number of smaller agreements were entered into, which were sufficient to concern the United States that it had been sidelined in a trade partnership with Canada.

However, Britain's own economic weakness during the 1930's meant that the Commonwealth preference system could not be fully exploited. Bennett pressed the United States as early as 1933, and a trade deal was completed between the two countries in 1935. One aspect of the agreement was that Canada relinquish some of the preferences it had negotiated at Ottawa in return for the lowering of U.S. tariffs. Although trade began to improve for Canada, it was still painfully slow. Bennett's government did not last beyond a single term.

Foreign Policy   One of the ways Canada wished to show its full independence from Great Britain was by refusing to be committed to any foreign policy deci-

Though Canada's relationship with Great Britain changed as it sought greater autonomy, Canada strongly supported Great Britain in World War II. Here, Leslie Hore-Belisha (in black hat and long coat), the British war secretary, interviews a Canadian machine-gun crew training in Britain in 1939. (Hulton Archive/Getty Images)

sion made by Britain without full consultation. Early during the 1930's, this was not significant. Britain and Canada were both members of the League of Nations, and Canadian diplomatic concerns barely existed outside London or Geneva, the seat of the league. The Canadian Department of External Affairs was small, as was its diplomatic corps, and depended greatly on information supplied by the British Dominions Office.

As the peace policies adopted by the League of Nations and by Great Britain began to unravel in the latter part of the decade, with the rise of Nazi Germany and Imperial Japan in particular, Britain became increasingly concerned as to what support it could expect from its Commonwealth in the event of hostilities. During World War I, Canada's loyalty to Britain had been strong but was severely tested, espe-

cially over the conscription issue. However, French Canadian opinion was not necessarily pro-British at any time, especially over issues such as relations with Italy and the Spanish Civil War, because pro-Catholic sympathies went hand-in-hand with far right-wing policies in Italy and Spain.

The King government, which had been reelected, put national unity ahead of outright support of Britain and so declined to commit itself to any future war. There was a strong pacifist and isolationist opinion supporting King. However, after the Imperial Conference in London, 1938, King was prepared to go to Germany and tell Adolf Hitler face-to-face that Canada would not stay neutral in the case of an outbreak of hostilities. Nonetheless, Canadian public opinion backed King as he supported British prime minister Neville Chamberlain in his peace negotiations with Hitler in 1938, negotiations that ultimately proved hypocritical and futile.

King also considered himself to be a go-between for Britain and the United States. U.S. isolationism in the early 1930's was beginning to thaw under President Franklin D. Roosevelt. King contacted the United States on Britain's behalf from 1935 onward. King and Roosevelt met at Chautauqua in 1936. At a famous meeting in Kingston, Ontario, in 1938, Roosevelt declared the United States would not stand by if Canada were invaded. In the light of Canada's demilitarization, this was a comforting gesture. Even so, King, only days after, made it clear that this did not weaken Canada's commitment to its British ties.

Even when war was finally declared in early September, 1939, the British were not fully certain Canada would do more than send economic help, supplies, and munitions. Whereas Australia and New Zealand took the British declaration of war as their own, King insisted on recalling the Canadian parliament to have a full debate. Although the vote, one week later, was practically unanimous in favor of supporting Britain's war effort, it was still a sign of Canada's determined independence.

When the first British and French expeditionary forces failed to withstand Nazi troops in spring, 1940, Canada responded to vastly greater demand for supplies and an all-out conflict in a strong way. It offered itself as the base for the British Commonwealth Air Training Plan, the main base for the training of Commonwealth air crews during the coming decade. Canada even supplied the equipment and finances for this venture largely by itself.

Other Commonwealth Links Canadian ties with Great Britain did not all concern trade and politics. Although British immigration lessened considerably, mainly because of the Depression and Canada's wish to protect its own workforce, there were still strong family ties between Canada and Great Britain. Canada hosted the first British Empire Games, at Hamilton, Ontario, in the summer of 1930. Eleven nations were represented; four hundred athletes participated in fifty-nine events. Canada did well, finishing second to England in the medals total. These games grew into the Commonwealth Games and had an enormous influence in binding together the postwar Commonwealth.

Canadians followed the British constitutional crisis of 1936-1937 over the Duke of Windsor (Ed-ward VIII) and his subsequent abdication over his proposed marriage to American divorcee, Wallace Simpson. When the new anointed king and queen, George VI and Elizabeth, decided to tour Canada in May, 1939, there was an outstanding welcome given to the royal pair, even in Quebec City, the area with the most French Canadians. The visit was a diplomatic success for Britain, securing Canadian support in any war in Europe.

Impact The ties between Canada and Great Britain changed considerably during the 1930's. The balance of relationships between Canada, Great Britain, and the United States inevitably tipped toward the United States in terms of trade and economic liaison. Nonetheless, at the end of the decade, when the call for support of Britain came as World War II broke out, Canadian commitment was total. Although military preparedness was at an all-time low, Canada rearmed itself and turned its industries to war-related production in an amazingly short time, even without conscription. Any show of isolationism disappeared overnight. As Canadians once again shipped to Britain to fight for the Commonwealth, the relationship between the two countries seemed as strong as ever.

David Barratt

Further Reading

Bothwell, Robert, Ian Drummond, and John English. *Canada 1900-1945.* Toronto: University of Toronto Press, 1987. Full account of Canada in the first part of the twentieth century, with several chapters dealing extensively with Canada's relationships with Great Britain during the 1930's.

Creighton, Donald Grant. *A History of Canada: Dominion of the North.* Cambridge, Mass.: Riverside Press, 1958. Chapter 9 deals with the 1930's, especially the effects of the Depression on Canada's trade policies with the Commonwealth.

Granatstein, J. L. *How Britain's Weakness Forced Canada into the Arms of the United States.* Toronto: University of Toronto Press, 1989. Granatstein, a leading Canadian historian, discusses Canada's economic split from England, which forced the country into closer ties with the United States.

Mackenzie, Hector. "'Arsenal of the British Empire'? British Orders for Munitions Productions in Canada 1936-1939." *Journal of Imperial and Commonwealth History* 31, no. 3 (2003): 41-73. Discusses the vexed question of Canadian ties with Great

Britain in the light of Britain wanting to protect its own industries.

Meehan, John. "Steering Clear of Great Britain: Canada's Debate over Collective Security in the Far Eastern Crisis of 1937." *International History Review* 25, no. 2 (2003): 253-281. Discusses the unrecognized importance of international relations of the Pacific sphere in the events leading to World War II.

Wittke, Carl. *A History of Canada.* 3d ed. New York: Appleton-Century-Crofts, 1941. Account of Canada's changing relationship with Britain during the 1930's.

See also   Agriculture in Canada; George VI's North American visit; Statute of Westminster; World War I debts; World War II and Canada.

■ Canadian minority communities

Definition   Ethnic groups not of Anglo-Saxon origin

The plight of the Canadian minority communities during the 1930's is a significant example of the nationalistic attitudes prevalent throughout the world before and during World War II.

The decade of the 1930's was a difficult period for most minority communities in Canada. The country had been populated primarily by British and French settlers. People of other races and nationalities had settled in Canada either as individuals or as small groups. As a result, the population of Canada was composed of three major groups: Canadians of British ancestry, French Canadians, and aboriginal peoples. The profitable fur trade created an attitude of tolerance between the native tribes and the British and French Canadians. In addition, Canada's enormous land mass and the location of aboriginal tribes away from urban areas permitted each group to live separately.

Although a certain amount of conflict and tension based on differences of language and religion always existed between the British majority and the French minority, the concentration of the French in the Quebec Province, created in 1867, and in Arcadia enabled the two communities to maintain their own lifestyles. In Quebec, the local French officials were in charge of issues such as education, property rights, and civil rights. This jurisdiction enabled them to preserve their cultural identity. The economic activities of the province were administered by the central government, which was controlled by the British Canadians. The three communities avoided social interaction with each other, spoke their own languages, and maintained separate religions and institutions. This situation set a precedent for the isolationism and segregation that was strongly entrenched in the Canadian mind-set when waves of immigrants began arriving during the late nineteenth and early twentieth centuries.

Canadians viewed the acceptance of immigrants from an economic standpoint. Admission of immigrants was considered a viable way of developing Canada's economy. The country needed farmers to settle the great prairies of western Canada; therefore, immigrants with farming skills were welcomed to Canada. The mining and logging industries were also in need of workers. Building the Canadian railways provided another incentive for admitting immigrants to Canada. From the 1880's to the 1920's, many immigrants arrived in Canada; these included Lithuanians and other eastern Europeans, Slavs, Italians, Jews, Chinese, Japanese, and people of African descent as well as minority religious sects adept at farming, such as the Russian pacifist Doukhobors and Mennonites.

The amount of assimilation possible for these groups of people was directly related to how much the immigrants were like Anglo-Saxons. During the 1920's, Canada developed a scale of desirability for immigrants. British and American immigrants ranked first and were readily given entry. People from western and northern Europe were classed second as preferred immigrants; those from eastern Europe were listed next, in the category of nonpreferred. Jews and southern Europeans were placed in a fourth class and required special permission to enter. Asians and black people were not welcome.

Thus, at the beginning of the 1930's, the majority of Canadians were Anglo-Saxon and Protestant and had a mind-set that Canada's population should be Anglo-Saxon and Protestant and follow Anglo-Saxon ideas in regard to politics and social customs. The French Canadians feared that the establishment of other minority groups in the country would weaken their position politically and culturally. The influx of other ethnic groups during the late nineteenth and early twentieth centuries had caused concerns about their own place in the country; consequently, they also were not welcoming to other nationalities and races. For the most part, both the British and the French Canadians viewed immigrants as not particularly desirable but as an asset to the economic development of the country. Isolation and separation of these minority communities was the accepted structure of Canadian society.

Effects of Economic Hardship and Unemployment
Because of the economic difficulties and high unemployment, ranging from 15 to 25 percent, that resulted from the Great Depression, minority communities were viewed unfavorably. If members of these communities were employed, they were taking jobs away from British and French Canadians. If they were unemployed, they were on the public charge and financially burdening the country.

Beginning in 1930, unemployed members of minority communities were deported because they were on the public charge. More than twenty-eight thousand individuals were deported between 1930 and 1935. After strong protests against deportation of the unemployed, the policy was modified. If the unemployed were fortunate enough to find employment before the date of their scheduled deportation, they could remain in Canada. However, preference in employment was given to British and French Canadians, especially to veterans of World War I.

Because of the difficulty of obtaining work and the low wages and harsh working conditions faced by most minority workers, many became active in labor unions or joined socialist or communist parties. In August of 1931, the Communist Party of Canada was declared illegal under the criminal code. Members were subject to revocation of their citizenship and deportation. By the fall of that year the federal government had made deportation for political affiliations a part of its regular policy. With this unfavorable view of minority communities in place, prejudice and discrimination intensified. Minority communities experienced even greater segregation economically, socially, and politically. Race and religion became causes for exclusion and persecution. The majority of British Canadians and French Canadians believed that the few available jobs should be filled by them, not by members of the minority communities. Many banks, retail stores, and insurance companies refused to hire anyone who was not of British or French ancestry. The discrimination spread to housing, and minorities were excluded from renting or buying property in many different neighborhoods. The Canadian courts maintained that employers and landlords had the right to exclude members of minority communities.

Discrimination Based on Race and Religion   In 1923, the Chinese Immigration Act (also known as the Chinese Exclusion Act) had been passed, which prohibited the immigration of Chinese to Canada; the act remained in force until 1947. Although they were willing to assimilate, the Chinese who were living in Canada during this period were isolated in Chinatowns. Jobs for Chinese were limited to the Chinatowns, and Chinese people were barred from a number of professions. The most widespread discrimination against Asians was in British Columbia. They were believed to be inferior and impossible to assimilate. The labor unions maintained that because Asians worked for lower wages, they took jobs away from white Canadians and also lowered the living standards in the communities where they lived. Consequently, they were not accepted as members of unions. Asians were also denied the right to vote and were not permitted to run for public office. They were also excluded from employment in civil service or as teachers. Black people and Asians were marginalized throughout Canada and suffered from discrimination in employment, education, and housing.

With the approach of World War II, the Doukhobors were disenfranchised because of their pacifist beliefs. As Canadians exhibited stronger senses of nationalism, the pacifist refusal to bear arms was interpreted as a lack of loyalty to Canada. Anti-Semitism had long been active in Canada, and during the 1930's, social discrimination against Jews increased. They were excluded from resorts, beaches, and recreational facilities. Quotas were placed on the number who could be admitted to universities. They were barred from a number of professions, and though not officially restricted from certain residential districts, they were not welcomed in them. Some more radical Canadians refused to patronize their businesses. In addition, they were the target of fascist and Nazi parties that had formed in the country. Anti-Semitism was particularly widespread in Quebec, where many Jews had settled.

During the 1930's, the disastrous state of Canada's economy and the rampant unemployment created a situation unfavorable for minority communities. They had been welcomed to Canada based on the idea that as farmers, miners, loggers, and railways workers, they would contribute to the development of the Canadian economy and improve the quality of life for Canadians. The Great Depression precluded economic expansion and improvement in living standards. To most Canadians, the minority communities were no longer an economic asset. In their view, minorities had become unwanted competition in an almost nonexistent job market and a burden to the country's welfare system.

Impact   During the 1930's, the minority communities of Canada had little influence politically, economically, or socially on the nation. The government policies of isolation and restriction marginalized these groups. The status of the communities changed from one of economic asset to that of a burden on the Canadian economy. The desire both to limit and to reduce the ethnic or non-Anglo-Saxon Protestant communities in Canada resulted in the closing of Canada's ports to refugees, whom the Canadians did not distinguish from immigrants. Coupled with the country's anti-Semitism, this decision proved disastrous for Jews fleeing the spread of the Nazi regime in Europe.

Nonetheless, the minority communities did leave legacies to future generations of ethnic and religious minorities in Canada and to Canada as a country. By enduring the hardships placed upon them during the Great Depression, they maintained a place in Canada for their descendants, who contributed to the ethnic diversity that developed in Canada after World War II.

Shawncey Webb

Further Reading

Berton, Pierre. *The Great Depression, 1929-1939.* Toronto: Anchor Canada, 2001. Thorough presentation of Canada during the Great Depression, including the country's policies, its public officials, and the plight of the average citizen and minorities. Provides the context necessary for understanding the situation of minority communities at the time.

Kukushkin, Vadim. *From Peasants to Labourers: Ukrainian and Belarusan Immigration from the Russian Empire to Canada.* Montreal: McGill-Queen's University Press, 2007. Looks at minority communities from the perspective that immigrants were useful to economic development.

Li, Peter S. *The Chinese in Canada.* 2d ed. New York: Oxford University Press, 1998. Investigates reasons for the entrenched Canadian view of Chinese as foreign.

Rosenberg, Louis. *Canada's Jews: A Social and Economic Study of Jews in Canada in the 1930's.* Montreal: McGill-Queen's University Press, 1993. Comprehensive study of the Jewish community's cultural, social, and economic aspects. Compares the situation of Jews to those of other religious and ethnic minorities.

Walker, Barrington, ed. *The History of Immigrants and Racism in Canada.* Toronto: Canadian Scholars Press, 2008. Good for information on racism during the 1930's, how it developed, and the changes that occurred after World War II.

Winks, Robert W. *The Blacks in Canada.* 2d ed. Montreal: McGill-Queen's University Press, 1997. Explores the black experience in Canada from 1620 to 1997. Chapters 10 and 14 address the 1930's.

See also   Anti-Semitism; Demographics of Canada; Fascism in Canada; Immigration to Canada; Jews in Canada; Religion in Canada; Unemployment in Canada.

■ Canadian regionalism

Because of the geographic vastness of Canada, tension between central control and regional forces based on separate identities and cultural differences has long existed. During the 1930's, this tension increased between the central federal government in Ottawa and the separate provinces, each with its own parallel political structures. The Statute of Westminster of 1931 enshrined this in constitutional terms.

Canadian regionalism has existed since the foundation of the country. It has been partly historically based, partly geographically. Historically, the beginnings of the country were French; Quebec, in lower Canada, has a French-speaking culture and Roman Catholic values and practices. In the eighteenth century, power shifted to the British colonial power with the foundation of Upper Canada, comprising part of present-day Ontario, and the reformation of the

Maritime Provinces (Nova Scotia, New Brunswick, and Prince Edward Island) as British, rather than French, colonies.

In the nineteenth century, westward and northward expansion led to the founding of the Prairie and Pacific coast provinces. Although these were English speaking, they were settled by independent-minded farmers and frontierspeople. By contrast, the northwestern territories were left to the Inuit, the aboriginal inhabitants of the land. Attempts were made to assimilate other original peoples into the colonists' European culture. Politically, all of this resolved itself in the formation of the Dominion of Canada, with its separate provinces to represent these regional differences.

Newfoundland, comprising the island of Newfoundland and the coasts of Labrador, was formed as a separate dominion in 1931. Later in the decade, it reverted to colonial status, with its affairs once again administered from Great Britain.

Maurice Duplessis, the premier of Quebec, was a strong regionalist, usually opposing the agenda of the Liberal federal government in Ottawa. (AFP/Getty Images)

Quebec During the 1930's   Catholic French speakers represented the strongest example of regionalism. Historically based in the province of Quebec, francophone culture maintained influence in pockets of other provinces, but these groups became assimilated into the larger anglophone cultures. In Quebec, this francophone regionalism was well formed institutionally, and it expressed its own identity strongly. However, during the 1930's, the province of Quebec was still anglophone in many areas, even in Montreal, and there was no real separatist movement.

The forces of regional identity took several different expressions. The most vocal group was the ultramontanists, who considered the control of the Roman Catholic Church to be vital educationally, culturally, and politically. As in Ireland, a country with Dominion status at the time, ultramontanist Catholicism promoted the continued authority of the pope and the Vatican as central in its mission to spread the Catholic faith. As in Ireland, the group was anti-industrial, agrarian, and family oriented. It sought to keep its traditional identity. It also was anti-Semitic and anticommunist, but so were other regional groups. Its strongest exponent was Henri Bourassa, a former politician and founder of the Nationalist League in 1903.

Another example of regionalism during the 1930's was represented by Maurice Duplessis, formerly a Conservative politician who became leader of the Quebec Conservative Party in 1933. In 1935, he established a coalition with a breakaway Liberal group, the Action libérale nationale, out of which grew the Union Nationale Party in 1936. This organization gained power in the provincial elections of that year in a landslide victory. Duplessis's politics grounded regionalism firmly into party provincial expression, standing in opposition to the federal Liberal Party in power in Ottawa.

The Western Provinces and Other Aspects of Regionalism   In the West, regionalism also took on a specifically political form along provincial lines. The best defined example of this was in Alberta, where the Social Credit Party governed the province from 1935 to 1971, through nine successive provincial elections. While there was no design to keep the party within a single province, in effect, this is what happened. The Co-operative Commonwealth Federation (CCF), another Western party, had a wider appeal with its socialist manifesto than the Social Credit Party, but found its power base in the three other Western provinces. Again, the effect was to place the provincial governments at odds with the federal government, dominated by the Liberal Party.

Regional movements also existed in the Maritime Provinces, especially as their resources were used by the central government. However, William Lyon Mackenzie King, the Liberal Party leader of the federal government, managed to compromise on their concerns, and no fully fledged regionalism developed.

Native Canadian tribes were minorities and were scattered throughout the country. However, the Inuit resided specifically in the undeveloped Northwest Territories. A federal policy of assimilation was still in force during the 1930's, though the 1930 Constitution Act did give more rights to Canadian aborigines. The term "First Nations" was not coined until the 1960's.

Impact The impact of the national-regional tensions was felt throughout the decade, though none of the tension developed into a separatist movement. However, the 1931 Statute of Westminster was developed differently for Canada than for other Dominions because of these unresolved tensions. For example, the London-based Privy Council retained its powers as Canada's final court of justice. At the end of the decade, the outbreak of World War II unified the country, especially as King took extreme care not to repeat the conscription debate that marred the internal politics of World War I.

David Barratt

Further Reading

Bothwell, Robert. *Canada and Quebec: One Country, Two Histories.* Rev. ed. Vancouver: University of British Columbia Press, 1998. One of the definitive books on francophone regionalism from a historical basis.

Lacoursière, Jacques, and Robin Philpot. *A People's History of Quebec.* Montreal: Baraka Books, 2009. Popular account of Quebec's development as a distinctive region.

Resnick, Philip. *Politics of Resentment: British Columbia Regionalism and Canadian Unity.* Vancouver: University of British Columbia Press, 2001. Explores what made British Columbia stand apart as a region and its role in the growing conversation over Canadian unity.

Wade, Mason. *Regionalism in the Canadian Community.* Toronto: University of Toronto Press, 1970. Part of a widespread exploration during the late 1960's of Canadian regionalism as it had developed since 1867.

See also Canadian minority communities; Native Americans; Urbanization in Canada.

■ Cancer

Definition Often fatal disease characterized by abnormal cell growth that can invade and destroy normal healthy tissue

By the 1930's, a decrease in prevalence or severity of infectious diseases resulted in medical research that focused on chronic diseases such as cancer. An increase in the incidence of certain forms of the disease, most notably lung cancer, stimulated research into its causes, treatment, and prevention.

During the nineteenth century, cancer was a relatively rare disease that was largely ignored by medical science. Cancer victims rarely died in hospitals, and characteristics of the disease were poorly understood by physicians. When President Ulysses S. Grant died from the disease, the prevailing view was that, while unfortunate in his case, the disease itself was of little concern to the general public. Two factors contributed to the increased interest in the disease during the first decades of the twentieth century. First, the ability to prevent acute illnesses among the young meant more persons lived to an age in which they would develop chronic diseases such as cancer. Perhaps more important, statistical analysis of disease morbidity and mortality provided evidence for the true prevalence of cancer.

Statistical Analysis of Cancer Mortality Mortality rates associated with most forms of cancer remained largely stable during the 1930's, with two notable exceptions. At the beginning of the decade, stomach cancer had the highest mortality rate among both men and women—between 40 and 45 persons per 100,000. Among men, colon and prostate cancers exhibited the next highest mortality rate, 20 per 100,000 persons. Among women, uterine cancer mortality was approximately equal with stomach cancer. With the exception of stomach cancer in both sexes, rates remained unchanged through the decade.

Mortality from stomach cancer began a sharp decline, which has continued. By 1940, the mortality rate had dropped by nearly one-half in both men and women. Reasons were, and remain, unclear. Similar changes had been observed in many regions of the world, which would seem to eliminate improved treatment as the cause.

The second notable change in cancer mortality during the 1930's was that associated with lung cancer. During the nineteenth century, lung cancer was a rare disease, one that most physicians had never observed. Not surprisingly, consumption of tobacco products was also low. The average cigarette smoker during the late nineteenth century consumed less than one-twentieth of a pound per year. By the beginning of World War I, that quantity had increased more than twentyfold and continued to increase through the post-World War II era. The increase in use was largely confined to men by the 1930's.

Increased tobacco use was reflected in a rise in lung cancer among men. In 1930, the mortality rate from lung cancer was below 5 per 100,000 persons. By 1940, the mortality rate had more than doubled, and it continued its steep rise into the twenty-first century. No comparable change in mortality among women was found during the decade.

Treatment of cancer during the 1930's was largely confined to surgical removal of the tumor; metastasis was considered a death sentence. William Stewart Halsted, a surgeon at Johns Hopkins University, applied the belief that cancer spread outward from the original tumor to the use of radical mastectomy, the removal of both breasts as well as associated tissue and nodes, for treatment of breast cancer. He felt any new appearance of the disease was unrelated to the original tumor. Treatment of breast cancer changed little in the subsequent three decades. Radiation treatment of cancer was limited in its effectiveness, as the treatment was as likely to cause cancer as cure it.

Establishment of the National Cancer Institute Early in 1937, articles published in three popular magazines of the day, *Fortune, Life,* and *Time,* noted the limited funding provided by federal sources for cancer research and stimulated a letter campaign to Congress requesting that the body address the situation. Recognition by the national government that research into the causes and prevention of disease required funding beyond the capabilities of private foundations resulted in the establishment of an agency dealing specifically with cancer. The National Cancer Act of 1937, enacted on August 5, of that year, established the National Cancer Institute as the principal research agency within the federal government for the study of causes, prevention, and treatment of cancer. In addition to receiving funding for research within the institute itself, the NCI was instructed to oversee research at other public and private institutions. A six-member advisory council was to be appointed by the surgeon general, with the surgeon general as chairman, to review research programs submitted to the institute for approval. The National Advisory Council had its first formal meeting in November of that year; the first fellowships for the study of cancer were awarded in January, 1938.

In 1944, the cancer institute became a division within the National Institute of Health. Shortly afterward, the research program overseen by the institute was divided into additional sections to oversee not only biological research but also the growing fields of cancer chemotherapy, epidemiology, and biochemistry.

Impact The increase in funding for cancer research that began during the 1930's eventually translated into an understanding of the underlying causes of the disease. The role played by the National Cancer Institute in the study of cancer has been substantial. The institute has helped fund the work of more than twenty Nobel laureates, with a significant proportion of the discoveries resulting in greater understanding of the genetic basis of most forms of cancer. By the 1930's, the fact that certain environmental factors such as chemicals or radiation could cause cancer to develop was known, but the molecular basis for the disease was completely unknown; in fact, the role of DNA as the basis for heredity was unknown. By the 1980's, researchers had determined that most cancers originate from mutations in units of DNA called oncogenes, genetic elements that regulate cell division.

Richard Adler

Further Reading

Aronowitz, Robert. *Unnatural History: Breast Cancer and American Society.* New York: Cambridge University Press, 2007. History of the disease, including the evolution of its treatment from the nineteenth century to the start of the twenty-first century.

Gaudilliere, Jean-Paul, and Ilona Lowy, eds. *Heredity and Infection: The History of Disease Transmission.* New York: Routledge, 2001. During the 1930's, the discovery was made that rabbit papillomas were associated with a type of cancer virus, representing the first discovery that mammalian tumors might have a viral etiology.

Grob, Gerald. *The Deadly Truth.* Cambridge, Mass.: Harvard University Press, 2002. Historical review of disease in the Americas. Description of the evolution of cancer as a rare disease to one that became increasingly common during the twentieth century.

Skloot, Rebecca. *The Immortal Life of Henrietta Lacks.* New York: Crown, 2010. While not directly associated with cancer of the 1930's, the story concerns HeLa cells, a line derived from cervical cancer cells removed from Lacks in 1951. In addition to the science of cancer, the author addresses the ethical implications of the use of such cells in viral and cancer research.

Wishart, Adam. *One in Three: A Son's Journey into the History and Science of Cancer.* New York: Grove Press, 2007. Set against the background of a father's fight against cancer; provides a view of the history behind understanding the disease. The increasing realization that began during the 1930's of the association between industrial pollutants and cancer represents a portion of his story.

See also   March of Dimes; Medicine; Sexually transmitted diseases.

■ Capone, Al

Identification   Leader of Chicago's largest criminal organization
Born   January 17, 1899; Brooklyn, New York
Died   January 25, 1947; Palm Island, Florida

Capone was the undisputed leader of organized crime in Chicago from the mid-1920's to the early 1930's. His flamboyant style and outspokenness made him a media celebrity and intensified the U.S. government's efforts to bring him to justice. His image and name are recognized worldwide and have become synonymous with the American gangster.

Al Capone was one of nine children born to Gabriele, a barber, and Teresina, a seamstress, both of whom emigrated from Naples, Italy, in 1893. Capone was reared in abject poverty and grew up in the notorious U.S. Navy Yard and Park Slope neighborhoods—highly criminogenic environments where many future members of organized crime honed their skills in thievery and violence. Dropping out of school in the sixth grade, Capone joined the Five Points street gang and quickly came to the attention of local organized crime bosses because of his pugilistic ability, extremely violent nature, and fearlessness.

Early Years   The young Capone was hired by crime boss Frankie Yale to be a bouncer in Yale's nightclub, the Harvard Inn. While working there, Capone made lewd comments to the sister of a low-level New York gangster, Frank Gallucio. To protect his sister's honor, Gallucio attacked Capone with a razor, cutting his face and jaw three times, leaving him with crooked, deep scars. These scars gave Capone the nickname of "Scarface."

Johnny Torrio, another Brooklyn-bred mobster and Capone's mentor, was called to Chicago to join the service of his cousin, "Big Jim" Colosimo, a politically connected street cleaner who ran the red light district. Colosimo anointed Torrio as his second in command. In New York, Capone ran afoul of Irish gangsters and the law, and he fled to Chicago at Torrio's urging. In 1919, Torrio and Colosimo opened a brothel together called the Four Deuces. Torrio enlisted Capone to work as a bartender and a bouncer, giving Capone his first entry into Chicago's underworld.

Prohibition and the Beer Wars   The advent of Prohibition opened up tremendous possibilities for gangsters. They had an opportunity to amass significant wealth and political influence. Smitten with his new, young wife, Colosimo was uninterested in taking advantage of this opportunity. Torrio decided that Colosimo was standing in the way of his own bootlegging aspirations and had to be eliminated for the sake of the organization. Allegedly, either Capone or Yale was the triggerman who killed Colosimo, who was shot in the vestibule of the Four Deuces while waiting for the delivery of a bootleg alcohol shipment.

Various gangs across the city entered the bootlegging business to compete with the Torrio-Capone

Gangster Al Capone at a football game in Chicago in 1931. (AP/Wide World Photos)

organization. Each one protected its interests in the production, distribution, and sale of illegal alcohol, using threats, beatings, bullets, and bombs. During the "beer wars," the streets of Chicago were strewn with the bodies of young men of various ethnic backgrounds, which largely defined their gang affiliations and territories. These groups were German, Irish, and Italian. Torrio recognized that bloodshed produced bad publicity and cut into the profits of all the gangs. As a strategy to curtail the rampant violence raging over the many bootlegging pursuits, Torrio proposed that the city be divided into north-south territories, each under the auspices of leading gangs. Torrio and Capone ruled over the South Side, and Dion O'Banion, Hymie Weiss, and Bugs Moran commanded the north side.

This peace among warring factions was short-lived, as each continued to encroach on the other's territory and profits. O'Banion and Weiss were killed in separate incidents; Capone was the target of frequent assassination attempts but managed to escape unscathed. Fortuitous to Capone's future was the near-fatal shooting of Torrio, which led Torrio to return to Italy and later to New York. He relinquished control of the Chicago Outfit to Capone in 1925. On February 14, 1929, Capone eliminated the vestiges of the North Side Gang in the infamous St. Valentine's Day Massacre, killing seven men in a garage. The mass murder received international attention, but it was never solved. Bugs Moran, the primary target of the attack, was not in the garage the morning of the shooting.

Height of Power and Descent At the height of Capone's power, his Chicago Outfit was reputedly earning $100 million of illegal income annually. Through systematic, widespread corruption, which included the bribing of Chicago mayor William H. "Big Bill" Thompson, Capone's organization stayed mostly free from legal scrutiny. It operated casinos, brothels, and speakeasies throughout Chicago and the surrounding suburbs. With his enormous wealth, Capone indulged in an opulent lifestyle that included custom clothing, imported cigars, gourmet food, rare liquors, and expensive jewelry. During the late 1920's, Capone became a major celebrity, entrepreneur, and philanthropist and garnered considerable media attention, appearing on the cover of *Time* magazine on March 24, 1930.

In 1931, Capone was indicted on several counts of income tax evasion. In the face of overwhelming evidence, his attorneys attempted to plea-bargain the case, but the presiding judge warned he might reject the prosecution's sentencing recommendation. Therefore, Capone withdrew his guilty plea. Following a lengthy trial, he was found guilty and sentenced to eleven years in federal prison. He also was sentenced to pay considerable fines, and liens were filed against his various properties. His appeal was denied.

In May of 1932, Capone was sent to the Atlanta Penitentiary, a tough federal prison, where he was nonetheless able to secure special privileges. To ensure that his prison activities and amenities were restricted, Capone was transferred to Alcatraz federal prison in California, where tight security and an uncompromising, incorruptible warden dictated that Capone have no contact with the outside world or receive any preferential treatment. His isolation from his criminal associates in Chicago and the repeal of Prohibition in December of 1933 dramatically reduced his power and prestige in the underworld.

Scarface and Free Enterprise

Al Capone once proudly said,

I make my money by supplying a public demand. If I break the law, my customers, who number hundreds of the best people in Chicago, are as guilty as I am. The only difference is that I sell and they buy. Everybody calls me a racketeer. I call myself a businessman.

In 1930, British journalist Claud Cockburn interviewed Capone. Cockburn asked what Capone would have done if he had not become a gangster. Capone replied, "[S]elling newspapers barefoot on the street in Brooklyn." Cockburn's interview is excerpted here.

He stood up as he spoke, cooling his finger-tips in the rose bowl in front of him. He sat down again, brooding and sighing. Despite the ham-and-corn, what he said was quite probably true and I said so, sympathetically. A little bit too sympathetically, as immediately emerged, for as I spoke I saw him looking at me suspiciously, not to say censoriously. My remarks about the harsh way the world treats barefoot boys in Brooklyn were interrupted by an urgent angry waggle of his podgy hand. "Listen," he said, "don't get the idea I'm one of these goddam radicals. Don't get the idea I'm knocking the American system. The American system. . . ." As though an invisible chairman had called upon him for a few words, he broke into an oration upon the theme. He praised freedom, enterprise, and the pioneers. He spoke of "our heritage." He referred with contemptuous disgust to Socialism and Anarchism. "My rackets," he repeated several times, "are run on strictly American lines and they're going to stay that way."

His vision of the American system began to excite him profoundly and now he was on his feet again, leaning across the desk like the chairman of a board meeting, his fingers plunged in the rose bowls.

"This American system of ours," he shouted, "call it Americanism, call it Capitalism, call it what you like, gives to each and every one of us a great opportunity if we only seize it with both hands and make the most of it." He held out his hand towards me, the fingers dripping a little, and stared at me sternly for a few seconds before reseating himself.

Source: Claud Cockburn, *In Time of Trouble: An Autobiography* (London: Rupert Hart-Davis, 1956).

Although Capone adjusted well to the prison environment, his health steadily declined. He had entered the tertiary stage of syphilis. He spent the last year of his sentence in the prison hospital, delusional and disoriented. Capone completed his term in Alcatraz on January 6, 1939, and was transferred to the Federal Correctional Institution at Terminal Island, California, to serve the remainder of his sentence for a misdemeanor conviction that was included in the larger tax-evasion case. He was paroled on November 16, 1939, spent a short time in a hospital, and then returned to his home in Palm Island, Florida.

Capone's control of and interests in the Chicago Outfit diminished after his release from prison. Because of the inexorable, unstoppable decline in his physical and mental health, he was no longer able to run the crime syndicate. Suffering from severe cognitive impairment and delusions, he often ranted about communists, foreigners, and Moran, who Capone steadfastly believed was still plotting to kill him from his Ohio prison cell. On January 21, 1947, Capone had a stroke. He regained consciousness and started to improve, but then contracted pneumonia. He suffered a fatal cardiac arrest the next day and died in Palm Island, Florida, on January 25, 1947.

Impact Al Capone was the quintessential Italian American gangster. Although he died in the 1940's, his image abounds on the Internet, and his dramatized persona has been featured in numerous films and television programs, starting with the 1932 classic film *Scarface* and including the 1987 film *The Untouchables*. Capone was highly successful in his illegal pursuits despite his humble beginnings, his brief tenure as a crime boss, and the fierce competition of rival criminal organizations. He solidified the power and control of the Italian American organized crime group in Chicago, which continued to maintain hegemony over vice, labor unions, and corrupt politics in the city.

Arthur J. Lurigio

Further Reading

Abadinsky, Howard. *Organized Crime.* Chicago: Nelson-Hall, 1985. Contains a chapter on organized crime in Chicago during Prohibition. The book's factual material is sketchy.

Allsop, Kenneth. *The Bootleggers: The Story of Prohibition.* New Rochelle, N.Y.: Arlington House, 1968. A history of the Prohibition era and its effects on organized crime. Allsop discusses the successes of Torrio and Capone in Chicago.

Bergreen, Laurence. *Capone: The Man and the Era.* New York: Touchtone, 1996. A 701-page biography of Capone. Provides a detailed history of the Prohibition era and uses Capone's life as a starting point for a larger history of the United States in the early twentieth century.

Helmer, William J., and Arthur J. Bilek. *The St. Valentine's Day Massacre: The Untold Story of the Gangland Bloodbath That Brought Down Al Capone.* Nashville, Tenn.: Cumberland House, 2004. Refutes the assumption that Capone ordered the murders to gain control of the Chicago crime syndicate.

Hoffman, Dennis E. *Scarface Al and the Crime Crusaders: Chicago's Private War Against Capone.* Carbondale: Southern Illinois University Press, 1993. Scholarly work that concentrates on attempts by honest Chicago merchants to rid their city of crime and to increase their own profits.

Iorizzo, Luciano. *Al Capone: A Biography.* Westport, Conn.: Greenwood Press, 2003. A comprehensive biography that tries to separate the myth of Capone from the reality of his life. Iorizzo examines organized crime in the United States to describe how someone such as Capone could rise to power and become a criminal legend.

Pasley, Fred D. *Al Capone: The Biography of a Self-Made Man.* Reprint. Salem, N.H.: Ayer, 1984. A 355-page biography with multiple biographical details. Does not contain an index, which makes fact-checking somewhat difficult.

Schoenberg, Robert J. *Mr. Capone: The Real and Complete Story of Al Capone.* New York: HarperCollins, 1992. A comprehensive biography following Capone from his early years as a delinquent to his rise to power.

See also Alcatraz Federal Penitentiary; Barrow, Clyde, and Bonnie Parker; Dillinger, John; Kelly, Machine Gun; Luciano, Lucky; Ness, Eliot; Nitti, Frank; Organized crime; Prohibition repeal.

■ Capra, Frank

Identification American film director
Born May 18, 1897; Bisacquino, near Palermo, Sicily, Italy
Died September 3, 1991; La Quinta, California

Capra revolutionized the film industry by creating the screwball romantic comedy and championing small-town American values in films that pitted the average man against corruption.

Frank Capra was born Francesco Rosario Capra in Sicily and moved to California with his family in 1903. Under pressure from his family to leave school and find work, he refused, believing that education was essential for success in the United States. He graduated from Throop College of Technology in chemical engineering.

While recuperating from the Spanish flu in 1919, Capra worked as a film extra for John Ford, beginning his motion-picture career. By 1920, Capra had collaborated on three short films; for the remainder of the 1920's, he worked with some of the biggest

Director Frank Capra relaxing on the set of You Can't Take It with You *in 1938.* (Time & Life Pictures/Getty Images)

names in film: Mack Sennett, Hal Roach, and Harry Langdon. His big break came in 1927, when Columbia Pictures hired him to direct feature-length films. Capra's comfort with technology, the result of his engineering background, allowed him to make the transition from silent films to talkies with ease.

Working with Barbara Stanwyck in 1931, Capra began developing his unique directorial style, characterized by requiring actors to speak quickly, overlapping one another's words, which condensed sixty-second scenes into forty seconds; this made films lifelike and compelling. He also streamlined filmmaking by filming all long shots at one time, all middle shots at another time, and all close-ups at another. He relied on planning and extensive rehearsals to decrease the number of filmed takes. Capra's greatest films, produced from 1934 to 1941, were either screwball romantic comedies, known as "Capra-corn" by detractors, or gritty portrayals of men fighting against tyranny and corruption, called "Capraesque."

The comedies usually dealt with men taming rich, selfish women, as in the case of *It Happened One Night* (1934). Many believe his work to be misogynistic, but Capra's female characters are usually strong, educated, and accomplished. The dramas portrayed the individual in conflict with a system; an example is *Mr. Deeds Goes to Town* (1936), in which a man who has inherited a fortune must protect himself from unscrupulous lawyers trying to rob him. His plan to help Depression-devastated people compels his attorneys to have him declared incompetent, because using the money for charity is a clear indication of insanity in the eyes of the greedy and powerful. In *Meet John Doe* (1941), an unscrupulous reporter, trying to get her job back, invents the story of a man who plans to commit suicide on Christmas Eve to highlight the world's cruelty. For money, an injured ballplayer pretends to be John Doe. In his honor, Golden Rule Clubs start up, and the Christmas spirit is reaffirmed until the fakery is revealed, causing an embarrassed and humiliated John Doe to attempt suicide. These pictures and others sided with the downtrodden and upheld American values but were not simplistic or naive, as is sometimes thought.

Capra was nominated for six Oscars and won three. As president of the Academy of Motion Picture Arts and Sciences, he introduced supporting acting, humanitarian, set design, and cinematography awards. During the 1940's, Capra focused on American war propaganda films, earning him the Distinguished Service Medal. In 1946, he was nominated for the best director Academy Award for *It's a Wonderful Life*. During the 1950's, he produced science shows for television, returning to Hollywood in 1959 and 1961 to direct his final two, unsuccessful, films.

Impact   Capra's influence is best seen in what have become known as Capraesque films, which depict the underdog fighting against seemingly insurmountable odds. In *Mr. Smith Goes to Washington* (1939), Capra showed that the man with small-town American values was the true good guy, the type of man all Americans should strive to be. Although beaten down by the Depression and oppression, Capra's heroes still had dignity and a belief in the American Dream. Although the films are sometimes misunderstood as sentimental and corny, they actually are realistic and gritty, dealing with suicide, despair, and loss of faith. Ultimately his characters prevail, but it often takes the help of another. Capra's films applaud the struggles of small-town inhabitants with old-fashioned American values in conflict with organizations intent on destroying and devaluing them.

Leslie Neilan

Further Reading

Capra, Frank. *The Name Above the Title*. New York: Macmillan, 1971.
Smoodin, Eric. *Regarding Frank Capra: Audience, Celebrity, and American Film Studies 1930-1960*. Chapel Hill, N.C.: Duke University Press, 2004.

See also   Academy Awards; Film; Ford, John; *It Happened One Night*; *Mr. Deeds Goes to Town*; *Mr. Smith Goes to Washington*; Screwball comedy; Thalberg, Irving.

■ Car radios

Definition   Radios specifically designed for installation in passenger automobiles

Shortly after the first automobiles were invented, people began attempting to design radios that could be used while driving in a car. Since radios in these early years used vacuum tubes, car radios and the batteries needed to power them were large and unwieldy. However, inventors persisted in their attempts to design smaller and better car radios.

Work began on portable radios during the 1920's. However, the first mass-produced radios that could be called car radios were marketed during the early 1930's. Given the technology of the times, these radios were cumbersome. A typical portable radio consisted of a box for the radio, a box including speakers, and a fairly heavy set of batteries. There also needed to be a long antenna. All of this was usually packed in a suitcase, making it portable.

When car radios were first developed, individuals who wanted radios in their cars usually adapted household radios for that use. Radios were not standard equipment in cars until much later in automotive history.

Since radios at this time had vacuum tubes with filaments in them, a power supply had to be able to heat the filament, and other power supplies, batteries, were employed to provide power to other radio parts. This meant that running a car radio off the car battery's power was difficult. The radio would rapidly use up the car's battery unless the car was kept running. Another problem with early car radios was that the technology used to power them often caused interference with the radio itself, causing static and difficult reception.

Eventually, different types of vacuum tubes were developed for use only in car radios, and technological difficulties began to be addressed. A number of manufacturers began to compete during the 1930's to offer the most compact and reliable car radio.

Paul and Joseph Galvin produced one of the first radios meant to be fitted into a car. In 1928, they began work on battery eliminators that would allow vacuum-tube-battery powered radios to run on household current. The Great Depression put an end to this endeavor, and they realized they had to find a new product.

The Galvins joined with inventors Bill Lear and Elmer Wavering and set the goal of developing a radio that could be installed successfully in cars. They finished a prototype by the 1930 car show in Atlantic City, New Jersey. Without funds for a booth to display their wares, they set up outside the convention center and demonstrated the radio installed in their car. They received enough orders to keep their company afloat.

In 1930, the Galvins also produced one of the first commercial car radios, which they called the Motorola. This was a joining of the word "motor" with the suffix "-ola," which was used in the brand names of other audio devices, such as the Victrola and Radiola. This model sold for about $120, which is equivalent to about $1,700 in the twenty-first century. The brand name Motorola continues to be used in the twenty-first century, although it is not used to refer to car radios.

Impact   The car radio is an automotive accessory that appears in almost every car. In the 1930's, the car radio moved from an unwieldy hobby device to a mass-produced item, albeit expensive at the time.

Mary C. Ware

Further Reading

Lind, Richard. *Evolution of the Car Radio: From Vacuum Tubes to Satellite and Beyond.* Washington, D.C.: Society for Automotive Engineers, 2004.

Rowan, Clem, and Carlos Altgelt. *When Car Radios Were Illegal: A History of Early American and European Car Radios.* Washington, D.C.: Society for Automotive Engineers, 1985.

See also   Automobiles and auto manufacturing; Business and the economy in the United States; Federal Communications Commission; Inventions; Radio in the United States.

■ Carter family

Identification   American country music group

A. P. Carter
Born   December 15, 1891; Poor Valley (now Maces Spring), Virginia
Died   November 7, 1960; Maces Spring, Virginia

Sara Carter
Born   July 21, 1898; Flat Woods, Virginia
Died   January 8, 1979; Lodi, California

Maybelle Carter
Born   May 10, 1909; Midway, near Nickelsville, Virginia
Died   October 23, 1978; Nashville, Tennessee

Performing together between 1927 and 1943, the Carter family exerted influence on generations of country music performers, primarily because of their distinctive sound and wide repertoire of Anglo-American folk songs, religious tunes, and country music songs. During the 1930's, the Carter family managed to speak to and befriend their listeners in a way that resonated with the daily experiences, struggles, and livelihoods of almost everyone across the United States.

From rural Virginia, the Carter family's down-home sound and folk-song sentiment spoke to a way of life that was rapidly disappearing during the 1930's. The Carters' rural ideals, however, flourished amid an increasingly depressed economy, the further separation of rural and industrial entities, and popular country music characterized by Jimmie Rodgers—a singer not afraid to experiment with alternative sounds and styles. In comparison with Rodgers, the Carter family depended on traditional folk melodies and successfully wove aspects of rural, preindustrial Appalachia into mainstream, modernizing American culture. Their songs became country music standards, and their unique musical style and sound have been highly envied and emulated since the group's exit from the public in 1943.

The Carter family was made up of three family members: A. P. Carter and Sara Carter, who were married between 1915 and 1939, and A. P.'s sister-in-law Maybelle Carter. Musically, this group consisted of Maybelle's virtuosic, distinctive guitar playing; Sara's rich, contralto voice and accompanying autoharp; and A. P.'s secondary high bass voice. This combination, with its unique use of women as lead vocalist and lead guitarist, allowed the Carters to create an instantly recognizable sound.

The Carter family's music reached a broad population throughout the 1930's. It could be heard often on wide-ranging, border-radio stations toward the end of the decade. Earlier, the Carters had traveled to Tennessee for a chance at public success, forging a relationship with the well-known businessman Ralph S. Peer, who showcased the group as part of the historically significant 1927 Bristol recording sessions. Under his tutelage, the Carter family recorded more than three hundred singles for several different companies between 1927 and 1941. They recorded for Victor (1927-1934, 1941), the American Record Company (1935), Decca (1936-1938), and Columbia (1940). Also, the family maintained a prolific recording career and occasionally performed live in local schoolhouses and churches. Through these varying venues, the Carter family was able to reach a large listening public and affect listeners in highly personalized forums.

The Carter family's songs tended to be about familial ideals, rural living, and country churches and were firmly grounded in the Anglo-American folksong tradition. With topics including love and longing, suffering, loss, and pain, the songs' appeal resonated with the everyday experiences of Americans during the difficult 1930's. Significantly, much of the Carter family's material was "collected" by A. P. on his periodic "song-hunting" trips, when he traveled into remote mountain homesteads, mills, factories, boarding houses, and coal mines. As a result of A. P.'s frequent trips, many folk songs that might otherwise have remained lost to mainstream American culture were discovered, transcribed, and recorded. Significantly, these songs appealed instantly to the listening public of the 1930's and have been widely circulated. The Carters' songs make up some of the most standard, oft-recorded repertory in the country music, bluegrass, and folk-song movements. "I'm Thinking Tonight of My Blue Eyes," "Little Darling, Pal of Mine," "Jimmie Brown the Newsboy," "Keep on the Sunny Side," "Engine 143," "Worried Man Blues," and "Will the Circle Be Unbroken" are some of the songs that have continued to affect musicians.

Impact While suddenly off the air in 1943 as American culture began to make drastic changes, the Carter family nonetheless continued to affect country music throughout the twentieth century and into the twenty-first century by means of its repertoire and ideals. The group's legacy is that it was able to sing about ordinary people and ordinary lives during a difficult decade.

April L. Prince

Further Reading

Hirshberg, Charles, and Mark Zwonitzer. *Will You Miss Me When I'm Gone? The Carter Family and Their Legacy in American Music*. New York: Simon and Schuster, 2002.

Kahn, Ed. "The Carter Family on Border Radio." *American Music* 14 (Summer, 1996): 205-217.

Malone, Bill. *Country Music USA*. 3d rev. ed. Austin: University of Texas Press, 2010.

See also Guthrie, Woody; Music: Popular; Radio in the United States; Recording industry.

■ *Carter v. Carter Coal Co.*

The Case U.S. Supreme Court ruling on
  congressional powers over commerce
Date Decided on May 18, 1936

In striking down the Bituminous Coal Conservation Act of 1935 in its Carter *decision, the Supreme Court ruled that production and manufacturing do not constitute "commerce," even when the manufactured products are subsequently shipped across state lines. Consequently, the U.S. Congress could not use its powers under the U.S. Constitution's commerce clause to regulate working conditions related to coal mining.*

The U.S. Congress designed the Bituminous Coal Conservation Act of 1935 (also known as the Guffey Act) to stabilize the coal-mining industry and promote interstate commerce by regulating labor conditions to ensure fair interstate competition. The production, distribution, and use of coal were said to "be affected with a national public interest" and to affect directly the general welfare. The federal law created a national commission to fix prices and regulate wages, hours, and working conditions of coal miners. It also provided that coal companies would be charged a tax set at 15 percent of their gross sales. Companies that accepted the board's regulations would receive a 90 percent tax rebate or "drawback." In May, 1936, the Supreme Court invalidated the law.

Justice George Sutherland wrote the opinion for the Court's five-member majority. He observed that the "tax" was not really a tax for revenue; it was a penalty that compelled compliance with the regulations. Those who complied with the act's provisions to receive the 90 percent drawback did not really "consent;" they were coerced into compliance to avoid monetary penalties. As such, the act could not be upheld as a valid exercise of congressional taxing powers.

Sutherland noted that enumerated congressional powers under the Constitution do not include a general power to promote the general welfare. The validity of the Bituminous Coal Conservation Act rested on the question of whether it was a legitimate regulation of interstate commerce. According to Sutherland, congressional powers extend to activities that directly affect interstate commerce. They do not, however, extend to the production and manufacture of products, even if these commodities are subsequently shipped out of state. Shipment is commerce, but manufacturing and production are local. Similarly, mining brings a commodity into existence, but commerce disposes of it. Labor conditions related to mining affect interstate commerce in indirect and secondary ways.

Impact Everything that moves in interstate commerce has a local origin. In *Schechter Poultry Corp. v. United States* (1935), the Supreme Court had ruled that poultry processing occurred *after* interstate commerce had ended. In *Carter,* the Court held that mining occurred *before* interstate commerce began. In both cases, the activities were local and therefore beyond the reach of congressional commerce powers.

Joseph A. Melusky

Further Reading

Baum, Lawrence. *The Supreme Court.* 10th ed. Washington, D.C.: CQ Press, 2010.

Lewis, Thomas T., ed. *U.S. Supreme Court.* 3 vols. Pasadena, Calif.: Salem Press, 2007.

Savage, David. *The Supreme Court and the Powers of the American Government.* 2d ed. Washington, D.C.: CQ Press, 2009.

See also Business and the economy in the United States; Congress, U.S.; Great Depression in the United States; New Deal; *Schechter Poultry Corp. v. United States*; Supreme Court, U.S.

CCC. See **Civilian Conservation Corps**

■ Chaplin, Charles

Identification English actor, director, producer,
  and film star
Born April 16, 1889; London, England
Died December 25, 1977; Corsier-sur-Vevey,
  Switzerland

Chaplin's films of the 1930's presented forceful critiques of social and economic inequalities and of the dehumanization experienced in the modern workplace while retaining Chaplin's immense popularity in the United States and around the world.

Charles Chaplin's films had always contained latent social criticism, but his work and his statements became more explicitly political during the 1930's.

While Chaplin's film success had made him one of the wealthiest entertainers in the film industry, his impoverished childhood in London had a lasting impact on his sympathy for the poor. His social critique is most evident in his likable screen character of the little tramp, a vagabond, who is caught between the aspirations of a well-to-do gentleman and the reality of his economic deprivation.

During the early 1930's, Chaplin struggled when faced with the advent of sound in film. The tramp character depended on the subtlety of the actor's distinctive pantomime, and Chaplin could not imagine transforming him into a speaking role. However, as economic inequalities and poverty grew during the Great Depression, the figure captured the sentiments of mass audiences in the United States and in Europe. Thus the tramp reemerged for the two films that Chaplin released during the 1930's: *City Lights* (1931) and *Modern Times* (1936). Chaplin solved the challenge of sound by focusing on music, which he composed himself, and on synchronized sound effects. This allowed him to preserve the tramp as a silent character while responding to the market demand for sound technology.

City Lights looked back on the social inequality of the Jazz Age as the tramp moved between the world of a millionaire and that of an impoverished flower girl. In *Modern Times*, Chaplin famously captured the alienation of the worker in the factory and depicted the deprivation of the unemployed and the poor. Both films featured Chaplin's trademark combination of physical humor, subtle pantomime, and pathos. While the films provoked the scorn of the powerful and wealthy, both became recognized as masterpieces in Chaplin's oeuvre.

After three long and difficult years spent working on *City Lights*, Chaplin left the United States for a tour of Europe and the Far East in February of 1931. The trip radicalized his political ideas as he felt the global repercussions of the Great Depression and met with a number of prominent politicians and intellectuals, such as Winston Churchill, Mahatma Gandhi, and George Bernard Shaw. Chaplin's political views took a progressive turn in favor of government control of the economy and labor protection legislation.

Following his return to the United States in May of 1932, he was confronted with the devastating social consequences of the Great Depression in the United States and gave up his reluctance to make po-

Actor and filmmaker Charles Chaplin in 1930. (Hulton Archive/Getty Images)

litical statements. He supported President Franklin D. Roosevelt's National Recovery Administration in 1933 and Upton Sinclair's campaign for governor of California in 1934. He worked for at least two years on *Modern Times*, which was his most political film at that time. After the release of *Modern Times* in 1936, Chaplin became even more political and turned his attention to antifascism. His desire to comment on the issue enabled him to relinquish his resistance to spoken dialogue film, and he embarked on the anti-Adolf Hitler satire *The Great Dictator* (1940), in which he played the double role of a Jewish barber and the dictator Hynkel.

Impact Chaplin's films and their popular appeal across nations and cultures exemplified the common humanity present during a time of economic crisis, international conflict, and war. Chaplin was one of the most influential comedians of the twentieth century, perfecting the use of pantomime in film and creating, with the tramp, one of the most iconic and most imitated celluloid characters. His star image declined in the United States during McCarthyism because of his left-leaning politics, and he was forced to leave the country in 1953. His reputation was restored during the 1960's when he was recognized as one of the first great auteurs of film history.

Tim Gruenewald

Further Reading

Robinson, David. *Chaplin: His Life and Art.* 2d rev. ed. New York: Penguin, 2001.

Schickel, Richard. *The Essential Chaplin: Perspectives on the Life and Art of the Great Comedian.* Chicago: Ivan R. Dee, 2006.

Weissman, Stephen M. *Chaplin: A Life.* New York: Arcade, 2008.

See also Academy Awards; *City Lights*; Film; *Modern Times*; National Recovery Administration; New Deal; Roosevelt, Franklin D.; Sinclair, Upton.

■ Charlie Chan films

Identification Series of films based on a fictional Chinese American detective from Honolulu

Dates 1926-1949

Although depicted as a rather stereotypical Chinese American who spouted pseudo-Confucian wisdom, the Charlie Chan character was the first ethnic Asian to be featured in a long series of films. Prior to and during his screen appearances Asian characters were most typically portrayed as villains (a result of the "yellow peril" campaign) or mocked as figures of fun. In contrast, Chan was usually depicted as a dignified and benevolent presence.

The character of the sagacious detective Charlie Chan was first developed in a series of novels by author Earl Derr Biggers. Transferred to film in 1926, the Chan character was initially seen in supporting roles in three silent films and was portrayed by one Korean and two Japanese actors. The first appearance of the detective in a starring role came in 1931 with *Charlie Chan Carries On*. He was played through 1937 by the distinguished Swedish actor Warner Oland, who already had had a lengthy career in silent cinema, and who brought a natural gravitas to the role. He had a slight Asian cast to his features and often played "Oriental" roles, usually villainous ones. His light and pleasant accent was neutral enough to be acceptable as that of an Asian to the undiscriminating ear.

One of the running jokes of the series was Charlie Chan's large family in Hawaii. A detective in Honolulu, he had so many children that his sons were usually designated as "number one," "number two," and so on. The actor playing his oldest son and bumbling, sometime assistant was Chinese actor Keye Luke. The production values of the initial films made by Twentieth Century-Fox were unusually high for a "B" series, and the stories often placed Chan in foreign settings such as Panama, Shanghai, London, Egypt, Paris, Rio de Janeiro, and Monte Carlo. The initial series, which had settings such as the Olympics, the racetrack, the circus, and the opera, was also buoyed by the casting of some well-known actors such as Boris Karloff and Leo G. Carroll. Even an unknown Rita Hayworth made an appearance.

Chan had a penchant for quoting what he called Confucian adages, such as "Mind like parachute, only function when open," "Suspicion often the father of truth," and "One grain of luck sometimes worth more than whole rice field of wisdom." In 1939, after Oland's death, the role of the series' title character was assumed by veteran character actor Sidney Toler. Toler, of Scottish ancestry, also had a naturally Asian cast to his features, and at first, the series retained its good production values and often superior stories. The casting of Victor Sen Yung (Number Two Son) as his father's primary assistant began to give the series a more comedic tone. In fact, the increasing comedy elements probably began a slide in the films' overall quality.

After Twentieth Century-Fox discontinued the series in the early 1940's, it was picked up by the low-rent Monogram Pictures Corporation. What were once excellent production values deteriorated into a melange of comedy and sometimes incoherent story lines that reflected the low budgets afforded to the series. The supposedly sagacious quotations became even more stereotypical and the dialogue ever more ridiculous, employing lines such as "You a chip off the old chopstick." The addition of broadly mugging comedy sidekicks—Mantan Moreland, who had started in the Toler-Fox series, and later Willie Best—did not improve matters. Following Toler's death, the series petered out with a few Roland Winters efforts; the last film in the almost continuous run beginning in 1931 was 1949's, *The Sky Dragon*. At least one television series was produced during the 1950's and later attempts at filming the character, in-

Warner Oland (third from left) as Chinese detective Charlie Chan in the 1937 film Charlie Chan at the Olympics. (The Granger Collection, New York)

cluding *Charlie Chan and the Curse of the Dragon Queen* (1981), served only to parody and cheapen the memory of the first memorable series during the 1930's.

Impact Although other Asian detectives appeared in brief film series—for example, Karloff as Mr. Wong and Peter Lorre as Mr. Moto—the most popular and imitated were the Charlie Chan films. The character, although hardly true to life, became beloved by film audiences and perhaps helped to bring a more positive image of Asians to the screen. During the Great Depression and World War II, the Chan films provided audiences with much needed escapism. The enduring worldwide popularity of Charlie Chan has been demonstrated by film productions in Spanish and Chinese, several radio series, a comic strip, and an animated television show.

Roy Liebman

Further Reading

Berlin, Howard. *The Charlie Chan Film Encyclopedia.* Jefferson, N.C.: McFarland, 2005.

_____. *Charlie Chan's Words of Wisdom.* New York: Wildside Press, 2003.

Hanke, Ken. *Charlie Chan at the Movies: History, Filmography and Criticism.* Jefferson, N.C.: McFarland, 1989.

Mitchell, Charles P. *A Guide to Charlie Chan Films.* Westport, Conn.: Greenwood Press, 1999.

See also Asian Americans; Film; Karloff, Boris; Mr. Moto films.

■ Chemistry

The period of the Great Depression was one of important developments and expansion in both traditional scientific disciplines, such as physical and organic chemistry, and new interdisciplinary fields, such as molecular biology. Building on European breakthroughs in quantum physics, American chemists such as Linus Pauling were able to create a new theory of the chemical bond that influenced structural chemistry and molecular biology. Industrial chemists created successful commercial products such as Freon and nylon.

During the first three decades of the twentieth century, most great discoveries in chemistry were made by Europeans; all but one of the Nobel Prizes in Chemistry during this time went to European chemists. In the 1930's, the situation remained essentially the same: Irving Langmuir was the only American to win the award during the decade, doing so "for his discoveries and investigations in surface chemistry." However, from the perspective of the history of chemistry, the Nobel Prizes have not always been an infallible indicator of progress in the field. Though often not recognized until the decades after World War II, during the 1930's, American chemists were fashioning the new ideas and experimental discoveries that not only transformed the field but also won for them many Nobel Prizes.

Physical Chemistry   During the 1930's, some of the most important discoveries in chemistry were made in interdisciplinary areas, especially in physics and chemistry. Because chemistry is a science largely dealing with the outermost electrons of atoms, and because quantum mechanics provided scientists with a powerful new tool for dealing with such electrons, quantum chemists were able to deepen their understanding of bonding between atoms, which involves the transfer or sharing of electrons. Quantum physicists had introduced the orbital as the electron's most probable location around the nucleus, but it was Pauling, steeped in structural chemistry, who introduced orbital mixtures, or hybridization, to explain the tetrahedrally arranged hydrogen atoms in the methane molecule. He also used hybridization to explain a series of increasingly complex inorganic and organic molecules.

In papers published throughout the 1930's, culminating in the influential book *The Nature of the Chemical Bond and the Structure of Molecules and Crystals: An Introduction to Modern Structural Chemistry* (1939), Pauling made use of the idea of resonance to explain why, for example, the flat, hexagonal structure of benzene required a hybrid of two atomic arrangements to account for the intercarbon distances. Robert S. Mulliken, a chemist who, like Pauling, had studied quantum mechanics in Europe, developed a rival approach, called the molecular orbital theory, that treated molecules not as fissioned but as fused structures, and it proved successful in explaining the spectroscopic properties of both simple and complex molecules.

Experimental chemistry followed a pattern similar to theoretical chemistry in which Americans built on and advanced ideas and inventions of Europeans. For example, Europeans had invented two techniques that proved extremely valuable in determining the three-dimensional structures of molecules: X-ray diffraction, which proved a powerful tool in elucidating the arrangements of atoms in crystals, and electron diffraction, which helped chemists understand the structures of gaseous and liquid substances. Instruments such as the ultracentrifuge and techniques such as electrophoresis and chromatography, with their associated technologies, had been developed by Europeans, but Americans made extensive use of them in separating complex mixtures into individual components for study. On the other hand, Americans were at the forefront in creating synthetic resins for use in ion-exchange columns, which proved adept in separating complex mixtures. Ion exchangers became widely available during the 1930's, allowing, for example, complex mixtures of proteins to be determined qualitatively and quantitatively.

Organic Chemistry   Like physical chemistry, organic chemistry had been dominated by Europeans, especially Germans, during the early decades of the twentieth century, but leadership began shifting to the United States during the 1930's. The ideas that Pauling had developed in physical chemistry proved to be applicable in organic chemistry. His creation of an electronegativity scale, which allowed chemists to measure the abilities of electrons to form certain chemical bonds, facilitated fertile insights into the nature, structure, and behavior of organic molecules. With organic chemists becoming increasingly interested in molecules from natural products, with their complex ring structures, Pauling's resonance theory deepened understanding of so-called aromatic compounds, with properties similar to those of the benzene ring. Organic molecules often possess asymmetric carbon atoms, leading to the formation of mirror-image pairs. For many natural products, only one member of the pair is biologically active. American organic chemists became leaders in this new field of stereochemistry.

Organic chemistry involves both analysis and synthesis, depending on whether a particular compound is broken down into its constituent parts or whether, and how, certain molecules are constructed from simple units. Sophisticated instruments and techniques, such as quantitative ultramicrochemical analysis, enabled organic chemists to analyze even small samples. Although quantum chemical ideas deepened synthetic chemists' understanding of their basic procedures, organic syntheses during the 1930's followed techniques developed in the first three decades of the century. An example of Nobel Prize-winning work done in the United States during the 1930's was the study of glycogen, the carbohydrate stored in the liver and in muscle, by Gerty and Carl F. Cori at the Washington University School of Medicine in St. Louis, Missouri. They elucidated how glycogen was synthesized and broken down in living things, and they were also able to make glycogen from glucose in vitro.

Inorganic Chemistry   Some historians of chemistry have characterized inorganic chemistry during the 1930's as "stagnant." When compared to the great advances in physical and organic chemistry, this was certainly true. Nevertheless, Pauling and his many coworkers were able to determine the basic structures of many silicate and sulfide minerals by using X-ray diffraction, and Pauling also developed a set of rules that enabled researchers to eliminate unlikely structures in their search for the correct one.

During the late 1930's, Herbert C. Brown began his work on the boron hydrides for which he later won a Nobel Prize. While most inorganic chemists

plied their trade with elements in the Earth's crust, a few, such as Harrison Brown at the California Institute of Technology (Caltech) and Harold C. Urey at the University of Chicago, became interested in the material in meteorites, helping to found the new field of cosmic chemistry.

Industrial Chemistry   Because of their isolation from Europe and especially Germany during World War I, and because of wartime demands, American chemical companies experienced accelerated growth, trends that continued during the 1920's and 1930's, though this growth was slowed by the Depression. Examples of companies that expanded during this time were DuPont, Union Carbide, Monsanto, and Allied Chemical. Another trend that characterized these companies was the realization of the importance of research and development of new and

Henry G. Knight, chief of the federal Bureau of Chemistry and Soils, demonstrating the manufacture of starch from sweet potatoes, a chemistry breakthrough, in 1937. (Library of Congress)

improved products. Government agencies sometimes collaborated with industry in helping to develop research. For example, in 1931, the U.S. Bureau of Standards joined with the American Petroleum Institute to study petroleum hydrocarbons systematically, leading such companies as Dow and Monsanto to make use of hydrocarbons in the manufacture of certain chemicals. Also important during the 1930's was the chemurgy movement, a joint effort of leaders in industry, academia, and agriculture to help solve the farm crisis by developing new industrial chemicals from the organic materials produced by farmers. Henry Ford was a leading figure in the movement.

During the 1930's, American companies created new products intended for the consumer, other firms, and the military. For example, Thomas Midgley, Jr., working for General Motors, developed difluorodichloromethane (Freon) as a safe refrigerant; it also found applications as a propellant in aerosol spray cans. Pharmaceutical companies introduced new drugs, some of which had been discovered in Europe. The sulfa drugs, which were effective against streptococcal and staphylococcal infections, came into wide use in Europe and the United States, especially since sulfanilamide was not patentable. Sulfanilamide's success led pharmaceutical companies to synthesize and test more than one thousand compounds for their possible therapeutic value. An advantage that American industrial chemists had over their European counterparts in creating plastics and synthetic textiles was that they accepted the existence of extremely long molecules (or macromolecules) in nature and the laboratory. Several successful commercial products subsequently came out of macromolecular research. For example, DuPont hired Wallace Hume Carothers, a chemist interested in polymerization. After studying such natural fibers as silk, Carothers mixed atopic acid and hexamethylenediamine to create nylon, which was commercialized at the end of the 1930's. However, because of World War II, it did not become a massive moneymaker until the postwar period. At times, companies such as DuPont depended on academic researchers. For example, the synthetic rubber neoprene was an outgrowth of studies on acetylene by Father Julius Arthur Nieuwland at Notre Dame University. Neoprene rubber turned out to be better than natural rubber in its durability and resistance to many chemicals.

Impact Compared to other professions, American chemistry did not experience many of the negative effects of the Depression. Chemistry programs at many universities and technical institutes continued to produce large numbers of graduates with bachelor's and doctoral degrees in chemistry, without substantial slumps in enrollment. These graduates found jobs through agencies such as the Works Progress Administration, organizations such as the Rockefeller and Carnegie foundations, and universities such as Harvard, Wisconsin, and Stanford that were able to maintain and occasionally increase faculty numbers. Pauling and other chemists built up illuminating bodies of work in theoretical and experimental chemistry that also led to the foundation of new fields such as chemical physics, molecular biology, and immunochemistry.

The increasingly creative work that American chemists did during the 1930's was utilized in World War II and the postwar decades, during which a preponderance of the Nobel Prizes were bestowed on U.S. chemists. During World War II, the organic chemist Louis Fieser at Harvard developed napalm, an incendiary used in bombs and flamethrowers. At Caltech, Pauling developed an oxygen meter that was used in submarines and airplanes. Industrial chemists working for Merck, Pfizer, and Squibb, with aid from the federal government, developed techniques for the mass production of penicillin, an antibiotic that saved the lives of many Allied servicemen. In the second half of the twentieth century, the groundwork formed by many American chemists during the 1930's ultimately resulted in the global superiority of U.S. chemistry.

Robert J. Paradowski

Further Reading

Brock, William H. *The Chemical Tree: A History of Chemistry.* New York: W. W. Norton, 2000. Thematic and disciplinary survey of chemistry from alchemy to environmental chemistry. Notes, bibliographical essay, and index.

Ihde, Aaron J. *The Development of Modern Chemistry.* Reprint. New York: Dover, 1984. Originally published in 1964; makes widely available a largely disciplinary approach to the history of modern chemistry. Encyclopedic rather than analytic; includes massive bibliographic notes, appendixes, and indexes of names and subjects.

Nye, Mary Jo. *From Chemical Philosophy to Theoretical*

Chemistry: Dynamics of Matter and Dynamics of Disciplines, 1800-1950. Berkeley: University of California Press, 1993. Investigates the interface between chemistry and physics; includes material on American physical chemistry during the 1930's. Glossary, bibliography, name and subject indexes.

Servos, John W. *Physical Chemistry from Ostwald to Pauling: The Making of a Science in America.* Princeton, N.J.: Princeton University Press, 1990. Emphasizes key figures such as Pauling and pivotal institutions such as the University of California at Berkeley in an account of the evolution of physical chemistry in the United States, including the significant decade of the 1930's. Notes and index.

Thackray, Arnold, et al. *Chemistry in America, 1876-1976: Historical Indicators.* Boston: D. Reidel, 1985. Intended as the first full-length, empirical history of American chemistry, emphasizes such themes as chemistry as an occupation, the chemical industry as context, and chemistry as a discipline. Amply documented with footnotes. Five appendixes, tables, bibliography, and index.

See also Education; Freon; Inventions; Nobel Prizes; Nylon; Pauling, Linus; Physics; World War II and the United States.

■ Chicago World's Fair

The Event International exposition
Also known as Century of Progress World's Fair
Dates May 27 to November 12, 1933; May 26 to October 31, 1934
Place Chicago, Illinois

The Chicago World's Fair provided the opportunity for agencies in the federal government to partner with large American corporations and scientific organizations to convince Americans and foreign visitors that American political and economic systems were stable despite prevailing financial circumstances.

During its two summer-to-fall runs, the Chicago World's Fair drew almost 49 million visitors, displayed modern consumer goods, and highlighted advances in technology, science, and medicine. The optimistic atmosphere of the fair belied the economic reality of the time, as the industrialized world fell deeper into a multiyear global depression.

The idea for a world's fair in Chicago began years earlier when wealthy businessman Rufus C. Dawes saw the success of the 1921 Pageant of Peace along Chicago's waterfront. Dawes thought that a larger fair would be even more economically successful for the city. The theme of the world's fair was "A Century of Progress 1833-1933." Dawes invited his brother, U.S. vice president Charles G. Dawes; business leader Lenox Lohr, president of the National Broadcasting Company (NBC); and Julius Rosenwald, president of Sears, Roebuck and Company, to join the fair's executive board. Based on its business and political connections, the executive committee raised enough funds to purchase $12 million in U.S. Treasury securities. The fair was budgeted at $100 million, but the $12 million in initial financing allowed fair executives to issue invitations of participation to various agencies in the U.S. and foreign governments and to domestic and international scientific and industrial corporations.

American companies including Ford Motor Company, Cadillac, and Lincoln constructed pavilions to showcase their automobile models. The U.S. Navy constructed a large pavilion depicting significant events in American naval history. General Motors furnished a fully functioning scale model of an assembly line. American railroads Union Pacific and Burlington showcased their high-speed "streamliner" trains. Burlington ran its brand-new Zephyr from Denver to the fair station in Chicago in record-setting time. Germany sent its airship *Graf Zeppelin*, which circled Chicago and then landed at an airfield near the fairgrounds.

Unlike the 1893 World's Columbian Exposition in Chicago, which stressed uniformity in white classical Greek design, the 1933-1934 fair showcased buildings in a variety of Art Deco styles painted a variety of colors. Various architects were responsible for specific areas of the fair. Buildings within each area reflected the "Century of Progress" theme in appropriate ways. Chicago's most famous architect, Frank Lloyd Wright, was not invited to participate. As a result, he was a vocal critic of the fair's architects and their buildings.

One of the hallmarks of the fair was the Homes of Tomorrow Exhibition, which contained every imaginable consumer-convenience product in twelve model homes. These homes were constructed using the most up-to-date materials and techniques. The consumer products included dishwashers and home

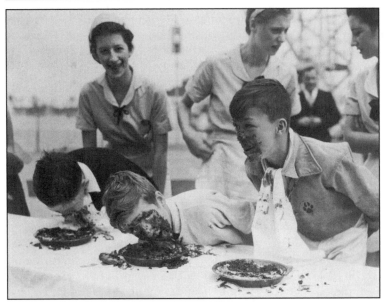

Boys compete in an old-fashioned pie-eating contest at the Chicago World's Fair in 1934. (©Bettmann/CORBIS)

air conditioners, both rarities in American homes at the time. Entertainment at the fair included a wild-animal park, singing and dancing shows that featured fan dancer and stripper Sally Rand, and singer Judy Garland. Fair executives persuaded Major League Baseball to stage its first all-star game in conjunction with the fair.

The fair closed on November 12, 1933, but President Franklin D. Roosevelt asked that the fair be reopened for the summer of 1934. He thought the fair was a great economic stimulus because it encouraged people to enjoy themselves as well as purchase cutting-edge consumer goods. By the time the fair closed permanently on October 31, 1934, the entire debt to produce the fair had been repaid. No government money was used to finance the fair; it was one of the few world expositions or fairs to pay for itself.

The fair was not without controversy, however. Women's contributions to American history and progress were ignored. Exhibits depicting Africa and African Americans were stereotypically demeaning. African Americans were denied employment at the fair and were refused admission and service when visiting the fair. Between the fair's closing in 1933 and its reopening in 1934, African American politicians and civil rights groups protested against the fair's discriminatory policies and practices. Legislation was hurriedly passed outlawing segregation and race-based discrimination at the fair. This successful publicity campaign and legislative approach to changing discriminatory practices became standard procedure for other civil rights cases.

Impact Neither the exhibits nor the buildings were intended to be permanent; however, some exhibits were donated to the Chicago Museum of Science and Industry. Profits from the fair were donated to cultural institutions in Chicago. The public and economic success of the event inspired other cities to mount their own "progressive" fairs. The 1939 New York World's Fair continued the "world of tomorrow" theme. More cities were working on fairs when World War II interrupted all such enterprises.

Victoria Erhart

Further Reading

Ganz, Cheryl R. *The 1933 Chicago World's Fair: A Century of Progress.* Urbana: University of Illinois Press, 2008. Studies the cooperation among business, the military, and science to promote a vision of a better future for ordinary Americans. The theme of progress through technology became standard for all later world's fairs and expositions.

Gleisten, Samantha. *Chicago's 1933-1934 World's Fair: A Century of Progress.* Chicago: Arcadia, 2002. Collection of advertising postcards and posters for the Chicago World's Fair, depicting numerous fair buildings and exhibits.

Schrenk, Lisa. *Building a Century of Progress: The Architecture of Chicago's 1933-1934 World's Fair.* Minneapolis: University of Minnesota Press, 2007. Examines materials and techniques for commercial and residential buildings displayed at the fair and the impact these innovative buildings had on mid-twentieth century American architecture.

See also African Americans; Airships; Baseball; Business and the economy in the United States; Civil rights and liberties in the United States; Great Depression in the United States; Home furnishings; Rand, Sally; Wright, Frank Lloyd.

■ Children's Hour, The

Identification Play about two young teachers accused of lesbianism
Author Lillian Hellman
Date First produced in 1934

Neither the Depression nor the word "lesbian" is mentioned in the play, but both are in the subtext of Lillian Hellman's play, which is concerned with the ruin of two teachers struggling to make a living by running a successful private school. The playwright demonstrates the dire consequences of assumption, as a community is provoked into believing the teachers have corrupted their children's innocence by setting an immoral example.

Hellman's first play produced on Broadway was a tremendous success. It ran for more than seven hundred performances and was acclaimed by critics, who regarded Hellman as a groundbreaking playwright exploring social issues and women's psychology in the context of the 1930's, a time when many writers were portraying previously taboo subjects on stage or challenging the political status quo. Like Clifford Odets's play *Waiting for Lefty* (1935), which dramatized a strike and explored the impact of economic injustice, *The Children's Hour* explored women's lives and careers with a candor that caused the play to be banned in Boston. The play was so controversial that Hellman had to change its plot when it was released as a film in 1936; it was retitled *These Three*, and the teachers are accused of engaging in a love triangle with the fiancé of one of the characters.

Karen Wright and Martha Dobie are in charge of a private school they have built on their own. Although the play does not explicitly say so, these two women have had trouble finding employment during the Depression and therefore have resorted to creating their own successful enterprise. However, their problem student, Mary, rebelling against the teachers' efforts to discipline her, tells her wealthy aunt that something unnatural has occurred between Karen and Mary. The outraged aunt promptly withdraws Mary from the school and makes sure that other parents in the community do so as well. Karen loses her fiancé, and a guilty Martha, wondering if perhaps she did have a romantic attachment to Karen, kills herself.

Impact Based on an actual case in nineteenth century Scotland, Hellman's play shifts the setting to the United States during the 1930's, a time of great anxiety because of the Depression and an unsettled society rife with calls for economic, political, and social change. Martha's self-doubt shows the influence of Freudian psychology, especially of the idea of the unconscious. At the same time, the play is protesting the structure of a society that permits the teachers no viable defense as soon as the rumors of their lesbianism are spread. Hellman intensified the Depression-era setting of the play in her film version of the play, showing an opening sequence clearly establishing that these two women are going to have trouble finding employment unless they start their own school.

Carl Rollyson

Further Reading

Griffin, Alice, and Geralding Thorston. *Understanding Lillian Hellman.* Columbia: University of South Carolina Press, 1999.
Rollyson, Carl. *Lillian Hellman: Her Life and Legend.* New York: iUniverse, 2008.

See also Hammett, Dashiell; Hellman, Lillian; Homosexuality and gay rights; Odets, Clifford.

■ Christie Pits riot

The Event Race riot Between Jewish and Nazi youths
Date August 16, 1933
Place Toronto, Canada

During the 1930's, many Jews settled in Toronto, where they faced discrimination from the locals. The Christie Pits riot occurred in 1933, in the midst of the Great Depression and the rise of Adolf Hitler and the Nazi influence on the world. The riot began after taunts at Jewish participants at a junior softball game.

In 1933, Jews were Toronto's largest ethnic minority group, accounting for 7 percent of the city's 682,000 residents. Jews lived in "the Ward" area of the city, west of Spadina Avenue. Many of the Jews worked in the garment district during the Depression years. They were unwelcome competition and were prohibited from area resorts, restaurants, hotels, and clubs. Signs at these locations read "Gentiles Only." Jews spent their free time at Kew Beach, though they experienced discrimination there as well. They were accused of littering the beach and changing in the open. Hitler had recently come to power in Germany, and the swastika, an icon appropriated by the Nazis, was emerging as a symbol of Jewish hate. To terrorize Canadian Jews, some non-Jewish Canadians formed groups such as the Swastika Club on Queen Street East.

The location of the riot was Willowvale Park, though the area was known as "Christie Pits" because it was a former quarry pit that had been turned into a park named "Christie," for a tanner who sold leather goods there. On August 16, the Christian, non-Jewish St. Peter's softball team from a church located at Bloor and Bathurst streets played the Jewish Harbord playground team. The Jewish team suffered through numerous insults. By the second game, a neighborhood gang called the Pit Gang waved a bed sheet with a swastika and chanted "Heil Hitler" when the Harbord team tied the game. Jewish supporters, many of whom were Italian and Roman Catholic, ran toward the gang with homemade weapons of sticks, chains, and pipes. The riot lasted about six hours.

Impact Although some people were seriously injured, there were no reports of anyone dying from the violence. The event was so shocking for the community that it marked the genesis of a new sensitivity and change in Toronto race relations. Soon thereafter, displaying a swastika was illegal in the city.

Camille Gibson

Further Reading

Comacchio, Cynthia R. *The Dominion of Youth: Adolescence and the Making of a Modern Canada, 1920-1950.* Waterloo, Ont.: Wilfrid Laurier University Press, 2006.

Levitt, Cyril, and William Shaffir. *The Riot at Christie Pits.* Toronto: Lester & Orpen Dennys, 1987.

Tulchinsky, Karen X. *The Five Books of Moses Lapinsky.* Vancouver, B.C.: Polestar, 2003.

See also Anti-Semitism; Canadian minority communities; Demographics of Canada; Great Depression in Canada; Immigration to Canada; Jews in Canada; Race riots; Racial discrimination; Unemployment in Canada; Urbanization in Canada.

■ Chrysler Building

Identification Skyscraper in Manhattan at the intersection of Forty-second Street and Lexington Avenue

Date Completed on May 28, 1930

Place New York, New York

Widely regarded as one of greatest modern structures in the United States, the Chrysler Building is a classic example of Art Deco architecture and is considered to be one of the world's best-designed skyscrapers. At the time of its completion, it was the tallest building in the world.

The Chrysler Building was designed by architect William Van Alen to house the Chrysler Corporation. Walter P. Chrysler, chairperson of the Chrysler Automobile Corporation, wanted to make his headquarters in New York instead of Detroit. Some details of the building, especially the gargoyles, were modeled after Chrysler automobile products, such as hood ornaments and hubcaps of the Plymouth. The building was completed on May 28, 1930.

Chrysler wanted the building to be the world's highest structure. Two other buildings, however, were in competition for this honor: the Manhattan Bank (later known as the Trump Building) and the Empire State Building. The building was taller than the Eiffel Tower, which had been built forty years earlier, but it was surpassed by the Empire State Building by more than 200 feet. Nevertheless, it won in style because it was the biggest example of Art Deco design. The interiors were lavish. Each part was exquisitely planned in detail.

Chrysler refused to pay Van Alen his fees because he believed he had entered into some dubious financial arrangements with some of the building's contractors. Van Alen sued but the matter was dropped. The design was world famous, but Van Alen never worked again on another major project. Chrysler, writing his autobiography in 1937, did not mention Van Alen. The design and lease for the Chrysler Building were sold to Chrysler. He maintained control until the 1950's, but the original name remains.

The Chrysler Building is easily identifiable, with a stainless-steel, stepped-dome top surmounted by a Spartan-like spire. The spire was a secret and installed in about ninety minutes. Part of it was hidden within the building's shell and was hoisted out of the top of the building and riveted into place.

New York City skyline, with the Chrysler Building in the center, viewed from atop the Empire State Building in 1932. (Library of Congress)

Impact   The Chrysler Building remains a New York City landmark. The base of the building is unremarkable; one would not notice much when passing by. However, when one views it from a distance, it is one of the highlights of the New York skyline.

Ski Hunter

Further Reading

Nash, Eric Peter, and Norman McGrath. *Manhattan Skyscrapers.* New York: Princeton Architectural Press, 1999.

Stravitz, David. *The Chrysler Building: Creating a New York Icon Day by Day.* New York: Princeton Architectural Press, 2002.

See also   Architecture; Empire State Building; Rockefeller Center.

CIO. See Congress of Industrial Organizations

■ City Lights

Identification   Silent film about a little tramp who falls in love with a blind girl who sells flowers
Director   Charles Chaplin
Date   Released in 1931

After the beginning of sound pictures in 1927 and the stock market crash of 1929, Charles Chaplin's last silent film beautifully combined humor and pathos to speak to Depression-era audiences. A box-office smash, City Lights *cemented Chaplin's reputation as the premier comic genius.*

One of the most unusual elements of *City Lights* is that it is essentially a silent film released after the Hollywood movement toward sound pictures had already started with *The Jazz Singer* (1927). In the midst of the nearly three-year production, Chaplin conservatively decided to keep *City Lights* silent, with the exception of certain sound effects and a musical score. He felt the little tramp character's universality and the international recognition of the pantomime would be compromised by dialogue and the difficulties of translation. His gamble paid off, and the film was a hit.

One of Chaplin's great innovations was the alternation and mixing of slapstick comedy with dramatic sentiment, creating tears of both laughter and empathy. *City Lights* exhibits the balance and blend of these two types of scenes in a "dialectic" perhaps better than any other film Chaplin made. Often in a scene, a comic slapstick moment serves as a "punch line" for a more serious mood. For example, in one scene, the tramp pretends to have left the blind girl with whom he is entranced; he sits down beside her while she fills a pail with water. The serious romantic mood of the tramp eyeing the girl is abruptly broken when the girl accidentally throws the water from the pail into the tramp's face. Other times the reverse effect occurs. In a masterpiece of comic farce, choreography, and ballet, the great boxing sequence exemplifies a chaotic orgy of mistakes. However, the hilarious mood is broken when the tramp is finally knocked unconscious, losing a last opportunity to make money to help the girl.

The film is bookended by a famous comic scene and a final, classic scene of drama and pathos. The film opens with the unveiling of a statue in the city. The speech of the mayor and others is represented by squawking gibberish. Finally, when the statue is unveiled, the little tramp is seen sleeping on the lap of the figure. Outraged by the tramp's desecrating presence, the authorities and the crowd order the tramp down from the statue. A sword on the statue impales the back of the tramp's pants, so that he is at first unable to move away. Eventually his nose touches the statue's huge extended hand—as if the tramp were "thumbing his nose" at the crowd.

Ever the perfectionist, Chaplin reworked, rewrote, and reshot the story until he came up with the last scene. Everything was then revised to prepare for that ending. This scene ties together the film's themes of blindness and insight, of class divisions, and of the surprising, ironical twists of fate. The tramp, who earlier had played the part of the millionaire to the girl and gave her the money to restore her eyesight, is released from jail and sees the girl in the flower shop. When the girl goes outside to give him a coin and a rose, she runs her hand on his clothes and recognizes him as her benefactor. The tramp asks if she can see now, and she answers yes. The camera holds a close-up and then fades out on the tramp's smiling face, a mixture of many complex emotions, just as her expression betrays a wealth of conflicting emotions. The scene is the capstone to a film masterpiece, accomplished with the understated acting and perfectionism in which Chaplin so much believed.

Impact   As star, writer, director, producer, editor, and musical composer, Chaplin remains the model for the ultimate auteur film artist. Both audiences and filmmakers alike consider *City Lights* Chaplin's greatest film. *City Lights* is usually on the American Film Institute's list of all-time best films.

Joseph Francavilla

Further Reading

Robinson, David. *Chaplin: His Life and Art.* New York: Da Capo Press, 1994.

Schickel, Richard. *The Essential Chaplin: Perspectives on the Life and Art of the Great Comedian.* Chicago: Ivan R. Dee, 2006.

Vance, Jeffrey. *Chaplin: Genius of the Cinema.* New York: Harry N. Abrams, 2003.

See also   Chaplin, Charles; Film; *Modern Times*; Motion Picture Production Code.

■ Civil rights and liberties in Canada

Some Canadians, primarily those affiliated with left-wing organizations, were deprived of civil liberties during the 1930's. However, a major civil liberties movement began during the decade.

A movement to defend civil liberties began in Canada during the 1930's as a reaction to the enforcement of Section 98 of the Criminal Code of Canada, enacted in 1919, which made it a criminal offense to belong to any organization advocating the use of force or violence to bring about a change in government. The law was broadly worded and carried a prison penalty of up to twenty years. During the first half of the 1930's, the law was used to harass left-wing political associations and labor unions. In 1931, the Royal Canadian Mounted Police, in cooperation with the Ontario Provincial Police, arrested eight leaders of the Communist Party of Canada in order to "strike a death blow at the Communist Party."

At the trial known as *Rex v. Buck*, the eight communist leaders were defended by the Canadian Labor Defense League (CLDL), a communist-led organization dedicated to defending the rights and liberties of workers and persons on the political left. Despite its class-based nature, the CLDL was one of Canada's earliest organizations devoted to individual liberties. Supporters of the group raised $160,000 for bail, organized large demonstrations, and collected a petition with 459,000 signatures calling for the repeal of Section 98. Many liberals and moderates who despised communism joined in the petition.

Eventually, the defendants were found guilty. They were given prison sentences of up to five years, and these sentences were later upheld on appeal. The publicity of the trial solidified support for free speech, and the eight convicted communists did not have to serve their full prison terms. Following the elevation of William Lyon Mackenzie King to prime minister in 1935, the Canadian parliament voted to repeal Section 98 in 1936.

Repression in Quebec In French-speaking Quebec, provincial premier Maurice Duplessis disagreed with the repeal of the law and was alarmed when communists and other left-wing groups began to distribute leaflets and hold open meetings. At his urging, the Quebec legislature passed the 1937 Act to Protect the Province Against Communist Propaganda, commonly known as the Padlock Act because it authorized local sheriffs to end meetings suspected of promoting communism and to place a padlock on the door of the meeting place for up to one year. During the first few months of the law's existence, police officers conducted more than one hundred raids. Because the act did not define the nature of communism, the provincial attorney general sometimes utilized it to prevent meetings of leftist organizations that were noncommunist. Jewish groups and Jehovah's Witnesses claimed that they were harassed under the law. The Padlock Act remained in effect until the Supreme Court of Canada ruled it unconstitutional twenty years later.

One of the unintended consequences of the Padlock Act was the 1937 establishment of Canada's first mainstream organization devoted to individual freedoms, the Canadian Civil Liberties Union (CCLU). The Montreal branch of the CCLU soon had more than one thousand members, and it generated considerable opposition to the Padlock Act throughout the province. Branches of the CCLU were soon created in Toronto, Vancouver, Ottawa, and Winnipeg. By its own bylaws, the CCLU was a nonpolitical organization devoted to "the rights of free speech, free press, free assembly, and other liberties." In contrast to the CLDL, the CCLU's goal was to enlarge liberties for all Canadians, regardless of their ideological views.

Bill of Rights and Wartime Repression In 1938, the Supreme Court of Canada initiated an important precedent when it struck down an Alberta provincial law restricting freedom of the press. In this case, *Reference Re Alberta Statutes*, the court held that the law violated the Canadian constitution, even though freedom of expression was not explicitly guaranteed in Canada's constitutional documents. In justification, the court noted that the British North America Act

of 1867 proclaimed that one of its purposes was to institute a constitutional system "similar in principle" to that of the United Kingdom. Based on this statement, combined with historical experiences, the court decided that Canada had an "implied bill of rights," which comprised a number of civil liberties, including freedom of expression.

In September, 1939, coinciding with Canada's entry into World War II, the Canadian parliament enacted the War Measures Act of 1939, which was implemented in a set of emergency measures called the Defense of Canada Regulations. The measures waived a number of traditional civil liberties, including the right to trial and the right of habeas corpus. The measures also authorized the government to place restrictions on speech and the press, to ban political and religious groups, to confiscate private property, and to detain without charge any person who might act "in any manner prejudicial to the public safety or the safety of the state." Through the remainder of the war years, the regulations were used to intern several thousand opponents of the war, particularly fascists, communists, outspoken critics of conscription, enemy aliens, and Canadians of German, Italian, and Japanese ancestry.

Impact Despite its libertarian tradition, Canada did not have a significant organized civil liberties movement until the 1930's. At the beginning of the decade, the country had legislation punishing people for their political affiliation. Soon after Section 98 was repealed in 1936, the province of Quebec enacted the repressive Padlock Act, which restricted rights of free speech and assembly over the following twenty years. Ironically, this law was the major impetus to the creation of Canada's first influential libertarian organization, the CCLU. In 1939, Canada enacted another repressive measure, the War Measures Act, but most of its impact occurred during the 1940's.

Thomas Tandy Lewis

Further Reading

Berger, Thomas. *Fragile Freedoms: Human Rights and Dissent in Canada.* Toronto: Clarke, Irwin, 1981. Standard work written by a British Columbia lawyer and jurist long one of Canada's leading voices for human rights.

Lambertson, Ross. *Repression and Resistance: Canadian Human Rights Activists, 1930-1960.* Toronto: University of Toronto Press, 2004. Contains excellent discussions of Section 98, the Padlock Act, and the War Measures Act.

Paulin, Marguerite. *Maurice Duplessis.* Montreal: XYZ, 2005. Colorful biography of the authoritarian premier of Quebec who was responsible for the Padlock Act.

See also Civil rights and liberties in the United States; Communism; Elections, Canadian; Fascism in Canada; World War II and Canada.

■ Civil rights and liberties in the United States

During the 1930's, individuals and groups took important steps in the areas of civil rights and civil liberties—particularly in terms of criminal procedure, free speech, and desegregation—that became commonplace to later generations.

A pair of landmark U.S. Supreme Court decisions during the 1930's signaled the movement toward greater procedural protections for criminal defendants; these foreshadowed the Warren Court revolution of the 1960's. In *Powell v. Alabama* (1932), the Court ruled that a group of young, indigent, illiterate, and uneducated African American defendants, who were facing the death penalty, were deprived of due process when the Court failed to appoint counsel, at the state's expense, to represent them. This was an important development; however, another thirty years passed before *Gideon v. Wainwright* (1963) extended the right to appointed counsel to all indigent defendants. Defendants in federal courts, on the other hand, soon reaped the benefit of *Powell v. Alabama* in *Johnson v. Zerbst* (1938), which ruled that all indigent federal defendants are entitled to appointed counsel.

In *Brown v. Mississippi* (1936), the Supreme Court ruled that confessions from defendants extracted through beatings or torture could not be used in trials. This too was significant because only four years earlier, the National Committee on Law Observance and Enforcement (also known as the Wickersham Commission) had found that police departments across the country gave criminal suspects the "third degree"—that is, used physical or mental pain to extract confessions. Although *Brown v. Mississippi* did not go as far as *Powell v. Alabama* did in defining the permissible terms of coercion, it laid the groundwork for more extensive judicial regulation during the 1960's, particularly the landmark decision of *Miranda v. Arizona* (1966).

Applying the First Amendment to the States The text of the First Amendment reads in relevant part, "Congress shall make no law . . . ," followed by a list of protected activities, including free speech and free exercise of religion. By its own words, therefore, the amendment appears to apply only to actions by the federal legislature and not the state governments. However, a series of cases during the 1930's continued an earlier trend of extending the civil rights protections in the Bill of Rights to the states. However, these cases were not explicit about the limitations on the states' ability to infringe upon free speech.

In *Stromberg v. California* (1931), the Supreme Court gathered these precedents to strike down a California law that prohibited the display of red flags (which were symbols of communism). Although the First Amendment mentioned only Congress, the Fourteenth Amendment's due process clause, which did apply to the states, the Court explained, contained a concept of liberty that included freedom of speech, including symbolic speech. *Near v. Minnesota* (1931) followed suit, extending freedom of the press to a newspaper that was seeking to reverse a lower court order forbidding it from publishing arguably slanderous material. Finally, in *Grosjean v. American Press Co.* (1936), the Court ruled that all "fundamental" rights in the Bill of Rights had been "incorporated" by the due process clause and that speech and press rights were fundamental. In other

---

Supreme Court Civil Rights and Liberties Decisions of the 1930's

- *Near v. Minnesota* (1931)
- *Stromberg v. California* (1931)
- *Powell v. Alabama* (1932)
- *Brown v. Mississippi* (1936)
- *Grosjean v. American Press Co.* (1936)
- *De Jonge v. Oregon* (1937)
- *Johnson v. Zerbst* (1938)
- *Missouri ex rel. Gaines v. Canada* (1938)

Lawyer Thurgood Marshall (left) speaks of behalf of his client, Donald Gaines Murray (center), who had petitioned to study at the University of Maryland School of Law but was denied admittance because of his race. (The Granger Collection, New York)

words, a case-by-case determination of whether a state's infringement of a specific kind of speech violated the First Amendment was not needed, because all speech was protected. The exact free press issue in *Grosjean v. American Press Co.* was whether a business tax targeted only against newspapers with a large circulation violated the free press guarantee of the First Amendment (as incorporated). Because a discriminatory tax could serve as a deterrent against newspapers, the tax could not stand. The next year, in *De Jonge v. Oregon* (1937), the Court decided that freedom of assembly also was fundamental. As a result, the Court reversed the conviction of a man who had merely helped run a meeting of the local Communist Party; there was no indication that either he or the group had intended to incite the violent overthrow of the government.

Beginning of School Desegregation Litigation   During the 1930's, the National Association for the Advancement of Colored People's (NAACP's) litigation strategy to integrate public schools took shape; the movement culminated in the landmark *Brown v. Board of Education* (1954) decision. Unlike *Brown*, which directly overruled the 1896 "separate but equal" distinction from *Plessy v. Ferguson*, these earlier cases did not challenge *Plessy v. Ferguson* so much as demonstrate that the particular facilities in question were not equal. The two leading lawyers in this litigation movement were Charles Hamilton Houston, dean of Howard University School of Law, and Thurgood Marshall, an NAACP attorney (and later the solicitor general of the United States and then an associate justice on the Supreme Court from 1967 to 1991).

In *Murray v. Pearson* (1936), the NAACP challenged the University of Maryland School of Law's policy of refusing to admit African American applicants because of their race. There were no public law schools in Maryland open to African Americans, so the state belatedly offered to raise funds to help pay for African American citizens of Maryland to study law at out-of-state schools. For a student who, like Donald Gaines Murray, wanted to practice law in Baltimore, however, studying at an out-of-state law school was not equal to studying at the University of Maryland, with two-thirds of its faculty composed of Maryland judges or prominent local lawyers. The Maryland appellate court upheld this ruling, and Murray was admitted to the Maryland law school.

Because *Murray v. Pearson* was a state law decision, it had no precedential effect outside Maryland, though courts in other states were free to follow it if they chose. The decision was an important psychological victory for the desegregation movement, which then focused on the University of Missouri law school. The state of Missouri had a public institution of higher education, known as Lincoln University, set aside for African Americans, but that school did not offer a law program. The plaintiff, a graduate of Lincoln, wanted to attend law school. Missouri offered him two choices: He could apply to Lincoln, which would develop its own law program for him, or he could attend an out-of-state law school, and the state would pay the difference between that school's tuition and what the University of Missouri would have charged him had he been able to attend.

In *Missouri ex rel. Gaines v. Canada* (1938), the Supreme Court tracked the Maryland appellate court's conclusion, with Chief Justice Charles Evans Hughes reasoning that Missouri had not provided an equivalent opportunity to Lloyd Gaines, because that required "legal education within the State." In short, Missouri had the choice of either providing an actual law school for African Americans—not a theoretical one, as was the case with Lincoln—or to admit African Americans to the single public law school in the state. The Gaines case was significant because it provided a foothold for the NAACP to attack a variety of other segregation practices by demonstrating that they too were separate and unequal.

Impact With the United States in the throes of the Great Depression during the 1930's, in retrospect, the decade may seem to have been an odd time for civil liberties to expanded, especially with an ideologically fractured Supreme Court seemingly occupied with fighting President Franklin D. Roosevelt's New Deal. Nonetheless, much of the famous Warren Court revolution of the 1960's—in many ways the high-water mark of judicial recognition of civil rights and liberties—had its roots in decisions from the 1930's.

Tung Yin

Further Reading

Cortner, Richard C. *A "Scottsboro" Case in Mississippi: The Supreme Court and Brown v. Mississippi.* Jackson: University Press of Mississippi, 1986. Detailed account of *Brown v. Mississippi*, the case that ruled coerced confessions to be in violation of the Constitution.

Currie, David P. *The Constitution in the Supreme Court: The Second Century, 1888-1986.* Chicago: University of Chicago Press, 1990. Academic but readable work that covers the background and rulings of the major Supreme Court decisions during the 1930's; also discusses insights into the personalities of the justices.

Epps, Garrett. *The First Amendment, Freedom of the Press: Its Constitutional History and the Contemporary Debate.* Amherst, N.Y.: Prometheus Books, 2008. Discusses the evolution of the freedom of the press and highlights the provision's ongoing significance in the twenty-first century.

Kluger, Richard. *Simple Justice: The History of Brown v. Board of Education and Black America's Struggle for Equality.* New York: Alfred A. Knopf, 1975. Definitive historical account of the desegregation movement.

Schwartz, Bernard. *A History of the Supreme Court.* New York: Oxford University Press, 1993. Readable summary of major Supreme Court decisions, organized chronologically.

See also African Americans; *Brown v. Mississippi; De Jonge v. Oregon;* House Committee on Un-American Activities; Jim Crow segregation; *Johnson v. Zerbst; Missouri ex rel. Gaines v. Canada;* National Association for the Advancement of Colored People; *Near v. Minnesota.*

■ Civilian Conservation Corps

Identification   New Deal program focused on the environment and rural development that provided jobs and training for thousands of unemployed men

Also known as   CCC

Date   Established March 31, 1933

Part of President Franklin D. Roosevelt's economic policies during the Great Depression, the Civilian Conservation Corps (CCC) combined technology and proven forestry methods to preserve swaths of the American environment and to improve agricultural regions through land management, all while teaching skills to an unemployed workforce.

As part of the New Deal, the Emergency Work Conservation Act created the CCC to solve two problems at once. Because the United States was in the middle of the Great Depression and unemployment peaked at about 25 percent, the CCC employed and trained thousands of men while also preserving some of the country's environmental assets, such as farmland and forests, using successful but labor-intensive methods.

Environmental Methods and the CCC   Like his cousin Theodore Roosevelt, a previous American president who helped to found the National Wildlife Refuge System, Franklin D. Roosevelt believed that some of the country's natural assets should be preserved for future generations. With the CCC, he wanted to stem catastrophic land erosion and preserve areas of wilderness.

The program acted as a sort of peacetime army of men who reforested areas throughout the United States, including states suffering from the effects of the Dust Bowl. These midwestern states needed trees to provide windbreaks and to halt wind and water erosion so that the plains and agricultural fields would not remain barren wasteland. Throughout the life of the program, more than 3 billion trees were planted and more than 84 million acres of agrarian land received new drainage measures to divert damaging, fast-moving water or stagnant water, therefore aiding farm production.

CCC Camps in Every State   CCC members had to be in good physical shape and enrolled for six-month stints. In order to be considered, applicants were required to be American citizens and unemployed. During the early years of the program, preference was given to unmarried candidates, most of whom were between eighteen and twenty-six years old. The CCC had the added benefit of lowering crime rates because it increased gainful employment opportunities and dispersed large jobless populations.

Because many of the proposed projects were in the more rural or Western areas of the country, many young men in the urbanized East were transferred to locations in other states. The War Department provided transportation, and the Agriculture Department and the Department of the Interior planned CCC projects. The Department of Labor selected candidates, relying on the established criteria.

In order to provide structure for the program, work camps were established in each state, in addition to Hawaii and Alaska, neither of which was yet a state. There were also work camps in the Virgin Islands and Puerto Rico.

By 1935, the CCC employed 500,000 men and had become known for stimulating local economies and for providing good forestry techniques, which

A Civilian Conservation Corps blacksmith, working in Maryland in 1935. (Library of Congress)

could help with fire prevention and flood control. The men built fire towers and used fire prevention methods in heavily forested areas, while also creating campgrounds and other recreational assets.

Because the CCC workers were spread throughout the country, they were also able to help in times of natural disasters. They helped rebuild communities after floods in several states. Long after a particularly devastating flood in southern Indiana in 1937, the towns still retained physical evidence of the disaster and remembered the work performed by the CCC. The CCC also helped repair destruction caused by blizzards and hurricanes, earning it gratitude from both local citizens and members of Congress.

Impact Congress eliminated funding to the CCC in 1941; the program's demise was the result of the need for soldiers during World War II and the low unemployment rate and was not based on problems with the CCC's work or mission. Bridges, roads, fire towers, campgrounds, and national parks constructed by the CCC have benefited millions of people throughout the country for many decades. The program helped reduce unemployment during a major economic crisis and provided a beneficial work history for the employees. The CCC had far-reaching and positive effects and proved to be a successful part of the New Deal.

Bonnye Busbice Good

Further Reading

Cohen, Stan. *The Tree Army: A Pictorial History of the Civilian Conservation Corps, 1933-1942*. Missoula, Mont.: Pictorial Histories, 1980. Collection of photographs detailing the types of forestry projects enacted by the corps.

Fleming, Thomas. *The New Dealers' War: F. D. R. and the War Within World War II*. New York: Basic Books, 2001. Overview describing Roosevelt's work to create new economic programs known as the New Deal in addition to the global issues concerning World War II.

Hill, Edwin G. *In the Shadow of the Mountain: The Spirit of the CCC*. Pullman: Washington State University Press, 1990. Describes camp life in the CCC and work that the organization performed.

Maher, Neil. *Nature's New Deal: The Civilian Conservation Corps and the Roots of the American Environmental Movement*. New York: Oxford University Press, 2008. Detailed account of the CCC's impact on modern environmentalism and how some of the practices became more widely used because of the training and success of the CCC.

Sypolt, Larry N. *Civilian Conservation Corps: A Selectively Annotated Bibliography*. Westport, Conn.: Praeger, 2005. Primary account of the CCC workers' environment and projects that also includes an explanatory overview of the program.

See also Dust Bowl; Great Depression in the United States; National parks; Roosevelt, Franklin D.; Roosevelt's first one hundred days; Unemployment in the United States.

■ Cleveland "torso" murders

The Event Unsolved murder, decapitation, and dismemberment of twelve victims, ten of whom have never been identified
Dates September, 1935, to August, 1938
Place Cleveland, Ohio

The Cleveland "torso" murders not only disturbed order in Cleveland and frightened residents but also frustrated and baffled law enforcement. The killer had no distinct pattern, left few clues for forensics, and performed the murders so that identifying most of the victims was impossible.

From 1935 to 1938 in Depression-era Cleveland, twelve men and women were murdered; most of their bodies were dumped in the impoverished area of the Cleveland Flats known as Kingsbury Run—a shantytown populated by the most indigent of the period. The victims were beheaded, which forensics teams determined was usually the cause of death, with evidence showing that most of the tightly bound victims had fought frantically against their restraints up to the last moments before death. The victims were also usually dismembered, and in some cases their bodies were treated with what was thought to be some sort of preserving chemical. The treatment of the bodies and the dumping of headless, limbless torsos made identification nearly impossible, and in all but two instances, the victims were never identified. Cleveland detectives could only surmise that these six men and four women were transients, drifters, or persons of ill repute with no family or associates to miss them when they disappeared. Furthermore, the manner in which the individuals, including Florence Genevieve Polillo and

Edward W. Andrassy, were mutilated led experts to markedly different conclusions about the identity of the murderer.

With the discovery of the first two "John Does" (dubbed "victim one" and "victim two," who was later identified as Andrassy), both headless, naked, washed, and drained of blood, detectives speculated that the killer was possibly a homosexual man with a deviant agenda. However, with the discovery of the third victim, Polillo, a forty-two-year-old Irish American, the profiling shifted. Detectives, led by the ambitious Eliot Ness, studied the fourth mutilated "body" of the "tattooed man." As the detectives considered whether the "lady of the lake" body was a victim of the same killer, they had to look beyond jealousy, revenge, or sexual deviance as motives.

Despite the similarity of the mutilations, which was also apparent in the next eight victims, no psychiatric profile could aid in tracking down the serial killer. Despite the numerous leads, and in spite of the occasional false, or falsely gained, confession, no grueling amount of superlative detective work brought police closer to capturing the murderer. With the limited knowledge and technology of 1930's forensics, Ness, seasoned detectives such as Sergeant James Hogan and Peter Merylo, skilled technicians such as Coroner Samuel R. Gerber, and many other experts in their fields could not come to any conclusion about who the "Mad Butcher of Kingsbury Run" was, what motivated his mad science, or where he could be found. Not until Ness finally ordered the shacks of the shantytown to be raided and burned down did the murders stop.

Impact The Cleveland "torso" murders, committed by the so-called Mad Butcher of Kingsbury Run, terrified citizens, brought more devastation to an already blighted area of Cleveland, and destroyed the lives of twelve presumably innocent victims. The murders put a drain on city resources, incited dissension in the ranks and rifts between and among politicians and police, and taxed and outwitted the limited forensic knowledge and technology of the time. Furthermore, they may have ruined the career of Ness, a man who had been the city's anticrime savior. As public safety director, Ness spent hundreds of hours personally interviewing the detectives on the case and the vagrants of Kingsbury Run, investigating crime scenes, consulting with forensic experts,

and neglecting his larger efforts of the 1930's fighting Prohibition bootleggers, racketeers, and corrupt police. When Ness ordered the shantytown to be destroyed, the initial results seemed to prove that Ness had found the answer to the mystery, because the murders stopped. However, because of his inability to identify either the murderer or most of the victims, Ness, the man who had captured Al Capone, was said to have been the Mad Butcher of Kingsbury Run's thirteenth "victim."

Roxanne McDonald

Further Reading

Badal, James Jessen. *In the Wake of the Butcher: Cleveland's Torso Murders.* Kent, Ohio: Kent State University Press, 2001.

Bellamy, John Stark, II. *The Maniac in the Bushes and More Tales of Cleveland Woe: True Crimes and Disasters from the Streets of Cleveland.* Cleveland: Gray and Company, 1997.

Nickel, Steven. *Torso: Eliot Ness and the Search for a Psychopathic Killer.* Winston-Salem, N.C.: John F. Blair, 2001.

Rasmussen, William T. *Corroborating Evidence II: The Cleveland Torso Murders, the Black Dahlia Murder, the Zodiac Killer, the Phantom Killer of Texarkana.* Santa Fe, N.Mex.: Sunstone Press, 2006.

See also Capone, Al; Crimes and scandals; *Dick Tracy*; Ness, Eliot; Nitti, Frank; Ohio Penitentiary fire; Ohio River flood.

■ Cohan, George M.

Identification American playwright, songwriter, and entertainer
Born July 3, 1878; Providence, Rhode Island
Died November 5, 1942; New York, New York

For more than one-quarter of a century, Cohan dominated American theater. In revolutionizing the concept of theater by creating the genre later known as musical comedy, Cohan became the first entertainment celebrity of the new century, known as much for staging successful theatrical productions as for penning dozens of hugely popular tunes.

George M. Cohan was born into a theater family; his parents were both vaudeville performers, and he was on stage before he was one. By twenty, he was writing stage plays that merged the best aspects of vaudeville entertainments, such as high-energy dancing and hummable tunes, and popular theater, such as sympathetic characters, simple sentiments, and upbeat resolutions. His more than forty frothy musicals dominated Broadway for the first two decades of the new century. His more than five hundred show tunes, including "Give My Regards to Broadway" and "Yankee Doodle Dandy," both from his landmark success *Little Johnny Jones* (1904), were a national sensation. Cohan achieved success in every aspect of the theater: He was a playwright, a composer, an actor, a dancer of enormous grace, and later a director and a producer.

By the late 1920's, however, Cohan's style of musical theater had lost its appeal. The era was far too skeptical for Cohan's naive lyrical celebrations of home and love and his snappy melodies. As the country lurched into the Depression, Cohan's unflappable optimism seemed at best out of place and at worst irrelevant. Ever the entertainer, Cohan understood his audience and understood his time had passed.

Cohan had frequently performed in his own musicals decades earlier, and during the 1930's, he returned to acting. He acted briefly in Hollywood, starring in a largely forgettable *The Phantom President* (1932), in which he played an affable song-and-dance man who agrees to campaign for a dull, if earnest, candidate for president with whom he shares a remarkable resemblance (Cohan played both roles). However, Cohan missed the spontaneity of the stage. He returned to New York and found immediate success playing the worldly, wise father in Eugene O'Neill's comedy *Ah, Wilderness!* (1933).

On June 29, 1936, President Franklin D. Roosevelt presented Cohan with a Congressional Gold Medal to recognize Cohan's remarkable contributions to the country's morale during World War I through his songs "You're a Grand Old Flag" and "Over There." Then, in 1937, Cohan performed a much-praised turn as Roosevelt in the Richard Rodgers and Lorenz Hart musical satire *I'd Rather Be Right* (1937). Typically, Cohan was not satisfied with the libretto and devised his own reading of the Roosevelt character, playing the wheelchair-bound executive as a gifted hoofer and including joyously exuberant dance numbers. Roosevelt himself expressed approval of the interpretation, and the show enjoyed a two-year run, including a grueling extended road production in which Cohan starred.

By the advent of World War II, Cohan had retired from performing after a diagnosis of inoperable stomach cancer. A Hollywood studio optioned the rights to Cohan's life story and, with a frail Cohan as production adviser and an irrepressible James Cagney in the lead, the 1942 musical blockbuster *Yankee Doodle Dandy* reintroduced Cohan to a new generation that embraced the unapologetic patriotism and sweeping optimism of Cohan's breezy melodies. Cohan lived just long enough to attend a New York showing of the film and to hear his songs embraced once again by a theater audience. He died at the age of sixty-four.

Impact The predominance of Cohan's style of light musical comedy had waned by the 1930's; however, his acting charisma was rediscovered via his stage performances during the period. This served to revitalize his song catalog, most strikingly those uptempo songs that helped lift the country's spirits during the Depression. Cohan embodied the brash confidence of the United States from the first decades of the twentieth century, even as the country was severely tested economically.

Joseph Dewey

Further Reading
Bordman, Gerald. *American Musical Theater: A Chronicle.* New York: Oxford University Press, 2001.
Kantor, Michael, and Laurence Maslon. *Broadway: The American Musical.* New York: Bulfinch, 2004.
McCabe, John. *George M. Cohan: The Man Who Owned Broadway.* Cambridge, Mass.: Da Capo Press, 1980.

See also Broadway musicals; Cagney, James; *I'd Rather Be Right*; Music: Popular; Roosevelt, Franklin D.; Theater in the United States.

■ Coinage

Definition Govenment-minted metal tokens that serve as money, a circulating medium of exchange for commercial transactions

Amid the Great Depression, the U.S. Mint reduced production levels, and American coinage ceased to feature gold coins and the silver dollar.

Entering the 1930's, U.S. coinage retained pennies, nickels, dimes, quarter-dollars, half-dollars, dollars, eagles, and double eagles. By the decade's end, the dollar, eagle, and double eagle had been replaced by similarly denominated units of paper currency.

The practice of placing presidential busts on coins began with the Abraham Lincoln penny in 1909. That practice accelerated during the 1930's. In 1932, the George Washington quarter was issued to honor the two hundredth anniversary of Washington's birth. Originally intended as a commemorative coin with low mintages at the Denver and San Francisco mints, the Washington quarter resumed as a regular-issue coin in 1934, replacing the Standing Liberty quarter last issued in 1930. In 1938, the Indian Head or Buffalo nickels was replaced by the Thomas Jefferson nickel, which was designed by Felix Schlag, winner of a public design contest. The Jefferson nickel featured Monticello, Jefferson's home, on the reverse side.

The Great Depression stifled demand for circulating coins, so there were several gaps in production. No mercury dimes were struck in 1932 and 1933. No pennies were struck in San Francisco from 1932 to 1934. The only Buffalo nickel minted between 1931 and 1933 was the low-mintage 1931-S. No quarters were struck in 1933. From 1930 to 1933, the only half-dollar was the 1933-S. Silver dollars were struck only in 1934 and 1935. Conversely, low mintages for particular dates and mints or mint errors stimulated collector demand. Low mintages brought attention to the 1931-S Lincoln penny and the 1938-D Walking Liberty half-dollar. The most spectacular error coin of the decade was the 1937-D three-legged Buffalo nickel.

The year 1933 signaled the end of gold coinage for regular circulation. At that time, it became illegal to own U.S. gold coins. Eagles had been struck in 1932 and 1933. Nearly one-half million 1933 double eagles were minted in Philadelphia. All were to have been withheld from circulation, but a few examples exist. One sold for $7.5 million at a 2002 auction.

Mints in Philadelphia, Denver, and San Francisco struck commemorative coins in great variety during the 1930's. The urge to raise money for public projects was too great to be resisted. Towns such as Lynchburg and Norfolk, Virginia; Albany and New Rochelle, New York; Bridgeport, Connecticut; Elgin, Illinois; and Columbia, South Carolina, were represented. States such as Arkansas, Connecticut, Delaware, Maryland, Wisconsin, and Texas commemorated anniversaries. Frontier personality Daniel Boone, Civil War battles at Gettysburg and Antietam, and the San Francisco Bay Bridge gained numismatic acknowledgment.

Impact The economic crisis of the 1930's limited production and banished gold, but it did not curb the imagination or artistry used on U.S. coinage. A modernizing society welcomed an increasingly modern coinage.

Myron C. Noonkester

Further Reading

Flynn, Kevin, et al. *The Authoritative Reference on Buffalo Nickels.* Irvine, Calif.: Zyrus Press, 2007.

Kelly, Richard G., and Nancy Y. Oliver. *A Mighty Fortress: The Stories Behind the Second San Francisco Mint.* Rev. ed. Hayward, Calif.: OK Association, 2004.

Lange, David W. *The Complete Guide to Buffalo Nickels.* 2d ed. Virginia Beach, Va.: DLRC Press, 2000.

_____. *The Complete Guide to Lincoln Cents.* Irvine, Calif.: Zyrus Press, 2005.

See also Bingo; Contract bridge; Hobbies; Marathon dancing; Monopoly; Postage stamps; Recreation.

■ Collier, John

Identification Commissioner of the Bureau of Indian Affairs under President Franklin D. Roosevelt
Born May 4, 1884; Atlanta, Georgia
Died May 8, 1968; Taos, New Mexico

Collier served as commissioner of the Bureau of Indian Affairs for twelve years (1933-1945), nearly all of Franklin D. Roosevelt's presidency and more time than any other person. Collier believed that Native American cultures and lands should be maintained but that they should be subject to the government's rules. The result of this synthesis was the Indian Reorganization Act (IRA), signed by Roosevelt in 1934.

John Collier's father was a lawyer, banker, and mayor of Atlanta. His mother, who was from New England, instilled in her son a love of literature and nature. Both parents died when Collier was a teenager. After a visit to the Taos Pueblo in New Mexico in 1920, Collier lived there for two years and developed an interest in the preservation of Pueblo culture and art.

Collier later took a lecturer position at San Francisco State College. In 1923, after he developed opposition to the Allotment Act, Collier played a major role in founding the American Indian Defense Association (AIDA), which presaged his later work in the Roosevelt administration. His belief that allotment was misguided was confirmed by issuance of the Meriam Report in 1928. Harold Ickes, Roosevelt's secretary of the interior, also had worked in the AIDA and, thus, appointed Collier as commissioner of the Bureau of Indian Affairs.

The Indian Reorganization Act, as designed by Collier, was the most fundamental and far-reaching piece of legislation related to Native Americans passed by Congress during the first half of the twentieth century. It eliminated the allotment system, which broke Native American lands into indi-

---

John Collier and Native Americans

In his book The Earth Shall Weep, *James Wilson describes Collier's passion for Native American rights.*

Collier's response to Native Americans belongs, undoubtedly, to the long European tradition of seeing the Indian as living in the "Golden Age": His description of aboriginal Californians, for example—"peoples joyously hospitable who seemed as free as birds, whose speech and colours were like the warbling and plumage of birds"—strikingly echoes Sir Francis Drake's account almost four centuries before.

Source: Wilson, James. *The Earth Shall Weep: A History of Native America.* New York: Atlantic Monthly Press, 1999.

Indian Commissioner John Collier, speaking at a Senate Indian Affairs Committee meeting. (Library of Congress)

vidual holdings, and established governments for some reservations under systems that were partially self-governing. The act also established hiring preferences for Native Americans within the Bureau of Indian Affairs. Although the act was criticized by some Native American groups, it also was widely acclaimed during the 1930's as a step beyond the repression of the nineteenth century. For example, this act allowed native peoples to resume their religious ceremonies openly, after a half-century of repression.

California was a major center of opposition to Collier's "Indian New Deal." One of the principal leaders of this opposition was Rupert Costo, a young Cahuilla who had attended college and had the respect of his people. Costo believed that the "Indian New Deal" was part of the effort to assimilate Native Americans. He called the Indian Reorganization Act the "Indian Raw Deal." By 1940, the act had received enough criticism to prompt congressional hearings to consider its repeal. As of that date, according to Native American law scholar Lawrence C. Kelly, 252 Native American nations and bands had voted on the act, including 99 small bands in California with a total population of fewer than twenty-five thousand. Seventy-eight groups had rejected it. Nationwide, thirty-eight thousand Native Americans voted in favor of IRA governments, while twenty-four thousand voted against them. Another thirty-five thousand eligible voters did not take part, most as a silent protest against the act.

Impact Through the Indian Reorganization Act, Collier's policies initiated a Native American resurgence to some degree. Some land was added to the national native estate, reversing a 150-year trend in the United States. While Collier was reviled frequently by political right-wingers for favoring native communalism over assimilation, he also encountered considerable criticism from many Native American people for ignoring their traditional systems of governance. Even while the Indian Reorganization Act was criticized, it stopped the allotment policies that had dismembered much of Native American's collective land base.

Bruce E. Johansen

Further Reading

Collier, John. *From Every Zenith*. Denver, Colo.: Sage Books, 1963.

Daily, David W. *Battle for the BIA: G.E.E. Lindquist and the Missionary Crusade Against John Collier*. Tucson: University of Arizona Press, 2004.

Philp, Kenneth R. *John Collier's Crusade for Indian Reform: 1920-1954*. Tucson: University of Arizona Press, 1977.

Stefon, Frederick J. "The Indians' Zarathustra: An Investigation into the Philosophical Roots of John Collier's New Deal Educational and Administrative Policies." *The Journal of Ethnic Studies*, Fall, 1983, 1-28.

See also Civil rights and liberties in the United States; Ickes, Harold; Indian Reorganization Act; Native Americans; Natural resources; Roosevelt, Franklin D.

■ Comic strips

Definition Illustrated cartoon stories syndicated in daily newspapers

During the 1930's, comic strips became more than ephemeral entertainment designed to fill space between advertisements. During this decade, strips developed iconic characters, and the creators of those strips infused them with powerful social, moral, and political messages that influenced broad swaths of the American public.

Richard Felton Outcault's *The Yellow Kid*, which debuted in the *New York World* in 1896, is generally credited as the first modern American comic strip.

The commercial success of *The Yellow Kid* led to a competition between Joseph Pulitzer, the publisher of the *New York World*, and William Randolph Hearst, the publisher of the *San Francisco Examiner*. Victory meant possessing the best slate of comic strips for the winning papers. As a result, between 1896 and 1930, the number of published strips multiplied rapidly. Syndication resulted, leading to the distribution of strips to papers nationwide.

This creative explosion produced some of the longest-running and most iconic strips in history. Many of these strips tended to reinforce traditional American values. One example is *Blondie*, a strip created by Chic Young that first appeared in the *New York American* on September 8, 1930. *Blondie* began as a gag strip following the adventures of dancing girl, Blondie Boopadoop. The narative focus changed three years later when Blondie married Dagwood Bumstead; the audience followed the young family's attempts to live the idealized American Dream. Although life was never perfect for the Bumsteads, their home was always happy because they kept the proper American values. This formula made *Blondie* one of the most popular and longest-lived strips of all time.

Another iconic strip that relied on reinforcing American values was Chester Gould's *Dick Tracy*. First published in the Detroit *Mirror* on October 4, 1931, *Dick Tracy* was a police procedural strip that followed the exploits of police detective Dick Tracy as he solved the violent crimes committed by one of fiction's most notorious rogue galleries. The content of *Dick Tracy* reflected the gangster-driven violence of Chicago during the 1930's; however, the strip's message was that good men, serving the forces of good, would always defeat evil.

Action-adventure, science-fiction, and pulp-fiction heroes were also popular subject matter for influential strips during the 1930's. These strips reinforced the mythic tale of the lone American hero driven by the desire for justice. Among the more iconic of these strips to debut during the 1930's were Alex Raymond's *Flash Gordon* (1934), Milton Caniff's *Terry and the Pirates* (1934), Lee Falk's *The Phantom* (1936), and Hal Foster's *Prince Valiant* (1937).

Strips during the 1930's also used powerful satire to convey social and political messages. The best known of this type was Al Capp's *Li'l Abner*, which was set in the hillbilly town of Dogpatch, Kentucky. First

Cover of the first comic book in which Superman appeared—the June, 1938, issue of Action Comics. *Superman was one of many comic-book characters to garner the attention of a Great Depression audience seeking diversion from the unsettling economic and cultural conditions of the era.* (Hulton Archive/Getty Images)

ridden streets of the Depression era. Gray's conservative beliefs were most evident in *Annie* stories about the New Deal, communism, and labor unions. The changing tone and message of the strip were so controversial that some media outlets called it racist and many newspapers stopped running the strip.

Strips for Disenfranchised Voices: The Black Press During the 1930's, the traditional newspaper industry ignored African American readers. To fill that void, a thriving Black Press evolved to disseminate news, sports, political opinion, and entertainment to African American readers. The largest void may have been in the depiction of black characters in mainstream comics. The depictions that did surface were generally stereotypically negative images that reinforced racist beliefs.

By the 1930's, black-owned and -operated papers such as the Chicago *Weekly Defender* and the Pittsburgh *Courier* ran strips of their own in which black characters were depicted realistically and devoid of stereotypes. A prime example of this was Bungleton Green, the longest-running character of all the black strips. Bungleton, who began in the *Defender* in 1920 as a lovable bum, was a character who constantly changed to reflect the difficulties of life as a minority in the United States. Through these strips, African Americans found a vehicle for the expression of ideas, which had been denied them in the mainstream newspapers.

published on August 13, 1934, by United Features Syndicate, *Li'l Abner* mixed slapstick, satire, and irony to question American values and politics. Capp's work became such a profound part of the American consciousness that terms such as "Sadie Hawkins Day," "Kickapoo Joy Juice," "Skunk Works," and "Shmoo" entered the American lexicon.

Other strips of the 1930's changed focus in order to take political stances. Harold Gray's *Little Orphan Annie,* which began in 1924 as a popular children's strip, had by 1931 transformed into a darker, adult-oriented, strip. Annie often found herself separated from the wealth of her adoptive father, Daddy Warbucks, leaving her alone in the cruel, violence-

Impact During the 1930's, comic strips not only became integral components of the American consciousness but also presented mature messages, moving from primarily gag strips to powerful vehicles for persuasive social, moral, and political messages.

B. Keith Murphy

Further Reading

Goulart, Ron. *The Adventurous Decade: Comic Strips in the Thirties.* New Castle, Pa.: Hermes Press, 2005. Provides a detailed history and selections of strips from the decade's key titles.

Gray, Harold. *Complete Little Orphan Annie.* Vol. 3. San Diego, Calif.: IDW, 2009. Compiles the *Annie* strips from April, 1930, through 1931, as Gray's conservative political voice first becomes evident.

Kane, Brian G. *The Definitive Prince Valiant Companion.* Seattle: Fantagraphics, 2009. History and synopsis of the strip combined with biographies of the creator, artists, and writers.

Perry, George, and Alan Aldridge. *The Penguin Book of Comics.* London: Penguin, 1971. Thorough study of the development of the comic form, from ancient pictographic writing through modern comic books.

Wright, Bradford W. *Comic Book Nation: The Transformation of Youth Culture in America.* Baltimore: Johns Hopkins University Press, 2003. An examination of the impact of comics on American popular culture.

See also *Apple Mary*; *Blondie* comic strip; *Dick Tracy*; *Flash Gordon*; *L'il Abner*; *Little Orphan Annie*; Newspapers, U.S.; Science fiction.

■ Commodity Credit Corporation

Identification   Federally owned corporation formed to stabilize the prices of U.S. agricultural goods

Date   Established on October 17, 1933

The Commodity Credit Corporation formed one portion of President Franklin D. Roosevelt's New Deal program to fight poverty in the rural United States during the Depression. It was designed to enable the production and marketing of commodities and to support commodity market prices through the intervention of government capital into agricultural markets. The Commodity Credit Corporation provided interest-free loans to farmers using commodities as security.

By the 1930's, American agricultural output far exceeded the available markets. Excess production of many commodities drove market prices to their lowest levels in centuries. As a part of the New Deal programs, President Roosevelt mandated that the government endeavor both to suppress production as a means of boosting commodity prices and to make loans to commodity producers to preserve their farms. Surplus crops would be purchased by the government at a price above the prevailing market price and would be stored. The proceeds of the sales to the government would be paid to farmers as government loans. As the market price for commodities rose, farmers could redeem their excess crops from the government at the government's purchase cost. Farmers then would repay their loans with the proceeds of crop sales, while pocketing the excess as profit. The program effectively functioned as a means of increasing price in the short term and stabilizing prices in the long term by providing a means to restrict supply while compensating farmers for their production. This program was originally designed for the cotton market but was soon extended into the wheat, corn, and other commodity markets. The Commodity Credit Corporation program fulfilled the hopes of many farmers' groups by providing a subtreasury economic system based on agricultural production.

Impact   The Commodity Credit Corporation marked the entry of the federal government into a system of price controls and supports for commodity production that in many way persists into the twenty-first century. This was achieved by creating a system of crop prices and market supports that closely resembles the framework suggested by farmers' organizations such as the Grange as early as the 1870's.

Patrick Callaway

Further Reading

Badger, Anthony J. *A Commonwealth of Hope: The New Deal Response to Crisis.* Baltimore: Johns Hopkins University Press, 2006.

Lawson, Alan R. *The New Deal: The Depression Years.* New York: Hill and Wang, 1989.

See also   Agricultural Adjustment Acts; Agriculture in the United States; Credit and debt; Dust Bowl; Farmers' organizations.

■ Communism

Identification   Political party and political movement

Date   Founded in February, 1919

The Communist Party USA (CPUSA) reached its peak of influence and membership as a militant party during the 1930's. The Great Depression drove many blue-collar workers and intellectuals to support the party because it supposedly offered an alternative to the poverty and unemployment of the Depression. Unionists, playwrights, novelists, and intellectuals either joined the party or supported its front groups.

The CPUSA entered the Depression in disarray. It was initially unable to profit politically from the widespread poverty and unemployment or from the sense that capitalism had failed. There were two major reasons for this. First, during the late 1920's there had been a series of splits and faction fights caused by the debates in the Soviet Union. Leon Trotsky had been expelled and forced into exile. Nikolay Ivanovich Bukharin had been defeated politically. Joseph Stalin finally took absolute power in the Soviet Union. Second, Stalin instituted the doctrine of "social fascism," the claim that noncommunist socialist parties were simply agents of capitalism and as bad as the fascists. Thus, the CPUSA lost members to departing "leftist" Trotskyists led by James Cannon,

who joined with noncommunist socialists to form the Socialist Workers Party in 1937, and "rightist" Bukharinites led by Jay Lovestone; others, dismayed and hurt by the infighting, dropped out of politics altogether. Furthermore, U.S. Communists refused to cooperate with socialists. This policy was disastrous in Germany, where Communists would not ally with the Social Democrats to oppose Adolf Hitler, and was also harmful to the prospects for the party in the United States.

The CPUSA pursued the policy of dual unionism in the early 1930's. This was a part of the ultra-left policy that included the doctrine of social fascism. Members of the CPUSA thought existing trade unions were too conservative and too influenced or

Joseph P. Ryan (center), head of the International Longshoremen's Association, flanked by U.S senators Arthur Vandenberg (left) and Royal Copeland in February, 1938. While testifying before the Senate Commerce Committee, Ryan claimed that communism was rampant throughout the leadership of the Congress of Industrial Organizations. (Library of Congress)

coerced by capitalist bosses to effect real social change. The party claimed that only in separate, parallel unions could a radical working-class movement be formed. Despite some heroic, if failed, strikes by miners in Pennsylvania, Ohio, and particularly Harlan County, Kentucky, and the success of a few unions of restaurant workers and longshoremen, the dual-union policy isolated Communists from most of the activist union members.

The Popular Front from 1935 to 1939   The triumph of Hitler and the Nazis' destruction of the Communist Party of German eventually led Stalin to shift to alliances with socialist parties, while still castigating heretical followers of Trotsky and Bukharin as saboteurs and traitors. Under the leadership of Earl Browder, the CPUSA embraced the Popular Front policy, allying with any progressives. Browder's policy led the party to embrace President Franklin D. Roosevelt's New Deal. This yielded great influence on popular movements and culture. It also led to major influence within mainstream unions. With the organizational drive of the Congress of Industrial Organizations, Communists and sympathizers held prominent positions within unions. Browder moved closer to compromise by declaring that "Communism is twentieth century Americanism."

The Spanish Civil War led many to support the Communist Party either as members or as fellow travelers. The Second Spanish Republic was under attack from the forces of Francisco Franco. The Western democracies withheld aid, while the German Nazis and Italian fascists supplied weapons to Franco. Only the Soviet Union gave aid to the Spanish democrats. U.S. drives for support were initiated by the Communists, and the Abraham Lincoln Brigade of American volunteers went to fight in Spain. One-half of this group died, and the survivors were persecuted by the Federal Bureau of Investigation during the Cold War.

Popular Front Communism and Culture   During the mid-to-late 1930's, Communist influence on the arts and culture was at its peak. Artists included the serious modern composer Aaron Copland, proletarian novelist Meridel Le Sueur, party cultural commissar Mike Gold, and leading African American writer Richard Wright. Plays such as Clifford Odets's *Waiting for Lefty* (1935) and *Awake and Sing!* (1935), which highlighted the plight of the working class in the Depression era, drew large audiences.

Numerous writers, such as major cultural critics Lewis Mumford and Edmund Wilson, who were not members of the party signed petitions and joined front groups. Communist musicologists and folk singers collected rural ballads and African American songs, influencing later American music. Woody Guthrie and Leadbelly (Huddie Ledbetter) were sponsored at party concerts. Hollywood figures such as Fritz Lang, Fredric March, and Oscar Hammerstein II supported Communist-front organizations. African American writers such as Langston Hughes and singers such as Paul Robeson allied with the party.

The CPUSA greatly influenced the African American community. The National Negro Congress was the most successful front group. The party was the only significant organization that held integrated meetings in the Deep South. A twenty-five-thousand-person march in Harlem, organized by the party, opposed the invasion of Ethiopia by Benito Mussolini's Italy.

Soviet Influence   A major burden borne by the CPUSA was its slavish following of Soviet policies. Even during the Popular Front, when domestic policies were indistinguishable from those of liberals, party members were obliged to support every foreign policy move of the Soviet Union. Some disagreement exists over the extent to which the CPUSA followed orders from Moscow. Most historians, particularly during the Cold War, saw the party as completely and robotically following Moscow's orders. There is no doubt that the major policy shifts of the CPUSA, from the ultra-left dual-union policy of the early 1930's to the Popular Front policy later in the decade to the isolationism and refusal to support war against the Nazis in 1939, were products of Soviet policy directives. Furthermore, the party and its liberal sympathizers defended Stalin's false accusations and executions of the old Soviet leaders. Some later historians have emphasized that local initiatives by party cells were often responses to local conditions and ethnic constituencies and were often ignored or winked at by the party leadership when successful, even if against official party line. However, this aspect of the party activities should not be overemphasized.

After the Roosevelt administration turned away from the New Deal following the recession of 1938, the CPUSA became vulnerable. The end of the

Popular Front period came with the signing of the Hitler-Stalin alliance in the Molotov-Ribbentrop Pact of August, 1939. Suddenly antifascism was no longer acceptable and many Communists left the party in anger or discouragement; a number became leading anticommunists during the Cold War at the end of the 1940's. The Dies Committee investigated the party for its isolationist position after the Hitler-Stalin pact, which put the party on the defensive.

Impact The CPUSA had its greatest impact during the 1930's. It affected many labor unions, political front groups, writers, composers, playwrights, and intellectuals. Some have claimed that post-World War II American culture was heavily influenced by the art forms of the Popular Front period, minus the leftist politics. The CPUSA declined from its eighty-thousand-member peak after the Hitler-Stalin pact but grew again in size, if not militancy, during World War II. The CPUSA's allegiance to the Soviet Union was to its advantage while the Soviets were a U.S. wartime ally but became a major detriment once the Cold War began. By the late 1950's, the CPUSA membership and influence had lessened considerably.

Val Dusek

Further Reading

Brown, Michael E., Randy Marin, Frank Rosengarten, and George Snedeker. *New Studies in the Politics and Culture of U.S. Communism.* New York: Monthly Review Press, 1993. Set of essays by leftists taking the view that many local activities of Communist cells and groups were often generated independently of Soviet orders.

Howe, Irving, and Lewis Coser. *The American Communist Party: A Critical History.* New York: Praeger, 1962. Treatment by two leading democratic socialists and anticommunists.

Klehr, Harvey. *The Heyday of American Communism: The Depression Decade.* New York: Basic Books, 1984. A thorough treatment, arguing that U.S. Communist policies were entirely responses to orders from Moscow and that many party members were involved in espionage for the Soviet Union.

Ottanelli, Fraser M. *The Communist Party of the United States: From Depression to World War II.* New Brunswick, N.J.: Rutgers University Press, 1991. A study focusing on the 1930's, attempting to strike a balance between accounts that claim all activities of the CPUSA were controlled from Moscow and accounts that emphasize grassroots initiatives.

Ryan, James G. *Earl Browder: The Failure of American Communism.* 2d ed. Tuscaloosa: University of Alabama Press, 1997. The most complete account of the leader of U.S. Communism during the Popular Front.

Storch, Randi. *Red Chicago: American Communism at Its Grassroots, 1928-35.* Urbana: University of Illinois Press, 2007. Centers the history of American Communism within the social fabric of Chicago.

See also Federal Theatre Project; Federal Writers' Project; Great Depression in the United States; Odets, Clifford; Socialist parties; Soviet Union; Spanish Civil War; Unemployment in the United States; Unionism.

■ Congress, U.S.

Definition Legislative branch of the U.S. federal government

Though Congress began the decade with a strong Republican majority, the Democrats took control through landslide victories in the elections of 1932, 1934, and 1936. The Democratic "New Deal Coalition" maintained control through and beyond 1939. President Franklin D. Roosevelt enjoyed noteworthy success in securing congressional cooperation for his legislative agenda, but this cooperation was not automatic and was often conditional, particularly as the 1930's wore on.

The Seventy-first Congress of the United States, convened from March 4, 1929, to March 4, 1931, comprised 56 Republican and 39 Democratic senators and 270 Republican and 164 Democratic representatives. The Farmer-Labor Party held one seat in each house of Congress; both officials were from Minnesota. The House leadership included Nicholas Longworth as Speaker, John Q. Tilson as majority leader, and John Nance Garner as minority leader. In the Senate, George H. Moses was president pro tempore, James E. Watson was majority leader, and Joseph Taylor Robinson was minority leader.

During the Depression, Congress's most significant legislative initiative was the Hawley-Smoot Tariff, which raised import duties to their highest level in more than one hundred years. The tariff was envisioned as a stimulus for American business. However, it provoked an international trade war and proved to be counterproductive.

President Franklin D. Roosevelt addresses Congress in 1939 during a celebration of the 150th anniversary of the first meeting of the legislative body. (©Underwood & Underwood/CORBIS)

The 1930 congressional elections resulted in noteworthy Democratic gains. The Republican majority in the Senate was cut to one vote, 48 to 47; the Farmer-Labor Party held one vote. The Democrats took control of the House, with 218 votes compared to the 216 and the one of Republicans and Farmer-Laborites, respectively. The Senate leadership remained intact, while in the House, Garner became Speaker, Henry T. Rainey became majority leader, and Bertrand H. Snell became minority leader. Making his entrance as a freshman senator was the colorful Louisiana demagogue Huey Long. The first female U.S. senator, Hattie Caraway, a Democrat from Arkansas, was installed on January 12, 1932.

This session of Congress failed to act upon "Bonus Army" demands that half of a bonus to World War I veterans mandated for disbursement in 1945 be paid at once, which led to the violent dispersal of the Bonus Army demonstrators on July 28, 1932, by General Douglas MacArthur. The relationship between Congress and the Herbert Hoover presidential administration became increasingly contentious as the Depression wore on. Differences arose not only between Hoover and members of the Democratic opposition but also among certain individuals within the Republican Party.

Hoover's interpersonal and negotiating skills were not the most developed; he was one of the few nonpoliticians to attain the presidency. He did not always respond to setbacks tactfully, such as in his rather unnecessarily acerbic veto of the Garner-Wagner Relief Bill of 1932. Shortly thereafter, the Emergency Relief and Construction Act was passed as a compromise measure. Hoover signed the act, opening the doors for government intervention into the economy on an unprecedented scale; this mildly prefigured the New Deal. However, the manner in which the initial bill was vetoed created festering resentment on both sides of the aisle and precluded productive collaboration between the executive and legislative branches.

Profound Change in Congress   The Seventy-third Congress, convened from March 4, 1933, to January 3, 1935, reflected the drastic turnabout of the 1932 elections. The Democrats assumed a commanding majority in the Senate, holding 59 seats compared to the 36 held by Republicans and the one held by Farmer-Laborites. In the House, Democrats held 311 seats, the Republicans 117, and Farmer-Laborites 5. (There were two vacant seats at the start of the 1933 session.) The Democrats retained control of both houses for the remainder of the decade. Key Pittman of Nevada became president pro tempore of the Senate. The majority leader was Robinson, and the minority leader was Charles L. McNary. In the House, Henry T. Rainey succeeded as Speaker when Garner became vice president, but he died on August 19, 1934; Joseph W. Byrns, Sr., was majority leader, and Snell became minority leader. This Congress worked hand-in-hand with Roosevelt to pass the flurry of legislation and authorization for programs known as the first one hundred days of the first New Deal. The most significant of these included the Civilian Conservation Corps Act, the Tennessee Valley Authority Act, the Glass-Steagall Bank Act, the Agricultural Adjustment Act, the Emergency Banking Relief Act, and the National Industrial Recovery Act.

When the Seventy-fourth Congress convened on January 3, 1935, Democrats had assumed a significant level of control over the Republicans in both houses: 69 to 25 in the Senate, with one member each from the Farmer-Labor Party and the Progressive Party; 322 to 103 in the House, with 7 Progressives and 3 Farmer-Laborites. The Senate leadership did not change, but in the House, Byrns, Sr., succeeded the late Rainey as the Speaker. However, he died on June 4, 1936, and was followed by William B. Bankhead of Alabama, who had been majority leader; John Joseph O'Connor replaced Bankhead as majority leader. This Congress was also exceptionally supportive of Roosevelt administration initiatives, particularly during what has been dubbed the

"second one hundred days" from June to September, 1935, or the "second New Deal." The most far-reaching piece of legislation passed by this Congress was the Social Security Act of 1935; other important measures included the Wagner Act and the Rural Electrification Act of 1936.

Congressional Reassertion   The Democratic Party maintained its overwhelming dominance in the Seventy-fifth Congress, convened from January 3, 1937, to January 3, 1939. In the Senate, the Democratic majority increased to seventy-six; the Republicans held 17 seats, the Farmer-Laborites 2, and the Progressives 1. In the House, Democrats had 334 seats, Republicans 88, Progressives 8, and Farmer-Laborites 5. Leadership changes occurred in the Senate and the House: Alben William Barkley of Kentucky became Senate majority leader on July 22, 1937, after Robinson's death; on January 3, 1937, Sam Rayburn of Texas became House majority leader. Even though President Roosevelt was able to secure congressional assent for most of his proposed measures—including the Miller-Tydings Fair Trade Act, the Civil Aeronautics Act, and the Fair Labor Standards Act—a serious rift occurred between Roosevelt and Congress over the Judiciary Reorganization Bill of 1937, better known as the court-packing plan. The plan was seen by most members of Congress as detrimental to the principle of separation of powers. The language in the bill was watered down, virtually nullifying the president's original intent. Afterward, there was a noticeable, though not overly substantial, waning of executive influence over Congress, and more assertive and ultimately more powerful congressional leaders such as majority leader Rayburn emerged.

During the 1938 congressional elections, the Republicans staged a comeback but stood far short of effectively challenging Democratic dominance in Congress. In the Senate, the Democrats held a majority of 69 to 23 Republicans, 2 Farmer-Laborites, 1 Progressive, and 1 Independent. In the House of Representatives, Democrats had 252 seats; the Republicans 177, the Progressives 3, and Farmer-Labor Party, the Labor Party, and the Nonpartisan League 1 each. Joseph W. Martin, Jr., of Massachusetts was made House minority leader after Snell retired.

The last significant legislative initiative of the 1930's was the Reorganization Act of 1939, which was designed to permit the president to appoint additional staff in the executive branch in preparation for a revamping of the organization. Also significant were the Hatch Act, which placed restrictions on governmental employees regarding participation in political activities apart from voting, and the Neutrality Act, which allowed U.S. citizens and the government to do business with opposing participants in World War II, if the business was conducted on a cash-and-carry basis.

Impact Congress was heavily dominated by one party or the other throughout the 1930's. However, given the volatility of the times and the shifting alignment of independent-minded personalities, skillful political management was a necessary trait for the president to possess. Hoover was not adept at this skill and was thus saddled with legislation sponsored by members of his own party that he personally opposed. Roosevelt, however, was a consummate political navigator. However, the very diversity of elements within the New Deal Coalition gave the various sessions of Congress that convened during the 1930's a pivotal role in shaping the country during the Depression era.

Raymond Pierre Hylton

Further Reading

Badger, Anthony J. *FDR: The First Hundred Days.* New York: Hill and Wang, 2008. Despite the book's title, the presidential initiatives during the first weeks of the first New Deal are not accorded exclusive treatment, and ample mention is made of the role played by congressional leaders.

Brinkley, Alan. *The End of Reform: New Deal Liberalism in Recession and War.* New York: Vintage Books, 1995. Focuses on the changing ideology from the first New Deal to the second New Deal, with Congress as an active, and not consistently subservient, player.

Folsom, Burton, Jr. *New Deal or Raw Deal? How FDR's Economic Legacy Has Damaged America.* New York: Threshold Editions, 2008. Revisionist appraisal that views the New Deal as a highly negative, rather than simply ineffective, force on the 1930's economy. Congress receives its share of criticism for either being manipulated by or ineffectively opposing Roosevelt's measures.

Jenkins, Roy. *Franklin Delano Roosevelt.* New York: Henry Holt, 2003. Jenkins is generally critical of Congress as too subservient during the early years of the Roosevelt administration but expresses respect for the more assertive role taken by Congress during the latter half of the 1930's.

Kennedy, David M. *Freedom from Fear: The American People in Depression and War, 1929-1945.* New York: Oxford University Press, 1999. Offers a noteworthy contrast between the interactions of President Hoover and President Roosevelt with a series of succeeding congressional leaders.

Mooney, Booth. *Roosevelt and Rayburn: A Political Partnership.* Philadelphia: J. P. Lippincott, 1971. Looks at Rayburn, an obscure but highly influential and effective House majority leader, and later Speaker, who was arguably the most powerful U.S. legislator from 1937 to 1961.

Patterson, James T. *Congressional Conservatism and the New Deal: The Growth of the Conservative Coalition in Congress, 1933-1939.* Lexington: University Press of Kentucky, 1967. Examines the most unpredictable, hardest-to-handle element in the New Deal Coalition and the beginnings of the southern Democrat-Republican alliance under the unlikely direction of Virginia's senator Carter Glass.

Schwarz, Jordan A. *The Interregnum of Despair: Hoover, Congress, and the Depression.* Urbana: University of Illinois Press, 1970. Detailed analysis that attempts to account for the failure of the Hoover administration's countermeasures against the Depression.

Shlaes, Amity. *The Forgotten Man: A New History of the Great Depression.* New York: HarperCollins, 2007. The author views the role of Congress during the Depression years as active but ambivalent. Prime focus is on the impact of the Depression on the "average" American.

Venn, Fiona. *The New Deal.* Chicago: Fitzroy Dearborn, 1998. Succinct and easily read volume that is useful in gleaning and connecting the basic events and personalities of the era.

See also Agricultural Adjustment Acts; Banking Act of 1935; Glass-Steagall Act of 1933; Gold Reserve Act of 1934; Hatch Act; Rayburn, Sam; Reorganization Act of 1939; Social Security Act of 1935.

■ Congress of Industrial Organizations

Identification   Federation of American industrial labor unions

Date   Committee of Industrial Organizations founded in November, 1935; became the Congress of Industrial Organizations in May, 1938

The most successful of the early labor organizations in the United States, the American Federation of Labor (AFL) concentrated on organizing skilled workers in craft or trade unions. Controversy within the AFL over the organization of industrial workers, including those who practiced no particular craft, finally led to a schism and the creation of the Congress of Industrial Organizations (CIO) in 1938. The CIO quickly came to rival the AFL in size and influence.

Organized labor in the United States suffered greatly during the early days of the Great Depression. Even before that, the number of union members declined even during the relatively prosperous 1920's. The passage of important labor legislation, including the Norris-La Guardia Act of 1932 and section 7a of the National Industrial Recovery Act of 1933 (later incorporated into the Wagner-Connery Act of 1935), gave new impetus to the labor movement. Within the dominant labor organization, the AFL, a growing conflict existed between the traditionalists, who held to emphasizing the organization of skilled workers in craft or trade unions, and others, who wanted to organize the mass of industrial workers, which included workers who practiced no particular job specialty and were often unskilled.

This conflict led to the creation of the Committee of Industrial Organizations within the AFL in November, 1935, led by John L. Lewis, who was the head of the United Mine Workers. Lewis had also been vice president of the AFL, but he resigned when the new committee formed. Controversy within the AFL over the issue of organizing industrial workers continued for months, with the old guard leadership of the AFL charging that the Committee of Industrial Organizations was virtually setting up a competing labor federation. In the summer of 1936, the AFL ex-

H. L. Queen (center), a worker at the Jones and Laughlin steel plant in Aliquippa, Pennsylvania, bites the hand of one of the union members assaulting him as he crosses the picket line of a strike called by the Congress of Industrial Organizations. (©Bettmann/CORBIS)

pelled ten industrial unions that had aligned with the committee. By 1937, unions associated with the committee represented 3.7 million workers; combined with the 3.4 million workers in the remainder of AFL, this meant that union membership had doubled since 1932. Further contributing to tensions within the AFL was the fact that many of the workers in these new industrial unions were unskilled or semiskilled; many were women and ethnic minorities. In May, 1938, a formal break occurred, and the Committee of Industrial Organizations became a stand-alone organization known as the Congress of Industrial Organizations (CIO). Lewis became the first head of the CIO.

Like the AFL, the CIO was an umbrella organization with many separate member unions. Besides Lewis, other significant figures during the early days of the CIO were David Dubinsky of the International Ladies Garment Workers Union, Sidney Hillman of the Amalgamated Clothing Workers Union, and Charles Howard of the International Typographical Union. While the AFL had often sought to maintain a nonpartisan stance, the CIO more clearly embraced the policies of President Franklin D. Roosevelt and his Democratic Party. Using new techniques such as the sit-down strike, in which workers occupied a factory or plant and refused to leave, the CIO succeeded in organizing unions in the automobile, steel, rubber, coal, textile, and electrical industries.

Impact The creation of the CIO enlarged and broadened the labor movement in the United States and began formal union organizing among the mass of industrial workers. Combined with the prolabor reform atmosphere of the New Deal, the organization of workers in the mass-production industries created a major change in the course of American labor history. By the late 1930's, the CIO rivaled the AFL in size. The creation of the CIO also contributed to the growing identification of organized labor with the Democratic Party. In 1955, as business and management seemed again to be taking the upper hand in labor relations in the post-World War II era, the AFL and CIO merged, creating a labor organization representing more than 16 million workers.

Mark S. Joy

Further Reading

Cohen, Lizabeth. *Making a New Deal: Industrial Workers in Chicago, 1919-1939.* 2d ed. New York: Cambridge University Press, 2008.

Galenson, Walter. *The CIO Challenge to the AFL: A History of the American Labor Movement.* Cambridge, Mass.: Harvard University Press, 1960.

Sinyai, Clayton. *Schools of Democracy: A Political History of the American Labor Movement.* Ithaca, N.Y.: Cornell University Press, 2006.

See also American Federation of Labor; Dubinsky, David; Great Depression in the United States; Labor strikes; Lewis, John L.; National Industrial Recovery Act of 1933; National Labor Relations Act of 1935; *National Labor Relations Board v. Jones and Laughlin Steel Corp.*; Unionism.

■ Consumers Union of the United States

Identification Nonprofit consumer testing and information organization
Also known as Consumers Union
Date Established February, 1936

Building on the groundbreaking work of the earlier Consumers' Research organization, the Consumers Union of the United States encouraged consumers to challenge the claims of manufacturers and their advertisers. Its magazine, Consumers Union Reports *(later known as* Consumer Reports*), was founded in May, 1936, and reports the results of product tests.*

The Consumers Union of the United States was established in 1936 by Arthur Kallet and other former employees of Consumers' Research, which began work in 1929. Kallet and Frederick John Schlink, founder of Consumers' Research, published a 1933 book titled *100,000,000 Guinea Pigs: Dangers in Everyday Foods, Drugs, and Cosmetics.* Consumers' Research was testing consumer products, but many of its researchers felt that the group should pay higher salaries, allow workers to unionize, and expand testing and reporting. Until the 1980's, Consumers Union and Consumers' Research were rivals. Both were independent, nonprofit laboratories, uncovering hidden dangers in food, cosmetic, and drug products and testing advertisers' claims against scientific reality.

During the 1930's, Consumers Union, after making the decision to test only products purchased rather than those donated by manufacturers, focused on small, inexpensive items. As donated funding and revenue from magazine subscribers increased, so did the budget for purchasing products and developing high-tech laboratories. Into the twenty-first century, *Consumer Reports* remained a well-known source of information and was relied on by consumers for its objective ratings of cars, major appliances, and smaller household items.

Impact In 1938, influenced by *100,000,000 Guinea Pigs* and by the work of consumer groups, Congress passed the U.S. Federal Food, Drug, and Cosmetic Act of 1938, launching federal oversight of product safety. Consumers Union empowered consumers by giving them unbiased, science-based information about the everyday products in their homes, enabling them to ignore or put into appropriate context the claims of advertisers. During the 1930's and for decades afterward, before the Internet enabled consumers to exchange information about products more easily, the reports issued by Consumers Union and other such groups provided the only access to such information.

Cynthia A. Bily

Further Reading

Florman, Monte. *Testing: Behind the Scenes at "Consumer Reports," 1936-1986.* Mount Vernon, N.Y.: Consumers Union, 1986.

Manion, Kevin P. *Consumer Reports.* Charleston, S.C.: Arcadia, 2005.

Mayer, Robert N. *The Consumer Movement: Guardians of the Marketplace.* Boston: Twayne, 1989.

See also Advertising in the United States; Congress, U.S.; Federal Food, Drug, and Cosmetic Act of 1938; Magazines; *100,000,000 Guinea Pigs*; Refrigerators; Unionism.

■ Contract bridge

Definition Card game for foursomes

Contract bridge became popular almost immediately after Harold S. Vanderbilt invented it on November 1, 1925.

Derived from whist, a British pastime created in the sixteenth century, contract bridge is a communication game between two sets of partners. After all fifty-two cards are dealt, thirteen to each player, each deal consists of three aspects: the auction, the play of the hand, and defense. Starting with the dealer, players bid in clockwise rotation to name the contract, the number of tricks to be taken in a specified trump suit or in no trump. There are thirteen tricks in the deck, four cards each. The winner of the auction, the declarer, plays both his or her own hand, which remains concealed, and his or her partner's hand, which is exposed as dummy, to try to make the contract. The other partnership defends, trying to prevent the declarer from succeeding.

The rapid proliferation of bridge resulted mainly from the work of Ely Culbertson, a flamboyant publicist who founded *The Bridge World*, the major magazine of bridge, in 1929, and Charles Goren, a lawyer who became a full-time bridge writer, player, and bidding theorist in 1936. While Goren's fame rested on his consummate expertise at the bridge table and his readable, intelligent books, Culbertson's came from his showmanship. Culbertson arranged, promoted, and participated in several famous demonstrations and contests, including the Culbertson-Sidney Lenz match, known as the "bridge battle of the century," from December, 1931, to January, 1932, and the Culbertson-P. Hal Sims match in March and April, 1935.

Impact Bridge fascinated millions of Americans throughout the 1930's. Mothers taught it to their children as a key to social success. On March 6, 1931, Myrtle Bennett was acquitted of murdering her husband in a fit of passion after he, as her bridge partner, failed to make his contract. The American Contract Bridge League was founded in 1937, as the merger of the American Bridge League and the United States Bridge Association, to govern the game, codify its rules, register its life masters, and organize national championships and other tournaments.

Eric v. d. Luft

Further Reading

Balfour, Sandy. *Vulnerable in Hearts: A Memoir of Fathers, Sons, and Contract Bridge.* New York: Farrar, Straus and Giroux, 2006.

The Official Encyclopedia of Bridge. 6th ed. Memphis, Tenn.: American Contract Bridge League, 2001.

Truscott, Alan, and Dorothy Truscott. *The New York Times Bridge Book.* New York: St. Martin's Press, 2004.

See also Bingo; Hobbies; Monopoly; Recreation.

■ Corrigan's wrong-way flight

The Event Journey from New York to Ireland by an American aviator who meant to fly to California
Date July 18, 1938
Places Long Island, New York, to Dublin, Ireland

Aviator Douglas Corrigan captured the imagination of Americans when he landed a plane in Dublin, Ireland. He had purchased the Curtiss-Robin monoplane for $325 and rebuilt the craft himself from scrap parts. He left from Long Island, New York, about twenty-eight hours before landing in Dublin without weather information, maps, a parachute, or a radio. Corrigan claimed to have misread his compass. He always maintained he was intending to fly to California.

Touching down at Dublin's Baldonnel Airport, Corrigan approached Irish airport workers, asking where he had landed. With an understated admission of his confusion, Corrigan initiated an unlikely chain of events that culminated in his sudden, worldwide celebrity.

A barnstorming pilot, a flying instructor, and an aviation mechanic, Corrigan had flown his plane nonstop from Long Beach, California, to New York, setting a solo record of 27 hours and 50 minutes for the 2,700-mile flight. Corrigan arrived in New York on July 10, 1938, which was the same day millionaire Howard Hughes and his crew departed the city on their around-the-world flight. Corrigan's accomplishment was overshadowed by the publicity surrounding Hughes's trip.

Corrigan had repeatedly requested permission for a transatlantic flight, but his aircraft was deemed unsuitable and given an experimental certification only. Because of his requests, many believed Corrigan was lying about not intending to cross the Atlantic. Corrigan, however, never admitted to misleading anyone. Instead, he claimed pilot error in misreading his compass.

It had been eleven years since Charles A. Lindbergh's first transatlantic flight in his plane, *Spirit of St. Louis*, which had been built in San Diego. Corrigan was a member of the team that had built Lindbergh's plane. In fact, Corrigan removed the chocks from the front of Lindbergh's plane as it left San Diego for St. Louis.

Impact In the intervening years between Lindbergh's famous flight and Corrigan's supposed mishap, several pilots, including Amelia Earhart and Wiley Post, had made a transatlantic flight. Few aviators, however, seemed to catch the spark of public recognition that Corrigan received. More than one million New Yorkers turned out for a ticker-tape parade to honor the errant pilot. Afterward, Corrigan flew his plane around the United States, where he was given awards and honored with parades in city after city.

Randy L. Abbott

Further Reading

Corrigan, Douglas. *That's My Story.* New York: E. P. Dutton, 1938.
Fyn, Chip. "The Story of Wrong Way Corrigan." *Fiddler's Green*, April, 2003.

See also Aviation and aeronautics; Earhart, Amelia; Hughes, Howard; Lindbergh, Anne Morrow; Post, Wiley.

■ Coughlin, Charles E.

Identification Roman Catholic priest and radio broadcaster
Born October 25, 1891; Hamilton, Ontario
Died October 27, 1979; Bloomfield Hills, Michigan

Coughlin was a pioneer in the development of radio as a channel of political communication and attracted a huge audience of avid listeners. Operating outside the two major political parties, he spoke for many Americans who felt victimized and powerless during the Great Depression.

Born the son of a Catholic church sexton who had come to Canada from the United States, Charles E. Coughlin earned a Ph.D. from Toronto University and was ordained a priest in 1916. After teaching at a Canadian college for several years and honing his skills as a preacher, he was given his own parish, the Shrine of the Little Flower, in Royal Oak, a suburb of Detroit. A few months later, on October 17, 1926, he made his first radio broadcast. Originally aiming his on-air remarks at children, he shifted his format to social and political commentary and, endowed with a distinctive speaking voice, a dramatic style of expression, and an aura of authority, he attracted an audience that eventually grew into the millions.

In 1930, Coughlin went on the air nationally over Columbia Broadcasting System (CBS), and after CBS dropped him because of complaints about his inflammatory rhetoric, he formed his own network that grew to twenty-seven stations in the Midwest and Northeast by 1932. Coughlin's radio talks reflected his staunchly anti-Communist and populist views, and after the Great Depression struck, he took on the role of champion of the downtrodden against the wealthy financiers, whom he saw as exploiters. He supported Franklin D. Roosevelt for president in 1932 but soon began to criticize and revile him. In 1934, he formed the National Union for Social Justice and began publishing a newspaper, *Social Justice*, to help build a political movement of his own. His strained relations with the president became clearer when he aggressively opposed Roosevelt's plan for the United States to join the World Court, and it is likely that his January, 1935, broadcast opposing the plan contributed to its rejection shortly thereafter by the U.S. Senate. In the 1936 presidential election, Coughlin threw his support behind the Union Party's candidate, William Lemke, only to see that third-party effort completely buried by Roosevelt's reelection victory.

As World War II drew closer, Coughlin's message became increasingly pro-German and anti-Semitic in tone, as he repeatedly identified Jews with the international bankers whom he blamed for the world's ills and defended Nazi Germany even as it repressed its own Jewish population. If it came down to a contest between fascism and communism, he

Bellicose Father Charles E. Coughlin, delivering a fiery radio address in 1930. (Hulton Archive/Getty Images)

Calls for Socialism

Speaking for those who felt left out of Roosevelt's New Deal, Father Charles E. Coughlin advocated the nationalization of banks, utilities, and natural resources, listing his tenets in a broadcast on November 11, 1934:

1. I believe in liberty of conscience and liberty of education, not permitting the state to dictate either my worship to my God or my chosen avocation in life.
2. I believe that every citizen willing to work and capable of working shall receive a just, living, annual wage which will enable him both to maintain and educate his family according to the standards of American decency.
3. I believe in nationalizing those public resources which by their very nature are too important to be held in the control of private individuals.
4. I believe in private ownership of all other property.
5. I believe in upholding the right to private property but in controlling it for the public good.
6. I believe in the abolition of the privately owned Federal Reserve Banking system and in the establishment of a Government owned Central Bank.
7. I believe in rescuing from the hands of private owners the right to coin and regulate the value of money, which right must be restored to Congress, where it belongs.
8. I believe that one of the chief duties of this government owned Central Bank is to maintain the cost of living on an even keel, and ar-

range for the repayment of dollar debts with equal value dollars.
9. I believe in the cost of production plus a fair profit for the farmer.
10. I believe not only in the right of the laboring man to organize in unions but also in the duty of the Government, which that laboring man supports, to protect these organizations against the vested interests of wealth and of intellect.
11. I believe in the recall of all non-productive bonds and therefore in the alleviation of taxation.
12. I believe in the abolition of tax-exempt bonds.
13. I believe in broadening the base of taxation according to the principles of ownership and the capacity to pay.
14. I believe in the simplification of government and the further lifting of crushing taxation from the slender revenues of the laboring class.
15. I believe that, in the event of a war for the defense of our nation and its liberties, there shall be a conscription of wealth as well as a conscription of men.
16. I believe in preferring the sanctity of human rights to the sanctity of property rights; for the chief concern of government shall be for the poor because, as it is witnessed, the rich have ample means of their own to care for themselves.

preferred fascism. As a result, Coughlin became the target of increasing pressure from leaders within the Catholic Church, notably his superior, Detroit archbishop Edward Aloysius Mooney, to silence him, and the U.S. government investigated him as a suspected Axis agent and purveyor of seditious propaganda. He stopped his radio broadcasts in 1940. Two years later, following the permanent suspension of the second-class mailing privilege of his newspaper *Social Justice*, and with the threat of a federal prosecution hanging over him, Coughlin ceased his political activities and confined himself to

serving as a parish priest until his retirement in 1966.

Impact   Coughlin demonstrated, like no other figure of his day, the political power of radio, and he was the prototype for the political talk-radio hosts who gained prominence in the United States half a century later. He also showed that radio, while it held great promise for educating the masses and improving the democratic process, was an instrument that could be adapted for rabble-rousing. Despite his large and devoted audiences, his ultimate failure was a clear indication that fascism never held the same allure for Americans that it did for many Europeans of his day.

Larry Haapanen

Further Reading

Carpenter, Ronald H. *Father Charles E. Coughlin: Surrogate Spokesman for the Disaffected.* Westport, Conn.: Greenwood Press, 1998.

Craig, Douglas. "Political Waves: Radio and Politics, 1920-1940." In *Radio Cultures: The Sound Medium in American Life,* edited by Michael C. Keith. New York: Peter Lang, 2008.

Warren, Donald. *Radio Priest: Charles Coughlin, the Father of Hate Radio.* New York: The Free Press, 1996.

See also Anti-Semitism; Elections of 1936, U.S.; Radio in the United States.

Court-packing plan. See Roosevelt's court-packing plan

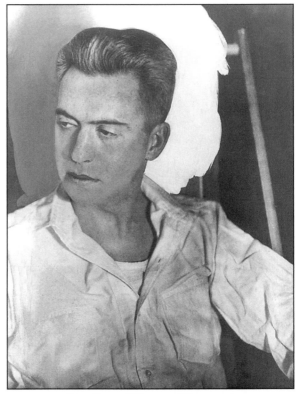

Hart Crane. (Library of Congress)

■ Crane, Hart

Identification American poet
Born July 21, 1899; Garrettsville, Ohio
Died April 27, 1932; at sea (Gulf of Mexico)

Crane was an American poet who wrote two important volumes of poetry at the beginning of the twentieth century: White Buildings (1926) and The Bridge (1930). His style is a unique fusion of orphic Romanticism, the style employed by Percy Bysshe Shelley, and dense, complex modernism, a style used by T. S. Eliot. Crane is also the heir to Walt Whitman, and The Bridge is similar to Whitman's Song of Myself (1855) in its ambition. It is a depiction of the American myth—its past, present, and future.

Hart Crane was born in Garrettsville, Ohio, where he was the only child of Clarence Arthur Crane (the candy maker who invented Life Savers) and Grace Hart Crane. The marriage of Crane's parents was strained, and Crane went to live with his maternal grandmother when he was in high school, eventually abandoning school altogether and running away to New York City at the age of seventeen.

For the following ten years, Crane alternated between odd jobs in New York and Cleveland, all the while writing many early poems in a highly original style, many of which were collected in his first volume of poetry, *White Buildings.* During this time, Crane also won the patronage of the philanthropist Otto Kahn, who provided Crane a sojourn on the Isle of Pines, Cuba, where Crane wrote many of his finest lyrics. In 1927, Crane moved into a building in Columbia Heights, Brooklyn, and through his window he could view the Brooklyn Bridge. While living there, Crane completed his masterpiece, *The Bridge.* In 1929, Crane lived under the sponsorship of Harry Crosby in Paris, where he began sinking into an alcoholic depression. On a Guggenheim Fellowship, Crane traveled to Mexico in 1931. During his return voyage to New York in 1932, he drowned himself off the Florida coast, three months shy of his thirty-third birthday.

Impact Crane's compact, metaphoric, and modernist style made him one of the most unique poetic voices of the early twentieth century. Although his style was not highly influential, he was respected by his contemporaries, with whom he frequently interacted, such as Sherwood Anderson, Malcolm Cowley, E. E. Cummings, Marianne Moore, Eugene O'Neill, and Gertrude Stein. Harold Bloom named him one of the seven greatest American poets, alongside Ralph Waldo Emerson, Whitman, Emily Dickinson, Wallace Stevens, Eliot, and Robert Frost.

Matthew Hoch

Further Reading

Bloom, Harold, ed. *Modern Critical Views: Hart Crane.* New York: Chelsea House, 1986.

Gabriel, Daniel. *Hart Crane and the Modernist Epic: Canon and Genre Formation in Crane, Pound, Eliot, and Williams.* New York: Palgrave Macmillan, 2007.

Hammer, Langdon, and Brom Weber, eds. *O My Land, My Friends: The Selected Letters of Hart Crane.* New York: Four Walls Eight Windows, 1997.

Mariani, Paul. *The Broken Tower: Hart Crane.* New York: W. W. Norton, 1999.

Reed, Brian M. *Hart Crane: After His Lights.* Tuscaloosa: University of Alabama Press, 2006.

Simon, Marc, ed. *The Complete Poems of Hart Crane: The Centennial Edition.* New York: Liveright, 2000.

Tapper, Gordon A. *The Machine That Sings: Modernism, Hart Crane, and the Culture of the Body.* New York: Routledge, 2006.

Uroff, M. D. *Hart Crane: The Patterns of His Poetry.* Urbana: University of Illinois Press, 1974.

See also Frost, Robert; Literature in the United States; O'Neill, Eugene.

∎ Crater disappearance

The Event Unsolved mystery of the sudden disappearance of New York state judge Joseph Force Crater
Date August 6, 1930
Place New York, New York

The unexplained disappearance of Judge Crater titillated the public, fueled speculation about political corruption, frustrated law-enforcement officials, and became the subject of countless comedy routines.

Joseph Force Crater had been elevated to the New York Supreme Court on April 8, 1930, by Franklin D. Roosevelt, then the governor of New York. In appointing Crater, Roosevelt had rejected the preferred candidate of the Democratic political ma-

chine, known as Tammany Hall. However, the appointment had the approval of U.S. senator and Democratic power broker Robert F. Wagner.

Crater and his wife, Stella, usually summered in Maine, but in 1930, the judge waited in New York City for court to adjourn before joining his wife. Later that summer, Crater spent two days in Atlantic City, New Jersey, and returned to Maine by way of New York City, where he visited Wagner briefly. Crater left for New York City again on August 3, and although he did not tell his wife the reason, he promised to be back by August 9, to celebrate her birthday.

According to Crater's court attendant, Joseph Mara, Crater spent much of August 6, filling briefcases and file folders with documents. He also asked Mara to cash two checks totaling $5,150 for him. Subsequently, he and Mara took a taxi to the Craters' apartment, where Mara left the documents. In addition, Crater arranged for a ticket to the revue *Dancing Partner* to be held at the Belasco Theatre at 111 West Forty-fourth Street. That evening, Crater dined at Billy Haas's restaurant at 332 West Forty-fifth Street with attorney William Klein and chorus girl Sally Lou Ritz. Shortly after 9:00 P.M., he left the restaurant, but accounts that he was seen climbing into a taxi were later determined to be mistaken, and his subsequent movements are a mystery. Crater's theater ticket was used, but it is not known by whom.

Crater's wife was disappointed when her husband did not return as planned but assumed that he had been detained by business. When she later questioned friends and colleagues, none claimed to have any knowledge of the judge's whereabouts. News of Crater's disappearance became public on September 3, provoking immediate talk of political scandal. Rumors circulated that judgeships were for sale for the equivalent of a year's salary; soon after, information surfaced that indicated Crater had cashed checks and converted stocks for just such an amount in May.

Police efforts to track Crater were unsuccessful, and a grand jury was unable to determine whether he was alive or dead. Stella Crater returned to the New York City apartment in January, 1931, and in a bureau drawer that had been overlooked by police found $6,619 in cash, a list in the judge's handwriting of companies and individuals who owed him money, and $30,000 in insurance policies listing her as beneficiary. However, neither she nor the police could locate the documents that Mara remembered leaving at the apartment. Only years later, on June 6, 1939, was Crater officially declared dead, allowing his wife to collect his life insurance.

Impact   Most assumed that political corruption lay behind Judge Crater's disappearance—a consideration that would have left officials reluctant to examine the case too closely. Whatever the circumstances, the event became a popular subject with comedians, and to "pull a Crater" was widely understood to mean "vanish." Over the decades, police received some sixteen thousand tips regarding the disappearance, and the case was not officially closed until 1979.

In 2004, journalist Richard J. Tofel discussed the decades-old rumor that Crater, who was known as "Goodtime Joe" outside legal circles, had died in a brothel and that his body had been quietly disposed of. In 2005, newspapers reported that Stella, who had died, had left papers stating that her late husband, Robert Good, had described Crater's fate on his deathbed. Good supposedly had been told by a New York City policeman and his taxi driver brother that they had murdered the judge and buried his body under the Coney Island boardwalk. However, the area in question had been excavated during the 1950's, and while there were initial reports that several bodies had been uncovered, the reports turned out to be incorrect.

Grove Koger

Further Reading

Crater, Stella. *The Empty Robe.* Garden City, N.Y.: Doubleday, 1961.

Rashbaum, William K. "Judge Crater Abruptly Appears, at Least in Public Consciousness." *The New York Times*, August 20, 2005, p. A1.

Tofel, Richard J. *Vanishing Point: The Disappearance of Judge Crater and the New York He Left Behind.* Chicago: Ivan R. Dee, 2004.

See also   Crimes and scandals; La Guardia, Fiorello Henry; Roosevelt, Franklin D.; Wagner, Robert F.; Walker, James J.

■ Credit and debt

The severe decline in prices between 1929 and 1933 greatly increased the burden of debts in the United States, leading to widespread home foreclosures and bankruptcies. These processes not only created misery for distressed debtors but also aggravated economic disorder. The federal government introduced many financial innovations designed to alleviate debt problems.

Much of the prosperity of the 1920's arose from business firms and households spending borrowed money. Booming construction was financed by a rapid increase in mortgage debt, which reached $37 billion by 1929. Consumer debt of $8.6 billion included many automobile loans. Ominously, more than $16 billion was owed in 1929 for loans on collateral for securities. This reflected the heavy speculation in stocks, financed by buying on margin.

Rapid decline in prices was under way by the beginning of 1930 and continued almost without stopping until early in 1933. By 1933, consumer prices had dropped by one-fourth. Furthermore, about one-fourth of the labor force was unemployed. Money wage rates declined roughly in the same proportion as prices.

Mortgage Defaults   As household incomes fell, many homeowners could not pay their debts. In 1934, a survey of twenty-two cities revealed that each had a default rate of 21 percent or more on residential mortgages. Half the cities had defaults in excess of 38 percent. Lenders, many of them financial institutions, had the option of taking title to the property and selling it. However, such activities glutted the market and drove down house prices. Consequently, many lenders allowed the residents to stay put. This simply shifted the burden to the lenders. Defaults on mortgages and other debts led to increased failures among banks and savings-and-loan associations. Distress also made lenders less able and less willing to make loans to finance new housing construction. The number of housing starts fell from 509,000 in 1929 to only 93,000 by 1933.

Farmers also experienced acute debt distress. Selling prices of farm products fell rapidly and by 1932 were less than half their levels of 1929. Farm incomes fell by about the same proportion, leading to increasing defaults. In 1929, forced sales of farm properties for tax and debt collection averaged about twenty per one thousand farms. By 1932, this figure was forty-two. By then, many creditors had given up trying to carry out foreclosures and forced sales. Efforts to make such collections drove down the price of farmlands.

The decline in stock prices was especially severe. By the summer of 1932, stocks had lost five-sixths of their 1929 peak values. Stockbrokers who had extended margin loans to investors pressured them to put up more of their own money and sold their stock collateral if they did not. This aggravated the decline in stock prices.

In general, the business sector struggled with debt problems. The railroads operated with an extremely high ratio of debt-to-revenue and assets. In 1929, they had $14 billion in bonds outstanding. Between 1929 and 1932, their operating revenues fell by one-half. Railroads as a group lost $121 million, leading many to default on bond interest payments.

Bank Failures Even in the prosperous 1920's, the country had experienced many failures among small rural banks. Failures among larger banks erupted in 1930. More than five thousand banks failed from 1930 to 1932. Their failures generated panic withdrawals of currency, further reducing bank lending power. Initially, many failures arose from speculation in stocks and real estate. However, as the Depression worsened, borrower defaults became an increasing source of failures. In the years before deposit insurance, bank failures deprived depositors of money they were counting on to finance their current consumption. The country's money supply declined sharply, falling from $44 billion at the end of 1930 to $34 billion two years later. All of the decline was in bank deposits, one of the most important forms of debt. When the authorities closed an insolvent bank, they initiated proceedings to collect debts owed to the bank, a process that aggravated the problems of those debtors. Also, the authorities sold off the banks' marketable assets, which worsened price declines for those assets. In an atmosphere of bank panic, even solvent banks were reluctant to extend new loans.

Ordinarily, a business-cycle recession reduces borrowers' demand for loan funds and thus leads to lower interest rates. These lower rates in turn help cushion the slump and promote increased borrowing and spending. However, the debt crisis of 1930-1933 created such a sense of risk and panic that interest rates of many risky bonds and other debts actually increased. Top-grade (Aaa) corporate bonds yielded 4.8 percent in late 1929, at which time the much-lower rated Baa bonds yielded about 6 percent. Aaa bond yields drifted slightly lower over most of 1930 and 1931. However, yields on bonds with higher risk moved higher after 1930. By September, 1931, Baa bonds were yielding 8 percent. By mid-1932, the Baa yields were more than 11 percent.

Bond yields rose because bond prices declined in response to panic selling. A survey of country banks revealed their bond holdings declined in value by 37 percent from 1928 to 1932. In combination with the drop in stock prices and in the market prices of houses and other real estate, the market value of the wealth of American households fell from $439 billion in 1929 to $331 billion in 1933. The fall in the value of marketable assets, the failure of higher-risk interest rates to decline, and the reluctance of lending institutions to make new loans all aggravated the 1929-1933 decline in spending by households and business firms.

Policy Interventions In January, 1932, Congress created the Reconstruction Finance Corporation (RFC) to make emergency loans to banks and other businesses. In 1932, the RFC extended about $1.5 billion in loans. In July, 1932, Congress created a system of regional Federal Home Loan Banks designed to lend to local mortgage institutions such as savings-and-loan associations. Their early operations were small. Beginning with Minnesota in 1933, several states adopted mortgage moratorium laws that greatly inhibited foreclosing on mortgaged homes and farms.

The inauguration of Franklin D. Roosevelt as president in March, 1933, brought many quick actions to deal with debt problems. A national "bank holiday" required all banks to close temporarily while each was evaluated for solvency. As they reopened, currency flowed back in. Convertibility of dollars into gold at a fixed price was suspended. In 1934, the price of gold was increased. As a result, gold flowed into the United States from the rest of the world, increasing bank reserves and contributing to reducing interest rates. Creation of the federal Export-Import Bank in 1934 promoted export expansion.

The Banking Act of 1933 created the Federal Deposit Insurance Corporation and provided for insurance of bank deposits beginning in January, 1934. This eliminated the risk of currency panic. Nonetheless, banks' perceptions of risk were still strong, and they were slow to expand loans even when they had abundant reserves. Instead, they bought low-risk debt claims, especially federal government securities. Deposit insurance was extended to savings-and-loan associations in June, 1934. In 1935, the Federal Reserve was given power to set minimum down payments on stock market margin loans.

In March, 1933, Congress created the Farm Credit Administration (FCA) to take over the numerous existing farm credit agencies, which were provided with additional funds. They supplied more than $2 billion in farm mortgage loans from 1933 to June, 1936. The FCA also administered extensive renegotiation of farm mortgages to improve borrowers' status. Additional farm credit facilities resulted from creation of banks for cooperatives, production credit associations, and the Commodity Credit Corporation.

To aid home-mortgage debts, the government established the Home Owners' Loan Corporation in June, 1933. Over its three-year lifetime, the corporation bought about one million mortgages for $3 billion, mainly from existing mortgage lenders. In June, 1934, Congress created the Federal Housing Administration with authority to insure home mortgages. Its influence led to widespread adoption of the amortized mortgage, with regular monthly payments of interest and principal. In 1938, the Federal National Mortgage Association (Fannie Mae) was established to provide a secondary market for mortgages.

All these federal programs greatly reduced risks associated with many types of loans. However, banks did not rush to expand loans. The number of banks had fallen from twenty-five thousand in 1928 to fourteen thousand in 1933. Their loans totaled $16.5 billion in mid-1933 and increased only to $17.4 billion by mid-1940. Banks channeled most of their funds into government securities arising from the growth of the public debt.

Public Debt In 1929, roughly equal amounts were owed by the federal government and by state and local governments. Their total debt of roughly $30 billion was just under one-fifth the size of net private debt. Between 1929 and 1933, net private debt declined from $162 billion to $128 billion, but government debt rose to $40 billion.

Public opinion viewed the national debt as undesirable, and national policy aimed to pay down the debt during periods of normal prosperity such as the 1920's. As the economic downswing worsened after 1929, government revenues declined and the administration of President Herbert Hoover engaged in deficit spending. Because of his strong commitment to "sound finance," President Hoover put through a large increase in tax rates in 1932, a policy that seriously worsened the downswing. During the presidential campaign of 1932, Roosevelt strongly criticized the deficits and promised to reduce them. After his election, he was responsible for many expenditure increases. However, he remained negative toward deficit finance and raised tax rates on numerous occasions. Even so, the national debt increased from $23 billion in 1933 to $40 billion in 1939. Over the same period, state and local government debts remained virtually unchanged, and private debt fell slightly.

Despite the enlargement of the national debt, the Treasury was able to borrow at extremely low interest rates. This reflected the stagnation of the private credit markets. The average interest cost of the national debt fell from 3.9 percent in 1929 to 3.4 percent in 1933 and 2.6 percent in 1939. Interest rates on short-term Treasury bills sometimes fell below 0.1 percent, reflecting banks' demand for riskless liquid assets. With the spread of Keynesian economics, the phobia against deficit spending was largely dispelled by 1940.

Impact The rapid decline in prices and in money incomes beginning in 1929 set off a debt crisis that inflicted much damage in its own right and made the economic downswing much more severe. The federal government adopted numerous policy innovations that expanded access to credit, reduced lenders' risks, and directed federal money into credit markets. The slow pace of economic recovery after 1933 reflected in part the unwillingness or inability of the private sector to borrow and spend more money.

For decades, observers praised such New Deal innovations as federal deposit insurance and the insuring and repurchasing of home mortgages. However, these programs became degraded over time. Deposit insurance became a cover for excessive risk-taking by lending institutions and contributed to the savings-and-loan crisis of the 1990's. The financial crisis of 2008-2009 arose in large part because government programs brought about excessive mortgage lending to borrowers with no reasonable hope of repaying. Fannie Mae was a major contributor to the crisis as a creator of toxic mortgage-backed securities.

The financial crisis of 2008-2009 was the most severe since that of 1929-1933. No intervening event had involved a comparable decline in household wealth. However, rapid and forceful federal interventions prevented conditions from matching those of the Great Depression. Incomes and prices did not decline as in 1929-1933. The real estate industry and the mortgage industry suffered, as did some homeowners.

Paul B. Trescott

Further Reading

Chandler, Lester V. *America's Greatest Depression, 1929-1941*. New York: Harper & Row, 1970. Leading monetary economist reviews all the financial aspects of the Depression in simple, readable terms.

Hart, Albert Gailord. *Debts and Recovery*. New York: Twentieth Century Fund, 1938. Extensive descriptive information on the extent of debts of various sectors and their problems, review of major financial intermediaries, and analysis of the economic and financial dimensions.

Homer, Sidney, and Richard Sylla. *A History of Interest Rates*. 4th ed. New York: John Wiley & Sons, 2005. Definitive historical review that places the experience of the 1930's into the long-term historical context, dramatizing the abnormality of the 1930's.

Stein, Herbert. *The Fiscal Revolution in America*. Chicago: University of Chicago Press, 1969. Examines the drastic revision in attitudes toward the national debt and federal fiscal policy that began in response to the Great Depression.

Trescott, Paul B. *Money, Banking and Economic Welfare*. New York: McGraw-Hill, 1960. College textbook that reviews fundamentals of credit and debt and relevant institutions, analyzing them in the context of the Great Depression.

See also　Banking; Banking Act of 1935; Business and the economy in the United States; Federal National Mortgage Association; Great Depression in the United States.

■ Crimes and scandals

Definition　Law violations and notorious acts that attract significant public attention

The decade of the 1930's is known for the Great Depression and bank failures. It is also marked by the infamous bank robbers who were at times considered folk heroes. During the first years of this decade, Prohibition fueled the growth of gangs. In 1933, the amendment creating Prohibition was revoked, making it legal to produce, sell, and drink alcohol again. The Bureau of Investigation (later known as the Federal Bureau of Investigation [FBI]) became a significant power during this time, waging a battle against the crime wave of the early 1930's.

The 1930's are infamous for flashily dressed gangsters and mobsters with colorful nicknames that referred to a physical attribute, a certain characteristic, or a talent. Some of these gangsters developed driving skills by delivering bootleg alcohol. They put those driving talents to work in the "getaway" car after robbing banks. Many of these gangsters thought nothing of driving hundreds of miles in a single day.

The FBI's Role in Crime Fighting　These interstate-traveling bank robbers gave J. Edgar Hoover an excuse to involve the FBI. The power held by the FBI and Hoover continued to grow when, in 1930, the responsibility for enforcing Prohibition laws fell to the Department of Justice. In 1931, Attorney General William Mitchell authorized the use of wiretaps in Prohibition cases. This authority was rescinded in the 1933 Department of Justice Appropriation Act. However, the growth of FBI powers continued in other ways. When the 1932 kidnapping of the "Lindbergh baby" led to the creation of the "Lindbergh Law," making kidnapping a federal offense, the FBI was given the authority to investigate kidnappings.

The advent of the automobile gave criminals the ability to travel long distances and cross state lines. The Thompson submachine gun, capable of firing eight hundred rounds per minute, contributed to the increase in bank robberies and gangland murders. Hoover created declared notorious criminals to be "public enemies" during the great crime wave of 1933-1934. This tactic improved the public image of the FBI, which had proved its ability to track these legendary bandits. At the beginning of this crime wave, the FBI was not permitted to use firearms and relied heavily on local law enforcement in making arrests. A deadly ambush at the Union Railroad Station in Kansas City, Missouri, in 1933 helped Hoover gain support for arming FBI agents.

Notorious Crimes and Criminals Al "Scarface" Capone was perhaps the most infamous Mafia criminal. He was well known for bootlegging, committing murders, and running rackets and was convicted on October 13, 1931, in Chicago for income tax evasion. He was sent to the U.S. penitentiary in Atlanta and later moved to the penitentiary at Alcatraz Island, where he was released in 1939 for health reasons. He lived the remainder of his life in Florida.

On February 15, 1933, Giuseppe Zangara, an alleged anarchist who claimed to hate all kings, presidents, and rich people, attempted to assassinate presidential candidate Franklin D. Roosevelt in the Miami area. Roosevelt was uninjured, but four bystanders were wounded and one other, Mayor Anton Cermak of Chicago, later died of his injuries. The results would have probably been more serious if Lillian Cross, a Miami housewife, had not grabbed Zangara's arm when he started shooting.

On March 1, 1932, Charles A. Lindbergh, Jr., the son of the world-famous aviator, was kidnapped from his crib in the family home near Hopewell, New Jersey. Although the ransom of $50,000 was paid, the baby's body was found several miles from the Lindbergh home on May 12, 1932. The kidnapping was investigated by the New Jersey State Police, the Bureau of Investigation, and the U.S. Treasury. The man accused of the kidnapping was Bruno Hauptmann, who had reportedly purchased gasoline with one of the $10 bills used to pay the ransom. Police were able to identify him through the license plate of his car. He was arrested on September 19, 1934. At the time of his arrest, he had another of the ransom bills in his wallet. A search of his residence led to the discovery of another $11,760 in ransom money. Police also found wood in the attic of Hauptmann's house that matched the wood used to build a ladder that the kidnapper had left at the scene. Hauptmann's trial started in January, 1935, and lasted six weeks. He was found guilty and was executed by electrocution on April 3, 1936.

On May 23, 1934, two bank-robbing, car-stealing killers were ambushed by law-enforcement officers in Bienville Parish, Louisiana. The two criminals were Clyde Barrow and Bonnie Parker. Although Parker and Barrow were generally considered small-time robbers, their history of "shooting it out" with the police and the number of police officers they had killed made them fugitives with a good deal of notoriety.

In November of 1934, sixty-five-year-old Albert Fish sent a letter to Mr. and Mrs. Albert Budd in which he described how he had strangled, cooked, and eaten their ten-year-old daughter, Gracie Budd, six years earlier. The letter's postmark led police to Fish, and they arrested him several weeks later. On December 13 of that year, Fish led police to Gracie's skull. Fish admitted to police that he had killed as many as one hundred children in thirty-three states during a forty-year period. In March of 1935, Fish was tried for and convicted of the murder of Gracie. He was sentenced to execution and died in the electric chair at Sing Sing Correctional Facility in New York in January of 1936.

Beginning in 1934, a series of dismembered bodies were found in the Cleveland area. The killings were called the Cleveland "torso" murders, and the killer was dubbed the "Mad Butcher of Kingsbury Run." The killer was credited with twelve murders during the 1930's. The case was investigated by the famous Eliot Ness, who, after cleaning up Chicago, became the public safety director of Cleveland. The "torso" killings remain unsolved.

On September 8, 1935, Senator Huey Long from Louisiana was shot by Carl Weiss, the son-in-law of Judge Benjamin Pavy, a political enemy of Long. Weiss was shot by the senator's body guards and died at the scene. Long died in a hospital two days later at the age of forty-two.

Scandals On August 6, 1930, Judge Joseph Force Crater, a womanizer who had been well connected with the corruption of Tammany Hall, the Democratic Party's political machine in New York, disappeared after leaving a restaurant and getting into a taxi. Judge Crater, who had been appointed to the New York Supreme Court by then-governor Roosevelt, was not reported seen after that night. In 1939, Crater was declared legally dead.

Eugenics, a movement to prevent mental and physical birth defects, gained supporters and legitimacy during the 1930's. A Supreme Court decision had upheld the concept of forced or involuntary sterilization supported by the argument that the mentally diseased, the feebleminded, or persons with epilepsy should not be permitted to have children. Eugenics was a driving force behind the Third Reich's "race hygiene" program, which had a traveling display that toured the United States from 1934 to 1935. The American Eugenics Society supported the same concepts of "pure" breeding that were designed to eliminate low intelligence and other defects that Nazi Germany used in its "pure Aryan race" program. In 1934, a California leader of the eugenics movement proudly proclaimed that German intellectuals were supportive of Adolf Hitler's implementation of a eugenics program.

On March 25, 1931, nine young black men, aged thirteen to twenty-one, were arrested near Paint Rock, Alabama, and charged with the rape of two young white women. During the trial, the defendants were denied adequate legal counsel. They were convicted with little evidence to support their guilt. The trial of the so-called Scottsboro Boys brought shame on the South and the nation. The verdict in the first trial of the teens was overturned in 1933. The Supreme Court decided that the indigent defendants were entitled to a competent defense counsel. On March 27, 1933, the Scottsboro Boys were tried again, this time with a change of venue. The jury again came back with guilty verdicts and set the penalty as execution by electrocution. In February, 1935, the Supreme Court again overturned the conviction, citing an exclusion of African Americans from the jury. After a series of trials, the state dropped charges against four of the men and later pardoned another four. One ended up serving time in prison.

In April, 1934, the FBI was ridiculed for the botched attempt to arrest John Dillinger and Baby Face Nelson, an event that ended in a shootout at Little Bohemia restaurant in Manitowish Waters, Wisconsin. During the shootout, Dillinger and Nelson fled the scene. The FBI killed an innocent bystander. One FBI agent was killed and another wounded. This emphasized the inexperience of the FBI as a crime-fighting agency. It proved to be a big embarrassment to the bureau and to Hoover.

In 1933, George Scalise, who had served time in prison and had ties to organized crime, became involved in the Building Services Employee International Union. In 1937, he won the presidential election of the national union, an event that was attributed to his ties to organized crime. The influence of organized crime on the labor unions grew

with Scalise's rise. From wiretaps, police gathered information that indicated Scalise was involved in sharing union revenues with Capone's former organization in Chicago. Scalise was convicted of extorting money from employers of his union employees.

On May 5, 1937, Metro-Goldwyn-Mayer executives held a party for 300 salesmen on one of the studio's film lots. Louis B. Mayer provided 120 young chorus girls and five hundred bottles of liquor. One young dancer, Patricia Douglas, who was then twenty years old, alleged that she was raped by a thirty-six-year-old salesman named David Ross. When the district attorney's office refused to indict Ross, Douglas filed civil charges against her attacker. Her suit was eventually dismissed.

On May 30, 1937, a Chicago incident, that later became known as the "Memorial Day Massacre" started as a labor protest. It ended with the police killing ten people and wounding another thirty, including an eleven-year-old boy and a baby. Steel Workers Organization Committee members were protesting working conditions at the Republic Steel Corporation in Chicago. Police responded to the crowd of protesters, a few members of whom had brought wooden sticks. When protesters pushed forward rather than dispersing as ordered by the police, the police responded with tear gas, clubs, and bullets.

Impact   During the 1930's, criminals took advantage of the growth of technology, which made new weapons available, and an improved automobile, enabling them to travel long distances to commit crimes. These factors were the framework for the growth of Hoover's national police force, the FBI, which was allowed to cross jurisdictional lines.

Gerald P. Fisher

Further Reading

Burrough, Bryan. *Public Enemies.* New York: Penguin, 2004. The author describes the characters that Hoover and his FBI labeled "public enemies" during the 1933-1934 crime wave.

Cogdell, Christina. *Eugenic Design: Streamlining America in the 1930's.* Philadelphia: University of Pennsylvania Press, 2004. The author chronicles the birth and growth of eugenics in the United States.

Fisher, Jim. *The Lindbergh Case.* New Brunswick, N.J.: Rutgers University Press, 1987. Complete coverage of the kidnapping, from the night it happened to the execution of the convicted murderer/kidnapper.

Helmer, William J. *The Complete Public Enemy Almanac: New Facts and Features on the People, Places, and Events of the Gangster and Outlaw Era, 1920-1940.* Nashville, Tenn.: Cumberland House, 2007. Contains biographical data and chronicles the crimes of the infamous gangsters of that era.

Keen, Mike. *Stalking Sociologists: J. Edgar Hoover's FBI Surveillance of American Sociology.* New Brunswick, N.J.: Transaction, 2004. This book discusses what the author refers to as surveillance of sociologists from the late 1930's to the 1960's.

Ruth, David E. *Inventing the Public Enemy: The Gangster in American Culture, 1918-1934.* Chicago: University of Chicago Press, 1996. The author looks at the use of the media to "create" gangsters.

Witwer, David S. *Shadow of the Racketeer: Scandal in Organized Labor.* Urbana: University of Illinois Press, 2009. Covers union corruption and racketeering during the 1930's.

See also Bonnie and Clyde; Civil rights and liberties in the United States; Cleveland "torso" murders; Coughlin, Charles E.; Gangster films; Lindbergh baby kidnapping; *Little Caesar*; Prohibition repeal; Roosevelt, Franklin D.; Unionism; *War of the Worlds, The* radio broadcast.

■ Curry, John Steuart

Identification American Regionalist painter
Born November 14, 1897; near Dunavant, Kansas
Died August 29, 1946; Madison, Wisconsin

Curry was one of the three major Regionalist painters who reacted against the style of internationalist modern art and painted rural subjects of the American Midwest in a dramatic, realistic style.

John Steuart Curry was born on his family farm and left home in 1916 to study at the Art Institute of Chicago. He admired the illustrator Harvey Dunn and in 1920 moved to Tenafly, New Jersey, to study with him. His training completed, he worked as a magazine illustrator in the New York area. He went to Paris in 1926 to perfect his drawing skills at the painter Vasily Shukhayev's Russian Academy of Arts. He returned to the United States in 1927 and settled in the art colony at Westport, Connecticut, where he

John Steuart Curry working below one of his own paintings in 1939. (Time & Life Pictures/Getty Images)

began to paint rural and farming scenes he recalled from his native Kansas. He began teaching in New York in 1932.

Curry's first fame came in 1928 with *Baptism in Kansas*, which shows a young woman being baptized in a cattle water trough. This painting attracted national attention and established Curry's reputation as a chronicler of rural midwestern life. Along with Thomas Hart Benton and Grant Wood, Curry was the subject of a December 24, 1934, *Time* magazine article praising the trio's realistic, homegrown art as a replacement for the unintelligible modern and experimental art from France.

Curry's paintings of the 1930's responded to the Great Depression by celebrating the mythic rural and farm life of Midwest. In a sympathetic, melodramatic, sentimental, and folksy style, his paintings record the spirituality, hard work, and heroism of those who lived and worked the land. Rejecting the abstraction of international modernist art, Curry painted everyday subjects in a highly realistic yet dramatic manner intended to reach a broad, popular audience.

The relation of people to nature provides the subject and dramatic motivation for most of his paintings, murals, drawings, and lithographs. Paintings such as *View of Madison with Rainbow* (1937) show the beauty and divine harmony of life in the Midwest.

Curry's paintings of floods, prairie fires, and storms show the struggle and conflict between people and the destructive forces of nature. His best-known painting, *Tornado over Kansas* (1929), shows a dramatic event on a Kansas farm: A heroic, protective father rushes his family into a storm cellar as a tornado approaches.

Curry did not shy away from showing the violence and brutality of life on a farm. Some of his scenes are of hogs killing a rattlesnake, a stallion and mule fighting in a corral, coyotes stealing a pig, and bulls fighting.

In 1936, Curry moved to Madison, where he was artist-in-residence at the University of Wisconsin. During that period, he painted numerous mural cycles about the westward migration for the Departments of Justice and the Interior as part of the New Deal's Federal Arts Project program that sponsored artists to paint murals for public buildings.

Curry's major commission, to paint murals for the Kansas State Capitol, came in 1937. Curry designed a series of murals to record the history of Kansas. One mural, *Tragic Prelude*, showed trappers, Spanish missionaries and conquistadors, and the abolitionist John Brown, whose raid on Harpers Ferry was a prelude to Kansas statehood and the Civil War. His depiction of John Brown, with wild eyes, flowing beard, and outstretched arms, allusions to the biblical Moses, is one of his best-known images. *Kansas Pastorale* showed the harmony and prosperity of a Kansas farmer and his family. The *Tragic Prelude*, with its towering figure of Brown, drew public objection for showing Kansas in a poor light. Disillusioned and frustrated by the reaction, Curry abandoned his ambitious cycle and returned to Wisconsin.

Impact Curry was one of the three major Regionalist painters who portrayed the rural life of the Midwest. Reacting against the abstraction and experimentalism of European modern art, Curry used a realistic style to reach a broad popular audience. However, the realist and homespun subjects of the 1930's soon appeared naive, sentimental, and isolated; as a result, his reputation, along with that of the other Regionalists, soon faded, as abstract art be-

came the dominant international style favored by the art world.

Thomas McGeary

Further Reading

Bertels, Alice Sue. *John Steuart Curry: The Road Home.* Overland Park, Kans.: Leathers, 2006.

Czestochowski, Joseph S. *John Steuart Curry and Grant Wood: A Portrait of Rural America.* Columbia: University of Missouri Press, 1981.

Dennis, James M. *Renegade Regionalists: The Modern Independence of Grant Wood, Thomas Hart Benton, and John Steuart Curry.* Madison: University of Wisconsin Press, 1998.

Guedon, Mary Scholz. *Regionalist Art: Thomas Hart Benton, John Steuart Curry, and Grant Wood: A Guide to the Literature.* Metuchen, N.J.: Scarecrow Press, 1982.

Junker, Patricia A. *John Steuart Curry: Inventing the Middle West.* New York: Hudson Hills Press, 1998.

Kendall, M. Sue. *Rethinking Regionalism: John Steuart Curry and the Kansas Mural Controversy.* Washington, D.C.: Smithsonian Institution Press, 1986.

Schmeckebier, Laurence E. *John Steuart Curry's Pageant of America.* New York: American Artists Group, 1943.

See also *American Gothic*; Art movements; Benton, Thomas Hart; New Deal; Wood, Grant.

■ Curtis, Charles

Identification Vice president of the United States under Herbert Hoover
Born January 25, 1860; Topeka, Kansas Territory (now in Kansas)
Died February 8, 1936; Washington, D.C.

Curtis actively promoted his indigenous and non-Native American heritages to achieve political fame as a proponent of allotment and progressivism and, as a result, served as the first Native American Senate majority leader in 1924 and as vice president from 1928 to 1932.

A Native American raised away from the Kaw reservation, Charles Curtis grew up Roman Catholic, learning French and English until the death of his mother Ellen Pappan in 1863. After his father, Owen Curtis, joined the Union army in 1863, Curtis was forced to live with his paternal grandparents until

1866, when he returned to Council Grove, Kansas, to live with his maternal grandmother on the Kaw reservation. During this time, Curtis learned the intricacies of reservation life, but he soon returned to Topeka. The Kaw were relocated to Indian Territory (now Oklahoma) in 1872, but Curtis refused to join the tribe, admitting later that he did not want to become a reservation Native American with no future.

In 1881, Curtis was admitted to the Kansas bar; in 1884, he was elected Shawnee County attorney. In 1892, Curtis was elected to Congress, and he joined the Senate in 1907. During his tenure, Curtis became an adamant supporter of the Indian allotment policy, work that resulted in the Curtis Act of 1898, which applied the Dawes Act to the Five Civilized Tribes in Indian Territory. Additionally, as chairperson of the House Committee on Indian Affairs, he drafted the 1902 Kaw Allotment Act, which forced his tribespeople into landless poverty. Beyond his work on the House Committee on Indian Affairs, Curtis forged political ties with prominent Republican leaders, garnering him membership on significant committees. Additionally, Curtis supported progressive issues, such as Prohibition, pensions for veterans, women's suffrage (or woman suffrage), and labor laws for children. He upheld a conservative veto of the 1927 McNary-Haugen Farm Relief Act to aid ailing farmers.

In 1928, Curtis ran for the Republican presidential nomination; however, because of limited finances, he accepted the vice presidential nomination. Curtis was not above utilizing the romantic images of tribalism when it suited him politically: While campaigning, he was accompanied by an Native American "princess" performer. Curtis's noteworthy political achievements preceded his role as vice president; his leadership faded following his election. He ignored the plights of Depression-era Americans, especially Native Americans. His political life ended with the 1932 election of President Franklin D. Roosevelt, and he worked as an attorney in Washington, D.C., until his death in 1936.

Impact   In addition to rising higher in American politics than any other person of Native American descent, Curtis was a leading advocate of Native American assimilation who helped pave the way for the dissolution of Indian Territory and tribal sovereignty.

Nathan Wilson

Further Reading

Unrau, William E. "Charles Curtis." In *The New Warriors: Native American Leaders Since 1900*, edited by R. David Edmunds. Lincoln: University of Nebraska Press, 2001.

_____. "Charles Curtis: The Politics of Allotment." In *Indian Lives: Essays on Nineteenth- and Twentieth-Century Native American Leaders*, edited by L. G. Moses and Raymond Wilson. Albuquerque: University of New Mexico Press, 1993.

_____. *Mixed-Bloods and Tribal Dissolution: Charles Curtis and the Quest for Indian Identity*. Lawrence: University Press of Kansas, 1989.

See also   Hoover, Herbert; Indian Reorganization Act; Native Americans.

■ Cyclotron

The Event   Lawrence designs and builds the first cyclotron
Date   January, 1931
Place   Berkeley, California

Ernest Orlando Lawrence designed and built a compact, circular particle accelerator. His cyclotrons achieved the high energies required to advance research in nuclear physics, nuclear chemistry, and nuclear medicine.

In 1911, Ernest Rutherford investigated the structure of atoms by measuring the deflection of alpha particles (helium ions) emitted by radioactive sources. Rutherford found that atoms have a small, positively charged nucleus surrounded by electrons. Later, Rutherford bombarded nitrogen atoms with alpha particles, transforming some into oxygen. Further progress on atomic structure and nuclear transformations required intense beams of ions with higher energies, which could be achieved using "linear accelerators," with each segment of the accelerator providing a small increase in energy. However, each increase in energy resulted in the accelerator becoming longer and more expensive.

Lawrence, a physicist at the University of California at Berkeley, designed a more compact, less costly accelerator than Rutherford's using a magnet to bend the ions into a nearly circular path. His accelerator, called a "cyclotron," consisted of a disk-shaped chamber split into two semicircular pieces called "dees." Each time the ions passed from one dee to the other, they received a small acceleration. As the ions gained energy, the radius of their path increased, so they spiraled outward. Their maximum energy was limited by the strength of the magnet and the diameter of the chamber.

Early in 1930, Lawrence and his assistant, graduate student M. Stanley Livingston, began building the first cyclotron, which was completed in January, 1931. Only 4.5 inches in diameter, it demonstrated the principle by accelerating hydrogen ions (protons) to an energy of 80,000 electron volts. By summer, they had constructed an 11-inch cyclotron that accelerated protons with one million electron volts.

Lawrence needed a stronger magnet to reach higher energy, but money for scientific research was difficult to obtain during the Depression. Another Berkeley professor, Leonard F. Fuller, vice president of the Federal Telegraph Company, provided an 80-

ton magnet his company was not using. This allowed Lawrence's group to build a 27-inch-diameter cyclotron in their "Radiation Laboratory." By 1936, that instrument was replaced with a 37-inch cyclotron, which accelerated protons to 8 million electron volts and alpha particles to 16 million electron volts.

Almost one century earlier, Dmitry Ivanovich Mendeleyev had brought order to the chemical elements, grouping them on the periodic table. Mendeleyev noted a gap between the element with forty-two protons and the element with forty-four protons. Experiments using Lawrence's 37-inch cyclotron filled this gap, producing the first man-made element, "technetium," named for the Greek word meaning "artificial." In 1936, Emilio Gino Segrè, an Italian physicist, visited the Radiation Laboratory, and Lawrence gave him a molybdenum foil that had been struck by high-energy ions. Segrè and Carlo

Ernest Orlando Lawrence (third from left) and his colleagues stand before the completed cyclotron in 1939. (SSPL via Getty Images)

Perrier observed radioactive decay in the foil, with a half-life inconsistent with any known element, and suggested it was the missing element.

In the mid-1930's, John Lawrence, a medical doctor, joined his brother's Radiation Laboratory to investigate the use of radioactive elements produced by the cyclotron in biology and medicine. This developed into the field of nuclear medicine. Radioactive elements are used in medical diagnostic procedures, and high-energy ions produced by cyclotrons destroy or slow the growth of cancerous tumors.

Lawrence's 60-inch cyclotron, completed in 1939, used a 220-ton magnet. Lawrence earned the Nobel Prize in Physics in 1939 for inventing the cyclotron and pushed for even bigger machines. His 184-inch cyclotron, employing a 4,000-ton magnet, was delayed by World War II. However, in 1946, it accelerated ions to energy of 100 million electron volts.

Cyclotrons remained the best source of high-energy ion beams for several decades, but their maximum energy was limited by relativistic effects, because the mass of an ion increases as its speed approaches the speed of light. To achieve even higher energy variations on Lawrence's circular accelerator, synchrocyclotrons, or synchrotrons, were developed to overcome relativistic effects.

Impact   Lawrence's invention of the cyclotron resulted in many developments in nuclear and particle physics, nuclear chemistry, and nuclear medicine. The design, construction, and operation of larger cyclotrons involved an increasing number of physicists, engineers, and chemists. This ushered in the era of "big science" in which research groups, frequently at government-funded national laboratories, undertake projects too large and too expensive to be funded by corporations or universities.

George J. Flynn

Further Reading

Childs, Herbert. *An American Genius: The Life of Ernest Orlando Lawrence.* New York: E. P. Dutton, 1968.

Heilbron, John L., and Robert W. Seidel. *Lawrence and His Laboratory: A History of the Lawrence Berkeley Laboratory.* Berkeley: University of California Press, 1989.

Taylor, Hugh Stott, Ernest Orlando Lawrence, and Irving Langmuir. *Molecular Films, the Cyclotron and the New Biology.* New Brunswick, N.J.: Rutgers University Press, 1942.

See also   Great Depression in the United States; Nobel Prizes; Nuclear fission; Physics.

D

■ Dance

During the 1930's, dance provided recreation and addressed social issues. The innovations by dancers and choreographers created new dance forms and made important contributions to the development of American culture.

As in the previous decade, dance during the 1930's continued to be dominated by rebellion, experimentation, and innovation. From the beginning of the twentieth century, dancers and choreographers had been searching for ways to create more personal and individualized self-expression through dance. In both performance and social dance, people were moving away from the concept of dance as a static form to be executed according to a set pattern. During the 1930's, the experimentation and innovation of the 1920's continued, and by the early 1940's, many dance forms had been recognized as valid; classical ballet began to accept movements and dance patterns that formerly had been expressly forbidden.

Ballet Neither the United States nor Canada had professional ballet companies during the early twentieth century. Ballet classes had been available in Canada but were primarily for children from wealthy families. During the 1930's, serious ballet teachers, such as Boris Volkoff and Gwendolen Osborne, opened studios in Canada. They produced talented dancers who had to go to Europe to dance professionally. In 1938, Gwyneth Lloyd and Betty Farrally founded a ballet club with the goal of creating a Canadian company. It took eleven years for their dream to be realized. Not until 1949 did Canada have its first ballet company, the Royal Winnipeg Ballet Company.

The ballet situation for Americans was similar to that of Canadians. Pursuing a career in ballet entailed moving to Europe. Those dancers who did so often returned to dance in the United States as members of touring European companies. Then,

Lincoln Kirstein, who wished to establish a ballet company in the United States, brought George Balanchine, a Russian choreographer who had worked with Sergei Diaghilev, to the United States. They opened the School of American Ballet on January 1, 1934, in New York. In 1935, the school's dancers performed their first season of ballet in New York as the American Ballet. Although the American Ballet was not the only ballet company performing in the United States during the 1930's, it was the only company composed of American-trained dancers performing ballets choreographed in the United States. In 1948, American Ballet became the New York City Ballet.

Modern Dance During the 1930's, many of the dancers and choreographers of the 1920's, such as Martha Graham, Doris Humphrey, and Charles Weidman, continued to explore expanded movements and themes in the dances they created. New dance companies formed, and dancers who had been students during the 1920's became choreographers. Alvin Ailey, a student of Graham, founded the Alvin Ailey American Dance Theater, which gave its first performance in 1930 in New York. In 1931, Hanya Holm established the New York Wigman School of Dance. New York was the center of modern dance activity, but in 1932, Lester Horton formed a dance group, the Lester Horton Dancers, in California. He combined elements from many different dance types. By 1934, his troupe was working in Hollywood films. That same year, the Summer School of the Dance began at Bennington University; Humphrey was a member of the faculty. The first American Dance Festival was held at Bennington. Founded by Katherine Dunham in 1936, Ballet Nègre performed dances that combined ballet with dance movements of African and Caribbean origin.

During the 1930's, modern dance reflected the reality of the period beset by the Great Depression and unemployment; it incorporated dark themes and concentrated on human suffering and struggle. In 1936, Graham choreographed *Chronicle*. The dance used dark costumes and settings and depicted depression and isolation. Touring continuously during the Depression, Humphrey and Weidman performed dances that dealt with social issues of the time. In works such as *How Long Brethren?*, Helen Tamiris not only depicted themes based on social concerns but also played an important role in the Federal Dance Project, which was initiated in 1937 as part of the Works Progress Administration's programs.

Popular Dance: Burlesque, Swing, Theater, and Film Dance continued to be an integral part of both Broadway productions and films. Sally Rand and Gypsy Rose Lee appeared in Hollywood films. In 1937, the dance group founded by Herbert White, Whitey's Lindy Hoppers, was featured in the Marx Brothers' film *A Day at the Races* (1937). Busby Berkeley choreographed innovative dance routines for the myriad films that he directed for Warner Bros. during the 1930's. First on Broadway with Clare Boothe Luce and later in films with Ginger Rogers, Fred Astaire popularized romantic ballroom dancing.

During the 1930's, burlesque concentrated more and more on striptease dancing, and the comedians and variety acts disappeared from the stage. However, the 1930's was a time of increased regulation of nude performance. The most successful dancers combined artistic qualities with the actual strip performance, and some of them actually appeared in body suits. Rand, with her fan and bubble dances, and Lee, with her aura of comic intellectualism, enjoyed nationwide popularity.

During the 1930's, social dancing was an extremely popular form of entertainment. Big bands and the associated music played by Glenn Miller, Tommy Dorsey, and others represented the popular dance music of the time period. The foxtrot and the waltz remained popular, but the swing dance became most popular. It had originated in Harlem and at the Savoy Ballroom. Swing dancing, also known as lindy hop and jitterbug, became the most popular dance of the time. It first found little acceptance among professional dance teachers, but its popularity with the general public was so great that in 1938, lindy hop and jitterbug competitions were included in the events of the Harvest Moon Ball. By the early

1940's, swing dance was taught in ballroom dance studios across the nation.

Impact Dance played an important role in the everyday lives of Americans during the 1930's. The combination of big band performances and swing dancing provided entertainment and a respite from the harsh economic conditions of the Great Depression. Dance on Broadway, in films, and in the burlesque theaters provided a fantasy world of escape.

In terms of ballet and modern dance, dance became a voice for change and reform. Dancers and choreographers redirected the focus of dance from the depiction of stories of romance and fantasy to those of the human condition as experienced by every individual. The experimentation in dance opened the way for eclectic dance styles.

Shawncey Webb

Further Reading

Anderson, Jack. *Dance*. New York: Newsweek Books, 1974. In-depth history of performance dance; includes photographs.

Franko, Mark. *The Work of Dance: Labor, Movement and Identity in the 1930's*. Indianapolis: Wesleyan, 2002. Excellent for its analysis of how dance reflected the social concerns of the 1930's.

Giordano, Ralph. *Lindy Hop to Hip Hop, 1901-2000*. Vol. 2. in *Social Dancing in America: A History and Reference*. Westport, Conn.: Greenwood, 2006. Discusses social dance in relation to economics, politics, and social mores. Emphasizes dance as a force for change and a social and cultural phenomenon.

Reynolds, Nancy, and Malcolm McCormick. *No Fixed Points: Dance in the Twentieth Century*. New Haven, Conn.: Yale University Press, 2003. A detailed history of dance in the twentieth century. Excellent for understanding the role of the 1930's dancers and choreographers in the development of later dance forms.

Thomas, Helen. *Dance, Modernity and Culture: Explorations in the Sociology of Dance*. New York: Routledge, 1995. Excellent for understanding innovative developments in dance during the 1930's. Coverage of dance companies of the 1930's and discussion of the role of women in making dance an accepted art form.

Walzak, Barbara, and Una Kai. *Balanchine the Teacher: Fundamentals That Shaped the First Generation of New*

York City Ballet Dancers. Gainesville: University Press of Florida, 2008. Excellent for understanding Balanchine's influence on American ballet and his creation of New York City Ballet.

See also   Astaire, Fred; Berkeley, Busby; Broadway musicals; Graham, Martha; Lee, Gypsy Rose; Rand, Sally; *Serenade*.

■ Davis, Bette

Identification   American film star
Born   April 5, 1908; Lowell, Massachusetts
Died   October 6, 1989; Neuilly-sur-Seine, France

Arguably the greatest female film actor of her generation, Davis rose to stardom during the 1930's, when she made forty films, and is remembered for her ability to play characters ranging from queens and cold-hearted murderers to harridans and sympathetic heroines.

Born in Massachusetts in 1908, Betty Davis, as she was then known, decided on a career in acting while attending high school. After appearing in a few plays, she changed her name to Bette and went on to study dance under Martha Graham and acting under John Murray Anderson. She had minor stage roles in New York, Baltimore, Philadelphia, and Washington, D.C.

Davis's first Broadway role, in *Broken Dishes* in 1929, brought her to the attention of Carl Laemmle at Universal Pictures in Hollywood. After taking screen tests, she was hired by the studio as a contract player in 1930 and soon appeared in six films. These first film roles earned her lukewarm acclaim, but she was noticed by the prominent actor George Arliss. Arliss secured her a leading part in his Warner Bros. film *The Man Who Played God* (1932). In that film, Davis played a woman in a romantic relationship with a much older man—a role that challenged her to strike a delicate balance between the naïveté of a young girl and the maturity of a woman who respects a great artist who has lost his hearing. In that film, she adopted a clipped, staccato manner of delivering lines that became one of the unique personal mannerisms that distinguished her from other female actors. After viewing the film's rushes, Jack Warner, the head of Warner Bros., offered Davis a five-year contract. Her next role was a small part in *So Big!* (1932), in which she played a renowned artist who is the love object of a snobbish son in a wealthy family. Davis later claimed that that acting job was one of her favorites.

After playing more than twenty character roles in mostly mediocre pictures, Davis finally got a chance to showcase her acting range when she was cast as the sluttish, cold-hearted waitress Grace Rogers in the RKO adaptation of the W. Somerset Maugham novel *Of Human Bondage* in 1934. She talked Warner into lending her to RKO to do the film and even aborted her pregnancy so it would not interfere with her taking on the role. She was determined to make audiences dislike her intensely, an approach to playing a character that would have caused most actors to decline the role. In scene after scene, she exhibited repressed rage, combining piercing dialogue

Bette Davis in a scene from the 1938 film Jezebel. *(AP/Wide World Photos)*

and animated facial expressions with choreographed body movements. The results were stunning. *Life* magazine called her performance the best ever by an American female actor, and she was nominated for an Academy Award for best actress.

The following year, Davis won an Oscar for her role as the hard-luck, alcoholic actor in *Dangerous* (1935). That performance was flamboyant and melodramatic and proved that Davis was a supremely skilled actor who commanded audience allegiance even in unsympathetic roles. In 1939, she won a second Oscar for her performance in the previous year's *Jezebel*. She would go on to receive eight more best-actress nominations in her career, including one for 1939's *Dark Victory*, but would not enjoy another win.

Impact Davis was an unlikely film star with her large, flashing, wide-set eyes framed by unruly hair. She was small in stature and comparatively plain looking. Her speech patterns were unique, a combination of New England pronunciations with precise diction and a staccato delivery. However, she won over both audiences and critics by showing conviction in her delivery of lines, which she coupled with striking facial expressions and body movements that accentuated her words, as if her performances were unrehearsed, though precisely choreographed. She crafted a kinship with audiences who identified with her common roots. Ultimately, she proved to be perhaps the greatest female actor of her generation and left an impressive body of work.

James R. Belpedio

Further Reading

Chandler, Charlotte. *The Girl Who Walked Home Alone: Bette Davis, a Personal Biography*. New York: Applause Theatre and Cinema Books, 2006.

Davis, Bette. *The Lonely Life*. New York: G. P. Putnam's Sons, 1962.

Higham, Charles. *Bette*. New York: Macmillan, 1981.

Leaming, Barbara. *Bette Davis*. New York: Cooper Square Press, 2003.

Ringgold, Gene. *The Films of Bette Davis*. New York: Bonanza Books, 1966.

See also Academy Awards; Astor, Mary; Film; Garbo, Greta; Harlow, Jean; Hepburn, Katharine; *Petrified Forest, The*; West, Mae; Wray, Fay.

■ Day, Dorothy

Identification Roman Catholic activist and cofounder of the Catholic Worker movement
Born November 8, 1897; Brooklyn, New York
Died November 29, 1980; New York, New York

Day's conversion to Catholicism in 1927 and her meeting with Peter Maurin in 1932 led her to start the Catholic Worker *newspaper and the Catholic Worker "houses of hospitality" to feed and clothe the poor.*

Dorothy Day, an activist and suffragist, began her career in journalism, dealing with issues of social justice and social activism. She was a part of the bohemian literary scene in New York City's Greenwich Village. The birth of her daughter, Tamar, in March of 1927, led her to convert to Catholicism. Day's religious interests only increased her sense of dedica-

---

Dorothy Day's Early Years

In The Long Loneliness *(1952), Dorothy Day details her life, including her earliest years of coming to terms with the ideas of God and "right and wrong."*

We did not search for God when we were children. We took Him for granted. We were at some time taught to say our evening prayers. "Now I lay me," and "Bless my father and mother." This done, we prayed no more unless a thunderstorm made us hide our heads under the covers and propitiate the Deity by promising to be good.

Very early we had a sense of right and wrong, good and evil. My conscience was very active. There were ethical concepts and religious concepts. To steal cucumbers from Miss Lynch's garden on Cropsey Avenue was wrong. And it was also wrong to take money from my mother, without her knowledge, for a soda. What a sense of property rights we had as children! Mine and yours! It begins in us as infants. "This is mine." When we are very young just taking makes it mine. Possession is nine points of the law. As infants squabbling in the nursery we were strong in this possessive stance. In the nursery might made right.

tion to the poor. Living in New York City during the 1930's, Day saw large numbers of people out of work and homeless, as the Great Depression swept across the country.

In 1932, Day met Peter Maurin, a Frenchman and former Christian Brother, living a life of voluntary poverty. His ideas inspired Day to start the Catholic Worker movement; she established a newspaper, which was sold for a penny, and set up "houses of hospitality" for those needing a place to stay. At Catholic Worker houses, residents share in chores and help make meals. Intellectual activities are also shared, as writers and others visit and lead discussions. Day died in 1980 in the Catholic Worker residence Mary House, in Manhattan's East Village, but the Catholic Worker houses and newspaper continue to thrive.

Impact   Day exemplifies the radical implications of Christianity. Choosing to live out the teachings of Jesus, Day was often criticized by those inside and outside the Catholic Church. Her cause for canonization has been brought forth at the Vatican.

Nancy Enright

Further Reading

Coles, Robert. *Dorothy Day: A Radical Devotion.* Reading, Mass.: Addison-Wesley, 1987.

Day, Dorothy. *Loaves and Fishes.* Reprint. Maryknoll, N.Y.: Orbis Books, 1997.

_____. *The Long Loneliness. The Autobiography of the Legendary Catholic Social Activist.* Chicago: Saint Thomas More Press, 1993.

See also   Breadlines and soup kitchens; Communism; Food stamps; Great Depression in the United States; Hoovervilles; Insull Utilities Trusts collapse; Labor strikes; Newspapers, U.S.; Religion in the United States.

■ Day of the Locust, The

Identification   Satiric novel about the Hollywood film industry
Author   Nathanael West
Date   Published in 1939

Set in Hollywood during the later years of the Great Depression, The Day of the Locust *lambastes film-industry people and their fans and dismantles the popular myth of the good life in a California paradise. It exposes a grotesque netherworld of decadence, despondency, madness, and mayhem.*

The Day of the Locust, Nathanael West's last novel, explores lost souls at the margins of the film world, centering on Tod Hackett, a "hack" artist who paints sets for films but aspires to produce a masterpiece depicting the burning of Los Angeles. Hackett befriends down-and-out vaudevillian Harry Greener and becomes sexually obsessed with Harry's teenage daughter Faye, a hard-boiled starlet who moonlights as a prostitute. Faye also finds funding through Homer Simpson, a trusting newcomer from the Midwest, who imagines that one day Faye will love him.

The book features other fictional Hollywood people, such as Claude Estee, a depraved producer with a taste for savage cockfights; Abe Kusich, a tiny hoodlum; Earle Shoop, a glitzy film cowboy; and Adore Loomis, a distressingly precocious child groomed for stardom by his overbearing mother. As Hackett completes his "Burning of Los Angeles" painting, his vision becomes eerily real when the frustrated Simpson erupts in rage after taunts by little Loomis; his violent retaliatory attack on the child triggers a horrible riot. His hopes and dreams betrayed, Simpson dissolves into the weltering chaos of the angry mob.

Impact   This scathing exposure of the California Dream and modern mass culture was not a commercial success at the time. However, *The Day of the Locust* became one of the canonical American novels of the twentieth century.

Margaret Boe Birns

Further Reading

Bernard, Rita. *The Great Depression and the Culture of Abundance: Kenneth Fearing, Nathanael West, and Mass Culture in the 1930s.* New York: Cambridge University Press, 2009.

Veitch, Jonathan. *American Superrealism: Nathanael West and the Politics of Representation in the 1930s.* Madison: University of Wisconsin Press, 1997.

See also Faulkner, William; Fitzgerald, F. Scott; West, Nathanael.

■ DC-3

Identification Commercial airplane designed by Douglas Aircraft Company
Date 1935

The Douglas Commercial 3 (DC-3) revolutionized air transportation. It was the first aircraft that allowed airlines to make a profit without any type of government subsidy. It has been called the most successful commercial aircraft of all time.

The DC-3 had an evolutionary design, tracing its origin from the DC-1 and DC-2. Its first flight, on December 17, 1935, was a milestone in commercial aircraft history. A product of the convergence of need and technology, the DC-3 resulted in unparalleled efficiency and reliability. Within a few years, it led to the disappearance of most other commercial aircraft then in operation.

Designed in response to Boeing's introduction of the revolutionary model 247 airliner, the DC-3 far surpassed all other commercial aircraft of the day. It was an all-metal, stressed-skin craft with a cantilevered, cellular wing. It incorporated retractable landing gear, variable pitch propellers, and streamlined engine cowlings. Seating twenty-one passengers, the DC-3 cruised at more than 192 miles per hour. Safety and passenger comfort were primary design considerations, and the DC-3 became the standard of the industry. Domestic and foreign airlines scrambled to replace their fleets, rendered obsolete, with the new design. By 1939, 90 percent of the world's air commerce was carried in the DC-3. The aircraft lowered the average passenger fare from 5.7 cents per mile to .0506 cent per mile. It carried twice the payload of other transports and cut cross-country travel time to less than seventeen hours. Ultimately, 803 civilian and 10,123 military variants were produced. The aircraft was utilized in every theater during World War II and was produced until 1946.

Impact The DC-3 rescued the airlines from bankruptcy. While not revolutionary in the sense that it created a new technology, it incorporated all of the technological innovations of the previous decades into one design and changed the face of air transportation. It was the plane that changed the world.

Ronald J. Ferrara

Further Reading

Boyne, Walter J. *The Smithsonian Book of Flight.* New York: Orion Books, 1987.
Christy, Joe, and Leroy Cook. *American Aviation: An Illustrated History.* New York: TAB Books, 1994.
Cunningham, Frank. *Sky Master: The Story of Donald Douglas and the Douglas Aircraft Company.* Whitefish, Mont.: Kessinger, 2007.
Ingells, Douglas J. *The Plane That Changed the World.* Fallbrook, Calif.: Aero, 1966.

See also Aviation and aeronautics; Hughes, Howard; Northrop, John Howard; Trans World Airlines; Transportation.

■ Dean, Dizzy

Identification Baseball player
Born January 16, 1910; Lucas, Arkansas
Died July 17, 1974; Reno, Nevada

For five years in the mid-1930's, Dean was the dominant pitcher in the National League. His outgoing persona and leadership of the St. Louis Cardinals' "Gashouse Gang" helped sustain baseball through difficult economic times.

The son of migrant workers, Jay Hanna "Dizzy" Dean spent his youth working in cotton fields in Arkansas and surrounding states. Following a two-year stint in the U.S. Army, Dean was signed by the Cardinals to a minor league contract in 1930. He joined the parent club in 1932 and quickly established himself as an overpowering strikeout pitcher.

From 1932 to 1936, Dean dominated the National League. As a rookie, the right-hander won eighteen games and led the entire major leagues with 191 strikeouts. In 1934, Dean won an astonishing thirty games; he won twenty-eight the following season. He led the majors in strikeouts from 1932 to 1935. Seemingly indefatigable, Dean averaged more than three hundred innings pitched from 1932 to 1936. He appeared in every all-star game between

1934 and 1937 and was the winning pitcher in 1934.

In 1934, the Cardinals overtook the New York Giants and captured the National League pennant. Known as the "Gashouse Gang" for their hard-nosed play, internal brawling, boastfulness, and frequent pranks, the Cardinals generated fan interest wherever they played. Particularly satisfying for Dean was that he was joined by his younger brother, Paul, who won nineteen games. In the World Series, against the formidable Detroit Tigers, each brother won two games, with Dean hurling a six-hit shutout in the deciding game.

In the 1937 all-star game, a line drive fractured Dean's toe. He came back from the injury prematurely, altered his pitching motion, and injured his arm. Dean's dominance was over. He retired in 1941 and began a long career in broadcasting.

Impact Colorful, talented, and competitive, Dean increased the profits and popularity of the small-market Cardinals and the National League in general. His thirty-win season in 1934 has not been equaled in the National League and has been tied in the American League only once, by Denny McLain in 1968. Dean was elected to the National Baseball Hall of Fame in 1953, the first year of his eligibility.

M. Philip Lucas

Further Reading

Alexander, Charles C. *Breaking the Slump: Baseball in the Depression Era.* New York: Columbia University Press, 2002.

Gregory, Robert. *Diz: Dizzy Dean and Baseball During the Great Depression.* New York: Viking Penguin, 1992.

Heidenry, John. *The Gashouse Gang.* New York: PublicAffairs, 2007.

See also Baseball; Foxx, Jimmie; Gehrig, Lou; National Baseball Hall of Fame; Ott, Mel; Ruth, Babe; Sports in the United States; Vander Meer, Johnny.

St. Louis Cardinals star Dizzy Dean, pitching during spring training in 1936. (AP/Wide World Photos)

■ De Jonge v. Oregon

The Case: U.S. Supreme Court ruling concerning the due process clause of the Fourteenth Amendment

Date Decided on January 4, 1937

The First Amendment, which guarantees freedom of assembly, applies only to the federal government. However, the Supreme Court found that state governments cannot make peaceable assembly a crime because of the due process clause of the Fourteenth Amendment.

On July 27, 1934, Dirk de Jonge, a member of the Communist Party USA (CPUSA), spoke at a party meeting in Portland, Oregon. The meeting was organized to protest police shootings of striking longshoremen and raids on workers' homes and halls. De Jonge spoke at the meeting and sold CPUSA publications. He did not advocate any type of unlawful conduct. He was prosecuted under Oregon's criminal syndicalism law, which made a crime of advocating any doctrine that supports unlawful acts to achieve political change or revolution.

The Supreme Court, by a vote of eight to zero, with one abstention, reversed De Jonge's conviction, noting there was no evidence that De Jonge had spoken in favor of unlawful acts or violence against government or industry. The Court said that under a republican form of government citizens have the right to meet and assemble peaceably regardless of the doctrine they advocate.

Impact The First Amendment prevents the federal government from violating the right to freedom of assembly. The *De Jonge* case made the right applicable at the state level by using the due process clause of the Fourteenth Amendment. This case was an early part of the movement to incorporate the Bill of Rights into the Fourteenth Amendment. The Court eventually made the entire Bill of Rights applicable at the state level, arguing they are fundamental rights that cannot be abridged.

Jerome Neapolitan

Further Reading

King, David C. *Freedom of Assembly.* Brookfield, Conn.: Millbrook Press, 1997.

Lewis, Anthony. *Freedom for the Thought That We Hate: A Biography of the First Amendment.* New York: Basic Books, 2008.

Tedford, Thomas L., and Dale A. Herbeck. *Freedom of Speech in the United States.* 6th ed. State College, Pa.: Strata, 2009.

See also Communism; *Palko v. Connecticut*; *Stromberg v. California*; Supreme Court, U.S.

"Peaceable Assembly for Lawful Discussion Cannot Be Made a Crime"

Reprinted below is an excerpt from the Supreme Court decision in De Jonge v. Oregon, *a case in which the defendant had been arrested and charged for his affiliation with the Communist Party USA and his participation in a meeting to protest police raids of workers' homes, among other injustices, called by the party.*

Peaceable assembly for lawful discussion cannot be made a crime. The holding of meetings for peaceable political action cannot be proscribed. Those who assist in the conduct of such meetings cannot be branded as criminals on that score. The question, if the rights of free speech and peaceable assembly are to be preserved, is not as to the auspices under which the meeting is held but as to its purpose; not as to the relations of the speakers, but whether their utterances transcend the bounds of the freedom of speech which the Constitution protects. If the persons assembling have committed crimes elsewhere, if they have formed or are engaged in a conspiracy against the public peace and order, they may be prosecuted for their conspiracy or other violation of valid laws. But it is a different matter when the State, instead of prosecuting them for such offenses, seizes upon mere participation in a peaceable assembly and a lawful public discussion as the basis for a criminal charge.

■ Demographics of Canada

Canadian demographic data from the 1930's demonstrate both long-term trends and the profound influences of the Great Depression and outbreak of World War II. The country was becoming more diverse and was urbanizing quickly. This process was more pronounced following World War II.

The most authoritative source for the study of demographics in Canada is the Canadian Bureau of Statistics' official census, which has been conducted every ten years since 1871. The seventh census was made in 1931, and the eighth occurred in 1941. Demographic scholars generally agree that Canadian censuses have been carried out on a nonpartisan basis and that the statistical results are generally reliable, although some groups invariably are undercounted. Under the Canadian constitution, the most compelling reason for the census is to determine representation to Canada's House of Commons. However, the census also serves to take stock periodically of the condition of the people and their affairs. The statistics in the census include the size of the population as well as local distribution, age, sex, nationality, language, racial origin, language, education, occupation, and employment.

Obtaining accurate statistics is not entirely possible for several aspects of individual years that occurred between the 1931 and 1941 censuses. This was particularly true for the crucial years between 1938 and 1941—a period in which the Great Depression ended and Canada entered World War II. By 1938, economic conditions appeared to be improving, and the outbreak of the war in 1939 produced a great demand for goods and services, thereby promoting significant gains in employment rates and living standards. In addition, a significant number of young persons joined the armed forces in 1939, and their expectations and fears had an impact on any number of important decisions, including decisions about education, marriage, and whether or not to have children.

Population Size and Growth　In the census of 1931, the Canadian Bureau of Statistics reported that the population stood at 10.4 million, which was an increase of 1.5 million people (or 18.08 percent) from the population of ten years earlier. In 1939, government statisticians estimated that the population was approximately 11.3 million. In the census of 1941, the bureau reported a population of 11.5 million, which was an increase of 1.1 million (or 10.89 percent) for the decade.

During the 1930's, Canada continued to have a birthrate significantly larger than its death rate; this circumstance was responsible for most of the population growth. The rate for the natural increase for the decade was about 7 percent less than during the previous ten years. The number of immigrants entering the country, however, declined much more dramatically. During the 1920's, a total of 1,166,004 persons immigrated to Canada, but during the 1930's, the number declined to only 140,361—a change of 88 percent.

If Canada's growth rate during the 1930's was significantly less than during the 1920's, the difference between the 1930's and the first two decades of the twentieth century was even greater. During the decade from 1900 to 1910, the population had increased by 34.17 percent, largely because of the immigration of 1.8 million people. During the decade

from 1911 to 1919, even with World War I, the growth rate was 21.94 percent. From a long-term perspective, the relative decrease in population growth during the 1930's was of limited impact. During the first four decades of the twentieth century, Canada's population increased almost threefold, making Canada one of the most rapidly growing populations within the British Empire.

Age Distribution　The age distribution of the population has a great impact on numerous aspects of any society, including economic growth, employment, medical care, birthrates, education, and crime rates. During the decades before the 1930's, Canada had a young population as a result of immigration and a relatively high birthrate, which was partially moderated by a relatively high death rate. During the 1930's, Canada experienced a pronounced aging of the population because of a lower birthrate, an extraordinary decline in immigration, and an increase in life expectancy.

Despite economic deprivation in Canada, the country's census bureau reported that the average life expectancy increased substantially during the 1930's. For the year 1931, the average life expectancy was 60.0 for men. By 1941, the average had grown to 63.0. The Depression, however, had a negative impact on the number of babies born in Canada. In 1931, the crude birthrate was 20.3 per one thousand people. In 1921, there had been 29.3 births per thousand. There was also a decline in the percentage of children ten years or younger. In 1921, Canada had 240 such children for every one thousand people. In 1931, the number declined to 212 per one thousand, and by 1941, the number had further declined to 182 per one thousand.

Sex Distribution　Many social theorists believe that an approximation of equality in the numbers of men and women is desirable for the promotion of social stability and the birthrate. In Canada, the large number of immigrants during the first half of the twentieth century resulted in a population that had significantly more men than women. Because of the dramatic decline in immigration during the 1930's, the disparity between the two sexes also decreased. In 1911, men outnumbered women by 60 per 100,000 people, compared with 36 per 100,000 people in 1931 and 26 per 100,000 in 1941.

The sex distribution of Canada varied greatly among the different regions and provinces of the country. In Quebec and parts of Ontario, immigration was too limited to interfere with the normal sex distribution of the population. The situation was different in the Western provinces and some of the territories. In 1931 in Quebec, for example, men outnumbered women by only 6 per 100,000 people, compared to 110 per 100,000 in British Columbia.

Marriage The marital characteristics of a society and its subgroups have a great impact on the economy and other social conditions. The Canadian Bureau of Statistics reported that about 75 percent of the population entered into marriage between 1871 and 1941. Most of the changes over the years were the result of four factors: the gradual aging of the population, the gradual retardation of early marriage, the level of prosperity, and a growing acceptance of divorce.

The Great Depression was a primary cause of the decrease in the percentage of persons who entered into new marriages. In fact, the lowest marriage rate ever recorded in Canadian history took place in 1932—5.9 per one thousand people. There had been an average of 7.3 marriages per one thousand in the years between 1926 and 1930, but the average number dropped to 6.4 per one thousand in the period from 1931 to 1935. During the late 1930's, as economic conditions improved somewhat, the percentage rate of marriages increased, reaching 7.9 per one thousand in 1938. The marriage rate grew significantly during the 1940's, reaching 10.9 per one thousand in 1946.

Divorces increased during the 1930's, but this appeared primarily to be a result of a long-term trend that began early in the twentieth century, although the Depression probably exacerbated the trend. In 1918, there were only 114 divorces in Canada, compared to 870 in 1930 and 2,088 in 1939. Most of the dramatic increase occurred in the provinces of Ontario and British Columbia. In 1939, for example, only 50 divorces were granted in the Quebec province, whereas 824 divorces were recorded in Ontario. Compared with later decades, divorces remained uncommon. In 1936, there were only 7.4 divorces per one thousand people, compared with 308.8 per one thousand in 1986.

Unemployment and Income The Great Depression, which began in 1929, greatly increased the number of unemployed Canadians, although the change in the unemployment rate in Canada was less dramatic

than it was in the United States. In the Canadian census of 1931, almost 21 percent of male wage earners reported that they were not working, and 8.8 percent of female wage earners said they were not working. Of all wage earners, 40.5 percent reported that they had lost time and money in comparison to previous years. The low point of the Depression was reached in 1933, when about 27 percent of wage earners were without work.

These official statistics, however, underestimated the persons unable to find work. The statistics did not include a number of groups, particularly farmers and self-employed workers, many of whom had almost no income. Canada did not have a national system of unemployment compensation, and local welfare varied greatly from place to place.

The number of unemployed Canadians became less severe during the second half of the decade. For the year 1936, the unemployment rate was 13.2 percent. For 1937, the rate declined to 10.7 percent. During 1938 and the first eight months of 1939, the unemployment rate increased to more than 14 percent. The outbreak of the war in September, 1939, however, had an immediate effect on Canadian business, and the unemployment rate declined to less than 11 percent during the last four months of 1939.

The per-capita incomes of Canadians decreased significantly during the 1930's. In 1928, the year before the Depression, the national per-capita income of the country was $543—an increase of more than one hundred dollars in ten years. By 1930, the Canadian per-capita income had declined to $436, and in 1933, it fell to a low point of $256. Per-capita incomes gradually increased to $395 in 1937; although incomes declined in 1938, the average income for 1939 was $400. During most of the decade, Canadian per-capita incomes were about 25 percent less than they were for the United States, in large part because of Canada's greater participation in primary activities, especially agriculture.

Urbanization During the 1930's, Canada experienced some growth in its urban centers, but the growth was small when compared with the growth of the previous two decades. The census of 1931 showed that 53.7 percent of the population lived in urban communities. By 1941, the urban population had grown to 54.3, but most of the growth occurred between 1938 and 1941. Except for the Great Depression, the movement toward more urbanization

Distribution of Canadian Population by Ethnicity

Numbers represent percentage of total population

Ethnicity	1901	1931	1941
French	30.71	28.22	30.27
English	23.47	26.42	25.80
Scottish	14.90	13.97	12.20
Irish	11.41	11.86	11.02
German	5.78	4.56	4.04
African ancestry	0.32	0.19	0.19
Chinese	0.32	0.45	0.30
Polish	0.12	1.40	1.45
Ukrainian	0.11	2.17	2.66
Japanese	0.09	0.22	0.20
Indian and Eskimo	0.03	1.21	1.09
Other Asian groups	—	—	0.14

Source: Canadian Bureau of the Census.

almost certainly would have proceeded more rapidly than it did. Urbanization meant a decline in the percentage of Canadians gaining their livelihoods in the agricultural sector. The decline in agricultural workers was relatively modest during the 1930's when compared with the decades of the 1920's and 1940's.

Racial and Ethnic Groups   Canada's ethnic makeup did not undergo any dramatic changes during the 1930's, although from a long-term perspective, the country was continuing to become more diverse. At the end of the 1930's, according to the census, 80 percent of the population reported that their ancestors had come from Great Britain or France. This compares with 83 percent in 1921, about 80 percent in 1901, and more than 92 percent in 1871. Beginning in the twentieth century, a great variety of European groups immigrated to Canada, but few constituted more than 1 percent of the total population. Throughout the 1930's, people of non-European ancestry continued to constitute only a small percentage of the Canadian population, even though the numbers had grown substantially since the beginning of the twentieth century.

Impact   Two particularly important events influenced Canada's demographics during the decade of the 1930's: the Great Depression and the beginning of World War II. For the decade as a whole, population growth was significantly less than the decades before and after, primarily because of a dramatic decline in immigration. The most important demographic variables of the 1930's were related to economic distress, especially the declines in employment, living standards, and incomes. Many aspects of Canadian demography, however, were primarily related to continuing, long-term trends that occurred during the first half of the twentieth century.

Thomas Tandy Lewis

Further Reading

Beaujot, Roderick, and Don Kerr. *Population Change in Canada.* 2d ed. Toronto: Oxford University Press, 2004. Well-written discussions of demographic variables, with consideration for the early twentieth century.

Berton, Pierre. *The Canada Year Book, 1941.* Ottawa: Minister of Trade and Commerce, [1945?]. Provides accessible summaries of the state of Canadian demographics at the outset of World War II and offers a useful comparison to the 1931 census for an overall outlook of the 1930's.

_____. *The Great Depression.* Toronto: McClelland & Stewart, 1990. Narrative account of Canada during the 1930's, with much statistical data integrated into the text.

_____. *Seventh Census of Canada, 1931.* Ottawa: Minister of Trade and Commerce, 1933. Multivolume works with a wealth of statistical information logically organized into useful categories.

Kelbach, Warren, and Wayne McVey. *Demographic Bases of Canadian Society.* Toronto: McGraw-Hill, 1979. Analysis of demographics and their impact, with some consideration of the 1930's and earlier.

Leacy, F. H., et al. *Historical Statistics of Canada.* Ottawa: Statistics Canada Marketing, 1983. Contains numerous tables of social, economic, and political topics.

See also   Advertising in Canada; Business and the economy in Canada; Canadian minority communities; Demographics of the United States; Housing in Canada; Immigration to Canada; Income and wages in Canada; Unemployment in Canada; Unemployment in the United States; Urbanization in Canada.

■ Demographics of the United States

The population characteristics of the United States during the 1930's were changing in a manner unlike previous decades because of the Great Depression. In the decades preceding the Great Depression, the United States experienced tremendous population and economic growth. This growth led to many changes within rural and urban communities and within the composition of the American family. The Great Depression impacted the demographic composition of the United States.

In 1930, the fifteenth census of the United States was conducted. These data were an assessment of the forty-eight states and the District of Columbia. There were 122,775,046 people living in the United States in 1930. In 1940, the population of the United States was 131,669,275. This represented a population increase of 6.8 percent during the decade of the 1930's. The population growth of the 1930's was much less than that of previous decades; this is considered a result of the Great Depression.

The 1930's represented a time of great social change in the United States. Many norms within society were no longer in place. Elements such as employment, family growth, and economic security that had been considered normal were in question for many Americans. The reconsideration of norms had a tremendous impact on the demographic transition of the United States during the 1930's.

Demographic Account of 1930   The U.S. Census examined five race and ethnicity categories in 1930. The official categories were: white, "Negro" (African American), Mexican, "Indian" (Native American), and Chinese. In 1930, the country was 88.7 percent white, 9.7 percent African American, 1.2 percent Mexican, 0.3 percent Native American, and 0.1 percent Chinese. Within the category of white, 77.8 percent were native-born citizens and 10.9 percent were foreign-born citizens. In 1930, 51 percent of the population were male and 49 percent were female. In terms of age of the population, 9 percent were under the age of five, 20.0 percent were between the ages of five and fourteen, 18 percent were between the ages of fifteen and twenty-four, 30 percent were between the ages of twenty-five and forty-four, and 23 percent were forty-five years of age and older.

The American Family During the 1930's   The examination of the American family is a key element in any demographic study. The 1930 census defined the family as a group of people who were related by blood, marriage, or adoption and who were all living together in one household. During the 1930's, "normal" families were defined as a husband and wife both present in the home. Normal families had the husband functioning as the head of household. The head-of-household label was attached to any person in the family who functioned as the primary income earner.

According to the 1930 census, approximately 30 percent of families consisted of one or two individuals. There was an extreme difference between families who were headed by men and those headed by women in terms of size. About 31 percent of the families headed by women were considered single-person families. In contrast, only 4 percent of the families headed by men were considered single-person families. In addition, 33 percent of the male-headed households had five or more people within the family. The figure for female-headed households with five or more people was only 15 percent.

In 1930, the median household size was 3.40 persons. Households with men as the head were much larger compared to households with those that had women as the head (3.56 to 2.22). Families with a married-male head of household were the largest families, with a median household size of 3.72. Southern families had the largest median household size at 3.67, followed by northern families (3.37) and Western families (2.92). The 1930 census also measured the difference between rural-farm, rural-nonfarm, and urban families. Rural-farm families had the largest median household size at 4.01, followed by rural-nonfarm families (3.27) and urban families (3.26). The findings for southern and rural-farm families are consistent with past literature regarding demographic transition. In 1930, much of the agricultural industry was located in the South. An incentive for rural-farm families to have large households is the potential increase in labor support that can result from having multiple people in the household. Because farming is labor intensive and involves many different jobs, large households provide more potential free laborers to do the necessary work.

In 1930, foreign-born families had the largest median household size at 3.74; native-born families had

3.35, and African American families had 3.15. African American families had the highest rate of broken homes (divorced, separated, or widowed) at 24 percent. In comparison, only 15 percent of white homes were considered broken. African American and native-born white families had similar patterns of family size across geographical locations; the largest families were located in the South, and the smallest families were located in the West. However, foreign-born families were largest in the North. This finding is consistent with research that examines patterns of foreign-born immigration. Research shows that foreign-born immigrants during the 1930's were most likely to migrate to large urban cities along the northern Atlantic coast or to the northern Great Lakes region. Foreign-born families were

also the most likely to have a large number of related persons (people who were not the husband, wife, or children) living in a household.

Economics and the 1930's American Family The Great Depression had a strongly negative impact on American families. Employment was scarce, and opportunities were few. Despite the hardship felt by many, bills and debts still had to be paid, and family members often turned to one another for support and assistance. The U.S. Census measured the number of gainful workers by family type. A gainful worker was any person who had been employed or was seeking employment in a legitimate wage-earning occupation. In 1930, 62 percent of families had one gainful worker, 21 percent had two gainful work-

Demographics shifted dramatically during the decade as many were displaced by the debilitating effects of the Great Depression. In this image, migrant workers prepare dinner on a makeshift stove at a government camp for migrants in Michigan. (Library of Congress)

ers, and 11 percent had three or more gainful workers. In comparison, only 6 percent of families in 1930 had no gainful workers. Female-headed households represented 56 percent of families without gainful workers, whereas broken-home families represented 57 percent of families without gainful workers. Three percent of African American families were without gainful workers; six percent of both native-born and foreign-born white families were without gainful workers.

Migration Patterns Within the United States The economic growth experienced in the decades prior to the 1930's drastically changed how people worked and where people lived. During the 1930's, in-country migration patterns were tracked by geographical location as well as urban, rural-nonfarm, and rural-farm distinctions. Employment was seen as the primary catalyst for in-country migration changes. People in the United States have always moved and relocated based on employment opportunities. As these opportunities changed, the demographic makeup of communities in the United States changed accordingly.

For decades, the majority of economic opportunities have been located in or near the center of urban communities. For example, 40 percent of people residing in urban areas during the 1930's had migrated from out of state. In comparison, 77 percent of people residing in rural areas were native residents of the state in which they were living. In the developing West, almost 70 percent of urban residents were out-of-state migrants, whereas in the South, approximately 75 percent of both urban and rural residents were state born. During the early 1930's, when people left home, the majority were leaving for urban cities. Nationally, nearly 70 percent of people who migrated out of state moved to urban communities. The most prevalent migratory shift was to the West; however, all states, with the exception of Alabama, Kentucky, Mississippi, and Tennessee, experienced significant levels of migration into the state. In the four aforementioned states, almost 90 percent of residents were state born. The size of a community appears to have a direct impact on migration patterns. The smaller the community, the more likely the residents were local and state born. In contrast, the more urban a community, the more likely the residents were foreign or nonstate born.

Changes in Migration Patterns Within the United States The domestic migration patterns that existed in the first part of the 1930's did not remain consistent throughout the latter portion of the decade. Between 1935 and 1940, the pattern of people moving from rural to urban areas in search of employment slowed tremendously. The impact of the Great Depression and the recession of 1937 stopped temporarily and reversed slightly the migratory demographic transition that had taken place during previous decades. For example, in 1940, three million fewer people lived in rural farm communities than in 1935. In previous decades, a majority of these people would have migrated to urban cities. However, between 1935 and 1940, approximately 75 percent of people who left the rural county they were living in moved either to another rural farm community within the same state or to a rural, nonfarm community (towns with fewer than twenty-five hundred people not reliant on farming). Urban cities across the United States declined in population during the last half of the 1930's. In contrast, rural, nonfarm communities were growing in size. Many of these rural, nonfarm communities were close in proximity to urban cities and were what were later considered suburbs.

Impact The 1930's were a unique time in the history of the United States. The effects of the Great Depression were experienced throughout society. For the first time in decades, families had to reevaluate how they planned family development, where they lived, and how and where they worked under the stressful economic environment of the Great Depression. This change in family life led to changes in the structure of many communities across the country. Families left the regions of the northern Atlantic and Great Lakes for opportunities in the West and rural, nonfarm areas. Families also developed at smaller and slower rates than in previous decades.

Despite the demographic changes that took place during the 1930's, the country eventually recovered economically, and families reverted to old behaviors. With the help of the New Deal and byproducts related to the war effort, the economic recovery of the United States led families back to urban areas and led to the post-World War II baby boom.

Jay Gilliam

Further Reading

Bogue, Donald J., Douglas Anderton, and Richard Barrett. *The Population of the United States.* 3d ed. New York: Free Press, 1997. Pioneering reference work that includes useful tables.

Carter, Susan B., et al., eds. *Historical Statistics of the United States: Millennial Edition.* 5 vols. New York: Cambridge University Press, 2007. Provides statistics about every field of American history and is available online.

Klein, Herbert S. *A Population History of the United States.* New York: Cambridge University Press, 2004. Chapter 5 charts major trends from 1914 to 1945.

U.S. Bureau of the Census. *The Statistical History of the United States: Colonial Times to the Present.* New York: Basic Books, 1976. Includes statistics related to changes in population, economics, and government.

Wright, Russell. *A Twentieth-Century History of the United States Population.* Lanham, Md.: Scarecrow Press, 1996. Analyzes census data from 1900 to 1990. Includes information about economic and social factors that shaped the United States during the 1930's.

See also   African Americans; Demographics of Canada; Great Depression in the United States; Housing in the United States; Immigration to the United States; Migrations, domestic; Resettlement Administration; Unemployment in the United States; Urbanization in the United States.

Depression. See **Great Depression in Canada; Great Depression in the United States**

■ *Design for Living*

Identification   Broadway comedy
Author   Noël Coward
Dates   January 24, 1933, to May, 1933

Design for Living ran for more than 135 performances and later became a staple of American theaters.

Design for Living was written in 1932 by British playwright Noël Coward, whose reputation had been established through popular Broadway hits *Hay Fever* (1925) and *Private Lives* (1931). It was intended to be a star vehicle for him, Lynn Fontanne and Alfred Lunt, his close friends and a married couple. The play depicts the relationships among three friends: Leo, a playwright (played by Coward); Gilda, an interior decorator (played by Fontanne); and Otto, a painter (played by Lunt). Although Gilda tries to forge a traditional relationship with each man, her need for a quality the other man possesses leads her to cheat on Leo with Otto, and on Otto with Leo. Unable to decide, she finds herself instead in a loveless marriage. Throughout, Gilda, Leo, and Otto struggle to find happiness despite repression by traditional expectations of fidelity and sexual mores. Ultimately, they decide to forge relationships among the three of them. The play ends suggestively with Gilda, Leo, and Otto falling onto a couch and laughing at the thought of what their futures hold.

When the play opened at the Ethel Barrymore Theatre on Broadway in 1933, Coward—who wrote, directed, produced, and starred in the production—basked in its popular and critical acclaim. Most critics gushed over the chemistry and performances of the three leading players, so much so that producers quickly raised ticket prices. Coward, who normally appeared in productions for three months or less, stayed in the production for five months.

Although the play was loosely based on the real-life love triangles throughout the marriage of Lunt and Fontanne, Coward had a difficult time getting the play produced in England because of its provocative themes and London's notorious censor. By the time it finally opened at the Haymarket Theatre on January 25, 1939, critics found it tame and even somewhat stylistically dated. It ran for 203 performances before ending as World War II began.

The bisexual undertones in the play seemed a bold step for the closeted Coward. Coward never came out publicly as a homosexual, because of his desire not to disillusion his audience and because of England's laws against homosexuality, which was considered a criminal offense until 1967. However, Coward's homosexuality is masked under the facade of heterosexuality, and this informs the connection among Leo, Otto, and Gilda. Like most of Coward's plays, *Design for Living* examines love, albeit a love that is brittle, repressed, and restless.

Though produced less frequently than some of Coward's other plays, *Design for Living* stands out for its bold examination of love, friendship, fame, and

Coward Comments

In his introduction to one of the earliest volumes collecting several of his plays, Noël Coward offers these comments about Design for Living:

Design for Living has been produced, published, and reviewed. It has been liked and disliked, and hated and admired, but never, I think, sufficiently loved by any but its three leading actors. This, perhaps, was only to be expected, as its central theme, from the point of view of the average, must appear to be definitely antisocial. People were certainly interested and entertained and occasionally even moved by it, but it seemed, to many of them, "unpleasant." This sense of "unpleasantness" might have been mitigated for them a little if they had realized that the title was ironic rather than dogmatic. I never intended for a moment that the design for living suggested in the play should apply to anyone outside its three principal characters, Gilda, Otto, and Leo. These glib, overarticulate, and amoral creatures force their lives into fantastic shapes and problems because they cannot help themselves. Impelled chiefly by the impact of their personalities each upon the other, they are like moths in a pool of light, unable to tolerate the lonely outer darkness, and equally unable to share the light without colliding constantly and bruising one another's wings.

The end of the play is equivocal. The three of them, after various partings and reunions and partings again, after torturing and loving and hating one another, are left together as the curtain falls, laughing. Different minds found different meanings in this laughter. Some considered it to be directed against Ernest, Gilda's husband, and the time-honoured friend of all three. If so, it was certainly cruel, and in the worst possible taste. Some saw in it a lascivious anticipation of a sort of triangular carnal frolic. Others, with less ribald imaginations, regarded it as a meaningless and slightly inept excuse to bring the curtain down. I as author, however, prefer to think that Gilda and Otto and Leo were laughing at themselves.

Source: Noël Coward, "Introduction," in *Play Parade* (Garden City, N.Y.: Garden City, 1933).

sexuality. During a time of financial unrest because of the Depression, *Design for Living* offered escapist entertainment through its presentation of upper-class lifestyles, easy wit, and thinly veiled risqué behaviors.

Impact   *Design for Living* was adapted for a 1933 film directed by Ernst Lubitsch, starring Fredric March, Gary Cooper, and Miriam Hopkins. The play was greatly revised and rewritten for the screen by Ben Hecht. Although not as widely revered as other Coward plays, *Design for Living* has entertained audiences through a number of revivals, including the first Broadway revival in 1984 at the Circle in the Square Theater, a sexually charged 1994 revival at the Donmar Warehouse Theater in London, and a 2001 Broadway revival starring Alan Cumming, Dominic West, and Jennifer Ehle.

Tom Smith

Further Reading

Coward, Noël, and Barry Day, eds. *The Letters of Noël Coward.* New York: Vintage, 2009.

Kaplan, Joel, and Sheila Stowel. *Look Back in Pleasure: Noël Coward Reconsidered.* London: Methuen, 2000.

Lahr, John. *Coward the Playwright.* London: Methuen, 1982.

See also   Film; Homosexuality and gay rights; Literature in the United States; Sex and sex education; Theater in the United States.

■ *Destry Rides Again*

Identification   Film about a pacifist lawman and saloon chanteuse who clean up a corrupt Western town
Director   George Marshall
Date   Released December 29, 1939

Destry Rides Again casts much of the world of the 1930's—Prohibition and its repeal, farm foreclosures, American isolationism—into the setting of a Wild West town in need of law and order.

In *Destry Rides Again*, director George Marshall and his screenwriters take three Western staples—the lawless frontier town, the gunfighter sick of guns, and the tough but golden-hearted sa-

In a scene from Destry Rides Again, *James Stewart pours a bucket of water on Una Merkel and Marlene Dietrich in an attempt to break up a fight between the two women.* (Hulton Archive/Getty Images)

loon girl—and transform them into a comic moral-ity play of American identity. The town of Bottleneck is run by a corrupt mayor and judge and a saloon owner and cardsharp, aided and abetted by saloon chanteuse Frenchy (Marlene Dietrich). The sheriff takes a sudden and permanent leave, leading the deputy to call in Tom Destry, Jr., played by James Stewart, to serve as deputy of the town that his father once served as sheriff before he was shot in the back.

The mocked, gunless, but crack shot, Destry, in-vestigating the disappearance of the previous sheriff and the landgrab schemes of the mayor and saloon owner, is alternately opposed and assisted by Frenchy, who is as eager a catfighter as he is a reluc-tant gunfighter. As Destry begins pinning the mur-ders and landgrabs on the town's corrupt leaders,

his father's old deputy is shot in the back. Destry, strapping on his father's six-guns, organizes towns-men to storm the barricaded saloon, while Frenchy organizes the women into a Carry Nation-style sa-loon-smashing mob. The forces of justice prevail, but Frenchy takes a bullet intended for Destry, leav-ing Destry—now the respected sheriff—available to marry the "good" girl.

Impact While the drinking and saloon-smashing scenes echo Prohibition's vexed history, the land-grab schemes—locals swindled out of their ranches through crooked card games—are a nod to Depres-sion-era farm foreclosures. Destry's initial pacifism, in a town where characters are identified as Russian, Chinese, French, and German ("Frenchy" is in fact

German), points to American isolationism amid a worsening world situation and the need for a strong sheriff to strap on his guns.

Howard V. Hendrix

Further Reading

Coyne, Michael. *The Crowded Prairie: American National Identity in the Hollywood Western.* New York: St. Martin's Press, 1998.

Lackmann, Ron. *Women of the Western Frontier in Fact, Fiction, and Film.* Jefferson, N.C.: McFarland, 1997.

Rollins, Peter C., and John E. O'Connor, eds. *Hollywood's West: The American Frontier in Film, Television, and History.* Lexington: University Press of Kentucky, 2005.

See also Agriculture in the United States; Foreign policy of the United States; Gambling; Isolationism; *Mr. Smith Goes to Washington*; Prohibition repeal.

■ Dewey, John

Identification American educator
Born October 20, 1859; Burlington, Vermont
Died June 1, 1952; New York, New York

A major contributor to the progressive education movement, Dewey was also considered the "Father of Experiential Education."

John Dewey was born in Vermont during the mid-nineteenth century. He was educated at the University of Vermont and was a public school teacher for several years. He received his doctorate degree from Johns Hopkins University and took a faculty position at the University of Michigan, where he taught from 1884 until 1894. He joined the newly formed University of Chicago during its early years, where he began the University of Chicago laboratory schools, where educational theorists could apply their ideas to the teaching of young children. During this period, he refined his beliefs in Pragmatic philosophy.

Dewey moved to the East in 1904 and began his connection with Columbia University and the Teachers College-Columbia University, a relationship that lasted for many years. He collaborated with other influential social scientists, philosophers, and educators to form the New School. He also served as the first president of the American Association of University Professors, which fought for academic freedom and rights of the professoriat from its inception in 1915.

Dewey is probably best known for his influence on the field of education, although he taught philosophy and considered himself a philosopher during most of his career. Dewey was a prolific writer, not only in the field of education but also in philosophy.

Dewey published more in a single year than many small college professors produce in twenty to thirty years. However, critics considered him to be not an especially talented writer. His works were ponderous and difficult to read. John Novak, an expert on Dewey, reportedly said that Dewey's works were like the Bible—often alluded to by both those who support them and those who confute them but seldom read.

In *Experience and Education* (1938), Dewey refutes binary thinking. For example, he felt that knowledge was both innate and external. In this work he also took on "progressive education," feeling that it was often a reaction to things that were wrong with education rather than a proactive move in the right direction. He felt his idea of "new education" should

John Dewey. (Library of Congress)

Books Written by Dewey During the 1930's	
1930	*Individualism Old and New*
1931	*Philosophy and Civilization*
1932	*Ethics* (2d ed.; with James Hayden Tufts)
1934	*Art as Experience*
1934	*A Common Faith*
1935	*Liberalism and Social Action*
1938	*Experience and Education*
1938	*Logic: The Theory of Inquiry*
1939	*Freedom and Culture*

be based on experience. He distinguished good experiences from bad, or noneducative, experiences.

Good experiences for learners, according to Dewey, included interaction and continuity. He felt an active mind should encounter the world to solve real problems—those that resemble problems from one's previous experiences. Thus, a teacher should be the person who provides the learner with these carefully selected experiences.

Dewey was active as a scholar throughout his life, even well into retirement. He contributed to politics, literature, and philosophy for twenty-three years after his formal retirement and maintained an active lifestyle until his death in 1952 at the age of ninety-two.

Impact As the "Father of Experiential Education," Dewey continues to have a major following. He is also known as one of the major proponents of progressive education, which was emerging as a powerful influence during the 1930's.

Mary C. Ware

Further Reading

Reed, Ronald F., and Tony W. Johnson. *Philosophical Documents in Education.* New York: Longman, 2000.

Westbrook, Robert B. *John Dewey and American Democracy.* Ithaca, N.Y.: Cornell University Press, 1991.

See also Education; Literature in the United States; Philosophy and philosophers.

■ Diary of a Country Priest, The

Identification Novel about an idealistic young French priest, struggling with difficult parishioners and serious illness
Author Georges Bernanos
Dates Published in France in 1936 as *Journal d'un curé de compagne*; English edition (translated by Pamela Morris) published in the United States in 1937

This book explores the struggles and spiritual progress of a dedicated young priest. Written from a perspective of serious faith, it can be considered a part of the Roman Catholic Literary Revival in Europe, which had an impact on a similar Catholic revival in the United States.

The Diary of a Country Priest explores the world of an earnest young priest in a country parish in France. Written as the priest's diary, the novel shows his self-doubt and suffering as he tries to minister to his parish. Nothing is obviously heroic about the struggles of this young priest. He is teased and generally mis-

---

The Country Priest's Despair

In the opening paragraphs of The Diary of a Country Priest, *the narrator's gloomy state of mind is evident:*

Mine is a parish like all the rest. They're all alike. Those of to-day I mean. I was saying so only yesterday to M. le Curé de Norenfontes—that good and evil are probably evenly distributed, but on such a low plain, very low indeed! Or if you like they lie one over the other; like oil and water they never mix. M. Le Curé only laughed at me. He is a good priest, deeply kind and human, who at diocesan headquarters is even considered a bit of a freethinker, on the dangerous side. His outbursts fill his colleagues with glee, and he stresses them with a look meant to be fiery, but which gives me such a deep sensation of stale discouragement that it almost brings tears into my eyes.

My parish is bored stiff; no other word for it. Like so many others! We can see them being eaten up by boredom, and we can't do anything about it. Some day perhaps we shall catch it ourselves—become aware of the cancerous growth within us. You can keep going a long time with that in you.

Source: Georges Bernanos, *The Diary of a Country Priest,* translated by Pamela Morris (New York: Macmillan, 1937).

treated by the young girls in his catechism class. His successful attempt to bring a bitter woman to repentance and peace is followed by accusations from her daughter that he caused her death by "upsetting her." In all these struggles, the young priest perseveres with humility and awareness of his own need for God's help.

Complicating the priest's spiritual and interpersonal struggles is physical illness. Unable to eat or drink anything beyond bread and wine, the priest is told by a doctor that he is dying of stomach cancer. The priest's last moments convey his faith and love; his final words express an awareness of the pervasive nature of grace.

Impact This book came to the United States in the middle of the Great Depression, when much suffering was sweeping across the country. Bernanos offers a depiction of redemptive suffering, a key concept in Catholic and Christian theology in general.

Nancy Enright

Further Reading

Comfort, Kathy. "Imperiled Souls: Metaphorical Representations of Spiritual Confusion in Georges Bernanos' *Journal d'un Curé de Campagne.*" *Renascence: Essays on Values in Literature* 57, no. 1 (Fall, 2004): 29.

Dorschell, Mary Frances. "Georges Bernanos: The Vocation of the Christian Writer." *Christianity and Literature* 55, no. 3 (Spring, 2006): 315.

Molnar, Thomas. *Bernanos: His Political Thought and Prophecy.* New York: Sheed and Ward, 1960.

See also Day, Dorothy; Literature in the United States; Religion in the United States.

■ *Dick Tracy*

Identification Comic strip about a big-city police detective and the criminals he faces
Artist Chester Gould
Date Launched on October 4, 1931

One of the most popular comic strips of the 1930's, Dick Tracy *led the rise of "hard-boiled" detective fiction and the romanticization of law enforcement in the decade's popular culture.*

Dick Tracy, the work of writer-artist Chester Gould, first appeared in 1931. It was syndicated by the Chicago Tribune Syndicate; the syndicate's editor, Joseph Patterson, gave Tracy his name. Gould's original title was *Plainclothes Tracy.* The square-jawed Tracy was a duty-bound and incorruptible plainclothes police officer, the scourge of evildoers in an unnamed midwestern city modeled on Gould's adopted home of Chicago. Gould may have taken inspiration from lawman Eliot Ness and his battle against Al Capone.

Tracy first joined the police force to discover who murdered his fiancé Tess Trueheart's father. In subsequent years, Tracy met and vanquished numerous criminals. The physical grotesquerie with which Gould endowed his criminals became one of the strip's hallmarks, but during the 1930's, Gould concentrated on more realistic villains, often loosely modeled on the bank robbers and other criminal celebrities of the decade. Among the earliest of the deformed villains was the hunchback Doc Hump, who appeared in 1934. Another early grotesque villain was the faceless The Blank, who appeared in 1937. Tracy's partner was comic relief character Pat Patton. *Dick Tracy* was morally unambiguous; Tracy represented good and criminals, including crooked officers, evil.

The strip had an unusually high level of violence for its time; Tracy was quick with his fists, and his pursuit of a criminal frequently ended in a shootout. Although Tracy was definitely a man of action, in contrast to the more cerebral model of the detective, Gould also incorporated forensic science into his plot lines. *Dick Tracy* was one of the first crime stories to emphasize crime-fighting as a job. Gould consulted with working police and criminologists to add verisimilitude to his tales. The violence of the strip and the regularity with which its villains met gory ends made introducing recurring villains difficult. One of the few recurring bad guys was Alphonse "Big Boy" Caprice, the crime boss ultimately responsible for the killing of Trueheart's father.

Tracy also had a private life, featuring a difficult relationship with Trueheart, who was sometimes jealous of Tracy's relationship with his job and was often the target of criminals who sought to bring down Tracy. He adopted a young street urchin, who was renamed Dick Tracy, Jr., and accompanied the senior Tracy on some of his adventures, setting a precedent for future child sidekicks, such as Batman's Robin and Captain America's Bucky.

The success of *Dick Tracy* led to a number of imitators, including *Radio Patrol* (1933), *Dan Dunn* (1933), *Secret Agent X-9* (1933), and *Red Barry* (1934). Tracy's adventures were collected in comic books and Big Little Books, which was a format of small, square, illustrated books introduced by Whitman Publishing to make use of scrap paper. This type of publication proved particularly conducive to Tracy, who starred in the first Big Little Book, *The Adventures of Dick Tracy* (1932), and dozens more. Like many comic-strip stars of the 1930's, Tracy crossed over to radio and film. A *Dick Tracy* radio drama first appeared in 1934. Gould's detective appeared in four serials from B-film giant Republic Studios: *Dick Tracy* (1937), *Dick Tracy Returns* (1938), *Dick Tracy's G-Men* (1939), and *Dick Tracy Versus Crime Inc.* (1941). The films portrayed Tracy as a Federal Bureau of Investigation officer rather than a policeman.

Impact   *Dick Tracy* brought a new hero into American popular culture—the big-city police officer. Subsequent "straight-arrow" fictional cops, such as Jack Webb's Joe Friday, can trace their ancestry to Gould's creation. Tracy was endlessly paid homage and parodied and went on to star in feature films, comic books, a video game, a postage stamp, and a short-lived television show. Gould retired on December 25, 1977, but *Dick Tracy* continued with different authors and artists.

William E. Burns

Further Reading

Maeder, Jay. *Dick Tracy: The Official Biography.* New York: Plume, 1990.

Roberts, Garyn G. *Dick Tracy and American Culture: Morality and Mythology, Text and Context.* Jefferson, N.C.: McFarland, 1993.

Walker, Brian. *The Comics Before 1945.* New York: Harry N. Abrams, 2004.

See also   *Apple Mary*; Capone, Al; Comic strips; Film serials; *Flash Gordon*; Ness, Eliot; Newspapers, Canadian; Newspapers, U.S.

Dies Committee. See **House Committee on Un-American Activities**

■ Dillinger, John

Identification   American bank robber
Born   June 22, 1903; Indianapolis, Indiana
Died   July 22, 1934; Chicago, Illinois

Dillinger was the best known and most celebrated outlaw of the 1930's, often regarded as a Robin Hood figure who stole from the rich but gave generously to the poor. He specialized in robbing banks at a time when financial institutions around the country were unpopular because many were collapsing, erasing depositors' savings, or foreclosing on homes, farms, and small businesses.

John Dillinger grew up in a middle-class family in Indiana, but he dropped out of high school, received a dishonorable discharge from the Navy, and pleaded

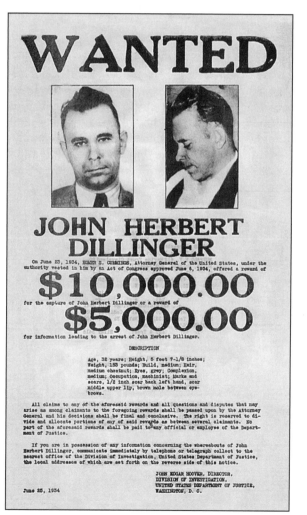

John Dillinger's "wanted" poster from 1934. (NARA)

guilty to robbing a grocery store—all by the time he was twenty-one years old. He served nearly nine years in prison before he was paroled in May, 1933.

Dillinger's subsequent crime spree lasted only fourteen months, but it quickly captured the imagination of a nation in the throes of economic depression. He and members of his gang robbed numerous banks throughout the Midwest. They also raided police stations to obtain weapons and fought their way out of several ambushes. In January, 1934, Dillinger was caught in Arizona and sent to prison in Indiana—only to escape several weeks later by cleverly using a fake gun. As the first criminal to be designated a "public enemy" by the Federal Bureau of Investigation (FBI), Dillinger was hunted nationally but seemed to have a sixth sense for evading capture. However, while leaving a Chicago movie theater in the company of a woman who had alerted the FBI, Dillinger was shot and killed.

Impact   Police and bank officials regarded Dillinger as a violent criminal, but the American public admired him as a folk hero—someone who robbed banks, not people, and did so with ingenuity and coolness under fire. Although there were several other Depression-era outlaws with whom the public sympathized, Dillinger received the most attention and acclaim. He has been lionized in films, television, and music.

James I. Deutsch

Further Reading

Girardin, G. Russell, with William J. Helmer. *Dillinger: The Untold Story.* Bloomington: Indiana University Press, 1994.

King, Jeffery S. *The Rise and Fall of the Dillinger Gang.* Nashville, Tenn.: Cumberland House, 2005.

Matera, Dary. *John Dillinger: The Life and Death of America's First Celebrity Criminal.* New York: Carroll & Graf, 2004.

See also   Barker Gang; Barrow, Clyde, and Bonnie Parker; Capone, Al; Crimes and scandals; Floyd, Pretty Boy; Gangster films; Kelly, Machine Gun; *Petrified Forest, The.*

■ Dionne quintuplets

The Event   Birth of quintuplets
Date   May 28, 1934
Place   near Callander, Ontario, Canada

In 1934, identical quintuplet girls were born in a farmhouse in a French-speaking community in Ontario, Canada. The seven-room homestead in which the girls were born had no electricity, gas, indoor plumbing, or hot water. The survival of the tiny infants, whose combined birth weight was 13 pounds 6 ounces, was considered a medical miracle and brought immediate media attention. People marveled that the quintuplets prevailed against all odds and were mesmerized by the little girls. Their amazing survival was sensational news during the Great Depression, and their upbringing under scientific scrutiny became both controversial and legendary.

Oliva and Elzire Dionne were already the parents of five children when they were surprised by the births of their quintuplet daughters: Annette Marie Lilianne, Cécile Marie Emilda, Émilie Marie Jeanne, Marie Reine Alma, and Yvonne Marie Edouilda. Their births were initially attended by midwives, as was the custom at the time, but the local doctor, Allan Roy Dafoe, was also called in to attend. The prognosis for the premature quintuplets was grim, but with Dafoe's supervision, incubators, and quality nursing care, the children thrived. Three months prior to the girls' births, Elzire had miscarried a sixth fetus.

Shortly after the quintuplets' birth, Oliva signed an agreement to have them displayed at the Chicago World's Fair. Instead, Dafoe quarantined the five babies, keeping them apart from even their other siblings. Careful medical examination documented the quintuplets' progress. With funding from the Red Cross, the Dafoe Memorial Hospital (later called Quintland), a nine-room nursery with modern conveniences, was built near the girls' original home. The children's early years were spent at the hospital under the watchful eyes of Dafoe, their main overseer. In March, 1935, the Ottawa government passed a protection act that made the children wards of King George V of England. The government-appointed guardians sought various opportunities to fund their care and to bring in revenue.

While their parents were strongly discouraged from visiting and bonding with their girls, millions of visitors flocked to observe the children. The quintuplets became a tourist attraction and a hot commodity for advertising a wide variety of products and were featured in several films, including *The Country Doctor* (1936), *Reunion* (1936), *Going on Two* (1936), *Quintupland* (1938), and *Five of a Kind* (1938). Souvenir stands sprang up and sold various quintuplet memorabilia. By the end of the 1930's, the Dionne quintuplets had become as well known as Shirley Temple.

Following a long legal battle that was supported by the Roman Catholic Church, Oliva reclaimed custody rights to his children. On November 17, 1943, the nine-and-one-half-year-old sisters rejoined their parents and siblings in a new home, but the adjustments were difficult for the five sisters. The hospi-

tal/nursery became a boarding school, Villa Notre Dame, which the girls attended, before enrolling in Catholic college. As adults, the quintuplets left their home and had little contact with their parents and other siblings.

In 1954, Émilie suffocated during an epileptic seizure. The four remaining quintuplets relocated to Montreal. On their twenty-first birthdays the girls received their inheritance but allowed their father to continue to oversee the majority of their funds. Yvonne and Cécile each graduated from nursing school. Annette and Marie worked in libraries. Annette, Cécile, and Marie each married, had children, and later divorced. Marie died of a blood clot or tumor of the brain in 1970. Annette, Yvonne, and

The Dionne quintuplets eating ice cream on their fourth birthday in 1938. From left to right: Émilie, Annette, Marie, Cécile, and Yvonne. (©Bettmann/CORBIS)

Cécile received an apology for their exploitation and a four-million-dollar compensation from the government of Ontario in 1998. Yvonne died from cancer in 2001.

Impact Throughout the 1930's, people were infatuated with the Dionne quintuplets. They became international celebrities and were exhibited as sensations during the Depression. While their uniqueness appealed to the masses, the controversy over how they were raised created hardship for the girls. Their peculiar upbringing led the girls to lead reclusive adult lives. Their original farmhouse became the Dionne Quints Museum.

Cynthia J. W. Svoboda

Further Reading

Blatz, William E., et al. *Collected Studies on the Dionne Quintuplets.* New York: Arno Press, 1975.

Brough, James. *"We Were Five": The Dionne Quintuplets' Story from Birth Through Girlhood to Womanhood.* New York: Simon and Schuster, 1965.

Nihmey, John, and Stuart Foxman. *Time of Their Lives: The Dionne Tragedy.* Elgin, Ottawa, Ont.: NIVA, 1986.

Talbot, Paul. *The Films of the Dionne Quintuplets.* Albany, Ga.: BearManor Media, 2007.

See also Business and the economy in Canada; Canadian minority communities; Chicago World's Fair; Great Depression in Canada; Housing in Canada; Psychology and psychiatry; Temple, Shirley; Unemployment in Canada.

■ Dorsey, Tommy

Identification Jazz trombonist and bandleader
Born November 19, 1905; Shenandoah, Pennsylvania
Died November 26, 1956; Greenwich, Connecticut

Dorsey is widely regarded as one of the most technically gifted trombonists of the swing era, and his popular dance bands of the 1930's were among the finest of his generation.

Tommy Dorsey, whose full name was Thomas Francis Dorsey, Jr., made numerous studio recordings with his older brother, Jimmy Dorsey, in New York from 1928 to 1933. The bands they assembled included several famous white jazz musicians, such as Jack Teagarden and Bing Crosby. "I'm Getting Sentimental over You" (1932), with its iconic trombone solo, is emblematic of Dorsey's style and quickly became a jazz standard.

The studio groups of the early 1930's served as a springboard for The Dorsey Brothers Orchestra, formed in 1934. The band signed with Decca Records and featured the vocals of Crosby and arrangements by Glenn Miller. Tunes such as "Every Little Moment" raised Dorsey's profile just as swing was emerging as a popular form of jazz. Frequent quarrels with his brother, capped by a well-known dispute over the tempo of "I'll Never Say Never Again," led Dorsey to leave the group in May, 1935, to launch his own ensemble.

Dorsey's new venture consisted of several musicians from Joe Haymes's swing band, and under Dorsey's leadership, the group quickly became one of the hottest in the country. Among the arrangers Dorsey employed were Paul Weston, Axel Stordahl, and, later, Sy Oliver. The band also engaged a number of talented musicians, including Jack Leonard, Johnny Mince, and Buddy Rich. In November, 1939, Dorsey met with Frank Sinatra and promptly signed him to his group, effectively launching the young singer's career. During the latter half of the 1930's, the band made regular radio appearances. Dorsey continued to work in radio well into the 1940's.

Impact Dorsey recorded nineteen number-one hits, and more than one hundred of the songs he recorded entered the *Billboard* charts during the 1930's and 1940's. He has been praised for his clear tone and smoothness of line on the trombone. As a bandleader, Dorsey employed a string of prominent musicians and arrangers and helped establish several rising artists in the business.

Joseph E. Jones

Further Reading

Levinson, Peter. *Tommy Dorsey: Livin' in a Great Big Way.* Cambridge, Mass.: Da Capo Press, 2005.

Sanford, Herb. *Tommy and Jimmy: The Dorsey Years.* Cambridge, Mass.: Da Capo Press, 1972.

Stockdale, Robert L. *Tommy Dorsey: On the Side.* Metuchen, N.J.: Scarecrow Press, 1995.

See also Basie, Count; Ellington, Duke; Fitzgerald, Ella; Miller, Glenn; Music: Jazz; Recording industry.

■ *Dracula*

Identification   Film about a vampire count from
Transylvania
Director   Tod Browning
Date   Released in the United States on February
12, 1931

Dracula, *the film adaptation of the Bram Stoker novel of
the same name, signaled the beginning of the modern era of
the horror genre. It solidified the position of Universal Studios as the premier producer of horror films and led to the
subsequent production of many legendary horror films such
as* The Wolf Man *(1941),* The Mummy *(1932), and*
Frankenstein *(1931). In addition, its release established
Bela Lugosi as one of the greats in the horror genre.*

Bram Stoker's novel, *Dracula,* while first published to
limited fanfare, is considered one of the greatest
gothic and macabre tales. *Dracula* was eventually
portrayed on the Broadway stage. Reportedly, female audience members fainted when Lugosi arose
from his coffin as the undead vampire count in the
1927 Broadway production of *Dracula.* Hollywood
producer Carl Laemmle was quick to see the economic potential of Stoker's *Dracula,* which was
drafted into a screenplay by writers Hamilton Deane
and John Lloyd Balderston. The story was taken to
the "big screen," and Hollywood
became enthralled with the undead count and the concept of the
vampire.

Dracula premiered on February 12, 1931, and brought horror
to talking films for the first time.
Laemmle correctly predicted the
mass appeal of films. Tickets sold
quickly and word spread among
filmgoers that *Dracula* was unlike
any film that preceded it. Newspapers in New York City wrote head-
line stories of audience members
fainting from fright.

Lugosi's portrayal was consid-
erably different from that of actor
Max Schreck as Count Orlock in
F. W. Murnau's *Nosferatu,* a 1929
German adaptation of the Stoker
novel. Unlike Schreck's Orlock,
Lugosi's Dracula was suave, sen-
sual, and alluring as the Transyl-

vanian nobleman with a taste for blood. While
Schreck's Orlock was a repulsive creature who over-
powered his victims with brute force or tricks of the
mind, Lugosi's Dracula swooped into unsuspecting
victims' bed chambers in the dark of night, smartly
attired in tuxedo and silken cape. Dracula would
gently wrap victims in his luxurious cape as bit into
their necks, draining them of their blood and transforming them into undead creatures of the night.

Impact   Dracula was more than mere entertainment. The film solidified Universal Studios' position
as the top producer of gothic and horror films. It
also established Lugosi as one of the greatest mon-
ster-movie actors of all time. It brought to the United
States a fresh and distinct sense of gothic horror. For
the first time, American audiences were treated to
the dark, lustful sensuality that was a part of the
broader landscape of gothic horror. This sensibility
became a hallmark of Universal Studios' horror
films in later years as *Dracula* gave rise to *Frankenstein,*
The Mummy, and *The Wolf Man.* These seminal works
of horror paved the way for growth and development in the horror genre; later filmmakers such as
Alfred Hitchcock, John Carpenter, and George
Romero attributed their inspiration to films such as
Dracula.

The vampire Dracula (Bela Lugosi) stalks Lucy Weston (Frances Dade) in the 1931 film.
(Hulton Archive/Getty Images)

The Hollywood portrayal of Dracula, his mountaintop castle, and the Transylvanian countryside are still copied in cinema worldwide. The transformation of the count into a bat has startled film audiences and readers of gothic horror for years. Since the initial release of *Dracula*, the film has been remade into more than 211 distinct titles.

Wendy L. Hicks

Further Reading

McNally, Raymond, and Radu Florescu. *In Search of Dracula: The History of Dracula and Vampires.* Boston: Mariner Books, 1994.

Spadoni, Robert. *Uncanny Bodies: The Coming of Sound Films and the Origins of the Horror Genre.* Berkeley: University of California Press, 2007.

Stoker, Bram. *Dracula.* New York: Fine Creative Media, 1897.

_____. *Dracula's Guest.* Portland, Oreg.: New Wave, 1914.

Yu, Eric Kwan-Wai. "Productive Fear: Labor, Sexuality, and Mimicry in Bram Stoker's Dracula." *Texas Studies in Literature and Language* 48, no. 2 (2006): 145-170.

See also Drive-in theaters; Film; *Frankenstein* films; Horror films.

■ Drive-in theaters

Definition Designated open-air screening areas where people could watch films from their automobiles

The drive-in theater was a new type of movie theater and moviegoing experience that eventually became a cultural institution.

During the early 1930's, Richard M. Hollingshead, Jr., was working as the general sales manager of the

Drive-in theaters, such as this one in Los Angeles, first appeared in the 1930's and quickly became popular settings for watching films. (Popperfoto/Getty Images)

Whiz Auto Products Company, located in Camden, New Jersey. Restless, bored, and infused with the desire to create something unique, he analyzed the consumer market and found that even during the lean economic times of the Great Depression, there were four things that people did not give up: food, clothing, automobiles, and films. Deciding to combine the last two, he experimented in the driveway of his home in Riverton, New Jersey. He nailed a film screen to a tree, put a film projector on his car hood, and used a sprinkler to simulate rain. With one car behind another, he determined the angle at which the second car would have to be for its passengers to be able to see over the first car. When he was satisfied, he obtained a 50-foot wide screen and a projector with sufficient power. RCA Victor Company provided "controlled directional sound," which meant sound emitting from three central speakers.

Hollingshead formed the Park-In Theatres company and, at a cost of about thirty thousand dollars, built the world's first automobile movie theater on Crescent Boulevard in Pennsauken Township, New Jersey. It opened on Tuesday, June 6, 1933. Admission was twenty-five cents per car and twenty-five cents for each person; cars with three or more people paid one dollar. The first film was *Wives Beware* (1932), starring Adolphe Menjou.

Although business was brisk the first night, attendance fell off and never recovered. Problems with the sound, viewing locations, unsynchronized sound and picture for those in faraway rows, and stifling heat with the windows up or insect swarms with them rolled down contributed to the decline in attendance. A few years later, Hollingshead sold the theater to a man who relocated it. Throughout the 1930's other drive-in theaters opened in places such as Texas, California, and Massachusetts.

Impact Although drive-in theaters were slow to catch on as a film-watching experience, they ultimately became extremely popular as American culture began to revolve increasingly around the automobile. Drive-ins not only became cultural institutions during the 1950's but also helped Hollywood survive the rise of television, when people were turning away from traditional movie theaters in favor of this new entertainment medium.

Russell Roberts

Further Reading

Liftin, Joan. *Drive-Ins*. London: Trolley, 2004.

McKeon, Elizabeth, and Linda Everett. *Cinema Under the Stars*. Nashville, Tenn.: Cumberland House, 1998.

Segrave, Kerry. *Drive-in Theaters*. Jefferson, N.C.: McFarland, 1992.

See also Academy Awards; Film; Horror films; Motion Picture Production Code; National Film Act of 1939 (Canada).

■ Dubinsky, David

Identification American labor leader
Born February 22, 1892; Brest-Litovsk, Russian Empire (now Brest, Belarus)
Died September 17, 1982; New York, New York

Dubinsky was the main force in creating the International Ladies Garment Workers Union (ILGWU), a key component of the American labor movement. He was also instrumental in strengthening both the American Federation of Labor (AFL) and the Congress of Industrial Organizations (CIO).

David Dubinsky was a Russian Jewish immigrant who came to the United States in 1911. He became president of the ILGWU in 1936 and held the post until 1961. He was elected to the national executive council of the AFL in 1934. In 1936, he helped form the CIO, an organization based on industries rather than crafts. He left the CIO in 1938 over a policy difference and led the ILGWU as an independent union until 1940, when the union again became part of the AFL.

As the Great Depression took hold during the early 1930's, the AFL fell into desperate straits. Its membership stood at only twenty-five thousand. Under Dubinsky's leadership, and using the New Deal National Industrial Recovery Act, the union grew tenfold. He introduced many innovations in the union to care for its members, including housing, pensions, and medical facilities. His honesty and loyalty to his members made him an ideal leader for the AFL.

Dubinsky was an ardent supporter of President Franklin D. Roosevelt and the New Deal. He said labor needed capitalism in order to thrive and worked hard to keep communists out of the American labor movement.

Impact Dubinsky's commitment to labor and his honesty made the ILGWU one of the strongest unions in the United States. His loyalty to the New Deal and anticommunism contributed to making the U.S. labor movement a partner with industry in strengthening the capitalist system.

Frederick B. Chary

Further Reading

Dubinsky, David, with A. H. Raskin. *David Dubinsky: A Life with Labor.* New York: Simon & Schuster, 1977.

Parmet, Robert D. *The Master of Seventh Avenue: David Dubinsky and the American Labor Movement.* New York: New York University Press, 2005.

See also American Federation of Labor; Business and the economy in the United States; Communism; Congress of Industrial Organizations; Fair Labor Standards Act of 1938; Income and wages in the United States; Labor strikes; Lewis, John L.; National Labor Relations Act of 1935; Unionism.

■ Du Bois, W. E. B.

Identification African American sociologist, civil rights activist, and editor

Born February 23, 1868; Great Barrington, Massachusetts

Died August 27, 1963; Accra, Ghana

In the 1903 publication of The Souls of Black Folk, *Du Bois proclaimed that the problem of the twentieth century was the problem of the color line, a statement that resounded throughout the century, profoundly shaping American's perceptions of race relations, while contouring the legacy of his life and work. A scholar, civil rights activist, and Pan-Africanist during the 1930's, Du Bois published extensively and was politically involved in the United States and abroad.*

By the 1930's W. E. B. Du Bois was an established and influential social scientist working as the editor of the magazine of the National Association for the Advancement of Colored People (NAACP), *Crisis*, which he had founded in 1910.

The 1930's were a time of controversy and creativity for Du Bois. His publication in 1935 of *Black Reconstruction in America, 1860-1880* was the culmination of his application of Karl Marx's economic class

model to the breakdown of post-Civil War Reconstruction. His basic argument was that Caucasians and African Americans, as laborers, failed to unify in common interest against upper-class Caucasians, thus creating substantial divisions among races and reinforcing racial ideologies of white superiority and black inferiority. Du Bois argued that these divisions and cleavages ultimately gave rise to southern segregation and Jim Crow laws, providing an explanation for the Reconstruction's failure. Though the book had little success in terms of sales, the unique argument he presented transformed the debate about Reconstruction. Whether critics and scholars found the argument compelling or dismissed it as far-fetched and radical, they agreed that the contours of the Reconstruction debate had changed.

The analysis Du Bois offered resonated with economic realities by paralleling Reconstruction and 1930's federal relief programs. These programs, such as the Federal Emergency Relief Act and the Works Progress Administration, had potential for great economic restructuring in the United States, but only if the impact of the programs was dispersed through the populace and not solely to upper-class Caucasians. The maturation of Du Bois's thinking and writing also evolved his best-known thesis, that African Americans continually battled a double consciousness—one of American ideals and black realities—and is reflected in his 1940 *Dusk of Dawn: An Essay Toward an Autobiography of a Race Concept.*

Influenced by the declining social and economic fortunes of African Americans he witnessed in the early 1930's, Du Bois asserted that African Americans should foster financial independence as a solution to the deepening economic crises brought on by the Depression. Many contemporaries of Du Bois, such as Marcus Garvey, reacted against his separatist claims, accusing Du Bois of espousing ideas he had once rejected. This tirade resulted in cleavages within the NAACP. As a result, Du Bois retired from his editorship of the *Crisis* in 1935.

Du Bois was also influenced by his continuing involvement with the continent of Africa and travels to Europe prior to and throughout the decade. He had long worked for a pan-African vision of black unity. This was based in his resolve that African Americans could not hope for equality while black Africans were repressed on the continent of Africa through exploitation by white Europeans and North Americans. In the mid-1930's, when Italian fascist dictator Benito Mussolini invaded Ethiopia, Du Bois advocated for a unified black race through American black solidarity with Ethiopians, publishing on the interconnections of African American and black Ethiopian in *Foreign Affairs*. By the end of the decade, Du Bois was aging, but remained an important figure in American life.

Impact   Du Bois brought a Marxist analysis to racial problems in the United States during the 1930's. He did this while contributing to a social agenda to better the economic situation of Americans, especially African Americans, during the decade. He visualized and promoted a global unity of oppressed African Americans within his social theories. While still best known for his 1903 *The Souls of Black Folk*, Du Bois dedicated his entire life to working on the problems created by the color line.

Sadie Pendaz

Further Reading

Gardullo, Paul. "'Just Keeps Rollin' Along': Rebellions, Revolts, and Radical Black Memories of Slavery in the 1930s." *Patterns of Prejudice* 41, nos. 3/4 (2007): 271-301.

Holt, Thomas C. "The Political Uses of Alienation: W.E.B. Du Bois on Politics, Race, and Culture, 1903-1940." *American Quarterly* 42, no. 2 (1990): 301-323.

Lewis, David Levering. *W.E.B. Du Bois, 1919-1963: The Fight for Equality and the American Century*. New York: Henry Holt, 2000.

See also   African Americans; Federal Emergency Relief Administration; Lynching; National Association for the Advancement of Colored People; Race riots; Racial discrimination; Works Progress Administration.

Duck Stamp Act of 1934. See **Migratory Bird Hunting and Conservation Stamp Act of 1934**

■ Dust Bowl

The Event   Drought and wind erosion that produced massive dust storms devastating the southern Great Plains

Dates   1932-1938

Places   Texas and Oklahoma panhandles, portions of Kansas, Colorado, and New Mexico

The Dust Bowl affected more than 400,000 acres of prairie, causing immense suffering among people and animals. It was the worst ecological disaster in the United States at the time and a stark example of the consequences of unregulated development at the expense of a fragile ecosystem. The U.S. government instituted many agricultural programs in response to the Dust Bowl, and the world as a whole learned valuable lessons in managing semiarid lands.

On April 14, 1935, the dawn broke on a clear and sunny day in the drought-stricken Oklahoma panhandle. Inhabitants enjoyed the respite from two years of dust storms. Then, abruptly, a darkening sky, fleeing birds, and crackling electricity signaled that another "black blizzard" was on the way. A seething wall of black dust, two thousand feet high and hundreds of miles wide, swept through the region at upwards of sixty miles per hour. The stinging, scouring grit destroyed vegetation, suffocated animals and people trapped in the open, and plunged the land into blackness so profound a person could not see objects one foot away. The high winds of the frontal system passed quickly, but dust remained suspended in the air for hours. Visiting the stricken area on April 15, Robert Geiger, a Denver reporter, coined the term "dust bowl."

Local dust storms were not novelties in the area, but severe regional storms appeared only during the 1930's, a result of the worst drought in recorded history combined with rapid expansion of wheat cultivation in the previous decade. The U.S. Soil Conservation Service recorded multiple regional dust storms from 1932 to 1938. In terms of intensity and duration, the worst year was 1935, followed by 1937. Effects could extend far beyond the core area. On May 9, 1934, a massive dust storm blanketed Chicago, dusted New York and Washington, D.C., and even reached ships hundreds of miles out in the Atlantic Ocean.

Living with dust was a constant battle. People endured dust in their homes, ate dust, and breathed it constantly. Medical facilities were overwhelmed by cases of dust pneumonia, and many people suffered from silicosis. No estimate exists of total fatalities, but if deaths from chronic lung disease and epidemics and malnutrition among refugees are included, it would be considerable. For most of the decade, cultivating crops in the Dust Bowl was impossible. Livestock starved or were destroyed by a government program that paid farmers five dollars a head for cattle.

The economic effects of the Depression were already apparent when the first dust storms hit and were exacerbated by the storms. Farmers who had borrowed heavily to buy land and machinery during the 1920's faced foreclosure when wheat prices dropped below production costs in 1931. Thus, they had no income, because of crop failure. After 1933, farmers had several options, including selling land directly to the federal government, accepting subsidies to take land out of wheat production and managing it to promote soil conservation, and borrowing money from the federal government to pay off old loans. Many families abandoned their land before subsidies were in place. Most of those who remained relied on some sort of federal aid to survive.

Background and Causes The southern Great Plains is a region of temperature extremes; high winds; and low, unpredictable rainfall. Until ranchers began arriving in the 1870's, it was an unbroken expanse of rich grassland. Within two decades of the ranchers' arrival, overgrazing had taken its toll, and a series of dry summers, severe winters, and poor markets forced drastic retrenchment.

The rancher's misfortune was the wheat grower's opportunity, or so it appeared. In the early twentieth century, many farmers moved into the former rangeland, where the rich, black prairie soil yielded bumper crops. Wheat prices rose rapidly during World War I, and patriotic propaganda proclaimed:

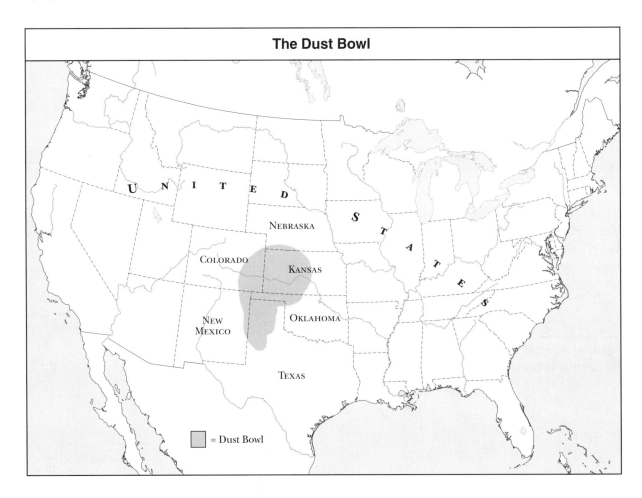

The Dust Bowl

"Wheat will win the war." Farming in the southern plains seemed both a sure avenue to financial security and a patriotic investment. About one-half of the people who embarked on cultivating the plains were owner-operators; investors made up the other half. To explain two decades of above-average rainfall, some alleged experts claimed: "Rain follows the plow." Between 1925 and 1930 farmers brought more than five million acres of virgin prairie into cultivation.

Introducing tractors and disc plows allowed a single farmer to cultivate ten times as much acreage as one who relied on horses and to convert pastureland to crops. Mechanization involved incurring debt. Credit was readily available through the system of Federal Land Banks, established in 1916.

In 1930, the price of wheat dropped abruptly. Farmers responded by plowing up more land, incurring additional indebtedness. The following summer was dry and hot, reducing yields to the point where a crop's value did not cover production costs. Many farmers opted not to plant, leaving fields fallow and exposed to the wind. Once erosion commenced, it gathered momentum. Surveying a dusty and nearly lifeless landscape in 1937, after four years of drought, many wondered whether the land would ever be productive again.

Okies and Dust Bowl Refugees   In the popular imagination, reinforced by John Steinbeck's novel *The Grapes of Wrath* (1939), the Dust Bowl was the principal cause of the mass migration of agricultural workers to California during the 1930's. This image is not entirely accurate. Although parts of the southern plains lost as much as 40 percent of their population, this was not a densely settled area. The bulk of the migrants were sharecroppers from farther east who had grown cotton, tobacco, and other labor-intensive crops before drought, falling commodity prices, and exhausted soil

The Dust Bowl Explained

In 2004, scientists at the National Aeronautics and Space Administration (NASA) determined the causes of the Dust Bowl disaster.

NASA scientists have an explanation for one of the worst climatic events in the history of the United States, the "Dust Bowl" drought, which devastated the Great Plains and all but dried up an already depressed American economy in the 1930's.

Siegfried Schubert of NASA's Goddard Space Flight Center, Greenbelt, Md., and colleagues used a computer model developed with modern-era satellite data to look at the climate over the past 100 years. The study found cooler than normal tropical Pacific Ocean surface temperatures combined with warmer tropical Atlantic Ocean temperatures to create conditions in the atmosphere that turned America's breadbasket into a dust bowl from 1931 to 1939. The team's data is in this week's [March 19, 2004] *Science* magazine.

These changes in sea surface temperatures created shifts in the large-scale weather patterns and low level winds that reduced the normal supply of moisture from the Gulf of Mexico and inhibited rainfall throughout the Great Plains.

"The 1930s drought was the major climatic event in the nation's history," Schubert said. "Just beginning to understand what occurred is really critical to understanding future droughts and the links to global climate change issues we're experiencing today." . . .

The researchers used NASA's Seasonal-to-Interannual Prediction Project (NSIPP) atmospheric general circulation model and agency computational facilities to conduct the research. The NSIPP model was developed using NASA satellite observations, including: Clouds and the Earth's Radiant Energy System radiation measurements; and the Global Precipitation Climatology Project precipitation data.

The model showed cooler than normal tropical Pacific Ocean temperatures and warmer than normal tropical Atlantic Ocean temperatures contributed to a weakened low-level jet stream and changed its course. The jet stream, a ribbon of fast moving air near the Earth's surface, normally flows westward over the Gulf of Mexico and then turns northward pulling up moisture and dumping rain onto the Great Plains. As the low level jet stream weakened, it traveled farther south than normal. The Great Plains dried up and dust storms formed.

Source: "NASA Explains 'Dust Bowl' Drought." National Aeronautics and Space Administration, March 18, 2004.

A father and his two sons walk through a dust storm in Oklahoma in 1936. Many chose to leave this part of the country because of the Dust Bowl and try their luck in California. (Library of Congress)

made it more profitable for owners of large farms to evict the tenants.

Compared to the stereotypical "Okies," Dust Bowl farmers were better educated, had early histories of success, and were more likely to believe that conditions would eventually improve. Those who held onto their land in the early years eventually benefited from federal programs designed to stabilize agriculture. They were paid by the acre not to grow wheat and could also be paid for labor on conservation projects.

Many Americans are familiar with the Dust Bowl through *The Grapes of Wrath*, Dorothea Lange's unforgettable photographs for the Farm Security Administration, the ballads of Woody Guthrie, and other outsider views. Though often of great literary and artistic quality, these conveyed an atmosphere of despair and hopelessness. Media coverage by local outlets and statements by local politicians present a somewhat different view. While not minimizing the severity of the crisis, they remain optimis-

tic and praise the often heroic efforts of individuals and communities to survive.

Recovery In the later 1930's, attention shifted away from relief and toward conservation efforts on both private and federal lands. Farming communities were organized into soil and water conservation districts, with elected boards, to promote good conservation practices on private lands. The government paid farmers to plow fallow land to minimize wind erosion and brought in crews from the Civilian Conservation Corps to replant barren ground to grass and create windbreaks. Few of the trees survived, but the grassland gradually regenerated. During World War II, both rainfall and wheat prices increased to the point where wheat farming on the least marginal lands was again profitable.

Over the course of the remainder of the twentieth century, the Dust Bowl area became a healthy prairie ecosystem, most of it devoted to cattle ranching, but some set aside in nature reserves. The revitalized prairie vegetation includes a number of deliberately introduced species, is less diverse, and is probably more vulnerable to disruption than the original virgin grassland. Only a handful of inhabitants remain who remember the Dust Bowl, an ecological disaster that peaked during the 1930's.

Impact The Dust Bowl provided a laboratory within which agricultural science could develop management practices for semiarid lands, set in motion a mass migration from the agricultural heartland to the coasts, and inspired a memorable body of literature, art, and folklore of enduring value. The farthest-reaching lessons of the Dust Bowl are those that are applicable to agriculture. The shifting population pattern is significant, but the Dust Bowl was not as responsible for this as is often believed.

Martha A. Sherwood

Further Reading

Bonnifield, Paul. *The Dust Bowl: Men, Dirt, and Depression.* Albuquerque: University of New Mexico Press, 1979. Emphasizes economics and criticizes New Deal agricultural policies.

Egan, Timothy. *The Worst Hard Time.* Boston: Houghton Mifflin, 2006. Based on interviews with Dust Bowl survivors; a vivid recreation of the human dimension of the disaster.

Grant, Michael Johnston. *Down and Out on the Family Farm: Rural Rehabilitation in the Great Plains, 1929-45.* Lincoln: University of Nebraska Press, 2002. Emphasis on economics and legislation and on areas outside the Dust Bowl that remained viable grain-growing regions.

Svobida, Lawrence. *Farming the Dust Bowl: A First-Hand Account from Kansas.* Lawrence: University Press of Kansas, 2007. Reprint of a 1941 memoir; the introduction puts the Dust Bowl in the context of the history of agriculture.

Worster, Donald. *Dust Bowl. The Southern Plains in the 1930's.* New York: Oxford University Press, 2004. An illustrated, objective account of all aspects of the Dust Bowl—human, ecological, political.

See also Agriculture in the United States; *Grapes of Wrath, The*; Great Depression in the United States; Guthrie, Woody; Heat wave of 1931; Lange, Dorothea; Migrations, domestic; Natural disasters; Natural resources; Steinbeck, John.

■ Dutch elm disease

Definition Disease caused by a fungus that kills elm trees

Dutch elm disease came to the United States from Europe in elm logs used in the furniture industry. American elms proved to be particularly susceptible to the disease. First identified in Ohio in 1930, the disease was found in seven eastern states by the end of the decade. Subsequently, it decimated elm trees throughout the United States and most of Canada.

Dutch elm disease quickly kills elm trees. Leaves of infected trees wilt, turn dull green and then yellow or brown, and may drop early. Young trees may die within months, while older trees may take two years to succumb. The disease is caused by a fungus (*Ophiostoma ulmi* or *novo-ulmi*) and is spread primarily by elm bark beetles. It can also be spread by root-to-root contact and contaminated pruning tools.

The disease originated in Asia and came to Europe during the 1910's. Its cause was first identified in 1921 in the Netherlands; hence its name. In the late 1920's and early 1930's, it came to the United States. In 1930, it was first identified in Cleveland, Ohio, where the outbreak was small and could have been controlled. However, in 1932, a major outbreak was discovered around New York City. In 1933, twelve hundred infected trees were identified within forty miles of the city, in parts of New Jersey, New York, and Connecticut. In 1934, more than seven thousand diseased trees were found in this area.

On October 21, 1933, an embargo barring the importation of elm logs was enacted. In addition, a domestic quarantine was instituted to prevent movement of elm plants or parts of plants beyond the outbreak area. The federal government created a program to identify and remove diseased trees. Scouts were hired under the Works Progress Administration and the Civilian Conservation Corps. However, resources were insufficient to halt the spread, which was exacerbated by the Great New England Hurricane of 1938. Hundreds of thousands of elms were destroyed and left to rot, providing a massive habitat for the elm beetles that carry the disease. By the end of the 1930's, more than five million elm trees had been removed in areas encompassing parts of New York, New Jersey, Connecticut, and Pennsylvania. Infected trees were also identified in Ohio, Indiana, and Maryland.

The federal program slowed the progression of the disease. Nonetheless, the disease spread up and down the East Coast of the United States and headed west, reaching the Rocky Mountains during the 1950's and the West Coast during the 1970's. At the beginning of the twenty-first century, it continued to spread north into Canada, although an aggressive campaign has kept the provinces of Alberta and British Columbia disease-free.

Impact   Prior to the 1930's, elm trees were planted along streets and walkways as windbreaks and shade-providing canopies. It was the preponderant urban tree at the time and many towns were proud of their elms, hailing themselves "Elm Cities." Because the American elm was particularly susceptible to the disease, the 1930's marked the beginning of the end of elm-lined streets, walkways, and parks in North America.

James L. Robinson

Further Reading

Campanella, Thomas G. *Republic of Shade: New England and the American Elm.* New Haven, Conn.: Yale University Press, 2003.

Sinclair, Wayne A., and Howard H. Lyon. *Diseases of Trees and Shrubs.* 2d ed. Ithaca, N.Y.: Cornell University Press, 2005.

See also   Civilian Conservation Corps; Great New England hurricane; Works Progress Administration.

■ Earhart, Amelia

Identification   Aviator and adventurer
Born   July 24, 1897; Atchison, Kansas
Died   July 2?, 1937; near Howland Island in the
Pacific Ocean

Earhart set many aviation records, wrote books, became a fashion icon, was the first woman to fly across the Atlantic Ocean, and became one of the world's most famous "missing persons" when she disappeared on July 2, 1937, while attempting to fly around the world.

Few figures have captured American hearts and imaginations as Amelia Earhart has. Born to Samuel Stanton Earhart and Amelia Otis Earhart, Earhart dedicated her life to the pursuit of adventure. Although arguably not the most talented of pilots, Earhart nevertheless set numerous aviation records. These included the altitude record for women (14,000 feet, in 1922); becoming the first woman to fly across the Atlantic (as a passenger, in 1928); becoming the first woman to fly across the Atlantic solo (in 1932); becoming the first woman to fly non-stop, coast-to-coast across the United States (in 1933); and numerous other distance, altitude, and speed records.

Early Years   Earhart's sense of adventure was encouraged and cultivated by her rather liberal mother. Earhart and her younger sister, Grace, were allowed to explore at will during their early childhood years.

Earhart's father was a railroad clerk in Atchison, Kansas. In 1914, he was fired from his job. In 1915, he secured a railroad clerk position in St. Paul, Minnesota, but he lasted only a short time at that position. Earhart's mother, desiring to provide more stability for her two daughters, moved with the girls to Chicago, Illinois, where they lived with friends. Earhart attended and graduated from Hyde Park High School in 1916. She briefly attended Ogontz Junior College before traveling to Toronto to visit her sister during the winter of 1917. Earhart completed Red Cross Nurses Aide training and began volunteering at the Spadina Military Hospital.

Aviation Adventures   In 1918, while attending the Canadian National Exposition in Toronto, Earhart watched a World War I ace put on a thrilling exposition in a biplane. Earhart was intrigued and later

Amelia Earhart at the front of her Lockheed Electra monoplane, which was under construction when this photograph was taken in 1936. (AP/Wide World Photos)

Amelia Earhart's Final Flight, 1937

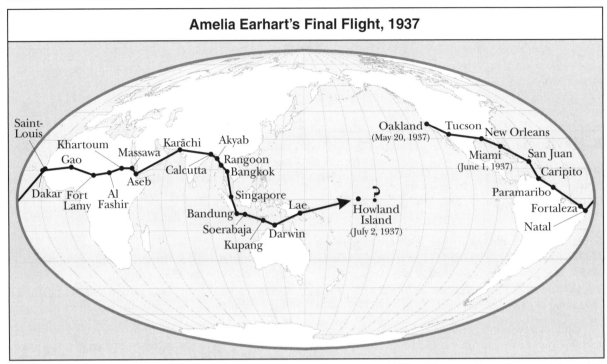

Amelia Earhart disappeared somewhere between Lae and Howland Island in July, 1937, while attempting to fly around the world.

credited the pilot with initiating her interest in becoming a pilot.

1n 1919, Earhart began attending Columbia University in New York City. She dropped out a year later to be with her parents, who had reconciled their differences and relocated to Southern California. On December 28, 1920, Earhart experienced her first flight in Long Beach, California. Although lasting only ten minutes, the flight was long enough to persuade her to pursue flying.

Earhart began her flight lessons on January 3, 1921. She purchased a Kinner Airster and completed her training in that airplane. On October 22, 1922, prior to receiving her pilot's license, Earhart set her first aviation record by flying her airplane to 14,000 feet, at that time the altitude record for women. On May 15, 1923, she became the sixteenth woman in the world to be issued a pilot's license.

The years from 1923 to 1928 were a time of upheaval and relocation for Earhart. An inheritance that she had been living off ran out, forcing her to sell her Kinner airplane and seek employment. In 1924, Earhart took a job as a teacher near Boston. She began writing aviation-related articles for local newspapers. These articles led to her gaining recog-

nition as an aviation advocate. She received an invitation to join an all-male crew in a flight across the Atlantic. On June 17, 1928, Earhart, as a passenger, flew from Trepassy, Newfoundland, Canada, to Llanelli, Wales. In doing so, Earhart became the first woman to fly across the Atlantic. George P. Putnam was the promoter of the flight. Putnam, married at the time, later divorced his wife and pursued Earhart. After refusing his offers of marriage on numerous occasions, Earhart finally accepted the proposal and married Putnam on February 7, 1931. Remaining in line with her independent character, Earhart refused to adopt the Putnam name.

The publicity that accompanied Earhart's transatlantic flight was the catalyst for numerous opportunities for her. She became a soft-spoken, yet highly effective, advocate of women's rights. Her short cropped hair and habit of wearing pants and leather jackets became an often mimicked fashion statement by women. In 1932, Earhart became the first woman to fly solo across the Atlantic when she piloted a Lockheed Vega from Newfoundland, Canada, to Culmore, Northern Ireland. Several more record-setting flights followed, culminating in Earhart's fateful attempt to circumnavigate the world in

1937. On June 1, Earhart and her navigator, Fred Noonan, set off from Miami, Florida, in a Lockheed Electra for an attempt at an equatorial circumnavigation of the Earth. On July 2, Earhart departed Lae, New Guinea, for the more than 2,500-mile flight to Howland Island, a tiny spot in the Pacific. She never arrived. Radio transmissions received by the U.S. Coast Guard cutter *Itasca* indicate that Earhart was close to Howland Island but was apparently unable to locate the small landmass. Earhart likely ran out of fuel and ditched in the sea. An extensive, multiday search by the U.S. Navy failed to locate any additional clues.

Putnam applied for a declaration of death, which was granted by a Los Angeles court on January 5, 1939. Although Earhart was declared legally dead, her legend and significant contributions to women and aviation have proven to be long lasting.

Impact   Earhart influenced generations of aviators, especially women aviators, with her groundbreaking sense of adventure and promotion of aviation. She became an icon for those who seek adventure and a role model for generations of women.

Alan Frazier

Further Reading

Butler, Susan. *East to the Dawn: The Life of Amelia Earhart.* Reading, Mass.: Addison Wesley, 1997. Biography focuses on Earhart's flights and politics.

Gillespie, Ric. *Finding Amelia: The True Story of the Earhart Disappearance.* Annapolis, Md.: Naval Institute Press, 2006. Uses documents of the International Group for Historic Aircraft Recovery to provide a logical explanation for the circumstances of Earhart's disappearance.

Long, Elgen, and Marie Long. *Amelia Earhart: The Mystery Solved.* New York: Random House, 1985. Dispels the conspiracy theories that surround Earhart's disappearance and uses detailed research to trace Earhart's final days.

Strippel, Richard. *Amelia Earhart: The Myth and the Reality.* New York: Exposition Press, 1972. Provides a look into Earhart's life and the circumstances of her death.

See also   Aviation and aeronautics; Hairstyles; Transportation; Travel.

■ *Ecstasy*

Identification   Czech film about a love triangle involving an old man, his young wife, and a young man
Director   Gustav Machatý
Dates   Released in Europe in January, 1933; released in the United States on December 24, 1940

Ecstasy, known as Extáze *in Czech and either* Ekstase *or* Symphonie der Liebe *(symphony of love) in German, is generally recognized as the first nonpornographic feature film to show full frontal female nudity and to present a woman's libido, erotic passion, and sexual frustration sympathetically. The sensuality of this soft, impressionistic, and intricately symbolic film was understated by later standards, but revolutionary in its own time.*

Under her real name, Hedy Kiesler, nineteen-year-old Hedy Lamarr portrayed Eva, the new bride of Emil, a kindly but inattentive, obsessive, and unresponsive gentleman, old enough to be her grandfather and either unable or unwilling to consummate their marriage. She leaves him, goes home to her father, and gets a divorce. One day, as she is skinny-dipping in a nearby stream, her horse runs off with her clothes on its back. While still naked, she meets Adam, a strapping young construction worker, who helps her get her horse and clothes back. Subsequent scenes with Adam depict their copulation and her orgasm. Events lead to Emil's suicide, Eva's guilt and despair, and Adam's shattered hopes.

Impact   *Ecstasy* defined for American censors and audiences the stereotype of the immoral foreign film. The usually lenient German censors delayed its release there for two years. American censors, after cutting or covering its nudity and severely muffling its erotic content, finally allowed the film to be shown in the United States in 1940, probably only because Lamarr, as the protégée of Metro-Goldwyn-Mayer magnate Louis B. Mayer, had recently become a popular Hollywood star. Such puritanical attitudes toward foreign films persisted into the late 1960's and early 1970's and resulted in American authorities banning or bowdlerizing many Swedish, French, Italian, German, and Japanese films whose producers tried to release them in the United States. The stereotype did not begin to dissolve until the American releases of the British surrealistic mystery

Blow-Up (originally titled *Blowup* in the United Kingdom) in December, 1966, and the Swedish sexual drama *I Am Curious (Yellow)* in March, 1969.

Eric v. d. Luft

Further Reading

Gardner, Gerald C. *The Censorship Papers: Movie Censorship Letters from the Hays Office, 1934-1968.* New York: Dodd, Mead, 1987.

Lamarr, Hedy. *Ecstasy and Me: My Life as a Woman.* New York: Bartholomew House, 1966.

Thomas, Alfred. *The Bohemian Body: Gender and Sexuality in Modern Czech Culture.* Madison: University of Wisconsin Press, 2007.

See also Film; Motion Picture Production Code; Pornography; Sex and sex education; *Ulysses* trial.

■ Education

The initial years of the Great Depression had little impact on educational opportunities and funding in the United States. However, traditional sources of funding that had fueled expansion during the previous decades began to decline, and federal support for public education increased to address youth issues and unemployment.

Prior to the Great Depression, most perceived education to be a significant pathway to prosperity and a greater quality of life. Economic growth enabled partnerships to form between commerce and education, which in turn provided adequate funding for schools and teacher salaries. School buildings became sources of pride for communities, and American colleges and universities expanded their campus facilities. However, by 1932, when the full effects of the Depression began to affect education, the benefits of studying and attaining a diploma or a degree soon gave way to hard economic realities. From the Depression through World War II, educational priorities declined and retrenchment became a common pattern in many communities throughout the nation.

Public Schools In the early years of the Depression, public education entities were stable. More than 50 percent of the nation's fourteen to seventeen-year-olds attended school, and that number rose to more than 65 percent by 1940. Teachers' salaries, though modest, remained steady, and only

funding for capital improvements was noticeably affected. The "Dick and Jane" books debuted in 1931, enabling schoolchildren and others to read in a simple and effective way. However, by 1932, budget cuts began, the impact of which was particularly felt by southern schools. Southern states had the highest birthrates and lowest expenditures per pupil in the country. In 1933, for example, every school in fifty of Alabama's sixty-seven counties closed. Schools met these challenges by shifting to shorter school calendars and school days and enacted other initiatives; nonetheless, many areas experienced a loss of up to 40 percent of pre-Depression funding.

In 1932, the U.S. Chamber of Commerce encouraged its membership to advocate eliminating evening schools and kindergarten, establishing shorter school days, and charging tuition for high school. That same year, President Herbert Hoover pledged undiminished support for public education, but replacement federal funding was insufficient, if available at all. The earlier support that education enjoyed from the corporate sector was gone. Furthermore, in many cases, corporations and educational entities clashed over issues of school curricula and educational philosophy. Though desiring to capitalize on the changing demographics of American society, progressivism in education, known as social reconstruction, created concern among business and community leaders that radical elements sought control of the nation's schools in order to redefine society. The notion of progressivism, first initiated by educators and philosophers in response to the failures of businesses and corporations in the United States, as evidenced by the economic conditions in which the country had been mired, created enmity between education and business that influenced both sectors for decades.

The National Education Association (NEA) remained the most significant group in determining educational policy. The NEA recognized the public's concerns about the state of education and identified curricular relevance and character education as worthy areas to emphasize. As certain business leaders feared, some in the NEA attempted to restructure education, working with the premise that schools had not served ordinary persons as well as they had served the wealthy. Though this movement never fully took hold during the decade and was essentially a moot point as the country braced for World War II, it did help cement an impression that

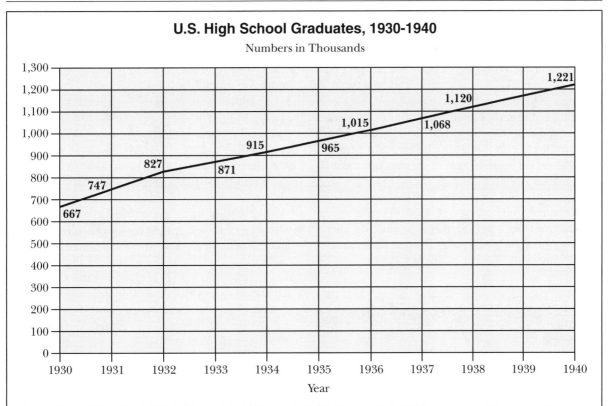

U.S. High School Graduates, 1930-1940

Numbers in Thousands

Source: Historical Statistics of the United States: Colonial Times to 1970. Washington, D.C.: U.S. Department of Commerce, Bureau of the Census, 1975, p. 379.

Note: Numbers for 1939 are unavailable.

educators were among the most liberal elements of society. In fact, twenty-one states required teachers to sign an oath of allegiance to American ideals.

Federal involvement in education increased during the Roosevelt administration in the form of several programs. The Civilian Conservation Corps (CCC) provided camps that involved young people in manual labor during the day and an evening program of practical education. In 1935, the National Youth Administration (NYA) encouraged school as a place for youth to be, offering six dollars per month to attend high school and promoting school service projects. During the 1930's, the film and radio industries provided education to the public. Concerned about the messages that films were disseminating, schools responded with the development of "appreciation" courses and study guides to help students select films with a positive benefit to their lives.

Challenges to the youth of the United States became the focus for the latter half of the decade. Seg-

regation persisted throughout the decade, and African Americans had fewer educational opportunities than Caucasians. Not only were school conditions for African Americans substandard in many cases, but also teacher quality and pay did not reflect the community standard for white students. However, one consequence of the Depression was that African Americans eventually received greater proportional benefits in education compared to Caucasians. Northern communities eliminated segregated schools if only to save money; southern communities sought to provide "separate but equal" conditions.

Some saw the growing restlessness of American youth as a bigger issue than the stock market crash, and schools began to implement counseling programs. As much as 40 percent of the nation's youth wanting to work could not finds jobs, so school remained the most viable productive setting for the country's young people. Nonetheless, most agreed on the necessity of some type of reform; therefore, school curricula moved toward a three-pronged approach: college preparation, vocational preparation, and life education. Though twenty-six states had legislation requiring instruction for special-needs children, only four were adequately funded. Attempts to extend ten years of public education to students regardless of economic condition gained momentum. Eventually, the secondary school enrollment for the decade grew to 6.5 million students by 1940, an increase of nearly 45 percent from ten years earlier.

As the Dust Bowl drove families westward, school enrollment patterns created challenges to developing communities. For example, Bakersfield, California, experienced a 300 percent increase in school enrollment from 1935 to 1940. By 1938, the federal government had spent almost $2.5 billion through the CCC, NYA, and the Works Progress Administration (WPA). However, the onset of World War II eliminated the issue of unemployed youth and delayed the return of educational funding for teacher pay and improved working conditions.

Colleges and Universities American colleges and universities had experienced a period of growth prior to the Great Depression, and, in some instances, as the result of large philanthropic gifts, institutional prestige was enhanced. Many saw the nation's colleges and universities as overtly liberal educational establishments. Many faculty members spoke openly and critically about issues affecting modern society; thus, the modern American university became characterized by a liberal workforce often at odds with what the country needed to escape from the economic challenges of the day. Because the wealthy remained able to afford the best educational experiences available, corporate sectors of the United States showed concern for the influences of higher education on the next generation of business leaders. Nevertheless, the leading institutions continued to prepare their graduates for places of service with established social institutions, such as business and professional sectors, and less so for roles as social reconstructionists. In general, higher education suffered less than other portions of the economy from the economic conditions because of the growth in facilities the previous decade. Furthermore, the high salaries of instructional staff could be supplemented with teaching assistants and postdoctoral fellows.

Most continued to consider a college degree a means to a better quality of life and representative of job security. For many, that meant a college should provide a residential experience and a range of extracurricular activities. However, progressive educators began to critique barriers to college for those from lower socioeconomic conditions and reductions in the disparity of educational experiences. During the 1930's, elite northeastern institutions continued to use the nonmerit criteria for admission. The College Education Examination Board developed college entrance exams, and the Graduate Record Exam became available for determining eligibility for postbaccalaureate opportunity. Graduate education progressed during the decade, as American universities earned worldwide recognition for

This Works Progress Administration flier promoting the importance of reading represented an ongoing effort to encourage the education of American youth. (Library of Congress)

the scientific research they conducted. In 1930, more than two thousand doctoral degrees were granted and more than fifty thousand students nationwide were enrolled in graduate programs of study.

College students became involved in various social issues, protesting mandatory Reserve Officer Training Corps courses and striking against exploitive work conditions. The Depression afforded a sobering reality that many jobs for which students had prepared might not be available or as lucrative as they had once been. In one sense, however, the ideals of American higher education flourished; higher education offered hope that the adversity of the Depression era could be overcome. By 1937, college attendance was 1,250,000, 500 percent above its 1917 level. Of the traditional college age group, 15 percent were enrolled in a postsecondary institution.

During this time, American colleges and universities compared their models of curriculum and professional preparation with European counterparts. In the previous decade, a decline occurred in the two-year model for state teacher's colleges, which increased the broader educational foundation for beginning teachers. College attendance patterns held steady through 1932 when they experienced their first drop since the onset of World War I. By 1934, national work-study programs were implemented through the Federal Emergency Relief Administration. The National Youth Administration, in addition to giving financial support for high school attendance, provided eligible college students fifteen dollars per month to help defray college expenses. Eventually, the rising numbers of high school graduates forced the development of other forms of postsecondary training. During the 1930's,

---

Canadian Postsecondary Education in the 1930's

In 1930, Canada's colleges and universities enrolled about thirty-three thousand students, or about 2.8 percent of the college-age population (less than one-tenth of the rate for the early twenty-first century). Although not all students came from affluent backgrounds, they were generally middle-class, and only a tiny minority came from the working classes. Almost no financial assistance for students was available in the country. With the beginning of the Depression, many students were forced to drop out, and graduation did not provide many job opportunities. In 1934, the University of Saskatchewan accepted promissory notes from one-third of the students, because of their inability to pay the fees. Between 1930 and 1935, the operating revenues of universities decreased between 30 and 40 percent, requiring cuts in programs and operating budgets. Nonetheless, enrollment rose by about 10 percent during the decade, and only a few small institutions were forced to close their doors. Despite the hard times, there were not many left-wing student groups, and the number of moderate students far outnumbered the radicals.

In comparison with many other professional groups, college professors did not do badly during the Depression. A 1937 national survey found that three-quarters of professors had incomes of more than $2,500; the average national wage at the time was about $965. Many universities, nevertheless, reduced professors' salaries, and the University of Manitoba suspended tenure in 1934. Universities hired almost no new full-time faculty, and teaching loads were usually increased to five or six courses. A substantial number of professors had left-wing ideas, and according to Michiel Horn's book *Academic Freedom in Canada: A History*, leftists who were outspoken were frequently vulnerable. While most of them were able to keep their jobs, some prominent professors, such as Eugene Forsy and Leonard Marsh at McGill University, were terminated.

Thomas Tandy Lewis

---

junior colleges began offering coursework in career and vocational fields and enabled students in their communities to choose between college and occupational programs of study.

Impact Eventually, American schools overcame the drastic effects of the Depression and emerged as institutions that shaped American ideals and character for the pupils attending them. Though tension remained as conservatives and business leaders wrangled over funding and curricular emphases, the influence of progressive educators remained a noticeable force. American higher education during the decade was evolving. Educational institutions underwent changes to or additions of junior colleges and research universities, public and private institutions, and agricultural schools and professional schools. As the country began to rebound economically at the end of the decade, states, alumni, and private philanthropy provided funding for colleges and universities, ensuring the importance of the institution of higher learning for the future.

P. Graham Hatcher

Further Reading

Gutek, Gerald. *Education in the United States: An Historical Perspective.* Boston: Allyn and Bacon, 1991. Covers topics such as child-centered progressivism and educational ideology.

Kliebard, Herbert. *The Struggle for the American Curriculum: 1893-1958.* 3d ed. New York: Routledge Farmer, 2004. Provides background to the debates that characterized educational philosophies of the Great Depression.

Lucas, Christopher. *American Higher Education: A History.* New York: Palgrave Macmillan, 2006. Provides an overview of the impact of the Depression on higher education, including financial, curricular, and campus-life issues.

Moreo, Dominic. *Schools in the Great Depression.* New York: Garland, 2006. Uses the press and periodicals of the time to examine the financial challenges faced in the New York and Seattle schools and the role of the WPA.

Thelin, John. *A History of American Higher Education.* Baltimore: Johns Hopkins University Press, 2004. Covers expansion of and reforms in higher education and popular images of campus life during the Depression.

Tyack, David, Robert Lowe, and Elizabeth Hansor. *Public Schools in Hard Times: The Great Depression and Recent Years.* Cambridge, Mass.: Harvard University Press, 1984. Examination of the impact of the Depression in Chicago, Detroit, and smaller school systems throughout the country.

Urban, Wayne, and Jennings Wagoner. *American Education: A History.* New York: Routledge, 2009. Covers school finance, governmental involvement, educational radicalism, progressivism, and teachers' roles during the Depression.

See also   Beard, Charles A.; Business and the economy in the United States; Dewey, John; Great Depression in the United States; National Youth Administration; Philosophy and philosophers; Radio in the United States; Unemployment in the United States; Works Progress Administration.

■ Einstein, Albert

Identification   German-born American physicist
Born   March 14, 1879; Ulm, Württemberg, Germany
Died   April 18, 1955; Princeton, New Jersey

Einstein developed the theory of relativity. He made several contributions to quantum mechanics but criticized the theory severely. He supported numerous leftist, pacifist, and racial-equality causes. He not only discovered the mass-energy equation that makes nuclear energy possible but also signed the letter to President Franklin D. Roosevelt that triggered work on the atomic bomb.

In December, 1930, Albert Einstein visited the United States, and in 1931, he taught at the California Institute of Technology in Pasadena. With the rise of Adolf Hitler in Germany in 1933, Einstein decided to stay in the United States and settled at Princeton's Institute for Advanced Study. He continued his unsuccessful search for a unified field theory extending his general relativity theory of gravitation to electricity and magnetism. He also made profound criticisms of the theory known as quantum mechanics, developed to describe the motion of subatomic particles, the implications of which were not fully realized until decades later.

Science   In 1935, Einstein published what became known as the "EPR" paper with Boris Podolsky and Nathan Rosen, entitled "Can the Quantum Mechanical Description of Reality Be Complete?," a question to which Einstein and his coauthors gave a negative answer. In the paper, they consider a correlated pair of electrons that travel far apart. Measuring the spin of one of the pair should produce the spin of the other, because such pairs have opposite spins. However, according to Niels Bohr's Copenhagen interpretation of quantum mechanics, the electron gets only a determinate spin when it is measured. If the electrons are at far ends of the universe from each other when the measurement is made, measuring one makes the other pop into the opposite spin, instantaneously. Thus, no causal connection traveling at the speed of light or less can tell the second electron that the first one is being measured or what its spin turns out to be. Einstein called this "spooky action at a distance." For Einstein, this showed quantum mechanics to be inherently incomplete. Decades later, this situation was seen simply as showing extreme "quantum weirdness" and "entanglement." More than three decades after Einstein's paper, a different version of this situation was experimentally tested, showing that subatomic particles really do behave in this strange fashion.

Einstein, despite earlier major contributions to quantum mechanics, always opposed the randomness of and the observer's influences on results of measurement resulting from the standard (Copenhagen) interpretation of the theory. He summarized his objections with "God does not play dice," and "God is sophisticated but not perverse." (The latter phrase stands above the entrance to the Princeton Institute for Advanced Study.)

Throughout this period, to the last day of his life, Einstein continued his unsuccessful search for a unified field theory to unite gravity and electromagnetism in a single geometrical theory. The public followed without understanding Einstein's heroic struggle. The *New York Herald Tribune* newspaper even published the long equations of one attempt, claiming, wrongly, that they formed a key to the riddles of the universe.

During his 1931 visit to Caltech, Einstein met with Edwin Powell Hubble, whose evidence on the red shift of light from receding galaxies showed that the universe is expanding from a small starting volume. This went against Einstein's preference for an unchanging universe, and he considered the cosmological constant he had earlier introduced to guarantee the universe's constant size to be the greatest blunder of his life.

In 1935, the same year as "EPR," Einstein also published, with Rosen, a paper on what was later called the "Einstein-Rosen bridge," a tiny tube that connected otherwise distant regions of space-time. This was a forerunner of what came to be called "wormholes" in physics and science fiction. Einstein never accepted the idea of large-scale black holes developed by Subrahmanyan Chandrasekhar and J. Robert Oppenheimer during the 1930's.

Politics Einstein was active in politics in addition to physics. Throughout the 1930's, he supported unions, equality of races, pacifism, and other causes on the left. At the beginning of the decade he wrote letters in favor of the Scottsboro Boys, a group of African Americans wrongly accused of raping a white woman who later recanted, and for Tom Mooney, a union organizer falsely imprisoned for murder. When African American singer Marian Anderson was refused a hotel room in 1937, Einstein had her stay at his house.

Einstein lent his support to various peace movements, to the Jewish Zionist cause, and to the Republican loyalists fighting Francisco Franco in the Spanish Civil War. In California, Einstein befriended the author and leftist political candidate Upton Sinclair, and supported the minimum wage and old-age pensions before they were realities in the United States. Einstein's letters of support and signatures on petitions for leftist causes caused opposition. A women's

Albert Einstein after being sworn in as an American citizen. (Library of Congress)

group tried to prevent his admission to the United States in 1932. The Dies Committee and the Federal Bureau of Investigation received letters falsely accusing Einstein of adherence to communism. Though a pacifist until Hitler's ascension, in August, 1939, Einstein codrafted and signed the letter to President Roosevelt that initiated the atomic bomb project.

Impact Einstein's work on special relativity led to the famous convertibility of mass into energy, which in turn led to the possibility of the atomic bomb. Einstein's theory of general relativity began to be extensively developed only during the 1960's, with theoretical developments such as black holes and wormholes and with new instrumental measurements and tests. The "EPR" article set the agenda for discussions about the foundations of quantum mechanics. Einstein's dream of a unified field theory was ignored by particle physicists during the last two decades of his life but was revived during the 1970's in string theory, which claims to unify gravity with the other forces in a single, geometrical theory. Einstein the humanist, civil libertarian, and Zionist was an inspiration to many around the world who supported democratic, pacifist, and leftist causes.

Val Dusek

Further Reading

Brian, Denis. *The Unexpected Einstein: The Real Man Behind the Icon.* Hoboken, N.J.: J. Wiley, 2005. Lends an intimate view of Einstein's life, thoughts, and personality based on interviews with friends and associates.

Einstein, Albert. *Out of My Later Years.* 1950. Rev. ed. Westport, Conn.: Greenwood Press, 1970. Covers Einstein's writings during the 1930's and 1940's. Highlights his stance on philosophical, political, social, and scientific issues.

Einstein, Albert, and Leopold Infeld. *The Evolution of Physics.* 1938. New ed. New York: Simon & Schuster, 1961. Highlights the period from the rise of the mechanical philosophy to relativity and quanta. Einstein's thoughts are clear and accessible.

Isaacson, Walter. *Einstein: His Life and Universe.* New York: Simon & Schuster, 2007. Addresses the importance of intellectual and individual freedom for Einstein and discusses how his rebellious nature formed his scientific imagination.

Robinson, Andrew, et al. *Einstein: A Hundred Years of Relativity.* New York: Harry N. Abrams, 2005. Released to commemorate the one-hundredth anniversary of Einstein's theory of relativity. Includes essays by prominent physicists.

See also Astronomy; Black hole theory; Civil rights and liberties in the United States; Immigration to the United States; Jews in the United States; Jim Crow segregation; Nuclear fission; Peace movement; Physics; Racial discrimination.

■ Elections, Canadian

During the early part of the twentieth century, Canadian domestic politics were typically dominated by the Liberal Party, especially under its leader, William Lyon Mackenzie King. For a short period during the early 1930's, this traditional dominance was broken by the Conservative Party, in the wake of economic depression. However, the Liberals soon reasserted themselves, though patterns of small-party support did vary considerably during the decade.

Canadian federal elections occur every five years, though a parliamentary session may be shorter if the government resigns for some reason. During the 1930's, federal elections were held in 1930 and 1935. Domestic politics in Canada is dominated by the two main parties, the Liberal Party and the Conservative Party, though smaller parties do attract considerable votes on a regional basis from time to time. The elections are only for the Canadian lower house, or House of Commons, in Ottawa, Ontario. There is an upper house, the Senate, whose members are appointed rather than elected. The governor-general appoints on the recommendation of the prime minister, based on a regional apportionment. There are also provincial elections, often but not always coinciding with the federal elections.

The 1930 Election The 1930 election was held as economic depression had brought the comparative prosperity of the 1920's to an end. The Liberals, under King, had taken credit for the prosperity; inevitably, they took much of the blame for the Depression. King was loath to admit the extent of unemployment or the financial assistance the provinces needed to combat this. The Conservatives had been renewed by their rich and vigorous new leader, Richard Bedford Bennett. The Conservatives grasped the extent of the Depression and campaigned hard on promises to grapple with it. Their aim was to break Liberal strongholds in the Western provinces and in Quebec; through a canny use of newspapers and the new medium of radio, they were able to do this.

There were 254 seats up for election for the seventeenth Canadian parliament. The Liberals lost twenty-six seats; the Conservatives gained forty-three, squeezing out the small third party, the Progressives, who were reduced to just three seats. The other small party, a local Alberta Farmers' Party, retained nine seats. In terms of the popular vote, the Conservatives gained 47.8 percent, the Liberals 45.5 percent. The Conservatives finished with 134 seats; the Liberals had ninety.

More significant than the national election was the change in traditional voting patterns in the provinces. In all of the Western provinces except for Saskatchewan, the Conservatives outvoted the Liberals, and in Liberal-dominated Quebec, they managed to win twenty-four seats. This left the Liberals with forty seats in Quebec, effectively one-half of their seats in the new parliament. The Conservatives had become a nationwide party.

The 1935 Election　Under Bennett, the Conservatives failed to manage the depressed economy. At first, Bennett had opted for high tariffs with little other intervention from the center. Later, he changed his policies to ones similar to President Franklin D. Roosevelt's New Deal policies. However, by then it was too late to reunite his divided party or convince the voters. The election result was an overwhelming defeat for the Conservatives.

Among the smaller parties, the Progressives and the Alberta farmers disintegrated but were replaced in the West by two other parties. The longer-lasting of these was the so-called Co-operative Commonwealth Federation (CCF) a non-Marxist socialist party, similar to certain Fabian elements of Great Britain's Labour Party. Formed in 1932 at Calgary, the party adhered to policies drawn up during the 1933 Regina Manifesto. Its leader was James Shaver Woodsworth, a

pacifist with parliamentary experience. The existence of a socialist party hampered the incipient Communist Party of Canada, which failed to garner more than a handful of votes throughout the decade.

The other small party to emerge was the Social Credit Party in Alberta, formed in 1932. It was based on a radical economic theory devised by William Aberhart, a fundamentalist radio preacher turned politician.

Because of the collapse of the Conservative vote, King's Liberals gained eighty-three seats, while the Conservatives lost ninety-five, ending up with a pal-

This political cartoon from a March, 1931, edition of the Montreal Star *depicts outgoing Canadian prime minister William Lyon Mackenzie King dropping off a basket filled with his administrations mistakes on the doorstep of the Richard Bedford Bennett administration, which was elected to power in 1930.* (Library and Archives Canada)

try thirty-nine seats, their lowest ever representation up to that date. The Social Credit Party swept Alberta, gaining seventeen seats, while the CCF had to be content with seven seats, even though they topped the polls overall in British Columbia. Apart from those two provinces, the Liberals won all the provinces, and their gains were especially large in Quebec. The Conservative representation was almost all based in Ontario.

Provincial Elections In Canada's constitution, drawn up at the passing of the British North America Act of 1867 (now known as the Constitution Act of 1867), various civic powers were divided fairly evenly between the federal parliament and the provinces. This meant that provincial elections, especially in the larger provinces, such as Ontario and Quebec, could have impact on the federal government. Often provincial premiers wielded considerable political power outside their own province; these included Ontario's Liberal Mitchell Hepburn and Quebec's Conservative Maurice Duplessis, who was premier five times after 1936.

Canadians often voted for one party at the federal elections and another at the provincial to maintain some sort of balance of power. During the 1930 election, this was hardly so. For example, Conservative provincial governments were returned in British Columbia in 1928, ahead of the national trend, and in Nova Scotia, where they only lasted three years. Against this, however, in the 1931 Quebec election, the Conservatives lost to the Liberals. However, in 1936, under Duplessis, the Conservatives managed to oust the Liberals after thirty-nine years.

In Alberta, the United Farmers Association (UFA) under John Edward Brownlee won in the 1930 provincial election, but scandal and economics brought the party down for good; it was replaced by the Social Credit Party in the 1935 election after a fourteen-year reign, a reflection of the Social Credit Party's success in the federal elections. In the Alberta parliament, the Social Credit Party gained fifty-six out of a possible sixty-three seats. Elsewhere, the CCF made more modest gains; for example, in the 1933 British Columbia elections, the party gained more than 30 percent of the popular vote.

Impact The pattern established at the 1935 election continued into the next decade. The main change was in the Conservative Party, which voted in a new leader, Robert Manion, in 1938. Perhaps taking a cue from the national government in the United Kingdom, he changed the Conservatives into the National Government Party, as the country entered World War II. However, the mood of the country was to stick to the tried and trusted Liberals, still under King, in 1940 and in subsequent elections. The National Government Party declined further, in Quebec especially, losing all their seats there in the 1940 elections. The smaller parties survived, although the Social Credit Party had to ally itself with a fifth party, New Democracy. Even so, it lost one-half of its seats in the 1940 election. All these smaller parties continued to draw support from the Western provinces only.

David Barratt

Further Reading

Brimelow, Peter. *The Patriot Game.* Toronto: Key Porter, 1986. Examines political voting patterns in Canada.

Morton, Desmond. *A Short History of Canada.* 6th ed. Toronto: McLelland & Stewart, 2006. Sound overall history that places the 1930's in a wider context.

Sayers, Anthony M. *Parties, Candidates, and Constituency Campaigns in Canadian Elections.* Vancouver: University of British Columbia Press, 1999. Systematic analysis of constituency campaigns, the nature of local political associations, and the selection of candidates.

Scarrow, Howard A. "Federal-Provincial Voting Patterns in Canada." *The Canadian Journal of Economics and Political Science* 26, no. 2 (May, 1960): 289-298. Examines theories of voting in national and local elections.

Soward, Frederic H. "The Canadian Elections of 1930." *The American Political Science Review* 24, no. 2 (November, 1930): 995-1000. Scholarly analysis of the 1930 campaign.

See also Demographics of Canada; King, William Lyon Mackenzie; Socialist parties.

■ Elections of 1930, 1934, and 1938, U.S.

The Events Congressional, state, and community elections held in even-numbered years between presidential elections

Dates November 5, 1934; November 5, 1938

Midterm elections are usually regarded as indicators of the success or popularity of the president elected (or reelected) two years previously. Voter turnout is generally lower in midterm elections, and often a party that has previously captured the presidency will lose seats in Congress. Presidential administrations rely on their parties to gain or keep seats in order pass their programs. During the 1930's, these elections were critical to the implementation of New Deal programs.

After nearly a decade of enjoying steadily increasing prosperity, American voters were alarmed by the unexpected world economic downturn triggered by the stock market crash of 1929, and they naturally turned against the incumbent Republican Party in the national elections throughout the 1930's. In the midterm elections of 1930, Republicans suffered their first major setbacks. By the time of Franklin D. Roosevelt's election to the presidency in November, 1932, more than fourteen million Americans were unemployed. By late summer of 1934, a few months before the midterm congressional elections, eleven million of these citizens had gone back to work; some were employed in the private sector, but most were employed by New Deal programs such as the Civil Works Administration, the Civilian Conservation Corps, the Public Works Administration, and the Federal Emergency Relief Administration.

The 1930 Election Occurring almost exactly one year after the great stock market crash of October, 1929, the midterm elections of November, 1930, represented the first of a series of major setbacks to the Republican Party, which had held the White House since 1921. Going into these elections, Herbert Hoover was in the second year of what would prove to be a one-term presidency, and his party had substantial majorities in both houses of Congress. Republicans had been popular during the boom years of the 1920's, but voters turned against them as the Great Depression was developing because of the apparent inability of the Republican-led Congress and the Hoover administration to reverse the na-

tional economic decline. The party was also in disfavor because of its support of the unpopular Hawley-Smoot Tariff Act that Congress had passed in June, 1930. That Republican-spawned law raised tariffs on imports to unprecedented levels to help protect domestic sales of American farm products, but it also prompted foreign retaliation against American exports and aggravated the national economic decline. The Republican Party was also losing supporters because of its identification with Prohibition, which was becoming increasingly unpopular. By late 1930, the Democrats were thus poised for major gains. In the November elections, Republicans lost eight Senate seats and fifty-two House seats to the Democrats but nevertheless retained narrow majorities in both houses. Voters were, however, discriminating, as virtually all the defeated Republican legislators were those identified with conservative economic policies. Most Republicans identified with liberal and progressive policies were reelected. In the national elections that were to follow, the Republicans would suffer broader losses, as the Democrats would go on to build large majorities in both houses.

The 1930 elections also had other important consequences. The Republicans lost six governorships to the Democrats and saw major declines in seats in state legislative bodies. Roosevelt's reelection as governor of New York helped ensure he would be the leading candidate for the Democratic presidential nomination two years later, when voters would turn against Republicans in much larger numbers.

The 1934 Election Roosevelt hoped to make the 1934 election a referendum on the New Deal, so he campaigned around the country at various sites where New Deal programs had put people to work, including Bonneville Dam and Glacier National Park.

The challenge for Roosevelt was to present the New Deal as a successful, moderate program that most Americans would perceive as something beneficial and not extreme. By 1934, the administration faced criticism from the left, which considered Roosevelt's policies to be insufficient for the poor and unemployed, and from the right, which perceived the policies to be too radical. Public figures such as Senator Huey Long, Francis E. Townsend, and Charles E. Coughlin had proposed alternatives to Roosevelt's policies that would have ostensibly done much more than the New Deal did for the poor and elderly. From the right, some Republicans and conservative Democrats accused the administration of trying to make the United States more like the Soviet Union.

California's Gubernatorial Election One example of the ways in which both extremes posed an electoral threat for the proponents of the New Deal came in the California gubernatorial election. Muckraking writer and social critic Upton Sinclair ran for governor as a Democrat, proposing the End Poverty in California program, which would have departed considerably from traditional economic and business practices. Sinclair hoped for Roosevelt's endorsement, but Roosevelt, fearful of doing anything that would prompt critics to label the New Deal as radical, quietly declined to help. Meanwhile, the California business community became alarmed. Louis B. Mayer, the head of Metro-Goldwyn-Mayer (MGM) motion pictures, launched a fund-raising campaign for Sinclair's Republican opponent Frank Merriam. MGM employees, including famous actors, who did not yet have a union, were required to contribute a day's salary to the fund. Sinclair was defeated, although a third-party Progressive Party candidate siphoned enough prolabor votes that the results might have been different in a two-person race.

Harry S. Truman's Election in Missouri Not all elections around the country were specifically focused on Washington, D.C. Some races depended more on the work of local political machines than on the president. One of these races was for one of the senate seats from Missouri, which changed hands in 1934, bringing future president Harry S. Truman to Washington, D.C. Truman had been a county judge in Missouri with loyalties to the Thomas Joseph Pendergast machine in Kansas City. After an unsuccessful gubernatorial campaign, he became the Pendergast candidate in the 1934 Democratic senatorial primaries. While he may have won the primary as the result of Pendergast's help, he also had statewide popularity because of his role as president of the county judges' association and because of his affiliation with the Masons. Roosevelt did not need to campaign in Missouri—in fact, Roosevelt took little notice of Truman until years later—because Truman's Republican opponent, Roscoe C. Patterson, made the New Deal an issue and campaigned against it, invoking threats of dictatorship, socialism, and communism.

Results of the 1934 Elections Usually the party of newly elected presidents loses seats in the following congressional election, and this was expected in 1934. Vice President John Nance Garner predicted the Democrats would lose only thirty-seven House seats, which would amount to a victory for the administration. Instead, the Democrats actually won nine House seats, while the Republicans lost fourteen; five others went to Progressive Party and Farmer-Labor Party candidates. In the Senate the Democrats increased their majority from fifty-nine to sixty-seven.

The results seemed to endorse the New Deal, and one critic of the administration called the election a coronation for Roosevelt. However, the election did not promise an easy time for additional New Deal legislation because some of the Democrats in Congress were conservative southerners, others were fairly militant young progressives, and others were more traditional progressives with ideas from earlier times. These different groups disagreed much of the time.

Prelude to the 1938 Election Despite continuing opposition on both the right and the left, Roosevelt remained popular and was reelected in a landslide in 1936, gaining a larger Democratic majority in Congress at the same time. However, a number of events threatened continued success in the congressional elections for 1938. After the 1936 elections the administration became more sensitive to charges of excess spending and began to reduce funding for some of the New Deal programs that had kept people employed. Also, the public became more cautious with personal spending, keeping more money in savings but out of circulation. The result was a recession in 1937.

Meanwhile, in 1936, the Supreme Court had begun to declare a number of New Deal programs unconstitutional. With his reelection campaign safely over, Roosevelt responded in 1937. In February, he announced a plan to speed cases through the federal courts, including the Supreme Court. This bill proposed allowing the president to appoint additional justices to the courts, depending on the number of sitting justices who were more than seventy years old. The passage of the bill would have allowed Roosevelt to appoint six additional justices to the Supreme Court of 1937, presumably creating a majority in support of New Deal programs. Congressional reaction was hostile, especially because Roosevelt had announced the plan without first alerting congressional leaders. John O'Connor, a Democratic congressman from New York and chairperson of the House Ways and Means Committee, stalled the bill for a long time; eventually the bill was buried in committee by a vote in the Senate of seventy to twenty.

Roosevelt's Purge Roosevelt decided to use the elections of 1938 as revenge. In that year he began to summon individual congressmen and senators to the White House in order to raise questions about whom he would and would not support in the fall elections. An even more aggressive move was his attempt to use the primaries of that year to purge the party of anti-New Deal Democrats. In a February primary in Florida, he endorsed Claude Pepper, who won by more than 100,000 votes. Emboldened by that success, he actively campaigned against five conservative Democratic senators who opposed his court-packing plan: Millard Tydings, Guy Gillette, Frederick van Nuys, Walter F. George, and Howard W. Smith. Campaigning against George in Georgia, he first reminded voters that as a founder of the spa at Warm Springs he was almost a resident. Then he called the incumbent "my friend" and a good person but not a good senator. In a 1938 fireside chat he used the word "conservative" to describe those who were unwilling to try new ideas when needed, and "liberals" for those who were willing to change with the times. More serious charges of election manipulation were reported in Scripps-Howard newspapers.

In Kentucky, Governor Happy Chandler was prepared to oppose incumbent Senator Alben William Barkley, a Roosevelt favorite, in the primary. Administration critics alleged that Works Progress Administration supervisors in Kentucky were forcing workers to support Barkley as a condition for continuation in the program. However, few historians have given this story much credence.

Results of the 1938 Elections Roosevelt's endorsements resulted in the defeat of John O'Connor and may have helped the reelection of future vice president Barkley from Kentucky and the election of Congressman, and future president, Lyndon B. Johnson from Texas. However, over all, the 1938 election was a setback for the New Deal. Republicans gained eight seats in the Senate and eighty-one in the House. The results made passage of additional New Deal legislation difficult. However, by this time, Roosevelt was already beginning to worry about Adolf Hitler and the situation in Europe, and he needed support from different divisions in Congress in order to begin quiet preparations for a possible war.

Impact The midterm elections of the 1930's led to different results and reflected vastly different moods in the country. The 1934 election increased the support in Congress of Roosevelt's administration and, with the results of the presidential election in 1936, made possible additional legislation, such as the Social Security program, to relieve the pain of the Depression. At the same time, these elections took some of the energy out of more radical plans by leaders such as Long and Townsend. By 1938, the country had become somewhat disillusioned with the New Deal, partly because of the disappointment caused by the recession of 1937. In addition, the results of the 1938 election reflected the country's bitterness over Roosevelt's efforts to manipulate the elections. Finally, the election of more Republican senators, who were mostly isolationist, complicated Roosevelt's efforts to prepare the country for the coming war in Europe.

Timothy C. Frazer

Further Reading

Badger, Anthony J. *The New Deal.* New York: Hill and Wang, 1989. Detailed look at the programs that figured prominently in the elections of 1934 and 1938.

Black, Conrad. *Franklin Delano Roosevelt: Champion of Freedom.* New York: Public Affairs, 2003. Although concerned mainly with foreign policy, the book offers insights on both elections. Its more than 1,100 pages are followed by a 27-page bibliography.

Brand, H. W. *Traitor to His Class: The Privileged Life and Radical Presidency of Franklin Delano Roosevelt.* New York: Doubleday, 2008. Detailed, highly readable biography of Roosevelt's entire life.

Dallek, Robert. *Harry S. Truman.* New York: Henry Holt, 2008. Primarily concerned with Truman's presidency but includes a readable summary of the Missouri senatorial primary elections of 1934.

Davis, Kenneth S. *FDR: The New Deal Years, 1933-1937.* New York: Random House, 1986. Events described herein mostly pertain to the election in 1934.

Ferrell, Robert H. *Truman and Pendergast.* Columbia: University of Missouri Press, 1999. Shows how local issues affected midterm elections, in this case, the Democratic primary. Speculates that machine votes may have helped Truman win the Democratic primary in 1934.

Flynn, John T. *The Roosevelt Myth.* New York: Devin-Adair, 1948. Although strident in his bias against Roosevelt, Flynn does provide some alleged details about how the Roosevelt administration supposedly attempted to use the 1938 Democratic primary elections to punish opponents of the New Deal, especially those who opposed Roosevelt's plan to pack the Court. However, the charges are not always well documented.

Fried, Albert. *FDR and His Enemies.* New York: St. Martin's Press, 1999. Public figures who worried Roosevelt the most, especially heading into midterm and presidential elections, were Coughlin, Long, John L. Lewis, Smith, and Charles A. Lindbergh. Fried outlines Roosevelt's responses to each.

Watkins, T. H. *The Great Depression.* Boston: Little, Brown, 1993. Discusses the elections of 1934 and 1938. Includes a summary of the California gubernatorial race in 1934.

See also Agricultural Adjustment Acts; Brandeis, Louis D.; Business and the economy in the United States; *Carter v. Carter Coal Co.*; Elections of 1932, U.S.; Elections of 1936, U.S.; Farmer-Labor Party of Minnesota; Fireside chats; Garner, John Nance; Supreme Court, U.S.

■ Elections of 1932, U.S.

The Event U.S. presidential and congressional elections

Date November 8, 1932

Franklin D. Roosevelt won the presidency by a landslide margin, and his Democratic Party assumed control of both houses of Congress. The Democratic Party's electoral triumph signaled the end of the dominance of the Republican Party as the majority political faction, dating to 1864, and the advent of a similar period of hegemony by the Democrats, lasting until 1968.

The Great Depression was the predominant issue during the 1932 election. The economic boom of the 1920's, so closely identified with the administration of President Calvin Coolidge, and thus with the Republican Party as a whole, had evaporated during the early months of the Herbert Hoover administration. Hoover, the secretary of commerce under Coolidge, had been elected overwhelmingly in 1928. Dubbed "the Great Engineer," Hoover had gained a reputation as an expert who could devise a solution to remedy any situation. His largely triumphal career had included outstanding accomplishments in the private sector before he catapulted to fame as the de facto director of the Committee for Relief in Belgium; official director of the United States Food Administration, 1917-1918; and secretary of commerce from 1921 until 1928. Riding the wave of prosperity and buttressed by his reputation as a problem solver, Hoover seemed unstoppable.

The stock market crash of October, 1929, and the ensuing Depression transformed the national political complexion. Hoover, though one of the more progressive individuals within the Republican Party, was nonetheless slow to grasp the true depth of the problem, and only belatedly realized that more was needed than conventional laissez-faire economic remedies. His appeals to volunteerism and his attempts to coax big business into reinvesting in the economy and maintaining existing levels in employment and salaries went largely unheeded, and his one innovative initiative, the Reconstruction Finance Corporation, proved to be belated and inadequate.

Republican and Democratic National Conventions

The Republicans convened for the purpose of nominating their electoral ticket from June 14 to 16, 1932, in Chicago, Illinois. Though Hoover had slumped in popularity and a general sense of apprehension and unease prevailed within party ranks, the president and his supporters dominated the party apparatus and would have been difficult to unseat. Those who wished to shake off the liability of an unpopular incumbent placed their hopes in former Maryland senator John Irwin France, but when he faltered in the primaries, some turned to Wisconsin candidate Senator John J. Blaine and former president Coolidge, who was the choice of the ultraconservatives, but who never indicated that he wanted the nomination. Hoover was nominated easily on the first ballot, garnering all but 22½ delegate votes, 13 of which went to his closest rival, Blaine. The in-

U.S. Electoral Vote, 1932

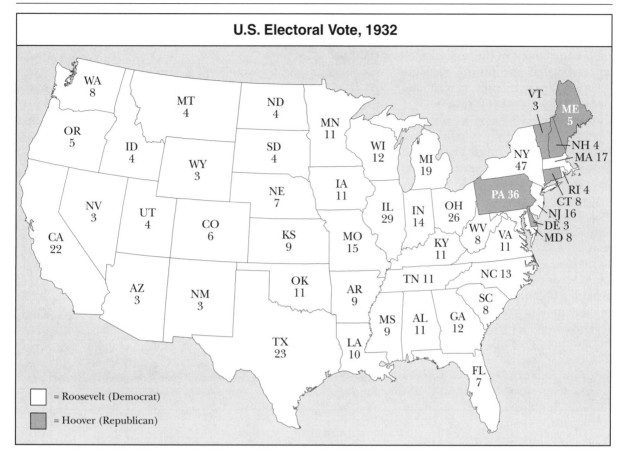

cumbent vice president Charles Curtis of Kansas was likewise renominated.

Chicago was also the site of the Democratic National Convention, which was held from June 30, to July 2, 1932. Unlike the Republican National Convention, the choice for president was not a foregone conclusion. Although the suave, charismatic governor of New York, Franklin D. Roosevelt, was the favorite, he faced strong opposition from Alfred E. Smith, the party's 1928 nominee, and Speaker of the House John Nance Garner of Texas. Smith was supported and bankrolled by the small but highly active, financially conservative branch of the Democratic Party and upset Roosevelt in the Massachusetts primary. Entering the convention, Smith and Garner, who had the backing of publishing tycoon William Randolph Hearst, were able to deny Roosevelt the first ballot nomination. However, the work of Roosevelt's "Brains Trust" advisory team coupled with an alleged political deal with Hearst and Garner, in which Roosevelt offered Garner the vice presiden-

tial nomination, set the stage for a dramatic fourth ballot switch to Roosevelt by the California delegation led by Senator William Gibbs McAdoo. This maneuver led to further defections to Roosevelt and gave the New York governor the nomination at 945 delegates to 190 for Smith. Garner was chosen as Roosevelt's running mate.

The Campaign and November Elections The Democratic strategy was to build their presidential candidate's credibility by instilling a sense of confidence in his commitment to revive the economy. The party also wanted to convey an overall sense of optimism, while not sounding either too conservative or excessively radical. Rexford Guy Tugwell, Raymond Moley, and other speechwriters followed this line of thinking and in doing so, devised some memorable, comforting, but vague phraseology: The promise of a "new deal" for the American people proved the most durable.

By contrast, Hoover seemed tired and listless, and

his campaign was disjointed. His mishandling of the Bonus Army March crisis contributed to the aura of malaise associated with his efforts. Hoover's perceived coldness toward the Bonus Army marchers' petition and his perceived weakness in allowing General Douglas MacArthur to exceed his orders and violently dismantle the group's tent city at Anacostia Flats may have struck the final blow to whatever slim chances his campaign might have had. His continued emphasis on self-help, limited governmental intervention, and a cooperative economic retrenchment along traditional lines came across as lame and too disinterested to effectively pull the nation out of its economic slump.

The November results revealed the full extent of the Republican debacle: The Democrats amassed 472 electoral votes and 22,821,277 popular votes as opposed to totals of 59 and 15,761,254 for the Republicans. The strongest third party candidacies were the Socialist Party, running perpetual candidate Norman Thomas, at 884,885 popular votes, and the Communist Party USA, led by William Z. Foster, at 103,307. In Congress, the Democrats achieved a veto-proof majority, gaining ninety-seven seats in the House of Representatives and thirteen in the Senate.

Impact So crushing was the Democratic victory that Roosevelt felt free to interpret the results as a mandate from the voters for change and experimentation, rather than as a strictly negative reaction against the Depression. The election became a license for the first one hundred days New Deal initiatives that followed. The generally moderate-liberal domestic agenda launched by Roosevelt prevailed as the Democratic agenda well into the years of the Lyndon B. Johnson administration. The Republicans' defeat was such that they remained a marginal force throughout the rest of the 1930's and did not recover their majority-party status until the 1946 elections or their occupancy of the White House until 1953.

Raymond Pierre Hylton

Campaign button for the 1932 Democratic candidate for president, Franklin D. Roosevelt. (Hulton Archive/Getty Images)

Further Reading

Badger, Anthony J. *FDR: The First Hundred Days.* New York: Hill and Wang, 2009. Though the book focuses primarily on the aftermath of the 1932 election, the opening chapter contains a clear and succinct account of the issues and personalities involved in the election.

Dickson, Paul, and Thomas B. Allen. *The Bonus Army: An American Epic.* New York: Walker, 2004. Definitive rendering of the Bonus Army events in Washington, D.C., which may have doomed the Hoover administration.

Ellis, Edward Robb. *A Nation in Torment: The Great American Depression, 1929-1939.* New York: Coward-McCann, 1970. Explains the causes behind the Republican debacle of 1932 but contains little about the process and mechanics of the election itself.

Kennedy, David M. *Freedom from Fear: The American People in Depression and War, 1929-1945.* New York: Oxford University Press, 1999. Paints Roosevelt's ability as a diplomat and conciliator as the reason for the Democratic victory.

McElvaine, Robert S. *The Great Depression: America, 1929-1941*. New York: Three Rivers Press, 1993. The account of the 1932 elections that follows the classic theory that the Democratic victory was a "sure thing." Highly critical of the role played by Smith but laudatory of the role played by Roosevelt's Brains Trust.

Schwarz, Jordan A. *The Interregnum of Despair: Hoover, Congress, and the Depression*. Urbana: University of Illinois Press, 1970. Provides a detailed chapter on the election and is told in an engaging style that focuses on the diverse personalities involved.

Shlaes, Amity. *The Forgotten Man: A New History of the Great Depression*. New York: HarperCollins, 2008. Takes a broad view of the events surrounding the 1932 elections; supplements the account of the political struggle with the salient social, intellectual, and economic currents.

See also Bonus Army March; Brains Trust; Elections of 1930, 1934, and 1938, U.S.; Elections of 1936, U.S.; Garner, John Nance; Great Depression in the United States; Hoover, Herbert; Long, Huey; Rayburn, Sam; Roosevelt, Franklin D.; Smith, Alfred E.

■ Elections of 1936, U.S.

The Event President Franklin D. Roosevelt was reelected, and Democrats increased their congressional majority

Date November 3, 1936

The 1936 election cemented the Democratic Party's dominance in American politics until 1968. Roosevelt's reelection confirmed his immense popularity with the American people and their support of his New Deal programs. The Republican Party continued to suffer from President Herbert Hoover's perceived failure to deal with the Great Depression; voters had little confidence in Republicans' ability to deal with the still-struggling economy.

On November 3, 1936, President Franklin D. Roosevelt of the Democratic Party faced reelection, as did the entire United States House of Representatives and one-third of the Senate. That summer, Roosevelt told one of his advisers, Raymond Moley, that he was the only issue in the campaign. The election was a referendum on Roosevelt's first four years as president. According to government statistics, when Roo-

sevelt became president on March 4, 1933, the unemployment rate was almost 25 percent, industrial production had declined almost 50 percent since 1929, gross domestic product (GDP) had been halved, and one-third of the nation's banks had collapsed. As president, Roosevelt inherited an economy in crisis with no sign of improvement.

New Deal and Roosevelt The New Deal had a mixed record in combating the effects of the Great Depression, but its programs had cut unemployment to 16.9 percent by 1936. Drawing on his charisma and public relations skills, Roosevelt instilled confidence among the American people in their president and government—something Hoover had failed to do. Campaigning for reelection, Roosevelt repeatedly made two points: First, the American people were better off in 1936 than they had been in 1932; and second, the improvements were the result of his New Deal programs, which provided aid to farmers, public works projects for the unemployed, Social Security for the elderly, and relief for banks that saved the financial industry from collapse.

Alluding to Republican president Hoover, who was almost universally despised by Americans as a failure, Roosevelt repeatedly warned of the danger of returning to what he called the old leadership, which had brought the country to the brink of disaster in 1932. Roosevelt also benefited from the unsettling effects of groups such as the American Communist and Socialist parties and demagogues such as Roman Catholic priest Charles E. Coughlin (who voiced anti-Semitic and profascist views on his weekly radio program) and U.S. Senator Huey Long, who promised to "share the wealth" by heavily taxing the rich and redistributing that wealth, thereby guaranteeing to every American a house, a car, a radio, and one thousand dollars. In comparison with the purveyors of such extreme ideologies, Roosevelt and the Democrats seemed a safe choice for most Americans.

Kansas governor Alf Landon, the Republican nominee for president in 1936, appealed to both conservative and progressive Republicans. An oil man and fiscal conservative who had balanced Kansas's budget, Landon had the support of business leaders. He also was a former member of the Bull Moose Party of Theodore Roosevelt and had sponsored measures similar to the New Deal programs during his term as governor. In addition, Republicans felt that Landon's farm-state background might help him win over Western farmers who had voted for Roosevelt in 1932.

Landon's campaign faced two major obstacles: how to combat the popularity of Roosevelt and the New Deal, and how to overcome the legacy of Hoover and convince the American people that the Republicans could do a better job dealing with the economy. Landon and the Republican Party denounced Roosevelt and the Democrats for spending recklessly, running huge budget deficits, and waging an assault on business and free enterprise. However, while denouncing the New Deal, the Republican Party also seemed to be endorsing it by supporting federal relief for the unemployed, Social Security for the elderly, aid to farmers, and the rights of workers to unionize. The campaign appeared ambivalent, if not inconsistent, about the New Deal: Endorsing it clearly was out of the question, but an outright rejection of the popular program would alienate more voters than it attracted. During the

presidential campaign, Landon therefore alternated between attacking the New Deal and supporting Roosevelt's plan, indicating he shared many of the president's political goals.

Compared with Landon, Roosevelt was in a much easier political situation in 1936. After Roosevelt was renominated by his party, he used his acceptance speech to denounce "economy royalists"—big business and the rich—and insist that Americans were fighting to save "a great and precious form of government," implicitly linking the salvation of the Americans with his presidency and the New Deal. Roosevelt ridiculed Republicans who claimed they could do what his administration had done, but cheaper and more efficiently, by reminding voters how much the economy had suffered under Hoover. Roosevelt also noted that conservative ideology demands that injustices be corrected to promote peace, thereby associating his New Deal policies with order and peace at a time of tremendous social upheaval.

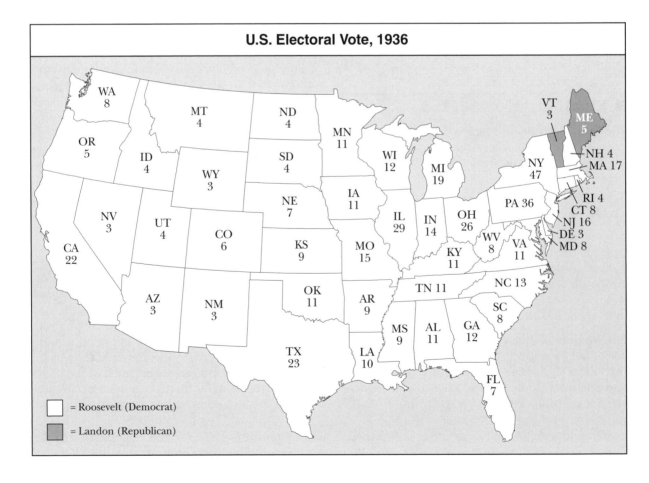

U.S. Electoral Vote, 1936

□ = Roosevelt (Democrat)
▨ = Landon (Republican)

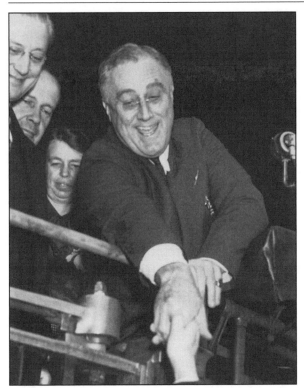

Franklin D. Roosevelt shakes hand with a policeman in Columbus, Ohio, in 1936, after earning his party's nomination for president in Chicago, as Eleanor Roosevelt watches from behind him. (AP/Wide World Photos)

Roosevelt was reelected in a landslide. He won by 27 million votes, carrying all but two states (Maine and Vermont) and winning 60 percent of the popular vote. Landon received only 16 million votes. Roosevelt captured the largest percentage of electoral votes since President James Monroe in 1820. In Congress, the Democratic Party retained control of both houses, gaining twelve seats in the House of Representatives to push its already sizable advantage to a 334-89 majority. The Democrats also gained six seats in the Senate, bringing their total to 75 seats (versus 17 for the Republicans).

Impact   The 1936 election cemented the Democratic Party's dominance in American politics until 1968 by uniting diverse groups into what has been called the New Deal Party System or Coalition. With the exception of business groups, which remained largely loyal to the Republican Party, Roosevelt and his New Deal programs rallied white Southerners, Northern African Americans, farmers, blue-collar and working class voters, intellectuals, and members of labor unions to vote Democratic for more than thirty years. The Democratic Party won all but two presidential elections between 1932 and 1968 and controlled Congress for all but four years (1947-1949 and 1953-1955). For this reason, Roosevelt is known as the Father of the Modern Democratic Party.

Stefan Brooks

Further Reading

Atler, Jonathan. *The Defining Moment: FDR's Hundred Days and the Triumph of Hope.* New York: Simon & Schuster, 2006. An account of how Roosevelt's policies during his first one hundred days in office restored people's trust in the government's ability to deal with the Great Depression.

Flynn, Kathryn. *The New Deal: A Seventy-fifth Anniversary Celebration.* Layton, Utah: Gibbs Smith, 2008. A detailed account of the major New Deal programs enacted during Roosevelt's presidency.

Leuchtenburg, William E. *Franklin Roosevelt and the New Deal, 1933-1940.* New York: Harper & Row, 2009. A comprehensive account of Roosevelt and the New Deal.

Shlaes, Amity. *The Forgotten Man: A New History of the Great Depression.* New York: HarperCollins, 2007. Conservative view of the New Deal, arguing that the New Deal failed and actually prolonged the Great Depression.

Smith, Jean Edward. *FDR.* New York: Random House, 2008. An expanded biography of Roosevelt.

See also   Elections, Canadian; Elections of 1930, 1934, and 1938, U.S.; Elections of 1932, U.S.; Great Depression in the United States; Landon, Alf; New Deal; Roosevelt, Franklin D.

■ Electric razors

Definition   Shaving devices powered by electric motors

By the late 1930's, electric razors were recognized as popular electronic gadgets for the modern man. They reduced much of the fuss of keeping well groomed; did not need water and cream; and were safe, convenient, portable, and reliable.

Canadian Jacob Schick invented the electric razor during the 1920's. Before marketing his invention, he had to wait for an electric motor to be developed that was small enough to fit into a handheld device and had the power to cut through a beard. By 1931, Schick had designed his first marketable razor, which consisted of an oscillating induction motor that drove a sliding cutter mounted inside of a slotted shearing head. That same year, he was granted a U.S. patent for his invention. By the end of 1931, he had sold more than three thousand of his prototype electric razors.

As the market for electric razors expanded, more companies were developing different electric razors, which led to many patent infringements and lawsuits. The Schick Model S was marketed in 1935. Two years later, more than 1.5 million were sold. The Sunbeam Shavemaster, the Rochelle Specialities Electro-Shav, and the Remington Close Shaver were on the market by the end of 1937. The Shavemaster used a universal brush motor with a foil shearing head. The Rolls-Razor Viceroy and Zenith electric razors emerged in Great Britain during the mid-1930's. In 1939, Royal Philips Electronics, based in the Netherlands, launched the first electric razors that used rotating cutters in the head. This razor was invented by electrical engineer Alexandre Horowitz, originally as a single-headed model known as the Philishave, then as a two-headed model. Cutting areas of the early electric razors were rather small, typically only about one-quarter of the size of modern razors.

Impact By 1937, more than 1.5 million electric razors were in use, with a market valued at more than $20 million. As a result of their versatility, electric razors became associated as much with travel as with domestic use. By the late 1930's, they were seen in hotels, trains, ocean liners, and airplanes. They became staples in many people's beauty repertoires. Gradually, the electric razor became a necessity for most men and women throughout the world.

Alvin K. Benson

Further Reading

Levy, Joel. *Really Useful: The Origins of Everyday Things.* Richmond Hill, Ont.: Firefly Books, 2002.

Zaoui, Myriam, and Eric Malka. *The Art of Shaving.* New York: Clarkson Potter, 2002.

See also Fads; Hairstyles; Inventions; Magazines; Physics.

■ Electron microscope

Definition Microscope that uses a beam of electrons instead of light to produce a highly magnified image

While the best light microscopes can achieve magnifications of up to two thousand times, electron microscopes can resolve images at magnifications up to two million times. Since electrons have a much smaller wavelength than electromagnetic radiation, the resolution of an electron microscope is one thousand times greater than a light microscope.

In 1928, German engineer Max Knoll led a team of researchers to improve the design of the cathode ray oscilloscope. In 1931, he and Ernst Ruska used two magnetic lenses to generate magnified images of mesh grids that were placed over the aperture of the anode. This was the first electron microscope. Later in the year, Reinhold Rüdenberg, scientific director of the Siemens company, patented an electrostatic lens electron microscope.

In April, 1932, Ruska proposed a new electron microscope, the transmission electron microscope (TEM), for direct imaging of samples inserted into the microscope. In a TEM, an accelerated, focused beam of electrons is partly scattered as it travels through an ultrathin specimen. The resulting image of the specimen carried by the scattered beam is magnified, focused with magnetic lenses, and recorded by an imaging device, such as a layer of photographic film. In September, 1933, cotton fibers were imaged at magnifications greater than those achieved using light microscopes.

In 1935, Knoll introduced the concept of a scanning electron microscope (SEM). In 1938, Manfred von Ardenne constructed a scanning transmission electron microscope (STEM) by adding scanning coils between two electrostatic lenses of a TEM. The first STEM imaged a zinc oxide crystal at a magnification of eight thousand times. Researchers at Siemens produced the first commercial TEM in 1939. After World War II, Ruska continued to improve the TEM and achieved magnifications of 100,000 times. The SEM was not substantially developed until the late 1960's. Ruska's microscope design is still used in modern, more advanced electron microscopes.

Impact Electron microscopes have become essential tools in biological and physical laboratories.

They are used for examining microorganisms, biological cells, medical biopsy samples, large molecules, crystalline structures, metallic surfaces, and other microscopic features. Industrial applications include inspection, quality assurance, and failure analysis of a variety of materials, such as proper fabrication of semiconductor devices.

Alvin K. Benson

Further Reading

Croft, William J. *Under the Microscope: A Brief History of Microscopy.* Hackensack, N.J.: World Scientific, 2006.

Egerton, Ray F. *Physical Principles of Electron Microscopy: An Introduction to TEM, SEM, and AEM.* New York: Springer, 2008.

See also Fluorescent lighting; Inventions; Medicine; Nobel Prizes; Physics; Polio.

■ Elixir sulfanilamide scandal

The Event   Mass-poisoning tragedy
Date   1937

Approximately one hundred American citizens, many of whom were children, died after consuming a liquid preparation of a popular antibiotic. The company that manufactured this elixir used a toxic, industrial solvent to dissolve the antibiotic but never tested its safety before distributing it. This enormous tragedy ignited a public outrage that spurred the writing and passage of the 1938 Federal Food, Drug, and Cosmetic Act.

In November, 1936, President Franklin D. Roosevelt's son, Franklin, Jr., was cured of a serious sinus and throat infection with the sulfur-containing antibiotic sulfanilamide. This initiated an enthusiastic demand for this "miracle" drug in the United States. In 1937, an exhaustive animal and clinical study published in the *Journal of the American Medical Society* endorsed sulfanilamide as a treatment for streptococcal infections. Soon thereafter competing brands of sulfanilamide flooded the American drug market.

In June, 1937, a salesman for the S. E. Massengill Company of Bristol, Tennessee, reported a demand for a liquid preparation of this popular antibiotic, because the solid form of the drug was distasteful. Sulfanilamide does not dissolve easily, but Massengill's head chemist, Harold Cole Watkins, found that

the clear, odorless, but highly toxic liquid diethylene glycol could dissolve it. Unbeknownst to Watkins, the Food and Drug Administration (FDA) had advised against the use of glycols in foods, and published reports from other labs that showed that diethylene glycol was toxic to laboratory animals. Watkins used raspberry extract and saccharine to sweeten the elixir and increase its palatability. Because the law did not require Massengill to test the safety or efficacy of the preparation before distributing it, the company tested only the color, taste, and smell of the solution before shipping it.

Beginning on September 4, 1937, Massengill shipped 633 commercial lots of elixir sulfanilamide and delivered some 671 samples to physicians nationwide. The product labels on the elixir containers failed to list any of the ingredients other than sulfanilamide.

The first reported elixir-related deaths were in Tulsa, Oklahoma, in early October. By mid-October, 1937, additional deaths were reported in the Deep South and Illinois. After consuming the elixir, patients initially experienced nausea and vomiting, followed by a progressive cessation of urine output, accompanied by severe back and abdominal pain, culminating in death two to seven days later. Autopsies revealed extensive kidney damage, and poisoning was suspected. The American Medical Association determined on October 12, 1937, that Massengill's elixir contained substantial amounts of diethylene glycol. Animal experiments conducted at the University of Chicago firmly established that diethylene glycol was the poisoning agent in the elixir.

On October 15, 1937, Massengill sent approximately 1,100 telegrams to elixir consignees that directed them to return all unused stocks at the company's expense, but failed to mention the toxicity of the product. That same day, FDA field inspectors began the herculean task of recalling and confiscating the distributed elixir bottles, even while reports of elixir-induced deaths continued to mount nationally. By the end of October, exacting searches helped recover 228 of the 240 gallons of elixir produced. The last elixir victim died on October 31. Overall elixir poisoning killed more than one hundred people, 30 percent of whom were children and infants.

Massengill paid more than one-half million dollars in claims, and the owner, Samuel E. Massengill, pled guilty to 174 counts of adulterating and misbranding elixir sulfanilamide. Nevertheless, the company refused to admit liability. On January 17, 1939, Watkins, the chemist who designed the elixir, committed suicide.

Impact The elixir sulfanilamide scandal eroded the foundational trust between patients and physicians. Massengill had used the public as guinea pigs for untested drug concoctions and was completely unwilling to admit that they had done anything wrong. The public was outraged.

This scandal also revealed the weaknesses in the 1906 Pure Food and Drug Act. The FDA had little authority to act and was only able to stop the distribution of the elixir bottles on a mislabeling charge, because elixirs normally contain alcohol and the Massengill elixir contained no alcohol. Otherwise, the FDA would have been powerless to confiscate the poisonous elixir. Congress responded by passing the 1938 Federal Food, Drug, and Cosmetic Act, which required companies to perform safety tests on their products and submit their results to the FDA before they were allowed to market them.

Michael A. Buratovich

Further Reading

Braithwaite, John. *Corporate Crime in the Pharmaceutical Industry.* London: Routledge & Kegan Paul, 1984.

Ghosh, Tapash, and Bhaskana R. Jasti. *Theory and Practice of Contemporary Pharmaceutics.* Boca Raton, Fla.: CRC Press, 2004.

Wax, Paul. "Elixirs, Diluents and the Passage of the 1938 Federal Food, Drug, and Cosmetic Act." *Annals of Internal Medicine* 122 (1995): 456-461.

See also Federal Food, Drug, and Cosmetic Act of 1938; Health care; Medicine; Roosevelt, Franklin D.

■ Ellington, Duke

Identification American jazz bandleader, composer, and pianist
Born April 29, 1899; Washington, D.C.
Died May 24, 1974; New York, New York

During the 1930's, swing dance bands reigned supreme in American culture. In contrast, Ellington composed and performed music of a different genre that consisted of a mixture of jazz and symphonic elements. He described it as simply "American music." His compositions were, paradoxically, both improvisational and carefully constructed with innovative concepts of harmony and orchestration. He was a jazz giant who influenced the musical world for all subsequent generations.

From 1927 to 1931, Duke Ellington's band enjoyed a steady engagement at Harlem's famous Cotton Club. Weekly radio shows and nightly white audiences provided Ellington with the exposure he needed. The band's performances at the Cotton Club included revues and vaudeville and burlesque shows and featured some of the greatest entertainers of the period, such as Florenz Ziegfeld, Jimmy Durante, Al Jolson, Ruby Keeler, and others.

From 1927 to 1937, Ellington maintained a highly successful partnership with Irving Mills, an agent and publisher. Mills managed recording sessions with Brunswick Records, Columbia Records, and Victor Records and promoted the band, while Ellington published jazz arrangements of popular songs by Hoagy Carmichael and Harold Arlen in addition to his own compositions.

Although the lingering Depression of the early 1930's affected musicians in the recording industry severely, Ellington survived by performing concerts on the road, which included trips to England in 1933 and mainland Europe in 1934. The resulting recognition and acclaim elevated Ellington and his music to an international level. Estimates indicate that in Ellington's career, his band performed more than twenty thousand concerts outside the United States.

At the height of Ellington's achievements, a devastating occurrence interrupted his career: His mother, Daisy, died of cancer in 1935. Ellington's sense of loss was deep and demoralizing. His despair was so great that it forced him to take a hiatus. To help ease his grief, he ordered $2,000 worth of flowers for Daisy's funeral and a half-ton iron casket that cost $3,500.

Jazz musician Duke Ellington at the piano during the early 1930's. (Redferns/Getty Images)

At the same time, the explosion in popularity of swing bands threatened to ruin Ellington's popularity. Ellington commented that swing music was business, whereas jazz was genuine music. His response to the craze was to form smaller combos from his big band and feature outstanding soloists by composing specific arrangements for them. Among the soloists were saxophonist Johnny Hodges, trumpeters Cootie Williams and Rex Stewart, and clarinetist Barney Bigard, all of whom became celebrated jazz artists. Composing for individual musicians within his band became one of Ellington's specialties.

In 1937, Ellington returned to the Cotton Club and ended his association with Mills. He signed with the renowned William Morris Agency and embarked on a European tour as the decade ended. In 1939, he hired Billy Strayhorn, a lyricist who quickly became his best friend, a prolific arranger, and substitute conductor and pianist as needed. Strayhorn's classical music background in French impressionism and talent for lyrics provided Ellington with an entirely different perspective that lasted into the next decade.

Impact   During the 1930's, Ellington composed countless hit songs, such as "Mood Indigo," "Sophisticated Lady," "Caravan," and "It Don't Mean a Thing If It Ain't Got That Swing." Ellington is widely viewed as one of the most outstanding American composers ever, mentioned in the company of Charles Ives. He composed more than three thousand songs, many of which are considered American classics, in not only jazz circles but also any category. His propensity for unusual instrumental combinations and his gift for melody dominated the music scene during the 1930's. As a composer, pianist, arranger, and bandleader for more than fifty years, Ellington left a legacy of American music that was universal in appeal.

Douglas D. Skinner

Further Reading

Cohen, Harvey G. *Duke Ellington's America.* Chicago: The University of Chicago Press, 2010.

Collier, James Lincoln. *Duke Ellington.* New York: Oxford University Press, 1987.

Howland, John Louis. *"Ellington Uptown": Duke Ellington, James P. Johnson, and the Birth of Concert Jazz.* Ann Arbor: University of Michigan Press, 2009.

Rattenbury, Ken. *Duke Ellington, Jazz Composer.* London: Yale University Press, 1993.

See also Basie, Count; Dorsey, Tommy; Fitzgerald, Ella; Goodman, Benny; Holiday, Billie; Miller, Glenn; Music: Jazz; Music: Popular; Recording industry; Shaw, Artie.

■ Empire State Building

Identification Skyscraper that was the world's tallest building for forty-one years, measuring 1,453 feet tall

Date Construction began March 17, 1930; opened to the public on May 1, 1931

Place Thirty-fourth Street and Fifth Avenue, New York City

The Empire State Building is one of the most famous structures in the world and was the world's tallest building for more than forty years, from 1931 until the completion of the North Tower of the World Trade Center in 1972.

The design for the iconic Empire State Building was created in two weeks by William F. Lamb of the architectural firm Shreve, Lamb and Harmon. Lamb was forced by city zoning regulations to develop "setbacks," or levels in the design where the building would gradually narrow to the central spire. This was meant to allow maximum street-level sunlight; this city requirement helped give the building its distinctive, slightly fragmented appearance.

The Empire State Building was the brainchild of a group of investors, including John Jakob Raskob and Pierre Du Pont and headed by former New York governor and presidential candidate Alfred E. Smith. Together the men formed Empire State, Inc., to oversee the financing and construction of the 37 million cubic foot, $24.7 million office tower. From the outset, the group wished the building to be the tallest in the world and every effort was made to ensure that the finished height remained a secret until the structure neared completion. This was because the Empire State Building was in direct competition to be the tallest with two other New York skyscrapers: 40 Wall Street (then known as the Bank of Manhattan Trust Building) and the Chrysler Building. In fact, both 40 Wall Street and the Chrysler Building briefly held the title of world's tallest building in 1930 and 1931. The Empire State Building's spire made it taller than the Chrysler Building. It held the distinction as the tallest building until 1972.

The Empire State Building at night during the early 1930's. (Hulton Archive/Getty Images)

Although the building was conceived and initial plans were begun before the onset of the Great Depression, the majority of the construction took place as the financial crisis worsened in the first years of the 1930's. Despite the unfortunate timing of the building's construction, it provided jobs for the nearly thirty-four hundred workers who contributed to its erection. Like other major construction projects of the period, the Empire State Building symbolized the feeling that the United States could recover from the Depression. Enthusiasm for the project helped it rise at the rate of four and one-half stories per week at its fastest.

When the Empire State Building opened, much of its office space was unrented, earning it the nickname the "Empty State Building." In an attempt to suggest full occupancy, workers were hired to turn lights on in the building during the night. The observation deck on the eighty-sixth floor took in nearly $2 million per year and helped keep the building solvent. The building quickly took on iconic status and was featured in the climactic scene of the 1933 film *King Kong*. The colored illumination at the top, one of the structure's most recognizable features, was first lit in 1932 in celebration of Franklin D. Roosevelt's victory over Herbert Hoover for president of the United States.

The building's spire was originally intended to serve as a docking point for dirigibles and other airships. However, despite a handful of attempts, the updrafts caused by the building itself proved to be too dangerous to the passengers attempting to disembark from the airships and so the idea was abandoned.

Impact The Empire State Building survived a turbulent first few years of operation to become a world architectural landmark and a valuable business property. The seven million man-hours involved in the building's construction were squeezed into a mere one year and forty-five days, a record for the completion of a building of its height. It is recognized globally as a symbol of New York City and is an example of Art Deco architecture at its best.

Shawn Selby

The Empire State Building: Facts and Figures

- *Completion time:* 410 days
- *Architect:* Shreve, Lamb & Harmon
- *Contractor:* Starrett Brothers and Eken
- *Construction man-hours:* 7,000,000
- *Cost including land:* $40,948,900
- *Cost of building alone:* $24,718,000
- *Site area:* 79,288 square feet
- *Foundation:* 55 feet below ground
- *Basement:* 35 feet below ground
- *Lobby:* 47 feet above sea level
- *Height to top of lightning rod:* 1,453 feet, 8$\frac{9}{16}$ inches
- *Floors:* 103
- *Steps:* 1,860 from street to 102d floor
- *Volume:* 37 million cubic feet
- *Weight:* 365,000 tons
- *Windows:* 6,500
- *Elevators:* 73
- *Exterior materials:* 200,000 cubic feet of Indiana limestone; 10,000 square feet of rose famosa and estrallante marble; 300,000 square feet of Hauteville and Rocheron marble for interiors
- *Plumbing:* 70 miles of pipe
- *Electricity:* 2,500,000 feet of electrical wire

Further Reading

Kingwell, Mark. *The Nearest Thing to Heaven: The Empire State Building and American Dreams.* New Haven, Conn.: Yale University Press, 2006.

Tauranac, John. *The Empire State Building: The Making of a Landmark.* New York: St. Martin's Griffin, 1995.

See also Airships; Architecture; Chrysler Building; *King Kong*; Smith, Alfred E.

■ *Erie Railroad Co. v. Tompkins*

The Case: U.S. Supreme Court ruling requiring federal courts to follow state precedent when jurisdiction is based on diversity of citizenship

Date Decided on April 25, 1938

The Supreme Court's decision in Erie Railroad Co. v. Tompkins *established that authority in federal diversity cases is state common law rather than federal general common law.*

Federal courts have jurisdiction to hear cases in which the parties are from different states and at least $75,000 is in dispute, making available an impartial forum to out-of-state litigants. A case regarding the determination of fault in a serious auto accident, for example, could be heard in federal court if the parties were from different states.

If no statute applies in a given case, the common law, consisting of previous cases, becomes the controlling authority. In *Swift v. Tyson* (1842), the Supreme Court held that a federal court in a diversity case could apply general principles and doctrines of jurisprudence, rather than the precedent of the state in which the case arose.

The Court addressed this issue again in *Erie Railroad Co. v. Tompkins* (1938). While trespassing near train tracks in Pennsylvania, Harry J. Tompkins was hit by a door extending from a passing train. The railroad was a New York corporation; thus Tompkins could sue in a federal court based on diversity of citizenship. According to Pennsylvania law, precedent liability to undiscovered trespassers lies only for "willful negligence." Tompkins argued that federal common law, which provided for liability to trespassers for simple negligence, should apply.

The Court ruled that applying federal common law to diversity cases is unfair and unconstitutional. It is unfair because persons in a state are entitled to the protection of that state's laws, including its common law; it is unconstitutional because federal common law is an arrogation by the federal judiciary of the states' power to determine their own common law.

Impact The *Erie Railroad Co. v. Tompkins* decision overturned the *Swift v. Tyson* decision and abolished federal common law in diversity cases. In federal diversity cases in which the authority for the decision is precedent, state precedent controls, preventing plaintiffs from suing in federal court to get more favorable precedent. This result was contrary to the trend of the 1930's, in which the federal government assumed power over matters that had previously been the domain of state government, especially in matters of commerce.

Howard C. Ellis

Further Reading

Purcell, Edward A., Jr. *Brandeis and the Progressive Constitution: Erie, the Judicial Power, and the Politics of the Federal Courts in Twentieth-Century America.* New Haven, Conn.: Yale University Press, 2000.

Tribe, Laurence H. *American Constitutional Law.* St. Paul, Minn.: West, 1999.

See also Black, Hugo L.; Brandeis, Louis D.; Four Horsemen vs. Three Musketeers; Hughes, Charles Evans; Supreme Court, U.S.

■ Europe

The U.S. government's commitment to foreign-policy neutrality was tested repeatedly by the fascist and Nazi regimes in Europe throughout the 1930's. By the end of the decade, the strict U.S. policy of nonintervention, combined with British and French appeasement, encouraged fascist forces in Spain, Italy, and Germany to demand more and grab more, and hence the policy actually hurt the victims of aggression more than the instigators.

American foreign policy until the mid-twentieth century was based on self-interest and military nonintervention. The geographic isolation of the United States, with vast oceans to the east and west and militarily weak neighbors to the north and south, only reinforced the U.S. tendency toward isolationism. Alliances and treaties that were part of European diplomacy were unnecessary to the United States because no immediate threats the United States existed. The fact that binding treaties between the Great powers of Europe had been among the main cause of World War I was clear evidence to Americans of the dangers of being party to such entangled agreements.

Geography, history, and culture compelled American politicians to justify and maintain U.S. isolation through the 1920's, continuing a foreign policy based on nonintervention. The Great Depression also contributed greatly to U.S. isolationism. The Depression was a worldwide event, and the United States, like all other industrialized nations at the time, turned inward to focus on its own domestic problems. As the democracies of Europe and the United States dealt with domestic crises and the antiwar sentiments of their populations, authoritarian nations such as Nazi Germany and fascist Italy took advantage of those preoccupations. Events in Europe throughout the 1930's challenged the U.S. government's commitment to neutrality and ultimately forced the United States to take sides.

Economic Interactions with Europe The Great Depression brought swift change to the free-market economic polices of the industrialized nations, making international cooperation difficult. The United States was among the first to react to the crisis with protectionist tariffs, which signaled to the rest of the world that the United States was unwilling to work with other countries. Other nations soon retaliated with protectionist policies of their own, causing further stagnation of the world economy. Attempts were made to solve some of the problems. For example, the Lausanne Conference addressed the question of Germany's crippling war debts, and the London Economic Conference of 1933 was intended to take action against the effects of the global depression by restarting international trade and stabilizing national currencies.

Unconstructive and uncooperative American actions at these meetings further illustrated American unwillingness to get involved in the affairs of the outside world during the 1930's, even on economic issues of global significance. This was particularly disappointing to the Europeans because the United States had benefited financially and politically from World War I and the destruction it had wrought on the economies of Europe. After the 1929 stock market crash European states had hoped that the U.S. government would take an active role in reviving the moribund global financial system. This was not to be the case, but soon political events in Europe overshadowed economic concerns, as the possibility of war grew as the decade progressed.

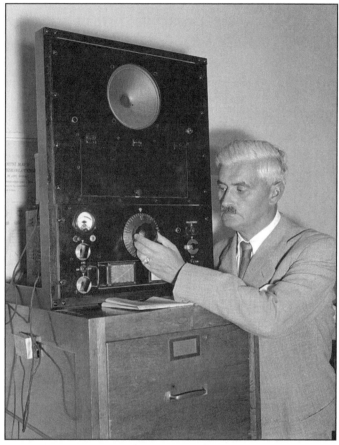

Karel Brejska, acting Czechoslovakian chargé d'affaires in Washington, D.C., listening to Adolf Hitler deliver a radio speech in September, 1938, as the tense political situation in Europe was becoming impossible for the United States to ignore. (Library of Congress)

European Crises, American Neutrality During the 1930's, dire economic circumstances, political protectionism, and finger-pointing made cooperation in the political arena difficult. In the United States the desire to withdraw from the international arena was even more pronounced because of Americans' isolationism. The Europeans and Americans worked on agreements that were supposed to lessen the chances of war. Even though the United States did not join the League of Nations, it was a signatory to a number of the accords, participating, for example, in the Geneva Disarmament Conference and both London Naval Conferences. At the same time, however, the rise to power and influence of militaristic, right-wing groups across Europe, whose fanatical worldviews were against negotiation and compromise, undermined international agreements.

continued on page 279

Western Europe, 1939

By 1939, Germany had already expanded its territory into Austria, Poland, and Czechoslovakia.

President Franklin D. Roosevelt ultimately remained true to American isolationism, extending the policy of nonintervention and dealing primarily with the Western Hemisphere. Neutrality became more difficult to maintain as the decade progressed because Germany was becoming an increasing threat to Europe and the existing, if imperfect, world order. Adolf Hitler came to power and almost immediately began to disrupt many of the international agreements of the 1920's and 1930's. For example, he demanded German rearmament and withdrew Germany from the League of Nations in the fall of 1933. Benito Mussolini, the fascist dictator of Italy, was not to be outdone and made moves to enhance Italian status that also weakened the League of Nations, such as the Italian invasion of Ethiopia in 1936. The outbreak of civil war in Spain, with fascist-nationalist forces attacking the republican government, also challenged American neutrality.

The U.S. reaction to events in Europe was to establish American neutrality as law. Collectively known as the Neutrality Acts, these were a series of acts passed by Congress between 1935 and 1939 that aimed to prevent the United States from becoming a participant in any foreign war. Though Roosevelt favored his administration's ability to embargo nations on a selective basis, Congress was controlled throughout the 1930's by isolationists. The Neutrality Acts were renewed each year and grew more stringent as the situation in Europe became more precarious and Japan's aggression in China continued. Congress initially forbade the sale of arms or munitions to any belligerent nation in 1935, but as crises continued to develop, the legislators adapted the laws to ensure American neutrality, even if it hurt U.S. allies and the victims of aggression. Ethiopia suffered under the Neutrality Acts, as did the Spanish Republicans, whose enemies were well funded and supplied by Germany and Italy. In late 1937, President Roosevelt was able to get a "cash and carry" clause into one of the Neutrality Acts of that year. This allowed the president to permit the sale of war materials to belligerents as long as the United States had nothing to do with the transport and the items were paid for in cash. This gesture was to aid Great Britain and France. By 1938, Congress and the public remained determined to stay out of the expected European war, even if Roosevelt wished to offer more active aid to U.S. allies. Despite further German landgrabs in 1938, the United States ad-

hered to its policy of nonintervention, allowing the "cash and carry" clause to elapse without renewal in early 1939. Not until the German invasion of Poland in September, 1939, and an impassioned plea from Roosevelt did Congress pass another Neutrality Act that included "cash and carry."

Impact   Initially dominated by the effects of the Great Depression and unresolved issues stemming from World War I, U.S. relations with Europe during the 1930's quickly became focused on avoiding any oncoming war. The crippling effects of the Depression on national economies, the protectionist policies adopted by the industrialized nations, and the mutual recriminations of governments over responsibility for the economic catastrophe encouraged a worldwide atmosphere in which domestic concerns and economic self-interest controlled negotiations and worked against compromise and mutual agreement. The fear and despair that made people in liberal democracies question their core beliefs and wonder whether capitalism was truly a bankrupt economic system was played upon by right-wing groups across Europe. This brought men such as Hitler to power. The British policy of appeasement, which the French followed unwillingly, was supported by the Americans by default; by claiming neutrality, the United States was, in reality, appeasing Germany and encouraging Hitler's expansionism. The Neutrality Acts backfired by rendering the United States powerless to aid its allies and friends, while at the same time, they had little effect on the aggressor nations. Ultimately, the unwillingness of the American public and Congress to become embroiled in another war gave Germany time to consolidate its territorial gains and build up its military and left the United States woefully unprepared, in all respects, when war finally came.

Megan E. Watson

Further Reading

Doenecke, Justus D. *From Isolation to War, 1931-1941.* Wheeling, Ill.: Harlan Davidson, 1991. A survey of U.S. foreign policy dilemmas during the 1930's, including discussion of the historiographical disagreements.

Doenecke, Justus D., and Mark A. Stoler. *Debating Franklin D. Roosevelt's Foreign Policies, 1933-1945.* New York: Rowman & Littlefield, 2005. Offers opposing views of Roosevelt's controversial policies with cogent and well-supported arguments.

Kennedy, David M. *Freedom from Fear: The American People in Depression and War, 1929-1945*. New York: Oxford University Press, 1999. Excellent source for students interested in a close examination of the United States during the 1930's.

Rhodes, Benjamin D. *United States Foreign Policy in the Interwar Period, 1918-1941: The Golden Age of American Diplomatic and Military Complacency*. Westport, Conn.: Praeger, 2001. A thorough study of the people and polices of the interwar years; essential reading for any serious student of U.S. foreign relations.

Sontag, Raymond J. *A Broken World, 1919-1939*. New York: Harper & Row, 1971. Highly readable and useful look at Europe in the interwar period.

See also Foreign policy of the United States; Germany and U.S. appeasement; International trade; Isolationism; League of Nations; London Economic Conference; Neutrality Acts; Spanish Civil War; World War I debts; World War II and the United States.

■ Evian Conference

The Event International conference on the issue of German and Austrian Jewish refugees
Dates July 6-15, 1938
Place Évian-les-Bains, France

Convened at President Franklin D. Roosevelt's behest, the Evian Conference met to discuss an international solution to the refugee problem created by Adolf Hitler's effort to make German territories free of Jews.

Following its establishment in 1933, the Nazi regime aimed at driving German Jews abroad, an objective frustrated by many Jews' reluctance to leave and other countries' refusals to accept refugees in a global depression. In the United States, strict immigration legislation combined with a mostly unsympathetic, wary public opinion on the issue of immigration limited President Roosevelt's options. Thus, when Germany's March, 1938, annexation of Austria escalated the Jewish refugee problem, Roosevelt invited thirty-three nations to an international conference, promising that no country would be expected or required to admit more immigrants than existing laws allowed.

Thirty-two governments sent representatives to the conference, held at the Hotel Royal in Évian-les-Bains, France, from July 6, to July 15, 1938. At the opening session, Myron C. Taylor, head of the American delegation, announced Washington's merger of German and former Austrian immigration quotas so as to allow 27,370 refugees into the United States per annum. Relieved that the Americans intended to do no more than fulfill existing quotas, delegates from other countries, one after the other, rationalized why their governments could not accept more immigrants. The exception was the representative of the Dominican Republic, who proclaimed his government's willingness to accept 10,000 Jews per year for a two-year period.

Evian's sole achievement was unanimous agreement to establish a permanent intergovernmental committee to continue the conference's work. Scheduled to begin meeting in London on August 3, this committee received the charge to ameliorate via negotiation existing conditions of forced immigration and to develop opportunities for the permanent settlement of refugees.

Impact The Evian Conference failed to solve the Jewish refugee crisis; the intergovernmental committee proved ineffective. Contemporaries, including the Nazi regime, ridiculed it, while scholars have characterized it as a mere public-relations ploy and a prime example of the world's failure to assist Europe's beleaguered Jews when many could still have been saved. Though these criticisms have merit, Evian transformed the plight of Germany's and Austria's Jews into an international issue and simultaneously highlighted the brutality of the Hitler government.

Bruce J. DeHart

Further Reading

Rosen, Robert N. *Saving the Jews: Franklin D. Roosevelt and the Holocaust*. New York: Thunder's Mouth Press, 2006.

Wyman, David G. *Paper Walls: America and the Refugee Crisis, 1938-1941*. Boston: University of Massachusetts Press, 1968.

See also Anti-Semitism; Foreign policy of the United States; Germany and U.S. appeasement; Hull, Cordell; Immigration to Canada; Immigration to the United States; Isolationism; Jews in Canada; Jews in the United States; *St. Louis* incident.

Executive Reorganization Act. See
Reorganization Act of 1939

■ Export-Import Bank of the United States

Identification   Official export credit agency of the
U.S. government
Date   Established on February 2, 1934

*During the early 1930's, the Export-Import Bank was able
to extend credit to exporters that private banks could not
because of their weakened positions during the Great Depression. Some critics argue that the bank contributed to
prolonging the Depression by interfering with the free
market.*

By signing Executive Order 6581 on February 2,
1934, President Franklin D. Roosevelt created the
Export-Import Bank of Washington, a new government agency, as part of the New Deal. Its purpose was
to make loans and loan guarantees that might be too
risky for private banks to offer, making it easier for
U.S. companies to trade with other countries. The
bank also supported American exporters by attempting to match the levels of financial support
that international trade partners gave their own citizens, enabling American companies to match or
beat the prices of their competitors. This allowed
firms to expand their markets internationally—an
important step in helping the U.S. economy recover
from the Great Depression.

The bank's first transaction was a $3.8 million
loan to Cuba so it could buy silver ingots from the
United States. In 1938, $22 million was loaned to
China to complete the Burma Road. Since the
1930's, the bank has loaned money to other nations
to build roads and industrial plants, helped fund the
reconstruction of Europe after World War II, and
has loaned money to troubled nations to help them
purchase American goods. In 1945, Congress re-
configured the bank as an independent agency, the
Export-Import Bank. Its name was changed again in
1968, to the Export-Import Bank of the United
States.

Impact   According to the bank's own figures, the
Export-Import Bank has supported U.S. exports
with a value of more than $400 billion since its
founding. Most of its support has gone to help American small businesses reach markets in developing
nations.

Cynthia A. Bily

Further Reading

Becker, William H., and William M. McClenahan.
*The Market, the State, and the Export-Import Bank of
the United States, 1934-2000.* New York: Cambridge
University Press, 2003.
Higgs, Robert. *Against Leviathan: Government Power
and a Free Society.* Oakland, Calif.: Independent In-
stitute, 2004.
U.S. Export-Import Bank Handbook. Washington, D.C.:
International Business, 2004.

See also   Banking; Business and the economy in
the United States; Foreign policy of the United States;
Great Depression in the United States; International
trade; New Deal; Roosevelt, Franklin D.

F

■ Fads

Definition   Popular products, activities, styles, and ideas

Although survival was paramount and resources were limited during the Great Depression, people also had more idle or leisure time for activities. As a result, many fads developed that entertained, consumed time, and helped people escape or forget the economy and their difficult lives.

The 1930's were preceded by the Jazz Age, or the Roaring Twenties, a period of economic prosperity and optimism in North America. Then came the stock market crash of 1929 and a major economic reversal. The Great Depression of the 1930's was a time of great financial hardship, increasing unemployment, and reduced income. By 1933, unemployment in the United States had reached 15 million, and 50 percent of home mortgages were in default. In Canada, the average income fell by one-half, and one-third of Canadians became unemployed. During the 1930's, many fads were cheap ways of passing time, and perhaps making some money, getting fed, or gaining some fame.

Games and Leisure   Pinball parlors provided an inexpensive pastime during the decade. In 1931, David Gottlieb introduced the first modern pinball machine, Baffle Ball, which was an immediate hit. Costing a penny per game, this coin-operated tabletop game used a wooden plunger to propel steel balls up into the play area to score points. The first year, Gottlieb sold more than fifty thousand units for $17.50 each. In 1932, the Ballyhoo and Whirlwind games appeared. In 1933, Harry Williams created a game called Contact, the first electrically powered pinball machine, which had colored lights and rang a bell to reward players. Colorful pinball art became a spin-off fad. By the end of the decade, pinball machines could be found in bars, candy stores, cafés, amusement arcades, and numerous other places.

A major recreational fad in 1930 was miniature golf, played by four million people on any given day. In this game, a player uses a putter to hit a golf ball across, under, around, and through various constructions or hazards on a playing surface and finally into holes. In 1930, Americans spent $225 million playing the game; about forty thousand miniature golf courses existed, in places such as highway filling stations, parks, empty lots, rooftops, and hotel courtyards. The Maples Inn in Pointe Claire, Quebec, had the first miniature golf course in Canada, where the sport became a favorite pastime.

Board games were the rage during the Depression years. The most popular game, Monopoly, was first distributed by Charles B. Darrow in 1934 and then sold to Parker Brothers, who introduced it on a broad scale in 1935. The goal of this real estate game is to travel around the board buying up properties and forcing the other players into bankruptcy. The last remaining player is the winner. The idea of becoming a real estate tycoon was appealing, and Monopoly was an immediate success, with more than twenty thousand sets sold in the first week of its release.

As people searched for easy ways to make money, gambling became widespread. Playing cards for cash and betting on horse races were popular pastimes. By the end of the decade, organized betting was legal in twenty-one states. Churches and charities held bingo parties regularly as fund-raisers. Also popular was the punchboard, a cardboard sheet with one thousand holes, each containing a ticket. Only one lucky ticket was the winner, and players could punch out a hole for a nickel, earning a chance to win $2.50. About fifteen thousand punchboards were produced daily by 1939. Contract bridge was an adult fad popularized by traditional bridge master Ely Culbertson. Tournaments were broadcast over the radio, and how-to books became best sellers. About twenty million people played the game, and more than fifty million decks of cards were sold during the Great Depression.

Language fads were fun and free. In the early 1930's, "Hooverisms" associated the President with the harsh conditions of the Depression. The shantytowns that housed the homeless on the outskirts of cities near railroad tracks were called "Hoovervilles," while the newspapers that hobos used as blankets were called "Hoover blankets." In 1933, Hoovercart rodeos began. Teams of mules hitched up to the back halves of dilapidated Model T Fords raced over an obstacle course. Another fad, the familiar knock-knock joke, consisted of a punster and recipient in a five-line call-and-answer exchange, ending with a punch line misusing the earlier response word or words. In 1936, "The Knock-Knock Song" was released, and the fad peaked that year.

Contests and Marathons   In 1933, Myron Scott invented the soap box derby, a popular youth fad. The original homemade cars were built out of old buggy wheels and soap boxes or other wood scraps. The early races drew more than thirty thousand spectators and hundreds of racers. The first official soap box derby was held in 1934 in Dayton, Ohio. Contestants were local champions from the Midwest.

Popular endurance fads included flagpole and tree sitting, whose participants collected money. The dance marathon was a huge spectator event. These public contests provided meals and small cash prizes for the desperate, competing couples, many of whom danced, walked, or shuffled to exhaustion for weeks at a time with only a fifteen-minute break each hour. There were also walking and talking marathons, kissa-thons, four-thousand-mile roller derbies, and six-day bicycle races. Numerous marathons revolved around consuming huge quantities of food, such as hot dogs, pies, eggs, clams, coffee, or spaghetti.

Soap Box Derby

(Archive Photos/Getty Images)

With assistants poised to provide a push off the starting line, a group of children sit inside their homemade soap-box cars, awaiting the start of the Wheeze Championship race along a residential street in Los Angeles. Though soap-box racing reached its popular peak during the 1950's and 1960's, ranking as a top-five sport in the United States, the event was a favorite pastime of the 1930's, a decade in which the first sanctioned race was held. The All-American Race, as it was named, was first held in Dayton, Ohio, in 1934, and was initiated by a staff photographer for the Dayton Daily News. After its introductory success in Dayton, the race was moved permanently to Akron, Ohio, where a state-of-the-art soap-box-derby track, Derby Downs, was constructed by the Works Progress Administration. The bodies of soap-box vehicles were usually made from wooden boxes and barrels, and the cars' speed and power were generated entirely from the pull of gravity, as none of the go-carts had engines. Construction of the soap-box carts highlighted the industrious spirit and the adaptability of American youth during the Great Depression.

Toward the end of the decade, swallowing goldfish became an intercollegiate fad. On March 3, 1939, Harvard University freshman Lothrop Withington, Jr., swallowed a live goldfish to win a ten-dollar bet. Withington, who was campaigning to become freshman class president, had invited reporters to witness this event. More than 150 people attended, and goldfish swallowing quickly spread, first to Franklin and Marshall College in Pennsylvania and then to other colleges. Imitators attempted to set new records for speed and the quantity of fish swallowed. In April, a Clark University student ingested eighty-nine goldfish. Some universities and towns banned the practice, various organizations protested the inhumane treatment of animals, and the U.S. Public Health Service raised health concerns. The fad lasted almost three months and then subsided.

Radio, Film, and Cultural Icons The 1930's were the Golden Age of Radio in North America. The radio was the center of most homes, and listening to the radio was an inexpensive form of entertainment, especially for families. Comedy, sports, news, music, and drama provided relief and escape from reality. By 1939, 80 percent of American homes had radios. Favorite programs included *Fibber McGee and Molly, Amos 'n' Andy,* and *The Green Hornet.*

One of the most popular radio programs in Canada was *The Happy Gang,* which presented jokes and music. Beginning in 1933, the Saturday night hockey games at Maple Leaf Gardens were broadcast nationally on Foster Hewitt's *Hockey Night in Canada* radio program. By 1934, there were more than one million listeners, and by 1940, there were more than two million regular fans. Other popular programs were *The Lone Ranger, The Burns and Allen Show* and *The Adventures of Gracie* with George Burns and Gracie Allen, and *The Jack Benny Show.*

During the 1930's, Hollywood was at its peak, with studios producing more than five thousand feature films during the decade. Millions of people went to the movies, where they could forget their problems and enter a fantasy world of romance, glamour, or adventure. Popular features included *Dracula* (1931), *The Wizard of Oz* (1939), Fred Astaire and Ginger Rogers films, and *King Kong* (1933), starring Canadian born Fay Wray.

Many fads revolved around film stars and characters, who were adored as cultural icons. Women bleached their hair to imitate Jean Harlow's trademark platinum blond hair. Screen idols Greta Garbo and Bette Davis set fashion trends in hats and dresses. Judy Garland's gingham dress in *The Wizard of Oz* became a fashion craze, and the best-selling sewing pattern was for a dress worn by Vivien Leigh

in *Gone with the Wind* (1939). Disney's lovable Mickey Mouse generated a whole industry of must-have products, such as stuffed dolls, watches, clothing, and costume jewelry.

From 1934 to 1939, the American child star Shirley Temple was an international box office attraction whose films grossed $5 million annually. She personified innocence, and her optimism was comforting to moviegoers. Young girls copied her ringlet curls, and the Royal Hawaiian Hotel invented a nonalcoholic Shirley Temple cocktail. In spite of the weak economy, Shirley Temple products were top sellers and included hair bows, polka-dot dresses, soaps, hats, bracelets, and dolls. In 1934, the Ideal Toy Company introduced Shirley Temple dolls dressed in costumes from her films. More than six million dolls, priced up to $30, were sold. Canada's top dollmaker, Reliable Toy Company of Toronto, Canada, was famous for its composition dolls, made of cornstarch, glue, and sawdust. Ideal Toys licensed Reliable to make the 18-inch composition Shirley Temple dolls for the Canadian market for five years. After the 1930's, Temple's popularity declined.

A highly endearing fad was the flirtatious cartoon character Betty Boop, created by animator Max Fleischer for Paramount Pictures's Talkartoons series. She first appeared in a small musical role in *Dizzy Dishes* (1930). In 1931, Betty Boop starred in *Betty Coed,* which was an instant hit, and she went on to appear in more than one hundred cartoons. She was the first animated siren, exuding both innocence and seductiveness. She had a Mae West figure, large dark eyes, and long eyelashes. Betty Boop usually wore strapless, short-skirted dresses. Her spit curls, high baby voice, and singing style were inspired by the flapper Helen Kane. Her trademark exclamation was "Boop-Oop-a-Doop." Betty Boop dolls, toys, and other products proliferated, and a comic strip began in 1934. However, the Motion Picture Production Code (also known as the Hays Code) censored the Betty Boop character, after which she became less sensual and her popularity declined. Her last film, *Yip Yip Yippy,* was released in 1939.

Impact The 1930's were years of economic turmoil and despair; nonetheless, an abundance of fads provided inexpensive entertainment and occasionally allowed people to make money. Numerous fads introduced during the 1930's left indelible marks on American culture. Among these were Monopoly and characters such as Mickey Mouse and Betty Boop.

Alice Myers

Further Reading

Calabria, Frank M. *Dance of the Sleepwalkers: The Dance Marathon Fad.* Bowling Green, Ohio: Bowling Green State University Popular Press, 1993. Analysis of the psychological, entertainment, and business aspects of this popular fad of the 1920's and 1930's.

Hoffman, Frank, and William G. Bailey. *Sports and Recreation Fads.* New York: Harrington Park Press, 1991. Includes stories examining 1930's fads, such as dance marathons, miniature golf, Monopoly, and drive-in theaters. Illustrated; bibliography and index.

Kyvig, David E. *Daily Life in the United States, 1920-1940: How Americans Lived Through the Roaring Twenties and the Great Depression.* Chicago: Ivan R. Dee, 2004. Political and social history, including details about leisure activities and fads, such as miniature golf, horseracing, and popular hairstyles.

Panati, Charles. *Panati's Parade of Fads, Follies, and Manias: The Origins of Our Most Cherished Obsessions.* New York: Harper-Perennial, 1991. This entertaining look at twentieth century fads includes a chapter on the "Swing Thirties." Illustrated with bibliography.

Walsh, Tim. *Timeless Toys: Classic Toys and the Playmakers Who Created Them.* Kansas City, Mo.: Andrews McMeel, 2005. Delightful history of toys and their creators from the first decade of the twentieth century through the 1990's. Includes interviews with industry leaders and 420 color photographs.

Young, William H., and Nancy Young. *The 1930s.* Westport, Conn.: Greenwood Press, 2008. History detailing every-day life and popular culture, including leisure activities, and fashion.

See also   Bingo; Contract bridge; Fashions and clothing; Hairstyles; Hobbies; Marathon dancing; Mickey Mouse; Monopoly; Recreation; Temple, Shirley.

■ Fair Labor Standards Act of 1938

The Law   Federal law that established a minimum wage, standardized work-week hours, and banned child labor

Also known as   Wages and Hours Bill; FLSA

Dates   Enacted on June 25, 1938; took effect on October 24, 1938

The Fair Labor Standards Act of 1938 was a product of the Great Depression. A landmark piece of legislation, it established for the first time in American history labor guidelines that guaranteed that American workers would be protected from labor exploitation. These mandatory standards included a federally mandated minimum wage, a maximum-hour workweek, and child labor age requirements.

The Fair Labor Standards Act (FLSA) targeted, among other issues, a competitive minimum wage for workers. In this 1939 picture, the Apparel Industry Committee meets to discuss raising the minimum wage from the twenty-five cents an hour set by the FLSA. (Library of Congress)

President Franklin D. Roosevelt was a strong proponent of establishing federal labor standards in an effort to end the exploitation of American workers. The fair labor standards legislation he supported was originally drafted by Secretary of Labor Frances Perkins in 1933 but was not brought before Congress during the president's first term in office.

During the 1936 presidential campaign, both the Democratic Party and President Roosevelt made higher labor standards a campaign issue. Following Roosevelt's reelection, the fair labor standards legislation drafted by Perkins was presented to Congress on May 24, 1937. Hugo L. Black of Alabama introduced it to the Senate, while William P. Connery, Jr., of Massachusetts introduced it to the House of Representatives. After more than a year of negotiations and debate, the Fair Labor Standards Act of 1938 was finally signed into law by President Roosevelt on June 25, 1938. In its final form, the bill set the maximum workweek at forty-four hours, set the national minimum wage at twenty-five cents per hour, and prohibited the employment of children under the age of sixteen. It became effective on October 24, 1938.

Impact The Fair Labor Standards Act of 1938 established federal standards for how American workers could be treated by their employers. Since then, it has been amended more than forty times. It continues to protect American workers from abusive working conditions.

Bernadette Zbicki Heiney

Further Reading

Kearns, Ellen C., and Monica Gallagher. *The Fair Labor Standards Act.* Washington, D.C.: Bureau of National Affairs, 1999.

Paulsen, George E. *A Living Wage for the Forgotten Man: The Quest for Fair Labor Standards, 1933-1941.* Selinsgrove, Pa.: Susquehanna University Press, 1996.

Repa, Barbara Kate. *Your Rights in the Workplace.* Berkeley, Calif.: Nolo, 2005.

See also   Black, Hugo L.; Elections of 1936, U.S.; Great Depression in the United States; Income and wages in the United States; Perkins, Frances; Roosevelt, Franklin D.

■ Fallingwater house

Identification   Architecturally innovative country house built over a natural waterfall
Architect   Frank Lloyd Wright
Date   Completed on July 22, 1937
Place   Bear Run, Pennsylvania

Considered the capstone of Frank Lloyd Wright's later career and the most innovative American residence of its time, Fallingwater exemplified the architect's belief in seamlessly blending nature with construction materials. In addition, the home showcased Wright's application of 1930's European modernism, along with his penchant for the bold and daring in architectural design.

Fallingwater might never have been built had Edgar Kaufmann, Jr., not read Wright's *Frank Lloyd Wright: An Autobiography* (1932). Highly impressed with Wright's approach to the creative process, Kaufmann brought the architect to the attention of his parents, Edgar "E. J." and Liliane Kaufmann, owners of the chain of Pittsburgh-based department stores

Architect Frank Lloyd Wright designed Fallingwater house for Edgar Kaufmann and his wife, Liliane. (AP/Wide World Photos)

bearing their name. While the senior Kaufmann and Wright met to discuss civic and commercial projects, Liliane's desire to build a weekend home on their Bear Run property came to light. The initial plans for what became Fallingwater were submitted by Wright in the fall of 1935.

Construction on Fallingwater began the following year. Apprentices from Taliesin, Wright's studio in Spring Green, Wisconsin, and engineers and builders from the Pittsburgh area executed the on-site work. As the name "Fallingwater" suggests, the home was constructed directly above the Bear Run waterfalls. Other innovative features included the retention of a natural boulder as part of the living room floor and the recurring motif of cantilevered terraces and ledges spanning all three floors. Americans learned of Fallingwater in early 1938 thanks to a feature article in the January 17 issue of *Time* magazine, an edition of *Architectural Form* dedicated to Wright, and an exhibit of photographs at New York's Museum of Modern Art.

Impact The aesthetics, innovation, and sophistication of Fallingwater provided a diversion for Americans, shifting their focus from economic depression and world conflict. Also, Fallingwater provided inspiration for Americans to consider living outside crowded metropolitan areas, thus serving as a catalyst for the future migration to the suburbs.

Cecilia Donohue

Further Reading

Hoffman, Donald. *Frank Lloyd Wright's Fallingwater: The House and Its History.* 2d rev. ed. New York: Dover, 1993.

Toker, Franklin. *Fallingwater Rising: Frank Lloyd Wright, E. J. Kaufmann, and America's Most Extraordinary House.* New York: Alfred A. Knopf, 2005.

See also Architecture; Gropius House; Wright, Frank Lloyd.

FARA. See **Foreign Agents Registration Act of 1938**

■ Farmer-Labor Party of Minnesota

Identification Political party
Date Established in August-November, 1918

The Farmer-Labor Party of Minnesota achieved dominance in the state in the first half of the 1930's. Under the leadership of Floyd B. Olson, who served as governor from 1931 to 1936, it stood as a major third-party response to the economic problems of the times. Olson gained a national reputation prior to his untimely death early in the second half of the decade.

The Farmer-Labor Party of Minnesota came into existence during the late summer and fall of 1918 and was a sometimes uneasy amalgamation of a number of different groups, including farmers and workers seeking moderate political and economic reforms and individuals of a more radical bent such as socialists, isolationists, and members of the radical farm organization known as the Nonpartisan League. During the 1920's, it achieved a modest level of success, electing Henrik Shipstead to the U.S. Senate in 1922 and three individuals to the U.S. House of Representatives and positioning itself as the chief rival of the Republican Party in the state. It attained its greatest level of prominence under the leadership of Olson.

Born in 1891, Olson began his political career in Minneapolis, where he served several terms as county attorney during the 1920's. After an unsuccessful run for the governorship on the Farmer-Labor Party ticket in 1924, he was elected to that office as a member of the Farmer-Labor Party six years later. Taking office during the early years of the Depression, Olson embarked on a moderate reform agenda during his first term. True to the ideals of his party, he sought legislation to strengthen the rights of organized labor, to postpone farm mortgage foreclosures, and to initiate a system of old-age pensions. He also launched extensive relief efforts as the economic hardships of the Depression increased. Like Franklin D. Roosevelt, Olson was a powerful speaker and used the new medium of radio to communicate directly with his constituents.

The combination of modest legislative successes and a high level of personal appeal gained Olson reelection in both 1932 and 1934. During this period, while frequently supporting Roosevelt and the New Deal, he continued to maintain the support of the radical wing of his party, which moved further to the left over time. To keep this latter alliance in place, his rhetoric in the 1934 campaign also took on a heightened radical tone. At the same time, his moderate, but basically prolabor, stand during the Minneapolis truck-drivers' strike in 1934 helped to gain him increasing national attention. Despite this popularity, however, he consistently rebuffed efforts to obtain his support for the formation of a national third party to oppose Roosevelt in the 1936 presidential election.

As the 1936 election approached, Olson decided to step down as governor and run for the U.S. Senate seat vacated by the death of Republican Thomas Schall the previous year. However, Olson died in August of that year.

In the period immediately following Olson's death, the Farmer-Labor Party triumphed in one more election, with left-leaning Farmer-Laborite Elmer Benson winning the governorship by a large majority in 1936. Under Benson's leadership, however, the internal divisions between the party's moderate and radical wings, which Olson had managed to control, helped lead to a devastating defeat by the Republicans in 1938. The party never again achieved success and eventually, following a purge of its radical left-wing element, merged with the Minnesota Democratic Party during the 1940's.

Impact Under the leadership of Olson, the Farmer-Labor Party of Minnesota was one of the most successful third-party movements at the state level during the 1930's. Eventually, the inherent conflicts within its membership proved too divisive for its future existence once Olson died. The party's meteoric rise and fall offers a good example of the volatile political climate of the decade.

Scott Wright

Further Reading

Gieske, Millard L. *Minnesota Farmer-Laborism: The Third Party Alternative.* Minneapolis: University of Minnesota Press, 1979.

Haynes, John E. *Dubious Alliance: The Making of Minnesota's DFL Party.* Minneapolis: University of Minnesota Press, 2009.

Mayer, George H. *The Political Career of Floyd B. Olson.* St. Paul: Minnesota Historical Society Press, 1987.

See also Communism; Elections of 1932, U.S.; Elections of 1936, U.S.; Great Depression in the United States; New Deal; Nonpartisan League; Roosevelt, Franklin D.

■ Farmers' organizations

Definition Agricultural groups formed to lobby the U.S. government for economic assistance during the Great Depression

Farmers' organizations served as advocacy bodies for rural and agricultural interests during the economic crisis of the 1930's. By organizing, farmers hoped to pressure the government into passing legislation and adopting policies that would support American farmers by providing price supports for crops, low-interest loans for farmers, and the ability to operate in the marketplace as collective cooperatives rather than as individuals.

Farmers' organizations during the 1930's drew on a long tradition of rural activism that sought to promote the interests of farmers within American society and economic structures. Throughout the economic crisis of the late nineteenth century, farmers' organizations such as the Grange and the Populists advocated for the development of an inflationary monetary policy, a subtreasury system that would allow farmers to more easily convert farm products into capital, and an equal relationship between individual farmers and railroads. As prosperity returned during the early years of the twentieth century, many of these goals receded; however, the complaints of many farmers did not entirely disappear. The collapse of the American economy in 1929 brought many of these simmering disputes back to the forefront. As a response, many farmers began to reorganize as political, social, and economic collectives in order to more effectively advocate for their interests.

One of the most important farmers' organizations was the Farm Bureau. The Farm Bureau was theoretically nonpartisan and did not formally endorse any candidate. However, as the 1932 election approached, the interests of the bureau were embraced by candidate Franklin D. Roosevelt. Roosevelt's association with Farm Bureau activist and subsequent secretary of agriculture Henry A. Wallace provided farmers with an advocate close to the center of government.

After the election, Roosevelt enacted many of the reforms sought by the Farm Bureau. As a part of his New Deal programming, Roosevelt signed the Agricultural Adjustment Act, which eased farm credit problems and provided support for agricultural prices. The Commodity Credit Corporation provided further support for price stabilization. This was achieved through the creation of an allotment system that mandated a diminished level of agricultural production. The Farm Bureau felt it was possible for these programs to be administered through the existing network of local and county agencies rather than through the creation of a new government-run bureaucracy. This advocacy fundamentally reshaped the execution of New Deal programming in the rural United States by creating political support for programs that benefited farmers, even if some programming adversely affected urban interests.

More radical farmers' associations shunned the Farm Bureau's method of political advocacy. Much like the Farm Bureau, the Farmers' Holiday Association demanded that the federal government suspend farm foreclosures, support an inflationary monetary policy, and guarantee that the prices paid for agricultural products would rise. Unlike the Farm Bureau, the Farmers' Holiday Association threatened a general strike of farmers if their demands were not met. The Farmers' Holiday Association believed in direct action as well. One judge who refused to halt farm foreclosures was assaulted by the crowd, compelling the governor of Iowa to declare martial law in some areas of the state. Many people feared that organizations such as the Farmers' Holiday Association could spark a general revolution in the United States.

The Depression also encouraged the growth of farmers' cooperatives. Cooperatives allowed farmers to band together in order to purchase needed materials such as gasoline in bulk, thereby saving each farmer money through participation in an economy of scale. The marketing and sale of agricultural goods also benefited from this economy of scale. Farmers' cooperatives were not political advocacy groups such as the Farm Bureau and did not spark violence like the Farmers' Holiday Association; however, economic cooperation was as vital to the survival of farms as political organization was.

Impact The farmers' organizations of the 1930's established many of the structures that influence American agriculture in the twenty-first century. Farmers' groups advocated for a system of farm price supports, marketing structures, and cooperative organizations that have remained a vital part of federal farm supports into the twenty-first century. In many rural areas, farmers' cooperatives allowed

for the continued existence of many family farms that would have otherwise disappeared when faced with competition from agribusiness.

Patrick Callaway

Further Reading

Badger, Anthony J. *A Commonwealth of Hope: The New Deal Response to Crisis.* Baltimore: Johns Hopkins University Press, 2006.

Kile, Oliver Merton. *The Farm Bureau Through Three Decades.* Baltimore: Waverly Press, 1948.

Schlesinger, Arthur J., Jr. *The Coming of the New Deal.* 7th ed. Boston: Houghton Mifflin, 1958.

See also Agricultural Adjustment Acts; Agriculture in Canada; Agriculture in the United States; Commodity Credit Corporation; Credit and debt.

■ Farnsworth, Philo T.

Identification American television inventor
Born August 19, 1906; Beaver, Utah
Died March 11, 1971; San Francisco, California

Philo Taylor Farnsworth read about early television systems in science and technology magazines as a child. In high school, he diagrammed an electronic scanning device that he developed into an operating system at the age of twenty-one. Farnsworth headed his own company, which was underfinanced and eventually outmaneuvered by Radio Corporation of America through legal challenges, thereby delaying the introduction of television broadcasting until his patents expired.

The concept of television broadcasting originated at the same time that inventors and scientists began experimenting with radio. In 1884, the German inventor Paul Nipkow developed the Nipkow Disk, a mechanical spinning wheel with a spiral of holes through which an image could be scanned. Using Nipkow's rotating disk, the Scottish inventor John Logie Baird sent thirty-line-resolution television signals over telephone lines during the 1920's. Around the same time, the American inventor Charles Jenkins demonstrated a similar system in the United States.

By the 1930's it was becoming evident that mechanical television scanning systems had limited capacity to produce high-resolution images. Other inventors were experimenting with competing elec-

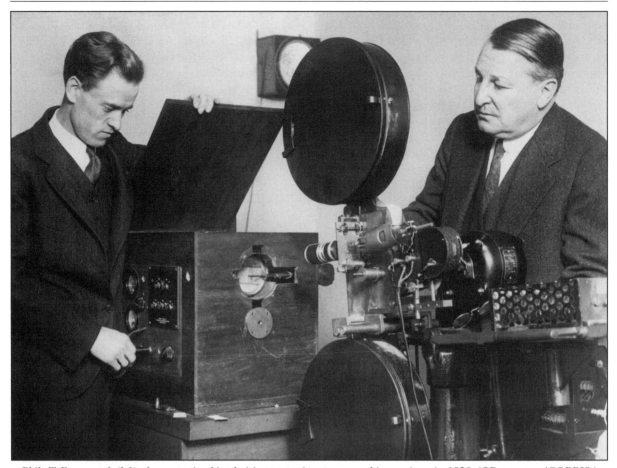

Philo T. Farnsworth (left), demonstrating his television transmitter to a consulting engineer in 1930. (©Bettmann/CORBIS)

tronic scanning systems that had the potential to achieve pictures with a resolution far exceeding that of mechanical systems. Farnsworth, an independent American inventor, and Vladimir Zworykin, a Russian immigrant who worked for Westinghouse and later the Radio Corporation of America (RCA), were competing inventors who conceived of moving images formed by electron beams scanning a scene.

The idea for Farnsworth's electronic television interlaced-line scanning process reportedly occurred to him as he plowed furrows into a potato field on his family's Idaho farm. He illustrated the scanning technique to his high school chemistry teacher: electron beams directed to scan across a scene, line by line, formed an image. This scanning process resembled the back-and-forth movement of a plow forming rows through a field.

Money, patents, and legal battles were destined to determine who would introduce public broadcast-

ing in America. Insufficient financial resources plagued Farnsworth throughout his career. Most of his financial support came from several California bankers who invested their personal funds. Farnsworth's competitor, RCA, was financially secure—a fact that gave Zworykin and his large staff an advantage with their television research.

After receiving his first patent in 1930, Farnsworth publicly demonstrated his cathode ray camera tube, the Image Dissector. At the time, Zworykin's Iconoscope tube was not yet fully reliable. Considering Zworykin a colleague, Farnsworth invited him to observe the Image Dissector at his San Francisco lab in 1930. Zworykin was impressed with what he saw and had replicas made of Farnsworth's device in an attempt to improve upon it. Determined to control the commercialization of television, RCA's David Sarnoff then arranged to observe a demonstration of the Image Dissector. RCA attempted to obtain

Farnsworth's patent, buy his company, and hire him in 1931. Although Farnsworth needed the money, he refused the RCA offer, preferring to work alongside his familiar lab assistants at Farnsworth Television, Incorporated.

The Philco Corporation, which also was interesting in television development, persuaded Farnsworth to work for it in Philadelphia in 1931. There the company conducted secret television research and acquired patents. However, the arrangement collapsed after two years. Farnsworth left Philco and established his own lab in Philadelphia.

As the developer of the only fully functioning electronic television system, Farnsworth was invited to Great Britain in 1934 by the inventor Baird. Farnsworth accepted fifty thousand dollars from Baird in exchange for a cross-licensing agreement and future royalty payments. Farnsworth eventually sold more stock to keep his business operating and in 1936 established television station W3XPF near Philadelphia, which transmitted 343 lines and 30-frame-per-second images. He filed numerous patent requests and completed a cross-licensing agreement with Bell Labs.

In 1938, the Radio Manufacturers Association recommended to the Federal Communications Commission (FCC) that a 441-line, 30-frame-per-second standard be adopted. Coincidentally, this was the same as the RCA system that Sarnoff would introduce and promote at the 1939 New York World's Fair.

Impact Farnsworth eventually succumbed to despondency and alcoholism as he recognized that the introduction of television broadcasting would happen without him. RCA made significant progress with its television development while obstructing his company with legal proceedings over patents. However, before commercial television's introduction, RCA was forced to pay patent royalties to Farnsworth for his Image Dissector.

Dennis A. Harp

Further Reading

Fisher, David E., and Marshall Jon Fisher. *Tube: The Invention of Television.* Washington, D.C.: Counterpoint, 1996. Comprehensive history of the development of television technology, profiling the various inventors and businessmen involved.

Kisseloff, Jeff. *The Box: An Oral History of Television, 1920-1961.* New York: Viking, 1995. Contains interviews with many people involved with the early days of television, including Farnsworth's wife and brother.

O'Shei, Tim. *Philo T. Farnsworth: Visionary Inventor of Television.* Berkeley Heights, N.J.: Enslow, 2008. Accessible biography covering Farnsworth's youth, career as an inventor, and struggles with RCA.

See also Armstrong, Edwin H.; Federal Communications Commission; Great Depression in the United States; Inventions; Radio trust; Television technology.

■ Fascism in Canada

Definition Canadian movements and groups that opposed democracy and embraced ultranationalism, racism, and authoritarianism

During the 1930's, several antidemocratic and xenophobic groups in Canada agreed with particular aspects of Italian fascism and German Nazism. Such groups, however, were relatively small and quite different from the European models.

Fascism in Canada consisted of a variety of fringe groups that advocated various ideological positions. Most fascists in Canada were radicalized by the economic hardships of the Great Depression, and they believed that the policies of the European fascists could bring about a return to prosperity. They usually sympathized with the hypernationalism of Adolf Hitler and Benito Mussolini, and a significant percentage agreed with Hitler's racist and anti-Semitic ideology. In general, however, members of these groups did not advocate that Canada adopt the kind of dictatorships that Mussolini and Hitler had established.

On August 16, 1933, the Christie Pits Park in Toronto was the scene of a six-hour confrontation between a large group of Jewish teenagers and an extremist, right-wing gang, called the Swastika Club, that displayed a large swastika flag following a softball game. Once the fighting began, hundreds of Jewish and gentile youths entered the park, fighting with fists and clubs. Although there were no reported deaths, scores of young men were seriously injured and many required medical attention. The incident underscored the pro-Nazi and xenophobic attitudes of a significant subculture of the Canadian population.

The best-known Canadian fascist was Adrien Arcand, a prominent French-speaking journalist who lived in Montreal. He edited several newspapers, including *Le Fasciste Canadien* and *Le Combat National.* In February, 1934, he founded the Parti National Social Chrétien (Canadian National Socialist Unity Party), and he referred to himself as the "Canadian füehrer." The party identified with the racist policies of Nazi Germany, and it called for the deportation of Canadian Jews to the Hudson Bay region. The party was also fervently anticommunist. It soon merged with the Canadian Nationalist Party, which was located in the Prairie Provinces. Arcand's enlarged party grew to about three thousand members, and it held a rally in Toronto that attracted almost four thousand sympathizers. In addition to expanding the party, Arcand was secretly employed as Prime Minister Richard Bedford Bennett's chief electoral director for the federal elections of 1935.

In June, 1938, Arcand joined with another white supremacist, John Ross Taylor, to establish the National Union Party; the organization later absorbed some of the swastika clubs located in Quebec and Ontario. Members of the National Union Party were required to take a pledge to support the government of Canada, to work for national unity, and to render strict obedience to Arcand.

Another noteworthy fascist leader was Charles Brandel Crate, who founded the Canadian Union of Fascists in 1933, with headquarters in Winnipeg, Manitoba. In contrast to the majority of fascists, Crate disagreed with Hitler's racist and anti-Semitic views, and his version of fascism emphasized Mussolini's program of corporatism, which attempted to use governmental intervention to coordinate the various sections of the economy. Only about two hundred persons attended the party's first meeting: The party remained much smaller than Arcand's organization, in part because so many fascists disagreed with Crate's disavowal of racism. Late in 1938, Taylor broke with Arcand's group and joined the Canadian Union of Fascists, becoming its secretary and chief organizer.

Impact After Canada declared war on Germany in 1939, the War Measures Act put an end to fascist activities. Crate dissolved the Canadian Union of Fascists and advised its members to obey the law. Crate

himself joined the Royal Canadian Navy, and he was never formally accused of disloyalty. In contrast, the National Union Party was banned in 1940. Arcand, Taylor, and a few hundred other sympathizers were interned as security threats for the duration of the war. After the restoration of peace, both men actively participated in various white supremacist activities, without much success.

Thomas Tandy Lewis

Further Reading

Betcherman, Lita-Rose. *The Swastika and the Maple Leaf: Fascist Movements in Canada in the Thirties.* Toronto: Fitzhenry & Whiteside, 1975.

Principe, Angelo. *The Darkest Side of the Fascist Years: The Italian-Canadian Press, 1920-1940.* Toronto: University of Toronto Press, 1999.

Robin, Martin. *Shades of Right: Nativist and Fascist Politics in Canada, 1920-1940.* Toronto: University of Toronto Press, 1992.

Salvatore, George T., ed. *Fascism and the Italians of Montreal: An Oral History, 1922-1945.* Toronto: Guernica Editions, 1998.

See also Anti-Semitism; Canadian minority communities; Coughlin, Charles E.; House Committee on Un-American Activities; Jews in Canada.

■ Fascism in the United States

Definition Antidemocratic American movements and groups that embraced ultranationalism, racism, and authoritarianism

During the 1930's, several antidemocratic and xenophobic groups in the United States agreed with particular ideas espoused by Italian fascists and German Nazis. Such groups, however, were quite different from the original European models.

The word "fascism" usually denotes the ideas and practices found in Italian fascism and German Nazism, although sometimes the word is used loosely as a pejorative label, referring to a variety of right-wing groups and persons. During the 1920's, the Fascist League of North America openly supported Benito Mussolini's policies, but because of growing opposition, the group was dissolved in 1929. During the decade of the 1930's, Mussolini continued to be highly respected by a large number of people, including

President Franklin D. Roosevelt. The majority of Americans, in contrast, perceived Adolf Hitler to be a dangerous dictator, and his anti-Semitic policies were particularly unpopular. A minority of Americans, particularly those of German ancestry, admired and defended Hitler's policies, and they organized themselves into a number of pro-Nazi organizations.

German-American Bund The German-American Bund was the largest and most important fascist organization in the United States. In May, 1933, the German government authorized Heinz Spanknobel, a German immigrant to the United States, to create a Nazi organization, which was called the Friends of New Germany. After the Department of State protested some of the group's anti-Semitic activities, Hitler advised German citizens in the United States to leave the Friends of New Germany. In March, 1936, members of the group established a new organization, the Amerika-Deutscher Volkerbund, translated as the German-American Bund, and they selected Fritz Julius Kuhn, a recent immigrant to the United States and veteran of the German army, to serve as the leader. The group was based in New York City, with branch offices in Chicago, Buffalo, and Milwaukee.

Supported openly by the German government until 1935, the German-American Bund appealed to many German Americans who were proud of their cultural heritage. The group copied many Nazi practices, including the use of Nazi marching songs, the greeting *sieg heil*, and the symbol of the swastika. The group's publications included pamphlets and a weekly newspaper, *Deutsche Weckruf* (German reveille). Kuhn's speeches and writings praised Hitler's Third Reich, and he denounced Jews, communists, and the Treaty of Versailles. Nevertheless, he claimed that he and other German-American Bund members were loyal to the U.S. Constitution and asserted that the institutions of the Third Reich were relevant only to Germany—not exportable elsewhere.

In 1936, Kuhn and four hundred bund members traveled to Berlin to attend the Summer Olympics, and the trip allowed Kuhn to have a ten-minute meeting with Hitler at the Reich Chancellery. According to Kuhn's account, Hitler praised the group's work and said, "Go back and continue your fight." By 1938, however, officials in Berlin had lost confidence in Kuhn's effectiveness, and Hitler or-

dered that German citizens withdraw from the group. When Kuhn traveled to Berlin to argue against the edict, Hitler refused to see him. Later that year, Kuhn faced hostile questions before the House Committee on Un-American Activities, which was chaired by Martin Dies, Jr. Then, Kristallnacht (the Night of Broken Glass), which highlighted Hitler's anti-Semitism, increased the opposition to the German-American Bund in the United States.

The German-American Bund reached an estimated membership of between five and ten thousand. At one point, Kuhn claimed that the membership was more than 100,000, but this is considered unlikely. A significant percentage of the members were German citizens. In an effort to attract young people, the bund organized recreational camps in a number of places, including Camp Siegfried on Long Island and Camp Hindenburg in Wisconsin. In February, 1939, the bund held its largest and most successful rally, when about twenty-two thousand supporters gathered in New York's Madison Square Garden. In front of a large portrait of George Washington surrounded by swastikas, Kuhn charged that President Franklin D. Roosevelt and the "Jew Deal" were part of an international anti-German conspiracy. The rally was interrupted by violent fistfights between hecklers and the bund's paramilitary troops.

A few months after the rally, the district attorney of New York, Thomas E. Dewey, arrested Kuhn and prosecuted him on charges of forgery and of misusing the group's funds. When the jury found Kuhn guilty of both forgery and larceny, the judge sentenced him to a prison term of between two and one-half years to five years. Under Kuhn's successor, Gerhard Kunze, the Bund rapidly lost members. After the outbreak of war in 1939, the bund was unable to stage public rallies because of popular opposition. On December 8, 1941, the executive committee voted to dissolve the organization.

Other Fascists and Semifascists The German-American Bund was not the only American organization during the decade that explicitly praised and imitated some of the rituals and ideology of Nazi Germany. In 1933, William Dudley Pelley, a fervent admirer of Hitler, organized the Silver Legion of America (commonly called the Silver Shirts), which grew to perhaps ten thousand members. In his publications, *Liberation* and *Pelley's Silvershirt Weekly*, Pelley combined millennial Christianity with an ideology of racism, extreme patriotism, and anti-Semitism. Another group, the Defenders of the Christian Faith, organized by Gerald B. Winrod, endorsed Hitler's anti-Semitic views and insisted on the veracity of the *Protocols of the Elders of Zion* (first published in English in 1919), which claimed to reveal a Jewish plot to take over the world.

A number of noteworthy authors defended selective policies of Hitler and Mussolini, expressing a great variety of interpretations and opinions. For example, Lawrence Dennis published *The Coming American Fascism* (1936), denouncing capitalism and arguing that the U.S. should adopt the economic arrangements of Hitler and Mussolini. Other profascist writers included George Sylvester Viereck, Joe McWilliams, Robert Edward Edmondson, and Elizabeth Dilling.

The message of anti-Semitism resonated with numerous Americans. Roman Catholic priest Charles E. Coughlin attracted a radio audience of about forty million with a message that combined anti-Semitic discourse with opposition to banks, Wall Street, and communism. His magazine, *Social Justice*, recognized the authenticity of the *Protocols of the Elders of Zion* and alleged that Marxist atheism was part of a Jewish plot. Similarly, fundamentalist preacher Gerald L. K. Smith, a leader of the Share Our Wealth movement, delivered virulent anti-Semitic speeches and advocated white supremacy. Coughlin and Smith rejected many aspects of fascist ideology, but their activities and speeches tended to legitimate the ideology among some right-wing Americans.

Although the number of thoroughgoing fascists remained relatively small during the decade, there was no shortage of antidemocratic and xenophobic movements. Numerous Americans, especially in the South, agreed with Hitler's notions about the inherent superiority of the white Aryan race. Since the 1860's, the best-known organization committed to white supremacy has been the Ku Klux Klan (KKK), which never attempted to hide its commitment to racism and anti-Semitism. The KKK had several million members during the 1920's, but during the 1930's, membership declined precipitously, and by 1939, when James B. Colescott assumed leadership of the group, it had only a few thousand members. Five years later, the organization was forced to disband for financial reasons. Scholars have disagreed about whether the word "fascist" should be applied to groups such as the KKK.

Impact Fascism was primarily a European phenomenon between World War I and World War II, and the ideology in its totality had limited appeal in the United States. Even the most prominent American organization, the German-American Bund, remained relatively small; it attracted a great deal of negative attention, thereby increasing the opposition of Americans to Nazi Germany. As World War II approached, there was little toleration in the United States for proponents of fascism. A number of fascist leaders and apologists, including Kuhn, Kunze, Viereck, and Pelley, were imprisoned on various charges during the war years. Approximately thirty prominent profascists, including Winrod and Dennis, were prosecuted under the Smith Act in the Great Sedition trial of 1944, which was eventually declared a mistrial. The military defeat of Italy and Germany greatly weakened the appeal of the fascist ideology, although a few fringe groups continued to adhere to it.

Thomas Tandy Lewis

Further Reading

Beekman, Scott. *William Dudley Pelley: A Life in Right-Wing Extremism and the Occult.* Syracuse, N.Y.: Syracuse University Press, 2005. Details the story of a forgotten defender of Nazi Germany.

Bell, Leland. *In Hitler's Shadow: The Anatomy of American Nazism.* Port Washington, Wash.: Kennikat Press, 1973. Highlights the story of the German-American Bund and the later American Nazi Party.

Diamond, Sander A. *The Nazi Movement in the United States, 1924-1941.* Ithaca, N.Y.: Cornell University Press, 1974. Scholarly work based on exhaustive research, asserting that no more than 10 percent of the German-American Bund's members were born in the United States.

Diggins, John P. *Mussolini and Fascism: The View from America.* Princeton, N.J.: Princeton University Press, 1972. Demonstrates that Mussolini was highly respected during the 1930's.

Horne, Gerald. *The Color of Fascism: Lawrence Dennis, Racial Passing, and the Rise of Right-Wing Extremism in the United States.* New York: New York University Press, 2006. Argues that Dennis's experiences with racial discrimination contributed to his support of fascism and criticisms of the United States.

MacDonnell, Francis. *Insidious Foes: The Axis Fifth Column and the American Home Front.* New York: Oxford University Press, 1995. Study of fears of Nazi spies between 1938 and 1942, arguing that such spies posed little risk and that fears were used for political purposes.

Remak, Joachim. "Friends of the New Germany: The Bund and German-American Relations." *Journal of Modern History* 29 (March, 1957). Scholarly article arguing that the German-American Bund did great damage to the image of Germany in the United States.

Smith, Gene. "Bundesfuehrer Kuhn." *American Heritage* 46 (September, 1995): 102-104. Biographical sketch and analysis of the leader of the German-American Bund.

Strong, Donald S. *Organized Anti-Semitism in America: The Rise of Group Prejudices During the Decade, 1930-1940.* Washington, D.C.: American Council on Public Affairs, 1941. Summary of eleven anti-Semitic organizations based largely on congressional investigations.

See also Anti-Semitism; German-American Bund; Jews in the United States; Jim Crow segregation; Racial discrimination.

■ Fashions and clothing

Fashions of the 1930's distanced themselves from the gamine looks of the 1920's, accentuating the curves of the body in both women's and men's fashions. As traditional designers were reeling from the Depression, American designers turned to ready-to-wear garments, creating a powerful industry and providing affordable fashion for the masses. Additionally, Hollywood became a guide for fashion and elegance.

Despite the harsh economic times, many women thought it their duty to be fashionable. The reality of everyday life was in juxtaposition to the glamour presented by Hollywood. Nearly all Americans needed practical dress for the day, when working, but wanted luxurious fashions for the evenings.

Fashion Design At the beginning of the 1930's, designers struggling to ride out the economic downturn reduced prices and switched from expensive decoration to more affordable alternatives. With dropping orders for couture, designers added ready-to-wear lines, which took advantage of washable fabrics. The switch to cheaper, mass-produced materials meant thousands of skilled workers in fashion-crafts areas lost their jobs. Economical fabrics were even introduced in evening clothing, when in 1931, Chanel showed thirty-five evening gowns in a variety of cotton fabrics.

After the Depression, New York and London encroached on Paris's domination of international fashion. New York became respected for ready-to-wear and leisure sports fashions, and the United States became the leader in the mass production of clothing in a standard set of sizes, utilizing technological improvements. Wholesale clothing became New York's leading industry and the fourth largest in the United States. As the mass production of garments rose, most designers were unknown; American design houses preferred to be linked to Paris.

Though the 1930's fashions tended toward mass-produced garments, designers were influenced by many trends. The angular style of Art Deco showed in motifs used in clothing and accessories. The mid-1930's brought about an interest in neo-Victorian, romantic fashions with padding, heavy ornamentation, and highly theatrical clothing. By the late 1930's, surrealism showed in designs with strange juxtapositions and extreme hats. As the swing-music craze swept the United States, the "jitterbug's" acrobatic dancing brought about a trend of clothing, with flared skirts, flat shoes, and looser trousers, that accommodated the movement.

Women's Fashions Designers of women's fashions rejected the waifish, linear silhouette of the 1920's and moved toward clothing that highlighted the female curves. Designers cast off the gamine dress and cloches of the 1920's and replaced them with clothing that emphasized femininity and restored the natural waist. Modern women were no longer of the leisured variety; they worked during the day and wanted extravagant fashion for the evening.

Brassieres offering natural shaping replaced the flat-chest look of the 1920's. The gentle shaping of the waist came from lightly boned and laced corsets or stretch undergarments. Pastel slips, camiknickers, and negligees were made in silks or rayon and complemented with lace and embroidery. Rayon stockings were replaced by nylon versions near the end of the decade.

Fashionable woman modeling a straw hat and halter top. (©H. Armstrong Roberts/ClassicStock/CORBIS)

Emphasis on the shoulders brought about a squared look. Upper sleeve puffs; cape sleeves; short, shoulder-covering capes; and tiny bolero jackets became highly fashionable. Skirts stayed slim but were longer and became fuller at the knee, cut to flare or with sewn-in pleats, later in the decade. Evening gowns were to the floor, afternoon garments were usually calf length, and day garments were a bit shorter. Unable to afford these longer 1930's fashions, many women resorted to adding strips of contrasting fabric or fur to the hems of their older skirts. For day wear, skirts were paired with blouses and sweaters shaped to be worn over the waistband.

Evening gowns became even more distinct from their daytime counterparts. Backless evening gowns allowed only the smallest of undergarments, and the smooth fabrics were cut on the bias to encourage curve-hugging silhouettes. Nineteenth century fashions, Grecian-inspired pleating, and sequins in evening dresses were trends that continued through the mid-1930's.

Though women's fashions tended toward the feminine form, men's wear continued to be adapted for women in the workplace. Tailor-made suits, with short jackets, were constructed of wool, linen, cotton, and tweed. Women's overcoats tended to be calf length and in the polo-coat style. Short leather and suede jackets were either belted at the waist or sported a band that stopped short of the hip.

As health clubs became synonymous with beauty regimens, the popular gym suits consisted of one-piece shorts suits, split skirts, or shorts paired with a slipover blouse. By 1937, sports suits for wearing to the beach, picnicking, or hiking allowed women the freedom of trousers, matched with jackets or knit tops. Trousers were worn beachside and, with full legs, even as informal evening attire.

Bathing suits became briefer and, with the help of elasticized fabrics, more formfitting. Both skirted and skirtless styles were created from wool and latex blends. Sunglasses with tortoiseshell rims became a popular craze, and sports clothing with halter necklines or removable straps aided in tanning.

Ladies' Accessories Accessories helped to personalize the American mass-produced garments. The Sears basic "Many-Way" dress showed women how to use accessories to create "a different dress for every day in the week." Catalogs and department stores carried all the little extras the modern woman needed to complete and update her outfit.

Hats continued to be popular in many styles, including sailor, fezzes, tricornes, berets, pillbox, and brimmed hats set at rakish slants. In the mid- to late 1930's, turbans became popular. Surrealist-inspired millinery creations showed up in high fashion and influenced the ready-made hats on the market.

The 1930's brought about a variety of shoe styles and materials, including various reptile, dyed-to-match satins, and metallic kid. Strappy sandals, slingbacks, and open-toed designs were created with lower heels for day and beachwear and higher heels for evening attire. Later, wedge soles and platform shoes were introduced.

Belts helped in accenting the natural waist; therefore, they were made with decorative clasps and belting made of leather or fabrics that matched the garments. Scarves were sold in a variety of colors, fabrics, and patterns that were printed, hand painted, or dyed. The envelope-style clutch purse became popular for a day accessory. For evenings, women carried small, neat bags.

Costume jewelry and gloves lent a measure of glamour to any lady's costume. Rhinestone, simulated pearls, and jabot jewelry, along with gloves in several lengths and fabrics, were sold in catalogs for the woman to accessorize within her budget.

Color and Materials During the early 1930's, color seemed to mirror the tough economic times. Subdued hues of black, navy, and earth tones were popular in day wear; black and pastel hues were fashionable for evenings. Later, vivid color became accepted and expected. Designers created looks in multiple bold colors, and even the beaches became awash in color. Navy-blue swimwear receded in popularity and was replaced by bold-colored suits, swim caps, and beachwear.

Though fine wools, linens, and silks remained highly fashionable fabrics, many fabrics were created. Nylon, rayon, metallic lamé, Rhabdophane, and cellophane were developed or improved during this time, and forward fashion designers worked them into their collections, often mixing them with natural fibers. By 1934, elasticized fabrics, using lastex (later called latex), were produced in a variety of styles, enabling top designers to create dresses with no fasteners and an assortment of new undergarments. Varieties of fur to fit all budgets were used in coats, jackets, animal-pelt scarves, and trimmings and were often dyed in bright colors. Plastic was also introduced into the fashion world to create accessories and colored zippers. For the first time, plastic was cheap enough for everyone to afford and stylish enough to be made into jewelry.

Hollywood Fashion Hollywood became a trendsetting place for fashion during the 1930's. Movies made fashion dramatic and reached everyday people in a way traditional fashion shows could not. Hollywood costume designers began to influence trends and showcase current fashions and hairstyles. Even children's clothing was influenced by the child stars of the day.

The commercialization of Hollywood fashions brought about manufacturers that marketed through department stores and mail-order catalogs. A leader in the catalog business, Sears, Roebuck and Company carried Hollywood fashion items and products endorsed by the film legends. Loretta Young, Fay

Wray, and Claudette Colbert all endorsed fashion products. The film fanzines also brought American fashion to people's homes, promoting Hollywood, and not Paris, as the center of fashion. Many of these magazines carried paper patterns for the home dressmaker and advertised their own lines of Hollywood styles.

Though many women could not afford the fashions of Hollywood, most could copy the accessories, hair, and makeup of their favorite stars. California was the world leader in cosmetics and the home of many makeup styles created for Hollywood. Marlene Dietrich popularized finely arched and penciled eyebrows for women. Also popular were false eyelashes and artificial nails. Max Factor, a studio employee, created his own brand of cosmetics. His beauty salons became the place where women could go to have their makeup and hair done by professionals. Magazine advertisements showed Hollywood stars giving step-by-step instructions on how to create these looks. This combined with the introduction of makeup products changed how a woman went about her toilet.

Men's Fashions European royalty and Hollywood influenced men's grooming through the 1930's. The men's look was sleekly tailored and reinforced by stars such as Cary Grant and Gary Cooper. British style included sophisticated tailored suits, while American leisure garments focused on the rugged man.

U.S. influence on men's summer and resort clothing created a more leisurely look. Blazers were paired with looser linen trousers. The shift toward a more relaxed American look was also evident in the abundance of sporty, soft-collared, polo-style shirts. Men's casual sweaters were worn both in cardigan style and as pullovers, made from wool and cotton.

Men's trousers were high waisted with wide waistbands that fit snugly at the hip and began to sport zipper closures instead of buttons. They had full legs, cuffed at the bottom and were made in a variety of fabrics, including cassimere, corduroy, serge, and tweed.

Dark colored suits, with squared shoulders, paired with a shirt and tie remained the norm for more formal occasions. Frederick Scholte, tailor to the Duke of Windsor, created the "London cut" or the "drape" suit to promote the athletic, masculine form. The cut of Scholte's suit came to be synonymous with the American style of suits during the 1930's. The jacket had broad shoulders and a breast pocket, was nipped in at the waist, and had lifted sleeves to give the desirable look of squared shoulders. The waistcoats were six button and short, though at the end of the 1930's, men left off the waistcoats in the summer. The trousers were high waisted, with doubled pleats, and the legs were cuffed. Double-breasted dinner jackets became more popular. Evening waistcoats were black and often backless, and trousers followed the daytime style, but without cuffs.

Gym clothing for men consisted primarily of pullover sweatshirts with or without hoods and sweatpants. Men's swim trunks were made from wool with zipper fronts or from Latex blends that pulled on. Most trunks had high-cut legs and were supported by belts. During this time, men stopped wearing shirts at the beach.

Men's raincoats were loose-fitting, belted, trench style, and created from cotton fabrics. Overcoats hit below the knee and were often double breasted in the beginning of the 1930's and single breasted by the late 1930's. Wools in solids and plaids, along with fur, were used in the creation of overcoats. Men began to turn up the collars of their coats to give the impression of the tough guy, made popular by Hollywood gangsters. Short overcoats had front zippers and were created in fabrics and leathers.

Hat styles for men included the fedora, with the brim down at the front and up in the back, and the trilby, a soft, felt hat with an indention on the crown. In men's shoes, Oxford styles were widely popular, as were the moccasin style, the Stratford, and the Dixie. Though leather was prominent, suede grew in popularity as a shoe material. Fashionable colored or patterned socks were held up with suspenders.

Impact Fashion of the 1930's brought back the curves of the body and extravagant dress for evenings. The United States led the way in creating the mass-produced clothing industry, and Hollywood brought fashion to the masses. Fashion designers eagerly made use of advances in technology, bringing new materials into common usage in the fashion industry.

Hannah Schauer Galli

Further Reading

Bailey, Margaret J. *Those Glorious Glamour Years: The Great Hollywood Costume Designs of the 1930's.* Secaucus, N.J.: The Citadel Press, 1982. Explores the fashion of the 1930's films, using photographs of the stars in costume to showcase Hollywood's influence on fashion.

Blum, Stella, ed. *Everyday Fashions of the Thirties as Pictured in Sears Catalogs.* New York: Dover, 1986. Composed of reproductions of Sears catalog pages from the 1930's.

Costantino, Maria. *Fashions of a Decade: The 1930s.* New York: Chelsea House, 2007. Examines the role of fashion during the 1930's and its relation to the Great Depression and Hollywood. Photographs and illustrations provide a firsthand look at the fashions and their cultural context.

Mendes, Valerie, and Amy De La Haye. *Twentieth Century Fashion.* London: Thames & Hudson, 1999. Overview of fashion from 1900 to 1999. The authors give a concise survey, using important fashion developments to denote chapters. Heavily illustrated.

Robinson, Julian. *Fashion in the '30's.* London: Oresko Books, 1978. Documents the styles of the 1930's. Original photographs and advertisements are used to illustrate the fashions.

See also Art movements; Dance; Fads; Hairstyles; Magazines; Music: Popular; Nylon; Unemployment in Canada; Unemployment in the United States.

■ Father Divine

Identification African American clergyman and leader of the International Peace Mission movement

Born May, 1879; Rockville, Maryland

Died September 10, 1965; Gladwyne, Pennsylvania

As the founder of the International Peace Mission movement, one of the most popular and colorful religious outreach efforts of the 1930's, Father Divine brought hope and inspiration combined with a practical communalism that directly improved the physical conditions of many individual lives in the black community.

The charismatic figure of Father Divine, born George Baker, a son of freed slaves born shortly after the Civil War, had become a well-known if controversial icon of the African American religious community by the 1930's. His early life in the Methodist

Church formed an awareness of deep spirituality and dedication to religious convictions that served as the foundation of his later public career.

Father Divine left home as a young adult. He began to work as an urban evangelist, aided by a strong speaking voice and compelling personal presence. By 1917, he had attracted a group of disciples, with whom he settled in a communal apartment in Brooklyn, New York, and took the name Reverend Major Jealous Divine. His preaching filled a void in African American communities, which were expanding rapidly as a consequence of the Great Migration. Many African Americans were accustomed to a structured religious institution as part of a normal life. Father Divine claimed to be God working directly for his followers and that the International Peace movement operated under heavenly sanction.

Moving to Long Island in 1919, Father Divine continued to espouse a theology marked by a belief in the equality of all in the sight of God and provided a haven from the social conditions to which African Americans were subjected. The International Peace Mission movement (so named for the common greeting used by Divine and all members to one another) was one of several religious cults to emerge during the early 1930's in Harlem, where unemployment reached 50 percent and housing conditions were substandard and overpriced. The existing mainstream African American churches of all denominations were unable to comprehensively address the myriad problems faced by their parishioners, providing an opportunity for other spiritual leaders to offer alternative options.

Father Divine's household left Brooklyn and moved into a house in Suffolk County on Long Island, where in November, 1931, local residents and the district attorney responded to a complaint based on the noise generated by the religious meetings. This began a lengthy legal proceeding that ended in January, 1933. The New York Supreme Court overturned the initial trial on grounds of judicial prejudice. This verdict helped to further Father Divine's career, and he abandoned Suffolk County, moving his headquarters to Harlem. Upon arriving, he be-

Father Divine speaking at his Crum Elbow estate in 1938. (Time & Life Pictures/Getty Images)

gan to address the massive needs of the poor by initiating public banquets. By the end of the decade, these had become a trademark of his ministry. He also acquired properties in New Jersey, Baltimore, and Bridgeport, Connecticut. He called on his followers to create a wide variety of businesses based on the communal model, ranging from restaurants to rooming houses. Because of this, many lived in better circumstances than they had previously known. The sheer volume of trade at many of the businesses helped to keep costs down for individuals. His followers also opened centers, termed "heavens," that showcased their lifestyle; these were located in California, Washington, New Jersey, and Pennsylvania.

Both the mainstream churches and many of the other independent evangelists active in the black community were wary of Father Divine's work. Notably absent from his early public life was work directly related to civil rights for African Americans. This changed after the Harlem riot of 1935, which massively damaged the community. In January, 1939, Father Divine held the first and only "Divine Righteous Government Convention," which highlighted political platforms that incorporated elements of Father Divine's doctrine. Segregation was a particular target of his sermons, as were many of the discriminatory practices against African Americans, such as the Jim Crow laws and lynching. While the total number of participants in the International Peace Mission community was never made public, the perception was that Father Divine could and did influence the minds and votes of millions, thus giving him substantial political authority, which he applied only in the service of his beliefs.

Impact   Father Divine's preaching and organizing focused on creating an environment and mode of life for his followers in which the racial division between black and white Americans was invalidated and the human dignity of each person was restored. His positions on universal equality and opposition to any form of race-based discrimination foreshadowed the later protests and activism of the Civil Rights movement.

Robert Ridinger

Further Reading

Burnham, Kenneth E. *God Comes to America: Father Divine and the Peace Mission Movement.* Boston: Lambeth Press, 1979.

Mabee, Carleton. *Promised Land: Father Divine's Interracial Communities in Ulster County, New York.* Fleischmanns, N.Y.: Purple Mountain Press, 2008.

Vaughn, Mina A. "Father Divine." In *African-American Orators: A Bio-Critical Sourcebook,* edited by Richard W. Leeman. Westport, Conn.: Greenwood Press, 1996.

Watts, Jill. *God, Harlem U.S.A.: The Father Divine Story.* Berkeley: University of California Press, 1992.

Weisbrot, Robert. *Father Divine and the Struggle for Racial Equality.* Urbana: University of Illinois Press, 1983.

See also   Civil rights and liberties in the United States; Race riots; Racial discrimination; Religion in the United States.

■ Faulkner, William

Identification   American novelist and short story writer
Born   September 25, 1897; New Albany, Mississippi
Died   July 6, 1962; Byhalia, Mississippi

Faulkner is generally regarded as the greatest American writer of prose fiction, and the 1930's represents the richest period of his productivity in terms of both quantity and quality. The ten books and dozens of short stories he published during the decade laid the foundation for the career achievement that earned him the Nobel Prize in Literature in 1950.

With the publication of his breakthrough fourth novel *The Sound and the Fury* (1929), William Cuthbert Faulkner began to attract a higher degree of critical attention. Until his ascendance, writers such as Ernest Hemingway and Dashiell Hammett had dominated the American literary scene of the 1920's by writing their stories and novels in a terse, deceptively plain prose style and with a rigorously

For author William Faulkner the 1930's was a prolific period in which he produced Light in August, As I Lay Dying, *and other literary classics. (©Bettmann/CORBIS)*

objective approach to handling point of view. Faulkner, however, wrote in an emotionally charged, ornately poetic style and experimented freely with a range of innovative techniques aimed at rendering the stream of consciousness of his characters as subjectively as possible.

While his book sales were never sufficient to generate much income during the 1930's, Faulkner won the respect of many critics and most of his creative peers with a series of groundbreaking novels, including such undoubted masterpieces as *As I Lay Dying* (1930), the first important American novel of the 1930's; *Light in August* (1932); and *Absalom, Absalom!* (1936). In an unparalleled display of artistic resourcefulness, Faulkner created an entirely different and original narrative structure for each of his major novels. *As I Lay Dying*, for example, is told through the stream-of-consciousness monologues of fifteen characters, including one section narrated from the point of view of a dead woman. *Light in August*, on the other hand, relies primarily on a convoluted handling of time, telling the story out of chronological order to intensify its impact. *Absalom, Absalom!* produces its distinctive effect through the layering of multiple consciousnesses, as characters attempt imaginatively to reconstruct the minds and thoughts of historical characters.

Even though Faulkner's achievements as a novelist have overshadowed his reputation as an author of short stories, he is also one of America's greatest writers of short fiction, and the decade of the 1930's was one of his most fruitful periods as a short story writer; twenty of his stories were published or accepted for publication from 1930 to 1932. His first publication in a national magazine, and his most widely anthologized and analyzed story, was "A Rose for Emily," which appeared in April, 1930. It was

---

"No Town nor City Was His"

At the beginning of the second chapter of Light in August *(1932), William Faulkner introduces the main character of his story, Joe Christmas, as seen through the eyes of Byron Bunch.*

Byron Bunch knows this—it was one Friday morning three years ago. And the group of men at work in the planer shed looked up, and saw the stranger standing there, watching them. They did not know how long he had been there. He looked like a tramp, yet not like a tramp either. His shoes were dusty and his trousers were soiled too. But they were of decent serge, sharply creased, and his shirt was soiled but it was a white shirt, and he wore a tie and a stiffbrim straw hat that was quite new, cocked at an angle arrogant and baleful above his still face. He did not look like a professional hobo in his professional rags, but there was something definitely rootless about him, as though no town nor city was his, no street, no walls, no square of earth his home. And that he carried this knowledge as though it were a banner, with a quality ruthless, lonely, and almost proud. "As if," as the men said later, "he was just down on his luck for a time, and that he didn't intend to stay down on it and didn't give a damn much how he rose up." He was young. And Byron watched him standing there and looking at the men in sweatstained overalls, with a cigarette in one side of his mouth and his face darkly and contemptuously still, drawn down a little on one side because of the smoke. After a while he spat the cigarette without touching his hand to it and turned and went on to the mill office while the men in faded and worksoiled overalls looked at his back with a sort of baffled outrage. "We ought to run him through the planer." the foreman said. "Maybe that will take that look off his face."

Source: Faulkner, William. *Light in August: The Corrected Text.* New York: Vintage International, 1990.

---

quickly followed by a series of masterpieces, including "That Evening Sun," "Red Leaves," "A Justice," and "Dry September," all of which were included in his first collection of short fiction, *These Thirteen* (1931), followed by a second collection, *Dr. Martino and Other Stories* (1934), generally regarded as the less successful of the two.

The line between Faulkner's short stories and novels is permeable, and critics continue to argue over the genre of such volumes as *The Unvanquished* (1938), which was assembled from seven linked stories, six of which had been previously published. Another "hybrid" novel, *The Wild Palms* (1939), which alternated chapters between two stories, became his best-selling book of the decade, and three short stories from the 1930's appeared in revised form in the novel *The Hamlet* (1940).

While magazine publications earned him substantially more money than his novels did, Faulkner was unable to support his family on his income from writing fiction, and in 1932, he began spending time as a contract writer for Hollywood studios, becoming a favorite of such directors as Howard Hawks. Faulkner always dreaded the work and the lifestyle, but it paid too well to turn it down; he spent extended periods of time during the 1930's as a screenwriter.

Impact Faulkner's originality and significance began to be widely recognized by critics and fellow writers during the 1930's, and by the end of the decade his reputation was so secure that he appeared on the cover of *Time* magazine on January 23, 1940. His radical experiments in form and technique, especially in his complex handling of point of view, and his densely poetic style influenced almost every major prose writer who followed him.

William Nelles

Further Reading

Atkinson, Ted. *Faulkner and the Great Depression: Aesthetics, Ideology, and Cultural Politics*. Athens: University of Georgia Press, 2006. Explores the relation between Faulkner's writing and the historical and cultural contexts of the Great Depression, focusing on the fiction of the 1930's.

Berland, Alwyn. *Light in August: A Study in Black and White*. New York: Twayne, 1992. The first book-length study of the novel summarizes the literary and historical contexts for general readers and provides a detailed reading of the narrative itself.

Blotner, Joseph. *Faulkner: A Biography*. 2 vols. New York: Random House, 1974. The most thorough and detailed of the many biographies of Faulkner runs more than two thousand pages and remains the foundation on which all other biographies are built.

Parker, Robert Dale. *Absalom, Absalom! The Questioning of Fictions*. Boston: Twayne, 1991. Surveys the literary and historical contexts of Faulkner's masterpiece and offers a chapter-by-chapter reading of the novel. Includes an appendix outlining the narrative chronology.

Peek, Charles A., and Robert W. Hamblin, eds. *A Companion to Faulkner Studies*. Westport, Conn.: Greenwood Press, 2004. Includes thirteen essays written expressly for the volume, organized by critical approaches. Includes a selective bibliography and useful index.

Skei, Hans H. *Reading Faulkner's Best Short Stories*. Columbia: University of South Carolina Press, 1999. Provides an overview of Faulkner's career as a short-story writer and detailed analyses of twelve of his greatest short stories.

Wadlington, Warwick. *As I Lay Dying: Stories out of Stories*. New York: Twayne, 1992. An accessible discussion of the first major American novel published during the 1930's, addressing its literary and historical contexts and critical reception.

See also Great Depression in the United States; Hammett, Dashiell; Hemingway, Ernest; Literature in the United States; Magazines.

FCC. See Federal Communications Commission

Federal Aid in Wildlife Restoration Act. See Pittman-Robertson Act of 1937

■ Federal Communications Commission

Identification Federal government agency regulating nonfederal government use of the radio spectrum and all interstate telecommunications

Date Established in 1934

Created by the Telecommunications Act of 1934, the Federal Communications Commission (FCC) is the preeminent government organization charged with regulating the telecommunications industry. This includes not only wire communications but also radio and television broadcasting. The FCC was formed as the country was recovering from the Great Depression; since then the commission's responsibilities and powers have increased.

Several circumstances led to the creation of the FCC in 1934. Telecommunications were becoming increasingly important, and the commission previously responsible for regulating broadcasting, the Interstate Commerce Commission, was overburdened with the regulation of the transportation industry. Furthermore, the country was slowly recovering from its most severe depression ever, and discontent existed with the way the huge telecommunications industry, principally the Bell System, had treated its employees. President Franklin D. Roosevelt's election led to a greater control of all industry, and the telecommunications industry was not exempt.

The FCC was charged with regulating "interstate" telephone companies. Although every telephone company, by virtue of its toll-line connection, is theoretically an "interstate" company, the 1934 law limited this definition. It defined so-called connecting companies, as opposed to interstate companies, as those that do not operate in interstate commerce except by virtue of their connections with other companies.

One of the first projects of the FCC was a massive investigation of the telephone industry. American Telephone and Telegraph (AT&T) constituted about 85 percent of that industry, so that is where the emphasis of the investigation was placed. The inquest went on for nearly three years and consumed vast amounts of money. The government spent $2 million, and AT&T spent $1.5 million. It was probably the most complete record of factual information on the operations of an important American business enterprise.

The general thrust of the government's case was that Western Electric, the manufacturing arm of the Bell System, was charging the Bell Operating Companies too much for their equipment. In this case the telephone subscriber ultimately paid, because the country's telephone rate structure was built upon the costs of the operating companies. The government concluded that those costs were inappropriately high.

FCC commissioner Paul A. Walker submitted a "Proposed Report" in April, 1938. Changes were made to the report, and in 1939, the FCC body approved a "Report on the Investigation of the Telephone Industry in the United States." Because World War II began several months later, the report

---

Section One of the Communications Act of 1934

For the purpose of regulating interstate and foreign commerce in communication by wire and radio so as to make available, so far as possible, to all the people of the United States a rapid, efficient, Nation-wide, and world-wide wire and radio communication service with adequate facilities at reasonable charges, for the purpose of the national defense, and for the purpose of securing a more effective execution of this policy by centralizing authority heretofore granted by law to several agencies and by granting additional authority with respect to interstate and foreign commerce in wire and radio communication, there is hereby created a commission to be known as the "Federal Communications Commission," which shall be constituted as hereinafter provided, and which shall execute and enforce the provisions of this Act.

---

was largely ignored. However, antitrust charges leveled against AT&T lingered for years and decades later led to the breakup of the Bell System.

The modern commission is directed by five commissioners appointed by the president and confirmed by the Senate. Commissioners serve five-year terms, and one of the commissioners is designated by the president as chairperson. Only three of the five members can be of the same political party, and none of them may have a financial interest in any commission-related business.

Impact　The role of the FCC increased as rapidly as the communications industry has. Areas of concern have included wire communications, wireless communications, radio and television broadcasting, and satellite communications.

Robert E. Stoffels

Further Reading

Brooks, John. *Telephone: The First Hundred Years.* New York: Harper & Row, 1976. Likely the most inclusive and important book dealing with the first one hundred years of the telephone industry.

Flannery, Gerald V. *Commissioners of the FCC, 1927-1994.* Lanham, Md.: University Press of America, 1995. Looks at the people who have served as FCC commissioners.

Paglin, Max D. *The Communications Act: A Legislative History of the Major Amendments, 1934-1996.* Silver Spring, Md.: Pike & Fischer, 1999. Emphasis on the changes that have been made to the Communications Act of 1934.

_____. *A Legislative History of the Communications Act of 1934.* New York: Oxford University Press, 1989. Compiled by the former general counsel and later executive director of the FCC; describes in detail the 1934 Communications Act.

See also Great Depression in the United States; Public Utilities Act; Rural Electrification Administration; Telephone technology and service.

■ Federal Emergency Relief Administration

Identification New Deal direct-relief agency for the unemployed
Also known as FERA
Date Established on May 12, 1933

The Federal Emergency Relief Administration (FERA) provided $3.1 billion in federal grants to states and localities between May, 1933, and December, 1935. Authorization for the FERA came from the Federal Emergency Relief Act that Congress passed in May, 1933. The FERA was the first direct-relief operation of Franklin D. Roosevelt's New Deal.

Planned by Harry Hopkins and Roosevelt the first week after Roosevelt's inauguration and passed by Congress during the first one hundred days of Roosevelt's administration, the FERA authorized immediate grants to states for relief.

When the Federal Emergency Relief Act passed in May of 1933, fourteen million people—more than one-fourth of the U.S. workforce—were unemployed. After directing the New York Temporary Emergency Relief Administration while Roosevelt was New York governor, Hopkins became the director of the FERA. The organization emphasized work relief, not handouts.

Congress allocated $500 million, one-half of which was available on a matching basis of one federal dollar for every three dollars the state had spent over the previous three months. Hopkins made the second half available on a discretionary basis because the Depression had impacted each state differently.

The State Emergency Relief Administrations submitted monthly reports that enabled Hopkins to allocate funds equitably; these state agencies typically distributed the funds on a monthly basis to the county relief committees. The FERA could assume control of a state's relief organization if it failed to comply with federal mandates.

State social workers visited homes, assessed needs, and determined other possible sources of income to establish eligibility. Relief applicants who were able to work usually performed some task; women and white-collar workers, however, were often more difficult to accommodate than the unskilled.

Additional relief became necessary for the winter of 1933-1934. On November 9, 1933, President Roosevelt created by executive order the Civil Works Administration (CWA), to provide short-term aid for the unemployed. Its $400 million went primarily to the states for soup kitchens, blankets, employment projects, and nurseries.

The temporary CWA disbanded in the spring of 1934, and Hopkins reorganized the FERA into three divisions: social service, public works, and rural rehabilitation. The FERA had three primary objectives: adequate relief, work for those on relief rolls, and a diversity of programs, including education. Some results included the creation of fishing cooperatives, freezing and processing plants on the coastal plain, a cattle program, a vagrancy program, and survey and research projects. The FERA helped reduce farm surpluses and redistribute food to the needy through food stamps, school lunches, and direct distribution.

The FERA provided work and education to more than fifteen million Americans. In March, 1935, the emergency education programs of the FERA were at their peak with more than 1,724,000 enrollees. More than forty-four teachers—many previously unemployed—began serving as educators. The education programs included general adult-education and literacy classes, vocational education and rehabilitation programs, aid to college students, and nursery classes for underprivileged preschoolers.

The FERA ended in December of 1935. The Works Progress Administration, the Social Security Board, and other New Deal agencies assumed its duties.

Impact Within the first two hours of its existence, the FERA distributed $5 million in relief funds. By December of 1935, the FERA had distributed more than $3 billion. The FERA provided work relief and education to millions of Americans. Furthermore, the agency established the idea that sufficient public relief from the government was a right of American citizens.

Anita Price Davis

Further Reading

Axinn, June, and Mark J. Stern. *Social Welfare: A History of the American Response to Need.* 7th ed. Boston: Pearson/Allyn and Bacon, 2008.

Brock, William Ranulf. *Welfare, Democracy, and the New Deal.* Reprint. Cambridge, England: Cambridge University Press, 1993.

Davis, Kenneth S. *FDR: The New Deal Years, 1933-1937.* New York: Random House, 1986.

See also   Great Depression in the United States; Roosevelt, Franklin D.; Roosevelt's first one hundred days; Unemployment in the United States; Works Progress Administration.

Joseph Caliway, a senior Food and Drug Administration chemist, in 1938. (Library of Congress)

■ Federal Food, Drug, and Cosmetic Act of 1938

The Law   Invested authority in the Food and Drug Administration to oversee the food, drug, and cosmetics industries

Also known as   FFDCA

Date   1938

Allowed for the regulation of food, drug, and cosmetics industries for purposes of safety and truth in advertising.

In 1937, the S. E. Massengill Co. distributed sulfanilamide that had been prepared with the solvent diethylene glycol, a toxic substance. Massengill had not performed any animal testing with the medication, instead releasing it directly to the public. Reports began to surface of deaths associated with this medicine, and more than one hundred people were believed to have died from this poisoning.

In response, Congress enacted the Federal Food, Drug, and Cosmetic Act in 1938 in order to protect the safety of the American people. Part of the law required companies to test their products on animals and submit reports to the Food and Drug Administration (FDA) before marketing their products.

Though the FDA already had some power in regulating the food and drug industry, the act extended this power to the cosmetics industry as well. Also, the

FDA was given the power to inspect facilities that handled or produced food, drug, or cosmetic products. The FDA could also determine safe levels for unavoidable substances that could cause potential harm. Furthermore, the FDA had the responsibility to set standards for the packaging of food, drugs, and cosmetics; this task included marking clearly ingredient lists, weights, and quality on packages.

Furthermore, the act removed a previous provision known as the Sherley amendment, giving the FDA power to prosecute mislabeled items whether or not the manufacturer intended to mislead the consumer. The responsibility for regulating advertising of these products fell to the Federal Trade Commission, under the Wheeler-Lea Act. The FDA maintained authority in the regulation of the advertising of prescription drugs.

Impact   Congress gave the FDA more power to regulate the food, drug, and cosmetics industries to ensure the safety of the products of these industries. This act has been amended several times as advancements have been made in each field.

Emily Carroll Shearer

Further Reading

Hilt, Philip J. *Protecting America's Health: The FDA, Business, and One Hundred Years of Regulation.* Chapel Hill: University of North Carolina Press, 2004.

Kay, Gwen. *Dying to Be Beautiful: The Fight for Safe Cosmetics.* Columbus: Ohio State University Press, 2005.

See also Advertising in the United States; Congress, U.S.; Elixir sulfanilamide scandal; Federal Trade Commission; Food processing; Medicine; Wheeler-Lea Act of 1938.

■ Federal Housing Administration

Identification Federal government agency providing insurance for home mortgages

Date Established on June 28, 1934

By providing government-backed insurance for loans to purchase homes, the Federal Housing Administration (FHA) expanded the availability of loans for Americans without requiring large down payments.

The Great Depression produced a dramatic decline in home ownership. Foreclosures of family homes became widespread, and estimates indicate that one-third of unemployed persons had earlier worked in the housing industry. One of the major causes for the decline in the housing industry was that the failure of thousands of banks made it extremely difficult for people to obtain mortgages. From the beginning of his presidency, Franklin D. Roosevelt was firmly determined to establish programs that would promote the building and ownership of private homes.

Roosevelt was especially interested in a program that would not require large expenditures and would not involve the government directly in financing or construction. To design such a program, he formed the President's Emergency Commission on Housing. The chair of the commission was Frank Comerford Walker, and members included Harry Hopkins, Frances Perkins, Rexford Guy Tugwell, and Henry A. Wallace. The group drafted a housing bill, which, despite considerable opposition from some banking and construction interests, was approved by Congress in June, 1934.

The National Housing Act established the FHA, which guaranteed home mortgage loans made by banks and other lending institutions. The act reduced down payments from 30 percent to 10 percent and extended the periods of payments from twenty to thirty years—conditions that made home ownership affordable for millions of Americans with modest incomes. In addition, the act created the Federal Savings and Loan Insurance Corporation, which provided insurance for deposits in savings-and-loan associations and home-loan banks.

Under the act, when an individual applied for a home mortgage, an FHA-approved lending institution would ask the borrower if FHA insurance was desired. If the down payment was small, the lender could insist that the borrower apply for the insurance. When insurance was desired, FHA employees assessed the conditions of the proposed loan, and if these met the necessary criteria, the FHA would then insure the lending institution against a loss of principal in case the borrower defaulted. Borrowers paid an insurance premium, and in return, they received two benefits: an external appraisal and usually a lower interest rate. The FHA was one of the few government agencies that operated entirely from its self-generated income, thereby costing taxpayers nothing.

The first administrator of the FHA was James Moffett, a conservative businessman. Under his leadership, the FHA was reluctant to insure new constructions, rental houses, and houses in blighted neighborhoods. Moffett also opposed the building of pubic-housing projects, and this opposition brought him into conflict with liberals in the Congress and the administration. In 1938, amendments to the National Housing Act substantially lowered requirements for down payments and raised financing limits, thereby allowing more middle-class families to obtain FHA-insured loans. Only after passage of the 1938 amendment did the FHA begin to aggressively finance the construction of new homes.

Impact The insurance program of the FHA helped to make home mortgages more accessible to persons of modest income, and it also helped to promote home construction and repair, thereby reducing unemployment. The FHA was more successful in financing the modernization of existing structures than in promoting the construction of new homes. Between 1934 and 1940, the FHA extended $4.07 billion in insured loans. This included more than 1.5

Howard Gray (left), head of the Federal Housing Administration, showing Secretary of the Interior Harold Ickes a map of low-cost housing projects in the United States. (Library of Congress)

million loans to repair or modernize homes and 494,474 loans to build new homes.

During its first thirty years, the major function of the FHA was to serve as an insuring agency for loans from private lenders, but after the late 1960's, its role expanded to include the administration of interest-rate subsidies and rent-supplement programs. By 2000, the FHA had provided insurance for 34 million mortgages. The FHA continued to function into the twenty-first century.

Thomas Tandy Lewis

Further Reading

Fish, Gertrude. *The Story of Housing.* New York: Macmillan, 1979.

Garvin, Alexander. *The American City: What Works, What Doesn't.* 2d ed. New York: McGraw-Hill, 2002.

Gelfand, Mark. *A Nation of Cities: The Federal Government and Urban America, 1933-1965.* New York: Oxford University Press, 1975.

Henderson, A. Scott. *Housing and the Democratic Ideal: The Life and Thought of Charles Abrams.* New York: Columbia University Press, 2000.

Jackson, Kenneth. "Race, Ethnicity, and Real Estate Appraisal: The Home Owners Loan Corporation and the Federal Housing Administration." *Journal of Urban History* 6 (August, 1980): 419-452.

Wood, Edith Elmer. *Slums and Blighted Areas in the United States.* College Park, Md.: McGrath, 1969.

See also Banking; Credit and debt; Federal National Mortgage Association; Great Depression in the United States; *Home Building and Loan Association v. Blaisdell*; Immigration to the United States; New Deal.

■ Federal National Mortgage Association

Identification Secondary-mortgage-market
financial institution
Also known as Fannie Mae
Date Established on February 10, 1938

The establishment of Fannie Mae gave birth to the secondary mortgage market. It has played a major role in making mortgage money available to home buyers in the United States.

President Franklin D. Roosevelt and the U.S. Congress created the Federal National Mortgage Association under the umbrella of the New Deal in 1938. The agency was established in response to a financial situation that was paralyzing the real estate marketplace and thereby further depressing the national economy.

By the mid-1930's unemployment and the resulting financial strain on families had pushed so many home mortgages into foreclosure that lending institutions were finding themselves short of the funds needed to continue making mortgage loans to prospective home buyers. From 1932 to 1936, bank loans dropped by almost $11 billion. The lack of available money from lenders dried up both home resales and new building starts.

In an effort to stimulate lending, Fannie Mae was given the ability to buy Federal Housing Administration-insured mortgages from the lenders who originally wrote the loans. Federal money was thus pumped into the economy through payment to the banks in return for the mortgages. In turn, the banks would have more cash to lend out. This procedure was justified as an expansion of the flow of mortgage money and therefore beneficial to the nation as a whole. It was done in an attempt to raise the ratio of home ownership across the nation and to stimulate the availability of affordable housing.

The business of selling mortgages to a third party is known as the secondary mortgage market. The Federal National Mortgage Association was the first financial organization to be created exclusively for this function. It began with only $1 billion in mortgage purchasing power, but it contributed to the realization of the American Dream for a whole generation of low- and middle-income citizens. Americans could buy homes with minimal down payments because banks were stimulated to lend when the Federal Housing Authority was willing to insure the loans. Furthermore, with Fannie Mae standing by, bankers knew that the loans could be sold quickly to a third party. In 1944, Fannie Mae's mortgage purchasing authority was expanded to include loans guaranteed by the Veterans Administration; it expanded even more in the following years.

For thirty years Fannie Mae held a virtual monopoly on the secondary mortgage market in the United States. Not until 1968 was it privatized by President Lyndon B. Johnson and removed from the national budget. At that point, it was designated a government-sponsored enterprise (GSE). Shares in the company were sold to private investors.

As the first financial institution in the secondary mortgage market, Fannie Mae forever changed the nature of lending in the United States. Without competition, it held unchecked power in the financial marketplace until another similar GSE, Freddie Mac, was created in 1970. Together they held as much as 90 percent of the nation's secondary mortgage market.

Impact The creation of the Federal National Mortgage Association not only stimulated the financial marketplace of the 1930's but also established lending practices that continued and expanded into the twenty-first century. Bankers were attracted to the prospect of writing long-term mortgages because they did not have to hold them for the long term. Mortgage loans looked less risky to lenders and therefore became more readily available to borrowers.

The expanding power of the secondary mortgage market has resulted, however, in tremendous financial complexity. By the end of the twentieth century, mortgages were bought and "bundled," sometimes with dissimilar properties grouped together, and the resulting packages were sold as mortgage-backed securities on the stock exchange. Often the trades were made without buyers' knowledge of the components of the bundle. Lack of federal supervision and accountability made Fannie Mae a significant contributor to the financial crisis of 2008.

Carolyn Janik

Further Reading
Calder, Lendol. *Financing the American Dream: A Cultural History of Consumer Credit.* Princeton, N.J.: Princeton University Press, 1999.
Frame, W. Scott. "The 2008 Federal Intervention to

Stabilize Fannie Mae and Freddie Mac." Atlanta, Ga.: Federal Reserve Bank of Atlanta, 2009.

Wallison, Peter, *Nationalizing Mortgage Risk: The Growth of Fannie Mae and Freddie Mac.* Washington, D.C.: AEI Press, 2000.

See also   Banking; Business and the economy in the United States; Credit and debt; Federal Housing Administration; Great Depression in the United States; Housing in the United States; New Deal; Recession of 1937-1938; Roosevelt, Franklin D.

■ Federal Power Commission

Identification   Independent commission of the U.S. government
Date   Established on June 23, 1930

The Federal Power Commission (FPC) was initially created as part of the Federal Water Power Act of 1920, and its jurisdiction continued to expand throughout the 1930's with the passage of additional acts of Congress. Its primary purpose was to regulate the construction, development, licensing, and pricing of hydroelectric power and natural-gas utilities.

Prior to the Federal Power Act of 1935, the primary purpose of the FPC had been the regulation and licensing of the development of hydroelectric power on public lands and navigable bodies of water within the United States and of any dams owned by the United States. The FPC had first been created by the Federal Water Power Act of 1920. However, this act had not established an independent commission. Not until June 23, 1930, was the FPC formally established as an independent and bipartisan committee. It consisted of five members nominated by the president; nominations required the approval of the Senate. The FPC's initial duties dealt with hydroelectric projects, fish and wildlife, natural gas, and interstate electrical utilities.

Throughout the years, the most important responsibility of the FPC has been the regulation of companies that trans-port and produce electricity and natural gas; this regulation ensures that consumers are protected from unfair prices. In order to accomplish this mission, the FPC has enacted surveillance programs using price schedules. Each year, at least two thousand of these price schedules are filed in order to meet the price regulation requirements of the FPC. In addition to filing price schedules each year, public electric and natural-gas utilities are required to provide thirty-days notice to the FPC if any changes in energy rates or energy charges occur. The FPC has the ultimate authority to change any energy price it deems to be unreasonable, and it also has the authority to monitor the usage of capital expenditures in daily operations.

In addition to monitoring energy prices in order to protect consumers and the economy, the FPC requires that applicants for licenses must comply with all state laws related to the construction or maintenance of any project involving electricity, fish and wildlife, or natural gas. These licenses may be issued

Clyde Seavey became the chairman of the Federal Power Commission. (Library of Congress)

for up to fifty years, and the FPC determines both the original cost of the project and any additions to the licensed project.

In 1935, Congress enacted the Federal Power Act in order to specifically support the development of rivers to supply flood control, energy generation, water for human consumption, fish and wildlife management, and recreation. The jurisdiction of the FPC was further expanded by the Tennessee Valley Authority Act, the Bonneville Act, the Fort Peck Act, the Public Utility Holding Company Act of 1935, the Flood Control Act of 1938, and the Natural Gas Act of 1938. In 1977, Congress reorganized the FPC into the Federal Energy Regulatory Commission after numerous problems such as the Organization of the Petroleum Exporting Countries (OPEC) embargo and power-grid outages occurred during the 1970's.

Impact   The Federal Energy Regulatory Commission has jurisdiction over sixteen hundred hydroelectric projects and the transmission and wholesale pricing of natural gas and electricity. It works with the U.S. Coast Guard. In 2005, the Energy Policy Act gave the commission the authority to impose penalties for any manipulation of the natural-gas and electricity markets. The decisions made by the commission are no longer subject to approval by Congress or the president; instead they are reviewed by the U.S. federal courts. The primary mandate for the commission continues to be the maintenance of reasonable and nondiscriminatory energy rates for U.S. consumers.

Jeanne L. Kuhler

Further Reading

Federal Power Commission. *Uniform System of Accounts Prescribed for Public Utilities and Licensees Subject to the Provisions of the Federal Power Act.* Ann Arbor: University of Michigan Library Press, 2009.

MacAvoy, Paul W. "The Effectiveness of the Federal Power Commission." *Bell Journal of Economics and Management Science* 1, no. 2 (1970): 271-303.

Seavy, Clyde L. "Functions of the Federal Power Commission." *Annals of the American Academy of Political and Social Science* 201 (1939): 73-81.

See also   Boulder Dam; Federal Power Commission; Grand Coulee Dam; National parks; Natural Gas Act of 1938; Public Utilities Act.

■ Federal Reserve Board

Identification   Entity that governs the central banking system of the United States
Date   Established on December 23, 1913

The Federal Reserve system became one of the federal government's most important economic agencies. As the central bank of the United States, it is the institution in which the federal government and private banks do their banking. The board was reorganized and its powers extended during the 1930's.

The original Federal Reserve Act of 1913 created a governing board of seven members. The secretary of the U.S. Treasury and the chairperson of the Office of the Comptroller of the Currency were ex officio members. The other five were to be appointed by the president, subject to Senate confirmation. Twelve regional Federal Reserve banks were created. They were authorized to issue currency, to make loans to banks, to conduct open-market operations in government securities, to hold reserve deposits of member banks, and to supervise the operations of member banks.

During the stock market boom of the late 1920's, conflicts appeared between the Federal Reserve Board in Washington, D.C., and the leadership of the New York Federal Reserve Bank. All involved were alarmed by the rise of speculation and feared that a general tightening of credit would damage the productive economy, which showed no signs of inflationary excess. The Federal Reserve did slow monetary growth after 1928, which contributed to the downswing. More serious, they failed to adopt vigorously expansionary measures after the downswing was under way, particularly when escalating bank failures provoked currency withdrawal from the banks. The worst monetary panic in American history occurred from 1930 to 1933, twenty years after the Federal Reserve had been created to eliminate bank panics.

The Federal Reserve Board's problems arose partly because it was responsible for maintaining the convertibility of dollars into gold at the fixed official price of $20.67 per ounce. European monetary disorders in 1931 led to gold withdrawals, and the Federal Reserve raised interest rates on loans to banks, producing an increase in bank failures. Those interest rates remained relatively high through the banking collapse of early 1933. The Federal Reserve could have expanded bank reserves by buying government securities in the open market—a policy advocated by the New York Federal Reserve—but the board failed to support sufficiently vigorous action.

President Franklin D. Roosevelt's decision to go off the gold standard in 1933 freed the Fed to take more expansionary actions. However, the monetary situation resolved itself. Currency flowed back into banks, and the Treasury's purchases of gold from other countries helped expand bank reserves and the money supply.

The Federal Reserve Board was authorized in 1933 to set maximum interest rates on bank time deposits and in 1934 to set margin (down-payment) requirements on credit-financed purchases of securities. More drastic changes came in the Banking Act of August, 1935. This law abolished the existing Federal Reserve Board and in effect dismissed all of its members. The Board of Governors, Federal Reserve System, was created. The ex officio status of the secretary of the Treasury and chairperson of the Office of the Comptroller of the Currency was removed. There were still to be seven members, serving overlapping two-year terms, removable only for specified cause. The new board had greater authority over discount rates and member-bank reserve requirements. The Federal Open-Market Committee (FOMC) was given statutory recognition. FOMC was to consist of the seven board members and five of the twelve presidents of the Federal Reserve banks, serving in rotation but always including New York. Headed by the chairperson of the board of governors, FOMC gradually became the most powerful element in the system.

President Roosevelt thus had the power to appoint an entirely new board. However, he reappointed Marriner Eccles, who had been chair of the previous board, and one other former member, M. S. Szymczak. The other five were newcomers. Eccles was a strong believer in expansionary monetary and fiscal actions.

The Federal Reserve used its authority over reserve requirements in a destructive manner. Alarmed by the gold-induced rise in member-bank excess reserves, it raised reserve requirements in August, 1936, and again in two stages in the Spring of 1937. In combination with a drastic deflationary shift in fiscal policy, these actions drove the economy into a painful recession in 1937. Early in 1938, the Federal Reserve reduced the requirements and bought securities in the open market to help restore easier credit conditions. Nevertheless, the economy remained far below full employment until the outbreak of war.

Impact   The Federal Reserve Board failed to bring about appropriate expansionary actions during the downswing of 1929-1933. The board was drastically reorganized in 1935, but again took inappropriate actions in 1936-1937, which contributed to the recession. However, its expanded powers came into full use during the 1950's and thereafter.

Paul B. Trescott

Further Reading

Chandler, Lester V. *American Monetary Policy, 1928-1941.* New York: Harper & Row, 1971.

Friedman, Milton, and Anna J. Schwartz. *A Monetary History of the United States, 1867-1960.* Princeton, N.J.: Princeton University Press, 1963.

Meltzer, Allan H. *A History of the Federal Reserve System. Vol. 1: 1913-1951.* Chicago: University of Chicago Press, 2003.

Shlaes, Amity. *The Forgotten Man: A New History of the Great Depression.* New York: HarperCollins, 2007.

See also   Banking; Banking Act of 1935; Business and the economy in the United States; Glass-Steagall Act of 1933; Great Depression in the United States; Recession of 1937-1938.

■ Federal Theatre Project

Identification   Federal make-work project for actors and dramatists that was part of the Works Progress Administration

Date   Established on April 8, 1935

The Federal Theatre Project changed the face of twentieth century American theater, first by decentralizing professional theater from urban centers to communities across the country. It employed thirteen thousand out-of-work artists in thirty-one states; encouraged diversity and experimentation in plays and productions; established quality professional theater with noncommercial interests; recognized theater of, by, and for the people, including previously marginalized groups such as ethnic minorities and children; and trained thousands of theater artists who went on to create imaginative, provocative theater and train others who followed.

In the wake of the Great Depression more than fifteen million Americans, including thousands of theater artists, found themselves out of work. By 1934, only five, of the previously seventy-five, legitimate theaters in New York City were open. In addition, talking films took over opera houses and theaters across the country, putting touring, summer stock, and vaudeville performers, designers, and technicians, as well as theater orchestras, out of work. Franklin D. Roosevelt proposed the Works Progress Administration (WPA) to Congress in an attempt to put people to work. When the legislation passed, Harry Hopkins, a close Roosevelt aide and head of the WPA, sought out Hallie Flanagan, a former college professor from Vassar College, to head the theater division because he wanted someone who could recognize the benefits as artistic, not commercial. Although she was reluctant, Hopkins promised her a "free, adult, and uncensored" theater. She took office in August, 1935.

Getting Organized Flanagan had toured Europe on a Guggenheim Fellowship and was impressed with the diversity and artistic integrity of the European theaters. She viewed her appointment as an opportunity to create a living theater that responded to a changing world. Even though her nearly $7 million budget was a small fraction of the $5 billion available, Flanagan set about her task, which she saw as the challenge of providing work to the unemployed while still maintaining high artistic standards.

Flanagan started by hiring twelve thousand people and appointing a deputy national director, to oversee administrative issues, and an assistant director, to handle royalties and equipment. She also established seven geographic areas of concentration, each with its own director, which included three city centers—New York, Los Angeles, and Chicago—and four large regions—East, West, Midwest, and South. All ten directors met regularly to discuss plays, policies, and ways to spread theater far and wide. Hopkins and Flanagan agreed not to compete with commercial theater; thus, Flanagan stressed the creation of alternative theater forms such as marionette, dance, and caravan as well as theater for children, high schools, and minorities.

Each region had various "units," depending upon available talent and the cultural make-up of its community. For example, there was a Spanish unit in Miami, a Yiddish unit in New York, and other ethnic groups in various areas who presented plays in their native languages. African American and children's theater units sprang up in several regions, and there were also units that focused on a particular type of performance, such as classical plays, vaudeville, and circus acts. Flanagan's interest in developing new drama spread into a variety of avenues, including the Living Newspaper, experimen-

Works Progress Administration poster, advertising a stage production of the "Negro Unit" of the Federal Theatre Project. (Library of Congress)

tal theater, and African American theater as well as imaginative productions of classic plays. Most famous of these productions were Orson Welles's and John Houseman's voodoo *Macbeth*, with a completely African Americans cast, and their modern-clothed production of *Julius Caesar.*

Federal Theatre troupes played in lodge halls, high school gymnasiums, church basements, old barns, abandoned store buildings, showboats, parks, and even on sidewalks and in makeshift tents. Most Federal Theatre Project productions were free or charged a nominal admission fee to help defray production costs. Flanagan envisioned a federation of theaters across the country answering the needs of their own unique communities. She held to her conviction that art should reflect the United States in all its diversity and not be the sole property of any one interest group.

In its short life, the Federal Theatre Project employed more than ten thousand artists per year, and gave more than sixty thousand performances of more than twelve hundred plays, which included nearly nine hundred major works and more than three hundred original plays, to an audience estimated at thirty million in forty states. A large percentage of the audience had never before seen a live theater performance. By 1939, the U.S. government had spent more than $45 million to pay the salaries of playwrights, directors, actors, designers, and technicians to produce plays, even though the pay was less than $25 a week.

The Demise of the Federal Theatre Project Despite its extraordinary accomplishments, the Federal Theatre Project had many enemies. Because some of the plays took critical stances on current political issues, they were considered "leftist" and came under intense scrutiny by conservatives in Congress and the print media. In 1939, the controversy over

---

Supporting Theater in Hard Times

Before the Federal Theatre Project came to an end in 1939, the project's director, Hallie Flanagan, presented a brief before the Committee on Patents of the U.S. House of Representatives on February 8, 1938. She began by stating the reasons the project was established:

Government support of the theatre brings the United States into the best historic theatre tradition and into the best contemporary theatre practice. Four centuries before Christ, Athens believed that plays were worth paying for out of public money; today France, Germany, Norway, Sweden, Denmark, Russia, Italy and practically all other civilized countries appropriate money for the theatre.

However, it was not because of historic theatre tradition, nor because of contemporary theatre practice that the Federal Theatre came into being. It came into being because in the Summer of 1935, the relief rolls of American cities showed that thousands of unemployed theatre professionals, affected not only by the economic depression but by the rapid development of the cinema and the radio, were destitute. The Federal Theatre came into being because Mr. Harry Hopkins, Administrator of the Works Progress Administration, believed not only that unemployed theatrical people could get just as hungry as unemployed accountants and engineers, but—and this was much more revolutionary—that their skills were as worthy of conservation. He believed that the talents of these professional theatre workers, together with the skills of painters, musicians and writers, made up a part of the national wealth which America could not afford to lose.

---

the Federal Theatre Project came to a head, gaining the attention of Martin Dies, Jr., the chair of the House Committee on Un-American Activities, who seized the opportunity to attack the Roosevelt administration and identified the Federal Theatre Project as part of the New Deal's propaganda machine and an arm of the Communist Party USA (CPUSA). Barred from making public comment in her own defense by the WPA administration, Flanagan was convicted in the court of public opinion before the Dies committee initiated its hearings. As a result, the House passed the Relief Bill for 1939-1940, calling for drastic changes in the WPA program that included severe cuts to arts funding, eliminating the theater project altogether, and requiring loyalty oaths intended to suppress political radicals.

Impact In the beginning, the commercial theater scoffed at the idea of a government-funded theater employing out-of-work artists, but within a few years, most critics hailed it as the biggest hit-producing enterprise in New York. The Federal Theatre Project launched the careers of many well-known performers, such as Joseph Cotten and Will Geer; writers, such as Eugene O'Neill, Arthur Miller, and Mary Chase; directors; designers; and technicians who influenced and inspired future generations.

The Living Newspaper was seen at the time as the most significant contribution of the Federal Theatre Project because it presented an original form for plays, incorporating current events and actual content of political speeches and/or newspaper reports into a multimedia performance with movement, amplified sound, and special lighting effects. It was lively, timely, entertaining, and labeled as dangerous by Federal Theatre Project adversaries, in response to which Flanagan asserted that good theater is, by its nature, dangerous.

The lasting influence of the Federal Theatre Project is undeniable. Theatrical trends that became commonplace in the American theater can trace their roots directly to the seeds planted by the Federal Theatre Project. During the 1940's, the regional theater movement took hold, creating high-quality professional theaters across the country, and the outdoor theater movement begun by Paul Green with *The Lost Colony* in 1937 gave rise to a movement of historical dramas and other outdoor productions. The Federal Theatre Project's fostering of new and uniquely American drama encouraged a whole generation of playwrights to explore its own voice; the project included plays by women, African Americans, Latinos, and other ethnic groups. Experimentation in scenic, lighting, costume, and sound design created new paths for theatrical designers and their imaginations. Flanagan always maintained that theater belonged to everyone, not as a luxury, but as a necessity.

Jill Stapleton Bergeron

Further Reading

Buttitta, Tony, and Barry Witham. *Uncle Sam Presents: A Memoir of the Federal Theatre 1935-1939.* Philadelphia: University of Pennsylvania Press, 1982. Firsthand account of Buttitta and his work with the Federal Theatre in New York, first as a reporter for the *Federal Theatre Magazine* and later as a press agent for several productions.

Flanagan, Hallie. *Arena.* New York: Duell, Sloan, and Pearce, 1940. Flanagan's complete, firsthand account of her work as head of the Federal Theatre Project; indispensable source for understanding the project from the inside.

Fraden, Rena. *Blueprints for a Black Federal Theatre, 1935-1939.* New York: Cambridge University Press, 1994. Presents the historical context of the African American units of the Federal Theatre Project while also exploring the problems in writing plays that tore down old stereotypes and redefined drama from an African American viewpoint.

Kazacoff, George. *Dangerous Theatre: The Federal Theatre Project as a Forum for New Plays.* New York: Peter Lang, 1989. Dedicated to exploring the organization's role in creating plays and redefining American drama throughout the country; limits coverage to "legitimate," professionally produced plays and musicals presented originally to American audiences and does not include the Living Newspaper, African American plays, or other forms of performances, such as pageants, puppetry, revivals, and so forth.

Mathews, Jane DeHart. *The Federal Theatre, 1935-1939: Plays, Relief, and Politics.* Princeton, N.J.: Princeton University Press, 1967. Focuses on the nature of the Federal Theatre as a national institution, namely its people and ideas, the forces that shaped it, problems it encountered, and its contributions to the country.

Schwartz, Bonnie. *Voices from the Federal Theatre.* Madison: University of Wisconsin Press, 2003. Contains firsthand accounts by prominent actors, producers, writers, and variety artists of the Federal Theatre; includes collection of photographs and a DVD containing additional photographs from productions and of Federal Theatre Project posters, interviews with key players, and a documentary film entitled *Who Killed the Federal Theatre?*

Whitman, Willson. *Bread and Circuses: A Study of Federal Theatre.* New York: Oxford University Press, 1937. The first book written about the project; gives an overview of the development of the Federal Theatre in the midst of its tenure. Perhaps most valuable are the bibliography, which chronicles the important periodical articles of the day concerning the Federal Theatre, and the appendix of plays produced across the country.

Witham, Barry B. *The Federal Theatre Project: A Case
Study.* New York: Cambridge University Press,
2003. Witham presents an excellent overview of
the Federal Theatre Project that includes coverage of the bus tours, Civilian Conservation Corps,
and the Living Newspaper; particular emphasis
on the Seattle African American unit and the production of *See How They Run.*

See also   Dance; Federal Writers' Project; House
Committee on Un-American Activities; New Deal;
Odets, Clifford; O'Neill, Eugene; Rice, Elmer; Theater in the United States; *War of the Worlds, The* radio
broadcast; Works Progress Administration.

∎ Federal Trade Commission

Identification   U.S. government agency created to
enforce consumer protection and antitrust laws
Date   Established on September 26, 1914

*As the main federal consumer protection agency, the Federal
Trade Commission (FTC) also enforces the antitrust laws
against illegal price fixing, monopolization, and
anticompetitive mergers. During the 1930's, the FTC was
involved with numerous acts and procedures that intended
to protect consumers from nefarious business and advertising practices.*

The FTC was created in 1914 as part of the Progres-
sive-era movement to prohibit cartels, trusts, and
monopolies. Unlike the Antitrust Division of the Justice Department, which functions primarily as a
prosecutor of civil and criminal antitrust cases, the
FTC was designed as an independent regulatory
agency that would bring cases to court, provide guidance to business as to what constituted fair and unfair competition, conduct research, and publish reports about different sectors of the economy and
various business practices.

Section 5 of the FTC Act prohibits "unfair methods of competition." In 1931, the Supreme Court in
a case called *Federal Trade Commission v. Raladam Co.*
interpreted this provision narrowly to prohibit only
those practices that harmed a competitor or competitors as a group. The agency thus could not regulate false advertising that harmed only consumers.

Congress reacted to this ruling by passing the
1938 Wheeler-Lea Act, which gave the FTC the additional power to regulate "unfair or deceptive acts
and practices." This law expanded the work of the
FTC to include both antitrust and consumer protection law and gave the FTC explicit authority to regulate false advertising.

The Wheeler-Lea Act also made important
changes to the enforcement powers of the FTC. The
law allowed FTC orders to become final and binding
without the need for any additional court action. Violations of an FTC order were subject to civil penalties or potentially contempt of court. Finally, the act
allowed the FTC to seek court injunctions to prohibit false and misleading advertising.

The 1930's brought other important changes to
the powers of the FTC and the scope of its regulation
of the economy. Congress passed the Robinson-
Patman Act, prohibiting price discrimination, which
meant charging similar customers different prices
for the same goods without an objective justification.
The FTC enforced this act vigorously for many decades. Congress also passed the first of many labeling acts, which required manufacturers of clothes,
furs, fabrics, and eventually other consumer goods
to label their products honestly, a practice that the
FTC continues to enforce.

Impact   Without the legal changes of the 1930's,
the FTC would have been a toothless tiger without
the powers or procedures to protect the economy
from anticompetitive business conduct and unfair
and deceptive acts and practices. Therefore, FTC actions during the decade were aimed at protecting
consumers.

Spencer Weber Waller

Further Reading
Kanwit, Stephanie W. *Federal Trade Commission.* 2
vols. St. Paul, Minn.: Thomson West, 2008.
Katzmann, Robert A. *Regulatory Bureaucracy: The Federal Trade Commission and Antitrust Policy.* Cambridge, Mass.: MIT Press, 1981.

See also   Advertising in the United States; Business
and the economy in the United States; Great Depression in the United States; Robinson, Joseph Taylor.

■ Federal Writers' Project

Identification   New Deal relief program
Date   Established on July 27, 1935

The Federal Writers' Project (FWP) was a public program that sustained writers and their writing during the Great Depression. It created materials that documented extensively the lives of ordinary Americans and the diverse places across the country that people called "home."

Initial relief programs of the New Deal, a period of economic and social reform, focused on unemployed blue-collar workers. Programs such as the FWP were created to employ people with other talents. The FWP was part of the Works Progress Administration (WPA), itself a part of Federal Project Number One (Federal One), which figured prominently in the New Deal. Federal One also included the Federal Music Project, the Federal Theatre Project, the Federal Art Project, and the Historical Records Survey.

Best known among FWP publications was a series of state guidebooks called the "American Guide Series," which focused on the forty-eight states and some American regions, territories, and certain cities. The guides followed a common format and included information about history, culture, cities and towns, government, natural resources, industry, and places of interest and significance. There was still room, however, for idiosyncratic particulars. Writers crisscrossed their areas, talking to people, gathering information, and generating text. Because travel by automobile was increasingly popular, guides also mapped out trips to encourage tourism, and photographs were included.

The series was federally funded, but states participated voluntarily. To be hired, writers had to document their unemployment; the term "writer" was interpreted loosely. If enough professionals were not found in an area, others were hired. Some had writing experience; some did not. Most were young people, often from working-class backgrounds, not necessarily with high school diplomas; many were women.

The WPA paid writers about twenty dollars a week for twenty to thirty hours of employment. Each state had a director, who organized staff and was responsible for the guide's printing and distribution. Some states joined with established publishers to create high-quality books; other states were more modest.

Estimates indicate the FWP supported more than six thousand people, including writers, editors, researchers, art critics, archaeologists, cartographers, and historians.

In addition to state guides, FWP materials included oral histories, books for children, pamphlets, local histories, radio scripts, and ethnographies. Through its Folklore Project, thousands of Americans—including those often marginalized—told their life stories, reflecting on experiences of immigration, social and ethnic customs, survival during the Depression, and other things. Frequently, the names of people and places were pseudonyms. Firsthand accounts included those by former slaves.

The FWP was a controversial program. Some questioned the wisdom of supporting artists, and there were bureaucratic battles. Although most of FWP publications were apolitical, the politics of many of its employees tended toward the Left. This irritated conservatives in the U.S. Congress, especially Martin Dies, Jr., a member of the House of Representatives from Texas, who led the House Committee on Un-American Activities and targeted the FWP because he believed its workers were trying to undermine the United States. In 1939, Congress discontinued FWP funding, citing the need for a larger defense budget. Because of conservative opposition during this time, some states hardly distributed their guides, while others continued to fund state guides themselves until the program ended in 1943.

Impact   FWP items archived in the Library of Congress number more than 300,000. Most deal with the guidebooks, which helped promote patriotism and have been called the country's first oral histories. Author John Steinbeck—a FWP participant who, during the 1960's, wrote about his own travels across the country working for the program—said that the collective accounting of the United States presented in the guidebooks was never equaled.

In addition to producing tangible products, the FWP had a significant influence on the development of young writers, many of whom later became well known. Having an income allowed them to pursue their own writing after hours, and some included FWP experiences in their later works. Although relatively few FWP writers were African American, a number of them went on to distinguished writing careers. In addition to Steinbeck, writers who worked for the FWP include Saul Bellow, John Cheever, Richard Wright, May Swenson, Loren Eiseley, Conrad Aiken, Margaret Walker, Eudora Welty (who was also a WPA photographer), Nelson Algren, Ralph Ellison, and Studs Terkel. Critics have suggested that in areas such as civil rights and women's rights, the FWP prefigured social changes that were to occur later in the century.

Jean C. Fulton

Further Reading

Brinkley, David A. *Soul of a People: The WPA Writers' Project Uncovers Depression America.* Hoboken, N.J.: John Wiley & Sons, 2009.

Mangione, Jerry. *The Dream and the Deal: The Federal Writers' Project, 1935-1943.* Syracuse, N.Y.: Syracuse University Press, 1996.

Weisberger, Bernard A., ed. *The WPA Guide to America: The Best of the 1930s America as Seen by the Federal Writers' Project.* New York: Pantheon, 1985.

See also Federal Theatre Project; Great Depression in the United States; New Deal; Roosevelt, Franklin D.; Works Progress Administration.

Stepin Fetchit on a film set in 1935. (Hulton Archive/Getty Images)

FERA. See Federal Emergency Relief Administration

■ Fetchit, Stepin

Identification African American film and stage actor and comedian
Born May 30, 1902; Key West, Florida
Died November 19, 1985; Woodland Hills, California

Fetchit was one of the first African American actors to be featured in sound films. Beginning in 1927 and continuing, with several interruptions, through the 1930's, Fetchit came to embody the image of the slow-witted, indolent black comic character developed during minstrel days. His off-screen behavior demonstrated a temperament and promotional savvy belying his screen image.

Stepin Fetchit was born Lincoln Theodore Monroe Andrew Perry and changed his name in the early 1920's, after more than a decade touring the black vaudeville circuit both alone and in tandem with various other performers. By 1927, his stage work had taken him to California, where he began working in films for most of the major studios. His portrayal of Gummy in *Hearts in Dixie* (1929) established his character as lazy, mumbling, and somewhat devious in his avoidance of work.

An acclaimed series of performances in various films was followed by a period of unemployment beginning in 1930. This was largely the result of his temperamental behavior and imperious attitude off screen. During this time he returned to the stage, even appearing on Broadway. A return to Hollywood resulted in successful appearances with Will Rogers (*Judge Priest* in 1934 and *The County Chairman* and *Steamboat 'Round the Bend* in 1935) and Lionel Barrymore (*Carolina* in 1934). In the late 1930's, Stepin Fetchit endured another period of banishment because of a series of scandals and negative publicity, but he returned to team with Hattie Mc-Daniel in *Zenobia* in 1939.

The Stepin Fetchit character became so well known that it was used in cartoons and even copied by other black actors. Stereotypical associations have harmed Fetchit's reputation, and he has been cited as a negative force in the development of African American characters in film. A revisionist theory is that he was responsible for opening the doors to actors of a later generation and that he was the first nonsubmissive black performer in Hollywood.

Impact Stepin Fetchit is a complex character: Seen as a throwback to a more racist time, he also looked forward to the era of black empowerment because of his refusal to cooperate with the demands of the Hollywood studio system. While his performances can be difficult for a modern audience to watch, they must be viewed in the context of the pre-civil rights era in the United States.

John L. Clark, Jr.

Further Reading

Bogle, Donald. *Toms, Coons, Mulattoes, Mammies and Bucks: An Interpretive History of Blacks in American Films.* 4th ed. New York: Continuum, 2001.

Watkins, Mel. *Stepin Fetchit: The Life and Times of Lincoln Perry.* New York: Pantheon Books, 2005.

See also African Americans; *Amos 'n' Andy*; Ford, John; McDaniel, Hattie; Rogers, Will.

FHA. See **Federal Housing Administration**

■ *Fibber McGee and Molly*

Identification Comedy radio show
Dates Broadcast 1935-1956, 1959

"Fibber McGee" and "Molly" were roles created by two former vaudevillians from the Midwest. The show, named for the title characters, was popular on a national network, and was a prototype of the situation comedy.

Fibber McGee and Molly creators Jim Jordan and Marian Driscoll (later Jordan) both grew up in Peoria, Illinois, where they met as teens at St. John's Church. They married in 1918 and worked on stage for a few

years. *Fibber McGee and Molly* debuted on April 16, 1935. It was written by Donald Quinn and starred the Jordans and a cast of regular characters: Mayor LaTrivia (Gale Gordon), the Old-Timer (Cliff Arquette), Doc Gamble (Arthur Q. Bryan), Teeny (Marian Jordan), Mr. Whimple (Bill Thompson), and Mrs. Abigail Uppington (Isabel Randolph). The show also featured regular guests ranging from Bea Benaderet and Herb Vigran to the Billy Mills Orchestra and the King's Men vocal group.

The show helped establish the structure of situation comedies, putting the boastful but kindhearted Fibber into harebrained situations that were indulged by the patient Molly. The program featured trademark lines or gags, such as Molly's "T'ain't funny, McGee!" and Fibber's legendary messy closet. The program grew steadily in popularity and was an established hit by the end of the decade.

After Marian Jordan died, Jim Jordan retired, making a few television and cinematic appearances. He guested on a 1976 episode of *Chico and the Man* and provided the voice for Captain Orville in Disney's film *The Rescuers* in 1977.

Impact *Fibber McGee and Molly* helped establish the formula for radio and television situation comedies and spawned spin-off series and motion-picture appearances. Radio featured *The Great Gildersleeve* series, starring Harold Peary, and *Beulah*, a popular show starring a succession of African American female actors. The Jordans played Fibber McGee and Molly in the films *This Way Please* (1937), *Look Who's Laughing* (1941), *Here We Go Again* (1942), and *Heavenly Days* (1944).

By the end of their radio career, the Jordans had performed on stage four thousand times and had done seven thousand radio shows. The duo did not make the transition to television; National Broadcasting Company's (NBC's) television version of *Fibber McGee and Molly* did not feature the couple and was canceled after one season. In 1983, the Jordans received a star on Hollywood's Walk of Fame. Jim Jordan died in 1988, and a year later, the couple was inducted posthumously into the Radio Hall of Fame.

Bill Knight

Further Reading

Maltin, Leonard. *The Great American Broadcast: A Celebration of Radio's Golden Age.* New York: New American Library, 2000.

Price, Tom, and Charles Stumpf. *Heavenly Days: The*

Story of Fibber McGee and Molly. Waynesville, N.C.: World of Yesterday, 1987.

Schulz, Clair. *Fibber McGee and Molly: On the Air 1935-1959.* Albany, Ga.: BearManor Media, 2008.

Simons, Mel. *Old-Time Radio Memories.* Albany, Ga.: BearManor Media, 2007.

See also   *Amos 'n' Andy*; Car radios; Film; Radio in Canada; Radio in the United States; *War of the Worlds, The* radio broadcast.

■ *Field Guide to the Birds*

Identification   First modern handbook for birders
Author   Roger Tory Peterson
Date   Published in 1934

The publication of Field Guide to the Birds *is partly responsible for an increased interest in bird-watching and in naturalism as a whole. Roger Tory Peterson is considered one of the founders of the modern environmental movement, and the publication of this guide was a seminal moment in this cause.*

Amateur ornithologist Peterson was twenty-six years old in 1934 when he combined his interests in art and science to write and illustrate his *Field Guide to the Birds.* The guide was a breakthrough in natural science, identifying North American birds through a series of clear paintings and descriptions based on readily observable characteristics of the animals in the field. The book was the first modern field guide designed to help amateur naturalists and hobbyists to identify animals in their natural habitats rather than relying on the conventional method of killing the animal for study in a laboratory or classroom. This method is sometimes called the Peterson Identification System in recognition of the author's contribution.

Peterson's book was turned down by four publishers before Houghton Mifflin took a chance on this unknown author and his unconventional work. It sold out a press run of two thousand copies in one week, indicating a public hunger for such a work. The publication of the guide was later recognized as an important event in the nascent environmental movement of the 1930's.

Impact   Spurred in part by the publication of this book, bird-watching became ever more popular as the twentieth century progressed and represented an expanding public interest in natural history and the outdoors. The *Field Guide to the Birds* has never gone out of print or out of fashion among bird enthusiasts. The success of the book led the author to become editor for Peterson Field Guides, a large series that includes guides to insects, mammals, plants, and rocks.

Janet E. Gardner

Further Reading
Carlson, Douglas. *Roger Tory Peterson: A Biography.* Austin: University of Texas Press, 2007.

Line, Les. "He Transformed Us into a World of Watchers." *National Wildlife,* February/March, 2002.

Weidensaul, Scott. *Of a Feather: A Brief History of American Birding.* San Diego: Harcourt, 2007.

See also   Book publishing; Hobbies; Migratory Bird Hunting and Conservation Stamp Act of 1934; Recreation; Wilderness Society.

■ Fields, W. C.

Identification   American film comedian and actor
Born   January 29, 1880; Darby, near Philadelphia, Pennsylvania
Died   December 25, 1946; Pasadena, California

One of Hollywood's most recognizable movie stars during the 1930's, Fields developed a unique curmudgeonly persona equally believable as an unscrupulous charlatan or a beleaguered, hard-drinking everyman. He memorialized such characters in a series of classic film roles from the early 1930's through the early 1940's.

W. C. Fields was born William Claude Dukenfield, the eldest of several children of poor English immigrants James and Kate Spangler Felton Dukenfield. Fields's father was a street vegetable vendor. Fields had a falling out with his father when, after witnessing a vaudeville performance of juggling, he practiced the art with the family produce. Fields ran away from home early and survived as a cardsharp and pool shark while honing his juggling skills.

As a teenager, Fields landed a job as an amusement park juggler before drifting into vaudeville in Atlantic City. Afterward, he worked vaudeville and burlesque circuits and in the early twentieth cen-

W. C. Fields (right) with ventriloquist Edgar Bergen and dummy Charlie McCarthy, in blackface, in the 1939 film You Can't Cheat an Honest Man. *(Archive Photos/Getty Images)*

tury, traveled Europe as a renowned humorous juggler of unusual objects (such as cigar boxes or hats). Fields's skills as a comic performer led to appearances with the Ziegfeld Follies (1915-1921), which led to a starring role in the hit 1923 Broadway musical *Poppy*. He soon was in regular demand for both short subjects, produced by Mack Sennett, and feature-length films in Hollywood.

By the early 1930's, Fields—easily identified by his tomato-shaped nose, distinctive nasal voice, sarcastic asides, and sharp characterizations of con artists, put-upon husbands, or typical working stiffs—had become a major film star. During the decade, he appeared in twenty-five films, more than one-half of his cinematic canon. Some of his most memorable roles and funniest comedic bits occurred in such films as *Million Dollar Legs* (1932), *You're Telling Me!* (1934),

The Old Fashioned Way (1934), *It's a Gift* (1934), *Man on the Flying Trapeze* (1935), and *You Can't Cheat an Honest Man* (1939). He also performed occasionally on-screen in more serious roles, notably as Mr. Micawber *in David Copperfield* (1935). As a successful actor with a proven audience, Fields was allowed to script films he headlined. He did so with surrealistic panache, using outrageous screenwriting pseudonyms (such as Mahatma Kane Jeeves) while creating unforgettable scoundrels (such as Larsen E. Whipsnade) to move through improbable plot lines.

Late in his career, Fields suffered various ailments associated with heavy drinking, a practice that had been part of his life since his vaudeville days and one to which he often referred in his films, and was confined to cameos in his final few celluloid appearances. During recuperations, he was a frequent guest on radio and became famous for sparring with Charlie McCarthy, Edgar Bergen's wooden dummy, in highly popular, insult-laden routines on the *Chase and Sanborn Hour.*

Fields, father of a son born in 1900 from his marriage to Harriet Hughes and another son born in 1917 to his girlfriend Bessie Poole, lived with actor Carlotta Monti during the last fifteen years of his life. He succumbed to complications from cirrhosis of the liver. After a yearlong stay in a sanatorium, Fields died at the age of sixty-six on Christmas Day, a holiday his grouchy characters professed to hate.

Impact Although Fields' film career spanned only twenty years, from 1924 to his final appearance in 1944, his best and best-remembered work was released between 1932 and 1941 and incorporated routines from his previous employment as a world-class comic juggler. A consummate entertainer who successfully made the transition from burlesque and vaudeville to stage, silent screen, talkies, and radio, Fields remains a cultural icon many years after his death. He has served as inspiration for countless impressionists and comedians, has been parodied in modern comic strips, and has been paid tribute in films and advertisements. Fields was also posthumously inducted into the Juggling Hall of Fame. In 1980, the U.S. Postal Service issued a commemorative stamp for Fields, on the one hundredth anniversary of his birth, an honor shared with iconic comedians Charles Chaplin and the Marx Brothers.

Jack Ewing

Further Reading
Anobile, Richard J. *A Flask of Fields: Verbal and Visual Gems from the Films of W. C. Fields.* New York: Darien House, 1972.
Curtis, James. *W.C. Fields: A Biography.* New York: Alfred A. Knopf, 2003.
Fields, Ronald, and Shaun L. Higgins. *Never Give a Sucker an Even Break: W. C. Fields on Business.* Upper Saddle River, N.J.: Prentice Hall, 2000.
Taylor, Robert Lewis. *W. C. Fields: His Follies and Fortunes.* New York: St. Martin's Press, 1989.

See also Chaplin, Charles; Film; Marx Brothers; Radio in the United States; Theater in the United States; West, Mae.

■ Film

The film industry came of age during the 1920's, and motion pictures were well established as the favorite American entertainment form by 1930. During the decade that followed, films became even further embedded in the fabric of American life as audiences embraced the introduction of sound, color, and a new generation of stars.

Although a popular myth holds that all Americans went to the movies in the 1930's to escape the drudgery of their daily lives, the relatively modest admission prices still were a luxury for many. As a result, the Hollywood studios lost money from 1930 to 1933. For example, Warner Bros. recorded a profit of $17.2 million in 1929 and a loss of $7.9 million in 1931, and the downward trend continued. Box-office receipts for early 1933 were down 40 percent from the same period in 1931; however, by the end of 1933, as the economy slowly improved, film attendance began to rise. Its rise continued for the rest of the decade, except for a slight dip during the 1937 recession. Weekly average attendance rose from seventy-five million in 1935 to ninety million in 1936. All studios showed profits by the summer of 1936. Audiences were attracted by the novelty of sound, glamorous new stars, and the treatment of new topics in diverse genres.

Technological Innovations Sound was one of the two main technological achievements in the film industry of the 1930's. After sound was introduced in 1927, the studios scrambled to make the transition from silent films to "talkies," a change hampered by the size and clumsiness of early recording devices. As a result, many films in the early 1930's have a conservative visual style because of the difficulty of moving the camera and the sound equipment simultaneously. Much more than in the silent era, Hollywood films resembled plays with wide shots of group interactions. Films shot on location, such as Westerns, had more flexibility with regard to camera movement because dialogue and sound effects were added later. While the legend that innumerable silent stars became unemployable because of the inadequacy of their voices and their inability to read lines might be an exaggeration, demand grew for stage-trained performers as dialogue became increasingly important. The similarity of their vocal styles and the artificiality of their enunciation also contributed to the stilted quality of early talkies. Too many characters, regardless of their socioeconomic backgrounds, spoke as if they had attended British public schools. Only with the rise of gangster films did characters begin to talk more naturalistically.

The second major technological development in American films was the introduction of color. Although the company Technicolor had been incorporated in 1922 and its two-color process had appeared occasionally in the silent era, the technology did not advance until Technicolor created its three-color process in 1932. This development led to *Becky Sharp*, the first completely Technicolor film, in 1935. *The Trail of the Lonesome Pine* was the first outdoor film shot in Technicolor in 1936. Color was used sparingly until 1939, when *Gone with the Wind* and *The Wizard of Oz*, both directed by Victor Fleming,

Two Technicolor cameras, costing $25,000 each, mounted on scaffolding on a film set in 1935. (Archive Photos/Getty Images)

demonstrated vividly that color films could look much better than they previously had.

The Hays Code   In 1922, U.S. postmaster general Will Hays was hired by the Hollywood studio bosses to help counter the rising power of state and local censors, whose actions posed a serious economic threat to the film industry. Aiming to purify American films, Hays eventually created the Motion Picture Production Code of 1930 to regulate the content of Hollywood films. This early version of the code was essentially ignored, however, and many films of the early 1930's had much stronger sexual content than films made later in the decade. Comedies of the voluptuous star Mae West, such as *She Done Him Wrong* (1933) and *I'm No Angel* (1933), were full of sexual innuendo, and in *Baby Face* (1933), Barbara Stanwyck played a young woman who uses sex to gain control of a bank.

In 1934, Hays strengthened the production code, which came to be known as the Hays Code, to try to avoid what he considered the lowering of viewers' moral standards. As a result of the enforcement of the Hays Code, strong restrictions were placed on sexual content, and characters who broke the law always had to be punished. Films were barred from depicting drug use and ridiculing religion, and urged to reinforce the sanctity of marriage and to tone down violence.

The Studio System   The Hollywood studio system, which had been evolving over the previous twenty years, solidified during the 1930's. After years of mergers among companies and the failures of smaller studios unable to compete with the larger enterprises, Hollywood became a smooth-running operation often referred to as the "Dream Factory." Metro-Goldwyn-Mayer (MGM), Paramount, Twentieth Century-Fox, and Warner Bros. were the most powerful studios, with Columbia, RKO, and Universal lagging slightly behind. United Artists was an influential distributor of films made by others, especially independent producer Samuel Goldwyn and British producer Alexander Korda. In addition, smaller studios such as Monogram and Republic turned out lower-budget films, mostly Westerns, mysteries, and adventure serials.

The heads of these studios were the most powerful people in Hollywood and often were seen as infuriating despots by the writers, directors, and stars who worked for them. The most dictatorial was Louis B. Mayer of MGM, whose tyranny was offset by Irving Thalberg, his well-respected production chief, who was thought to have a creative sensibility similar to that of his subordinates. Thalberg died in his prime in 1936, but not before establishing MGM as the dominant studio for glamorous, prestigious productions that showcased stars such as Clark Gable and Greta Garbo. All Hollywood studios of the time depended heavily upon novels and plays as sources of material, but none more than MGM, as Mayer considered adaptations of well-known literary works as the best possible films.

Paramount, best known for its highbrow comedies, operettas, and exotic costume dramas, was the first studio to recognize that directors were the true artists of the medium. The studio gave nearly free reign to filmmakers such as Cecil B. DeMille, Josef von Sternberg, and Ernst Lubitsch, who was rewarded for his successes by becoming Paramount's production manager in 1935.

Under the guidance of Jack Warner, Darryl F. Zanuck, and Hal Wallis, Warner Bros. made films that aimed to accurately depict the economic realities facing ordinary Americans. In addition to producing films that were blatantly socially conscious, such as *I Am a Fugitive from a Chain Gang* (1932) and *Wild Boys of the Road* (1933), Warner incorporated social commentary into its most successful genre, the gangster film. The criminals played by Humphrey Bogart, James Cagney, Edward G. Robinson, and others were not merely vicious killers but also products of their time. Audiences identified with them because the gangsters were striking back at the uncaring and the powerful. Even the lavish backstage musicals, with inventive choreography by Busby Berkeley, focused on the struggles of the performers to overcome their modest circumstances.

The long-established studio Fox merged in 1935 with Twentieth Century, a production company formed two years earlier by Zanuck, after leaving Warner, and Joseph M. Schenck. Twentieth Century-Fox took longer to establish an identity, focusing on Tyrone Power vehicles, musicals starring Alice Faye and Norwegian ice-skater Sonja Henie, and family films with child star Shirley Temple, the top box-office draw of 1938 and arguably the most popular performer of the decade.

Harry Cohn was perhaps the most ruthless and despised of studio bosses as he slowly elevated Co-

lumbia from low-budget efforts to major status, aided considerably by the films of Frank Capra, such as *It Happened One Night* (1934). Universal struggled financially more than the other studios, making profits primarily from horror films directed by Tod Browning and James Whale and starring Boris Karloff and Bela Lugosi and from musicals featuring teenage singer Deanna Durbin. RKO, also financially shaky throughout most of its existence, was notable for several films starring Cary Grant and Katharine Hepburn and for its Fred Astaire-Ginger Rogers musicals.

The restlessness of the 1930's was epitomized by the peregrinations of producer David O. Selznick, Mayer's son-in-law. After bouncing from MGM to Paramount to RKO and back to MGM, Selznick finally followed the lead of Goldwyn and became an independent producer. Striving to achieve an enormous popular and artistic success, Selznick finished the decade by making *Gone with the Wind* (1939), seen by many as the ultimate producer's film.

Producers and studio executives dominated Hollywood in the 1930's perhaps more than in any other era; directors and especially screenwriters complained of being badly treated by the powerful studios, which were intent on turning out a uniform product as quickly and cheaply as possible. Novelist F. Scott Fitzgerald was especially miserable during his time at MGM, complaining to producer Joseph L. Mankiewicz, "Oh, Joe, can't a producer ever be wrong? I'm a good writer—honest."

Genres and Stars A multitude of film genres thrived in the 1930's. While Westerns were mostly cheap, modest efforts aimed at undiscriminating audiences, more substantial efforts arrived late in the decade with Henry King's *Jesse James* (1939) and particularly John Ford's *Stagecoach* (1939). Although soap operas, referred to at the time as women's pictures, often were maudlin and melodramatic, they offered juicy roles for actors such as Bette Davis, Irene Dunne, Barbara Stanwyck, and Garbo.

Better musicals would be made in later decades, but few would match the pure joy of the Astaire-Rogers and Berkeley musicals of the 1930's. While many supposedly prestige films, notably costume and historical dramas, have not held up well, and others have become dated because of their stereotyping of women and racial minorities, the Universal horror films and Warner gangster films, such as *Little*

Caesar (1931) and *The Public Enemy* (1932), were among the best ever made in these genres and can be seen as metaphors for the turmoil of the time.

The decade's most lasting achievement, however, might be its screwball comedies, which began mid-decade and lasted into the 1940's. With stars such as Grant, Hepburn, Dunne, Stanwyck, Jean Arthur, Claudette Colbert, Melvyn Douglas, and Carole Lombard, films such *The Awful Truth* (1937) and *Bringing Up Baby* (1938) appear wittier, sexier, and more modern than anything else Hollywood created in the 1930's. They offered pure escapism while demonstrating that those who considered themselves society's best could be as bumbling and foolish as ordinary citizens.

Impact   Despite the hard economic conditions prevailing throughout North America through most of the 1930's, that decade may have experienced the greatest number of significant advances of any period in film history. The decade coincided with the fundamental shift of films from an essentially silent art form to one in which sound became an integral part of cinematic language. The second great technological change was the introduction of color. That change began later and evolved more slowly than the introduction of sound and would never displace black-and-white films altogether, but it would eventually prove equally revolutionary. The decade also saw the development of distinct genres that would shape filmmaking for the decades to follow. Westerns were refined during the 1930's; horror films, gangster films, and musicals arose during the decade; and screwball comedies emerged as perhaps the decade's most innovative creation.

Michael Adams

Further Reading

Balio, Tino. *Grand Design: Hollywood as a Modern Business Enterprise, 1930-1939*. Reprint. Berkeley: University of California Press, 2007. Excellent overview of the economic consequences of sound, censorship, exhibition practices, and the star system.

Bergman, Andrew. *We're in the Money: Depression America and Its Films*. Chicago: Ivan R. Dee, 1992. Future screenwriter and director examines how socioeconomic conditions affected such genres as crime films and women's films.

Bordwell, David, Janet Staiger, and Kristin Thompson. *The Classical Hollywood Cinema: Film Style and Mode of Production to 1960*. Reprint. London: Routledge, 1996. Describes how studio production methods and technology combined to create film style, with emphasis on the impact of sound.

Buhle, Paul, and Dave Wagner. *Radical Hollywood: The Untold Story Behind America's Favorite Movies*. New York: New Press, 2002. Engaging examination of political content in films, the influence of the New Deal, and the work of screenwriters later blacklisted during the McCarthy era.

Crafton, Donald. *The Talkies: American Cinema's Transition to Sound, 1926-1931*. History of the American Cinema 4. New York: Scribner, 1997. Provides information on the technological and economic aspects of the development of sound, how actors made the transition, and how audiences responded.

Leff, Leonard J., and Jerold L. Simmons. *The Dame in the Kimono: Hollywood, Censorship, and the Production Code from the 1920s to the 1960s*. New York: Grove Weidenfeld, 1990. Detailed look at the impact of Will Hays and the Production Code Administration.

Sarris, Andrew. *"You Ain't Heard Nothin' Yet": The American Talking Film: History and Memory, 1927-1949*. New York: Oxford University Press, 1998. Thorough overview of the era by a major film historian, with analysis of studio styles, genres, and major directors and actors.

See also   Academy Awards; Drive-in theaters; Film serials; Gangster films; *Gone with the Wind*; Horror films; Motion Picture Production Code; Screwball comedy; Western films; *Wizard of Oz, The*.

■ Film serials

Definition   Episodic action films

During the Great Depression families looked for inexpensive entertainment. Film serials and the action and melodramatic features with which they played in second-tier film houses fit this bill. In fact, film serials became a staple of the Saturday matinee.

First called the chapter play, the serial was popular in France during the World War I era. It required the audience to return to the theater for each new episode. In 1914, the former comedian Pearl White starred in *The Perils of Pauline*, a twenty-episode serial produced by the American branch of Pathé Frères, a

French film company. She made three more silent serials between 1914 and 1920, firmly establishing the genre in the United States.

By 1930, the conventions of the film serial were well settled. The story was told in twelve episodes. The audience was totally familiar with the format for each of these episodes, which had a running time that was a fraction of that of a feature film. At its conclusion, the hero is faced with a predicament that can mean only certain death. The next Saturday, the audience returns to find, as it expected, that the hero has effected a miraculous escape, only to get into a similar predicament by the end of the episode.

The conflict in each serial is good versus evil, with no subtlety employed. The faces of the character actors who played the villains became familiar, even if their names did not. Serials remained popular through the 1940's, and Republic Pictures dominated the field. Columbia Pictures, Universal Pictures, and several independent producers also made serials. *King of the Carnival*, released by Republic in 1955, and *Blazing the Overland Trail*, released by Columbia in 1956, were among the last of the film serials. The genre had finally succumbed to the popularity of television and the changing tastes of the audience.

Serials were a specialty of the smaller studios, known in the business as "Poverty Row," that produced low-budget action films, primarily in the Western genre. These played in small film houses to which major productions were seldom released. However, some performers who later became major stars appeared in serials early in their careers. Foremost among these was John Wayne. He had already played the lead in a few Western films, but in two serials for Mascot (later Republic Pictures), he played contemporary characters. In *Shadow of the Eagle* (1932), he was a daredevil skywriter doing battle with a mysterious villain, the eponymous Eagle. In *The Hurricane Express* (1932), Wayne was again an airplane pilot, this time in pursuit of a villain known as "the Wrecker." Using villains such as these was a standard device of the 1930's serial. A master criminal known only by a cryptic title matches wits with the hero, who must battle the villain's henchmen, played mostly by the same actors from serial to serial. The audience knows the mastermind will not be unmasked until chapter 12.

Shortly before emerging as the top film cowboy of the 1930's, Gene Autry appeared in the Mascot serial *The Phantom Empire* (1935). The serial was a curious blend of two of the most popular action genres of the day—the B-Western and science fiction and fantasy. Autry played himself, a modern-day singing cowboy who operates Radio Ranch, a dude ranch from which he broadcasts a daily radio program. Associated with him is a group of youngsters who don costumes to become the adventurous Junior Thunder Riders. Autry and two of his sidekicks are kidnapped and taken to the scientifically advanced underground empire of Murania, ruled by the evil blond Queen Tika. Adding to the conflict is the presence of a gang of crooks led by a villainous scientist, Professor Beetson. His intent is to seize both Radio Ranch and the rich radium deposits of Murania. In short, *The Phantom Empire* features virtually every plot device to be found in a 1930's serial.

Buster Crabbe, an Olympics swimmer in 1928 and 1932, winner of bronze and gold medals, starred in the serial *Tarzan the Fearless* in 1933; then he played the title role in the iconic serial of the decade. The futuristic *Flash Gordon*, released by Universal in 1936, contained thirteen episodes, one more than the customary number. Flash strives to save the whole world from a collision with the planet Mongo, ruled by the cruel emperor Ming, a Fu Manchu character. (Ethnicity was frequently used to underscore villainy during the period.) Crabbe also portrayed Buck Rogers and later made a successful series of B-Westerns playing an upright Billy the Kid. From the beginning, there was an affinity between the low-budget Western and the serial, and many actors worked tirelessly in both.

Impact   The serials of the 1930's were pure escapist fare. Good and evil were clearly defined, and good always emerged triumphant. This result was psychologically reassuring to an audience suffering through a problematic economic period. Additionally, serials were affordable because they played as part of the least expensive theatrical programs.

Patrick Adcock

Further Reading

Barbour, Alan G. *Cliffhanger: A Pictorial History of the Motion Picture Serial.* New York: A&W, 1977. Chapter 1 crowns Crabbe the "King of the Serials." Chapter 17 concludes with "The Final Fade-Out."

Lahue, Kalton C. *Continued Next Week: A History of the Moving Picture Serial.* Norman: University of Oklahoma Press, 1964. Although devoted to the silent serials from 1914 to the last four produced in 1930, the book discusses all the conventions of the film serial firmly in place by that year.

Rainey, Buck. *Serial Film Stars: A Biographical Dictionary, 1912-1956.* Jefferson, N.C.: McFarland, 2005. Lists details of major films, as well as life before and after the films, for 446 serial performers.

Stedman, Raymond William. *The Serial: Suspense and Drama by Installment.* Norman: University of Oklahoma Press, 1971. Chapters entitled "At This Theater Next Week" and "Perilous Saturdays" capture the Saturday matinees.

Weiss, Ken, and Ed Goodgold. *To Be Continued . . .* New York: Crown, 1972. Brief analyses of selected serials from 1929 through 1956.

See also   Drive-in theaters; Film; *Flash Gordon*; Motion Picture Production Code; Tarzan films; Western films.

■ Fireside chats

The Events   President Franklin D. Roosevelt's informal radio broadcasts to the nation

Date   March 12, 1933-June 12, 1944

Throughout the 1930's, Roosevelt adroitly used informal radio addresses to educate the American people about his initiatives to ease the pressures of the Great Depression. He spoke confidently about his New Deal reforms, veered into unsuccessful clashes with the Supreme Court and Democratic Party critics, and rallied public support for American entry into what would become World War II.

On March 12, 1933, only eight days after his inauguration as president of the United States, Franklin D. Roosevelt held the first of the thirty "fireside chats" he would broadcast over the radio during his long tenure in office. In his first broadcast, he focused on the national banking crisis, an economic catastrophe that had emptied the vaults of thousands of financial institutions and threatened the savings of millions of Americans. He

began this chat with an intimate, "Good evening, friends" that exuded confidence and warmth. He then went on to explain the "banking holiday" that Congress had recently mandated and assured listeners that it was still "safer to keep your money in a reopened bank than under the mattress."

Roosevelt delivered his radio presentations with heavy doses of optimism and reassurance. He often mentioned his own family and forged personal links with listeners, who hungered for a president who would speak to them plainly about the bleak Great Depression and the need for a fresh approach. Roosevelt began developing his mastery of the increasingly powerful medium of radio after he became governor of New York in 1929. Radio became an educational tool for Roosevelt, who used it especially effectively from the White House to explain his legislative initiatives.

Roosevelt followed up his first chat with a May 7, 1933, broadcast, in which he explained his flurry of legislative proposals for restricting agricultural production, reviving the industrial foundation of the nation, redeveloping the ravaged Tennessee River Valley, and putting unemployed young men to work

Franklin D. Roosevelt understood the power of communicating with the American public via the medium of radio, and his fireside chats became means of explaining his political agenda and calming the nation during a time of economic uncertainty. (FDR Library)

Roosevelt's First Fireside Chat

In the first of thirty national radio broadcasts—his "fireside chats"—on March 12, 1933, President Franklin D. Roosevelt spoke about the state of the country's banking system. In his other fireside chats, which continued until June 12, 1944, Roosevelt addressed such topics as the Dust Bowl and the war in Europe.

We had a bad banking situation. Some of our bankers had shown themselves either incompetent or dishonest in their handling of the people's funds. They had used the money entrusted to them in speculations and unwise loans. This was of course not true in the vast majority of our banks but it was true in enough of them to shock the people for a time into a sense of insecurity and to put them into a frame of mind where they did not differentiate, but seemed to assume that the acts of a comparative few had tainted them all. It was the government's job to straighten out this situation and do it as quickly as possible—and the job is being performed.

I do not promise you that every bank will be reopened or that individual losses will not be suffered, but there will be no losses that possibly could be avoided; and there would have been more and greater losses had we continued to drift. I can even promise you salvation for some at least of the sorely pressed banks. We shall be engaged not merely in reopening sound banks but in the creation of sound banks through reorganization. It has been wonderful to me to catch the note of confidence from all over the country. I can never be sufficiently grateful to the people for the loyal support they have given me in their acceptance of the judgment that has dictated our course, even though all of our processes may not have seemed clear to them.

After all there is an element in the readjustment of our financial system more important than currency, more important than gold, and that is the confidence of the people. Confidence and courage are the essentials of success in carrying out our plan. You people must have faith; you must not be stampeded by rumors or guesses. Let us unite in banishing fear. We have provided the machinery to restore our financial system; it is up to you to support and make it work.

It is your problem no less than it is mine. Together we cannot fail.

in government conservation projects. He gave two more fireside chats in 1933, each time returning to radio to garner public support for his New Deal. On each occasion, he spoke clearly, optimistically, and informally, and provided a personal touch by pointing out that his own wife, Eleanor Roosevelt, and his children had a shared stake with all Americans in reform and economic regulation. These chats ranged from fifteen minutes to forty-five minutes in length, each conveying the importance of a concerted effort to combat the Great Depression.

On June 28, 1934, Roosevelt reviewed the efforts of Congress and stated that he believed in "practical explanations and in practical policies." Three months later, he shifted themes to analyze America's role in world affairs. In April, 1935, he rallied public support for his Works Progress Administration, confidently proclaiming that "Fear is vanishing." On September 6, 1936, he lamented the drought conditions prevailing in the Midwest and launched into a defense of what would be his futile effort to reform the Supreme Court six months later.

Issues and Themes Roosevelt usually focused his fireside chats on domestic issues, such as his legislative agenda. He discussed a wide range of reforms designed to restructure the national economy, give organized labor more clout, and combat unemployment. Occasionally, however, he immersed himself in partisan politics. On June 24, 1938, for example, he gave an address that attempted to "purge" the Democratic Party of lawmakers who were not of his liking. The latter presentation demonstrated the limits of his powers of persuasion, as most of the candidates whom he backed lost in that year's midterm elections.

By the end of the decade, Roosevelt's chats turned from the economy and his domestic political foes to the more sinister demons who lurked around the globe. On September 3, 1939, two days after World War II began in Europe, Roosevelt spoke of the aggression of Adolf Hitler and other foreign dictators: "I have said not once, but many times, that I have seen war and that I hate war."

Impact As commander in chief of U.S. military forces during World War II, Roosevelt used his powerful radio presence to continue educating the American people about their enemies. Every U.S. president since Roosevelt's time has utilized modern technology to communicate directly with the nation about pressing legislative policies and international challenges, and they all owe something to Roosevelt's example.

Joseph Edward Lee

Further Reading

Broun, Robert J. *Manipulating the Ether: The Power of Broadcast Radio in Thirties America.* Jefferson, N.C.: McFarland, 1998.

Buhite, Russell D., and David W. Levy, eds. *FDR's Fireside Chats.* New York: Penguin Books, 1992.

Leuchtenburg, William E. *In the Shadow of FDR.* Ithaca, N.Y.: Cornell University Press, 1983.

Winfield, Betty Houchin. *FDR and the News Media.* Urbana: University of Illinois Press, 1990.

See also Foreign policy of the United States; Germany and U.S. appeasement; Great Depression in the United States; Isolationism; Neutrality Acts; New Deal; Recession of 1937-1938; Roosevelt's first one hundred days; Unemployment in the United States.

■ Fitzgerald, Ella

Identification African American jazz vocalist
Born April 25, 1917; Newport News, Virginia
Died June 15, 1996; Beverly Hills, California

Fitzgerald's musical influence was so widespread that label heads, industry leaders, and her peers crowned her "the First Lady of Swing." Fitzgerald changed the sound of jazz music and impacted the 1930's with her unique voice and style and her worldwide appeal.

Ella Fitzgerald was discovered in 1934 as a teenage talent-show contestant. However, her contributions to the swing era began long before most of the world even knew what swing was. Managed by legendary swing drummer William Henry "Chick" Webb, Fitzgerald's career took off soon after she won amateur night at the famous Apollo Theater in Harlem, New York. She was only fifteen years old when Webb became her advocate; he decided to be her legal guardian to guide her career. At the time, Fitzgerald was homeless and had just run away from a reform school because her caretakers were physically abusive.

One of the biggest hits of the entire decade—and the biggest of Fitzgerald's entire career—was "A-Tisket A-Tasket." She sang a soulful version of the song to lift Webb's spirits during a hospital stay. Arranger Van Alexander reworked the song for recording, and at only twenty-one years old, Fitzgerald, with her jazzy rendition of the nursery rhyme, had cemented her place in the music industry. The album sold one million copies, hit number one, and stayed on the pop charts for seventeen weeks. Within months of the release of "A-Tisket A-Tasket," Fitzgerald became known as "the First Lady of Swing," and later, "the First Lady of Song."

One of the greatest artists of the Great Depression and war years, Fitzgerald spent two years as bandleader of Webb's orchestra after his death and renamed the Savoy Eight "Ella Fitzgerald and Her Famous Band." Her vocal versatility eventually earned her yet another title, "Queen of Scat," establishing her as a jazz modernist. Her unique talents afforded her the opportunity to break down racial barriers. Many white jazz and swing artists of the Depression era were quick to praise her. Even veteran performers, such as singer Fred Astaire, took notice, even if it were only to criticize Fitzgerald for being "too breathy" during many of her performances.

The Mills Brothers, Louis Armstrong, and Benny Goodman were just a few of the talented musicians that collaborated with Fitzgerald during the early years of her career. Often paired with her label mates on Decca Records, she performed with the same artists that she enjoyed and admired. The pairings resulted in an integration of jazz and pop, something that did not happen often during the Depression years. During the days of Bing Crosby, Charlie Parker, and Dizzy Gillespie, Fitzgerald created her own brand and made a lasting impression on the artists of the 1930's and the 1940's who helped develop the sound of the war years.

Impact Fitzgerald was one of the first women jazz artists to perform with an earthy resonance. She was a mezzo-soprano who often sang exclusively in the world's great concert halls, but Fitzgerald was never known for making hit records. She was, however, most popular for bebop-inflected scat singing, even though she was a product of the swing era and could not sing the blues. Fitzgerald took advantage of becoming a swing sensation—many of her recordings had the words "swing" or "swinging" in the title. Her approach to music, unique use of falsetto, rocking riffs, and deep and throaty vocals changed the face of music during the war years.

Ramonica R. Jones

Further Reading

David, Norman. *The Ella Fitzgerald Companion.* Westport, Conn.: Praeger, 2004.

Giddins, Gary. *Faces in the Crowd.* New York: Oxford University Press, 1992.

_____. *Visions of Jazz: The First Century.* New York: Oxford University Press, 1998.

See also Armstrong, Louis; Basie, Count; Goodman, Benny; Holiday, Billie; Music: Jazz.

F. Scott Fitzgerald. (Library of Congress)

■ Fitzgerald, F. Scott

Identification   American novelist
Born   September 24, 1896; St. Paul, Minnesota
Died   December 21, 1940; Hollywood, California

Fitzgerald was the voice of the Jazz Age, chronicling life during the 1920's. By the 1930's his reputation had diminished, and his descent into alcoholism contributed to his untimely death. After his death, he became renowned as the writer of the major American novel, The Great Gatsby *(1925).*

One of the greatest American writers, F. Scott Fitzgerald had written numerous short stories and three major novels by 1925, including *The Great Gatsby,* considered by many the greatest American novel. His work was naturalistic and timely, describing the lives of the young and rich during the Roaring Twenties. Making upwards of $25,000 a year, Fitzgerald was as much one of his characters as their portrayer.

However, by the beginning of the 1930's, Fitzgerald's life was falling apart. Zelda Sayre, his wife and inspiration for much of his work, began to succumb to schizophrenia, experiencing her first breakdown in 1930. She continued to be institutionalized and released from various facilities from 1930 through 1936. Fitzgerald, always a big drinker and famous for

drunken rampages, sank into alcoholism partially as a response to Zelda's illness. Unable to concentrate on his fourth novel, Fitzgerald relied on money from writing short stories to support himself. However, because he always felt that his talent was wasted on short stories he sank further into depression as the 1930's continued. He tried screenwriting, moving to Hollywood in 1931, but that proved fruitless. In 1932, Zelda published *Save Me the Waltz,* which told the same story that Fitzgerald was working on for his novel. He was furious that she stole his material, and this rift between them was never healed. By 1934, *Tender Is the Night,* Fitzgerald's story of a psychiatrist and his mentally ill wife, was published to good reviews, but his increasing dependence on alcohol was taking its toll on his health.

During 1936 and 1937, Fitzgerald hit what he considered to be the bottom; he was essentially unemployed, Zelda was back in an institution, and he believed himself incapable of writing anything of value. Labeling this period "the crack-up," Fitzgerald produced a series of three essays for *Esquire* in which he candidly exposed his weaknesses and analyzed his drunkenness and failures. At first received poorly as too truthful, they became an important firsthand glimpse into the life of one of greatest American writers.

Fitzgerald returned to Hollywood in 1937 as a screenwriter, getting a writer's credit for only one script, *The Three Comrades*, although he worked on others as well. He lived the rest of his life in Hollywood even though Metro-Goldwyn-Mayer fired him in 1938. While in Hollywood, Fitzgerald worked on his fifth novel, *The Love of the Last Tycoon*, about film mogul Irving Thalberg, but never finished it. He died of a massive heart attack in 1940 at the age of forty-four. A collection of seventeen comic stories about his Hollywood experiences, *The Pat Hobby Stories* (1962), and *The Last Tycoon* (1941) were published posthumously.

Impact At the time of his death, Fitzgerald's literary reputation was poor. His work had been eclipsed by his public drunkenness and dissipation, and he died considering himself a failure. However, time has reinterpreted his legacy, and Fitzgerald is considered to be one of the finest American writers of the twentieth century. He captured the textures of his times and left a vibrant portrait of life during the 1920's, creating the era as much as he was created by it. *The Great Gatsby* has influenced generations of writers and continues to be a critical and popular success. The short stories of which he was so ashamed are also highly regarded and anthologized, further securing his reputation.

Leslie Neilan

Further Reading

Bruccoli, Matthew Joseph. *Some Sort of Epic Grandeur: The Life of F. Scott Fitzgerald.* 2d rev. ed. Columbia: University of South Carolina Press, 2002.

Tate, Mary Jo. *A Critical Companion to F. Scott Fitzgerald: A Literary Reference to His Life and Work.* New York: Facts On File, 2009.

See also *Day of the Locust, The*; Hemingway, Ernest; Literature in the United States; Thalberg, Irving; West, Nathanael.

■ Flash Gordon

Identification Science-fiction/fantasy comic strip and film series

Dates Comic strip first published in 1934; film serials released in 1936, 1938, and 1940

The Flash Gordon *comic strip defined the look for action/adventure strips during the 1930's. Along with Buck Rogers, the character helped to popularize the growing genre of science fiction, and the three film serials were among the most popular and profitable produced in the decade.*

Combining the futuristic science fiction of *Buck Rogers* with the fantasy elements of Edgar Rice Burroughs's *Tarzan* series, *Flash Gordon* told the story of Flash, a star polo player, and Dale Arden, who inadvertently blast off on a rocket ship with a scientist, Dr. Hans Zarkov. The ship lands on the planet Mongo, ruled by the evil emperor Ming the Merciless. Together, the three heroes form alliances and forge rivalries with the wild and fantastic inhabitants of Mongo while fighting the forces of Ming and trying to escape the planet.

Unlike many of the daily strips, Alex Raymond's *Flash Gordon* only appeared once a week in large, color spreads in Sunday newspapers. Raymond included vibrant colors, romantic layouts, and exotic

Buster Crabbe (left) as the title character in Flash Gordon's Trip to Mars *with Dale Arden (Jean Rogers) and Happy Hapgood (Donald Kerr).* (Hulton Archive/Getty Images)

details, making many of his rival strips look crude in comparison. The strip inspired three film serials, *Flash Gordon* (1936), *Flash Gordon's Trip to Mars* (1938), and *Flash Gordon Conquers the Universe* (1940), all starring Buster Crabbe, an Olympic swimmer, as Flash. While most film serials were cheaply produced, the *Flash Gordon* serials were among the most expensive ever made, providing fans of science fiction with one of the only examples of successful filmmaking in the genre.

Impact Even more than its predecessor *Buck Rogers*, the *Flash Gordon* strip and serials defined the pulp science-fiction hero for the twentieth century. Raymond's imaginative layouts for the comic strip influenced almost every artist of adventure strips thereafter. The comic strip continued for decades, and the character went on to inspire toys, collectibles, a radio drama, television shows, cartoons, comic books, and a feature-length film; furthermore, it helped provide the look and feel of George Lucas's *Star Wars* (1977).

Thomas Gregory Carpenter

Further Reading

Kinnard, Roy, Tony Crankovich, and R. J. Vitone. *The Flash Gordon Serials, 1936-1940*. Jefferson, N.C.: McFarland, 2008.

Roberts, Tom. *Alex Raymond: His Life and Art*. Silver Spring, Md.: Adventure House, 2008.

See also Astronomy; Aviation and aeronautics; Comic strips; Film; Film serials; Science fiction.

■ Fleming, Victor

Identification American film director
Born February 23, 1889; Banbury Ranch (now near present-day La Cañada Flintridge), California
Died January 6, 1949; Cottonwood, Arizona

As the most forceful of Metro-Goldwyn-Mayer's (MGM's) stable of directors, Fleming directed many of the most popular and lasting films of the decade, including Gone with the Wind *(1939) and* The Wizard of Oz *(1939).*

Originally an automobile mechanic, Victor Fleming entered the film business as a stuntman and quickly progressed to cinematographer and, finally, to director during the silent era. Along with fellow directors Clarence Brown, Jack Conway, W. S. Van Dyke, and Sam Wood, Fleming helped MGM become the major Hollywood studio of the 1930's, as it emphasized lavish production values and prestigious films. Fleming is generally seen as possessing a more distinctive, personal style than his colleagues.

Fleming also helped create major stars, as with Clark Gable and Jean Harlow in the risqué adventure *Red Dust* (1932). He guided Harlow in one of her best comedies as a temperamental movie star, reportedly inspired by Fleming's relationship with Clara Bow, in *Bombshell* (1933), a forerunner of the screwball comedies popular later in the decade.

Fleming's adventure films during the decade included *Treasure Island* (1934) and *Captains Courageous* (1937), which his strongly masculine sensibility kept them from becoming merely mawkish children's films. Spencer Tracy earned an Academy Award for the latter and costarred with Gable, who based his screen persona on Fleming's rugged personality in *Test Pilot* (1938), arguably the director's most personal film.

Fleming is best known for making two of the most popular films ever in the same year. He replaced George Cukor on *Gone with the Wind* and helped give it the epic scope needed to transcend its soap-opera essence, thereby earning his only Academy Award. The fourth director to work on *The Wizard of Oz*, Fleming suggested the inclusion of the song "Follow the Yellow Brick Road" and fought to retain "Over the Rainbow."

Impact Sometimes described as the Steven Spielberg of his era, Fleming became MGM's most reliable director of prestigious films becuse of his ability to identify and resolve potential production problems. Able to deliver what the public wanted without condescension, Fleming helped MGM maintain its status throughout the 1930's.

Michael Adams

Further Reading

Harmentz, Aljean. *The Making of the Wizard of Oz*. New York: Alfred A. Knopf, 1977.

Sragow, Michael. *Victor Fleming: An American Movie Master*. New York: Pantheon Books, 2008.

See also Academy Awards; Film; Gable, Clark; *Gone with the Wind*; Harlow, Jean; McDaniel, Hattie; Screwball comedy; Thalberg, Irving; Tracy, Spencer; *Wizard of Oz, The.*

■ Flint sit-down strike

The Event Forty-four-day strike by the United
Automobile Workers against General Motors
Corporation
Dates December 30, 1936, to February 11, 1937
Place Flint, Michigan

*In the midst of the Great Depression, during times of record
unemployment and weakened unions, Flint sit-down strikers triumphed against the world's wealthiest industrial corporation, General Motors (GM). The concessions gained by
the strikers demonstrated the ability of working-class individuals to overcome seemingly insurmountable odds
against giant corporations through group solidarity and
collective bargaining and paved the way for unionization
of the automobile and other mass-production industries in
the United States.*

December 30, 1936, marked the beginning of the
most famous sit-down strike in U.S. history. GM's
lack of collaboration with the United Automobile
Workers (UAW), utilization of labor spies, mistreat-
ment of workers, low salaries, acceleration of production lines, and threats of layoffs contributed to
auto workers' refusal to vacate the Fisher 1 and
Fisher 2 plants. The passage of the 1935 Wagner Act
had legalized collective bargaining, facilitating workers' willingness to participate in the strike in Flint, a
community where the majority of households were
dependent upon GM for their livelihood.

The workers organized within the plants, establishing numerous committees dealing with issues of
strike strategy, food, safety, education, and entertainment. Daily meetings took place and care was taken
to maintain the excellent condition of the property.
Labor classes and plays were held, an orchestra was
assembled, and makeshift basketball courts were devised by taking the bottoms out of wastebaskets. Men
barricaded the buildings and made makeshift beds
from the parts of disassembled cars.

Outside the plants, committees were formed at
union headquarters to deal with security and relief
measures, food preparation for several thousand
strikers inside the plants and on the picket lines, and
publicity for the strikes. Since Flint was a "GM-
owned" town, strikers had to contend with coverage
from the local *Flint Journal* and radio station that denounced the strikers and blamed the strike on the
work of communists and socialists. While communists and socialists were key players in the strike, the

majority of strikers were driven by their concern for
decent working conditions rather than by political
ideologies. GM organized the Flint Alliance in an effort to persuade the public that the majority of citizens were opposed to the strike. Area churches were
hesitant to take on the strikers' cause, and strikers'
children were given school assignments denouncing
the strike.

Women played an instrumental role in the
strike's success by forming the Women's Auxiliary
and the Women's Emergency Brigade. The latter
group was founded by Genora Johnson after the
"Battle of Bulls Run" on January 11, 1937. On that afternoon, company guards stormed Fisher 2 as food
was being handed in the gate to strikers. Despite
freezing temperatures, GM officials turned off the
heat, police threw gas bombs, and strikers retaliated
by using fire hoses and throwing bottles and any object at hand. When the police began shooting and in-
juring strikers, Johnson yelled to the women of Flint
to join the fight against the cowardly police. After
the plant was successfully secured by the strikers,
Johnson began recruiting volunteers for the brigade. On February 1, 1937, the brigade played an
important role in the capture of GM's largest plant,
Chevrolet 4. This helped bring the strike to an end
in large part because union officials had leaked information that a sit-down strike was to occur at Chevrolet 9. With company resources diverted to plant 9,
a successful takeover of plant 4 occurred while brigade members formed an outside barricade. Largely
because of the efforts of Governor Frank Murphy
and the Congress of Industrial Organizations (CIO)
president John L. Lewis, on February 11, 1937, an
agreement was reached recognizing the UAW and
granting it sole rights to organize for six months in
other GM plants. Returning strikers were promised
protection from discrimination and harassment.

Impact The immediate impact of the Flint sit-down
strike was extensive. Strikes occurred across the nation, resulting in increased wages and improved
working conditions. UAW membership increased
dramatically. On March 2, 1937, United States Steel,
in an effort to avert a strike, signed a contract with
the CIO.

The sit-down strike afforded several benefits over
conventional strikes by preventing replacement
scabs and affording workers more security and negotiating power. Though sit-down strikes were eventu-

Striking auto workers in Flint use a chalkboard to count the number of days their strike has lasted. (NY Daily News via Getty Images)

ally outlawed, the Flint strike continues to serve as an example of the power inherent in group solidarity.

Maureen Moffitt Wilt

Further Reading

Barnard, John. *American Vanguard: The United Auto Workers During the Reuther Years, 1935-1970.* Detroit: Wayne State University Press, 2004.

Fine, Sidney. *Sit-Down: The General Motors Strike of 1936-1937.* Ann Arbor: University of Michigan Press, 1969.

See also Automobiles and auto manufacturing; Great Depression in the United States; Income and wages in the United States; Labor strikes; National Labor Relations Act of 1935; Unionism.

■ Floyd, Pretty Boy

Identification Bank robber and kidnapper
Born February 3, 1904; Bartow County, Georgia
Died October 22, 1934; near Wellsville, Ohio
Also known as Charles Arthur Floyd

Floyd was a notorious kidnapper and bank robber. He is credited with introducing the machine gun and armored vests to the outlaws of Oklahoma.

In 1911, Charles Arthur "Pretty Boy" Floyd moved with his family from Georgia to Oklahoma, settling in Akin. He had a degree of infamy prior to the start of the "great crime wave" of 1933-1934. In 1930, he was paroled from a prison in Missouri, where he had served time for the robbery of a Kroger store in St.

Pretty Boy Floyd. (Courtesy, F.B.I.)

Louis in 1925. In 1931, he joined some of his prison friends and began robbing banks in Oklahoma. The press in Oklahoma wrote about Floyd, who was reported to have killed eleven men, comparing him to "Billy the Kid." The director of the Federal Bureau of Investigation (FBI), J. Edgar Hoover, believed that Floyd was a ruthless killer who played a major role in the Kansas City Massacre at the Union Station in Kansas City, Missouri, during which four lawmen, one of whom was an FBI agent, were killed.

East Liverpool police officers Glenn Montgomery, Chester Smith, and Herman Roth were with FBI special agents Melvin Purvis and Sam McKee in the shootout that led to Floyd's death. While Floyd lay on the ground dying, Agent McKee asked him about the Union Station shootout. Floyd refused to comment on his involvement and, other than the use of an expletive, died without a statement. His funeral in Akin on October 28, 1934, was described by some as a media circus. Some people brought picnic lunches to the cemetery; some were drinking.

Impact The FBI indicted Floyd and several others for their involvement in the machine-gun killing of four law-enforcement officers and their prisoner at the Union Station in Kansas City, Missouri, on June 17, 1933. This shooting reportedly influenced President Franklin D. Roosevelt to reappoint Hoover as the director of the FBI. It influenced the push for legislation to make killing a federal agent a federal crime and to the arming of FBI agents.

Gerald P. Fisher

Further Reading

Burrough, Bryan. *Public Enemies.* New York: Penguin Books, 2004.

King, Jeffery. *The Life and Death of Pretty Boy Floyd.* Kent, Ohio: Kent State University Press, 1999.

Toland, John. *The Dillinger Days.* Cambridge, Mass.: Da Capo Press, 1995.

See also Alcatraz Federal Penitentiary; Barrow, Clyde, and Bonnie Parker; Capone, Al; Gangster films; Kelly, Machine Gun; Prohibition repeal.

■ Fluorescent lighting

Definition Light produced by fluorescence, typically from a gas-discharge tube that uses electricity to excite mercury vapor

Fluorescent lighting is produced by fluorescent lamps that convert electrical power into useful light much more efficiently than incandescent lamps. The savings in energy costs offset the higher initial cost of fluorescent lamps. For the same amount of light, fluorescent lighting uses only about one-fifth of the electrical current used for incandescent lighting.

By the end of the 1920's, all of the key components for fluorescent lighting had been discovered, invented, and developed, including glass tubing, inert gases to fill the tubes, electrical ballasts, competent electrodes, mercury vapor for luminescence, an effective way of generating reliable electrical discharge, and fluorescent coatings that could be energized by ultraviolet light. The 1930's became the decade for launching the commercial development of fluorescent lighting.

In 1934, renowned physicist Arthur Holly Compton reported on the successful experiments that he had conducted on fluorescent lighting for General Electric in Great Britain. Shortly thereafter, after extensive experimentation, George E. Inman and others produced a prototype fluorescent lamp at the engineering laboratory of General Electric in Nela Park, Ohio. An electrical ballast (a large inductor) sent a surge of current between the electrodes to form an arc in the lamp that excited mercury vapor atoms to produce ultraviolet light. The ultraviolet light excited fluorescent phosphor coatings to generate visible light.

Sales of fluorescent lamps commenced in 1938 when four different sizes of tubes were marketed. In 1939, General Electric and Westinghouse demonstrated the advantages of fluorescent lighting at the New York World's Fair and at the Golden Gate International Exposition in San Francisco. After Inman's U.S. patent application for fluorescent lighting met several delays, General Electric purchased the patent application of Friedrich Meyer, Hans Spanner, and Edmund Germer, who had invented an experimental fluorescent lamp in 1927, for $180,000 in 1939. Although legal battles continued, General Electric had the necessary patents to gain a preeminent position in the emerging fluorescent lighting market.

Impact As fluorescent lighting became popular and affordable, it replaced the old, hot incandescent bulbs and became the major way of lighting cities. By 1951, more light was produced in the United States by fluorescent lighting than by incandescent lighting.

Alvin K. Benson

Further Reading

Hordeski, Michael Frank. *New Technologies for Energy Efficiency.* Lilburn, Ga.: Fairmont Press, 2002.

Karlen, Mark, and James Benya. *Lighting Design Basics.* New York: John Wiley & Sons, 2004.

See also Chemistry; Inventions; Magazines; New York World's Fair; Physics.

■ Food processing

Definition Techniques used to transform grains, vegetables, fruits, meats, and fish into marketable goods appropriate for human consumption

During the 1930's, many new techniques in food processing were developed, including automated meat packaging, brine injection, freeze-drying, chemical preservatives, quick freezing, spray-drying, and lacquered canning for vegetables and fruits. These techniques made possible the wide variety of processed food items available in supermarkets.

Food processing involves any activities that take place after foods have left the primary producer and before they reach the consumer. Thus, these processing methods include canning, milk pasteurization, fermentation, extraction of flour and juices, osmotic dehydration, drying, heating, freezing, high pressures, controlled and modified atmospheres, hydrogenation of oils, blanchers, bleachers, automation of meat packaging, addition of new ingredients, and many food preservation techniques. These food preservation methods range from simple refrigeration and freezing to freeze-drying, chemical preservation, and irradiation.

Advances in Refrigeration and Freezing Hunters in prehistoric times were the first to use snow and ice to preserve meat. A physicist and chemist named Ibn Sina invented the first refrigerated coil in the eleventh century. William Cullen invented artificial refrigeration in 1748. During the nineteenth century, several inventions were made in the field, including the cooling compression system by Jacob Perkins in 1834 and the first ice-making machine by James Harrison in 1857. The "Monitor-Top" refrigerator was manufactured by General Electric, and more than one million of these were sold to households during the first years of the 1930's. Although many of these units continue to work, mass production of these refrigeration units did not continue because they used sulfur dioxide or methyl formate. Both of these chemicals are toxic and harmful to human eyes.

During the 1930's, Freon replaced sulfur dioxide and methyl formate because of its lack of toxicity; additionally, it is nonflammable. Freon is the brand name that the manufacturing company DuPont gave to the chemical called dichlorodifluoromethane, with formula CCl_2F_2. Other manufacturers have given this chemical trade names such as Daiflon, Flon, Flugene, Genetron, Arcton, Algofrene, and Racon.

Dichlorodifluoromethane is a member of a subclass of chemicals referred to as hydrochlorofluorocarbons, which includes other chemicals that also have been used as refrigerants and aerosol propellants since the 1930's. These are more often referred to by their common names, which consist of the prefix of Freon followed by numbers indicating the number of carbon atoms minus one, the number of hydrogen atoms plus one, and the number of fluorine atoms. Thus, the dichlorofluoromethane developed by DuPont during the 1930's was referred to as Freon-12 to indicate one carbon atom, no hydrogen atoms, and two fluorine atoms. Freon is useful because of its ability to flow into the compressor as a vapor that can then be compressed to become a superheated vapor. This can then cycle through the coils of the compressor, through a valve, and eventually pull heat from the box area of the refrigerator, keeping it cool. Freon-12 has been phased out because of concerns related to the depletion of the ozone layer. However, its introduction during the 1930's into refrigerators allowed ordinary consumers to expand their daily diet to include many perishable items and opened the door to many new processed food items, including frozen foods and ice cream.

Frozen food became available to consumers during the 1930's as a result of several technological advances, including rapid or "quick" freezing, refrigerated retail cabinets, and spray-drying. Many new products became available to consumers at supermarkets, and many of these products continue to be popular. Birds Eye frozen foods; Ballard Biscuits, which produces refrigerated biscuit dough packaged in cardboard tubes; Nescafé instant coffee; and Dairy Queen ice cream are among some of the familiar brand names that originated during the 1930's as a result of these technologies. Birds Eye frozen foods owes its name to Clarence Birdseye, who is given credit for the development of the first commercially available frozen foods, which ranged from frozen vegetables and frozen juice concentrates to the mass-marketed "TV dinner" products.

Drying Techniques for Food Preservation Improvements in food drying began during the 1930's. In spray-drying, a partial vacuum is used to dehydrate foods while simultaneously pulling water out and gently heating the food. Dehydration had been used to enhance transport and storage of foods by reducing the volume and to prolong storage life by inhibiting microorganisms and enzymes dependent on water for their growth.

Fruit and instant coffee have been prepared by this method of drying either by using a flow of air hot enough to cause vaporization or via projection onto hot metallic plates. This process is also known as lyophilization or cryodesiccation. Because vacuum is applied, the destructive toughening, loss of taste, and shrinkage that normally would occur when the food is heated do not happen. The tray freeze-drier

functions by freezing the food while it is fixed in place and while the surrounding pressure is reduced to the range of a few millibars. Then the latent heat of sublimation value is used to determine the amount of heat needed. This process is referred to as the primary drying phase, and it removes any unbound water molecules. These unbound water molecules then collect and resolidify in either a cold condenser chamber or a condenser plate in order to prevent the water from damaging the vacuum pump. A secondary drying phase removes water molecules that are bound to the food by increasing the temperature even more, according to the food's individual adsorption isotherm. The pressure is lowered in order to facilitate desorption of the water molecule. Together these two drying phases remove 96 to 99 percent of the water content, thus significantly decreasing the ability of microorganisms to cause spoilage.

Food Preservation Advances Using Chemical Preservatives By functioning as an antioxidant, ascorbic acid (vitamin C) is an important food preservative that gained usage during the 1930's. Chemically, it reduces the nitrate in cured meats to nitrogen oxide as it becomes oxidized to dehydroascorbic acid, thus preventing the formation of cancer-causing nitrosamines. During this process the ascorbic acid also prevents the fading of the red color associated with fresh meats, because it prevents the breakdown of fats in the meat that create the brown color and rancid smell. When ascorbic acid is added to bread and becomes oxidized to dehydroascorbic acid, it facilitates the formation of the intermolecular disulfide bonds in gluten. These bonds enhance the volume and texture of a loaf of bread. This application was discovered during the 1930's and continues to be used.

Carrageenan had been used in China as early as 600 B.C.E. but gained widespread usage during the 1930's as a food additive to thicken dairy products, including milk shakes, yogurt, and ice cream, and in processed meats to increase their volume by enhancing water retention. Thus, its general usage has been as a stabilizer and thickening agent. Its application as a thickening agent has been made possible because of its large, helical, polysaccharide structure, which has enough flexibility to form a variety of gels at room temperature. It acquired its name from the Irish village of Carragheen, where it was isolated from a type of red seaweed. Thus, it has often been called Irish moss. Its usage has been discouraged because of possible harmful effects ranging from upset stomach to gastrointestinal cancer. Other food gums that functioned as stabilizers found usage in a wide range of products—including frozen foods in TV dinners, ice creams, salad dressings and sauces—with improved taste and storage for transport to supermarkets.

Vitamin B_6, sodium benzoate, and bacteriophages also became important food additives during the 1930's. Vitamin B_6 gained widespread usage to prevent the deoxyribonucleic acid (DNA) damage that can result from a vitamin B_6 deficiency. With food additive number E211, sodium benzoate began to be used during the 1930's for its bacteriostatic and fungistatic properties. Along with other food additives, including sunset yellow (E110), ponceau 4R (E124), quinoline yellow (E104), allura red (E129), and carmoisine (E122), sodium benzoate has been under study by the Foods Standards Agency for links to hyperactive behavior. However, sodium benzoate continues to be used as a preservative in acidic foods including pickles, jams, carbonated beverages, and salad dressings. Bacteriophages, viruses capable of killing bacteria, were introduced into pharmaceuticals and foods during the 1930's but have declined in usage since then because of health concerns.

Additional Food Processing Advances   During the 1930's, polyphosphates began to be added to food to facilitate the reverse osmosis procedure that is important to the processing of fruit juices, milk, and other beverages. The Grindrod direct steam-injection method was developed during the 1930's to facilitate the sterilization of various beverages, including vegetable juices, milk, and frozen orange juice. In this method high heat is applied, followed by the application of vacuum and rapid cooling, as an improvement to the early process of pasteurization.

Impact   Early food processing began in ancient times with cooking, adding salt to preserve food, and the discovery that cold temperatures slowed the spoilage of food. Since then, food processing has evolved to include not only fermenting and pasteurization but also automated meat packaging with brine injection, freeze-drying, and chemical preservatives. Many of the most important advances in food-processing techniques were developed during the 1930's. These technological improvements allowed for the invention of many common food

products that remain in use, such as Campbell's Chicken Noodle and Cream of Mushroom soups, Pet Evaporated Milk, Spam, Kraft Miracle Whip, and Kraft Macaroni and Cheese Dinner.

Jeanne L. Kuhler

Further Reading

Brimelow, C., and D. Vadehdra. "Chilling." In *Vegetable Processing*, edited by D. Arthey and C. Dennis. London: Blackie, 1991. Provides information on frozen-food preparation.

Fellows, P. J. *Food Processing Technology: Principles and Practice*. 3d ed. London: CRC Press, 2009. Contains historical information related to mechanical developments for the meat- and poultry-processing industries and the development of brine-injection technology.

Holdsworth, S. D. *Aseptic Processing and Packaging of Food Products*. London: Elsevier, 1992. Provides additional information regarding refrigeration.

Welch, R. W., and P. C. Mitchell. "Food Processing: A Century of Change." *British Medical Bulletin* 56, no. 1 (2000): 1-17. Overview describing changes that occurred in food processing throughout the twentieth century.

See also   Agriculture in the United States; Chemistry; Federal Food, Drug, and Cosmetic Act of 1938; Freon; Frozen-food marketing; Instant coffee; Refrigerators; Supermarkets; Vending machines.

■ Food stamps

Definition   Coupons that can be exchanged for food

During the late 1930's, there was an oversupply of some agricultural goods and there were individuals without the means to buy food. The food-stamps program was envisioned as a program to bridge this gap and solve both problems at once.

Secretary of Agriculture Henry A. Wallace and his associate, Milo Perkins, viewed the food-stamps program as a unique way to solve two problems created by the Great Depression. Because of widespread unemployment, many people did not have sufficient income to purchase food. Because of the need to keep farmers employed, subsidies had been provided to farmers to grow food; this had created a sur-

Worker at the Bureau of Engraving and Printing inspects the first batch of food stamps to be produced. (Library of Congress)

plus. Wheat, for example, was stored in warehouses and barns, while hungry people did not have enough to eat. Surplus food generally causes the prices of that food to go down, creating a situation among farmers in which it costs more money to grow crops than they could get from selling them. For that reason, the government had purchased the surplus but was simply storing it.

Wallace and Perkins created a system in which qualifying individuals could purchase paper stamps that would allow them to buy certain foods. They were also given 50 percent of the value of their purchase price in other stamps, with which they could obtain surplus items at no cost. For example, if a person bought six dollars' worth of stamps, that person received six dollars' worth of one color of stamp, which could be used to buy any food, and three dollars' worth of another color stamp that could be redeemed for certain food items that were in oversupply.

The first user of food stamps is thought to be Mabel McFiggin, who reportedly bought butter, eggs, and fruit with the stamps. From the program's inception until 1943, approximately twenty million people used food stamps. Most who have studied the program have felt that it did a good job of considering the interests of both farmers and individuals in need of governmental assistance. It also diversified and improved the diets of those participating. Over the four years, the program cost the government $262 million.

Wallace and Perkins instituted specific features for food stamps. Initially, the program was considered experimental and was to end when it was no longer needed. Only individuals on relief could qualify for the food stamps. These people were allowed to buy an amount of food stamps that equaled their usual food expenses.

When large surpluses and major unemployment ended, the program ended. Even critics of later food-stamps programs have generally considered the Depression-era program to have been a success because of its short time frame and its beneficial outcome.

Impact Between 1939 and 1943, the food-stamps program helped destitute farmers and unemployed and underemployed individuals by keeping prices of surplus foods up, and it is therefore considered one of the successful economic measures of the era. Also, the successes of the program allowed for similar ones to be implemented later in the twentieth century.

Mary C. Ware

Further Reading

DeLorme, Charles D., Jr., David R. Kamerschen, and David C. Redman. "The First U.S. Food Stamp Program: An Example of Rent Seeking and Avoiding." *American Journal of Economics and Sociology* 51, no. 4 (October, 1992): 421-433.

Landers, Patti S. "The Food Stamp Program: History, Education, and Impact." *Journal of the American Dietetic Association* 107, no. 11 (November, 2007): 1945-1952.

Poppendieck, Janet. *Breadlines Knee Deep in Wheat: Food Assistance in the Great Depression.* New Brunswick, N.J.: Rutgers University Press, 1986.

See also Agricultural Adjustment Acts; Agriculture in the United States; Dust Bowl; Unemployment in the United States.

■ Football

Definition   Team sport contested by two eleven-member teams attempting to advance a ball by running, passing, or kicking to the opposing teams' end zones

The 1930's proved to be a time of great change for football. What had been a regional sport based in the Northeast and Midwest began to proliferate, with regards to media attention, across the country. In addition, the rise of the professional game challenged the dominance of college football. These elements helped it become the dominant spectator sport in the United States.

Football during the 1930's was not a novel sport. However, it grew in exposure as the result of two factors. First, more college teams began receiving attention, especially in areas that had been underappreciated. Second, the fledgling National Football League (NFL) was able to bring more stability to its organization. At first, the NFL was considered to be in direct competition with college football, but it grew into a complementary sport and offered fans an alternative outlet for watching the sport.

The College Game   The 1930's were an era of transition for college football, as many aspects of the game shifted. Many teams that became traditional powers established their legacy during this decade. In contrast, some of the established powers, such as the University of Chicago and Princeton University, began slipping out of the national spotlight. At the time, the sport did not have many of the unified qualities that existed in later versions. Teams rarely traveled across the country to play one another. The lack of head-to-head games created a situation in

Future U.S. Supreme Court justice Byron "Whizzer" White, a halfback for the University of Colorado, rushes for a touchdown in the 1938 Cotton Bowl game against Rice. (AP/Wide World Photos)

Rose Bowl Game Scores, 1930-1939

Year	Winner	Loser	Score
1930	University of Southern California (USC)	Pittsburgh	47-14
1931	Alabama	Washington State	24-0
1932	USC	Tulane	21-12
1933	USC	Pittsburgh	35-0
1934	Columbia	Stanford	7-0
1935	Alabama	Stanford	29-13
1936	Stanford	Southern Methodist University	7-0
1937	Pittsburgh	Washington	21-0
1938	California	Alabama	13-0
1939	USC	Duke	7-3

which several teams could be considered national champions. Many of the champions were so declared solely because they finished first in their conferences. The exception was the Rose Bowl game, which did feature teams from across the country playing at the end of the season in Pasadena, California. The Rose Bowl was instrumental in accelerating football's overall growth with two surprising games in the late 1920's. Both games featured teams from the South playing teams from the West Coast, and in both games, the southern teams won. The sport, which had succeeded through regional action, began to unify nationally.

As the sport grew in popularity, many universities and colleges began to invest more money in their teams. While this had been evident in the rise of the "superstar" coaches, such as Amos Alonzo Stagg, Knute Rockne, and Fielding Harris Yost, more teams began placing added emphasis on gathering quality athletes and improving their facilities. Stadiums began to increase in size as a result of the growing desire of fans to see the games. College campuses were not the only places seeking to benefit from the increase in fans; in 1930, the Atlantic City Auditorium held a legitimate indoor game that was attended by a sizable crowd. While night games had been in existence since the early 1900's, the novelty of an indoor game brought more attention to the sport.

The growing exposure for the college game helped to establish other teams in different areas of the country. The Rose Bowl wins by southern teams created interest in this region. Texas, which had been considered its own region, also began to rise in prominence thanks to the exposure. Two games in the South, University of North Carolina versus University of Virginia and the University of Georgia versus the University of Auburn, had been played since 1892, but because no teams from the South had beaten any of the established powers, the teams of the region had been considered inferior. Teams from the West experienced a similar rise in prominence during this time.

A number of other aspects contributed to college football becoming more prevalent during the decade. Recognizing and following the success of the Rose Bowl, four other bowls came into existence: the Orange Bowl, the Sugar Bowl, the Sun Bowl, and the Cotton Bowl. These games provided the opportunity for teams from varying regions to play each other. In conjunction with the rise of other bowl games was the development of the Associated Press poll, in which writers voted on the ranking of the top teams. This practice of ranking teams was the beginning of what evolved into the Bowl Championship Series.

Another factor contributing to the success of the college game was the creation of the Heisman Memorial Trophy Award, commonly called the Heisman Trophy. Named after the former coach, John Heisman, the award is presented to the most outstanding player in college football. Known first as the Downtown Athletic Club Trophy, the name was changed in 1936 when Heisman died. The first winner was Jay Berwanger from the University of Chicago. This award created additonal interest for fans, and the accompanying media exposure helped to make the award a fixture for the game.

An element that was instrumental in producing greater interest in the college game was the rise of the forward pass. The play had been in existence for some time; however, rules were in place that discouraged it. The removal of these rules helped to open up the game. Some coaches resisted using the play, but, overall, the forward pass began to infiltrate the game, and fans found it to be an exciting element.

The Rise of the Professional Game The NFL had been considered inferior to the college game. The league was formed during the 1920's and therefore had little history. Also, the league struggled with stability, which compromised its status. Most of the teams that had entered the NFL at its inception had failed, and many felt that the league would never survive. At the time, the NFL was unstructured: Some teams played more games than others, and no system existed for the allotment of players to the teams. In addition, many of the teams were formed in small towns in the Midwest and had neither the facilities nor the draw in fan interest. The league persisted, however, and continued to field teams that were willing to play, even if their existence was tenuous.

By the mid-1930's, a number of changes had begun. For example, most teams, with the exception of the Green Bay Packers, played in major cities. The ability to draw fans from the cities helped the league gain more attention. The overall game was developing to appease fans. Unlike the college game, the NFL embraced the forward pass, even if the results were mixed. The passing game, along with what was considered a faster pace than in the college game, helped to make the league more attractive to fans.

In 1935, a draft system was implemented, in which the teams chose in reverse order of their finish in the previous season. The first draft pick in the NFL was the first Heisman winner, Berwanger, who was selected by the Philadelphia Eagles. Berwanger never played in the NFL, choosing to go into journalism instead. In 1936, all teams played the same number of games, a change that helped organize the NFL. The league continued to battle for fans, but it had began to garner a following. The draft created

a way for the league to carry fan interest from the college game to the professional one.

The NFL also capitalized on the fact that most of its teams had access to a built-in fan contingency. The ability to use the major outlets of communication provided the NFL a way to reach those fans quickly through both radio and print. In 1939, the NFL televised its first game, featuring the Brooklyn Dodgers and Philadelphia Eagles. Roughly one thousand fans witnessed the event.

By the end of the decade, the NFL had begun to be a viable operation. In the 1939 season, attendance exceeded one million. The championship games gained in exposure, and the game grew in acceptance. During this time, the league laid a foundation on which it could build.

Impact The development of the professional game of football offered a new outlet for fans. The establishment of this league helped solidify the country's love of football. Both college and professional football suffered during World War II, but both came back strongly, with the NFL gaining more market share. Fans have long debated which form of the game is better, but spectatorship for both has continued to rise. The 1930's can be considered one of the most influential periods in the growth of football.

P. Huston Ladner

Further Reading
Danzig, Allison. *The History of American Football: Its Great Teams, Players, and Coaches.* Englewood Cliffs, N.J.: Prentice-Hall, 1956. One of the early and preeminent texts on the history of the rise of football.

MacCambridge, Michael. *America's Game: The Epic Story of How Pro Football Captured a Nation.* New York: Random House, 2004. A sweeping survey of football that begins prior to World War II, portraying how football grew into the most popular American sport.

Oriard, Michael. *Brand NFL: Making and Selling America's Favorite Sport.* Chapel Hill: University of North Carolina Press, 2007. Oriard offers a sweeping depiction of professional football.

Peterson, Robert. *Pigskin: The Early Years of Pro Football.* New York: Oxford University Press, 1997. Details the rise of the professional game during the 1920's to the championship game in 1958.

Watterson, John. *College Football: History, Spectacle, Controversy.* Baltimore: Johns Hopkins University

Press, 2002. Offers a comprehensive examination of the growth of college football beginning in 1875.

Whittingham, Richard. *Rites of Autumn: The Story of College Football.* New York: Free Press, 2001. With a foreword from Roger Staubach, this book offers a survey of the college game. There is an accompanying DVD.

_____. *What a Game They Played: An Inside Look at the Golden Era of Pro Football.* Lincoln: University of Nebraska Press, 2001. This book focuses on the rise of professional football from the 1920's through the 1940's.

See also   Baseball; Basketball; Boxing; Ice hockey; Tennis.

■ Ford, Henry

Identification   Auto manufacturer
Born   July 30, 1863; Springfield township (now Dearborn), Michigan
Died   April 7, 1947; Dearborn, Michigan

Ford's activism against the administration of President Franklin D. Roosevelt and his anti-Semitic, pro-Nazi sympathies led to a decline in his popularity in the United States, while his erratic handling of business matters had a negative effect on the Ford Motor Corporation during the decade.

In 1930, Henry Ford was the most recognizable figure among American automobile manufacturers. By that time, however, he was largely an absentee owner at Ford Motor Company, after installing his son Edsel as president in 1919. In 1930, he intervened to help the company counter the effects of the Great Depression, certain it was a temporary aberration in the business cycle. He raised wages to seven dollars per day and announced plans for a $25 million plant expansion. These efforts were short-lived, however; the company eventually succumbed to the general economic downturn. Meanwhile, Ford busied himself with a number of scientific, agricultural, and historical projects, most notably the Thomas Edison Institute, created to honor his hero, and Greenfield Village, an outdoor museum located near Detroit.

Many who had once thought highly of Ford found him eccentric and unpredictable during the 1930's. That side of Ford's personality emerged dur-

ing the midst of the country's banking crisis in 1932. Ford was asked by representatives of President Herbert Hoover to assist in saving the Union Guardian Bank, where his company had significant deposits, by leaving his funds on deposit and providing an additional loan. In December, 1932, Ford agreed; however, weeks later he changed his mind, and the bank failed. Ford also made no secret of his disdain for President Franklin D. Roosevelt and the New Deal. He was reluctant to support any of the president's initiatives and loathed what he saw as welfare programs designed to give handouts to the unemployed.

In 1935, Ford took steps to protect his fortune from depletion by a new law that placed onerous taxes on large estates. The Ford Foundation was created to be the beneficiary of most of the wealth of Henry, his wife Clara, and their son Edsel upon their deaths. A division of company stock ensured that the family would continue to control company operations even after the bulk of the stock transferred to the foundation.

Although Ford seemed to be occupied with other interests, he regularly interjected himself in decisions at the automobile company he founded. However, he was often out of touch with engineering developments and new management practices, and his directives were often counterproductive. During this period, Ford came increasingly under the influence of Harry Bennett. Officially the head of the Services Division, Bennett gained exceptional power at the company while Ford attended to other interests. His high-handed tactics drove a wedge between Ford and Edsel, hampering company operations. Ford would tolerate no criticism of Bennett, however, so the company continued to see losses in sales to manufacturers who offered more reliable cars with more desirable features.

Throughout his life, Ford made no secret of his racist and anti-Semitic views. During the 1920's, he had expressed his opinions in the *Dearborn Independent*, a paper he owned. He also published *The International Jew*, a set of pamphlets outlining what he perceived as a threat to the United States from Jewish business interests. In the following decade, he continued to rail against Jewish interests in government and banking and openly displayed disdain for African American workers at his company. After 1933, Ford's ideas and writings came to be viewed most favorably in Germany by leaders of the new government under Adolf Hitler. While Hitler built his war machine, Ford expressed strong views on keeping the United States out of any conflict in Europe. The highlight, or low point, of Ford's relationship with the Nazis came in 1938, when Hitler awarded him the Grand Cross of the Order of the German Eagle.

Impact Ford's constant meddling in the operations at Ford Motor Company, especially his abrupt demands for reversals of many decisions made by his son and other company executives to promote innovation, took its toll on the business. During the decade, Ford Motor Company slipped to third among major manufacturers, behind General Motors and the Chrysler Corporation. Ford's admiration for Germany and his loathing for Roosevelt's New Deal made him a reluctant participant in efforts to support the Allies when war broke out in Europe in 1939. That recalcitrant attitude was not shaken until his own country entered the conflict two years later.

Laurence W. Mazzeno

Further Reading

Bak, Richard. *Henry and Edsel: The Creation of the Ford Empire.* Hoboken, N.J.: John Wiley & Sons, 2003.

Brinkley, Douglas. *Wheels for the World: Henry Ford, His Company, and a Century of Progress.* New York: Viking Press, 2003.

Gelderman, Carol. *Henry Ford: The Wayward Capitalist.* New York: Dial, 1981.

See also Anti-Semitism; Business and the economy in the United States; Ford Foundation; Germany and U.S. appeasement; Greenfield Village; Labor strikes; Roosevelt, Franklin D.; Unionism.

■ Ford, John

Identification American film director
Born February 1, 1894; Cape Elizabeth, Maine
Died August 31, 1973; Palm Springs, California

The winner of six Academy Awards for best picture, Ford was one of the most highly lauded and influential filmmakers of the twentieth century. Although none of his Oscars was awarded for the Western films he made, he is regarded as the founder and pioneer of the Western genre. His film version of John Steinbeck's The Grapes of Wrath *(1940) is a rare example of a film that is equal in power to the literary classic on which it was based.*

Born Sean Aloysius O'Feeny, John Ford had a long career as a filmmaker, beginning in the silent era. By the advent of synchronized sound, he was already established as a director, working with and contributing to the latest innovations of the industry. *Men Without Women* (1930) was the first film to depict life on a submarine utilizing a real submarine for the set. John Wayne, who became more closely associated with Ford than any other actor, worked as a stuntman in this film. *Up the River* (1930) followed in the same year; the film was a prison story Ford rewrote with Dudley Nichols to include comic elements.

Ford worked with some of the most prominent actors of the era, utilizing Will Rogers in three films. *Dr. Bull* (1933) took advantage of Rogers's unique style in scenes in which Rogers adjusted the script to convey the personality of his character. Boris Karloff was one of the men under siege in the Arabian Desert in *The Lost Patrol* (1934), a film that concentrated on a group of men functioning as a tight team in a perilous situation, and the first film that included Victor McLaughlin, a prominent member of the Ford "stock company." Max Steiner's score won the Academy Award.

Laughlin's performance as the title character of *The Informer* (1935) was one of the reasons that Ford's stature rose from competent professional to one of the leading filmmakers in Hollywood. The apparent authenticity of the setting in Dublin, which was actually painted sets on a studio lot; the gripping rendition of the Irish Civil War; and McLaughlin's legendary performance were key elements in the formation of Ford's signature style. *The Prisoner of Shark Island* (1936) told the story of Samuel Mudd (played by Warner Baxter), the doctor who treated John Wilkes Booth. *Mary of Scotland* (1936), with Katharine Hepburn as the tragic Mary Stuart, and a cinematic version of Sean O'Casey's play *The Plough and the Stars* (1936), with Barbara Stanwyck, were the second and third films Ford directed in a typically industrious year of filmmaking. He followed that with *Wee Willie Winkie* (1937), one of Shirley Temple's first films.

Three of the films that Ford made at the end of the decade remain enduring American classics. For *Stagecoach* (1939), Ford drew Wayne out of a series of minor roles and nondescript characters to play the "Ringo Kid," who is a passenger on a stagecoach traveling through hostile territory in New Mexico in 1884. Ford shot the film in Monument Valley, the setting for his best-known Westerns and a location that became a visual correlative for a mythic vision of the frontier. Wayne's iconic performance began the concept of the westerner as a representation of an epic American hero, and the blend of romance, action, and intricate character interaction represented all of Ford's strengths as a filmmaker.

Ford cast Henry Fonda as Abraham Lincoln in *Young Mr. Lincoln* (1939), a film based on Lincoln's life as a "jackleg lawyer from Illinois," in Ford's words, prior to his presidency. Fonda's heartfelt, intelligent, and unaffected performance as Lincoln offered a humane and vastly appealing conception of an individual's struggles through hard times at the moment of economic depression in the United States. It anticipated Fonda's unforgettable role as Tom Joad in *The Grapes of Wrath*, which was in production as the decade ended. Ford's final film of the 1930's was *Drums Along the Mohawk* (1939), which re-created a revolutionary-war setting in anticipation of the forthcoming World War II; Fonda played the main character.

John Ford, the pioneering filmmaker who directed Stagecoach *and many other 1930's films, relaxing aboard a yacht in 1934.* (AP/Wide World Photos)

Impact The films that Ford directed during the 1930's were instrumental in the development of the medium in the first decade of talking pictures. Every filmmaker since then has had to compare his own work to Ford's.

Leon Lewis

Further Reading

Gallagher, Tag. *John Ford: The Man and His Films.* Berkeley: University of California Press, 1986.

Grant, Barry Keith. *John Ford's "Stagecoach."* New York: Cambridge University Press, 2003.

McBride, Joseph. *Searching for John Ford: A Life.* New York: St. Martin's Press, 2001.

See also Academy Awards; Film; *Informer, The*; *Stagecoach*; *United States v. Curtiss-Wright Export Corp.*; Western films; *Young Mr. Lincoln*.

■ Ford Foundation

Identification Philanthropic organization
Date Established January 15, 1936

Establishing the Ford Foundation provided Henry Ford a vehicle for avoiding payment of high estate taxes and eventually made available significant funds to support charitable causes worldwide.

The Ford Foundation was created in part as an act of spite by automaker Ford. In 1935, the U.S. Congress, encouraged by President Franklin D. Roosevelt, passed a law establishing high tax rates on estates of wealthy Americans. Estates of more than $50 million were to be taxed at 70 percent. Ford despised Roosevelt and his New Deal policies and was adamant that the family fortune—estimated by some to exceed $1 billion—should not be seized by the federal government when he died. Ford was equally determined that the Ford Motor Company remain a family business and not become a publicly traded corporation.

Almost as soon as the new law passed, Ford directed company attorneys to determine how to circumvent the new tax. Attorneys proposed the establishment of a foundation into which the three members of the Ford family who together held 100 percent of the company's shares would bequeath the bulk of their holdings when they died. The Fords divided their stock into two classes: Five percent of each member's holdings would be Class B stock, with voting privileges; the remaining 95 percent, designated Class A, carrying no voting privileges, would be willed to the foundation. As a consequence, the foundation would receive nearly all of the Fords' wealth, but the family could retain control of the company through the Class A shares, which would be bequeathed to children and grandchildren when the three principal shareholders died. Although Ford had never been particularly generous with his fortune, he was willing to see it set aside for the public good rather than pass into the federal Treasury.

Impact Although the immediate impact of the creation of the Ford Foundation was minimal, when Henry, Edsel, and Clara Ford died the bulk of their estates was transferred into the foundation, where it created the largest single nonprofit in the United States. Since the 1950's, the foundation has been a world leader in sponsoring educational and social-services programs. At the outset of the twenty-first century, it was still the largest private foundation in the United States, with assets of approximately $11 billion in 2008.

Laurence W. Mazzeno

Further Reading

Brinkley, Douglas. *Wheels for the World: Henry Ford, His Company, and a Century of Progress*. New York: Viking Press, 2003.

Lacey, Robert. *Ford: The Men and the Machine*. Boston: Little, Brown, 1986.

See also Automobiles and auto manufacturing; Ford, Henry; Income and wages in the United States; Revenue Acts; Roosevelt, Franklin D.

■ Foreign Agents Registration Act of 1938

The Law Federal legislation to counter the growing influence of propaganda in the United States from communist, fascist, and Nazi governments

Date Enacted on June 8, 1938

Also known as McCormack Act of 1938; FARA

The act is a disclosure statute that requires persons acting as agents of foreign principals in a political or quasi-political capacity to make periodic public disclosure of their relationship with the foreign principal as well as their activities, receipts, and disbursements in support of those activities.

The Foreign Agents Registration Act (FARA) was the first legislative attempt by the U.S. government to counter the growing influence of propaganda from communist, fascist, and Nazi governments that circulated within the United States during the 1930's. In response to German propaganda in the lead-up to World War II, the act originally required sources to be properly identified to the American public as an attempt to limit the influence of German agents in the United States. The legislation's original title was the McCormack Act, in recognition of its primary sponsor, Democratic representative John W. McCormack of Massachusetts.

Section 4 of the act contains the provisions relating to the filing and labeling of political propaganda by persons required to register under the act. The original intent of these regulations applied to political propaganda disseminated by U.S. mail and to interstate or foreign commerce in the interests of the foreign principal. Individuals and organizations that disseminated propaganda or participated in related activities on behalf of another country had to file public reports with the U.S. Department of State. Although there were exemptions in the legislation on commercial, religious, scientific, artistic, and academic bases, the act was mainly used to prohibit unlabeled political propaganda—whether print, radio broadcasts, or telecasts—from coming into the United States or to limit access to political materials hostile to the United States.

Since 1938, the act has been amended several times, including a general revision in 1942 and major amendments in 1966. Administration of the act was the responsibility of the U.S. Department of

State until it was transferred to the U.S. Department of Justice in June, 1942. The term "political propaganda" was deleted as a result of the Lobbying Disclosure Act of 1995 and was replaced by "informational materials."

Impact The Foreign Agents Registration Act of 1938 has been the foundation for the regulation of foreign representatives. Its purpose is to protect legislative and executive processes in the United States from covert foreign influence.

Martin J. Manning

Further Reading

Foreign Agents Registration Act of 1938, as Amended, and the Rules and Regulations Prescribed by the Attorney General. Washington, D.C.: United States Department of Justice, 1986.

Luneburg, William V., and Thomas M. Susman. *The Lobbying Manual: A Complete Guide to Federal Law Governing Lawyers and Lobbyists.* 3d ed. Chicago: American Bar Association, 2005.

Smith, Grant F. *America's Defense Line: The Justice Department's Battle to Register the Israel Lobby as Agents of a Foreign Government.* Washington, D.C.: Institute for Research, Middle Eastern Policy, 2008.

See also Communism; Congress, U.S.; Foreign policy of the United States; Germany and U.S. appeasement; Magazines.

■ Foreign policy of Canada

During the 1930's, Canadian foreign policy objectives were torn between North America and the British Commonwealth. U.S. isolationism pulled in one direction; greater participation in the British Commonwealth of Nations pulled in another. Canada's support for the League of Nations became conflicted. As the threat of European war increased, Canada hoped to have only a marginal role in any future conflict. Above all, the Great Depression was an underlying cause of Canadian weakness. The desire to maintain unity between the French- and English-speaking parts of Canada was a strong incentive for disengagement with international affairs and was a primary cause of Canada's unreadiness when war actually came.

William Lyon Mackenzie King's Liberal Party government fell in 1930 to the Conservative Party, led by Richard Bedford Bennett. Bennett was more open

to a connection with the United States than King was; King was a traditionalist and therefore loyal to the British Commonwealth. Bennett had control over the ministry of external affairs in Ottawa, the Canadian capital, and his pro-American policy was ably backed by Oscar D. Skelton, undersecretary of state for external affairs. Skelton had a deep suspicion that Great Britain would use Canada in the same way it had during World War I. However, Bennett kept the ministry of external affairs and the cadre of Canadian diplomats small.

Relationships with the United States In response to the economic depression following the Wall Street crash of 1929, the United States had set up enormous trade barriers against most other countries, including Canada, in the form of tariffs under the Smoot-Hawley Act. Canada responded with its own barriers. Canada's international trade fell from $2.5 billion to $1.25 billion between 1929 and 1931. The Ottawa Conference of 1932, at which Commonwealth countries tried to establish a system of trade preferences, added to American fears that the Canadian market was closed to the United States and that Britain was bidding to dominate world trade.

As the decade went on, the United States was not excluded by the Commonwealth as much as had been feared. American investment in Canada increased, and negotiations over a common use of the St. Lawrence Seaway began in 1931; the two sides reached an agreement in 1932, though the seaway was not completed until 1959. By 1935, the tariff war with the United States was largely over. In a 1938 trade agreement, Canada traded off some Commonwealth preferences for greater entry into U.S. markets. By 1939, U.S. companies and investors supplied 60 percent of all foreign capital, compared to the 36 percent that came from the United Kingdom.

U.S. president Franklin D. Roosevelt and reelected prime minister King met about common defense policy in August, 1938. Roosevelt declared that the United States would not allow any foreign force to invade Canada. Practical results of the conference were a regular meeting of Canadian and American defense chiefs and some joint discussions over Pacific Ocean and St. Lawrence River coastal defenses.

Relations with the Rest of the World Apart from direct relations with the United States and the British Commonwealth, Canada had its relations with the rest of the world largely mediated through the

Canadian prime minister William Lyon Mackenzie King (left) hosts American president Franklin D. Roosevelt (center) and the latter's son James Roosevelt in Quebec in 1936. The United States became an important international ally of Canada in an era in which the latter sought to establish political autonomy from Great Britain. (AP/Wide World Photos)

League of Nations. In fact, only with Japan and France did Canada have separate diplomatic contact at embassy level. Few Canadian diplomats showed the skills of Vincent Massey or Lester B. Pearson. During the 1920's, Canada had shared something of the early idealism of the League of Nations but also shared its weakness during the 1930's, as the will to take decisive action evaporated.

Three foreign crises faced Canada in the League of Nations in the 1930's: the Japanese takeover of Manchuria in September, 1931; the Italian invasion of Ethiopia in 1935; and the German march into the Rhineland in 1936. Only in the case of Italy did the Canadian delegate, Walter Riddell, take a strong line on the question of sanctions, but he was immediately undermined by the King government. In some of these cases, as with the 1936 Spanish Civil War,

French Canadian sentiment was at odds with Anglo-Canadian sentiment. In order to keep national unity, the Canadian government preferred a hands-off approach. In this, King was heavily dependent on his leading French Canadian minister, Ernest Lapointe, his minister of justice. A mood of isolationism, paralleling that in the United States, helped the Liberal government in this determination.

As the decade progressed and the threat of war in Europe grew, Canada hoped any such war would be brief and that its role would be merely to supply munitions and other war supplies. This view was shared by both the British and the American governments. Canada largely supported British prime minister Neville Chamberlain's efforts toward peace and negotiation, or appeasement, with Adolf Hitler during 1938-1939. However, despite Canada's obvious reluctance to commit itself to a war, Prime Minister King did meet with Hitler in 1938, as part of one of his rare tours of Europe, and told him face-to-face that Canada would not remain neutral regarding German expansionism. However, King, like Chamberlain, misjudged Hitler as a person and failed to see the danger his leadership presented. Even after the German takeover of Czechoslovakia, Canada remained uncertain of Nazi intentions.

Impact   As a result of Canada's noninterventionist policy, when World War II started in September, 1939, Canada was woefully unprepared militarily. However, Canada voted to declare war within a week of the British and French declaration, leaving no doubt about its support for the Commonwealth. Canada's contribution to the effort was far greater than envisaged, in terms of both supplies and manpower. The speed with which Canada responded to these changed circumstances showed that its economy and industrial sector had not been fatally broken by the earlier depression. With the continuing promise that there would be no conscription, it also showed the level of national unity in the country and that Canada was capable of defending itself without U.S. participation.

David Barratt

Further Reading

Bothwell, Robert, Ian Drummond, and John English. *Canada, 1900-1945.* Toronto: University of Toronto Press, 1987. One of the fullest historical accounts of Canada's development through the first half of the twentieth century, covering its foreign policy and other aspects of government.

Crawley, Terry. *Marriage of Minds: Isabel and Oscar Skelton Reinventing Canada.* Toronto: University of Toronto Press, 2003. Traces Skelton's important influence in prying Canada away from its British connections to form a more North American identity.

Creighton, Donald Grant. *Dominion of the North: A History of Canada.* Cambridge, Mass.: Riverside Press, 1958. Chapter 9 deals closely with the relationship between the Depression and Canada's foreign policies.

Granatstein, J. L. *Canada's War: The Politics of the Mackenzie King Government 1939-1945.* Toronto: University of Toronto Press, 1990. Discussion of the Liberal Party government's attitude to the impending conflict in Europe.

_____. *How Britain's Weakness Forced Canada into the Arms of the United States.* Toronto: University of Toronto Press, 1989. Part of the 1988 Joanne Goodman Lectures. Granatstein, a leading Canadian historian, shows how Canada had to shift its foreign policy from one that was Anglo-oriented to one that relied on the United States.

MacFarlane, John. *Ernest Lapointe and Quebec's Influence on Canada's Foreign Policy.* Toronto: University of Toronto Press, 1999. Traces the influential role Lapointe, minister of justice in King's government from 1935 to 1941, played in keeping Quebec in and Canada out of policies that would have caused disunity.

Meehan, John David. *The Dominion and the Rising Sun: Canada Encounters Japan 1929-1941.* Vancouver: University of British Columbia Press, 2004. Traces Canada's international relationship with Japan leading up to Japan's entry into World War II.

Wittke, Carl. *A History of Canada.* 3d ed. New York: Appleton-Century-Crofts, 1941. An old but full history that traces Canada's international relationships.

See also   Geneva Disarmament Conference; Immigration to Canada; Inter-American Conference for the Maintenance of Peace; League of Nations; London Economic Conference; London Naval Treaty; St. Lawrence Seaway Treaty; Soviet Union; Spanish Civil War; World War II and Canada.

■ Foreign policy of the United States

American democracy underwent severe tests in the 1930's, both at home and abroad. While faced with the greatest economic depression in its history, the United States was forced to confront growing threats to its interests in Europe and East Asia. Despite overwhelming isolationist sentiment in American society, the American people came to realize by the end of the decade that they bore unshakable responsibilities for world peace and the survival of democracy.

Through much of the 1930's, both the American public and the U.S. government showed great reluctance to assume responsibility for or leadership in global affairs. U.S. foreign policy in this decade was characterized by isolationism, withdrawal from international commitments, hesitation in the face of overseas crisis, and slow response to rising threats to world peace. Such behavior was largely attributable to American disenchantment with the settlement of World War I and the unprecedented economic difficulties at home.

Effects of the Great Depression The 1930's opened with Western nations sliding into the Great Depression. A stagnant economy, persistent unemployment, and other related domestic issues kept the governments of major democracies preoccupied. The U.S. government likewise focused its attention on the exigencies at home. Its foreign policy often reflected domestic needs even at the expense of international cooperation. With the support of President Herbert Hoover, in June, 1930, the U.S. Congress passed the Hawley-Smoot Tariff Act, which limited the import of commodities, especially sugar and textiles, to protect domestic industry. The crash of the stock market seriously hampered American programs such as the Young Plan, designed to stabilize the European economy by pumping U.S. dollars into European banks. Because of the magnitude of the Depression, other U.S. measures meant to salvage the world economy, such as the one-year moratorium on intergovernmental debts and reparations from 1931 to 1932, proved largely ineffective.

During the majority of his first term in office, President Franklin D. Roosevelt was engrossed in dealing with the dire economic situation at home. Through a variety of government-sponsored programs known as the New Deal, his administration tried to alleviate the impact of the Great Depression on the American people. In these years, Roosevelt showed even less interest in international economic cooperation than had his predecessor. At the London economic conference in June, 1933, for example, American leaders disappointed their allies by refusing to commit the U.S. government to restoring the international gold standard, for fear that it would further destabilize the U.S. economy. Moreover, the Roosevelt administration endorsed the Silver Purchase Act of 1934, which was aimed at reestablishing silver as the basis of the U.S. dollar. American purchases of silver at an artificially high price on domestic and foreign markets sucked large amounts of the metal from countries such as China and Japan, which in turn exacerbated the economic difficulties in those countries.

In the Western Hemisphere, both the Hoover and Roosevelt administrations sought to rebuild amicable relationships with their neighbors to promote regional cooperation. The Roosevelt administration, in particular, pursued the Good Neighbor Policy, by which it disavowed military intervention in Latin America. Under the principle of nonintervention, the U.S. government repealed the Platt Amendment of 1902, thereby acknowledging Cuba's full sovereignty. It also withdrew American troops from the Caribbean region except for the Panama Canal Zone and sought to increase trade with its neighbors through a series of negotiations, even though the volume of exchange in the Western Hemisphere did not grow significantly in this period.

Shackles of Isolationism While the Great Depression played a major role in shaping U.S. foreign policy in the 1930's, isolationist sentiment also prevented the United States from actively participating in international affairs. Although isolationism had always been a component of U.S. foreign policy, American involvement in World War I and the American public's disenchantment with the postwar settlement drove isolationism to new heights. This shift in public sentiment occurred at a time when events threatened to drag the nation back into costly entanglements overseas.

The first challenge to the United States came in East Asia in September, 1931, when the Japanese Kwantung Army launched an attack on Chinese troops in Manchuria and, despite the outcry from the international community, went on to occupy the entire region by the end of the year. Although shocked by this show of aggression, the Hoover administration did no more than urge Japan's government to respect China's territorial integrity.

Secretary of State Henry L. Stimson, in response to the Chinese government's appeal for U.S. intervention, pointed out that the Japanese action in Manchuria had violated the Kellogg-Briand Pact, which outlawed war, and the Nine-Power Treaty, the signatory nations of which vowed to honor the Open Door principle with regard to China. However, President Hoover refused to use economic sanctions against Japan for fear of provoking that nation's anger. His administration was glad to see the League of Nations tackle the Manchurian crisis but refrained from participation.

Although the League of Nations sent the Lytton

Commission to China and adopted its report, which condemned the Japanese action, its actions had little effect. The American policy of nonrecognition—that is, the refusal to accept any agreement between China and Japan that ran counter to the Open Door principle—fared no better. When the Japanese set up the *Manchukuo,* a puppet regime, in Manchuria in 1932, they simply ignored American protests.

From 1931 to 1937, the U.S. government had little leverage over Japan, as no other power in East Asia would commit itself to the Americans' Open Door principle. Between 1933 and 1937, while American leaders maintained a façade of friendship with Japan, the Japanese continued their encroachment into Chinese territory. Through a combination of military strikes and diplomatic coercion, Japan took much of North China into its de facto sphere of influence.

In Europe, the United States faced similar challenges, and its policy there showed similar characteristics to that in East Asia. The challenges to the United States in Europe were the weakness of its democratic allies and the rise of totalitarian regimes in Italy, Germany, and Russia that not only rejected democratic values and destroyed democratic institutions but also harbored imperial ambitions.

In Germany, public resentment over the Treaty of Versailles, continuing economic depression, and mass unemployment under the Weimar Republic gave rise to widespread discontent and political radicalism. The Great Depression dealt the final blow to the Weimar Germany. In 1933, Germany fell under the rule of the Nazi party headed by Adolf Hitler. While pursuing a highly repressive policy against political opposition and a racist policy toward the Jews at home, the Nazi government first sought to revise

As the political and military situations in Europe grew less stable, the United States moved away from its isolationist stance. In this picture, American ambassadors to France, Germany, and Italy—as well as Acting Secretary of State Sumner Welles (second from left)—convene at the White House to meet with President Franklin D. Roosevelt. (Library of Congress)

the Versailles settlement and then to alter the balance of power in Europe altogether. In Italy, the Fascist party, after seizing power amid widespread economic chaos and social unrest in the early 1920's, established one-party rule under dictator Benito Mussolini. The government reorganized the nation's economy under a corporatist model and pursued a foreign policy that was virulently nationalist and openly expansionist.

In the face of growing disorder in global relations, isolationism became law in the United States. To prevent future involvement in international crises, the U.S. Congress passed three neutrality acts between 1935 and 1937. In August, 1935, it passed the First Neutrality Act, which put serious restraints on the president's power to take any diplomatic initiative that might lead the country into overseas conflicts. The law gave the Roosevelt administration an excuse for inaction when the League of Nations called for sanctions against Italy, which launched an aggressive war against Ethiopia in October. To reinforce the neutral position of the United States in a volatile international environment, Congress passed the Second Neutrality Act in February, 1936. The new legislation not only renewed the First Neutrality Act but also expanded it by adding new limits to the power of the president and by prohibiting American banks from lending money to belligerents. Just one week after the Second Neutrality Act went into effect, German troops marched into the Rhineland in violation of the Treaty of Versailles.

In July, 1936, a civil war broke out in Spain between the troops of the republican government and rebels under General Francisco Franco. The United States, together with Great Britain and France, adopted a policy of nonintervention. In January, 1937, Congress passed a resolution that prohibited the U.S. government and American citizens from providing arms to the combatants in the Spanish Civil War. In contrast, both Hitler and Mussolini openly assisted the rebels in toppling the elected government. The policy of Western democracies toward the Spanish Civil War not only cost them a possible ally in future conflicts but also betrayed the weakness of their leadership. In the same year, Hitler and Mussolini entered into an anticommunist alliance. One year later, the Berlin-Rome-Tokyo Axis was formed, which signaled the beginning of a very dangerous era.

At this critical juncture, the American public still doggedly clung to its hope for world peace. Isolationist sentiments among the American people prompted Congress to pass the Third Neutrality Act. This act made it illegal for American citizens even to travel on belligerent ships. It prohibited the sales of arms and war matériel unless the warring countries paid cash for them and transported them on their own ships. In the winter of 1937-1938, when Congress debated the Ludlow Amendment, which would have required a national referendum before a declaration of war unless American soil was under direct attack, Japanese militarists were committing heinous crimes in China's fallen capital, Nanking. If not for the vehement rejection of Roosevelt, the amendment could have further restrained his administration response to aggressor nations.

Rising to the Challenge of Aggression   Public opinion in the United States began to change gradually in late 1937. The outbreak of hostilities between Japan and China in July of that year and the ensuing war between the two countries exposed the futility of the U.S. government's East Asian policy. Roosevelt, too, was apparently shocked by the virulent nature of Japanese imperialism. In a speech in Chicago in October, he openly condemned the Japanese aggression and urged the international community to come together to quarantine the lawlessness in East Asia. Still, the president's message was not enough to spur a lethargic public into action. Outside the United States, however, world opinion turned decisively against the Japanese. The League of Nations condemned Japan for violating the Nine-Power Treaty and the Kellogg-Briand Pact. At a meeting in Brussels, members of the organization called on the United States to join them to thwart further Japanese aggression. However, the U.S. government again refused to get involved.

Despite the efforts of the British and French to preserve peace in Europe by making concessions to Hitler, a global war loomed in the summer of 1938. After the Munich Conference in September, Germany annexed the Sudetenland of Czechoslovakia with the connivance of Britain and France. In early 1939, German troops invaded and occupied the rest of Czechoslovakia. In the same year, Italian troops overran Albania. Britain and France finally realized the futility of appeasement and decided to take a stand against the aggressors. Roosevelt made a last plea to Hitler and Mussolini in April, 1939, asking them to refrain from further expansion for ten years. His plea was rejected. Meanwhile, when Japan announced its intention to create the Greater East Asia Co-Prosperity Sphere in late 1938, the Roosevelt administration began to look for ways to counter the Japanese plan. It provided an aid package worth twenty-five million dollars to the Chinese government.

On September 8, 1939, Nazi Germany invaded Poland. Ten days later, the Russian Red Army entered Polish territory, too. These actions marked the beginning of World War II. The Roosevelt administration, although wary of repeating the difficult entanglement of World War I, made its position clear. As far as the administration was concerned, ending the arms embargo was the only hope to keep America out of the war. After much debate, Congress passed the Fourth Neutrality Act, which relaxed the earlier position of the United States by allowing the Allies to buy American war matériel on a "cash-and-carry" basis. Meanwhile, the administration remained quiet about the Russian invasion of Poland in mid-September and Finland in December to avoid pushing Joseph Stalin closer to Hitler.

Impact The global events of the 1930's, especially the rise of totalitarian regimes and the aggressive acts of Japan and Germany, exposed the shortsightedness of America isolationism. These events forced the United States to reconsider its retreat from internationalism and passivity toward international crises and eventually provide assistance to its allies in Asia and Europe. By abandoning isolationism, the American people moved irrevocably toward a fight for peace, justice, and national honor.

Peng Deng

Further Reading

Adler, Selig. *The Uncertain Giant, 1921-1941: American Foreign Policy Between the Wars*. New York: Harper & Row, 1965. A popular survey of the role of the United States in Europe between World Wars I and II.

Cole, Wayne S. *Roosevelt and the Isolationists, 1932-1945*. Lincoln: University of Nebraska Press, 1983. Discusses the relationship between Roosevelt and the isolationists from the perspective of the latter.

Dallek, Robert. *Franklin D. Roosevelt and American Foreign Policy, 1932-1945*. 1979. Reprint. New York: Oxford University Press, 1995. Defends Roosevelt's foreign policy, showing the president as a master politician who had to consider both domestic and diplomatic objectives.

DeConde, Alexander. *History of American Foreign Policy*. 3d ed. New York: Charles Scribner's Sons, 1978. Comprehensive history of foreign policy throughout the nation's history, with a substantial section on the 1930's.

Glantz, Mary E. *FDR and the Soviet Union: The President's Battles over Foreign Policy*. Lawrence: University Press of Kansas, 2005. Discusses changing U.S. policy toward the Soviet Union in 1933.

Pastor, Robert A. *Congress and the Politics of U.S. Foreign Policy, 1929-1976*. Berkeley: University of California Press, 1980. Argues that the passage of Hawley-Smoot can be explained by Republican predilections to turn to tariffs during times of economic stress. Provides a good, nontechnical discussion of the evolution of tariffs after Hawley-Smoot.

Rhodes, Benjamin D. *United States Foreign Policy in the Interwar Period, 1918-1941: The Golden Age of American Diplomatic and Military Complacency*. Westport, Conn.: Praeger, 2001. In-depth examination of American diplomacy during the period covered includes discussion of the neutrality laws passed in the 1930's. Features selected bibliography and index.

See also Germany and U.S. appeasement; Isolationism; Japanese military aggression; League of Nations; Neutrality Acts; Spanish Civil War.

■ *Fortune* magazine

Identification American business magazine
Publisher Henry Luce
Date First published in February, 1930

A periodical focusing on successful business ventures, Fortune magazine was launched only four months after the New York stock market crash triggered the Great Depression. Nevertheless, the magazine remained successful despite the economic turmoil that encompassed the American business world throughout the 1930's. Fortune incorporated new literary figures as its contributors and featured innovative visual perspectives, providing a fresh example for the periodical business.

First issued in February, 1930, *Fortune* magazine was launched by Henry Luce, the same businessman who cofounded *Time* magazine. *Fortune* was created as a magazine about business for businesspeople. Luce estimated that the cost to begin the magazine would be close to $400,000, but large amounts of advertising would help offset this initial cost. Demonstrating advertisers' confidence in the magazine, *Fortune* boasted 779 advertisements during its first year in circulation, and it sold for one dollar per copy.

The product of what Luce referred to as the "experimental department," made up of *Time*'s business writer Parker Lloyd-Smith and a researcher named Florence Horn, *Fortune* was a mash of new ideas. It received its name mostly because Luce's wife preferred it to other suggestions. Quickly becoming popular, *Fortune* managed to succeed even during the economic decay in the 1930's. Debuting with 30,000 subscribers, the magazine increased its circulation to nearly 460,000 by 1937, grossing almost $500,000 that year.

Contrary to normal practices for business magazines, Luce did not recruit experienced businesspeople to be his magazine's writers. Instead, he focused on hiring promising young literary figures, such as Archibald MacLeish and John Kenneth Galbraith, because he felt that their perspectives would add literary depth to the business world. In addition to new written perspectives, *Fortune* became known for its innovative visual perspectives as well. *Fortune* had artistic covers and advertisements, incorporating the works of Antonio Petruccelli, Ervine Metzl, Walter Buehr, Ernest Hamlin Baker, and others.

Fortune's largest competitor during the 1930's was *BusinessWeek*, founded in 1929, which aimed at the same audience: business executives. Both magazines remained widely read and successful throughout the Great Depression and in the years after, despite economic setbacks in nearly every field of business. Most believe that the accelerated growth of advertising is what made this success possible, giving magazines the revenues they needed in order to retain a profit.

Fortune became famous for its annual listings of corporations worldwide. Lists such as the "Fortune 500," which ranks the world's companies by gross revenue, are widely consulted by both businesspeople and the general public.

Impact   In a depressed economy, *Fortune* rose from the minds of successful businesspeople and reached out to those with similar interests and investments. The magazine turned profits despite the economy, proving that some businesses were able to conquer financial challenges exacerbated by the Great Depression. *Fortune* tells stories of struggling businesspeople who manage to make ends meet in spite of these financial challenges, and it remains one of the most popular business magazines in the United States. *Fortune* has endured numerous economic recessions, which makes its continued popularity and prosperity all the more intriguing.

Joanna L. Thaler

Further Reading
Abrahamson, David. *Magazine-Made America: The Cultural Transformation of the Postwar Periodical.* Cresskill, N.J.: Hampton Press, 1996.
Augspurger, Michael. *An Economy of Abundant Beauty: Fortune Magazine and Depression America.* Ithaca, N.Y.: Cornell University Press, 2004.

See also   Advertising in the United States; Art movements; Business and the economy in the United States; Great Depression in the United States; Health care; Income and wages in the United States; *Life* magazine; Magazines.

■ *Forty-second Street*

Identification   American musical film
Director   Lloyd Bacon
Date   Released in 1933

Forty-second Street *marked a turning point in American film musicals as choreographer Busby Berkeley's lavish, precision style became the standard against which other 1930's musicals were judged. The film also launched the Warner Bros. careers of popular songwriters Al Dubin and Harry Warren and marked the film debut of dancer Ruby Keeler.*

The central theme of *Forty-second Street* is the desperation of Julian Marsh (Warner Baxter), once a successful director of Broadway shows, who must have another hit to solve his financial problems. With the promise of a new show and popular leading lady Dorothy Brock (Bebe Daniels), whose wealthy benefactor promises to back the show, the demanding Marsh drives his cast and crew, despite a serious

Dancers watch as Warner Baxter (second man from left) points at Ruby Keeler in a scene from Forty-second Street. *(The Granger Collection, New York)*

heart condition. Two backstage romances complicate the show, one between Dorothy and Pat Denning (George Brent), a former partner who now shuns show business, the other between newcomer Peggy Sawyer (Keeler) and singer Billy Lawler (Dick Powell). A crisis ensues when the backer threatens to pull out his money after Dorothy drunkenly insults him at a pre-opening party. When Dorothy later breaks her ankle, Marsh is forced to take the advice of chorine Anytime Annie (Ginger Rogers) and make the talented but unproven Peggy the star. After a night of physically and emotionally exhausting rehearsals with Marsh, Peggy leads the show to success, thus freeing Dorothy to return to Pat and saving Marsh from ruin.

The continued popularity and significance of *Forty-second Street* are based more on Berkeley's staging of the production numbers than on its story line,

which was already a cliché by 1933. Audiences marveled at the songs; the lavish, movable sets; and the dozens of dancers. Among the production numbers, which include "Young and Healthy" and "Shuffle Off to Buffalo," the standout is the six-minute-long title song, which begins with Keller singing about the history of the bohemian street and doing a tap dance against a painted background. She then exits on the running board of a taxi, singing about the "naughty, bawdy, gaudy, sporty Forty-second Street" as the stage opens up to vignettes that include cars, mounted policemen, and various characters who dance and sing. The scene continues with the murder of a young woman, as Powell sings the refrain from the window of a speakeasy. The number continues with precision lines of male and female tap dancers, finally ending with Keeler and Powell atop a set of a skyscraper.

Impact Although not the first film musical, *Forty-second Street* was the first to be a top-ten box-office hit. Also, it earned two Academy Award nominations, including one for best picture. Beyond that, the film was the most important style setter for future 1930's musicals. The Great Depression fanned audiences' desire for escapist fare, and the musicals Berkeley choreographed and later directed at Warner Bros. captured the audience's imagination. His highly choreographed, precision musical-production numbers became increasingly grand and more complex, even as he moved to Technicolor musicals at Twentieth Century-Fox and Metro-Goldwyn-Mayer during the 1940's and early 1950's.

Patricia King Hanson

Further Reading

Fumento, Rocco, ed. *Forty-second Street*. Madison: Wisconsin Center for Film and Theater Research/University of Wisconsin Press, 1980.

Hirschhorn, Clive. *The Hollywood Musical*. New York: Crown, 1991.

Hoberman, J. *Forty-second Street*. London: BFI, 1993.

Siegel, Marcia B. "Busby Berkeley and the Projected Stage." *Hudson Review* 62, no. 1 (2009): 106-112.

Thomas, Tony, and Jim Terry, with Busby Berkeley. *The Busby Berkeley Book*. Greenwich, Conn.: New York Graphic Society, 1973.

See also *Awake and Sing!*; Berkeley, Busby; Broadway musicals; *Grand Hotel*; *Green Pastures, The*; *Hellzapoppin'*; *I'd Rather Be Right*; Music: Popular; *Porgy and Bess*; *Top Hat*.

■ Four Horsemen vs. Three Musketeers

The Event Infighting of U.S. Supreme Court members

Dates 1933-1937

Place Washington, D.C.

Between 1933 and 1937, the U.S. Supreme Court declared unconstitutional much federal and state economic legislation. Four members of the Supreme Court—later dubbed the "Four Horsemen"—consistently opposed economic legislation. Three other justices—nicknamed the "Three Musketeers"—regularly supported such legislation.

In 1932, in the midst of the Great Depression, Democrat Franklin D. Roosevelt was elected president of the United States. Roosevelt promised the American people a "New Deal," a complex package of economic reforms intended to stimulate the economy and reduce unemployment. Many of these reforms were later declared unconstitutional by the U.S. Supreme Court, where a majority of justices held a restrictive view of federal regulatory power. In *Schechter Poultry Corp. v. the United States* (1935), a unanimous Court struck down the National Industrial Recovery Act of 1933, which authorized the president to set standards for wages, hours, and working conditions. The Court found that the activity in which the corporation was engaged was intrastate commerce and, therefore, outside the scope of Congress's regulatory power over interstate commerce.

By 1936, the consensus among the justices on the issue of federal economic intervention had shattered. The Agricultural Adjustment Act of 1933, designed to raise farm prices by limiting production, was declared unconstitutional, by a six-to-three margin, in *United States v. Butler* (1936). In *Carter v. Carter Coal Co.* (1936), the Court, by a five-to-four margin, struck down the Bituminous Coal Conservation Act of 1935, which set minimum prices for coal and provided for collective bargaining to achieve fair wages. Both acts were invalidated in part because they authorized Congress to regulate activity that did not qualify as interstate commerce. In both of the aforementioned cases, Justices Willis Van Devanter, James C. McReynolds, Pierce Butler, and George Sutherland—the "Four Horsemen"—were in the majority. Also in both cases, Justices Louis D. Brandeis, Harlan Fiske Stone, and Benjamin N. Cardozo—the "Three Musketeers"—dissented. In *United States v. Butler*, the "Four Horsemen" were joined by Chief Justice Charles Evans Hughes and Justice Owen J. Roberts; the latter provided the fifth vote in the Carter case.

Prior to this time, Van Devanter, McReynolds, Butler, and Sutherland had not been identified as a voting bloc, often taking separate positions on constitutional issues. However, during the 1935 term, the four often traveled together to and from the Court, presumably strategizing. In response, Brandeis, Stone, and Cardozo met weekly at Brandeis's residence. These strategy sessions promoted the image of each group as a voting bloc. More times than not, Roberts agreed with the "Four Horsemen," thus providing the fifth and decisive vote, with Hughes joining the "Three Musketeers."

As a result, many New Deal statutes were struck down.

Much state economic legislation was similarly invalidated. *Morehead v. New York ex rel. Tipaldo* (1936), for example, declared a New York minimum-wage law for women and children violative of the liberty protected by the due process clause of the Fourteenth Amendment. The split among the justices was a familiar one—the "Four Horsemen" and Roberts in the majority, the "Three Musketeers" and Hughes in dissent.

Impact In February, 1937, following his landslide electoral victory, Roosevelt sent to Congress a bill to increase the number of justices. His stated reason for the "court-packing plan" was that the older justices were unable to attend to the workload. What he really wanted was a Court majority that would uphold economic legislation. The plan was soon rendered moot. The following month, in *West Coast Hotel Co. v. Parrish* (1937), the Court voted five to four to uphold Washington State's minimum-wage law. Two weeks later, by the same vote, the justices upheld the National Labor Relations Act in *National Labor Relations Board v. Jones and Laughlin Steel Corp.* (1937). The "Three Musketeers" and Hughes found a fifth vote in the person of Roberts. Journalists christened Roberts's change "the switch in time that saved nine (justices)."

Between 1937 and 1941, Van Devanter, Sutherland, Butler, and McReynolds retired. Each was replaced by a Roosevelt nominee. The former justices did not become widely known as the "Four Horsemen (of Reaction)" until the 1950's. This characterization was meant to categorize them as obstructionists, and it has largely persisted. In most rankings of Supreme Court justices, Van Devanter, McReynolds, and Butler are considered "failures." By contrast, Brandeis, Stone, and Cardozo are ranked as "great."

Richard A. Glenn

Further Reading

Cushman, Barry. *Rethinking the New Deal Court: The Structure of a Constitutional Revolution.* New York: Oxford University Press, 2002.

Solomon, Burt. *FDR v. Constitution: The Court-Packing Fight and the Triumph of Democracy.* New York: Walker, 2009.

White, G. Edward. *The Constitution and the New Deal.* Cambridge, Mass.: Harvard University Press, 2000.

See also Brandeis, Louis D.; *Carter v. Carter Coal Co.*; Hughes, Charles Evans; *National Labor Relations Board v. Jones and Laughlin Steel Corp.*; Roberts, Owen J.; Roosevelt's court-packing plan; *Schechter Poultry Corp. v. United States*; Supreme Court, U.S.; *United States v. Butler*; *West Coast Hotel Co. v. Parrish.*

■ Foxx, Jimmie

Identification American baseball player
Born October 22, 1907; Sudlersville, Maryland
Died July 21, 1967; Miami, Florida

Foxx played for the Philadelphia Athletics (A's) and Boston Red Sox and is considered by many to be the right-handed successor to Babe Ruth. He hit 534 home runs in his career while maintaining a high batting average. Short in stature and humble and generous by nature, Foxx was nevertheless one of the most feared hitters in the American League.

A sports star at Sudlersville High School, Jimmie Foxx excelled in track, soccer, and baseball. In 1924, he dropped out of school to sign a minor league baseball contract. He eventually became the first baseman of the A's in 1928.

From 1929 to 1931, the A's dominated the American League, winning two of three World Series. Foxx, nicknamed "the Beast" and "Double X," blossomed into a star. With revenues declining as the result of the Depression, A's owner Connie Mack dismantled the team, and in December, 1935, the Red Sox purchased Foxx's contract. Foxx's hitting helped the Red Sox contend with the New York Yankees by the end of the decade.

Foxx's accomplishments during the 1930's rivaled anyone's in baseball. Foxx led Major League Baseball in home runs four times, hitting 58 in 1932. From 1930 to 1939, he averaged 41.5 home runs and 124 runs batted in (RBI) per year. He led the American League in RBI three times. His batting average was regularly better than .330; he won the American League batting championship in 1933 and 1938 with averages of .356 and .349. The Baseball Writers Association voted Foxx the American League most valuable player three times. By 1942, age and heavy drinking had diminished Foxx's skills. Ill-prepared financially for retirement in 1945, Foxx held numerous jobs in and out of baseball until his death in 1967.

Philadelphia Athletics first baseman Jimmie Foxx—the American League's most valuable player in 1932, 1933, and 1938. (Archive Photos/Getty Images)

Impact Neither Jimmie Foxx nor Hank Greenberg of the Detroit Tigers ever topped Ruth's record of 60 home runs in a season, though fans expected one of them to accomplish the feat. Ted Williams, who achieved great fame with the Red Sox, claimed no one "hit a ball harder" than Foxx. Foxx was inducted into the National Baseball Hall of Fame in 1951.

M. Philip Lucas

Further Reading

Daniel, W. Harrison. *Jimmie Foxx*. Jefferson, N.C.: McFarland, 2004.

Gorman, Bob. *Double X: The Story of Jimmie Foxx— Baseball's Forgotten Slugger.* New York: Bill Goff, 1990.

Millikin, Mark R. *Jimmie Foxx: The Pride of Sudlersville.* Lanham, Md.: Scarecrow Press, 2005.

See also Baseball; Dean, Dizzy; Gehrig, Lou; National Baseball Hall of Fame; Ott, Mel; Ruth, Babe; Sports in the United States; Vander Meer, Johnny.

■ *Frankenstein* films

Identification Films about a scientist's attempt to create living human beings from stitched-together body parts taken from dead bodies

Director James Whale

Date *Frankenstein* released on November 21, 1931; *Bride of Frankenstein* released on May 6, 1935

During the early 1930's, Universal Pictures was fighting for its financial life when it single-handedly created a new filmmaking genre—sound horror films. The success of Frankenstein *and* Bride of Frankenstein *made Universal a major Hollywood studio and helped establish the horror film and various conventions associated with it as cinematic staples.*

The first of a series of horror films inspired by Mary Shelley's century-old novel, *Frankenstein: Or, The Modern Prometheus* (1818), *Frankenstein* (1931) and *Bride of Frankenstein* (1935) were landmark films in several respects. First and foremost, they firmly established horror as a reliable film genre along with other types, such as Westerns, comedies, and dramas. The films rescued tottering Universal Pictures from financial disaster and helped it hold its own against other Hollywood studios. The two films made the British-born actor Boris Karloff—who played the artificially created monster (Frankenstein was the scientist)—one of the biggest film stars in the world and stamped him as the successor to the deceased Lon Chaney as a genius of characterization and a master of disguise. The films also made household names out of several others who were involved with their production, such as director James Whale, actors Colin Clive and Dwight Frye, and Universal make-up artist Jack Pierce.

***Frankenstein* Sets the Horror Bar** *Frankenstein* opens with Henry Frankenstein (Clive) and his hunchbacked assistant Fritz (Frye) lurking in a cemetery spying on a funeral in progress. It soon becomes apparent that they have been robbing graves to harvest "fresh" body parts for Frankenstein's experiments in trying to reanimate a man he has stitched together from body parts collected from other corpses. When finding a suitably noble brain proves a stumbling block, Fritz is sent to steal one from a university; however, he mistakenly takes a "criminal" brain. Meanwhile, Frankenstein's fiancé, Elizabeth (Mae Clarke), anxious for news of him, visits his laboratory along with Frankenstein's friend and university instructor, Dr. Waldman (Edward Van Sloan). After they witness a spectacular life-giving electrical storm, Frankenstein basks in triumph as his creation comes to life. However, his elation is short-lived when he realizes his creation, more monster than man because of its criminal brain, displays murderous tendencies and kills his tormentor, Fritz.

Waldman persuades the exhausted Henry to attend to his wedding plans while he destroys the monster. Instead, however, the creature murders Waldman, escapes, and terrorizes the countryside. The townspeople of the nearby village pursue the creature, with Frankenstein leading one group. When Frankenstein becomes separated from his companions, he confronts the monster alone. The creature overpowers him and carries him to a nearby windmill, from the top of which he throws off Frankenstein. The townspeople then burn the windmill to the ground, apparently killing the monster. In the final scene, Henry is shown alive, recuperating with Elizabeth by his side.

Bride of Frankenstein After a brief prologue, *Bride of Frankenstein* picks up exactly where *Frankenstein* ended—at the site of the burned-down windmill. It soon emerges that the monster is not dead, merely badly burned. After he kills some villagers, he once again is loose in the countryside. Meanwhile, Frankenstein is visited by a former teacher, Dr. Pretorius (Ernest Thesiger), who shows him a collection of tiny people he has created. He then suggests that he and Frankenstein collaborate to create a mate for the monster. Meanwhile, the monster is taken into

Boris Karloff (right) as the monster, with Elsa Lanchester in the 1935 film Bride of Frankenstein. *(Archive Photos/Getty Images)*

the isolated home of a blind hermit (O. P. Heggie), who welcomes him as a friend and teaches him a few words of English. When their idyllic existence is interrupted by hunters, the monster again stumbles into the forest. When he happens upon the body-snatching Pretorius, the two hatch a scheme designed to force Frankenstein's cooperation in making a mate for the monster.

The monster kidnaps Frankenstein's fiancé, Elizabeth (now played by Valerie Hobson), forcing Frankenstein to cooperate with Pretorius. In another spectacular laboratory sequence that outdoes the first in terms of machinery buzzing, sparking, and flashing, the monster's covered-in-bandages companion, Elsa Lanchester (who also plays Mary Shelley in the film's prologue), is brought to life. However, the moment her bandages are removed and she sees her eager but terrifying mate, she gasps and utters a few strangled cries. All this proves too much for the monster, who lets Frankenstein and Elizabeth leave but then pulls a lever that blows the entire laboratory and everybody in it to smithereens.

Impact   The two films could not be more different. *Frankenstein* is a serious attempt at a horror film, with plenty of shocks and scares. The atmosphere is moody and grim, and even without a swelling orchestral accompaniment to punctuate the moment, numerous shots are creepy and frightening solely on their own merit. Far from being merely a simple cautionary tale about a man trying to play God, the film evokes a visceral fear of such simple devices as blind corners, slowly opening doors, and ominous thunderclaps. The use of sinister shadows, sparking electrical equipment, a torch-waving village mob, and Clive's near-hysteria performance as a mad scientist established horror film conventions that scores of later films would slavishly follow and audiences learn to expect.

In contrast, *Bride of Frankenstein* rarely even tries to inspire fear. Instead, owing to director Whale's boredom or frustration at making yet another horror film, he substitutes black humor and camp for terror. It has been said that the line between laughter and fear is slight, and Whale walks that line between both worlds nicely. By filling the film with over-the-top images and characters, the director both parodies the horror film and laughs at some of the conventions he himself helped to establish only a few years earlier. Whale had explored this avenue two years ear-

lier in *The Invisible Man* (1933), but in *Bride* he took it on directly. Perhaps to his chagrin, the resulting film established yet another horror film staple—the horror film as winking jest, with campy characters, snappy one-liners, and outright gags—that would again be imitated by later generations of filmmakers.

Russell Roberts

Further Reading

Brunas, Michael, John Brunas, and Tom Weaver. *Universal Horrors: The Studio's Classic Films, 1931-1946.* Jefferson, N.C.: McFarland, 1990. A critical examination of every horror film produced by Universal in the 1930's and 1940's, presented chronologically with insightful commentaries, many photographs, and useful appendixes.

Lindsay, Cynthia. *Dear Boris.* New York: Alfred A. Knopf, 1975. Intimate, readable biography of Karloff, the most famous portrayer of Frankenstein's monster, by a longtime friend.

Nollen, Scott A. *Boris Karloff: A Critical Account of His Screen, Stage, Radio, Television, and Recording Work.* Jefferson, N.C.: McFarland, 1991. Well-organized and documented historical and critical analysis of Karloff's complete body of work. Includes a full filmography and bibliography.

_____. *Boris Karloff: A Gentleman's Life.* Baltimore: Midnight Marquee Press, 2005. Biography written with the cooperation of Karloff's daughter covers all aspects of the actor's life.

Riley, Philip J., ed. *Frankenstein: The Original Shooting Script.* Absecon, N.J.: MagicImage Filmbooks, 1990. Part of the publisher's film script series, this volume contains the entire script of the first *Frankenstein* film, along with numerous photographs and informative commentary. Other volumes in this series including the scripts of *Bride of Frankenstein* and three other *Frankenstein* sequels.

Shelley, Mary, *Frankenstein: Or, The Modern Prometheus.* New York: Modern Library, 1984. Modern edition of the 1818 novel on which the *Frankenstein* films were based.

Underwood, Peter. *Karloff: The Life of Boris Karloff.* New York: Drake, 1972. Biography that includes a detailed, anecdotal account of the making of *Frankenstein.* Includes photographs, selected bibliography, discography, and filmography.

See also   *Dracula*; Film; *Freaks*; Horror films; *Invisible Man, The*; Karloff, Boris; *King Kong*.

■ *Freaks*

Identification Film about people with physical anomalies who are displayed as curiosities in a traveling circus
Director Tod Browning
Date Released on February 20, 1932

Depression-era Americans were drawn to films that featured marginalized characters, such as dispossessed Oklahomans in The Grapes of Wrath *(1940), gangsters in* Scarface *(1932), and even a gigantic simian antihero in* King Kong *(1933). However, when prominent Hollywood director Tod Browning, fresh from his success with* Dracula *(1931), released* Freaks, *the film was a spectacular failure that effectively ended his career.*

With a screenplay by William Goldbeck and Edgar Allan Wolf, based on a 1923 short story by Tod Robbins, *Freaks* tells the story of the trapeze artist Cleopatra, who, though in love with the strongman Hercules, agrees to marry the midget Hans because of the fortune he has inherited.

Cleopatra (Olga Baclanova) and Hercules (Roscoe Ates) intend to poison Hans (Harry Earles) after the marriage and claim his wealth. However, the circus "freaks"—who include, among others, microcephalic people (commonly known as "pinheads"), a limbless man, conjoined "Siamese" twin sisters, and a hermaphrodite—constitute a tightly knit community intensely loyal to one another. "Offend one and you offend them all" was a widely repeated line in the film's publicity. After Cleopatra cannot hide her repulsion for her husband's friends, the "freaks" become suspicious and discover the plot. During a late-night rainstorm, they hunt down the conspirators and wreak ghastly vengeance: Hercules is castrated, and Cleopatra is mutilated.

Impact Many of Browning's most popular films featured protagonists who existed outside respected society—drifters, criminals, show-business people. His biggest success, the Bela Lugosi version of *Dracula*, featured a foreign monster and was set in an insane asylum. However, with *Freaks*, Browning went too far. Americans of the 1930's might have identified with the excluded and disenfranchised and might have fantasized about the freedom of a criminal lifestyle, but *Freaks* proved too dark and too grim for most moviegoers. Although it later came to be perceived as a classic, at the time it incited the wrath of local film watchdog committees. Browning lived into the 1960's and made a few more films, but he never again enjoyed success or prestige in Hollywood.

Thomas Du Bose

Further Reading

Mark, Gregory William. *Women in Horror Films, 1930s.* Jefferson, N.C.: McFarland, 2005.
Skal, David J., and Elias Savada. *Dark Carnival: The Secret World of Tod Browning.* New York: Anchor, 1995.

See also *Dracula; Frankenstein* films; Horror films; *King Kong.*

■ Freon

The Event Discovery of a practical refrigerant fluid that would revolutionize refrigeration equipment
Date Developed in April, 1930
Place Dayton, Ohio

Throughout the early twentieth century, refrigeration equipment relied on dangerous toxic and flammable working fluids such as ammonia, sulfur dioxide, and methyl chloride. The discovery of dichlorodifluoromethane—which would become better known as Freon—a nontoxic and nonflammable fluid, made possible safer refrigeration equipment for home appliances and vehicles. Many years later, however, Freon was found to pose a dangerous threat to the atmosphere.

The substance that would eventually be called Freon—a trade name of the DuPont corporation—was prepared by Frédéric Swarts in Belgium as part of his research on organofluorine chemistry during the late nineteenth and early twentieth centuries. However, neither Swarts nor anyone else found a use for that compound until 1930.

During the late 1920's, Charles F. Kettering, the head of engineering at General Motors, asked Lester Keilholtz, the chief engineer at the company's Frigidaire home appliance division, to start a program of research to find a better working fluid for refrigerators. Keilholtz passed that challenge along to Thomas Midgley, Jr., a chemical engineer who had previously solved the problem of "knocking" in automobile engines by developing lead additives for gasoline. Midgley was led to dichlorodi-fluoromethane by an analysis of boiling-point trends relating to the chemists' periodic table. With the help of A. L. Henne, he prepared a small sample of the first Freon by reacting carbon tetrachloride with antimony trifluoride. The resulting fluid soon found practical applications in refrigeration units, air conditioners, and other cooling devices.

Impact   Refrigerators and air conditioners using Freon were more compact and safer to use around the home. These advantages made these appliances desirable as never before, and millions of units were eventually sold worldwide. In addition, other uses were found for Freon in aerosol propellants, foaming agents for plastic, and other areas. It was not until much later that the accumulation of Freon in the atmosphere was shown to be detrimental to the earth's ozone layer.

John R. Phillips

Further Reading

Christie, Maureen. *The Ozone Layer: A Philosophy of Science Perspective.* New York: Cambridge University Press, 2001.

Edwards, Jonathan. "The Man Who Poisoned Air." *Chemistry World* 5, no. 7 (July, 2008).

Goldwhite, Harold. "April, 1930: Midgley Introduces Dichlorodifluoromethane as a Refrigerant Gas." In *Great Events from the Twentieth Century, 1901-1940,* edited by Robert F. Gorman. 6 vols. Pasadena, Calif.: Salem Press, 2007.

Midgley, Thomas. *From the Periodic Table to Production: The Life of Thomas Midgley, Jr., the Inventor of Ethyl Gasoline and Freon Refrigerants.* Corona, Calif.: Stargazer, 2001.

Parson, Edward A. *Protecting the Ozone Layer: Science and Strategy.* New York: Oxford University Press, 2003.

Thevenot, Roger. *A History of Refrigeration Throughout the World.* Translated by J. C. Fidler. Paris: International Institute of Refrigeration, 1979.

See also   Air pollution; Chemistry; Food processing; Inventions; Physics; Refrigerators.

■ Frost, Robert

Identification   American poet
Born   San Francisco, California; March 26, 1874
Died   Boston, Massachusetts; January 29, 1963

The best-known American poet of his time, Frost published his first major collection of poems during the 1930's.

Robert Lee Frost's first volume of poetry published in the United States, *A Boy's Will* (1915), resulted in immediate recognition as a popular poet. By the time he won the Pulitzer Prize, the first of four, for *New Hampshire* in 1923, he was already regarded as one of the leading writers in the United States. The publication of the first edition of his *Collected Poems* in 1930 was an event of considerable literary and cultural significance, and Frost began the decade pleased with his prominence and concerned that those critics who had disparaged his work would renew their attacks on his first collection.

Frost's concern about an adverse critical response was compounded by his worries about his family. His daughter Marjorie suffered a mental breakdown, his son Carol's wife was diagnosed with tuberculosis, and his daughter Leslie was expecting her second child while in the final stages of a divorce in 1930. Frost felt responsible for some of his children's emotional turmoil and was anxious to assist them financially in troubled times. For this reason, he was ready to accept appointments at various universities and to take advantage of a growing interest in workshops, conferences, and readings. The award of the Pulitzer Prize in 1930 for *Collected Poems* helped to offset some negative reviews, as did his election to membership in the American Academy of Arts and Letters. Frost's reputation was enhanced when he received his ninth honorary degree, from Columbia University. However, his worries about his family continued, and when his daughter Marjorie contracted puerperal fever giving birth, Frost wrote to the anthologist Louis Untermeyer, "We are going through the valley of the shadow with Marjorie, I'm afraid"; her death left Frost bereft.

The Poet as Public Figure   By 1935, Frost had become sufficiently experienced as a speaker that his frequent appearances at universities were attracting increasingly larger, supportive audiences. His first lecture in the Charles Eliot Norton series at Harvard in March, 1936, drew more than one thousand people. They greeted him with raucous applause that startled but delighted him and made him more confident about a forthcoming volume of poetry. In the seven years after he had published *West Running Brook* (1928), he had placed poems in many periodicals and realized that he had enough for a book. His travels across the country to visit his children had given him a perspective beyond the well-known New England landscape that had been the foundation for his work and led to the title *A Further Range* for his book. In the spring of 1936, *A Further Range* was announced as the Book-of-the-Month Club choice for June, an important designation because it meant an initial printing of fifty thousand copies for the club. The book won Frost his third Pulitzer Prize for poetry.

The Trials of Existence In an effort to ease the strain of moving from one part of the country to another, which was affecting his wife Elinor's health and psychic stability, Frost decided to purchase a home in Gainesville, Florida, where he had been spending some time in the winter and where his daughter Leslie had settled. On March 18, 1938,

Robert Frost's reputation as a preeminent American poet grew during the 1930's. (Time & Life Pictures/Getty Images)

Elinor suffered a heart attack and died two days later. This was a kind of conclusion to the middle stages of Frost's life, and Frost sought to mark his loss with a visit to the Derry, New Hampshire, farm where he and Elinor had begun their married life. It was Frost's intention to place his wife's ashes on the land there, but a somewhat unsettling conversation with the occupants of the farm changed his mind. In a break with his origins as a poet of New England, after his daughter Leslie denied his request to move in with her, he began a series of residences in locations designed to facilitate his vision of himself as a poet and spokesman for a national cast of mind. The dedication of *A Further Range* conveys his feeling about his marriage and his life's work to that point.

> To E. F./for what it may mean to her that beyond the White Mountains were the Green; beyond both were the Rockies, the Sierras and in thought the Andes and Himalayas—range beyond range even into the realm of government and religion.

A Further Range includes several of the mature poems that reflect Frost's development of a philosophical perspective drawn from the demands of his work, his desire to help his family, and his determination to gain recognition as a national poet of his era. "Neither Far out, Nor in Deep"—superbly described by Helen Vendler as "the incorrigible human attraction to the unfathomable beyond"—is an example of Frost's ability to encapsulate a primal truth about human experience in direct, terse, and evocative language. "Iris by Night" recalls Frost's friendship with Edward Thomas in England as a joining of kindred spirits in a moment of ecstatic revelation amid the wonders of the natural world. A sharp mind and a hopeful heart, the subjects of these poems, are examples of the themes that made Frost a towering figure in American life many decades after their composition.

Impact In addition to achieving a heightened type of celebrity for a poet, Frost wrote several poems that remain a part of familiar American cultural experience. The "voice" that he developed represents a kind of rural wisdom that many Americans cherish and admire.

Leon Lewis

Further Reading

Hall, Donald. "Vanity, Fame, Love, and Robert Frost." In *Their Ancient Glittering Eyes: Remembering Poets and More Poets.* New York: Ticknor and Fields, 1992. Revealing account of the Hall's contacts with Frost during the crucial decades of the latter's creative and public life.

Lentricchia, Frank. *Modernist Quartet.* New York: Cambridge University Press, 1994. Contains illuminating readings of many of Frost's most powerful poems.

Parini, Jay. *Robert Frost: A Life.* New York: Henry Holt, 1999. Intelligent, well-balanced biography, offering incisive comments about Frost's poetry and a judicious assessment of his character and psychological foundation.

Pritchard, William H. *Frost: A Literary Life Reconsidered.* 2d ed. Amherst: University of Massachusetts Press, 1993. Thoughtful, revealing discussion of the poet's work in conjunction with a solid accounting of his life and times.

Thompson, Lawrance. *Robert Frost: The Years of Triumph, 1915-1938.* New York: Holt, Rinehart and Winston, 1970. Packed with factual material, but clouded by Thompson's animus against the poet.

See also   Crane, Hart; Literature in the United States; MacLeish, Archibald; *Our Town*; Steinbeck, John.

■ Frozen-food marketing

Definition   Methods used to bring the frozen-food industry into mainstream American culture

The development of frozen foods ultimately changed American eating habits. Formerly perishable fresh produce and meats could be safely stored for later use when frozen. When thawed and prepared, they could be enjoyed year-round with no loss in quality of texture or taste.

During the early 1920's, inventor Clarence Birdseye perfected a method of quick-freezing that preserved the freshness and flavor of foods for future consumption. In 1925, he began selling packaged frozen fish fillets from his factory in Gloucester, Massachusetts. By the end of the decade, when he sold his General Foods Company and his patented process for more than $20 million to the Postum Company (later General Foods Corporation), Birdseye was flash-freezing a whole range of products, including fruits, vegetables, and meats. As part of the transaction with Postum, Birdseye was retained to conduct research and development. Divided for easy comprehension, his distinctive surname became a brand name for the frozen products. In 1930, the new owners began test-marketing Birds Eye frozen-food products. They had several major obstacles to overcome.

The first difficulty was consumer resistance to frozen foods in general. The usual method of freezing foods—by immersion in ice or by spraying with a saline solution—as an alternative to drying or smoking meats or canning fruits and vegetables had been employed for decades. However, slow-freezing not only permits bacterial growth but also causes undesirable chemical reactions in many foodstuffs, resulting in mushy, tasteless products that are a pale imitation of fresh varieties. Thus, it is no wonder potential customers initially viewed Birds Eye products with deep suspicion.

A second problem was proper storage of the new frozen goods once they were taken home. Though a practical refrigerator had been introduced in 1915, most American families relied upon the icebox, which was nothing more than an insulated cabinet into which a large block of ice was inserted to keep foods cooled. Iceboxes did not contain separate freezer compartments and could not produce the low temperatures required to keep prefrozen foods from thawing.

A third drawback was the inability of most retailers to display frozen products in-store. Freezer cases were available, but at a cost of one or two thousand dollars apiece, they were a major investment for supermarket owners struggling to keep their heads above water during the Depression. Furthermore, refrigerated trucks and railcars to haul frozen products from manufacturer to retailer did not yet exist.

Luckily for General Foods, consumers drawn by newspaper ads to carefully selected test markets in the northeastern United States quickly took to the concept of frozen foods. By the mid-1930's thirty million pounds of Birds Eye products were sold annually, though 90 percent of the total was purchased for industrial and institutional use. By the end of the decade, when the first precooked frozen meals were introduced, 150 million pounds of frozen Birds Eye foods were sold annually.

Simultaneously, the refrigerator had become a must-have appliance in American homes. What had cost $600 in 1920 had fallen in price to $275 ten years later, and dealers were offering liberal payment plans. By 1940, refrigerators, replete with separate freezer compartments, retailed for about $150, and more than one-half of all American families owned one. Deep freezers were introduced at about the same time.

General Foods took the lead in resolving the retailing issue during the mid-1930's by introducing a low-cost, 500-pound capacity freezer cabinet with a self-contained compressor built in. The company offered it for rental at just ten dollars per month. By the end of the decade, refrigerated trucks were introduced to transport products to distant markets, and more than twelve thousand supermarkets had frozen-food displays in place.

Impact Because of rationing and conversion of manufacturing facilities to the production of combat matériel during World War II, the impetus of frozen-food marketing was interrupted. Nonetheless, the convenience of the new product had caught on. Postwar advancements in refrigeration technology aiding preservation and transport, combined with significant changes in lifestyle, made the wide variety, the storability of seasonable products, and the ease of preparation of frozen foods a permanent part of the American culture.

Jack Ewing

Further Reading

Evans, Judith, ed. *Frozen Food Science and Technology.* Oxford, Oxfordshire, England: Wiley-Blackwell, 2008.

Kurlansky, Mark. *The Food of a Younger Land: A Portrait of American Food—Before the National Highway System, Before Chain Restaurants, and Before Frozen Food, When the Nation's Food Was Seasonal.* New York: Riverhead Trade, 2010.

Platt, Richard. *Eureka! Great Inventions and How They Happened.* New York: Kingfisher, 2003.

See also Agriculture in the United States; Business and the economy in the United States; Food processing; Freon; Inventions; Refrigerators; Supermarkets.

■ Functions of the Executive, The

Identification Nonfiction book offering a theory of organizational behavior
Author Chester Irving Barnard
Date Published in 1938

Chester Irving Barnard's book helped to shape subsequent theories of business and public organizations and the role of executive leadership. It remains in print and is often the starting point for other discussions of organizational theory. In particular, it emphasizes the importance of informal as opposed to formal organization in any consideration of organizational effectiveness.

Barnard spent nearly forty years with American Telephone and Telegraph, culminating in service as the president of New Jersey Bell Telephone Company. In addition, he served on numerous governmental boards. His practical experience was complemented by his association with the theorist George Elton Mayo. Barnard's work demonstrated the limitations of previous organizational theory, most notably the scientific management school of thought. *The Functions of the Executive* helped to forge the human relations school of thought, which emphasized the importance of interpersonal relations in any theory of organizational behavior.

Organizational theory prior to Barnard focused on the individual rather than the organization and stressed the use of economic incentives as motivators for human behavior. Drawing on the lessons gained from the Hawthorne experiments, Barnard emphasized that workers were often motivated by more than pay and negative punitive measures. He developed a theory that showed how complex organizations developed and implemented goals in a rational manner that individual did not always follow. Barnard maintained that economic incentives were less important, once a bare minimum was reached, than ideas of group identity and personal satisfaction. This latter point became the foundation for what came to be known as the human relations school of management.

Barnard went beyond earlier theorists who emphasized formal lines of authority in organizations. While accepting that formal authority was important, he indicated that informal relationships in an organization had important influences on how workers behaved. Neglect of informal organization could lead an organization to fail in his view. However, he neglected the possibility that informal relationships could have negative consequences for an organization.

Impact   *The Functions of the Executive* was not a perfect work. Its extreme functionalism, which indicated that an organization was functional for all involved, missed important aspects of organizational behavior. Nonetheless, the book led to different ways of looking at organizational behavior. Later theorists built on Barnard's work in constructing better developed theories of organizations.

John M. Theilmann

Further Reading

Perrow, Charles. *Complex Organizations.* 3d ed. New York: Random House, 1986.

Shafritz, Jay, J. Steven Ott, and Yong Suk Jang, eds. *Classics of Organization Theory.* 6th ed. Florence, Ky.: Wadsworth/Cengage, 2007.

See also   Advertising in Canada; Advertising in the United States.

■ Fundamentalist-Modernist conflict

Definition   Debate among Protestant theologians about the literal interpretation of the Bible

By 1930, historical criticism of the Bible had spread from universities to seminaries intent upon maintaining academic credibility without sacrificing a distinctively Christian worldview. Some theologians contended accommodations to secular scholarship would be ruinous to the faith, so they prepared for combat with advocates of the liberal approach to Scripture. Consequences of this dispute left Protestants sharply divided.

Princeton Theological Seminary became the major defender of orthodoxy early in the twentieth century, and its scholars continued to lead that effort until 1929, when they lost control. An exodus of professors committed to the Bible as God's infallible word led to the formation of Westminster Theological Seminary in Philadelphia to continue the struggle against Modernist departures from orthodoxy.

By the opening of the 1930's, the concept of fundamentalism had come to identify Protestants who affirmed full confidence in Scripture and espoused

all doctrines derived from subscription to its authority. A series of booklets, *The Fundamentals: A Testimony to the Truth,* began appearing in 1915, and Baptist editor Curtis Lee Laws introduced the term "fundamentalist" in 1920. Although the controversy affected numerous denominations, it was most pronounced with Presbyterians and Baptists, among whom it caused deep divisions.

Concurrent with disputes in seminaries, reports about Modernism among foreign missionaries agitated further unrest, especially when it became evident that Pearl S. Buck, Presbyterian appointee in China, had abandoned orthodoxy and was promoting a syncretism between Christianity and traditional Chinese philosophies. Although Buck resigned from the Presbyterian mission in 1933, the furor she had helped to inflame had only begun. Comparable disputes among Baptist missionary personnel agitated congregations of that affiliation too.

One of the most influential leaders of the Modernist movement was Henry Sloan Coffin, professor and president of Union Theological Seminary, in New York, the academic fountainhead of liberal scholarship, from 1926 to 1945. Through his influence in the Presbyterian Church, USA, Coffin promoted the view that accommodations to the contentions of culture were essential for the survival of Christianity, for such concessions alone would make it attractive to modern people. Coffin regarded religious experience as the foundation of faith and the basis for preaching. He saw the Bible as a product of evolving religious insights rather than specific divine revelation. Partly because of the eloquence of spokespersons such as Coffin, Modernism gained supporters in Presbyterian ranks, a development which led conservatives to reach beyond their own denomination to find support; Baptists often joined with Presbyterians to defend historic beliefs they held in common.

Baptist concern about theological issues had been growing at least since the start of the twentieth century, but 1930 proved to be a crucial year in provoking disputes among members of the denomination. Wealthy Baptist churchman John D. Rockefeller funded a project to examine the entire missionary enterprise, and seven denominations participated in the study. Harvard University professor William Ernest Hocking, a liberal Congregationalist, led a "layman's inquiry" about Christian efforts in East Asia. The report, *Re-thinking Missions* (1932), portrayed Christianity as part of an emerging world religion, and it urged missionaries to promote fraternity among religions by refraining from proclaiming divisive doctrines such as the exclusive saviorhood of Christ.

Reactions to *Re-thinking Missions* ranged from enthusiastic endorsements to stern rejections, with John Gresham Machen, founder of Westminster Theological Seminary, leading the conservatives. Machen regarded the report of Hocking's committee as abominable syncretism and a betrayal of Christianity, and he criticized other orthodox leaders who responded to it temperately. Buck, on the contrary, hailed *Re-thinking Missions* and urged all mission agencies to adopt its recommendations. When the general assembly of the Presbyterian Church, USA approved the leadership and policies of its board of foreign missions, Machen announced some conservatives would form an Independent Board of Presbyterian Foreign Missions (IBPFM) to preserve the historic faith. Publication of *Re-thinking Missions* occurred at a time when church leaders and missionaries were debating the relevance of believing in Jesus' virgin birth, a doctrine liberals found incredible but conservatives considered indispensable. At the same time Buck declared her inability to affirm belief in a personal God.

A pivotal figure in these disputes was Robert E. Speer, secretary of the IBPFM, who in spite of his avowed belief in all cardinal doctrines of Christianity, refused to acknowledge deviations from the faith among missionaries of his church. Other leading conservatives denounced *Re-thinking Missions* but did not support Machen's IBPFM. In 1934, the Presbyterian general assembly ordered all members of that board to resign. Those who refused were suspended from the ministry of the church.

Meanwhile in Baptist circles the fundamentalist-Modernist conflict was equally intense. The Northern Baptist Convention had suffered a division in 1925, when seceding congregations formed the General Association of Regular Baptist Churches, and a larger schism was yet to come. Baptist congregations, being fully autonomous, left the convention in growing numbers; eventually that body lost one-half of its membership. Once more, reports of Modernism among missionaries in China aroused concern, and William Bell Riley, a pastor in Minneapolis, had discovered departures from orthodoxy in China as early as 1923. Thereafter, efforts to obtain assurance that the denominational Board of Foreign Missions would appoint only persons of conservative belief encountered opposition from denominational leaders.

When a Baptist missionary in China published a book denying Jesus' virgin birth, bodily resurrection, and second coming, conservatives demanded removal of all mission personnel who did not espouse historic Christian teachings. Such efforts continued through the decade of the 1930's, but they were not successful. In 1943, the fundamentalists organized the Conservative Baptist Foreign Mission Society (CBFMS) to operate within the Northern Baptist Convention but independent of its control. The orthodoxy of appointees was to be assured by subscription to a statement of faith. The CBFMS made China one of its major fields. In 1947, frustrated fundamentalists formed the Conservative Baptist Association of America, another costly secession from the Northern Baptist Convention.

Impact Although fundamentalists and Modernists seldom any longer attack each other with the vigor displayed during the 1930's, the issues dividing them remain, and the antithesis they reflect shows the conflict is unresolvable. The preeminent fundamentalist leader Machen made this clear in his book *Christianity and Liberalism* (1923), which portrays the two schools of thought as competing religions.

James Edward McGoldrick

Further Reading

Buck, Pearl S. *Is There a Case for Foreign Missions?* New York: John Day, 1932. Displays the author's syncretistic beliefs, which forced her split from the fundamentalist elements of Christian theology.

Dollar, George W. *A History of Fundamentalism in America.* Greenville, S.C.: Bob Jones University Press, 1973. A thorough account with a useful biographical index.

Hocking, Ernest W., ed. *Re-thinking Missions.* New York: Harper & Brothers, 1932. The document that propelled fundamentalists into action.

Loetscher, Lefferts A. *The Broadening Church.* Philadelphia: University of Pennsylvania Press, 1957. A liberal historian's erudite analysis; opposite to the perspective of Machen.

Longfield, Bradley J. *The Presbyterian Controversy.* New York: Oxford University Press, 1991. A work of careful scholarship and fair judgments by a Presbyterian historian.

Macartney, Clarence E. *The Making of a Minister.* New York: Channel Press, 1961. An autobiography of a learned Presbyterian pastor deeply involved in the controversy.

Machen, J. Gresham. *Christianity and Liberalism.* Reprint. Grand Rapids, Mich.: William B. Eerdmans, 2009. The classical scholarly defense of orthodoxy that has received applause from partisans on both sides of the conflict.

Poteat, Gordon. *Stand by for China.* New York: Friendship Press, 1940. The work of a Modernist missionary who caused much controversy.

Tulga, Chester E. *The Foreign Missions Controversy in the Northern Baptist Convention.* Chicago: Conservative Baptist Fellowship, 1950. An eyewitness account from a participant in this conflict.

Utzinger, J. Michael. *Yet Saints Their Watch Are Keeping.* Macon, Ga.: Mercer University Press, 2006. Examines fundamentalist perceptions of the proper nature of the church from 1887 to 1957.

Ward, Keith. *What the Bible Really Teaches.* London: SPCK, 2004. A liberal critique of conservative beliefs.

See also Buck, Pearl S.; Religion in Canada; Religion in the United States.

G

■ Gable, Clark

Identification American film star
Born February 1, 1901; Cadiz, Ohio
Died November 16, 1960; Hollywood, California

Gable personified the romantic hero in Hollywood films of the 1930's and 1940's. His career included more than seventy films, but he is best known for his portrayal of Rhett Butler in Gone with the Wind *(1939), a Civil War epic that provided escapism for fans during the Depression.*

William Clark Gable was born at the beginning of the twentieth century and rose to stardom at a time when the concept of a romantic hero was widely accepted and admired. As a young man, Gable used an inheritance to pursue his dream of an acting career. He worked in small theaters across the Midwest until he arrived in Portland, Oregon. There he met Josephine Dillon, an older woman who, as his acting coach, groomed him to be a romantic leading man. She paid for dental and cosmetic surgery and guided him to better posture and voice control. After a period of training, they went to Hollywood, where she became his manager and his first wife. He had small parts in silent films and did some work on stage. With the beginning of the Depression in 1930, many plays were canceled, and work as an actor was difficult to obtain.

In 1930, Gable and Dillon divorced, and he married again within a few days to Ria Langham, a Texas socialite. Gable began his rise to stardom with a supporting role in *A Free Soul* (1931). He was a hit and was never cast in a supporting role again. At this time, he was under contract to Metro-Goldwyn-Mayer (MGM) and was an important member of its group of male stars whose studio image was rugged and manly. He played opposite Joan Crawford in *Dance, Fools, Dance* (1931) and Greta Garbo in *Susan Lenox (Her Fall and Rise)* (1931). He costarred with Crawford again in *Possessed* (1931), and the two began a long love affair. In 1932, he starred with Jean Harlow in *Red Dust*, the role that made him MGM's most important star. Harlow and Gable made several more films together: *Hold Your Man* (1933), *China Seas* (1935), *Wife vs. Secretary* (1936), and *Saratoga* (1937). She died in 1937 during the production of the final film.

After Gable refused several roles, he was loaned to Columbia Pictures, a lesser-ranked studio. He was not the first choice for male lead, but he was cast in *It Happened One Night* (1934) with Claudette Colbert. His performance earned him an Oscar for best actor

Clark Gable during the early 1930's. (Hulton Archive/Getty Images)

in 1934. He returned to MGM an even bigger star and played Fletcher Christian in *Mutiny on the Bounty* (1935), said to be one of his favorite roles. This earned him another Academy Award nomination in 1935.

During the 1930's, Gable acted in a number of popular films. His popularity grew through his variety of roles and romances with his leading ladies both on and off screen. In 1938, Ed Sullivan named him the "King of Hollywood" in his newspaper column. This title helped his career, but it was not his favorite accolade.

Gable earned a third Academy Award nomination in 1939 for his role as Rhett Butler, the debonair leading man in *Gone with the Wind*, with Vivien Leigh as Scarlett. Although he is best known for this role, he was initially the second choice. Gable was wary of the high expectations for any actor taking on this iconic role but yielded to the pressure and the influence of Carole Lombard, whom he married in 1939. The resulting film became an American classic.

In later years, Gable joined the Army Air Forces in World War II, flying in combat missions. After Lombard's death, he married twice more. He refused character roles as he grew older. His last performance, opposite Marilyn Monroe in *The Misfits* (1961), is said to have been the cause of his final and fatal heart attack. He died in Los Angeles in 1960.

Impact   Gable was the representative leading man in American film during this era. He was the essential romantic hero who could be gruff and manly as well as smooth and debonair. He was the "king" of Hollywood during the 1930's.

Dolores Amidon D'Angelo

Further Reading

Bret, David. *Clark Gable: Tormented Star.* New York: Carroll and Graf, 2008.

Harris, Warren G. *Clark Gable: A Biography.* New York: Harmony, 2005.

Spicer, Chrystopher J. *Clark Gable: Biography, Filmography, Bibliography.* Jefferson, N.C.: McFarland, 2002.

See also   Academy Awards; Garbo, Greta; *Gone with the Wind*; Harlow, Jean; *It Happened One Night*; McDaniel, Hattie; *Mutiny on the Bounty*.

■ Gambling

Definition   Wagering on any game or activity of which the outcome is unknown, including horseracing, craps, slot machines, lotteries, dice, and poker.

Gambling during the 1930's was significant for two reasons. First, states passed laws to legalize gambling in order to generate revenue for state and local economies struggling during the Great Depression. Second, Americans began to embrace gambling as a socially acceptable form of entertainment.

The Great Depression had a devastating impact on local and state economies across the United States. Given the dire times, states explored any and every opportunity to increase their economic standing. Gambling was identified as a possible revenue generator if legalized because it could be taxed by the state. States enacted myriad gambling laws, including pari-mutuel betting, slot machines, and casino gambling. The gambling legislation passed by select states during the 1930's inspired the remaining states to legalize gaming practices by the end of the decade.

The end of Prohibition coupled with the legalization of gambling in certain states prompted a shift in the way Americans viewed gambling. Previously, gambling had been condemned by religious groups and polite society. Consequently, gamblers were labeled people of ill repute, and gambling activities were largely relegated to back rooms and other clandestine locations. However, Americans viewed the legalization of gambling as an endorsement from the state; thus, the stigma that had been associated with gambling gradually dissipated. This allowed Americans to adopt a more accepting attitude toward gambling because the activities were available to "upstanding" citizens in reputable commercial establishments and were monitored by the state.

Impact   Legalization of gambling practices that took place during the 1930's paved the way for economic growth of local and state economies and also spurred a change in the social conscience of Americans that allowed gambling to be embraced as a legitimate form of entertainment.

Legalized gaming operations have often resulted in job opportunities at the local levels, increased tourism, and an increase in tax revenue at the local and state levels. Nevada may be the best example of the economic impact gambling has had on a state economy. Casino gaming was legalized in Las Vegas in 1931; according to the American Gaming Association, in fiscal year 2008, Nevada reported $924.5 million in tax contributions from its 266 casinos, which employed 202,216 people.

Brenda Vose

Further Reading

Giacopassi, David, and B. Grant Stitt. "Assessing the Impact of Casino Gambling on Crime in Mississippi." *American Journal of Criminal Justice* 18, no. 1 (1993): 117-131.

Haller, Mark H. "Policy Gambling, Entertainment, and the Emergence of Black Politics: Chicago from 1900 to 1940." *Journal of Social History* 24, no. 4 (1991): 719-739.

McMillen, Jan, ed. *Gambling Cultures*. London: Routledge, 1996.

Rosecrance, John. *Gambling Without Guilt: The Legitimation of an American Pastime*. Belmont, Calif.: Brooks/Cole, 1988.

Schwartz, David G. *Roll the Bones: The History of Gambling*. New York: Gotham Books, 2006.

See also Anti-Racketeering Act of 1934; Capone, Al; Crimes and scandals; Luciano, Lucky; Organized crime; Recreation.

■ Gangster films

Definition Films about criminal gangsters and their underworld

Movies featuring gangsters flourished during the 1930's, and the actors appearing in them were among the stars of the period. Audiences during the Depression seemed drawn to these outlaws, who, despite the odds, succeeded at the American Dream of becoming rich and famous.

The gangster in films of the 1930's came directly out of the newspaper headlines of the 1920's. Because the American public was willing to break the law to obtain alcoholic beverages, Prohibition provided the perfect opportunity for organized crime to expand and accumulate the money that gave gangsters clout, both economically and politically. Although crime has always been an equal opportunity employer, by the mid-1920's Al "Scarface" Capone was the most famous mobster in the United States

and came to represent the gangster to many Americans. However, things changed with the election of Franklin D. Roosevelt, because one of the first things he did as president after his inauguration in 1932 was to repeal the Eighteenth Amendment. With alcohol legal again, the character of the rumrunner passed into history but remained alive and well in films.

Pre-1930's Gangster Films The early history of the gangster film lacks examples to study, because it has been estimated that around 90 percent of all silent films have been lost or destroyed. Most film historians, however, single out two silent films as iconic representations of gangster films: D. W. Griffith's *The Musketeers of Pig Alley* (1912) and Josef von Sternberg's *Underworld* (1927). Griffiths's film is atmospheric for its time, portraying the urban environment as it is fought over by rival gangs of thugs. The main gangster turns out to be a rather honorable fellow when he helps out a starving violinist and his wife. The central gangster in *Underworld*, Bull Weed (George Bancroft), amid the murder and mayhem meted out to his fellow gangsters, achieves redemption of sorts by sacrificing himself so that his girl, Feathers (Evelyn Brent), can be with her lover, Rolls Royce (Clive Brook), the alcoholic lawyer Weed pulled out of the gutter. These two silent films portray gangsters as capable of violence but not defined by it; there is a soft side to them that disappears in the early 1930's.

The Early 1930's Three films from the early 1930's defined the gangster film: Mervyn LeRoy's *Little Caesar* (1931), William Wellman's *The Public Enemy* (1931), and Howard Hawks's *Scarface* (1932). Whatever sentimentalism was present in the films of the 1920's is absent here. All three trace the rise and fall of the gangster figure. Little Rico, Tom Powers, and Tony Camonte are all ruthless killers and use violence to achieve the power after which they lust. In all three films the central characters, and in some cases, their gangs, are clearly of immigrant backgrounds: Italian in *Little Caesar* and *Scarface* and Irish in *The Public Enemy*. The films feature energetic, charismatic actors, who became stars as a result. In all three, the gangster achieves wealth and power but pays for his wrongdoing by the end of the film. In addition, these films feature the city. The urban landscape was often overlooked by Hollywood, but these films juxtapose the evils and dynamism of the city. All were made before the stricter enforcement of the motion picture code by the Hays Office.

Little Caesar sets the pattern for subsequent gangster films. Rico "Little Caesar" manages to murder his way to the top of the criminal organization in a large city; the character clearly is based on Capone. Rico, played with snarling perfection by Edward G. Robinson, is a low-level hood with limited intelligence and few social graces. He is awed by the opulence of his boss and wants it for himself. His ambition and drive mimic the values needed to achieve the American Dream cherished by most of the moviegoing audience. His methods leave something to be desired; in the end, he must atone for his moral transgressions, and he dies in the gutter.

Tom Powers, of *The Public Enemy*, decides that the illegal track is the way to fame and fortune. As with *Little Caesar*, the central character, played with verve by James Cagney, exhibits an energy that is attractive if also questionable in its violence. Like Rico's, Tom's rise demands a fall, and he, too, dies in the end.

Tony "Scarface" Camonte, of *Scarface*, is played by Paul Muni, a stage actor who also did films; the character is driven to succeed by some seriously dark desires. In a key scene, Tony handles a submachine gun for the first time and sprays bullets with abandon; he will spray chaos and violence until he dies in another hail of bullets at the film's end. On his rise, Tony appropriates his boss's lifestyle, his operations, and his girl. He speaks with an accent, typifying the immigrant theme in these early gangster films.

The violence, various sexual improprieties, and morally questionable values of these early 1930's films were halted as early as the release of *Scarface*, which was delayed in order to do some cutting and to insert a scene depicting a group of concerned citizens who demand the end of this criminal behavior. Furthermore, the film was released with the subtitle: "The Shame of the Nation." The popularity of these films and the actors who starred in them created a problem for the studios when the Hays Office instituted guidelines for Hollywood films that restricted use of language, nudity, sexuality, and violence in

Paul Muni (center) brandishes a machine gun in the 1932 gangster film Scarface. *(Hulton Archive/Getty Images)*

films. As a result, Warner Bros., a studio that had pioneered these action-oriented productions, ceased to make them.

The Depression helped to popularize the gangster figure who became successful despite his outsider status. For people without jobs, many of whom hated banks and political and legal authority, the success of the gangster character, especially as played by attractive actors, may have been a bit too enticing. In any event, by the middle of the decade, with Prohibition over, the Roaring Twenties fading from memory, and Capone and others in jail, the gangster film declined.

The Late 1930's   By the late 1930's, films such as *Dead End* (1937), *Angels with Dirty Faces* (1938), and *The Roaring Twenties* (1939) marked a decided change in the portrayal of the gangster, by downplaying his attractiveness and stressing his failure in the end. In addition, the growing concerns about the international situation, the lessening impact of the Depression, and the decrease in immigration all contributed to Hollywood's move away from crime films set in the city by increasingly emphasizing historical dramas, fantasy films, and films with political themes. Gone were the early days of unbridled expression of violence, sex, and crime. However, the gangster film did not disappear entirely and flourishes in the twenty-first century in much the same form as those of the early years of the 1930's.

Impact The gangster films of the 1930's initially were subversive in their depiction of violence, sex, and American values. The Depression was raging and a great deal of social unrest existed in the United States. The gangster, portrayed by such engaging Hollywood actors as Robinson, Cagney, and Muni, became attractive enough to engender public outcry. That, coupled with the tightening censorship of the Hays Office, forced studios to shut down production of such films. The gangster character was both softened and demonized by the end of the decade. In spite of such changes, the gangster figure originally created on film in the early 1930's continues to provide potent subject matter for films and television. American audiences find something attractive about the gangster's outlaw status, abrogation of the rule of law, and freedom from societal norms.

Charles L. P. Silet

Further Reading

Baxter, John. *The Gangster Film.* New York: A. S. Barnes, 1970. Contains an encyclopedic listing of actors, directors, and topics associated with the gangster film.

Leitch, Thomas. *Crime Films.* New York: Cambridge University Press, 2002. Focuses on a critical, cultural, and historical overview of crime films, with chapters on individual crime films.

McArthur, Colin. *Underworld USA.* New York: Viking Press, 1972. Explores genre, iconography, development, and background of crime films in the early chapters.

Rafter, Nicole, ed. *Shots in the Mirror: Crime Films and Society.* New York: Oxford University Press, 2000. Rafter and her other contributors divide crime films into categories, such as cop, prison, and courtroom, that trace the history of crime in the films.

Shadoian, Jack. *Dreams and Dead Ends: The American Gangster Film.* New York: Oxford University Press, 2003. Examines the gangster film by topics, including a chapter on the "Golden Age" of Hollywood that features the "classic" 1930's gangster films.

See also   Cagney, James; Film; Gangster films; *Little Caesar*; Motion Picture Production Code; Muni, Paul; Robinson, Edward G.

■ Garbo, Greta

Identification   Swedish-born American film star
Born   September 18, 1905; Stockholm, Sweden
Died   April 15, 1990; New York, New York

The beautiful Garbo was a leading film star during the 1930's whose major roles won her critical acclaim. She brought quiet strength and a forceful presence to several notable black-and-white films.

After making ten silent films during the 1920's, Greta Garbo, born Greta Louisa Gustafsson, debuted in talking pictures in 1930. *Anna Christie* (1931), adapted from a Eugene O'Neill play, was much publicized by her Metro-Goldwyn-Mayer studio, which took out a large advertisement in *Variety* stating: "Garbo Talks." Audiences loved her voice, which was rich, full, and throaty.

In 1932, Garbo played one of her most memorable roles as Grusinskaya, an aging ballerina, in *Grand Hotel.* Her performance was so outstanding that she overshadowed her famous costars: Joan Crawford and John and Lionel Barrymore.

Anna Karenina premiered in 1935 and again featured a superb performance by Garbo. It won her a best actress award from the prestigious New York Film Critics Circle. However, at this point, as the Great Depression deepened, American film audiences were enamored with Shirley Temple and happy musicals. Since Garbo acted in serious dramas, often with tragic endings, her box-office numbers dropped slightly.

Camille, released in 1937, is considered to be Garbo's greatest role; she played a famous Parisian courtesan of the 1840's. Garbo appeared to be at the height of her personal beauty during the filming and had a forceful intensity on the screen. She was nominated for an Academy Award for this role but did not win.

Film icon Greta Garbo in 1937. (AP/Wide World Photos)

Garbo's last major film, in 1939, is a lighthearted, witty satire featuring Soviet officials visiting Paris. Promotions for *Ninotchka* (1939) used the phrase: Garbo Laughs. Audiences were delighted with her comedic talent, and she again received an Academy Award nomination but did not win. In 1941, at the age of thirty-six, she completed one final film.

Impact   Garbo has been remembered for her five greatest film roles. At the height of her career during the 1930's, she presided over a phenomenon known as "Garbomania." Her fan base was extensive in both the United States and Europe. Her style choices, such as wearing slacks and donning the "Garbo bob," influenced women's fashions and hairstyles.

Patricia E. Sweeney

Further Reading

Daum, Raymond. *Walking with Garbo: Conversations and Recollections.* New York: HarperCollins, 1990.

Payne, Robert. *The Great Garbo.* New York: Praeger, 1976.

Robinson, David, and Paul Duncan. *Greta Garbo.* London: Taschen, 2007.

Sands, Frederick, and Sven Broman. *The Divine Garbo.* New York: Grosset and Dunlap, 1979.

Vieira, Mark A. *Greta Garbo: A Cinematic Legacy.* New York: Harry N. Abrams, 2005.

See also   Academy Awards; Fashions and clothing; Film; *Grand Hotel*; Hairstyles; O'Neill, Eugene; Temple, Shirley.

■ Garner, John Nance

Identification   Vice president of the United States during Roosevelt's first two terms

Born   November 22, 1868; Red River County, near Detroit, Texas

Died   November 7, 1967; Uvalde, Texas

Drawing on nearly thirty years of legislative experience, John Nance Garner, as Franklin D. Roosevelt's first vice president, secured passage of significant elements of Roosevelt's New Deal programs and became, save for Roosevelt himself, the most influential American politician of the 1930's. Garner's growing rift with the administration during Roosevelt's second term defined the decade's schism between proactivist New Deal liberals and more cautious conservative Democrats.

From his arrival in Washington, D.C., in 1903, representing a newly carved congressional district in Texas, one larger than many states, Garner relished the machinery of legislation and the practical work of closed-door negotiations. Although a practicing lawyer, Garner had never completed law school— poor health curtailed his education at Vanderbilt University. However, with his charisma and his maverick personality, Garner won several state elections until he was chosen to represent the massive district whose creation he had supervised.

Career Before the Vice Presidency   For nearly three decades in the House, Garner, a conservative Democrat, mastered the legislative process, extending the scope of his influence and rising steadily within the Democratic leadership, first on the powerful House Ways and Means Committee, then as minority leader from 1929 to 1930, and finally, in 1930, as Speaker of the House. With the economic catastrophe of the burgeoning Depression and the floundering Hoover administration, Garner, with the support of powerful newspaper magnate William Randolph Hearst, positioned himself as the Democratic presidential nominee for 1932. Because Garner disdained the idea of campaigning, the juggernaut support for upbeat New York governor Franklin D. Roosevelt took the convention to a fourth ballot when Garner released his delegates, most prominently Texas and California, to Roosevelt. In return, Roosevelt, to avoid a party split, offered the vice presidency; Garner reluctantly agreed, believing that Speaker was a far more influential post. On November 8, 1932, Garner became the thirty-second vice president of the United States.

The Vice Presidency For Roosevelt's first term, Garner set aside his own conservative misgivings over the reach of Roosevelt's New Deal initiatives and steered the president's ambitious legislative agenda through Congress. Indeed, as Speaker during Hoover's last year in office, Garner had proposed similar public-works legislation as a way to address the crippling unemployment rates. Few vice presidents had come to office with Garner's legislative background, his colorful personality, and his influence in both houses of Congress, specifically the large bloc of southern conservative Democrats. Although he famously disparaged his own office, Garner worked the congressional corridors to guarantee Roosevelt's economic recovery programs.

Perhaps because, Garner was setting his sights on the 1940 Democratic nomination, his second term as vice president was fractious. Garner spoke openly of his disagreements over what he saw as the excess of Roosevelt's agenda, specifically the looming reality of deficit spending to finance the government recovery initiatives. He objected strongly to both Roosevelt's bald attempts to influence congressional races in 1938 and his ultimately disastrous attempt to expand the Supreme Court to fifteen members. Garner came to be seen as the public leader of the party's loyal opposition. In fact, Roosevelt and Garner seldom spoke in their last two years together.

When Roosevelt decided to pursue a third term, Garner challenged him, in large part because he objected to a three-term presidency. However, Garner's problems with labor, concerns about his age, and the perception that he was a party malcontent doomed his candidacy. Roosevelt beat him handily and selected Henry A. Wallace, his agriculture secre-

tary and a vociferous supporter of the New Deal, as vice president. When his term ended in 1941, after a public career of forty-six years, Garner retired to Texas and never returned to Washington, D.C.

Impact Although his selection as vice president may have been motivated by politics, Garner proved an invaluable part of the New Deal initiatives. He understood Washington, D.C., in ways that Roosevelt, a governor and hence an outsider, did not. Roosevelt inspired the nation, but Garner secured the congressional support that turned the programs into law during Roosevelt's historic first one hundred days. In that, Garner redefined the role of the vice presidency and established the office as a legislative enabler of an Administration's agenda. In his split with Roosevelt, Garner put beliefs above party loyalty. He believed that Roosevelt's politics would lead to a welfare state and that Roosevelt himself was accumulating excessive political power. In challenging a sitting president, Garner was the precursor of maverick southern conservative Democrats; although retired to Texas, Garner maintained his associations with that wing of the Democratic Party and lived to see the rise of one of its disciples, Texan Lyndon B. Johnson.

Joseph Dewey

Further Reading

Alter, Jonathan. *The Defining Moment: FDR's One Hundred Days and the Triumph of Hope.* New York: Simon & Schuster, 2007. Important assessment of the first one hundred days that places Garner's legislative achievement within a broad historic context.

Cohen, Adam. *Nothing to Fear: FDR's Inner Circle and the Hundred Days That Created Modern America.* New York: Penguin, 2009. Meticulous account of the backroom negotiations that secured Roosevelt's initial programs. Credits Garner's arm-twisting and his understanding of the legislative process and examines Garner's misgivings over Roosevelt's policies.

Fisher, O. C. *Cactus Jack: A Biography of John Nance Garner.* Waco, Tex.: Texian Press, 1978. The most important biography of Garner. Provides a vivid account of Garner's early years in the outback of Texas and how they shaped his Washington, D.C., persona.

Neal, Steven. *Happy Days Are Here Again: The 1932 Democratic Convention, the Emergence of FDR, and*

How America Was Changed Forever. New York: Morrow, 2004. Significant account of Garner's most ambitious political year—specifically how he negotiated his way onto the national ticket and ensured the election of Roosevelt.

Smith, Jean Edward. *FDR.* New York: Random House, 2008. Landmark biography that provides a fascinating look at the stormy relationship between Roosevelt and Garner.

See also   Congress, U.S.; Elections of 1932, U.S.; Elections of 1936, U.S.; Great Depression in the United States; Labor strikes; Recession of 1937-1938; Reorganization Act of 1939; Roosevelt's first one hundred days; Unionism; Wallace, Henry A.

Gay rights. See **Homosexuality and gay rights**

■ Gehrig, Lou

Identification   American baseball player
Born   June 19, 1903; New York, New York
Died   June 2, 1941; New York, New York

Gehrig's power hitting made him one of the greatest first basemen in baseball history and one of the most significant sports figures of the 1930's. He played a pivotal role in establishing the New York Yankees as an enduring baseball dynasty.

Lou Gehrig, born Ludwig Heinrich Gehrig, a left-handed first baseman, achieved baseball superstar status during the 1920's, but ten of his full or partial seventeen major league seasons occurred during the 1930's. Although the Yankees, with whom he spent his entire major league career, emerged as baseball's preeminent franchise during the 1920's, the team won an additional five World Series championships during the 1930's.

During the decade of the Great Depression, Gehrig accumulated the largest component of his career batting statistics with 347 of his 493 home runs, 1,358 of his 1,995 runs batted in (RBI), and 1,802 of his 2,721 hits. His cumulative 1930's batting average of .343 slightly exceeded his career mark of .340. He led the American League in several categories during the 1930's, including batting average in 1934 (.363); home runs in 1931 (46), 1934 (49), and 1936

Lou Gehrig in 1936, the year in which he won the second of his two American League most valuable player awards. (AP/Wide World Photos)

(49); and RBI in 1930 (174), 1931 (184), and 1934 (165). In these and other categories, Gehrig's single-season and career offensive totals ranked among the game's highest at the time of his retirement. A triple crown winner (finishing first in batting average, home runs, and RBI) in 1934, Gehrig received the American League's (AL's) most valuable player award in 1936; he had previously won the award in 1927.

Despite his achievements, Gehrig stood, to a significant degree, in the shadow of more celebrated teammates throughout most of his career. The home runs of Babe Ruth transformed the game and made Ruth the game's dominant figure before Gehrig even reached the major leagues. Although Ruth and Gehrig gave the Yankees arguably the most potent one-two batting duo in baseball history, the former clearly pervaded newspaper and fan attention until his release by New York following the 1934 sea-

---

Gehrig's Farewell to Baseball

Fans, for the past two weeks you have been reading about the bad break I got. Yet today [July 4, 1939] I consider myself the luckiest man on the face of this earth. I have been in ballparks for seventeen years and have never received anything but kindness and encouragement from you fans.

Look at these grand men. Which of you wouldn't consider it the highlight of his career just to associate with them for even one day? Sure, I'm lucky. Who wouldn't consider it an honor to have known Jacob Ruppert? Also, the builder of baseball's greatest empire, Ed Barrow? To have spent six years with that wonderful little fellow, Miller Huggins? Then to have spent the next nine years with that outstanding leader, that smart student of psychology, the best manager in baseball today, Joe McCarthy? Sure, I'm lucky.

When the New York Giants, a team you would give your right arm to beat, and vice versa, sends you a gift—that's something. When everybody down to the groundskeepers and those boys in white coats remember you with trophies—that's something. When you have a wonderful mother-in-law who takes sides with you in squabbles with her own daughter—that's something. When you have a father and a mother who work all their lives so you can have an education and build your body—it's a blessing. When you have a wife who has been a tower of strength and shown more courage than you dreamed existed—that's the finest I know.

So I close in saying that I may have had a tough break, but I have an awful lot to live for.

---

loid headlines. Even when Gehrig hit four home runs in a game in 1932, a rare feat, sports pages headlined the retirement of New York Giants manager John McGraw. Although Gehrig was the highest paid player in the game from 1935 to his 1939 retirement, the adverse economic impact of the Great Depression on baseball kept his peak salary of $39,000 well below what he would have earned in a more prosperous era.

Gehrig's signature achievement was the record for most consecutive games played (2,130), a mark that long appeared unapproachable. It stood until broken by Cal Ripken, Jr., of the Baltimore Orioles in 1995. From June 1, 1925, until April 30, 1939, Gehrig was a constant in the Yankee lineup, playing hurt if necessary when confronted by illness or injury. Hitting an anemic .143, Gehrig asked Yankees manager Joe McCarthy to scratch him from the lineup prior to the May 2, 1939, game. Gehrig, suffering from the muscle-wasting and inevitably fatal amyotrophic lateral sclerosis (which came to be known as Lou Gehrig's disease), never played again. On July 4, 1939, at Lou Gehrig Day at Yankee Stadium, he displayed notable courage and eloquence, proclaiming himself, despite a "bad break," "the luckiest man on the face of this earth." Gehrig's emotional farewell to baseball elevated him to iconic status, prompting a retrospective appreciation of his athletic greatness and exceptional character. By special election, he was named to the National Baseball Hall of Fame in 1939. Gehrig died from the disease that now bears his name on June 2, 1941.

son. In contrast to the dramatic, charismatic, and bombastic Ruth, Gehrig was introverted and socially inept. Without Ruth, Gehrig, despite his usual outstanding personal performance, failed to lead the Yankees to the AL pennant in 1935. Then, center fielder Joe DiMaggio, lionized beyond any previous rookie, joined the Yankees in 1936, pacing the team to the first of a then record four consecutive World Series championships.

While the muscular Gehrig, nicknamed "The Iron Horse" and built like the collegiate football player he once was, embodied physical power, his strength appeared more stolid than aesthetic. Conversely, DiMaggio, in motion, projected a graceful physical elegance, balletic and compelling. Gehrig led an exemplary life, both on and off the playing field, but it seemed relatively colorless, not the material of tab-

Impact Gehrig endures in history and public consciousness as a great athlete and a role model of American masculinity. His modest demeanor, baseball achievements, and courage grant him a heroic stature.

William M. Simons

Further Reading

Alexander, Charles C. *Breaking the Slump: Baseball in the Depression Era*. New York: Columbia University Press, 2002.

Eig, Jonathan. *Luckiest Man: The Life and Death of Lou Gehrig*. New York: Simon & Schuster, 2005.

Kashatus, William C. *Lou Gehrig: A Biography*. Westport, Conn.: Greenwood Press, 2004.

See also   Baseball; Dean, Dizzy; Foxx, Jimmie; National Baseball Hall of Fame; Negro Leagues; Ott, Mel; Ruth, Babe; Sports in the United States; Vander Meer, Johnny.

■ General Theory of Employment, Interest and Money, The

Author   John Maynard Keynes

Identification   Groundbreaking and controversial book on the sources of and possible solutions to economic depressions

Date   Published in 1936

Considered by many scholars as the masterpiece of twentieth century economic thought, Keynes's The General Theory of Employment, Interest and Money *grew out of his continued investigation and theorizing on connections among consumers, investors, business and banking policies, national governments, and uncertainty in business booms and busts. Keynes argued that national governments must intercede in the business and banking spheres to revive economies during severe economic depressions and aid in fiscal recovery efforts.*

John Maynard Keynes had long been a student of probability and uncertainty in areas ranging from national economies to consumer behaviors. As a professor of economics at Cambridge University, Keynes developed his theories on business cycles, investments, and savings. Keynes conceived of economies as continually evolving structures in which individual decisions to save, spend, or invest profits or wages could affect the entire national fiscal health. With the onset of the Great Depression in 1929 and 1930, Keynes observed that markets and economies were not self-correcting, as economists had maintained since the nineteenth century. There was no "invisible hand" that would magically solve unemployment or reenergize the stock markets or banks.

He argued that only national governments had the ability to revitalize business, trade, and employment during severe downturns.

In early 1931, he began writing his analysis of why economies boom and collapse and how individual and corporate behaviors shape these cycles. Keynes became economic adviser to the British government and traveled to the United States to meet with President Franklin D. Roosevelt and his economic advisers in 1934. The almost complete collapse of the American fiscal and economic structure shocked Keynes, and he fully supported Roosevelt's National Industrial Recovery Act. However, Keynes warned that American government spending was too little to propel business and banks into motion, nor would this practice solve mass unemployment. With the worldwide Depression continuing in intensity, Keynes, recalling his meetings with economic leaders in the United States and both businesses and governments seeking remedies to high unemployment and losses of investments and profits, completed *The General Theory of Employment, Interest and Money* in 1936.

The General Theory of Employment, Interest and Money is filled with pages of algebraic formulas, interspersed with acute observations. What Keynes determined is that economies, as with all things created and controlled by humans, are unpredictable and volatile. Human behavior and human nature can affect fiscal cycles as much as interest rates, industrial output, and international trade. What Keynes argued in *The General Theory of Employment, Interest and Money* is that there are several paradoxes and contradictions in capitalism. These contradictions can lead to robust fiscal security or complete collapse. According to Keynes, there are two types of economic actors, "hoarders" and "spenders." "Spenders" keep money flowing with purchases of goods and services but then lack savings to fall back on should a recession or depression occur. "Hoarders" plow most of their profits and wages into savings or financial investment vehicles (stocks and bonds), thereby depriving businesses and wage-earners of their money. The paradox Keynes highlighted in this dichotomy was that both "hoarders" and "spenders" had the ability to affect entire national economies, but neither had the ability to survive economic downturns. "Hoarders" would lose savings tied up in stocks and private accounts, and "spenders" would have no extra money to spend. Moreover, the perceptions and confidence of individual wage-earners, consumers, businesses, and bankers would all play into national and international economies. If there were little confidence in recovery, people and businesses would simply save their money, if they had any, and cut production. What was needed was an outside stimulus to kick-start spending. That is where governments could enter the marketplace, creating employment and wages, resetting interest rates, restructuring banking and loan practices, and providing social confidence in the system.

Impact   *The General Theory of Employment, Interest and Money* was hotly debated during the late 1930's and remains a controversial text. Though Keynes firmly believed in capitalism and private enterprise, he realized that under some conditions such as those of the Great Depression, government intervention was not only desirable but also necessary for economic recovery. Though he supported both British and American government recovery efforts during the 1930's, Keynes believed that the Depression was so severe that only massive government spending— more than any of the British or American leaders had proposed—could help the economic recovery.

Tyler T. Crogg

Further Reading

Blackhouse, Roger E., and Bradley W. Bateman. *The Cambridge Companion to Keynes.* New York: Cambridge University Press, 2006.

Heilbroner, Robert L. *The Worldly Philosophers: The Lives, Times, and Ideas of the Great Economic Thinkers.* New York: Touchstone Books, 1986.

Skidelsky, Robert. *The Economist as Savior, 1920-1937.* Vol. 2 in *John Maynard Keynes.* New York: Penguin Books, 1992.

See also   Great Depression in the United States; Income and wages in the United States; Inflation; National Industrial Recovery Act of 1933; National Recovery Administration.

■ Geneva Disarmament Conference

The Event   International gathering to discuss disarmament or arms limitation

Also known as   World Disarmament Conference; Conference for the Reduction and Limitation of Armaments

Dates   1932-1934

Place   Geneva, Switzerland

The Geneva Disarmament Conference was the largest international conference ever held up to that time. Irreconcilable security interests among the many conference delegations resulted in the lack of an arms agreement.

After World War I, world leaders sought to reduce the number of available armaments to avoid another catastrophic war. They successfully negotiated naval treaties at the Washington Naval Conference in 1921-1922 and the London Naval Conference in 1930. The high cost of arms races and the economic difficulties of the Great Depression greatly contributed to the call for arms reductions. President Herbert Hoover strongly supported the idea of a disarmament conference for economic reasons.

Planning for the Geneva Disarmament Conference, or World Disarmament Conference, began in 1926. In January, 1931, the League of Nations summoned the conference to begin in a year. The conference opened at Geneva on February 2, 1932, and was formally known as the Conference for the Reduction and Limitation of Armaments. The conference began under the chairmanship of former British foreign secretary Arthur Henderson. At the conference, delegations from fifty-nine countries, including non-League of Nations members the United States and the Soviet Union, attempted to form agreements for arms reductions. The U.S. delegation was led by Norman Davis and included Hugh S. Gibson, Senator Claude Swanson, and Hugh Wilson.

The conference quickly ran into difficulties. The Japanese invasion of Manchuria was a major problem for the League of Nations and collective security. Moreover, the European powers were not in the mood for arms agreements. France, the strongest military power on the continent, feared German rearmament. Germany had been placed under arms restrictions by the Treaty of Versailles in 1919. French delegates demanded security against Germany before agreeing to an arms-limitation treaty. France sought American and British commitments to the defense of Europe. Great Britain, on the other hand, wanted French disarmament and an American commitment to the defense of Europe.

The United States made several proposals at Geneva. In June, 1932, President Hoover suggested a one-third reduction in all armies and battle fleets. He also urged the abolition of large mobile guns, tanks, and chemical weapons and the prohibition of aerial bombardment. However, the American delegation hesitated on the idea of committing the United States to any permanent verification procedures. Then, in May, 1933, President Franklin D. Roosevelt proposed the abolition of modern offensive weapons. He also indicated that the United States was willing to consult with other nations in a crisis that might lead to war. However, the U.S. Senate opposed dropping U.S. neutrality for international cooperation.

Meanwhile, the German delegation argued that if the other powers did not disarm to the German level, then Germany had the right to rearm without restrictions. Talks quickly came to a standstill, and the conference was adjourned from June to October, 1933.

In the autumn, Adolf Hitler demanded the immediate right to build weapons prohibited by the Treaty of Versailles and to increase the size of the German army. After strong French objections, on October 14, 1933, Hitler withdrew Germany from the World Disarmament Conference, and one week later, he announced that Germany was withdrawing from the League of Nations. The Geneva Conference dragged into 1934 without any evident results. The conference had failed. Proposal after proposal was unsuccessful because of irreconcilable security interests.

Impact   The failure of the Geneva Conference led to German rearmament. Germany was secretly rearming, and in March, 1935, Germany announced openly that it would rearm. Germany created an air force and initiated conscription to create an army of one-half million men. Germany was challenging the League of Nations and the restrictions of the Treaty of Versailles. Aggressive German actions led to the remilitarization of the Rhineland in 1936. A militarily powerful Germany annexed Austria and the Sudetenland in 1938 and took further aggressive ac-

tions that led to the outbreak of World War II in Europe in 1939.

William Young

Further Reading

Adamthwaite, Anthony. *Grandeur and Misery: France's Bid for Power in Europe, 1914-1940.* London: Arnold, 1995.

Bennett, Edward W. *German Rearmament and the West, 1932-1933.* Princeton, N.J.: Princeton University Press, 1979.

Marks, Sally. *The Illusion of Peace: International Relations in Europe, 1918-1933.* London: Macmillan, 1976.

Offner, Arnold A. *The Origins of the Second World War: American Foreign Policy and World Politics, 1917-1941.* 2d ed. Malabar, Fla.: Robert E. Krieger, 1986.

Steiner, Zara. *The Lights That Failed: European International History, 1919-1933.* New York: Oxford University Press, 2005.

See also   Asia; Canada and Great Britain; Europe; Foreign policy of the United States; Germany and U.S. appeasement; Isolationism; Japanese military aggression; League of Nations; London Naval Treaty; Manchuria occupation.

■ George VI's North American visit

The Event   British king's month-long tour of Canada and the United States

Dates   May 17 to June 17, 1939

Places   Quebec, Ontario, Manitoba, Saskatchewan, Alberta, British Columbia, New York, Pennsylvania, Maryland, Virginia, Delaware, New Jersey, New York, and Washington, D.C.

This was the first visit by a ruling British monarch to the United States. Its purpose was to bolster Canadian morale and to foster a closer relationship between Great Britain and the United States in the face of Adolf Hitler's aggressive foreign policy and territorial acquisitions. The royal couple dispensed with certain forms of protocol in an attempt to appear down-to-earth.

George VI's North American visit had been carefully planned by the British Foreign and Commonwealth

Office to connect with Canada and undercut the isolationist mood in the United States. Both Canadian prime minister William Lyon Mackenzie King, who acted as minister in attendance on the visit to give the impression that George VI's visit was as Canadian king, and President Franklin D. Roosevelt had requested that George VI visit their countries. The royal party sailed from England on May 6, 1939; the Atlantic crossing took much longer than expected because of ice in the North Atlantic, and the king and queen disembarked at Wolfe's Cove, Quebec, on May 17, 1939.

Formal ceremonies were held at Quebec, Montreal, Ottawa, and Toronto, but the royal couple walked among the people, some of whom even hugged and kissed their majesties. The king and queen moved by train across Canada to British Columbia and made the return trip back to Niagara Falls, Canada, where they crossed the Canadian-American border the night of Wednesday, June 7, 1939. After brief greetings from Secretary of State Cordell Hull, the couple continued on to Washington, D.C., arriving at Union Station the morning of June 8, 1939, where President Roosevelt and First Lady Eleanor Roosevelt greeted them.

The king and queen's two-day visit in Washing-

U.S. president Franklin D. Roosevelt (right) speaks seriously to the young King George VI during the latter's trip to North America in 1939. (AP/Wide World Photos)

ton, D.C., was a whirlwind of personal appearances, official functions, and constant changes of clothes in the 90-degree-plus heat. Important appearances on day one included a garden party at the British embassy and a state dinner at the White House, which featured contralto Marian Anderson, the first African American to perform at the White House. On day two, June 9, 1939, there were ten engagements in eleven hours, highlighted by visits to Mount Vernon and a Civilian Conservation Corps site and wreath laying at Arlington National Cemetery. The royal couple traveled overnight by train to New Jersey and from New Jersey to New York City on the USS *Warrington*. Stops in the city included the New York World's Fair and Columbia University before a drive to the Roosevelts' home at Hyde Park on the Hudson River.

The atmosphere at Hyde Park was much more relaxed, with cocktails, dinner, and conversation between the king and president about politics and the defense of the Western Hemisphere. On Sunday, June 11, 1939, the couples attended services at St. James Episcopal Church, and later the president drove the king and queen to the controversial "hot dog picnic." Desirous of presenting a common touch, Roosevelt had the humble hot dog included in the menu. Many felt that it was beneath their majesties' royal dignity, but the king and queen handled it with aplomb. After an exchange of gifts with the Roosevelts, the king and queen boarded a train for Canada, and the return voyage landed them in England on June 22, 1939.

Impact The royal visit helped boost Canadian morale and improved British-American relations in the months immediately preceding the outbreak of World War II in Europe. Although Roosevelt and George VI established an amicable working relationship, it did not produce any substantial benefit for the British. The president's promises of support had to be weighed against the backdrop of a strong isolationist mood in the U.S. Congress. Many Americans, while charmed by the royal couple, remained suspicious that the visit presaged further American entanglements in European affairs.

Mark C. Herman

Further Reading

Reynolds, David. "FDR's Foreign Policy and the British Royal Visit to the United States." *The Historian* 45, no. 4 (1983): 461-472.

Swift, Will. *The Roosevelts and the Royals.* Hoboken, N.J.: John Wiley & Sons, 2004.

See also Canada and Great Britain; Canadian regionalism; Civilian Conservation Corps; Europe; Foreign policy of Canada; Foreign policy of the United States; King, William Lyon Mackenzie; Neutrality Acts; Roosevelt, Eleanor; Roosevelt, Franklin D.

■ George Washington Bridge

Identification Bridge spanning the Hudson River, connecting New York and New Jersey
Date Completed October 25, 1931
Places New York and New Jersey

The George Washington Bridge had the longest main span of any bridge in the world when it opened. The original plans called for the steel towers of the bridge to be covered in concrete with granite for aesthetics, but the economic realities of the Great Depression left the towers bare, inadvertently creating one of the most striking landmarks of New York City.

Run by the Port Authority of New York and New Jersey, construction of the George Washington Bridge began in 1927 under the watchful eyes of chief engineer Othmar Ammann and architect Cass Gilbert. The bridge, originally known as the Hudson River Bridge, was dedicated in 1931.

At its opening in 1931, the bridge featured the longest main span in the world at 3,500 feet and had a total length of nearly 5,000 feet. Constructed of steel, the towers of the bridge are 570 feet tall, and the bridge was able to withstand the weight of two railroad lines. Four cables suspended the bridge, each with a diameter of one yard. The total cost for building the bridge was $59 million, and twelve men lost their lives during construction.

The bridge originally featured six lanes of traffic; more were added later. The original plans left the possibility for a lower traffic deck, which was added during the 1960's. New York governor Franklin D. Roosevelt presided over the dedication of the bridge, which held the record as the longest suspension bridge until 1937, when the Golden Gate Bridge opened in San Francisco. During the first year of operation, an estimated 5.5 million vehicles crossed the bridge.

Impact In addition to providing a convenient commuting option for people living in New Jersey and working in New York, the George Washington Bridge became a landmark in New York City and is known as one of the most beautiful bridges in the world.

Jennifer Hardiman Shearer

Further Reading

Rockland, Michael Aaron. *The George Washington Bridge: Poetry in Steel.* Camden, N.J.: Rutgers University Press, 2008.

Whitney, Charles S. *Bridges of the World: Their Design and Construction.* Mineola, N.Y.: Dover, 2003.

See also Architecture; Automobiles and auto manufacturing; Roosevelt, Franklin D.; San Francisco Bay bridges.

◼ German-American Bund

Identification Organization representing German-American interests and promoting Nazi ideology

Also known as Amerikadeutscher Volksbund

Date April, 1936

The German-American Bund generated a great deal of alarm among many Americans, who saw the Bund's public, uniformed demonstrations and anti-Semitic propaganda as clear indications that the organization represented a Nazi "fifth column" in the United States. The House Committee on Un-American Activities used such alarmist sentiment to investigate the Bund, setting a precedent for future actions against perceived internal enemies in the United States.

The German-American Bund was founded in April, 1936, by Fritz Julius Kuhn, a naturalized American citizen who remained the driving force of the movement throughout its existence. The Bund's membership considered themselves loyal Americans who maintained strong ties to Germany. The organization's official objectives were to fight against "Jewish Marxism," to retain German language and customs, and to promote positive relations between the United States and Germany. The Bund tried to emphasize its members' loyalty to the United States by displaying the American flag and portraits of George Washington alongside those of Nazi Germany and Adolf Hitler.

The Bund was the successor of a previous movement, the Friends of New Germany, which, like the Bund, promoted Nazism and friendship between the United States and Germany. Because of increasing concerns about international perceptions of Germany as the nation began to rearm and work toward repealing the various strictures imposed by the Treaty of Versailles, the Nazi government ordered all German nationals to withdraw from membership in the Friends of New Germany in October, 1935. Kuhn organized the remnants of that group into the German-American Bund, which attempted to portray itself as an inherently American movement by requiring U.S. citizenship as a prerequisite for membership.

Structurally, the Bund was modeled after the Nazi Führerprinzip (führer principle) of leadership, with Kuhn serving as the organization's Bundesführer. Like the Nazi Party's Sturmabteilung (SA) and Schutzstaffel (SS), the Bund had a uniformed, paramilitary wing called the Ordnungsdienst (OD), which provided security for Bund functions, including public speeches and demonstrations. Unlike their Nazi counterparts, however, members of the OD did not carry firearms. The Bund also included a women's auxiliary and youth groups modeled after the Hitler Youth. At Camp Nordland, New Jersey, youth groups participated in a variety of activities, including sports, the singing of traditional German songs, and education in Nazi principles.

The majority of the Bund's membership was in New York and New Jersey, although there were several chapters across the country in cities such as Chicago and Los Angeles. Many members of the Bund were immigrants who had experienced the harsh privations of World War I and its aftermath. These immigrants tended to feel a particularly powerful connection to Germany, and many saw their time in the United States as temporary. Although Kuhn claimed a national membership of more than twenty thousand, later evidence presented to the Dies Committee suggested the Bund never had more than eight to ten thousand official members.

Impact The German-American Bund provided its members with a sense of community and connection to the German fatherland. Despite efforts to portray itself as an American movement, the Bund

Officials of the German-American Bund, including leader Fritz Julius Kuhn (right), meeting to dedicate a flag at the Plattduetsche Volksfest Park in New York in 1938. (AP/Wide World Photos)

came under the increased scrutiny of the U.S. government and public because of its adherence to the trappings of Nazism, including military-style uniforms and vocal anti-Semitism. In 1938 and 1939, the Dies Committee (later renamed the House Committee on Un-American Activities) conducted a series of hearings in which the Bund was identified as an extension of the German Nazi Party despite Adolf Hitler's general disdain for the movement as potentially damaging to German relations with the United States. In 1939, Kuhn was deported to Germany following his conviction for embezzling party funds, and the Bund fell into a rapid decline until its official disbanding on December 8, 1941, a day after the Japanese attack on Pearl Harbor.

Aaron D. Horton

Further Reading

Canedy, Susan. *America's Nazis: A Democratic Dilemma.* Menlo Park, Calif.: Markgraf, 1990.

Gross, Ruth, ed. *Traveling Between Worlds: German-American Encounters.* College Station: Texas A&M University Press, 2006.

Kazal, Russell. *Becoming Old Stock: The Paradox of German-American Identity.* Princeton, N.J.: Princeton University Press, 2004.

See also   Anti-Semitism; Demographics of the United States; Germany and U.S. appeasement; House Committee on Un-American Activities; Immigration to the United States; Jews in the United States; Racial discrimination; World War II and the United States.

■ Germany and U.S. appeasement

Definition   U.S. foreign policy from 1933 to 1939 that sought to placate Nazi Germany and avoid military entanglements in Europe

The United States, Great Britain, and France initiated policies appeasing German chancellor Adolf Hitler in the belief that by doing so, they could prevent war. The policies were unsuccessful; eventually, Great Britain, France, and the United States all entered World War II against Germany.

Hitler's designation as German chancellor on January 30, 1933, and Franklin D. Roosevelt's inauguration as U.S. president on March 4, 1933, initiated twelve years of parallel rule that ended in the latter stages of World War II. Germany and the United States experienced tense relations prior to the outbreak of European hostilities on September 1, 1939. In the United States, foreign policy decisions were made on the basis of widely shared views, such as isolationism, a feeling of security based on geographic distance, distrust of foreign alliances or "entanglements," fear of immigration, a desire to handle the economic woes of the Great Depression, and a revulsion of the horrors of World War I. These concepts guided how the Roosevelt administration dealt with Germany.

Within his first year in office, Hitler made provocative moves that tested the United States. His anti-Semitic rhetoric became official policy that turned into physical violence. He canceled German debt to the United States. He rearmed the German military, criticized the Treaty of Versailles, and withdrew from the League of Nations. Roosevelt sought to address economic and domestic issues. This caused an ineffective policy that reinforced Hitler's view that the United States was weak. Early attempts to engage Hitler in disarmament and "collective security" talks failed.

In 1935 and 1936, a series of events connected to the revision of the Treaty of Versailles heightened international tensions. In January, 1935, inhabitants of the Saar area voted overwhelmingly to return to Germany, an action that emboldened Hitler. In March, 1935, Hitler announced the creation of an air force and the reintroduction of the draft, unilateral violations of the treaty. In June, 1935, in a bilateral violation, Great Britain and Germany signed a naval agreement granting Germany a navy 35 percent as large as Britain's. Because the United States

was not a signatory to the treaty, these actions did not elicit a significant American response. Isolationism held sway. The U.S. Senate rejected a proposal for the United States to join the World Court at The Hague, and Congress passed the first of several Neutrality Acts that prohibited the United States from trading with belligerents, but the laws failed to designate between aggressor or victim nations or nations assisting victims. German reoccupation of the Rhineland in March, 1936, was yet another violation of the treaty, but since it did not involve any American interests, no response was forthcoming.

Roosevelt's quarantine speech of October 5, 1937, which called for a "quarantine" of aggressor nations, was ignored by Hitler. Nonetheless, in an-

German chancellor Adolf Hitler salutes in the background as SS (Schutzstaffel) troops goose-step during a parade in Germany in 1938. The United States spent the better part of the decade ignoring the Third Reich's move toward domination of Europe. (The Granger Collection, New York)

other example of appeasement, the United States replaced its ambassadors in Berlin. Ambassador William Dodd, whose anti-Nazi comments were well known, was recalled in December, 1937, and was replaced by Hugh Wilson, who had little sympathy for the plight of the Jews and actually attended the 1938 Nazi Party rally at Nuremberg, something Dodd had refused to do.

In 1938, Hitler completed the Anschluss of Austria and then applied pressure on Czechoslovakia to relinquish the Sudetenland border area that contained many Germans. The United States tried unsuccessfully to involve Germany in the July, 1938, Evian Conference concerning refugee issues. When the Sudetenland issue was resolved through the Munich Agreement of September, 1938, which ceded the Sudetenland to Germany, the height of appeasement was reached. Most British, French, and Americans were relieved that war had been averted. The infamous Kristallnacht of November 9 and 10, 1938, highlighted the Nazis' barbaric anti-Semitism and prompted the recall of Ambassador Wilson. German violation of the Munich Agreement with the incorporation of the remainder of Czechoslovakia in March, 1939, and German pressure on Poland for territorial concessions resulted in war on September 1, 1939, when Germany invaded Poland. British and French declarations of war on Germany ended their appeasement policies. U.S. isolation and neutrality ended with the Japanese attack on Pearl Harbor on December 7, 1941, and Germany's declaration of war on the United States several days later.

Impact American appeasement and attempts at conciliation and engagement were rejected by Hitler. The ineffectiveness of the League of Nations, which the United States had not joined, further emboldened Hitler to pursue aggressive foreign policy that violated international law and the territorial in-

The Rhineland

= The Rhineland

tegrity of a number of European nations. Attempts to appease Hitler did not prevent the United States from fighting Germany in World War II.

Mark C. Herman

Further Reading

Mayers, David. "Neither War nor Peace: FDR's Ambassadors in Embassy Berlin and Policy Toward Germany, 1933-1941." *Diplomacy and Statecraft* 20 (2009): 50-68.

Offner, Arnold A. *American Appeasement: United States Foreign Policy and Germany, 1933-1938.* Cambridge, Mass.: Belknap Press of Harvard University Press, 1969.

See also Congress, U.S.; Evian Conference; Foreign policy of the United States; Geneva Disarmament Conference; Isolationism; League of Nations; Neutrality Acts; Quarantine speech; Roosevelt, Franklin D.; World War II and the United States.

■ Gershwin, George

Identification   American composer, pianist, and
   conductor
Born   September 26, 1898; Brooklyn, New York
Died   July 11, 1937; Hollywood, California

*George Gershwin bridged many gaps in music at a time
when popular music was rarely associated with the concert
hall. His beginnings in piano and popular music were combined with later education in concert music, and during
the 1930's, he developed into the most universally known
composer of American concert music and popular songs.*

George Gershwin, born Jacob Gershvin, was of
Jewish-Russian heritage. He started his musical studies at the age of twelve and by the age of fifteen had
already started a career in music as a "plugger," a
salesman of songs for mainstream use, for a publishing company called Remick's. This position led to
significant developments in his piano skills, and he
eventually cultivated a reputation as the finest pianist at Remick's. Gershwin found employment and
greater compositional outlets as a pianist on Broadway after leaving Remick's in 1917. This led to his
first full Broadway score, *La La Lucille*, in 1919. By
1920, his first nationally popular song, "Swanee," began to create a greater source of income. Working
often with his brother Ira Gershwin as his lyricist, he
continued a lifelong output of popular songs and
Broadway shows.

Gershwin's first fame as a serious composer came
with the creation of *Rhapsody in Blue* (1924) for piano and orchestra. The composition, which was revolutionary for its successful integration of jazz styles
with orchestral music, garnered Gershwin the status
of the man who brought jazz to the concert hall.
While never leaving popular songs and Broadway,
Rhapsody in Blue marked a change in Gershwin's output of music, as he moved toward composition for
the concert hall. The most notable of his late 1920's
work include Concerto in F for Piano and Orchestra
(1925) and the tone poem *An American in Paris*
(1928).

By the 1930's, Gershwin had reached enormous
popularity worldwide and was earning considerable
sums of money through royalties and performances
of his compositions but still continued to study composition from several notable teachers (Rubin
Goldmark, Wallingford Riegger, Henry Cowell, and
Joseph Schillinger). His major works of the period
included five full Broadway productions—*Strike Up
the Band* (1930), *Girl Crazy* (1930), *Of Thee I Sing*
(1931), *Pardon My English* (1933), and *Let 'Em Eat
Cake* (1933)—four film scores—*Delicious* (1931),
Shall We Dance? (1937), *A Damsel in Distress* (1937),
and *The Goldwyn Follies* (1938)—and several works
for the concert hall—*Second Rhapsody* (1931), *Cuban
Overture* (1932), and *Porgy and Bess Suite* (1935).

During this time, he also composed the opera
Porgy and Bess (1935). Although somewhat controversial initially, it was the pinnacle of Gershwin's
composing career and became regarded as the most
important American opera of the twentieth century.
Based on the novel *Porgy* (1924) by DuBose Heyward, the opera centers on the fictional story of the
poor black residents of "Catfish Row" in Charleston,
South Carolina, and like the book, the dialogue contains the colloquial speech of the residents. Gershwin's "folk opera," as he called it, contained jazz and
blues musical styles combined with the color of a
large orchestra.

Gershwin had already become part of the elite society in arts and business of New York before signing

George Gershwin. (Library of Congress)

Music Composed by George Gershwin in the 1930's

Musical theater:
- *Girl Crazy* (1930)
- *Of Thee I Sing* (1931)
- *Let 'Em Eat Cake* (1933)
- *Pardon My English* (1933)
- *Porgy and Bess* (1935)
- *The Show Is On* (1936)

Orchestral works:
- *Cuban Overture* (1932)
- *Second Rhapsody* (1932)
- *Variations on "I Got Rhythm"* (1934)
- *Catfish Row* (1936)

Songs:
- "I Got Rhythm" (1930)
- "Let's Call the Whole Thing Off" (1937)
- "Nice Work If You Can Get It" (1937)
- "They Can't Take That Away from Me" (1937)
- "Our Love Is Here to Stay" (1938)

---

a contract with RKO Pictures in Hollywood for himself and Ira in 1936. There he produced many popular compositions; the best-known of which was *Shall We Dance?*, which featured Fred Astaire and Ginger Rogers.

Gershwin's early death at the age of thirty-eight was sudden, with little indication other than dizziness and headaches. He collapsed into a coma on July 9, 1937. Doctors diagnosed Gershwin with a brain tumor and sought consultation from medical personnel from around the country to determine a prognosis for immediate surgery. Gershwin passed away several hours after an unsuccessful attempt to remove the tumor on July 11, 1937. His untimely death cut short what had already been an illustrious and compositionally varied career.

Impact   Gershwin's influence on music and American society can scarcely be overstated. His music continues to be performed by leading artists and elite orchestras across the globe. His memorable and widely known melodies make his music immediately identifiable, and they continue to be used in mainstream media culture such as television and films.

Gershwin is considered to be the first composer to bridge the gap between popular music and concert halls, and his combination of African-inspired hymnody, rhythm, and jazz with concert instrumentation and form allowed him to become one of the most popular composers of the twentieth century.

L. Keith Lloyd

Further Reading

Alpert, Hollis. *The Life and Times of Porgy and Bess: The Story of an American Classic.* New York: Alfred A. Knopf, 1990.

Hyland, William G. *George Gershwin: A New Biography.* Westport, Conn.: Praeger, 2003.

Jablonski, Edward. *Gershwin.* New York: Doubleday, 1987.

Pollack, Howard. *George Gershwin: His Life and Work.* Berkeley: University of California Press, 2006.

See also   African Americans; Astaire, Fred; Broadway musicals; Dance; Music: Classical; Music: Jazz; Music: Popular; *Porgy and Bess*; Recording industry.

■ Glass-Steagall Act of 1933

The Law   New Deal legislation created to protect bank depositors from speculative practices contributing to thousands of bank failures

Also known as   Banking Act of 1933

Dates   Enacted on June 16, 1933; repealed in 1999

In an effort to end the banking industry's speculative excesses, which contributed to thousands of bank failures in the early 1930's, the Glass-Steagall Act severed the business of commercial banking (collecting deposits) from that of investment banking (underwriting securities).

Passed as part of the New Deal, the Glass-Steagall Act sought to quickly address the thousands of bank failures that occurred nationwide in 1932 and 1933. The act was sponsored by Senator Carter Glass, a Democrat from Virginia, and Representative Henry Bascom Steagall, a Democrat from Alabama, and was passed in two parts. The first part, enacted in February, 1932, strengthened the Federal Reserve's hand in regulating the nation's banking system. In the months that followed, however, thousands of insolvent banks closed, and pressure mounted for additional legislation to permanently address the country's banking woes. The second Glass-Steagall Act—the one most historians refer to by that term—was enacted to end the involvement of commercial banks in the risky practice of securities underwriting, or the buying and selling of new stocks and bonds.

While underwriting was highly lucrative for the banks, it often put bank customers' deposits at risk. Underwriting also resulted in great inflation of the perceived value of stocks and bonds that were issued. Once this false price inflation became apparent, securities prices fell, contributing greatly to the 1929 stock market crash and ensuing bank failures.

The act prohibited commercial banks' involvement in investment banking practices, relegating the banks to their traditional lines of business: collecting deposits and making loans. The act also prohibited investment banks from collecting customers' bank deposits and created the Federal Deposit Insurance Corporation, which guarantees bank customers' deposits.

Impact   By ending the mingling of the business of commercial banking and investment banking, the Glass-Steagall Act was able to effectively return stability to the U.S. banking sector. Eventually, it restored the trust of the American public in their local banks.

Gregg Wirth

Further Reading

Benston, George J. *The Separation of Commercial and Investment Banking: The Glass-Steagall Act Revisited and Reconsidered.* New York: Oxford University Press, 1990.

Cohen, Henry. *The Glass-Steagall Act: A Legal Overview.* Washington, D.C.: Congressional Research Service, 1982.

McKinney, J. "Financial Free-for-All." *Black Enterprise* 30, no. 11 (2000): 197-201.

See also   Bank Holiday; Bank of United States failure; Banking; Banking Act of 1935; Business and the economy in the United States; Federal Reserve Board; New Deal.

■ "God Bless America"

Identification   Popular patriotic song invoking divine guidance
Composer   Irving Berlin
Date   Debuted on radio November 11, 1938

As the spread of fascism raised fears of war in Europe, Americans embraced an anthem reaffirming God's support of the nation's values, traditions, and destiny. The song became the signature tune of its first radio performer, Kate Smith.

Irving Berlin wrote this song as an Army sergeant in 1918 while preparing a military musical revue entitled *Yip Yip Yaphank.* At the time, he felt the song did not fit the needs of the show and put it aside. Twenty years later, with Adolf Hitler on the ascendancy and Japan rising to greater power in Asia, Berlin, himself a Jew and creator of some of the most beloved patriotic songs of World War I, believed the United States needed a patriotic reawakening to prepare for possible confrontation even while celebrating peace.

Berlin pulled the older work from his files, revised some lines, and gave it to Kate Smith, a radio singing star, to introduce on her popular weekly show *The Kate Smith Hour.* The song debuted on November 11, 1938, then widely recognized as Armistice Day, a holiday devoted to the memory of those who died in World War I and the goal of international peace.

Smith, a woman who weighed more than two hundred pounds, performed the song with conviction. The tune begins as a gentle hymn but swells into a strident march as it moves toward the last lines, and Smith's matronly presence and firm resolve as she built to the last high note, which she always hit a cappella in her clear strong soprano, conveyed righteous strength. The song was an immediate hit throughout the nation and was the song Americans associated with World War II.

Impact   Through the rest of the twentieth century, *God Bless America* continued as one of the most revered patriotic songs in the United States. Its increased usage after the terrorist attacks of September 11, 2001, and its subsequent adoption for seventh-inning-stretch performances in professional baseball demonstrate its ongoing popularity in the twenty-first century.

Scot M. Guenter

Further Reading

Collins, Ace. *Songs Sung Red, White, and Blue: The Stories Behind America's Best-Loved Patriotic Songs.* New York: HarperCollins, 2003.

Phillips, Kimberley Ann. "Keeping a Record of Life: Women and Art During World War II." *OAH Magazine of History* 19, no. 2 (March, 2005): 20-24.

Smith, Kathleen E. R. *God Bless America: Tin Pan Alley Goes to War.* Lexington: University Press of Kentucky, 2003.

See also   Foreign policy of the United States; Jews in the United States; Peace movement; Radio in the United States; "Star-Spangled Banner"; World War II and the United States.

■ Goddard, Robert H.

Identification   Physicist and rocket engineer
Born   October 5, 1882; Worcester, Massachusetts
Died   August 10, 1945; Baltimore, Maryland

Honored as the "father of spaceflight and American rocketry," Goddard was one of the most prominent pioneers of rocket science and spaceflight theory. He received 214 patents for his inventions related to spaceflight. His greatest engineering contributions were made during the 1920's and 1930's.

As a boy, Robert Goddard was an avid reader, particularly of popular science-fiction novels. This peaked his interest in space exploration. While attending Worcester Polytechnic Institute, he began experimenting with rockets in the basement of the physics building. In 1919, his treatise on rocket propulsion, *A Method of Reaching Extreme Altitudes*, was published by the Smithsonian Institution. On March 16, 1926, he launched the first liquid-fueled rocket from a site in Auburn, Massachusetts.

With funding from the Guggenheim family, Goddard moved to Roswell, New Mexico, in 1930, a place where he could conduct his research without endangering others. In 1932, he tested a rocket controlled by a gyroscope mounted on gimbals that electrically controlled steering vanes in the exhaust. By 1934, he was experimenting with rockets that were up to 4.5 meters long. The rockets were powered by gasoline and liquid oxygen pressurized with nitrogen. Using his gyroscopic guidance system, one of his rockets achieved supersonic velocity and

Robert H. Goddard. (NASA)

reached an altitude of 2.3 kilometers on May 31, 1935.

Between 1936 and 1937, Goddard worked on massive rockets that were designed to reach high altitudes. Because of engine burn-through, he returned to smaller rockets and reached an altitude of 2.7 kilometers on March 26, 1937. He reduced rocket weight by using thin-walled fuel tanks reinforced with high-tensile strength wire. Although Goddard did not reach the extreme altitudes he had hoped to achieve, he set the stage for future rocket development and space exploration.

Impact   Goddard developed and patented numerous technologies later used in large rockets, ballistic missiles, and earth-orbiting satellites and for interplanetary exploration, including gyroscopic guidance systems for rockets, film cooling of rocket engines, and a variable-thrust rocket motor. He demonstrated the necessity for using liquid fuel to sustain rocket propulsion and the principle that a rocket provides thrust in a vacuum. The National

Aeronautics and Space Administration named the Goddard Space Flight Center in Greenbelt, Maryland, in his honor.

Alvin K. Benson

Further Reading

Clary, David A. *Rocket Man: Robert H. Goddard and the Birth of the Space Age.* New York: Hyperion, 2004.

Streissguth, Thomas. *Rocket Man: The Story of Robert Goddard.* New York: Carolrhoda Books, 1995.

See also   Astronomy; Aviation and aeronautics; Inventions; Physics; Rocketry.

■ *Gold Clause Cases*

The Cases   Challenges to a New Deal law that struck down gold clauses in contracts

Date   February 18, 1935

The cases challenged the constitutionality of New Deal inflationary monetary policies.

On April 18, 1933, President Franklin D. Roosevelt took the United States off the gold standard; on May, 12, he devalued the dollar by nearly 41 percent. On June 5, Congress passed a law abrogating clauses in private and government contracts that mandated payment in gold. Several court cases challenged this law. The Supreme Court ruled against the plaintiffs in three such cases, with opinions by Chief Justice Charles Evans Hughes.

Norman v. Baltimore and Ohio Raiload involved a private contract calling for payment in gold. Repeating his argument in a 1911 case, Hughes ruled that private contracts are subject to federal laws and cannot cancel out their effects. In 1937, the plaintiff in *Holyoke Water Power v. American Writing Paper* sought payment in the equivalent gold value. Justice Benjamin N. Cardozo ruled against the plaintiff, citing the *Norman* precedent as controlling.

Perry v. United States involved a gold clause for a World War I Liberty Bond. In a hair-splitting decision often compared to *Marbury v. Madison*, Hughes ruled this abrogation of a federal contract unconstitutional but also ruled that lower prices largely canceled out the reduced value of the dollar, leaving no damages to recover. Justice Harlan Fiske Stone agreed with the result in a concurring opinion, claiming that the issue of damages made the consti-

tutionality of the abrogation irrelevant, though he considered abrogation deplorable and dishonorable.

Nortz v. United States concerned gold certificates. Hughes ruled that the question of their redemption in gold was made irrelevant by the ban on private gold possession. Even if the certificates were redeemed for gold, the owners would have to turn in the gold to the government.

Justice James C. McReynolds led the four conservative justices in bitter dissents from the three decisions, denouncing the abrogation of gold clauses as a dishonorable, arbitrary violation of contractual rights. He argued that they would debase the currency, and that legitimate congressional goals cannot excuse inappropriate actions.

Impact   The Court upheld inflationary New Deal money policy and delayed its collision with the administration. Roosevelt had decided to refuse to enforce the decisions if they favored the plaintiffs.

Timothy Lane

Further Reading

Pusey, Merlo J. *Charles Evans Hughes.* Vol. 2. New York: Macmillan, 1951.

Ross, William G. *The Chief Justiceship of Charles Evans Hughes, 1930-1941.* Columbia: South Carolina University Press, 2007.

Smith, Jean Edward. *FDR.* New York: Random House, 2007.

See also   Four Horsemen vs. Three Musketeers; Hughes, Charles Evans; Inflation; New Deal; Roosevelt's first one hundred days; Supreme Court, U.S.

■ **Gold Reserve Act of 1934**

The Law   Federal law making the possession of gold illegal

Also known as   Thomas Amendment

Date   January 30, 1934

This law was enacted both to stimulate the U.S. economy and to ensure that one currency standard, the U.S. dollar, would be used for commerce.

In response to the Great Depression, President Franklin D. Roosevelt proposed Executive Order 6102 on April 5, 1933, an order that required all people to exchange their gold coins, gold bullion, and gold-backed currency for money that was not redeemable in precious metals. On January 30, 1934, Congress passed the Gold Reserve Act of 1934, also known as the Thomas Amendment, which amended the original act of May 12, 1933, making it illegal to possess any gold currency. Thus, all gold coinage was withdrawn from circulation and was kept in the form of bullion.

All gold was to be housed and protected under military control at Fort Knox, Kentucky, and at other military bases. In addition to the general public, the Federal Reserve was also to surrender all of its gold. The act also authorized the president to devalue the gold dollar so that it would have no more than 60 percent of its existing weight. However, while people received $20.67 an ounce in paper money issued by the Federal Reserve, the Federal Reserve was paid in gold certificates, which were assigned no specific monetary value. Thus, the Treasury owned all U.S. gold reserves, and no one else inside the United States was permitted to possess any gold except by the express authorization of the Treasury. The act helped increase the value of gold to $35 an ounce in 1934, producing close to a $3 billion profit for the government.

Impact The Gold Reserve Act helped stimulate the U.S. economy after the Great Depression. Additionally, the law helped prevent the hoarding of massive gold supplies by private citizens, ultimately allowing the government to establish the dollar as the sole economic standard.

Paul M. Klenowski

Further Reading

Eichengreen, Barry. *Golden Fetters: The Gold Standard and the Great Depression, 1919-1939.* New York: Oxford University Press, 1992.

Friedman, Milton, and Anna Jacobson Schwartz. *A Monetary History of the United States, 1867-1960.* Princeton, N.J.: Princeton University Press, 1963.

See also Banking; Business and the economy in the United States; *Gold Clause Cases*; Securities and Exchange Commission.

Golden Gate Bridge. See **San Francisco Bay bridges**

■ Golf

During the Great Depression years, golf began to change from a recreational activity for the wealthy to a sport in which professionals could earn their livings.

In 1930, the great Bobby Jones retired from golf at the age of only twenty-eight after winning what, at that time, was considered the Grand Slam of golf. During that year, the four tournaments constituting the Grand Slam were the U.S. Open, the British Open, the U.S. Amateur Championship, and the British Amateur Championship. Jones was considered to be the greatest golfer that the United States had produced, and his departure from the game created a void that a new breed of competitive golfers would have to fill.

Another leading golfer of the time was Gene Sarazen, a fiery competitor who knew how to win. In 1930, he won the Miami Open for the fourth consecutive time. By accomplishing this, Sarazen tied Walter Hagan's record for the most consecutive wins at a single tournament. As a sign of the future commercial growth of the sport, Sarazen earned ten thousand dollars for winning the Agua Caliente Open played in Tijuana, Mexico. During most years of the 1930's, however, the leading money winners earned less than that amount for the entire year.

The Professional Circuits From 1930 to 1967, the Western Open was considered a major championship on the women's tour. The only professional female golfer to win the Western Open during the 1930's was Helen Hicks, in 1937. However, by the late 1930's, the legendary, multisport athlete Babe Didrikson Zaharias and Patty Berg were beginning to make their marks on women's golf. Nevertheless, it took a long period of time for professional women's golf to win popular acceptance.

While the women's tour did not gain public or corporate recognition for many decades, the men's tour began to grow dramatically during the 1930's. In 1930, the proposal was made to expand the men's tour to a year-long event. However, the Great Depression hampered this initiative, and many professional tournaments either had to cut the amounts of prize money they offered or had to drop cash prizes altogether. Also during the 1930's, a slowdown in the construction of new golf courses occurred. These cost-cutting trends meant professional golfers strug-

Gene Sarazen (left), Tommy Armour (center), and Walter Hagen walk the links at a Miami golf tournament in 1933. (AP/Wide World Photos)

gled to earn livings, especially during the first half of the decade.

New Stars, Rules, and Courses Players such as Sarazen, Leo Diegel, Denny Shute, Tommy Armour, Horton Smith, Billy Burke, and Craig Wood dominated golf during the first half of the 1930's. Smith beat Wood by a single stroke at the first Augusta National Invitational in 1934. Jones and Alister Mackenzie had designed the course at Augusta National Golf Club, which opened in 1933 and held its first tournament one year later. The tournament was initially called the Augusta National Invitational, but its name was changed to the Masters in 1939. When Smith won the tournament in 1934, he received a prize of only $1,500. By the end of the decade, the leading golfers on the tour included Sam Snead, Jimmy Demaret, Jimmy Thompson, Ben Hogan, Byron Nelson, Paul Runyan, and Henry Picard. Hogan had become a professional golfer in 1930 at the age of seventeen. In 1938, Snead set a record for earnings in one year with $19,534. To set that record, he had to win eight tournaments during the year.

During the early 1930's, both the United States Golf Association (USGA) and Great Britain's Royal and Ancient Golf Club of St. Andrews (R&A) ruled on such matters as regulation ball size, which golf clubs were legal for tournament play, and how tournaments were to be scored, but the ruling bodies of these organizations did not always agree on what was best for the game. In 1931, the USGA approved increasing the diameter of balls from 1.62 to 1.68 inches, while reducing their weight from 1.62 to 1.55 ounces. The new balls proved unpopular with players, so the USGA kept the larger diameter but restored the 1.62-ounce weight. Meanwhile, the R&A decided not to alter the size or weight of the golf ball.

Sarazen worked on a new design for the sand wedge. He added weight to the lower back of the club, which helped him to power balls out of sand traps. He first used the club at the 1932 British Open, which he won. While Sarazen's design set the standard for future sand wedges, Jones developed a concave-faced wedge; however, it was banned from tournament play. Another concern for the governing groups was how many clubs golfers should be allowed to carry during tournament play. Caddies often complained about the large numbers of clubs they had to carry around courses. Some players made their caddies carry golf bags with as many as twenty-five clubs. In 1938, the USGA mandated that golfers could have a maximum of fourteen clubs in their bags in tournament play.

Another major transition in the golf game during the 1930's was a shift from hickory-shafted to steel-shafted clubs. In 1914, steel shafts had been banned by both the USGA and the R&A, but by the end of the 1920's, steel shafts had been legalized. In 1936, Johnny Fischer was the last golfer to win a major championship using hickory-shafted clubs.

Impact While the Great Depression hindered the growth of professional golf in the 1930's, by the end of the decade, the game was becoming a mainstay in American culture. However, international competition was curtailed with the outbreak of war in Europe in 1939. Because of the growing popularity of golf, corporate sponsorship increased during the late 1930's. Great players left their marks on the game during the decade, and golf further elevated its status as a serious, professional sport with the standardization of rules and the construction of an increasing number of magnificent courses.

Jeffry Jensen

Further Reading

Barkow, Al. *The Golden Era of Golf: How America Rose to Dominate the Old Scots Game.* New York: St. Martin's Press, 2000. Writing for dedicated American golf fans, Barkow gives a detailed account of each decade.

Jerris, Rand, with Rhonda Glenn, David Normoyle, and Marty Parkes. *Golf's Golden Age: Robert T. Jones, Jr., and the Legendary Players of the '10s, '20s, and '30s.* Far Hills, N.J.: United States Golf Association, 2005. Includes portraits of the major golfers of the period and discusses how the game was made better by their presence.

Kirsch, George B. *Golf in America.* Urbana: University of Illinois Press, 2009. In addition to essays covering the golfers who have made the game great, Kirsch includes a history of how golf has grown into a vast, worldwide phenomenon.

Peper, George, Robin McMillan, and James A. Frank, eds. *Golf in America: The First Hundred Years.* New York: Harry N. Abrams, 1988. Overview of the game that includes discussions of the important players, the evolution of equipment, and the boom in the number of golf courses.

Wind, Herbert Warren. *The Story of American Golf: Its Champions and Championships.* New York: Farrar, Straus, 1948. Careful and colorful look at the growth of American golf up to the 1940's.

See also   Recreation; Sarazen, Gene; Sports in Canada; Sports in the United States; Tennis.

■ *Gone with the Wind*

Identification   Novel and its film adaptation about a Southern belle during the American Civil War and Reconstruction period
Author of novel   Margaret Mitchell
Director of film   Victor Fleming
Dates   Novel published in 1936; film released in 1939

Gone with the Wind was the biggest and fastest selling novel in American publishing history. Americans identified themselves with the trials of Southerners during the Civil War and found in the novel strength and endurance to cope with the hardships of the Great Depression. The book created a powerful Southern myth of honor, strength, endurance, and courage. The film version made the novel even more popular.

Immediately after its publication in June, 1936, *Gone with the Wind*, a Civil War novel by former journalist and Atlanta socialite Margaret Mitchell, became the biggest American best seller on the U.S. literary scene. Six months later, in a country constrained by the financial difficulties of the Great Depression, it had sold one million copies. Though its high price for the time (three dollars) was perceived by its publisher, Macmillan, as a threat to its marketability, it did not stop anyone from buying the novel. People saw their own penuries mirrored in those of the war-torn South. The novel stayed on *The New York Times* best-seller list for more than two years. The popularity of the novel was such that it generated all kinds of memorabilia bearing the protagonists' names.

In her only novel, Mitchell rewrote the stories about the Civil War she had heard and combined them with some autobiographical overtones to create an epic tale of love and courage in her native Atlanta. On the eve of the American Civil War, Scarlett O'Hara, a sixteen-year-old Southerner, is rejected by the man she loves, Ashley Wilkes, and decides to marry another instead. Soon a war widow, she moves to Atlanta, where she gets acquainted with Rhett Butler, a blockade runner. The end of the war brings starvation and poverty for the O'Haras. Scarlett is forced to marry her sister's suitor to save the family's plantation. Later, widowed again and still in love with Ashley, she marries Rhett, who truly loves her. Still later, with Ashley's wife dying, Scarlett realizes she really loves Rhett, but he abandons her, tired of waiting for her.

Clark Gable (left) and Vivien Leigh embracing in an iconic scene from the 1939 film Gone with the Wind. *(The Granger Collection, New York)*

Critical acclaim followed the release of the novel, and *Gone with the Wind* was favorably compared with William Makepeace Thackeray's *Vanity Fair* (1848) and Leo Tolstoy's *Anna Karenina* (1877) and *War and Peace* (1869). *Gone with the Wind* won the Pulitzer Prize, beating, among others, William Faulkner's *Absalom! Absalom!* (1936), another Civil War novel. Its film rights were sold for $50,000, the highest bid ever paid in Hollywood at the time.

Mitchell refused to have anything to do with the film production, afraid that her zealous fans would blame her for any potential mistake or inaccuracy in the film, even though she was begged to write the screenplay. The screenplay was written by a series of writers, including F. Scott Fitzgerald. Talk about who should be cast for the main roles became a favorite national pastime, with magazines extensively covering the issue. One magazine poll determined that Clark Gable was the people's choice to play Rhett Butler, against Mitchell's own wishes. Vivien Leigh played Scarlett O'Hara. The premiere in Atlanta received national and international press coverage. Readjusting figures to twenty-first century prices,

Gone with the Wind remains the highest-grossing film ever. It won eight Oscars, including a supporting actress award for Hattie McDaniel for her performance of Mammy; she became the first African American to win an Oscar.

The novel became popular abroad as well, especially as World War II swept through Europe. During the Spanish Civil War, American soldiers read it at campsites at night. Regardless of which side soldiers were fighting for, they interpeted the novel as representative of their own cause and sufferings, though the ideological tenets of the Spanish Civil War had nothing to do with those of the American one.

Impact   *Gone with the Wind* has sold more than twenty-eight million copies worldwide and has been translated into twenty-seven languages. The novel remains in print, and television reruns of the film are frequent. Two authorized sequels have been published, *Scarlett* (1991) by Alexandra Ripley and *Rhett Butler's People* (2007) by Donald McCaig, as well as a parody told from the points of view of Gerald O'Hara and Mammy's illegitimate daughter, titled *The Wind Done Gone* (2001) by African American writer Alice Randall. There are also several biographies of Margaret Mitchell. The process of writing the novel and the consequences of its immediate success inspired a television film, *A Burning Passion: The Margaret Mitchell Story* (1994).

M. Carmen Gomez-Galisteo

Further Reading

Curran, Trisha. "*Gone with the Wind*: An American Tragedy." In *The South and Film*, edited by Warren French. Jackson: University of Mississippi Press, 1987. An exploration of why *Gone with the Wind* was considered the greatest American film ever in a poll by the American Film Institute.

Edwards, Anne. *Road to Tara: The Life of Margaret Mitchell, Author of "Gone with the Wind."* London: Orion, 1996. Biography of Mitchell explores events in her life often omitted in earlier biographies, such as her first marriage.

Faust, Drew Gilpin. "Clutching the Chains That Bind: Margaret Mitchell and *Gone with the Wind*." *Southern Cultures* 5, no. 1 (1999): 6-20. An examination of how Scarlett defies social expectations and boundaries in regard to Southern womanhood.

Flamini, Roland. *Scarlett, Rhett, and a Cast of Thousands. The Filming of "Gone with the Wind."* New

York: Collier Macmillan, 1975. An exhaustive analysis of the complicated process of adapting *Gone with the Wind* for the screen.

Haskell, Molly. *Frankly, My Dear: "Gone with the Wind" Revisited.* New Haven, Conn.: Yale University Press, 2009. A defense of both the book and the film in terms of the critical neglect they have experienced.

Pyron, Darden Asbury, ed. *Recasting: "Gone with the Wind" in American Culture.* Miami: University Presses of Florida, 1984. Collection of essays analyzing aspects such as the reception and literary standing of *Gone with the Wind* and issues involving such topics as the Civil War, racism, ideology, and gender roles.

See also Academy Awards; Film; Fitzgerald, F. Scott; Fleming, Victor; Gable, Clark; Great Depression in the United States; Literature in the United States; McDaniel, Hattie.

■ Good Earth, The

Identification Novel about a peasant family in rural China
Author Pearl S. Buck
Date Published in 1931

Pearl S. Buck's first novel, The Good Earth, *was a huge best seller and established her reputation. Her depiction of the struggles of Chinese peasants drew the attention of readers during the Great Depression, a time when so many endured similar hardships.*

The Good Earth tells the story of the struggles of Chinese peasants against poverty, famine, and abuse by the elite. The story follows the life of the humble farmer Wang Lung, from his wedding day to his death. He marries O-Lan, who is a slave in a great house. She has no beauty, and Wang Lung has no love for her during most of their marriage.

Wang Lung feels a great bond with the land and will not part with his farm even when famine forces him to flee to a southern city to beg. During an uprising by the poor, he hesitates to steal, but when the beggars plunder a wealthy estate, he takes money from a man who offers a bribe in return for his escape. He is able to return to his land and to restock his farm. He prospers, buys more land, and in time becomes wealthy.

O-Lan gives Wang Lung sons (and little-valued daughters), and her character and skills contribute greatly to the family's success. However, Wang Lung fails to appreciate her fully until she lies dying. When Wang Lung takes a concubine, O-Lan endures humiliation.

Impact *The Good Earth's* huge popularity can be attributed in large part to Buck's compelling subject. The plight of the poor farmer and the starving city beggar is narrated in brilliant detail, as is the somewhat decadent life the family leads after they gain wealth. The novel is composed like a saga and has a biblical cadence. The family is Chinese, but their story seems universal. The novel affirms the value of simple people. Buck won a Pulitzer Prize for *The Good Earth* and was awarded the Nobel Prize in Literature in 1938.

Charlotte Templin

Further Reading

Conn, Peter. *Pearl S. Buck: A Cultural Biography.* New York: Cambridge University Press, 1996.

Doyle, Paul A. *Pearl S. Buck.* Rev. ed. Woodbridge, Conn.: Twayne, 1980.

Pam, Eleanor. "Patriarchy and Property: Women in Pearl S. Buck's *The Good Earth* (1931)." In *Women in Literature: Reading Through the Lens of Gender,* edited by Jerilyn Fisher and Ellen S. Silber. Westport, Conn.: Greenwood Press, 2003.

See also Asia; Buck, Pearl S.; Fundamentalist-Modernist conflict; Literature in the United States.

■ Good Neighbor Policy

Identification U.S. government foreign policy pledging that the United States would not interfere in the domestic policies of other nations of the Western Hemisphere
Date Announced on March 4, 1933

The Good Neighbor Policy represented a shift in relations between the United States and Latin America. Since the time of the Monroe Doctrine (1823), the United States had viewed itself as possessing the right to interfere in the domestic affairs of Latin American nations. Instead of exerting military and political pressure on Latin American nations, the United States sought improved economic agreements to ensure mutual cooperation with Latin American nations.

On March 4, 1933, Franklin D. Roosevelt delivered an inauguration speech in which he stated firmly that his foreign policy would be that of a "good neighbor." The president emphasized that the United States would respect the rights of other nations throughout the world. On April 12, 1933, Roosevelt gave a speech before the Pan American Union, outlining his policy based on mutual respect and nonintervention toward Latin America. The Good Neighbor Policy lasted for approximately a decade and helped to foster better relations between the United States and Latin America.

In early 1933, following Roosevelt's pledge to respect the rights of other nations and not to interfere in their domestic affairs, violence broke out in Cuba. Roosevelt sent Under Secretary of State Sumner Welles to Cuba in an effort to convince the dictator Gerardo Machado y Morales to resign. He refused but was ousted by the Cuban army in August, 1933. Welles chose a new president for Cuba, but he was overthrown in September, and a government seeking reform took power. The United States continued to try to change the government, eventually succeeding in January, 1934, when Fulgencio Batista y Zaldívar overthrew the previous government.

Following this inauspicious beginning to the Good Neighbor Policy, the Roosevelt administration moved firmly toward a nonintervention policy for the remainder of the 1930's. In December, 1933, the United States agreed formally to the principle of nonintervention, laid out in the Seventh International Conference of American States. Based on the Good Neighbor Policy, all nations were considered juridical equals, despite size differences among nations. By August, 1934, Roosevelt removed the last of the U.S. soldiers in Haiti, who had been stationed there following the occupation of Haiti by United States forces in 1915. The United States used the opportunity to increase trade with Latin American nations through a series of reciprocal trade agreements.

Throughout the 1930's, the United States avoided interfering in the domestic affairs of Latin American nations and sought to treat Latin American countries with greater equality. In 1938, Mexico decided to nationalize the foreign oil companies operating in Mexico. The Mexican government offered to provide compensation to U.S. oil companies, who refused the terms and sought intervention from the U.S. government, particularly by placing an embargo on all Mexican goods. However, the U.S. government refused to become involved, and the oil companies eventually were forced to settle with the Mexican government. From its inception through the 1930's, the Roosevelt administration sought to stand by its pledge to not interfere in the domestic affairs of other nations.

Impact The Good Neighbor Policy represented a fundamental shift in relations between the United States and Latin America. The move was welcome in much of Latin America, particularly because the United States had previously been heavily involved in interfering in the domestic affairs of other nations. Despite this welcomed change, Latin Americans also noted that a significant majority of leaders in Latin America, particularly the Caribbean basin, were dictators. The Good Neighbor Policy, with its precepts of nonintervention and noninterference, allowed these dictators to remain firmly in power throughout the 1930's.

Additionally, being a "good neighbor" had its limits. Following American entrance into World War II in 1941, the United States made demands on a number of Latin American nations regarding individuals with German ties living in their countries. The countries headed by dictators in Latin America often chose to surrender these people, often citizens with few ties remaining with Germany, to the United States for internment. After World War II, the United States moved away from the Good Neighbor Policy back to a policy of interventionism.

Michael W. Cheek

Further Reading

Pike, Frederick B. *FDR's Good Neighbor Policy: Sixty Years of Generally Gentle Chaos.* Austin: University of Texas Press, 1995.

Roorda, Eric. *The Dictator Next Door: The Good Neighbor Policy and the Trujillo Regime in the Dominican Republic, 1930-1945.* Durham, N.C.: Duke University Press, 1998.

Smith, Peter H. *Talons of the Eagle: Latin America, the United States, and the World.* 3d ed. New York: Oxford University Press, 2008.

See also Foreign policy of the United States; Great Depression in the United States; Haiti occupation; Latin America and the Caribbean; Roosevelt, Franklin D.